THE HISTORY OF MODERN WARFARE

To my Mother and Father, brought together by war.

THIS IS A SEVENOAKS BOOK

Text and design © Carlton Publishing Group 2007

This edition published in 2007 by SevenOaks
an imprint of the Carlton Publishing Group
20 Mortimer Street
London W1T 3JW

10 9 8 7 6 5 4 3 2 1

A CIP catalogue record for this book is available from the British Library.

ISBN: 978 1 86200 463 4

Executive Editor:	Stella Caldwell
Project Editor:	Gareth Jones
Senior Art Editor:	Gülen Shevki-Taylor
Editor:	Bobby Gainher
Design:	Vicky Holmes, Zoë Dissell
Picture Research:	Steve Behan
Production:	Lisa Moore

Printed and bound in Dubai

THE HISTORY OF
MODERN WARFARE

PAUL BREWER

SEVENOAKS

Contents

INTRODUCTION - Reporting War

Stories of wars have been reported going back to the dawn of history. The famous Vulture Stela of ancient Mesopotamia records a war between the cities of Lagash and Umma. The war correspondent, as a chronicler of the events of a conflict as they happen, is largely a creation of the rise of newspapers during the nineteenth century.

Roger Fenton used this mobile dark room to develop his images from the Crimean War.

At first, news of wars was collected somewhat haphazardly. Often, the newspapers simply repeated the dispatches from the armies in the field as received and published in official government sources. Occasionally, such as during the Napoleonic Wars (1803–15), officers participating in the campaigns would send letters to editors describing what they had seen. There were also reports written by people who did not necessarily accompany the armies, but spoke to participants or collated information from local newspapers.

In the 1830s, Charles Lewis Gruneisen wrote battlefield reports for the London-based *Morning Post* on a civil war fought in Spain. In some respects he was the earliest war correspondent, although he did not continue in this work, instead becoming a music critic. George W. Kendall, editor of the *New Orleans Picayune*, also had some claim to being a war correspondent. He accompanied US armies during the war in Mexico, although he had some difficulty separating himself from the conflict. He was an early advocate of

the annexation of Texas by the United States, and fought with a Texan unit against the Mexican army in the opening campaigns of the war, as well as accompanying the main American military force during its campaign to capture the capital, Mexico City.

Traditionally, the title of "the first war correspondent" is awarded to William Howard Russell, commissioned by *The Times* of London to accompany the allied armies during the Crimean War.

Russell had been working for the *The Times* since 1841, and effectively established the basic principles of war reporting for those who would follow in his footsteps. He was present at battles, and described both the broad outline of an engagement and also the sense of battle as experienced by those participating in the actual fighting. He gathered his information by questioning those who were willing to speak to him – officers and other ranks alike. His dispatches proved immensely popular, and also were an effective tool for enabling politicians to tackle the aristocratic incompetence that severely hampered the efforts of the British army in the campaign. He became a full-time journalist, a published author and developed a second career as a sought-after lecturer.

However, Russell's success also highlighted the failings of the war correspondent. The Crimea was only one theatre of the war and not the most important one. His depiction of an incompetent officer class damning its men to avoidable misery and failing to offer them the kind of leadership needed to win battles through effective tactics, guaranteed the enduring view of that war as one of British military mismanagement. In fact, while the army floundered in the Crimea, the Royal Navy fought a two-year campaign of considerable innovation in the Baltic that effectively defeated Russia.

While Russell established the operating practice of war correspondents, photographers also made some steps during the Crimean War towards creating a photo-journalism of war. At first, war photography was hampered by the unwieldy equipment that was mid-nineteenth-century technology. Nonetheless, Roger Fenton, James Robertson and Charles Langlois all took pictures that offered those who saw them a glimpse of what a real war looked like. Subsequently, Felice Beato took some dramatic images of the aftermath of battles in India and China during the Mutiny and the Second Opium War.

In spite of these pioneering efforts, the real breakthrough for war photography came in the American Civil War. Numerous photographers accompanied the Union armies and Matthew Brady in particular

Sir William Howard Russell, war correspondent of *The Times*.

US and British troops and journalists take shelter in trenches in the Kuwait desert, 2003.

created a shock with his exhibition of "The Dead of Antietam". At the time, American papers listed names of those killed in battle, but the exhibition, in New York, made a terrific impact. These were silhouettes that represented the names, in all the ghastly postures of the dead who had lain in the open for some hours or even days after they had perished. War photography needed to capture a visual reality of war, not simply be restricted to images of uniformed men beside tents or cooking in the open as if they were some kind of reunion jamboree of former boy scouts.

Such was the impact of dispatches by Russell or exhibitions organized by Brady, that generals were quickly aware of the need to control the work of war reporting. In the closing days of the Crimean War, the British commander-in-chief ordered the expulsion of any correspondent who disclosed military secrets. What was deemed secret was left up to the soldiers to determine. Brady was criticized for damaging the morale of citizens who paid for the war through taxes and by offering up their kin to meet the same fate as the Dead of Antietam. War correspondents and photographers, however, were still able to go about their work.

The nature of war correspondents' work has remained much the same, even though printing, radio, television and computers have brought new technologies to deploy on the reporting of war. The development

of printing methods that could reproduce photographs created the picture newspaper, and opened up photography to a wider audience than could attend an exhibition in a gallery. Film stunned viewers when they saw Geoffrey Malins's and John McDowell's documentary *The Battle of the Somme*. Edward R. Murrow enabled listeners in the United States to hear the sound of bombs falling on London. The nightly news in 1960s America delivered pictures of the conflict in Vietnam direct to American homes. Today, war-blogs are written by individuals actively involved in the American occupation of Iraq, and allow internet surfers to get first-hand accounts of what is going on there, almost immediately. During the invasion, reporters were able to use wireless computer technology to submit reports "live from the front".

The effect of all this information has led to widespread censorship and to a certain degree of manipulation by armed forces. A popular American correspondent of the Second World War was Ernie Pyle, who attained folkloric status as he reported in homey Middle American tones about the lives, and occasionally the deaths, of the men in the field. Pyle made a point of referring to a soldier's home town and state when he mentioned them, which of course drew the locality's residents into the war in a subtle way, and encouraged the home front in the war effort.

Rather more amazingly was the work of Peter Arnett during the Gulf War. Arnett had come to fame as a war correspondent during the Vietnam War and his presence in Baghdad throughout the bombing illustrated how the global audience was targeted by the Iraqi government through the means of an enemy alien. This incredible use of the enemy's media against itself continued during the US invasion of Iraq in 2003. War correspondents have gone from being regarded as spies – Gruneison was nearly executed – to being an important part of a state's propaganda campaign.

Chronicle of War attempts to strip away the manipulation and propaganda provided by mere reprints of wartime press reports, while retaining the immediacy and the context that a daily newspaper published in wartime might reveal. It is this context that is often lost on armchair theorists: for example, given the bad situation confronting the Confederacy in mid-1863, even a victory by Lee's army at Gettysburg may have accomplished little more than extending the war by a few weeks.

In this spirit, I hope that *Chronicle of War* will help the reader toward a better understanding of the "whys" of naval and military history in general.

Paul Brewer

On 13 September 1847 the castle of Chapultepec to the west of Mexico City was stormed by American forces, leading to the fall of the Mexican capital. Chapultepec's capture opened the way to American assaults to the north-west and west of the city.

Halls of Montezuma fall to US troops in conquest of Mexico City

On 13 September 1847, a US army commanded by General Winfield Scott successfully stormed the Mexican defences to the west of Mexico City. The Mexican capital fell at dawn on 14 September.

The key to the Mexican defences facing the Americans was the castle of Chapultepec, which housed the country's military academy and stood on top of a hill that reached some 200 feet (61 m) above the surrounding terrain.

The Americans launched a three-pronged assault on the position. The first regiment to assault the walls was forced to hold its position for some time while waiting for scaling ladders to allow them to ascend. The 9th, reinforced by two additional regiments from the Volunteer Division of the American army, and the arrival of the scaling ladders, finally captured Chapultepec at around 9.30 a.m. When the Stars and Stripes appeared in place of the Mexican tricolour over the walls of Chapultepec, the commander of the Mexican army, General Antonio López de Santa Anna commented, "If we were to plant our batteries in Hell the damned Yankees would take them."

General Scott's plan of attack assumed that after the fall of Chapultepec, fresh troops would push north then west to enter the city, while the Volunteer Division would make a feint attack directly west toward the Garita de Belén. General John A. Quitman, however, pushed his attack home, at heavy cost to both his men and his staff. The Garita de Belén fell, but not the main barracks for the Mexican garrison of the city, the Ciudadela, overlooked it and prevented any further advance.

Scott's main assault, regular army troops under Brigadier General William Worth, successfully captured the Garita de San Cosme. The Mexicans had not expected the Americans to attack here and only makeshift sandbag defences were set up hurriedly after the fall of Chapultepec. These did not delay the American attackers' advance for long, and at nightfall the Garita de San Cosme was captured; American soldiers set up camp in the Alameda, a great park on the western edge of the city itself.

The city government did not want a house-to-house defence of the capital, and requested Santa Anna to leave. He respected their wishes and withdrew to Guadalupe Hidalgo, leaving Scott and his men to occupy the city the next day.

The battle was witnessed by one of the earliest recorded war correspondents, George W. Kendall, founder and editor of the New Orleans *Picayune*.

MEXICAN-AMERICAN WAR

DATES:	1846-48
COMBATANTS:	United States of America vs Mexico
FORCES ENGAGED:	USA, 60,000; Mexico, 40,000
CASUALTIES:	USA, 17,435; Mexico, 25,000
RESULT:	US victory

Radetzky marches on Italian rebels

An Austrian army commanded by Marshal Josef Radetzky defeated the Piedmontese Army at Custozza, a town near Lake Garda in the north of Italy, in a three-day battle that began on 24 July 1848. The battle represented a serious blow to Italian nationalists who had rebelled against their Austrian overlords in Milan and other cities in the north of the Italian peninsula.

The Piedmontese monarch, King Charles Albert, had mobilized his army after a rebellion in Milan chased out

> *The battle represented a serious blow to Italian nationalists who had rebelled against their Austrian overlords.*

the Austrian garrison in March 1848. Piedmont was the only state in Italy ruled by an Italian secular authority, and as such became a natural focus for those Italians who wanted an Italian national government.

The Piedmontese captured the city of Peschiera before blockading another Austrian fortress-city, Mantua. Radetzky led his forces against the centre of the Piedmontese positions, and pushed them off a range of hills that commanded the general area on the 23rd. Over the following two days, the Piedmontese attempted to recapture these hills but were driven off with heavy losses. They then retreated back to Piedmont, harassed by the Hapsburg cavalry the whole way. An armistice was agreed, with Radetzky willing to accept a return to the situation before the revolution in Milan.

Austrian Marshal Josef Radetzky von Radetz crushed the hopes of Italian nationalists to liberate Lombardy and Venezia from Austrian control in the summer of 1848.

IN BRIEF

❧ In Spain, a rebellion by supporters of the Carlist succession to the Spanish throne led to the inconclusive Battle of Pasteral in Catalonia in early 1849. The rebels found little support for their cause outside Catalonia and Aragon. The Carlists were a conservative group largely opposed to the liberal-minded regime established under the main line of the Borbón monarchs of Spain.

Chilean government wins at Loncomilla

A **civil war in** Chile, launched by the losers in a recent presidential election, ended in victory for the government forces.

The struggle was caused by political tension between the ruling authoritarian conservatives, and an emerging young liberal and wealthy bourgeoisie. For ten years, Chile had been run by a conservative former general, Manuel Bulnes Prieto. In 1851, a new election for president was held, and Bulnes' hand-picked successor, Manuel Montt Torres, emerged victorious. Five days before the inauguration of Montt in September 1851, some liberals, in the provinces of Biobío, in the central south, and Coquimbo, north of the capital Santiago, rebelled.

The defeated liberal candidate, José Maria de la Cruz Prieto, assembled an army made up of veterans of frontier campaigns against the Indians, militia troops from Biobío and Araucanian Indians. He fought against the regular Chilean army at Loncomilla on 8 December 1851 and suffered a crushing defeat in one of the bloodiest battles of Chilean history, with over 3,500 casualties.

IN BRIEF

⊰⊱ The duchies of Schleswig and Holstein, between Denmark and the German states, launched a rebellion against their Danish overlords in early 1848. The Prussian government supported the rebels, but the Danes received support from Sweden and Russia. Fighting in the conflict was largely restricted to the duchies themselves. In 1850, a settlement was achieved under which the two duchies remained part of Denmark, although with increased powers to their parliaments.

Shell guns blast Ottoman fleet as Crimean War begins

An **Ottoman fleet** was destroyed at Sinope, on the Black Sea coast of Turkey, by a Russian squadron, on 30 November 1853. This action is notable for being the first use of shell guns in naval warfare.

A dispute over the role of Russia's Tsar in protecting Christians in the Ottoman Empire resulted in a war between Russia and the Ottoman

> *The Russians opened fire on the Ottomans and within a couple of hours had destroyed all but one of the opposition. Some 3,000 Ottomans perished, and Admiral Osman Pasha was taken prisoner. Russian losses were limited to about 300.*

Empire that broke out in July 1853 when a Russian army crossed the Danube border and occupied the largely Christian principalities of Moldavia and Wallachia. The move provoked a general European crisis, as the French, under Napoleon III, had been agitating to replace the Russian Tsar as protector of Christians in the Ottoman Empire.

The Ottoman army checked the Russian advance, although no major battles were fought. The most influential event occurred in the war at sea.

A Russian squadron cruising off the Turkish coast discovered that their Ottoman counterparts had anchored in the port of Sinope in order to shelter from bad weather. The Russian commander, Vice Admiral Pavel Nakhimov, took the decision to attack. The Ottomans – 12 ships in total – were deployed in the typical crescent formation they adopted in port. Nakhimov ordered his ships – eight vessels, six of them larger than any of the Ottoman vessels – to sail into the harbour in a two-line formation. The Russians opened fire on the Ottomans and within a couple of hours had destroyed all but one of the opposition. Some 3,000 Ottomans perished, and Admiral Osman Pasha was taken prisoner. Russian losses were limited to about 300.

The Russian achievement shocked both France and Britain, to whom the Ottoman Empire turned for support. On 28 March 1854, Britain and France declared war on Russia, thus beginning the Crimean War.

CRIMEAN WAR

DATES:	1853-56
COMBATANTS:	Britain, France, Ottoman Empire, Sardinia-Piedmont vs Russia
FORCES ENGAGED:	Allies (estimate), 370,000; Russians (estimate), 400,000
CASUALTIES:	Allies, 145,000; Russia, 250,000
RESULT:	Allied victory

On 30 November 1853, Russian warships used shell guns to utterly destroy a Ottoman squadron at the Black Sea port of Sinope, thus beginning a new era in naval warfare.

Britain and France have the upper hand in war with Russia

After nine months of conflict, Britain and France have the strategic advantage in a war with Russia, the allies' strategy having been advanced on two fronts, in the Baltic and in the Black Sea.

The war began as a military expedition to drive the Russians out of Moldavia and Wallachia, but the Russian Tsar withdrew his troops even before the arrival of British and French forces.

The allied army, numbering about 60,000, then landed at Kalamata Bay, in the Crimea, in September 1854. The objective was to capture the main Russian naval port in the Black Sea, at Sevastopol, but Russian defenders blocked their route at the Alma river. The allies attacked, but did not co-ordinate their moves properly. As a result, the British suffered needlessly heavy casualties in driving the Russians out of their position.

Although Sevastopol was placed under siege in October, the Russian commander at the Alma, Prince Menshikov, kept part of his army in the field. On 25 October, he led a raid against the British base of Balaclava, on the right of the allied siege lines. The Russians succeeded in capturing allied positions on the Causeway Heights overlooking Balaclava and their cavalry advanced against the port, but they were defeated by the "Thin Red Line" of the 93rd Highlanders. Meanwhile, another cavalry force directed at the rear of the British siege lines was engaged by the British Heavy Brigade and driven off.

British troops scale the heights overlooking the Alma river during the Battle of Alma that opened the way for the Allied forces to lay siege to the Russian port of Sevastopol on 20 September 1854.

The Battle of Balaclava is best remembered, though, for a British military disaster. The Russians were removing the guns from the redoubts the Ottomans had defended along the Causeway Heights. The British commander, Lord Raglan, sent an order to the Light Brigade to stop the Russians doing so. Its commander, Lord Cardigan, did not have the same view of the battlefield, and the only guns he could see were those positioned by the Russians in the valley between the Causeway Heights and the Sapoune Heights. Disastrously, he charged these, and lost half his command in a needless effort.

Eleven days later, on 5 November and in thick fog, Menshikov attacked the British again, at Inkerman. The Russians suffered extremely heavily in this battle and it marked the end of Menshikov's career. As winter settled in, both sides turned their attention to the siege.

Florence Nightingale and Mary Seacole

News of the horrific conditions experienced by wounded British soldiers in the Crimea during the autumn of 1854 led to two enterprising women arriving to offer help. Florence Nightingale was the daughter of a wealthy family who rebuffed their concerns about her social status to embark on a career as a nurse. She arrived in Scutari, the site of the main British hospital in Turkey,

and established a much more hygienic environment for the wounded cared for there. However, overcrowding and the proximity of sewers condemned her efforts to a degree of futility, as the death rate was unaffected by her efforts. A sanitary commission sent out in March 1855 reduced the death rate more effectively.

Mary Seacole was a woman of

Scots-Jamaican descent, who had run "hospitals" known as "hotels" for cholera victims in Panama. In January 1855, Seacole set up a similar establishment for officers in the Crimea, as well as tending to the wounded on the battlefields of the war. Unlike Nightingale's hospital, Seacole's "hotel" was a private initiative that charged for its services.

The Light Brigade: who blundered?

The Charge of the Light Brigade has achieved mythical status as a military blunder. Ever since the day it happened, there has been heated debate as to who was responsible.

Lord Raglan, the British commander-in-chief, created confusion by sending two separate orders without specifying the same details in the second order as he had done in the first.

Lord Lucan, the commander of the British cavalry, did not interpret the order correctly, nor did he question the interpretation put on it by the aide who brought it to him. However, he did not have the same view of the battlefield as Lord Raglan.

Lord Cardigan, the commander of the Light Brigade, did not discuss the order with Lucan, but did point out that he would be leading his men into a distinctly disadvantageous situation. Furthermore, he failed to keep in contact with the Heavy Brigade, advancing on his right.

Captain Louis Nolan, the aide who brought the order, gave an over-emotional display in explaining Lord Raglan's intent to Lord Lucan, possibly directing Lucan's gaze in the wrong direction.

Richard Caton Woodville's painting shows British cavalrymen of the 17th Lancers, one of five regiments in the Light Brigade, charge the Russian guns at Balaclava on 25 October 1854.

IN BRIEF

❦ In China, a major rebellion broke out when a Christian-inspired sect, opposed to idolatry, formed a military organization that defeated an attempt by the imperial authorities to destroy them in December 1850. In the following year, Hung Hsiu-ch'üan, the sect's leader, who believed himself to be the Younger Brother of Jesus Christ, proclaimed himself the Heavenly King and established the Kingdom of Heavenly Peace. (Heavenly Peace is the English translation of T'ai-ping, which gave the rebels their name.) In March 1853, the Taipings took over Nanking, which they made their capital. A subsequent attempt to capture Peking failed, marking the high-water mark of the rebellion.

The Taiping Rebels fought ferociously against Imperial troops.

The decisive naval war in the Baltic

Allied plans to launch a naval attack on the Russian capital, St Petersburg, together with the threat of Austria joining the war on the allied side, convinced Tsar Alexander II that continuing the war into 1856 would lead to total Russian defeat. At a meeting of his council of advisers on 29 January 1856, he ordered his ministers to negotiate for peace.

The French and British had sent a large fleet to the Baltic in 1854, which compelled the Russians to withdraw their own vessels into the fortified ports of Sveaborg and Kronstadt. With the coming of winter, when the sea would freeze over, the allied squadron withdrew. In 1855, however, it returned and this time used floating batteries and mortar-equipped gunboats to destroy the Russian dockyard facilities at Sveaborg.

The success of the Sveaborg operation inspired the Great Armament – a collection of newly built batteries and gunboats specifically designed to bombard a fortified naval dockyard into submission – which targeted both the main Baltic naval base at Kronstadt and the nearby capital St Petersburg. Faced with the threat of this, the Russian government concluded it had no choice but to seek an end to the war.

The Russian defences after the surrender of Sevastopol on 9 September 1855 included guns on naval carriages deployed on the landward side of the port.

The capture of the fort at Kinburn on 17 October 1855 was the last major operation in the Baltic Sea, and involved the use of armoured floating batteries.

Sevastopol falls after lengthy siege

After a siege lasting nearly a year, the garrison of the Russian naval base of Sevastopol abandoned it to the allied armies on 11 September 1855. The evacuation was caused by the capture of the Kornilov Redoubt, a key position on the Malakoff Hill overlooking the city, during an allied assault.

The French had pushed forward their trenches to within 84 feet (26 m) of the Russian defences, and synchronized their assault using watches. Although the fighting was hard, by throwing a whole corps into the assault – some 10,000 men – the French simply overwhelmed the defenders.

The allied success has come after months of frustration. Following a failed assault on Sevastopol in October 1854 and the Russian assault on the allied siege lines in November of the same year, both sides devoted more of their effort to coping with the harsh weather than to pursuing the siege aggressively. Disease and bad weather had badly affected the allies. The ordinary British soldier suffered terribly, especially compared to his French counterpart, who had at least been provided with timber huts. One British regiment, the 28th Foot, 783 strong when it embarked for the Crimea, lost 265 men dead to disease, malnutrition and exposure alone, before any losses to enemy action.

When the late Russian Tsar, Nicholas, learned of the difficulties the weather was causing the allied troops his confidence had risen. He believed that "Generals January and February" would transform the Russian chances of victory dramatically. However, his generals in the field were less enthusiastic about their chances and, after the failure of a probe at Eupatoria on 17 February, a new commander, Prince Dmitri Gorchakov, was appointed.

The siege was an impressive engineering effort on both sides. There had been a number of major assaults on the Russian defences prior to the final one, and the one of 18 June 1855 in particular was intended to capture the city for the allies. Some 10,000 men from both sides were killed or wounded in this attack.

A Russian attack on the French in August, at the Tchernaya river, was intended as a last attempt to break the siege. If it failed, Gorchakov believed nothing could save Sevastopol. Reinforcements from the rest of Russia arrived in the Crimea after long marches across the Ukraine and were barely fit

The French had pushed forward their trenches to within 84 feet (26 m) of the Russian defences, and synchronized their assault using watches. Although the fighting was hard, by throwing a whole corps into the assault – some 10,000 men – the French simply overwhelmed the defenders.

for service; the same problems of deaths through disease and lack of supplies affected the Russians as the allies.

As it was, the attack failed miserably, in part because Gorchakov did not expect it to succeed. It was a gesture, not a serious attempt and was followed by a 20-day allied bombardment that ended with the assault and capture of the Kornilov Redoubt.

Stubborn Ottomans aid allied victory in Crimean War

The Ottoman armed forces, having begun their war with Russia badly, eventually played an important role in the allied victory.

The Ottomans fought on three fronts in the war. Their first campaigns were against the Russians in the principalities of Moldavia and Wallachia. Here, they managed to halt the Russian advance, although they could not on their own reverse the Russian occupation of these vassal states of the Ottoman Empire.

The Ottomans were also involved in an offensive into the areas of Georgia and Armenia controlled by Russia. Here the Ottomans experienced less success than they did in the Balkans. In 1854, three battles resulted in the Ottomans being forced back into the city of Kars. However, this strongpoint would defy the Russians until after Sevastopol had fallen, in part owing to the efforts of a British officer seconded to the Ottomans, Nova Scotian-born William Fenwick Williams.

The garrison managed to keep the Russians out of Kars from the beginning of the siege in June 1855 until the end of it in November the same year.

Ottoman artillery pounds Russian positions around the town of Kars in the Caucasus Mountains. The Russian siege of the Ottoman-defended town lasted a total of five months.

Rebellion in India challenges British rule

A major uprising in the subcontinent of India attempted to bring an end to British rule in India, using the Mogul emperor as their figurehead. The backbone of the uprising was provided by the native troops employed by the British East India Company, who mutinied against their officers and took up arms against the British. The mutiny was largely restricted to the Ganges valley between Delhi and Bengal.

Such was the fear of "a fate worse than death" that British officers attacked by mutineers were known to kill their wives before using the last bullet on themselves.

On 10 May 1857, two regiments of native troops, part of the British East India Company's army in India, rebelled against their officers and launched the biggest challenge to British rule in India since the victory at Plassey had established British control of the subcontinent in 1757. There was a rumour among the troops that rifles issued to them used cartridges greased with the fat of cows and pigs, animals whose consumption was forbidden to the Hindu and Moslem soldiers in the ranks. Regardless of whether this was true, the rumour united traditional rivals in hostility toward their officers. The initial uprising occurred at Meerut, 40 miles (64 km) from Delhi, where a garrison of about 4,000 troops was equally divided between Indian and British forces.

The rebels marched on Delhi, where the last Mogul emperor, Bahadur Shah Zafar, lived. Bahadur had been told by the British authorities that he would be the last emperor and that after his death his sons would not be allowed to inherit his throne. Bahadur accepted this with good grace, but his sons were less enthusiastic. When the native troops, or sepoys, arrived in Delhi, Bahadur found himself pushed into the position of figurehead for the rebellion.

The rebels also got support from the heir to the other great pre-British Indian state, the Maratha Confederacy. The adopted son of the last head of state, Nana Sahib, lived near the garrison town of Cawnpore. When the native troops of that locality mutinied, he joined them, and may have been connected with the subsequent massacre there. Other rulers backing the uprising included the Rani of Jhansi and the Emir Haji Imdadullah.

The British forces in India first sought to topple Bahadur Shah Zafar with troops drawn from the garrisons at Meerut and Simla, who marched slowly from their bases towards the traditional northern Indian capital, Delhi. One reason for the slowness of their advance was the desire to 'punish' Indians by pillaging and murdering in all the towns and villages along the route. The rebels were defeated in the field on 8 June at Badli-ke-Serai, and the British reached Delhi on 1 July, where they began a partial blockade, the assault being delayed until the arrival of the siege train on 4 September. Further reinforcements had

> The rebels were defeated in the field on 8 June at Badli-ke-Serai, and the British reached Delhi on 1 July, where they began a partial blockade.

been on the march from other garrisons in India during the preceding two months, so that by 14 September, the day of the assault, a substantial army of 15,000 had been built up. The imperial palace was occupied by troops loyal to the British on 21 September and Bahadur Shah Zafar was captured, as were his sons. The latter were shot in cold blood by a British officer, Major William Hodson, and their heads were presented by Hodson to Bahadur.

Meanwhile, the European members of the garrison at Lucknow managed to hold out against the rebels. Shortly after news of the Meerut garrison's mutiny reached Lucknow on 14 May 1857, General Henry Lawrence, the commander there, fortified the Residency in order to make a stand until relief should come. He managed to disarm or chase out of the garrison compound all disloyal troops, but the whole of the former kingdom of Oudh, of which Lucknow was the capital, was in revolt.

Lawrence had done his work badly, and the entire Residency was vulnerable to rebel musket and artillery fire. Casualties among

The Secundra Bagh, Lucknow: still littered with skeletons months after the relief in November 1857.

In February 1858, two British forces moved against Lucknow and Jhansi, both of which fell to the British: Lucknow in March and Jhansi in April. From Lucknow, the British concentrated on driving the remaining rebels north toward Nepal, but by then the Rani of Jhansi had joined with Tantia Tope to

Tantia Tope's was the first force dealt with. He attempted to recapture Cawnpore, but was defeated in battle on 6 December 1857.

form the most powerful force remaining to the rebels.

The rebels tried to make a stand at Kunch on 6 May 1858, and at Kalpi on 22 May, but were beaten twice, retreating in the direction of Gwalior, a city controlled by a native prince loyal to the British. This the rebels occupied at the beginning of June and the victor of Kunch and Kalpi, General Sir Hugh Rose, advanced to recapture it. On three successive days of fighting, 17–19 June, Rose eliminated the last main field army of rebels. The Rani of Jhansi was killed but Tantia Tope escaped to wage a campaign of guerrilla warfare that lasted until he was captured in April 1859. His execution on 18 April 1859 can be taken as the last act of the Indian Mutiny. British rule was firmly re-established, but the former regime of the East India Company was replaced by one directly controlled by the government in London.

the defenders were heavy, including Lawrence himself on 4 July 1857.

Control of Oudh was important to challenging British rule in India, with a major centre of rebellion next to the Great Trunk Road between Delhi and Calcutta, but the rebels here were unable to co-ordinate their activities with resistance elsewhere. A rebellion at Allahabad failed owing to the prompt arrival of British troops under General Henry Havelock, who recaptured Cawnpore on 17 July, pausing here before leaving to relieve Lucknow in mid September. But this force was not large enough to break out again and it took the arrival of a second column of reinforcements to enable the defenders of Lucknow to escape.

Relief of Lucknow

When British troops reached Lucknow on 18 November 1857, the garrison was able to evacuate the Residency it had defended for six months and rejoin the main British forces at Cawnpore, along the Great Trunk Road. British resistance kept the rebels from seizing control of this important road and separating the two main centres of British military strength in northern India.

In December 1857, there remained three main concentrations of rebels: in Oudh, Lucknow was still in rebel hands; in Jhansi,

the Rani there controlled an important force; and Cawnpore was threatened by a large, but untrained, army led by Tantia Tope.

Tantia Tope's was the first force dealt with. He attempted to recapture Cawnpore, but was defeated in battle on 6 December 1857, which was the last chance the rebels had of gaining control of part of the Great Trunk Road.

The weapons of the Mutineers' armies included modern British rifles and Indian elephants.

French, Piedmontese drive Austrians out of Milan

An allied army of French and Piedmontese soldiers has successfully fought and outmanoeuvred their Austrian opponents out of the capital of the kingdom of Lombardy-Venetia, which they entered triumphantly on 8 June 1859. The liberation of Milan is the result of an allied victory in the Battle of Magenta on 4 June 1859. The war is the result of the ambitions of the King of Piedmont, Vittorio Emanuele II of the House of Savoy, which has ruled the Piedmontese kingdom from Turin since 1720, and other Italian nationalists. Austria controlled Lombardy-Venetia, directly ruled by the Austrian emperor, Franz Josef II.

After a secret agreement between the French emperor, Napoleon III, and the Piedmontese prime minister, the Count Cavour, was reached in 1858, both Piedmont and Austria began looking for an excuse to go to war. Austrian leaders rightly believed that if they could force an aggressive act by Piedmont, Napoleon III would stay neutral in any resulting war – but they made a mistake. Piedmont had been increasing the size of its army as well as arming militia

groups of Italian nationalists when, on 23 April 1859, the Austrian government presented its Piedmontese counterpart with an ultimatum: the Piedmontese were to disarm the militia and reduce the size of their armed forces; only three days were granted for an answer. Instead, the Piedmontese declared war on 26 April, and Austria ended up appearing as a bully. Napoleon III immediately joined Piedmont, and French troops began arriving in Genoa on 3 May.

The Austrians had assembled a sizeable army, which crossed the River Ticino into Piedmont on 8 May. However, heavy rains and a lack of enthusiasm on the part of its commander, Marshal Count Gyulai, led to a withdrawal.

The first battle of the war between allied and Austrian forces took place at Montebello on 20 May, when the outnumbered allies, through sheer aggressiveness, defeated the Austrians. A similar result occurred at the Battle of Palestro on 30 May.

Magenta, about 12 miles (20 km) west of Milan, was the first major battle of the war between the main armies. The Austrians had established a position on

Giuseppe Garibaldi wearing the Red Shirt that became the symbol of his volunteer corps fighting for Italian unity.

the heights overlooking the River Ticino. At the centre of the Austrian position was the road leading to the town of Magenta. Napoleon III adopted a plan involving a crossing of the Ticino under fire, while part of the French army advanced on the right flank of the Austrians, from the north. The battle soon degenerated

French troops charge through the streets of Magenta during the battle of 4 June 1859. Their high morale was a key to their victory. At one point, the Austrians had been so confident they had halted the French that they telegraphed word of their victory to Vienna.

into a disjointed engagement as neither commander had sufficient control of his troops. The Austrians fought hard, especially in house-to-house fighting in Magenta, but French aggression and superior leadership on the part of sergeants and junior officers triumphed.

Marshal Gyulai regarded the defeat as far more significant than it actually was, and ordered a complete withdrawal of his army from Lombardy, retiring to an area known as the Quadrilateral, in the western Veneto and eastern Lombardy.

ITALIAN INDEPENDENCE WAR OF 1859

DATES: 1859
COMBATANTS: France and Piedmont vs Austria
FORCES INVOLVED: Allies, 200,000; Austria, 250,000
CASUALTIES: Allies, 25,000; Austria, 29,000
RESULT: Allied victory

IN BRIEF

⁂ A war between Persia and Britain broke out after the Persian army occupied the Afghan city of Herat. The British bombarded the port of Bushire, on the Persian Gulf, and landed a small army which defeated a Persian one at Kooshab in February 1857.

⁂ In April 1857, in West Africa, the African leader El Hadj Umar Tall, of the Toucouleur kingdom, launched a war against the Khasso that brought him into conflict with French plans to expand westward from Dakar and north from Niger. He attacked the Khasso at Medina fort, but after a 97-day blockade, a French force led by General Louis Faidherbe arrived with supplies to break the siege in July 1857.

⁂ On 1 May 1857, the self-proclaimed president of Nicaragua, American William Walker, surrendered to opponents of his regime. He was handed over to the American authorities and left the country. Walker had been invited to Nicaragua by one of the factions in a civil war there in 1855, but instead of helping his allies win, he defeated their enemies and took power for himself. In 1860 he then turned his attention to Honduras, where he was captured and shot in September 1860.

⁂ In Venezuela, the Federal War broke out in February 1859, between the oligarchical central government and a mixture of peasant and regional leaders. The war began with victories for the rebels, but then degenerated into a guerrilla war where small groups banded together temporarily to fight battles or simply to burn and pillage areas controlled by the opposition. The war was ended in 1863, with a victory for the rebels.

French African colonial troops were an important part of the army General Louis Faidherbe used to build an empire in West Africa.

Bloody victory at Solferino creates Red Cross

The allied army of Piedmont and France achieved a major victory over their Austrian opponents at the Battle of Solferino on 24 June 1859. In subsequent treaty negotiations, the Austrian emperor ceded Lombardy to the king of Piedmont.

The battle was a bizarre mix of intention and blundering. Franz Josef II, the Austrian emperor, dismissed the defeated commander of the Battle of Magenta on 17 June and took titular command of his army in the field, whilst yielding actual authority to a council of generals. When the generals requested an offensive that the emperor was not happy about he conceded to their expert knowledge.

The advancing allies, expecting no opposition, were surprised to find the Austrians crossing the Mincio river on 22 June 1859. The Austrians were able to occupy all the dominating high ground around Solferino before the allies could organize their attacks.

The battle was effectively a savage melee across a front of about 5½ miles (9 km). A Swiss observer, Henri Dunant, remembered: "Austrians and allies trampled each other under foot, slaughtered each other on a carpet of bloody corpses, smashed each other with rifle butts, crushed each other's skulls, disembowelled each other with sabre and bayonet."

By nightfall, the Austrians were in a retreat that was only saved from being a rout by the actions of General Count Von Benedek, whose rearguard action delayed the allied pursuit.

Dunant's published memoir of the battle and its aftermath, including the makeshift hospitals that tried to save as many wounded as they could, led to a Geneva conference and the founding of the International Red Cross in 1863.

Emperor Napoleon III of France gives orders to one of his subordinates during the battle of Solferino, 24 June 1859. *The Battle of Solferino, 24th June 1859* (oil on canvas), by Adolphe Yvon (1817-93).

British, French storm China

On **18 October** 1860 a British force set fire to the Old Summer Palace of China and burned it to the ground, bringing to an end a two-year conflict that had its origins in 1856.

In that year, Chinese officials seized a British-registered ship, the *Arrow*, which led to the bombardment of the Taku forts at Tientsin in 1858, and a treaty that improved the rights of Westerners to trade with China. However, Chinese unwillingness to complete all the formalities required by this treaty led to further armed action on the part of Britain and France against China. The Taku forts were again bombarded, and this time a significant military force was landed in August 1860. These troops carried out a successful assault on the Taku forts on 21 August before advancing on Peking, the Chinese imperial capital. This was reached on 26 September and the city surrendered on 6 October.

The victorious soldiers looted the Summer Palace of the emperor, and on 18 October, following the negotiation of a further treaty that ratified the unfinished formalities of the 1858 treaty, they were ordered to burn it.

Chinese soldiers lie dead around the defences of one of the Taku forts that guarded the port at Tientsin until their capture by French and British forces on 21 August 1860.

IN BRIEF

❧ A brief war between Spain and Morocco in 1859–60 broke out after the Moroccans raided the outskirts of Ceuta and Melilla, cities controlled by Spain. When the Spanish invaded in order to seize territory from Morocco they defeated the Moors at Castillejos on 1 January 1860, and subsequently laid siege to the city of Tétuan. A second battle on 23 March 1860 resulted in another Spanish victory, after which the Moors agreed to a peace treaty, granting Spain all its demands.

❧ A revolution in the Kingdom of the Two Sicilies, in southern Italy, in April 1860, led to the invasion of the kingdom by Italian nationalist Giuseppe Garibaldi and his thousand Redshirts. On 20 July, Garibaldi's army defeated their Neapolitan enemies at the Battle of Milazzo, which ended resistance to him on the island of Sicily. His army then invaded the peninsular part of the kingdom on 19 August. The final victory was won at the Volturno on 2–3 October 1860. In late October, the kingdom of the Two Sicilies voted to join the House of Savoy's Kingdom of Italy.

❧ In Colombia, an important battle occurred at Manizales on 28 August 1860. The fighting was part of an uprising against the central government started by secessionist leaders in the Valle de Cauca, west and south-west of Bogotá. After some initial success, the rebels were defeated.

America begins Civil War

The festering crisis over control of Fort Sumter, in the middle of the harbour of Charleston, South Carolina, was resolved on 13 April 1861 after the fort surrendered following a 36-hour bombardment. The fort had been occupied

The crisis began on 21 December 1860, when the legislature of the state of South Carolina formally seceded from the United States of America.

by a garrison of US troops, while its attackers were members of the armies of rebellious American states that had formed the Confederate States of America.

The crisis began on 20 December 1860, when the legislature of the state of South Carolina formally seceded from the United States of America. Six other states joined South Carolina by the beginning of February 1861 and their governments began occupying federal buildings within their borders almost immediately.

The commander of the US fortresses defending Charleston harbour led the other Federal garrisons to Fort Sumter on 27 December 1860, conceding the rest of the fortifications to South Carolina. The Rebel government, acting in support of South Carolina, assembled an army at Charleston and batteries trained their guns on Fort Sumter. On 4 April 1861, the recently inaugurated president of the United States, Abraham Lincoln, ordered the sending of supplies to the garrison, but South Carolina officials were warned of the approaching supply ship. Faced with this news, the commander of the Rebel troops, General P.G.T. Beauregard, issued an ultimatum to the defenders of Fort Sumter, requiring them to evacuate the fort. When they refused, the bombardment commenced at 4.30 a.m. on 12 April.

The Confederate "Stars and Bars" flag flies over Fort Sumter, the fort in Charleston harbour that triggered the outbreak of a civil war.

Yankee soldiers from the 79th New York, taken prisoner in the battle along Bull Run, pose for the camera at a Rebel prison in Charleston Harbor.

Federal advance to Richmond beaten at Bull Run

The army of the Rebel government of the Confederate States of America won a significant victory over the forces of the United States at the Battle of Bull Run on 21 July 1861. The Federal forces had advanced from Washington DC against the main Rebel army in Virginia, which was protecting the Confederacy's new capital at Richmond, as it was generally believed on the Federal side if Richmond was taken, the Confederacy would collapse.

The Rebel forces arrayed themselves along Bull Run, a stream that ran between the towns of Centreville and Manassas. General Irvin McDowell, the Federal commander, did not realize, as he advanced, that the main Rebel force, the Army of the Potomac, commanded by General P.G.T. Beauregard, had been reinforced. The Confederate Army of the Shenandoah had evaded the Federal army confronting it. Each side numbered around 30,000 on the day of battle.

Both sides had intended to attack, using an identical plan. Their left wings would make a feint attack, while their right wings would try to outflank the enemy. By virtue of moving first, McDowell took the initiative. Beauregard attempted to get his army going forward, but the commander of the Army of the Shenandoah, General Joseph E. Johnston, realized that the Federal forces had taken the initiative, and the Rebel plan was abandoned.

Fierce fighting occurred on Henry House Hill, just west of Bull Run. The Rebel commanders rushed reinforcements there and a confused action was terminated when Rebel troops dressed in blue – the most common colour of uniform at this time among Federal troops – were mistaken for Federal troops and captured a key Federal artillery position. The Federal forces eventually began a rout that only finished once they had got past Centreville.

The Federal casualties amounted to around 3,000 men; the Rebels lost just under 2,000.

Wilson's Creek battle restores Rebel hopes

Rebel sympathizers in the divided border state of Missouri received a fillip on 10 August 1861, when Rebel forces defeated a smaller, but better-equipped, Federal army at the Battle of Wilson's Creek. The Federal commander, fiery General Nathaniel Lyon, whose efforts during previous months had secured St Louis and eastern Missouri for the Federal cause, was killed in the battle.

Lyon was opposed by an army made up of the Missouri State Guard, commanded by General Sterling Price, and the Confederate Army of the West, commanded by Brigadier General Ben McCulloch.

Lyon's plan was too complex: to send a large column on a flanking march to appear behind the Rebel forces deployed near Wilson's Creek; while this manoeuvre was being carried out, Lyon himself would attack the Rebel front with his main body. He counted on his better-equipped troops to force a successful end to the battle.

In the event, the flanking column was stopped and defeated by McCulloch's Rebels, while Price's Missourians fended off Lyon's assaults. As the Rebels gained the upper hand in the battle, Lyon was killed attempting to rally his men. The Federal forces kept better order than they had managed during their retreat from Bull Run. Missouri is now territorially, as well as politically, divided.

Troops under General Lyon (Federal) and Colonel Sigel (Rebel) at the Battle of Wilson's Creek on 10 August 1861.

IN BRIEF

❧ The Federal Navy scored a major strategic success on 7 November 1861 when a squadron of ships bombarded two Rebel forts at the entrance to Port Royal Sound in South Carolina. Troops were then landed from accompanying transports to occupy the forts and take control of the surrounding area. A naval base was established which enabled the blockade of the southern ports in South Carolina and Georgia, proclaimed by President Lincoln on 19 April to become effective.

Ironclads fight for first time

The CSS *Virginia* (left) and the USS *Monitor* (right) traded fire for several hours before the Rebel vessel withdrew. Both ships suffered largely superficial damage.

On 9 March 1862, two ships armoured with iron on their hulls engaged in combat, the first such fight in history. The CSS *Virginia* of the Rebel navy and the USS *Monitor* of the Federal navy traded shots for around three hours before the *Virginia* broke off the action and retired to its base at Norfolk, Virginia.

The *Virginia* went into action for the first time only the previous day, 8 March, having been built using the hull of the USS *Merrimack*, a frigate that had been scuttled and burned along with many of the other buildings and stores of Gosport Navy Yard on 19–20 April 1861. But the engines and hull of the *Merrimack* were still seaworthy, so Rebel builders erected a wooden roof sheathed in iron plates on the hull. The ship was armed with ten guns: one in the bow, one astern and the remainder as broadsides. A iron ram 2 feet (60 cm) long was installed on the bow.

Having been rebuilt, the *Virginia* was taken almost straightaway into action by her commander, Franklin Buchanan. Buchanan sailed her out of Norfolk with the high tide on 8 March 1862 and headed for the nearest enemy, five large wooden warships that lay to the north in Hampton Roads. She sank two of them, the *Cumberland* and the *Congress*. With the tide falling fast, two of the other Federal vessels ran aground, but the *Virginia* drew too much water to finish them off. She retreated to Norfolk, in order to repair leaks, planning to return as the tide rose the next day.

Overnight, however, the Federal answer to the *Virginia* arrived. The USS *Monitor* was a more innovative ship, having been designed as an ironclad from the very beginning, and was equipped with a revolving turret in place of the traditional broadside armament.

The battle began around 9 a.m. on 9 March. The *Virginia* approached the USS *Minnesota*, a wooden ship like the *Cumberland* and *Congress*, that had run aground. The *Monitor* was all that stood between the two ships, but it proved to be enough. The *Virginia*'s smokestack had been riddled by shots the day before, making it difficult to keep her engine's boilers running, thus allowing the *Monitor* to out-manoeuvre her. Quickly discovering that her guns could not penetrate the armour of the *Monitor*, the *Virginia* tried to ram, but the boiler problems and the lack of the 2-foot- (60-cm-) long ram (lost in the *Cumberland* the day before) meant the blow had little effect. The battle ended in a draw.

Outnumbered Federal force crushes Rebel foe

General Samuel Curtis defeated a Rebel force superior in numbers at the Battle of Pea Ridge, in northern Arkansas, on 8 March 1862. The effect of this victory has been to eliminate any serious threat to take Missouri out of the Federal.

Curtis's opponent was General Earl

A Federal corporal in full equipment. The Rebels could only envy such plenty.

Van Dorn, who combined three forces in the Confederate Army of the West: General Ben McCulloch's Arkansas and Texas division, General Sterling Price's Missouri troops and a brigade of Native Americans recruited from the Choctaw, Creek and Cherokee who lived in Indian territory to the west of Arkansas. Curtis had advanced against Price during the previous winter, forcing the badly supplied Missouri contingent out of the state and into northern Arkansas.

Van Dorn devised a plan involving a night march that would place his force to the rear of Curtis's men. Although he was successful, he then divided his army hoping to turn both flanks of the Federal position, but Curtis split his forces as well. The force led by McCulloch was stopped trying to attack the main Federal position well before Van Dorn and the rest of the army was in action. McCulloch and his second-in-command were killed, and his third-in-command was captured.

Van Dorn and Price, meanwhile, did not press their attacks hard enough, in part owing to the clouds of gunpowder smoke that hung over the battlefield – neither side could see the other properly.

By nightfall, the Rebels had gained nothing, and were short of supplies, with the Federal Army between them and their supply wagons. The Federal attack the next day caused the Rebels to retreat in disarray.

Two Rebels, one holding a pistol, photographed as a memento for their families. In 1861, in both north and south, Americans rushed to volunteer on the assumption the war would be short.

IN BRIEF

◈ General Ulysses S. Grant achieved a key victory by capturing two Rebel forts in Tennessee. The first of these forts, Fort Henry, surrendered on 6 February 1862, after gunboats had subjected it to a lengthy bombardment. At nearby Fort Donelson, after a Rebel attempt to break out had failed, its commander, General John B. Floyd, escaped from the fort, leaving most of his troops to surrender to Grant on 16 February.

◈ A sizeable French fleet, accompanied by British allies, joined Spanish forces at the Mexican city of Vera Cruz on 8 January 1862, launching an invasion of Mexico at a time when the United States was engaged in its Civil War. The French, British and Spanish were seeking a resumption of Mexican payments on foreign debt, which the Mexican government had suspended on 17 July 1861.

Ironclads and the steel navy

The celebrated Battle of Hampton Roads started a new era in naval warfare, in which armour was challenged by guns and shells, and which persisted until the development of aircraft and submarines altered combat at sea still further.

Dents in the turret of the USS *Monitor* prove the ability of iron armour to keep out the shot fired by powerful guns at close range.

The CSS ***Virginia*** and the USS *Monitor* were by no means the first ironclad warships. The first such vessels, built by the French Navy and used in the Crimean War, were floating batteries – barges mounting guns whose sides were covered with iron plates. It was a simple step to add the plates to a steam warship, and the French built the first such ironclad, the broadside ironclad *Gloire*, one of a class of three ships.

When the *Gloire* entered service in 1860, the British Royal Navy was the largest fleet in the world. They were aware of what the French were building and were already at work on their own version. Whereas the French ship was a wooden-hulled ship with armour plates arranged in a belt along her sides – like the floating batteries – the British class, the Warriors, were iron-hulled with a similar, if shorter, belt of armour.

The use of armour on warships coincided with a number of other important changes to naval warfare, each change having some influence on the others. The development of naval shell guns, first used at the Battle of Sinope in 1853, seemed to threaten wooden ships. Armour was the counter to this, but the long belts needed to cover the length of a ship's side were expensive. It was

more efficient to put the guns in a turret that could swivel to cover both broadsides of the ship, which reduced the number of guns needed and allowed the armour protection to cover them completely. The first warship to have a turret, the USS *Monitor*, also was involved in the first battle between ironclad warships, the Battle of Hampton Roads in March 1862.

The cumulative effect of all these changes was ultimately to revolutionize ship design. At one end of this revolution lay the Battle of Sinope, fought between ships clearly resembling the battle fleet led by Lord Nelson at Trafalgar; at the other end lay HMS *Colossus*, which entered service in 1886 and was a turret ship almost completely without masts.

Although the American Civil War was the first conflict to feature a battle between ironclads, the lack of a significant iron industry in the Rebel states, and of any

substantial pre-war navy, meant that most battles involving ironclads involved no more than one or two Rebel ones. The main naval battles all involved a fleet attacking a

> The first warship to have a turret, the USS *Monitor*, also was involved in the first battle between iron-clad warships, the Battle of Hampton Roads in March 1862.

defended port, such as the battles of New Orleans (1862), Mobile Bay and Charleston (both 1864). The first battle between fleets of ironclads occurred in European waters, during the Seven Weeks' War in 1866 which involved Austria, Prussia and Italy. The Italians had 12 ironclads, the

Part of the crew of the USS *Monitor* gets some fresh air in port. The *Monitor* warship suffered from poor ventilation, and its low freeboard made it unsuitable for operations in high seas.

The Peruvian ironclad *Huascar* engages two Chilean vessels, the *Blanco Encalada* and the *Cochrane*, during the battle of Angamos on 8 October 1879. The *Huascar*'s ability to manoeuvre was severely compromised after her helm was damaged by Chilean gunfire early in the battle.

Austro-Hungarians seven. Since gunfire seemed to lack the penetration against armoured vessels sufficient to sink them, success came from ramming enemy ships. The Austro-Hungarians sank two of the Italian ironclads, while suffering no losses, although ships on both sides were badly damaged by gunfire. The Austro-Hungarians' ramming tactics influenced naval warfare for decades after.

There were few battles involving ironclads in the years that followed, although those that did occur were carefully studied. One engagement, the Battle of Callao, between Peru and Spain, resembled those of Mobile Bay or Charleston in the American Civil War, with a fleet of ocean-going ships attacking a defended port. Both sides had ironclads, but these did not engage each other heavily. In 1877 a battle between two British wooden warships and the mutinous crew of Peruvian ironclad *Huascar* ended in a draw. The effectiveness of iron armour was clear. Over 400 shots were fired at the *Huascar*, 50 struck her, but only one penetrated the armour. Peru was involved in the next major actions involving ironclads, in the War of the Pacific (1879–84). The *Huascar* engaged her Chilean opponents in two battles, the naval Battle of Iquique and the Battle of Angamos. Only the second

involved ironclads on both sides and ended with the capture of the *Huascar*, which was heavily outnumbered six ships to one.

The lack of much combat meant that numerous different theories were applied to ship design, making the Ironclad Era one of the most fascinating to look at in terms of sheer visual variety. The arrangement of the guns was a major matter for debate. Some ships were fitted with turrets, while

> The first naval action involving a steel warship was fought during a civil war in Brazil in April 1894, when a torpedo sank the battleship *Aquidaban* during a night action.

others had either a broadside battery or some kind of central area known as a barbette or citadel, with the upper deck often considerably narrower than the main deck to allow a degree of gunfire forward. Sailing rigs were not retained out of love of tradition, as is sometimes implied. For most ships, the availability of coal to feed their boilers was by no means assured if they were far from their home ports, so sails

provided extra motive power that might otherwise have been lacking.

By the time the *Huascar* was captured, the revolution in naval affairs had advanced further. The advantages of iron hulls over non-iron ones were well established – the main disadvantage lay in the great weight of iron, which kept the speeds of ships low. However, steel provided a lighter alternative to iron, with most of the same advantages, and naval shipbuilders began adopting steel hulls for their designs. The first large steel-hulled ship was the French battleship *Redoutable*, which was completed in 1878.

The first naval action involving a steel warship was fought during a civil war in Brazil in April 1894, when a torpedo sank the battleship *Aquidaban* during a night action. Later that same year came the first battle between steel warships, during the Sino-Japanese War of 1894–95, when two small squadrons fought off the island of Phung-Do in the Yellow Sea in July 1894. The Japanese sank one vessel and damaged the other. The result was never in doubt, for the Japanese ships were considerably more modern. A larger fleet engagement occurred in September at Yalu, when the Japanese defeated a Chinese fleet containing two battleships, although at heavy loss to themselves.

Grant triumphs in bloodbath

In a fierce two-day battle on 6–7 April 1862, General Ulysses S. Grant and his Federal army triumphed over an attacking Rebel force that had initially caught him at his camp next to the Tennessee river by complete surprise. The Rebel army is in retreat toward its main military base in the area, Corinth, Mississippi, having lost its commanding officer, General Albert Sidney Johnston, mortally wounded on the battlefield.

Shiloh has been the largest battle in the history of the United States, involving a total of 65,000 Federal soldiers and 45,000 Rebels, with over 20,000 killed, wounded or missing.

When the Rebel attack began on the morning of 6 April, it overran regiments and brigades that were in no position to give one another mutual support. Rebel divisions, however, had become mixed up and were unable to press home their advantage effectively. The fighting began before dawn, and as the sun came up the intensity redoubled, with the thump of artillery joining in the roar of muskets.

The Federal forces grudgingly gave ground toward their main base at Pittsburg Landing. Local successes opened gaps in the Federal lines as regiments withdrew under heavy pressure. Some of the most ferocious fighting occurred in an area that became known as the Hornet's Nest, where a division of Federal troops under General Benjamin Prentiss resisted from a sunken road that gave them some protection from the Rebel artillery. Prentiss and his

Shiloh has been the largest battle in the history of the United States, involving a total of 65,000 Federal soldiers and 45,000 Rebels, with over 20,000 killed, wounded or missing.

men withstood twelve Rebel charges and being bombarded by over sixty pieces of artillery. Johnston was shot during the battle here, but instead of getting prompt medical attention, which might have saved his life, he remained fighting and bled to death.

The fighting at the Hornet's Nest lasted until about 5.30 p.m., when the 2,000 survivors (including Prentiss) surrendered. The main Federal line of defence had been established in the rear, where reinforcements were arriving from the sixth of Grant's divisions and Don Carlos Buell's nearby Army of the Ohio. As night fell, the battle petered out and the two armies rested in the full knowledge that it would be resumed the next day, in spite of them both having suffered casualties far beyond their expectations. Federal General Sherman reportedly said to Grant, "Well Grant, we've had the devil's own day, haven't we?" Grant replied: "Yes. Lick 'em tomorrow, though."

The Rebels had no chance to renew their attacks in the morning. The Federal forces struck first, well supported with artillery. General P.G.T. Beauregard, who succeeded Johnston, withstood the onslaught for half the day, before ordering his men to withdraw in the early afternoon. The dispirited Rebels retreated back to Corinth, the apparent success of the first day having vanished overnight.

A Federal battery deployed in the woods near Pittsburg Landing in 1862. Federal guns broke up the Rebel attacks and saved the day for Federal commander General Ulysses S. Grant.

Union secures upper Mississippi river

Federal ships and soldiers have co-operated to secure control of the Mississippi river between St Louis and Memphis, a major setback to Rebel ambitions in Missouri and western Kentucky. The fall of mutually supporting Rebel positions at Island No. 10 in the Mississippi river and New Madrid, Missouri, in early 1862 opened the way to Memphis for the powerful Federal gunboat fleet.

The Federal advance on New Madrid, Missouri was in part motivated by the desire to disrupt a planned meeting of the state's secessionist legislators on 3 March. General John Pope took 12,000 troops and advanced from Commerce, Missouri at the beginning of the month. However, the Rebel garrison was dug in and received some support from a flotilla of gunboats on the Mississippi, which was able to subject the single Federal probe made by Pope's forces to a ferocious crossfire. Pope called for siege guns to support him.

A fierce artillery duel resulted in a loss of nerve by the Rebel commanders, who chose to evacuate New Madrid on 13 March.

As well as New Madrid, Island No. 10 was also a target for Federal operations, in this case by a flotilla of ironclad gunboats and mortar rafts. The Rebels had established three batteries on the island, and also a fort known as The Redan on the opposite Tennessee shore. The Redan defeated an attempt by three of the gunboats to batter it into submission on 17 March. A pause in operations then ensued until, on two nights in early April, two gunboats successfully ran past the Rebel guns at Island No. 10 and reached New Madrid, where they joined with Pope's forces. During the preceding month, Federal engineers had built a canal through a bend in the river, allowing four transport ships to pass below the island. With gunboats and transports, Pope was able to cross the Mississippi and approach Island No. 10 from the eastern shore. The Rebel forces in the area, now cut off from reinforcement or retreat, surrendered on 8 April.

Federal ironclads and mortar gunboats shell Island No. 10 in the Mississippi river.

Jackson beaten at Kernstown

General Thomas J. "Stonewall" Jackson, whose determination saved the day for the Confederacy at the Battle of Bull Run last year, suffered a repulse when he attacked Federal forces at Kernstown, Virginia, on 23 March 1862.

Jackson's attack attempted to turn the right flank of the Federal position. However, he lacked the strength to achieve a decisive breakthrough and was stalled by heavy Federal musketry. In the end, the brigade commander on the spot called the attack off, and Jackson was forced to retire from the field.

Although it was not clear at the time, the battle was in fact a strategic victory for the Confederacy. The forces Jackson engaged were intended to join the Army of the Potomac, but were instead kept in the Shenandoah Valley to prevent Jackson from attacking Washington DC.

Federal and Rebel troops trade volleys in the woods near Kernstown on 29 March 1862. The Rebels were forced to retreat.

Farragut's daring wins New Orleans

The largest city in the Rebel states, New Orleans, was brought under the guns of a Federal fleet after Commodore David Farragut succeeded in taking his ocean-going ships up the Mississippi river to the site of the city on 24 April 1862.

The plan of the attack was the idea of Farragut's foster brother, Commander David Dixon Porter, who presented the idea to US Secretary of the Navy, Gideon Welles, in November 1861. The key to Porter's scheme rested on a flotilla of schooners that would use 13-inch mortars to bombard the forts guarding the approach up the Mississippi to the Rebel city. Forts St Philip and Jackson stood on opposite banks and theoretically blocked the river, with the crossfire of their guns, 70 miles (113 km) from New Orleans. Porter's bombardment was intended to do sufficient damage to the batteries so that the approaching squadron could run past any remaining defenders and reach the docks of the city.

Farragut began the operation by getting his ocean-going warships, of which he had 20, into the Mississippi by entering the river's "passes" – the five outlets into the Gulf of Mexico – on 7 March 1862. Farragut's movement was slowed by the mud of the Mississippi, which gathered in the passes, requiring constant dredging to allow ships with a draught of 19 feet (6 m) to enter. It took two weeks, with the help of the steamers intended to tow Porter's sailing schooners up the river, to get all his ships through the second pass.

Porter's mortars went to work on 15 April with some ranging shots and the main bombardment began three days later, once all his barges had been moored in position. Porter expected the reduction of the two forts to take 48 hours, but in fact, the bombardment had still failed to achieve its desired effect after five days. Farragut now decided to take his ships to New Orleans by running past the forts under the cover of night. A barrier of chains and hulks the Rebels had erected to block the river was breached and Farragut ordered his ships to make ready for the run in the early morning of 24 April.

The sides of Farragut's ships were daubed with mud; anchor chains were hung along the hulls in order to provide some armour against enemy shot; and the decks were whitewashed to make objects more visible in the darkness.

The Rebel guns opened fire from the forts at 3.40 a.m. as the first Federal vessel was sighted. Porter's mortars also opened up, helping to drive some of the Rebel gunners away from their weapons.

Since the aim of the operation was to pass the forts, Farragut's ships did not spend time bombarding the Rebel positions, but instead concentrated their efforts on getting past them while sustaining as little damage to themselves as possible: they took measures such as sailing as close as 100 feet (30½ m) to the river bank, so that the Rebel guns could not be depressed at a low enough angle to cause any damage.

The naval battle that followed was more of a brawl than an organized engagement. The small Rebel flotilla had been built on the cheap, based on ramming rather than firepower, their tactics being to charge an enemy ship and then back off. These tactics were almost uniformly unsuccessful, as only one Federal vessel was sunk, while all but two of 11 Rebel vessels were sunk or ran aground.

Flag Officer David Farragut's fleet proceeds towards Forts Jackson and St Philip, guarding the approaches to New Orleans, on the night of 24/25 April 1862.

Winchester, Virginia, at the head of the Shenandoah Valley, changed hands several times during the first two years of the Civil War, and was the site of "Stonewall" Jackson's victory on 25 May 1862, which diverted Federal strength away from an attack on the Rebel capital at Richmond.

Stonewall Jackson's masterclass in valley

An outnumbered Rebel army in the Shenandoah Valley, commanded by General "Stonewall" Jackson, has outmanoeuvred and outfought three separate Federal forces during May and June 1862.

Jackson began his campaign by going in circles. He had been sent to the Shenandoah to keep Federal troops

President Lincoln tried to set a trap, sending two separate forces into the valley, aiming to cut Jackson's line of retreat.

from reinforcing the army threatening the Rebel capital of Richmond. His first act therefore was to march as if he was going to Richmond, but he turned round, came back into the valley and attacked a Federal force at McDowell on 8 May.

Jackson then moved north up the valley, turned east then west again to strike at a detached Federal force at Front Royal on 23 May. He pursued a retreating Federal force to Winchester, at the head of the valley, and defeated it there on 25 May.

President Lincoln tried to set a trap, sending two separate forces into the valley,

aiming to cut Jackson's line of retreat, but Jackson moved too fast for them and eluded the trap. He attacked one of the forces on 9 June at Port Republic, but his exhausted soldiers were unable to defeat the enemy quickly and Jackson did not press an attack against the other force as it withdrew northwards.

JACKSON'S SHENANDOAH VALLEY CAMPAIGN

DATES:	May–June 1862
COMBATANTS:	United States of America vs Rebel Confederate States of America
FORCES INVOLVED:	Union, 25,000; Rebels, 17,000
CASUALTIES:	Union, 7,000; Rebels, 2,500
RESULT:	Rebel Victory

Methodical Halleck captures Corinth

Halleck's Federal forces advance from their entrenchments against Rebel forces occupying their defences around the key railroad centre of Corinth, Mississippi during the fighting in May 1862.

General Henry Halleck: "Old Brains" to his comrades in the US officer corps.

The continuing success of Federal forces in the Mississippi Valley region was crowned by the capture of Corinth, Mississippi, on 30 May 1862, following the evacuation of the town by the Rebel army based there. Major General Henry Halleck, the commander of the Department of the Mississippi, took personal command of the three armies deployed on the operation.

Halleck had very definite ideas about how war should be fought, and put them into practice in a short campaign that began on 29 April. His armies advanced slowly, stopping early each day to dig considerable entrenchments to protect them against a night or dawn attack that not only never came but was never considered by the Rebel commander, General P.G.T. Beauregard. Consequently,

Halleck took over three weeks to march 20 miles (32 km) from his original base at Shiloh to Corinth.

Beauregard found his situation difficult. The area around Corinth was ill-suited to defence, and the place itself was unhealthy, with disease spreading rapidly among the large concentration of Rebel troops who had been there since retreating from Shiloh in early April. Furthermore, the many wounded from the Battle of Shiloh strained the limited hospital facilities there to breaking point. To make matters worse, food was running out and symptoms of malnutrition began to appear among Beauregard's men. The Rebel general therefore decided to abandon Corinth and did so on the night of 29/30 May, using a carefully crafted plan of deception that suggested he was about to attack.

McCLELLAN'S PENINSULAR CAMPAIGN

DATES:	April–August 1862
COMBATANTS:	United States of America vs Rebel Confederate States of America
FORCES ENGAGED:	Union, 155,000; Rebels, 95,500
CASUALTIES:	Union, 15,849; Rebels, 20,614
RESULT:	Rebel victory

McClellan retreats, Richmond is saved

A massive Federal army commanded by General George C. McClellan suffered a minor defeat on 27 June 1862 at the Battle of Gaines' Mill and is now withdrawing from a position threatening the Rebel capital of Richmond, Virginia. McClellan's army of 90,000 had been less than 10 miles (16 km) away, beaten off by the aggressive operations of General Robert E. Lee's army of 65,000 men.

McClellan's attempt at Richmond began in late March when he began assembling his forces at Fort Monroe. However, on 5 April, the day after starting his advance from the fort, McClellan brought it to a halt when it encountered a small Rebel army, a little more than a tenth the size of his own, entrenched around Yorktown. McClellan prepared for a long siege, bringing up heavy artillery.

On 3 May, two days before McClellan's grand bombardment, General Joseph E. Johnston ordered the Rebel force to withdraw. McClellan now moved much of his forces by water to a new position to the north-east of Richmond, either side of the Chickahominy river. Yet again he failed to attack. Instead, at the end of May, General Johnston struck at the left of McClellan's position, where a kink in the Federal line allowed an attack on three sides. The Battle of Fair Oaks, on 31 May, was handled badly by the Rebels, who were unable to co-ordinate their attacks effectively. A substantial part of the troops available did not even participate in the battle. Worse still,

General Johnston was badly wounded and a substitute commander attempted to continue the fight on a second day. That same day, 1 June 1862, a new commander was appointed to the Army of Northern Virginia, General Robert E. Lee, who broke off the battle, with both sides claiming victory. McClellan shifted most of his army to the south side of the Chickahominy.

Lee reorganized his forces, and sent his cavalry on a spectacular, if ineffective, ride around the Federal army between 12 and 15 June. McClellan responded by preparing to move his army again. He also ordered a limited assault on Rebel positions near Fair Oaks on 25 June. This was the beginning of the Seven Days' Battles. The Battle of Oak Grove, near Fair Oaks, was inconclusive, although Federal troops occupied the battlefield at the close of the day.

Lee had been planning an attack of his own and McClellan's limited operation did nothing to push him off his stride. On 26 June he struck at the Union V Corps, attacking around Mechanicsville, Virginia. Lee's complicated plan quickly unravelled and Stonewall Jackson, who had recently arrived from the Shenandoah Valley, was inexplicably timid so that the Rebel attack failed to achieve anything. However, Lee did not give up and renewed the assault the next day. The third battle of the Seven Days, Gaines' Mill, lasted the whole day and ended with the Federal line collapsing. The Union V Corps retreated from the battlefield.

Mexicans celebrate defeat of French

On 5 May 1862, a Mexican army defeated the French invaders at the Battle of Puebla, to the east of Mexico City, forcing them to retire towards Vera Cruz, the coastal city serving as the base for a French invasion of Mexico. On hearing of the defeat, Napoleon III decided to send sizeable reinforcements to the army in Vera Cruz.

The Mexicans had required the French army – which had been allowed to move inland in order to avoid the yellow fever that was endemic around Vera Cruz – to return to that coastal city. Only sick soldiers were allowed to remain in the highlands. However, General Charles Latrille de Lorencez decided to attack the Mexicans when they claimed some of these sick soldiers were healthy.

The French army, about 6,000 strong, forced the pass at Las Cumbres de Alcuzingo on 28 April 1862. General Lorencez then advanced on the town of Puebla, where General Ignacio Zaragoza had taken up a strong defensive position on the Cerro de Guadalupe, with its fort and fortified convent. Although Zaragoza had about 4,000 soldiers, many of them poorly trained militia, the French attack failed, their only success coming in driving off a Mexican cavalry attack that attempted to return a retreat into a rout.

French soldiers deploy for battle against the Mexicans, the infantry advancing in companies.

Memphis falls to gunboats

Following a victory over a Rebel flotilla of river gunboats, men from Federal vessels entered the city of Memphis, Tennessee, and raised the Stars and Stripes on 6 June 1862.

After the Federal capture of Island No. 10, the city of Memphis was the next key objective along the Mississippi river. Federal armies had already advanced along the Tennessee river to threaten the key railway junction at Corinth, Mississippi, through which passed the most direct railway connecting Memphis with the eastern Confederate States. However, any Federal advance along the Mississippi had to contend with two Rebel forts: Fort Randolph and Fort Pillow. Pillow was the further north of the two and was threatened by Federal gunboats.

However, on 10 May the main Rebel riverine flotilla, the River Defense Fleet, attacked and badly damaged two Federal vessels by ramming, thus delaying their approach to the fort. Events on land

With the strong current flowing in their favour, the Federal rams caused havoc among the Rebel boats, even before the gunboats could come up in support... The Rebel flotilla was swept aside in a couple of hours.

led to the abandonment of the forts, following the evacuation of Corinth in late May; however, the Rebels remained confident that their boats would defeat

any attempt to advance along the river as far as Memphis.

On 6 June, the Federal squadrons advanced on the city, with two boats designed exclusively as rams augmenting the main squadron of gunboats. The Rebels had no idea these rams existed, anticipating using ramming tactics themselves to defeat the Federal flotilla before its considerable superiority in firepower could take effect. With the strong current flowing in their favour, the Federal rams caused havoc among the Rebel boats, even before the gunboats could come up in support. The Rebel flotilla was swept aside in a couple of hours and it only needed four men to enter Memphis to reclaim the city for the Federal government.

The Federal rams of Colonel Charles Ellet and the armoured gunboats of Captain Charles Davis engage a Rebel flotilla off Memphis, Tennessee, on 6 June 1862.

Lee loses battles, wins campaign

Rebel General Robert E. Lee has achieved a strategic triumph over his opponent, Federal commander George McClellan, in spite of losing three battles in succession.

After the Battle of Gaines' Mill, on 27 June, McClellan withdrew. On 29 June, Lee attacked a rearguard at Savage's Station but was beaten back.

Badly worded orders prevented Lee's next attack at White Oak Swamp on 30 June from being effective. The fighting carried on until darkness fell, when two Federal generals rode into the Rebel lines and were captured.

Lee's aim in these battles was to catch part of McClellan's army and destroy it, but the repeated failure of his orders to be carried out meant that he had now lost his chance. The Federal forces had reached Malvern Hill, which overlooked their main supply base at Harrison's Landing. Lee believed that one all-out

The Federal army massed its batteries to provide the firepower that blunted the Rebel assaults during the battle of Malvern Hill on 1 July 1862.

assault might cause a Bull Run-style rout, which in the circumstances would be fatal to the Federal army. On 1 July 1862 the attack ran into a strong Federal position at Malvern Hill. Federal artillery in particular caused heavy casualties and Lee called off the operation, having lost many irreplaceable men and having gained little.

Over the three days of the retreat to Malvern Hill, the Federal forces lost around 11,000 casualties and prisoners, while the Rebels suffered nearly 10,000.

Vicksburg resists Farragut

Commodore David Farragut abandoned his operations around Vicksburg, Mississippi, on 24 July 1862 when the falling waters of summer threatened to ground his ocean-going vessels over 200 miles (322 km) upriver from the Gulf of Mexico. Vicksburg occupies a strong position, difficult to attack by land. With the city being the last major Rebel-held crossing point between the eastern and Trans-Mississippi regions, Federal strategists believed that the city might be vulnerable to attack from the river. Farragut was ordered to try.

On 18 May, Farragut tried to cannonade the Rebel batteries defending Vicksburg into submission, but when this proved

ineffective he temporarily withdrew his ships south again, returning over a month later, this time with the mortar schooners used against the New Orleans forts. He also intended to co-ordinate operations with the river gunboat force that had captured Memphis and sent word for to its commander, Commodore Charles H. Davis, to come down the river to join him.

Davis and his gunboats arrived on 1 July and for several days the two squadrons bombarded the Mississippi city, but to no real effect. Once the Federal commander in the area, General Henry Halleck, refused to attack by land, the attempt to take Vicksburg was doomed to failure.

In July 1862 the CSS *Arkansas* defied the near total Federal command of the Mississippi.

America's bloodiest day

The families of the United States of America, torn apart by Civil War, suffered heavy blows as long casualty lists emerged each month of the year 1862, but none was as long as that of 17 September 1862. The dead and wounded in the fields around the town of Sharpsburg, Maryland, reached a total 26,193 men.

The battle marked the end of General Robert E. Lee's attempt to carry the war into Maryland, well known as a state where many had sympathy with the Rebels. A victory here might even have convinced foreign powers such as Britain and France to grant official recognition to the Confederate government.

Lee's plans were undone by the carelessness of a staff officer who dropped an order intended for one of the divisions of Stonewall Jackson corps in a field. Later some Federal soldiers found the envelope containing the order and it

On 17 September, McClellan unleashed his attacks but they were unco-ordinated and Lee was able to shift his forces from unthreatened sectors to reinforce the threatened one.

passed up the chain of command rapidly until it was in the hands of General George McClellan. McClellan planned to mass his Army of the Potomac near Antietam Creek and attack part of Lee's army at the town of Sharpsburg.

McClellan took too long planning his attack and allowed Lee to gather reinforcements at Antietam. On 17 September, McClellan unleashed his attacks but they were unco-ordinated and Lee was able to shift his forces from unthreatened sectors to reinforce the threatened one. The Federal soldiers pressed home their attacks and at about 1 p.m. had opened a gap in the centre of the Rebel line. The soldiers who had made the gap had been too heavily engaged to continue and reinforcements were needed. Although two corps were available, inexplicably neither was used. Instead, the remainder of the Federal effort of the day was spent on a diversionary attack across Antietam Creek.

The Dunker Church was a key landmark on the Rebel left during the battle of Antietam on 17 September 1862, defended by the men of Stonewall Jackson's corps.

Lee triumphs at old battlefield

General **Robert E.** Lee led his Rebel Army of Northern Virginia to victory over the Federal Army of Virginia on the old battlefield of Bull Run on 29–30 August 1862. He is now poised to advance north and draw the remaining Federal forces away from Richmond.

The Army of Virginia, numbering 50,000 soldiers, was formed from the separate Federal commands that had faced "Stonewall" Jackson in the Shenandoah Valley in the spring, and given to a general fresh from victories in the west, General John Pope. Lee

Pope, outnumbered by Lee's united army, took a gamble of his own, believing he could defeat Jackson before the rest of Lee's army could arrive to help.

confronted the problem of how to deal with Pope at the same time as stopping General George B. McClellan's 90,000 soldiers at Harrison's Landing from advancing on Richmond. Once President Lincoln ordered McClellan to join forces with Pope, Lee had his chance and shifted his army north-westwards to attack Pope before McClellan could get there.

By 25 August Lee had concentrated his forces against Pope, although they were still widely separated. Pope, outnumbered by Lee's united army, took a gamble of his own, believing he could defeat Jackson before the rest of Lee's army could arrive to provide help.

Pope attacked Jackson near the Bull Run battlefield of the year before, but unwisely sent his divisions in as soon as they arrived on the battlefield, instead of waiting for them to deliver the kind of co-ordinated blow that would probably have driven Jackson out of his position.

Pope tried again on the second day of battle, using troops from his left flank to attack Jackson's position. What he did not realize was that the forces facing his left consisted of a larger corps than Jackson's, that of General James Longstreet. Timing his blow to perfection, Longstreet swept away Pope's left wing, delivering a crushing blow that threw Pope's army into retreat.

Officers and their wives of the 19th Georgia Infantry. The regiment fought in the railroad cut that bore the brunt of the Federal assaults on the first day of the Second Battle of Bull Run.

OBITUARY

FREDERICK TOWNSEND WARD (1831–1862)

The mortal wounding of Frederick Townsend Ward, founder and commander of China's Ever-Victorious Army, occurred while he was attacking the city of Tz'u-chi on 21 September 1862. Ward may have been shot on the orders of a Chinese general.

Ward was born in Salem, Massachusetts, and was sent to sea as the second mate on a clipper ship at the age of 16. He made several trips to China, where in 1860 he was serv-ing on a gunboat engaged in fighting piracy. His activities brought him into contact with the wealthy business leaders of Shanghai, who were concerned at the effect a long-drawn-out civil war between the Imperial government and the Taiping Rebels was having on their affairs. He was asked to organize a mercenary army on their behalf, made up of Westerners in China.

Ward's small force fought alongside Chinese imperial forces with mixed success. He was badly wounded in one engagement in the summer of 1860, and while he was recuperating developed the idea of forming a Chinese military force trained in Western-style warfare. He led the Ever-Victorious Army into battle in January 1862. The force's name proved to be no hyperbole, with Ward becoming famous and a Chinese citizen. Ward also developed a riverine auxiliary force, enabling the Ever-Victorious Army to use the rivers effectively in its campaigns against the Taiping, making up for the poor-quality roads in China.

Ward died of his wounds on 22 September 1862.

Slaughter before the stone wall

A view across the Rappahannock toward the Rebel positions, with Fredericksburg in the middle distance, and Marye's Heights just beyond, in front of which so many Federal soldiers fell.

The dominance of the Rebel Army of Northern Virginia continued as the Federal army suffered a heavy defeat at the Battle of Fredericksburg, in Virginia, on 13 December 1862. In perhaps the most bitter loss of them all so far, Federal soldiers were sent on a suicidal assault against a prepared enemy on higher ground.

The battle was part of a campaign launched by the new commander of the Army of the Potomac, General Ambrose Burnside. Burnside had taken on the job reluctantly, not considering himself suited to the responsibility. However, once in charge he made some significant changes to the army's organization and displayed great energy in leading it into battle.

The key to Burnside's plan was to cross the Rapahannock river rapidly at Fredericksburg, but after his army reached the opposite bank, it was delayed for two weeks waiting for the pontoons needed to build a bridge. This gave the time for General Robert E. Lee to rush his army to the heights overlooking Fredericksburg.

In spite of this initial failure, Burnside was still determined to attack. His plan now called for the main effort to take place against the Rebel right, south of Fredericksburg. The attack from the town was intended to prevent Lee from repositioning troops. In the end, the whole plan – not a good one, in any case – was bungled by Burnside's subordinates, who mismanaged both attacks. The troops crossing the field between the town and the heights suffered particularly heavily, as they were forced to march across open ground while under fire the whole time. Federal casualties amounted to 12,653, the Rebels only 5,309.

The Battle of Perryville

The largest battle of the war in Kentucky took place on 8 October 1862 and ended in a Rebel victory. Yet, owing to the curious events of the day, the Rebel commander preferred to retreat rather than risk a heavy defeat.

In August 1862, in conjunction with General Lee's coming invasion of Maryland, two Rebel forces – those in East Tennessee, some 19,000 men, and the Confederate Army of Tennessee, of just over 25,000 – began marching independently towards Kentucky. The East Tennessee force, commanded by General Edmund Kirby Smith, moved rapidly so that at the beginning of September they were at the state capital, Frankfort, and began preparations to

As the two armies manoeuvred for favourable positions, the bulk of Buell's troops bumped into just under half of Bragg's men at Perryville. The fighting began over access to water, on the night of 7 October. The next day, the Rebels attacked the left of the Federal position.

inaugurate a Confederate governor. Smith's army was dispersed to defend the state. On 4 October, as the inauguration was under way, a small Federal force attacked. General Don Carlos Buell and the 60,000-strong Army of the Ohio had returned from central Tennessee to drive the Rebels out of Kentucky.

General Braxton Bragg, the Army of Tennessee's commander and overall senior officer in Kentucky, pulled back in the face of Federal superior numbers. As the two armies manoeuvred for favourable positions, the bulk of Buell's troops bumped into just under half of Bragg's men at Perryville. The fighting began over access to water, on the night of 7 October. The next day, the Rebels attacked the left of the Federal position, utterly unaware that almost twice as many soldiers lay within 2½ miles (4 km) – but neither did Buell.

The Battle of Perryville was notorious for the "acoustic shadow" that prevented its sounds carrying across to the main Federal headquarters. The Federal forces, a third of whom were new recruits, suffered heavily from the Rebel attacks and gave ground. Bragg at first planned to attack them next day, then realized how the odds were stacked against him, and began retreating back to Tennessee.

The rolling terrain around the Perryville battlefield created acoustic conditions that prevented a sizeable portion of the Federal army from realizing that a major battle was being fought.

Western Union victories

On 19 September 1862, a battle was fought at Iuka, Mississippi, between General Sterling Price and General William S. Rosecrans. Price was trying to prevent Federal troops in northern Mississippi from being withdrawn to reinforce Kentucky. However, General Grant sent Rosecrans to find Price first and defeat him. Price instead attacked Rosecrans, but the attack was beaten off.

After defeat at Iuka, Price joined General Earl Van Dorn for an attack on Corinth, Mississippi, a former Rebel base that had been captured by the Union the previous spring. In a two-day fight on hot Indian summer days, 3–4 October 1862, the attacking Rebels were badly defeated by General Rosecrans.

Across the Mississippi, an 11,000-strong Rebel army commanded by General Thomas Hindman attempted to drive the main Federal army out of Arkansas. At the battle of Prairie Grove on 8 December 1862, both sides fought to a standstill, but Hindman withdrew after nightfall.

General Earl Van Dorn was an aggressive commander, shot dead, not on the battlefield, but on the streets of a Tennessee town by an aggrieved husband.

A bloody new year

Federal and Rebel armies clashed at the Battle of Stones River over the New Year of 1863 in central Tennessee, when General Braxton Bragg's Army of Tennessee attempted to defeat a larger Federal force commanded by General William S. Rosecrans near the town of Murfreesboro.

Both armies camped near one another on 30 December 1862 and adopted the same plan, but Bragg's men attacked first on the morning of 31 December, thus taking the initiative from Rosecrans. As at Shiloh, the Rebels made rapid gains until they encountered a division ready to stand and fight. General Philip Sheridan's unit stood firm, repelling major assaults from three sides while occupying a cedar forest that became known as the Slaughter Pen. By the end of the day on 31 December, Bragg's attack had driven the Federal army into a tight u-shape.

On New Year's Day, both armies rested, tending their wounded. The battle resumed on 2 January, when Bragg sent one of his corps to attack a division that Rosecrans had placed on some high ground overlooking his left wing. The attack was successful until the Rebels came within range of a battery of 45 guns, lined up hub to hub, positioned to protect the troops on the heights. The guns fired steadily, ripping huge gaps in the Rebel lines and forcing them to retreat.

Bragg originally believed he had won a victory, but ordered the withdrawal of his army on 3 January when it seemed that Rosecrans was steadily receiving reinforcements.

General William S. Rosecrans (seated centre, holding sword) with the staff of the Federal Army of the Cumberland. Rosecrans' forces were attacked at Stones River, but fought off the Rebel army under General Braxton Bragg.

Action at Grand Gulf

The USS *New Ironsides* entered service in August 1862 and began operating off Charleston, South Carolina, in early 1863.

Federal **Mississippi gunboats** failed to destroy the Rebel batteries at Grand Gulf, Mississippi, after a five-hour bombardment on 27 April 1863, the operation being part of General Ulysses Grant's campaign to capture Vicksburg.

Porter's gunboats divided into two groups, three attacking the strong position to the north of the town and four the southern battery. Both batteries had been constructed on high ground, but only the northern battery was well equipped with heavy guns.

Grant had abandoned any attempt to capture Vicksburg from his base of operations to the north of the city, around Memphis and Corinth. Instead, he took most of his army, crossed to the western bank of the Mississippi, and made his way below Vicksburg to a town opposite Grand Gulf, named Hard Times. The gunboats, commanded by Admiral David Dixon Porter, ran past the guns of Vicksburg by night, to rendezvous with Grant's army. Initially, Grant hoped to cross the river at Grand Gulf, even though the Rebels had placed strong batteries on hills overlooking the town.

Porter's gunboats divided into two groups, three attacking the strong position to the north of the town and four the southern battery. Both batteries had been constructed on high ground, but only the northern battery was well equipped with heavy guns. The southern battery was successfully subdued by the four gunboats, which then joined the other three vessels in their attack. But even after five hours, the Federal gunboats had no apparent effect on the Rebel battery and had themselves been damaged.

Bombardment of Charleston

An **attempt to** gain control of Charleston harbour through a bombardment by Federal ironclads failed on 7 April 1863. Rear Admiral Samuel Du Pont had a powerful fleet at his disposal, consisting of the large USS *New Ironsides*, an armoured frigate, seven monitors and the USS *Keokuk*, an ugly armoured-casemate ship.

The Federal squadron sailed up the main ship channel, which carried them between Fort Moultrie and Fort Sumter. The lead monitor, the USS *Weehawken*, pushed a raft that would be used to sweep aside any torpedo mines, but as she neared the bombardment position, lookouts spotted a very dangerous obstacle, consisting of nets and cables studded with torpedo mines. The Federal squadron halted and the Rebel batteries opened fire.

The guns blazed away for about an hour and the *New Ironsides* and the *Keokuk* were heavily battered, while the monitors got off more lightly. The *Keokuk* had to pull out of the action after firing only three shots, so badly damaged that she sank the next day. After about an hour, the rest of the Federal squadron withdrew.

Outnumbered Lee triumphs, loses Stonewall

A heavily outnumbered Rebel army has performed a daring manoeuvre to achieve a crushing victory at Chancellorsville in northern Virginia.

The Federal commander, General Joseph Hooker, had marched and skirmished his way to a strong position

Both sides suffered losses of over 10,000 men in the three days of fighting. Among the wounded was Jackson, who died of pneumonia on 10 May.

on 2 May 1863. At this point, the Rebel army, numbering 60,000 soldiers and commanded by General Robert E. Lee,

was in danger of being trapped on two sides by the Federal forces. Lee, however, sent General Stonewall Jackson, with the greater portion of his army, around the Federal right flank, before attacking the totally unprepared Union XI Corps. Now it was the Federal army that was apparently trapped. However, a detached Federal force in front of Fredericksburg launched an attack as the troops around Chancellorsville withdrew from the trap. The Rebels were not strong enough to prevent the Federal withdrawal and deal with the threat to their own right flank.

The Rebel army now divided itself once again and halted the Federal advance from Fredericksburg. Both sides' losses totalled almost 30,000 men in the three days of fighting. Among the wounded was Jackson, who died of pneumonia on 10 May.

An artistic depiction of the battle of Chancellorsville shows Rebel troops emerging from woods in an attack on a Federal line.

Grant finds the back door to Vicksburg

General Ulysses Grant's victories in the West during 1862–63 secured the control of the Mississippi river from Illinois to Mississippi.

O n **18 May** 1863, a Federal army put under siege the last Rebel-held strongpoint along the Mississippi river. General Ulysses S. Grant, after a masterful spring campaign following a difficult winter, is poised to capture his second Rebel army of the war.

After a couple of false starts in the winter, Grant adopted the most risky of options when he marched his army down the western bank of the Mississippi. Federal gunboats and supply vessels, operating under the cover of darkness, also sailed past the Vicksburg defences on the nights of 16 and 22 April 1863. With the help of these vessels, Grant crossed the Mississippi on 30 April at Bruinsburg.

Now able to approach Vicksburg from the south, Grant advanced quickly east to Jackson, which he captured on 14 May after a battle near the town with Rebel defenders. He then turned west and defeated a second Rebel army in battles at Champion's Hill and the Big Black River Bridge on 16 and 17 May. The Rebel army retired behind the Vicksburg defences, hoping that a relief force would raise the siege.

Battle of Brandy Station

Federal cavalry attacked their Rebel counterparts near Brandy Station, Virginia, on 9 June 1863, and achieved an early success before being driven back across the Rappahannock river. The day before the battle, the Rebel cavalry commander, General J.E.B. Stuart, presented his men in review before General Robert E. Lee. Stuart was so focused on this proud event that he failed to detect the movement of the Federal cavalry towards Culpeper Court House, as ordered by General Joseph Hooker in an attempt to regain some kind of initiative over the Rebels who had beaten his army a month ago at Chancellorsville. The battle focused on control of Fleetwood Hill, where sabres flashed as cavalry launched massed charges against their counterparts.

Stuart was so focused on this proud event that he failed to detect the movement of the Federal cavalry towards Culpeper Court House.

After a 12-hour battle, the Federal forces were unable to gain control of Fleetwood Hill and retired.

Puebla falls to French

The French invasion of Mexico resumed in the spring of 1863 as a much-reinforced army advanced inland to lay siege to Puebla on 16 March. Instead of surrounding the city, the French targeted specific parts of the defences in order to secure a breach which they could subsequently use to force the surrender of the rest of the town. However, the Mexicans defended doggedly, using churches and monasteries as strongpoints. A Mexican attempt to relieve the siege on 5 May failed, and the relief force itself was surprised in its camp at night shortly after by a French attack. On 17 May Puebla at last fell to the French. The way to Mexico City was now open.

Copperheads

The citizens of Federal states were by no means united on the need to defeat the secessionist southern ones. A political faction, called Copperheads by Federal sympathizers, after a venomous North American snake, was active in Ohio, Indiana and Illinois – states where many had family ties with the south. Clement Vallandigham was the most prominent Copperhead. In May 1863 he spoke against the war, falling foul of a military order issued by the local commander, General Ambrose Burnside, against "declaring sympathies for the enemy". Vallandigham was tried by a military court, and sentenced to prison, although eventually President Lincoln commuted his sentence to exile in the Confederacy.

A Federal cavalryman crosses the Hazel river near Brandy Station. The Federal cavalry surprised the Rebels, for the first time during the war in the Eastern theatre.

The French Foreign Legion

On 30 April 1863, the 3rd Company, 1st Battalion, of the French Foreign Legion left its camp at Chiqui-huite, near Vera Cruz, to accompany a convoy coming up from the port of Vera Cruz to the French army laying siege to Puebla. The convoy not only included rations and equipment for conducting the siege, but also a substantial amount of gold, some 3 million francs' worth.

Foreign Legion officers from the 1st Regiment, photographed in North Africa, circa 1900. Most officers were French, but the enlisted men were supposed to be foreign, although many French signed up claiming citizenship of a French-speaking country.

The coastal region of Mexico around Vera Cruz suffered badly from yellow fever and many legionnaires had gone down with the disease. The result was that only 62 men out of the company of 120 were fit for service, and they were joined by three officers who volunteered for duty with the company from battalion headquarters. The commander was Captain Danjou, who had lost his left hand during the Crimean War and had had it replaced with a wooden one.

Danjou assembled his men at 11 p.m. on 29 April and led them out after midnight. At 7 a.m. they stopped to brew coffee and eat breakfast but before they could eat they discovered that a large body of Mexican cavalry was approaching them. Estimating their number at around 800 strong, Captain Danjou realized he could not outrun them, nor could he defeat them in the open, so he ordered his men back up the road to a farm known as the Hacienda Camarone.

The cavalry caught up with them just a few hundred yards short of the building and Danjou ordered the forming of a square, the traditional infantry defence against cavalry. The square successfully fended off a Mexican cavalry charge, but the horsemen continued to ride around the formation. With bayonets fixed, the legionnaires charged toward the buildings and most made it to the hacienda, escaping the lances of the Mexicans.

Danjou and his men fought the whole day from the hacienda in an impossible position. The Mexicans already outnumbered them ten-to-one at the outset of the battle, but were then joined by 1,200 infantry. Although many of the Mexican soldiers had better rifles than the French, the French marksmanship was far superior. Numbers, however, gradually told.

Danjou himself was hit in the chest around 11 a.m. He realized that so long as the Mexicans were attacking his men they could not go after the convoy so, before he died, he insisted that his men swear an oath never to surrender.

The survivors of Danjou almost kept the oath. Their resistance continued until a little after 6 p.m. when there were only six left alive and fighting. Three of these were killed in the final assault, leaving three to surrender, provided they were allowed to keep their weapons. The Mexicans granted the request. "These are not soldiers, but devils," commented the Mexican commander, Colonel Francisco de Paula Milan. Approximately 300 Mexicans had been killed and many more were wounded in the fighting.

The founding of the Legion

The French Foreign Legion, founded in 1831, still marks Camerone Day each year on 30 April. Captain Danjou's wooden hand is kept like a sacred relic, having been eventually recovered from Mexico. For the Legion, Camerone is the perfect expression of their dedication to fighting.

The Legion was founded as a unit of

> Danjou assembled his men at 11 p.m. on 29 April and led them out after midnight. At 7 a.m. they stopped... but before they could eat they discovered that a large body of Mexican cavalry was approaching them.

foreign mercenaries intended for service in the conquest of Algeria. Predominantly officered by Frenchmen, the rank and file are been drawn from numerous countries, although many French join while claiming nationality of a French-speaking country such as Belgium or Switzerland.

For much of its career it has been associated with the French empire, and in particular with North Africa. In the English-speaking world, the image of the Legion remains one to a foreign country unto death.

However, the Foreign Legion remains an important element of the French military. In recent decades it has acted as a rapid reaction force deployed in defence of France's national interests, particularly in Africa. In 1978 it parachuted out of relative obscurity into Kolwezi to rescue Europeans in this Zairean province threatened by anti-government Rebels. It has also participated in peacekeeping in Kosovo, in the liberation of Kuwait in 1990–91, and in anti-terrorist operations in Djibouti and Afghanistan.

The Legion's history is also entwined with France's military history since its foundation, including some of the moments of greatest sacrifice and defeat, as well as heroic defence. Foreign legionnaires, in spite of their charter barring them from service in France, fought in the Franco-Prussian War of 1870–71, in battles around Orleans. During the First World War, the Legion fought at Verdun and elsewhere. Included among those who served with the Legion in this war was the American poet Alan Seeger, whose poem "Rendezvous with Death" proved eerily prophetic.

The Second World War was a mixture of highs and lows for the Legion. The creation of the Vichy French regime led to a quandary. Legally, it was the legitimate government of France, although General Charles de Gaulle's Free French movement offered a risky alternative for those opposed to German aggression. As some of the Legion's rank and file included Germans who had fled Hitler, it is not surprising that the Legion provided an important component of de Gaulle's forces. Vichy legionnaires and Free French legionnaires fought one another in Syria in 1941, and the defence of Bir Hakeim against the Germans in North Africa by the 13th Demi-Brigade has been embraced by the Legion as another moment of glory in their history.

Danjou and his men fought the whole day from the hacienda in an impossible position. The Mexicans already outnumbered them ten-to-one at the outset of the battle, but were then joined by 1,200 infantry.

After 1945, the Legion's history became somewhat chequered. They experienced a bitter defeat at Dien Bien Phu in Indochina in 1954, and also took part in the brutal Algerian Independence War. After de Gaulle chose to grant independence to Algeria in 1961, some members of the Foreign Legion joined the Generals' Putsch that attempted to overthrow de Gaulle's government.

The Legion's headquarters were based in Algeria, but, following the country's independence, the Legion was forced to move to southern France and Corsica.

Captain Jean Danjou's defence of the Hacienda Camarone against Mexican nationalists is commemorated each year by the Legion.

of a blue-coated or khaki-clad, hard-bitten loner striding across Saharan sands in order to forget or escape some secret past. Some people might even now be surprised to learn the unit still exists, and still nurtures its peculiar *esprit de corps* of hard-fighting loyalty

French Foreign Legion soldiers spring across the Libyan desert during the battle of Bir Hakeim in 1942. Like the nation itself, the Legion divided between the Free French and the Vichy French.

The bloodiest battle in American history

The little Pennsylvania town of Gettysburg was the setting of the first major defeat of Rebel General Robert E. Lee's Army of Northern Virginia. The battle arose out of a Rebel advance on the town as one of Lee's divisions marched to Gettysburg on 1 July 1863. There they encountered Federal forces, initially only cavalry. However, both sides moved reinforcements in the direction of the firing, and soon a major battle developed. At nightfall on 1 July, the Federal forces had been pushed out of their initial positions to the west of the town, and now occupied a fishhook-shaped line of hills to the south.

Lee planned a double envelopment, first attacking the far south of the Federal line, anchored on the hills of Little Round Top and Big Round Top. A second assault took place later in the day against the northern end of the Federal line, at Cemetery and Culp's hills. General George Meade, the Federal commander of the Army of the Potomac, was happy with his strong defensive line and focused his efforts on shifting reinforcements to counter the Rebel attacks. The fighting on the Round Tops was crucial to the battle, for if the Rebels had captured Little Round Top, the Federal position could not have been held. However, a valiant defence masterminded by the 20th Maine Regiment's commander, Colonel Joshua Chamberlain, secured the feature for the Federal.

The Rebels returned to the attack on 3 July, this time with a massive frontal assault against the centre of the Federal lines at Cemetery Hill. Pickett's charge ended in a costly failure, although the leading elements of his attack penetrated the Federal line. After three days of heavy losses, Lee decided to retreat. His invasion to the north had been intended to carry the war into Federal states and secure a victory that might have disheartened Northerners enough for them to agree to a peace treaty. However, the invasion ended in a battle that had cost 51,000 American casualties.

The gates of Cemetery Hill after the battle of Gettysburg in July 1863. The hill was a crucial part of the Federal line, and could have been captured by the Rebels on the first day of the battle had they attacked.

Grant conquers Vicksburg

Morgan rides into prison

Federal troops camp on the lawn of Castle Hill mansion, once part of the Rebel defences of Vicksburg, Mississippi. The Rebels withstood a six-week siege, under constant bombardment.

O**n 4 July** 1863, a three-month siege ended with the surrender of Vicksburg, Mississippi, the "Gibraltar of the West", to a Federal army commanded by Major General Ulysses S. Grant.

During the siege, Grant's army made two assaults on the Rebel lines, on 19 and 22 May, but both were repulsed with heavy losses. The earthwork fortifications around Vicksburg were very strong and it was not surprising that Grant's assaults failed. However, Grant said that "The troops believed they could carry the works in their front, and would not work so patiently in the trenches if they had not been allowed to try."

Grant's army began its lengthy siege operations. Their main effort initially went on an underground mine detonated on 25 June. Grant's soldiers stormed the resulting crater, but the Rebel defenders fought off the assault in ferocious hand-to-hand fighting.

The failure of this attack did nothing to relieve the Rebel garrison or the people of Vicksburg. The trenches and city were subject to constant bombardment, so many of the population hid in caves that were a geological feature of the area and offered more protection from shellfire than houses. Food was in short supply, people ate rats and some soldiers were near starvation.

With signs of an impending major assault, the commander of the Rebel garrison, General John C. Pemberton, met with Grant on 3 July and surrendered the next day.

A**24-day cavalry raid** into Indiana and Ohio led by Rebel General John Hunt Morgan ended on 26 July 1863 with the capture of his men and himself.

The raid was intended to disrupt the supply lines of the Union Army of the Cumberland, which a month earlier had begun advancing south-east from central Tennessee towards the city of Chattanooga, the main base for the Rebel Army of Tennessee. Morgan selected some 2,500 cavalrymen to carry out the raid and advanced into Kentucky at the beginning of July 1863.

After several fights with Federal troops in Kentucky, Morgan crossed the Ohio river into Indiana, his force having been reduced by about a third. His plan now was to travel up the Ohio river valley, crossing back to the south side somewhere in West Virginia.

General John Hunt Morgan's raid provided dramatic newspaper copy, but contributed little to the Rebel cause.

The Federal response to Morgan was managed by General Ambrose Burnside, who called out local militia and deployed his troops to block the most likely routes Morgan would take heading south. Morgan succeeded in evading Burnside's forces for the most part, although he did need to fight a battle at Corydon, Indiana, against militia, whom he defeated on 9 July.

Morgan's force tried to cross the Ohio at Buffington Island on 19 July, but about half of his remaining force was captured, leaving some 700 men under Morgan's command. These, in turn, surrendered near Salineville, Ohio, seven days later.

IN BRIEF

❧ Federal troops failed in an attempt to capture Morris Island, part of operations against the Rebel city of Charleston, in July 1863. A force commanded by Major General Quincy Gillmore twice assaulted Fort Wagner on 11 and 18 July, the latter attack led by the African-American 54th Massachusetts Infantry. General Gillmore concluded that a third assault would end in similar failure and resorted to a siege of Fort Wagner.

Bragg wins a battle

General Braxton Bragg, whose war record has been less than exemplary up to now, succeeded in defeating a Federal army at the Battle of Chickamauga on 19–20 September 1863. The defeated Federal force is in retreat to Chattanooga.

The Rebel Army of Tennessee, under General Bragg, which has thus far compiled a disappointing record in the war, can now claim a victory over the Union Army of the Cumberland, commanded by General William S. Rosecrans.

Rosecrans, in a two-phase campaign, had driven Bragg's men back from their positions around Murfreesboro and into northern Georgia between June and August, with very few casualties. Faced with this crisis, Rebel President Jefferson Davis shifted a corps from the Army of Northern Virginia to help Bragg.

Bragg attacked Rosecrans at Chickamauga in September, hoping to defeat a part of the Federal army. What Bragg did not know, however, was that Rosecrans had been concentrating his forces here.

On the first day, both sides seemed unaware of just how strong the enemy was. General George H. Thomas, one of Rosecrans' corps commanders, opened the battle attacking what he thought was a small cavalry force, while Bragg brought up more and more troops, thinking he was fighting about a third of Rosecrans' army. Both sides had a better idea of what they faced by nightfall and prepared for a tough battle on the second day, 20 September, which was hard-fought with heavy casualties. Bragg's attempt to turn Rosecrans' flank failed, but Rosecrans blundered and opened a large gap in his line that Rebel troops advanced into and the whole right of the Federal line collapsed. General Thomas' corps, however, stood firm and prevented the Rebels from pursuing effectively. The battle resulted in 16,000 Federal and 18,000 Rebel casualties.

A Federal general gestures to members of his staff during the battle of Chickamauga. General George Thomas was the only commander to emerge with much credit from the fighting, as his command held firm against Rebel attacks to cover the withdrawal of the rest of the army.

Rebels Run from Chattanooga

The Union Army of the Cumberland, in an astonishing attack on a strongly fortified Rebel position near Chattanooga, Tennessee, drove the Rebel Army of Tennessee from the field on 25 November 1863.

After its defeat at Chickamauga, the Union Army of the Cumberland retreated to Chattanooga. General Braxton Bragg and the Army of Tennessee followed and laid siege to the place, hoping to starve the Federal troops out. At the beginning of October, Bragg sent his cavalry on a lengthy raid to the north of Chattanooga, achieving a major success when they captured around 500 supply wagons, which greatly limited the amount of supplies that could be transported into the besieged city.

President Lincoln, recognizing the gravity of the situation, ordered General Ulysses S. Grant to Chattanooga, together with reinforcements from the

Army of the Potomac and the Army of the Tennessee.

Grant used the reinforcements to open a supply line to the city. Rebel troops controlled the road and river to the west, and Grant successfully concentrated his offensive actions here. The 'cracker line' soon improved the rations available to the Federal defenders. Grant then prepared a plan to defeat Bragg in the field, by attacking the besieging army on either flank. On 24 November, Federal troops successfully captured Lookout Mountain, overlooking the town to the west, although fighting to the east of Missionary Ridge, the centre of the Rebel line, did not go so well. On the 25th, attacks on both flanks bogged down so Grant ordered some of the Army of the Cumberland to advance on Missionary Ridge as a diversion. However, the Federal forces not only captured the first of three lines of Rebel trenches, but eventually swept the Rebels out of all three and delivered a crushing blow to the Rebel army, shouting 'Chickamauga, Chickamauga' at the routing Rebel forces as they surmounted the ridge.

A Federal 200-lb (90-kg) gun on Missionary Ridge after the capture of the heights during the battle of Chattanooga, the Tennessee city being turned into a major advanced supply base.

IN BRIEF

❧ Repeated Federal bombardments of Fort Sumter in August and September 1863 were capped by an attempt to storm the fortress on the night of 9/10 September. Some 400 troops (including 100 marines) in 20 barges set out, but only seven reached the beach at the fort. The Rebels defending the fort lit up the beach with a locomotive headlamp, greeting the troops who disembarked with heavy rifle fire and hand grenades. The attempt failed.

❧ Fort Wagner, outside Charleston Harbor, South Carolina, was abandoned by Rebels on the night of 6/7 September, after Federal troops had dug trenches to within 100 yards of the fort's defences.

❧ A Federal army commanded by General Ambrose Burnside occupied the city of Knoxville, Tennessee, on 3 September 1863.

❧ On 5 October 1863, the Rebel-built submersible craft CSS *David* made a night torpedo attack on the USS *New Ironsides* outside Charleston harbour. The *David* escaped, despite the torpedo's explosion swamping her engines. The *New Ironsides* was badly damaged and forced to leave the blockading squadron to return to port for repairs.

The Rebel vessel CSS *David* in harbour. The long tube on top is actually her funnel.

War in the wilderness

General Ulysses S. Grant was defeated by General Robert E. Lee in the Wilderness, near Chancellorsville, Virginia. This three-day battle on 5–7 May 1864 marked the opening of the summer campaigning season and the first confrontation between the two best generals to emerge during the war.

Grant marched out of winter quarters on 3 May across the Rapidan and toward the Wilderness, where the year before Lee had won a tremendous victory over the Army of the Potomac.

Meanwhile, Lee moved to intercept Grant in this tangled, uncultivated countryside, where Grant's superiority in artillery would count for less.

Lee had to go into battle with only two-thirds of his army, while Grant had only about half of his full forces. Although neither commander was ready for action, the armies clashed on 5 May. The battle started on the Federal left, where General

This two-day battle on 5–6 May 1864 marked the opening of the summer campaigning season and the first confrontation between the two best generals to emerge during the war.

Gouverneur Warren's V Corps faced General Richard Ewell's II Corps. They fought themselves to a standstill before reinforcements arrived. On the Federal right, General Winfield Scott Hancock's corps made considerable gains, pushing the Rebels back during the afternoon until nightfall ended the day's fighting.

The battle resumed on 6 May, with Hancock continuing to drive the Rebels back, but at midday, the rest of Lee's army arrived. General James Longstreet's I Corps counter-attacked and soon forced Hancock to withdraw, to the extent that all of his hard-gotten gains of the day before were given up. Rebel troops even infiltrated a gap in the centre of the Federal line along an unfinished railway cutting and seemed poised to divide the Federal army in two. However, by this time units on both sides were too mixed up, visibility was too obscured by smoke for any attacks to be effective and the battle came to an end.

General Ulysses S. Grant took the Federal army across the Rapidan river here at Germanna Ford to destroy General Robert E. Lee's Rebel army, to the relief of President Abraham Lincoln, who was tired of his generals concentrating their efforts on capturing Richmond.

A Prussian regimental band in camp during the war against Denmark in 1864. The Prussians and Austrians heavily outnumbered the Danish forces.

Prussia, Austria attack little Denmark

The Danes suffered a heavy defeat in the Battle of Dybbøl on 18 April 1864, at the hands of a Prussian army. The Prussians outnumbered the Danes by more than three to one, but could not achieve a decisive victory owing to the gallant charge of the Danish 8 Brigade, and the bombardment by the Danish ironclad *Rolf Krake* which prevented them from crossing Åls Sound.

The war between Prussia, the dominant power in northern Germany, and its ally Austria, the nominal leader of the German Confederation, against Denmark, was over the fate of the duchies of Schleswig-Holstein. The duchies had been controlled by the kings of Denmark by treaty since the fifteenth century, but nationalist Germans had come to resent that the majority German population of Holstein, as well as the minority community in Schleswig, were under Danish rule. When the Danes formally proclaimed Schleswig to be an integral part of Denmark in November 1863, war became likely. German troops crossed the border into Holstein in December, and in February 1864, Austrian and Prussian soldiers crossed the Eider river into Schleswig.

The first major battle of the war was fought at Mysunde on 2 February, when the Danes beat off an attack. Their position had to be evacuated in the face of a superior enemy force, and a new defensive line was established around Dybbøl, just west of the Danish archipelago. The Danish position was besieged and after a lengthy bombardment lasting from mid-March until 18 April, the Prussians succeeded in driving them out to the island of Åls.

Red faces on Red River

A mishandled campaign along the Red River in Louisiana ended with Federal defeat and the apparent trapping of a riverine flotilla at Alexandria, Louisiana. When General Nathaniel P. Banks, commander of the Army of the Gulf, arrived in the town on 25 April 1864 he discovered the river level far too low for his gunboats to continue on down to the Mississippi.

Banks was ordered to advance up the Red river from southern Louisiana and capture Shreveport, Louisiana. He came within 35 miles (56 km) of the town when he was defeated in the Battle of Mansfield at Sabine Crossroads on 8 April 1864. The next day he fended off the Rebel pursuit of his retreating army at the Battle of Pleasant Hill and continued his withdrawal until he reached Alexandria.

Federal forces assault Rebel positions along the Cane river during the Red River Campaign.

IN BRIEF

⚜ The defeat of a 500-strong Maori army, at Te Ranga, New Zealand, on 21 June 1864, by British forces, was the last battle of the Waikato War. An eight-hour bombardment preceded the assault by 300 British troops but a 230-man Maori garrison had built bomb-proof shelters and drove the British off with heavy casualties. The Maoris, however, withdrew, and were followed by British patrols that located the main Maori force at Te Ranga.

Grant moves south

Three days of attacks at Spotsylvania Court House have ended with some 32,000 casualties to both armies. Union General Ulysses S. Grant has resumed his Army of the Potomac's march south after breaking off the action on 18 May 1864, shadowed by General Robert E. Lee's Army of Northern Virginia.

After the Battle of the Wilderness, Grant abandoned the battlefield and was expected by both the Rebels and his own men to head back north of the Rapidan river, but he resumed the march in a south-easterly direction, to the surprise of his men.

Once Lee realized what was happening, he sent a force of troops to Spotsylvania, an intersection of three roads, to block the southward advance. Lee's men reached the junction first and began digging defensive positions.

After some preliminary skirmishing, the battle opened on 10 May. The Rebel position was shaped almost like an upside-down "U", and Grant attacked it at the apex of the 'Mule Shoe'. The assault was an innovative one conducted by Colonel Emory Upton who rushed the Rebel entrenchment with 12 regiments drawn up in four lines, without pausing to fire until the men were almost in the trenches themselves.

As the Rebel line gave way the first Federal line turned left and right to widen the breach, while the second line passed through to continue the assault. Although this was successful, the failure of follow-up units to come to Upton's support led to him eventually withdrawing.

Grant was impressed with Upton's attack and decided to attempt a similar, but larger assault, this time using a whole corps (81 regiments). Rain delayed the start of it and Lee momentarily assumed that Grant intended to march around his right flank again. But instead, General Winfield S. Hancock's II Corps struck at the apex of the Rebel position and

again the Rebels were forced out of their trenches. A counter-attack restored some of the lost ground and

the battle turned into a desperate hand-to-hand struggle over an area of ground that became known as the Bloody Angle, forcing Lee to give up the ground and withdraw to a new fortified position behind the old one.

A ferocious battle raged around Spotsylvania Court House in May 1864 as Lee's forces defended an entrenched position against Federal attacks.

Children go to war

A **charge by the** Cadet Battalion of the Virginia Military Institute on 15 May 1864 at the Battle of New Market captured a Federal field piece and contributed to the victory of the Rebel forces under General John Breckinridge. The Union Army of West Virginia under Major General Franz Sigel, was part of a three-pronged attack into Virginia, masterminded by General Ulysses S. Grant.

Sigel had about 6,000 men and encountered a slightly smaller force under the command of General Breckinridge. Sigel stood to receive the Rebel attack and found himself outflanked by cavalry in his original position. The Federal forces withdrew to a second line, half a mile

A cavalry attack on the advancing Rebels was broken up by Rebel artillery firing canister, and Breckinridge sent his troops forward once more to chase the Federal forces away again.

(0.8 km) behind his original position. The second line fared little better. A cavalry attack on the advancing Rebels was broken up by Rebel artillery firing canister, and Breckinridge sent his troops forward once more to chase the Federal forces away again. The battle ended with a long-range artillery duel.

IN BRIEF

✍ On 11 May 1864, the Ever-Victorious Army, a Western-trained Chinese force commanded by a British officer, Major Charles Gordon, captured the main military base of the Taiping rebels at Chanchufu. This effectively brought the Taiping rebellion to an end.

OVERLAND CAMPAIGN	
DATES:	May–June 1864
COMBATANTS:	Union vs Rebel Confederate States of America
FORCES ENGAGED:	USA, 120,000; Rebels, 60,000
CASUALTIES:	USA, 55,000; Rebels, 32,000
RESULT:	Union victory

Åls falls to Prussians, Danes seek peace

A trumpeter appearing in a mural commemorating the battle of Åls in June 1864. The Danish army stood and fought here to protect the approaches to the capital, Copenhagen.

T **he attempt by** little Denmark to resist both Prussia and Austria over control of Schleswig-Holstein came to an end in June 1864 after the fall of Åls to a Prussian assault on 29 June 1864. With negotiations between the two sides already having begun in Britain in April, it was only a matter of time before the Danes agreed to peace terms that would allow both halves of the duchy to pass into German control.

Control of Åls was important to the defence of the Danish capital, Copenhagen. However, the defeat of the combined Austro-Prussian fleet in the Battle of Heligoland on 9 May 1864 meant that any assault by the

Prussians would have to take place without naval support. The Prussians, who had succeeded in battering the Danes at Dybbøl with their artillery, began a long preparatory barrage of the Danish defences on 26 May. A month later, on 29 June, the Prussian assault began. The Danish warship *Rolf Krake* bombarded the flotilla of small craft the Prussians had assembled, and for some time it looked like the assault would fail disastrously. But minor damage led to the *Rolf Krake* having to retire and the Prussians were able to land on Åls. Once again, Prussian numerical superiority proved decisive and Åls had to be abandoned.

Grant pays butcher's bill for winning position

On 15 June 1864, the Army of the Potomac stood outside the city of Petersburg, Virginia. General Ulysses S. Grant fought the overland campaign from the Rapidan river in northern Virginia all the way to this important rail junction south of Richmond. He now threatened to cut off Lee's supply line to the rest of the Confederacy or to capture Richmond if Lee moved south to protect them. Grant had paid a heavy price to get this far, having lost as many as 65,000 casualties, although Rebel General Robert E. Lee had paid a similarly heavy price – 35,000 from an army half the size of Grant's. This has been the heaviest death toll in American military history for a single campaign.

Grant had paid a heavy price to get this far, having lost as many as 65,000 casualties, although Rebel General Robert E. Lee had paid a similarly heavy price – 35,000 from an army half the size of Grant's.

After withdrawing from Spotsylvania Court House, Grant repeated his manoeuvre round the right flank of Lee's army, only to be stopped by Lee again at North Anna on 23 May. This was perhaps Lee's strongest position of the campaign, as a river would divide Grant's army should he wish to attack. Grant realized the error he had made after a couple of early probes and disengaged before heading south again to Cold Harbor, but then made a bad error. He believed that Lee's army was "whipped", and gambled that one decisive attack might sweep it away. Instead, on 3 June he exposed his men to a slaughter comparable to the carnage at Fredericksburg – a decision he will regret for the rest of his life. Nine days of static trench skirmishing followed before Grant took his army off to Petersburg.

A burial party at work on the Cold Harbor battlefield. Grant's Overland campaign resulted in many casualties in a short space of time, but was a major strategic victory for the Federal army.

General William T. Sherman (standing with hand on gun barrel) together with some of his staff. Sherman's advance on Atlanta relied on manoeuvre to force the Rebels out of their positions.

Federal forces besiege Atlanta

The Federal western armies under the command of General William Tecumseh Sherman have begun their assault on the important city of Atlanta, having fought three battles around it at the end of July 1864. However, with powerful fortifications around the Georgian city, both sides face a stalemate.

Sherman's orders at the outset of the spring 1864 campaigning season required him to defeat the Rebel Army of Tennessee and capture Atlanta as part of a series of attacks planned to put pressure on the Rebel armies of the Confederate States of America at all points. Sherman commanded three separate armies – the Army of the Cumberland, the Army of the Tennessee and the Army of the Ohio – with a total strength of just under 100,000 men.

Sherman repeatedly manoeuvred around the left wing of his opponent, General Joseph Johnston, as he moved from his base at Chattanooga towards Atlanta. In May and June the two commanders fought several battles, as each probed the other's defences in search of a weak point that could be exploited. Resaca on 14–15 May, Adairsville on

17 May and New Hope Church on 25 May were the main engagements as Johnston repeatedly withdrew before Sherman could cut him off from his base. The biggest action occurred at Kennesaw Mountain, on 27 June, where Johnston's army occupied fortified entrenchments and Sherman attempted a rare frontal assault, believing that the length of front was too long for an army of the size Johnston commanded. The Federal soldiers were beaten back, however, suffering 3,000 casualties, the heaviest losses of the campaign so far.

Johnston was forced to withdraw when Sherman once again sent part of his army on a flanking march. Now only 4 miles (6½ km) from Atlanta, Johnston was removed from command by Jefferson Davis, the Rebel president, and replaced by General John B. Hood, an aggressive Texan. Hood attacked Sherman's forces twice – at Peachtree Creek on 20 July and in the Battle of Atlanta on 22 July – but both times the Rebels were forced back with heavy casualties. Sherman now tried another flanking manoeuvre, only for it to be halted by some of Hood's men in the Battle of Ezra Church on 28 July.

Duel in the Channel

A Rebel and a Federal warship arranged a combat off the French coast at Cherbourg on 19 June 1864, resulting in victory for the USS *Kearsarge* over the CSS *Alabama*. The Federal victory brought to an end the raiding career of the *Alabama*, which had captured or sunk shipping valued at an estimated $5 million – at a time when the average monthly wage of a newly enlisted Federal sailor was $12 per month.

The *Alabama* had arrived in Cherbourg while the *Kearsarge* was at Flushing in the Netherlands. When word of the Rebel raider's presence in the French port reached the commander of the *Kearsarge*, Captain John A. Winslow took his ship to intercept her. Winslow and the *Alabama*'s captain, Raphael Semmes, had been friends in the pre-war navy, and even shared accommodation during the Mexican War of 1846–48.

Semmes, whose ship desperately needed some maintenance and repair work, had little choice but to fight his way past the *Kearsarge* and find another port where work could be done on her. Semmes chose to engage the Federal ship, hoping to keep his opponent at long range where his guns would have an advantage. The battle lasted about an hour and a half, with the two ships circling round seven times before the close-range effectiveness of the Federal sailors' fire proved decisive. With his vessel sinking by the stern, Semmes gave the order to abandon ship.

Captain Raphael Semmes on the CSS *Alabama*. His cruise was ended by the USS *Kearsarge* off the French port of Cherbourg.

Surprise disaster in crater

On 30 July 1864, an innovative attack using an explosive mine to destroy Rebel trenches around Petersburg, Virginia, ended in catastrophe for the Federal attackers, forcing General Ulysses S. Grant's Army of the Potomac to continue its siege of the Rebel Army of Northern Virginia, commanded by Robert E. Lee.

Federal troops first probed the Petersburg defences on 9 June, when a force commanded by General Benjamin Butler, advancing from Fort Monroe on the coast, attempted to capture the city, but failed when its cavalry were defeated by a militia consisting of teenagers and old men.

Grant's first attempt came six days later, when an attack by part of his army breached the Rebel defences. However, the army had suffered so heavily in the May battles that its commanders were loath to risk the lives of their men. Rebel deceptions convinced the Federal commander on the spot that the enemy was stronger than in reality, so he waited for reinforcements, losing the opportunity to capture the city at once. However, three more days of fighting were to follow as Lee brought up reinforcements, at the same time as a new, more defensible, trench line was constructed behind the original one.

In July, a plan was adopted to tunnel under the Rebel defences in one sector and detonate 4 tons (3.6 tonnes) of gunpowder. After the explosion, Federal troops would charge through the breach in the lines and take Petersburg. In the event, the operation failed miserably as Federal troops got trapped in the crater and were gunned down by Rebel troops and artillery lining the rim and firing down into them. Over 4,000 Federal soldiers were casualties in what Grant described as "the saddest affair I have witnessed in this war".

Trenches around Petersburg. The lengthy siege of the Virginian city was largely marked by sitting in trenches, with occasional assaults such as the battle of the Crater on 30 July 1864.

President Abraham Lincoln watches from Fort Stevens as Washington comes under assault from the Rebel army of General Jubal Early. The raid succeeded in drawing some troops from Grant's army closely engaged with the Rebels at Petersburg.

Early's raid on Washington

Rebel troops from the Shenandoah Valley launched an offensive that brought them to the outskirts of Washington DC, but on 14 July 1864 General Jubal Early, their commander, ordered his men to retire. Federal reinforcements arrived rapidly from Grant's army, giving Early no chance of success.

Early had arrived in the Shenandoah Valley after a Federal army had advanced nearly to Lynchburg in mid-June, and General Robert E. Lee sent reinforcements to protect this vital source of supplies for his army. The Rebels now had superior numbers and the Federal forces withdrew toward West Virginia as Early advanced, leaving no substantial organized military force between himself and Washington.

Early's army crossed the Potomac on 6 July 1864. On 9 July, he confronted a Federal army at Monocacy, Maryland, made up of raw recruits and militia. Just before the battle, a division of the Army of the Potomac's VI Corps, which had been ordered to the Washington area in response to Early's sortie, arrived, only to be pushed aside by Early in a frontal attack. All that now stood between Early and Washington was some cavalry, with which his own mounted troops skirmished over the next two days.

On 11 July, Early arrived outside the city, where the fortifications appeared to him to be "feebly manned". He ordered his troops to prepare for a probing attack, but as they were forming up a column of dust signalled the arrival of Federal reinforcements, who filed into Fort Stevens, opened fire with the forts' guns and sent out skirmishers. During the night, two more Federal corps arrived. Early chose to withdraw and succeeded in evading his Federal pursuers.

Lincoln goes to war

One of the witnesses to the fighting outside Washington City on 12 July was President Lincoln himself. Having spent several years co-ordinating the movement of hundreds of thousands of men into positions where they were the target of Rebel bullets, Lincoln took this single opportunity he had during the war to share in the danger. Foolhardily, he stood on the parapet which Rebel sharpshooters had been firing at, in order to catch a glimpse of the enemy. Another later to become famous American, serving as a captain in the 20th Massachusetts, spotted the president and shouted, "Get down, you damn fool, before you get shot." An amused Lincoln took future Chief Justice Holmes's advice.

Admiral David Farragut's forces race past Fort Morgan guarding the entrance to Mobile Bay. The Federal fleet was deployed in two lines, with the armoured monitors closer to the Rebel batteries. The USS *Tecumseh* is sinking after striking a Rebel torpedo (floating mine).

"Damn the torpedoes"

A **Federal squadron commanded** by the victor of New Orleans, Admiral David Farragut, defeated the Rebel naval defenders of Mobile in the Battle of Mobile Bay on 5 August 1864. Farragut's squadron now occupies Mobile Bay, awaiting the arrival of Federal soldiers to take over this important Rebel-held port.

Farragut had to lead his ships past two forts either side of the entrance to the bay, and then defeat the most powerful of all Rebel ironclads, the CSS *Tennessee*. The *Tennessee* mounted six powerful guns and had a thickly-armoured casemate resembling the CSS *Virginia*, but her engines were woefully underpowered for the weight of the vessel.

The Rebel defence was based on a chain of floating mines, known as torpedoes, that stretched between the two forts. Farragut

In Mobile Bay, a ferocious mêlée erupted between Farragut's mix of monitors and wooden ships, and the Tennessee. *Badly outnumbered and unable to manoeuvre, it was only a matter of time before the* Tennessee *was pounded into submission.*

believed that by moving at high speed through the harbour entrance, he could escape heavy damage from the forts' guns.

The Rebels hoped that the torpedoes would cause the Federal ships to stop under the guns, and that heavy damage would enable the small defending squadron to defeat the larger Federal force.

As Farragut's ships reached the torpedoes, one of them, the monitor USS *Tecumseh*, detonated a torpedo and sank quickly. His ships slowed down but Farragut ordered, "Damn the torpedoes, full speed ahead," and the squadron entered the bay.

In Mobile Bay, a ferocious mêlée erupted between Farragut's mix of monitors and wooden ships, and the *Tennessee*. Badly outnumbered and unable to manoeuvre, it was only a matter of time before the *Tennessee* was pounded into submission.

Atlanta falls to Sherman

"**Atlanta is ours,** and fairly won," reported General William T. Sherman to President Lincoln on 2 September 1864. Using the same skill at manoeuvre that has marked his whole campaign against the Rebel army defending Atlanta, Sherman has managed to get the Rebels to leave their entrenchments, leaving his army free to march into the city.

He achieved this by probing at the main supply line used by General John B. Hood's Army of Tennessee, which was well dug in around Atlanta. On 26 August, Sherman pulled almost his entire army out of the siege works and sent it on a long march to target the Macon Railroad at two points: Rough-and-Ready and Jonesborough. Hood at first thought Sherman was in retreat but then realized the truth and rushed half his army to Jonesborough, where battle was joined on 31 August. The Federal forces were held, but the railway was still cut at Rough-and-Ready. With his supply line interrupted, Hood had no choice but to abandon the city.

The railroad yards of Atlanta after their destruction in the fire that damaged the city badly. The fire was set by the retreating Rebel troops abandoning this vital railway junction.

Sheridan in Shendandoah

General Philip Sheridan arrives in the midst of the battle of Opequon Creek, on 19 September 1864, to urge his troops on.

A Federal army now dominates the Shenandoah Valley after its victory at Fisher's Hill on 21–22 September 1864. General Philip Sheridan finally achieved what no other Federal commander has managed to do in the entire war – both defeat and drive the Rebels out of the valley. He is now preparing to devastate this rich agricultural region.

After Early had withdrawn from Washington, he first moved through central Maryland, his cavalry force even racing into Pennsylvania, burning the town of Chambersburg when the citizens proved unable to pay a ransom of $500,000 on 30 July 1864. Early returned to Virginia in August.

Early's raid forced Grant to withdraw troops from his army in front of Petersburg, Virginia, and he sent Sheridan, his cavalry commander, to take charge of the newly created Army of the Shenandoah, of 50,000 men, more than twice the 18,000-strong force commanded by Early. Sheridan proceeded uncharacteristically cautiously at first so that Early was able to ensure that the harvest was gathered in at the end of August. The two armies first clashed at Winchester, at the northern end of the valley, at the Battle of Opequon Creek on 19 September, in which Sheridan drove Early out of a strong position, both sides suffering heavy casualties. Three days later, Early had located himself in another strong position at Fisher's Hill. This time Sheridan used a whole day to manoeuvre part of his army into position on the flank of Early's lines, and the late-afternoon attack carried the Rebel defences with relative ease.

A dejected General Robert E. Lee with his son Custis (left) and his aide Lieutenant Colonel Walter Taylor after the surrender at Appomattox Court House.

Lee surrenders – Civil War ends

General **Robert E. Lee** surrendered his Rebel army on 9 April 1865, having abandoned Petersburg and having been chased across Virginia by the Federal army commanded by General Ulysses S. Grant.

Lee had to abandon Petersburg after the defeat of part of his army that he had sent to Five Forks – along which ran his last supply route from Petersburg to the south, the South Side Railroad – on 1 April 1865. Once out of the trenches, he moved in a south-westerly direction toward Lynchburg, Virginia, in an attempt to escape the much larger Federal army. After capturing Petersburg, Grant was able to advance northward to capture Richmond,

the Rebel capital, which had been abandoned by the Rebel government on April 2.

At Appomattox Court House the Army of Northern Virginia found Federal troops both to their front and rear. Virtually surrounded, Lee opted to surrender rather than fight to the death.

On 26 April 1865, General Joseph E. Johnston surrendered his Rebel army at Bennett's Place, North Carolina, to General William T. Sherman. Johnston had tried to evade Sherman until Lee could come and join him, but the surrender of Lee removed even this last hope. The last major Rebel force, the Trans-Mississippi Department, surrendered on 26 May 1865.

Hood's folly

After suffering a disastrous defeat at Nashville, Tennessee, on 16 December 1864, Rebel General John B. Hood retreated to Tupelo, Mississippi, and resigned his command on 23 January 1865. The Rebel Army of Tennessee has more or less ceased to be an effective force in the field.

Hood's mistake was to wage a campaign against the supply lines of the Federal army commanded by General William T. Sherman. Hood had discussed this idea with President Jefferson Davis when he visited the Rebel commander at his headquarters. At the time Sherman was still at Atlanta, but he planned to leave the Georgian city and march to the coast at Savannah, destroying everything in his path.

Once Sherman was on the move, Hood turned north and advanced into Tennessee. He gambled that he could defeat the Federal forces left there and gather new recruits for his army from Tennessee and Kentucky. Unfortunately, almost everything went wrong for Hood, in part thanks to his own miscalculations, when he launched a futile frontal attack on a Federal army at Franklin, Tennessee on 30 November, leading to the deaths of six of his generals and over 6,000 of his men. His outnumbered opponent retreated to Nashville, where Hood's army was badly beaten and routed off the field.

General John Hood's bravery was never in doubt, but his desperate assaults on Federal positions in Tennessee destroyed his army.

Marching through Georgia

General William T. Sherman reviews his army at Savannah, after he had completed his "March to the Sea". Sherman succeeded in causing serious devastation to northeastern Georgia, but he allowed a Rebel army to outflank his position at Atlanta and advance into Tennessee.

A **Federal army commanded** by General William T. Sherman reached the Georgian port of Savannah on the Atlantic coast on 22 December 1864. Sherman telegraphed Lincoln: "I beg to present you as a Christmas gift the City of Savannah."

Sherman had become increasingly frustrated by Rebel strategy after capturing Atlanta. Instead of offering battle, both the Rebel cavalry and the Army of Tennessee concentrated their efforts on harassing Sherman's lengthy supply line, which stretched all the way from northern states such as Ohio and Illinois to Atlanta, passing through Nashville and Chattanooga. Such a long line required the diversion of a large part of Sherman's army to protect it, so long as he was stationary in Atlanta. However, he realized that if he sent part of his army back into Tennessee, and marched with the rest to the coast, the problem would be solved. Those on the march could live off the rich agricultural land of northern Georgia, while those sent back to Tennessee would have a much shorter supply line and be able to use more of their numbers in combat.

Grant, in overall command of the Federal war effort, agreed and gave permission for Sherman's "March to the Sea". Sherman divided his army into two columns, marching about 60 miles (96 km) apart. On the way, they took anything they needed with them, at the same time destroying everything else.

The consequence was a swathe of savage devastation across Georgia. With few Rebel soldiers in the area, Sherman faced no resistance and captured Savannah after a long artillery bombardment.

IN BRIEF

❧ On 12 October 1864, a Brazilian attempt to influence Uruguayan domestic politics became an invasion when Brazilian soldiers crossed into Uruguay. Paraguay had offered to mediate in the dispute and, angered by the Brazilian act, captured a Brazilian ship on the River Paraguay. On 13 December, Paraguay declared war on Brazil, and on 18 March 1865 on Argentina, which had refused to allow its troops to cross its territory, and on Uruguay.

❧ On 15 January 1865 a combined assault by Federal ships and infantry captured the Rebels' Fort Fisher, outside Wilmington, North Carolina. The fort had been almost impregnable for most of the war, being built from sand and grass that just absorbed the impact of shells. It was well equipped with artillery and well defended with landmines and other explosive devices.

Prussian victory overthrows European order

Prussian troops advance in a thick skirmish line during the Battle of Königgrätz (also known as the Battle of Sadowa) in July 1866. The battle was a model of concentrating an army's strength by drawing together separately marching columns.

The **Prussian army** achieved an astonishing victory over the Austrian army in the Battle of Königgrätz (Sadowa) on 3 July 1866. The victory marks the passing of political supremacy in Germany after 400 years from the Austrian Hapsburgs to the Prussian Hohenzollerns.

The Prussians fought an extremely well-organized campaign, relying on the staff work of Field Marshal Helmuth von Moltke, who was able to use railways and telegraphs to gather his army together quickly and invade Bohemia. Using a concentric advance by three separate armies, they caught the Austrian forces at Königgrätz. By handling their forces aggressively the Prussians got the upper hand although it took the arrival of reinforcements in mid-afternoon to secure a decisive Prussian victory.

SEVEN WEEKS' WAR

DATES:	1866
COMBATANTS:	Austria vs Italy and Prussia
FORCES ENGAGED:	Austria, 160,000; Italy, 150,000; Prussia, 140,000
CASUALTIES:	Austria, 30,000; Prussia, 10,000; Italy, 8,000
RESULT:	Prussian and Italian victory

Austrian naval victory

The **Austrian navy** won a surprising victory over the Italian fleet at the Battle of Lissa on 20 July 1866, after Italy had joined Prussia in a war against Austria, only to experience defeats on land and sea.

The Austrian fleet was heavily outnumbered by the Italians and also less well equipped with artillery, so the fleet commander, Admiral Wilhelm von Tegetthoff, decided to get to close quarters and rely on ramming enemy ships in order to defeat them. The Italians, by contrast, seemed to have had no clear plan, choosing to improvise once battle was joined.

At the outset of the battle the Italians held an advantage, as Tegetthoff allowed their line-ahead formation to cross the T of his fleet's formation. But the Italians did not recognize their advantage and Tegetthoff was able to get close enough to ram several ships. Two large Italian ironclads were sunk, before the Italians withdrew.

The *Re d'Italia* sinks after being rammed by the Austrian flagship *Erzherzog Ferdinand Max* in the battle of Lissa, 20 July 1866.

Battle of Four Nations

A panoramic view of the Battle of Paso de Patria on 24 May 1866, showing Argentine troops in the foreground advancing on the Paraguayan positions.

The largest battle in Latin American history took place amid the Paraguayan swamps of Tuyutí on 24 May 1866, when an allied army of Uruguayans, Brazilians and Argentines defeated a smaller Paraguayan army. Over 60,000 troops were involved in the action.

Paraguay had experienced a number of defeats since June 1865 and some 7,000 of her soldiers were captured in

Brazil in September 1865. Following this success, the allies agreed to an invasion of Paraguay. The Paraguayans had constructed key fortifications at the confluence of the Paraná and Paraguay rivers.

When the allied army reached Tuyutí, their camp was subjected to constant skirmishing attacks by the Paraguayans. With indiscipline and disease also hampering the plans of the allied commander, General Bartolome Mitre, the Paraguayan dictator, Francisco Solano López, decided to attack the allied camp.

The battle began at 11.30 a.m. on 24 May and lasted until 4 p.m. The Paraguayan troops advanced resolutely, in spite of some difficult terrain, but their inferior numbers and hard going in parts of the battlefield eventually told against them. About half the army was lost. The allies suffered almost as heavily, but their army numbered 35,000 against the Paraguayans' 23,000.

IN BRIEF

❧ An Italian army was defeated at Custozza on 24 June 1866, during the Seven Weeks' War. The outnumbered Austrian forces engaged the separate parts of an Italian army divided on its march by the terrain, driving them back.

A Brazilian river squadron defeated a smaller Paraguayan force on 11 June 1865, in the Battle of Riachuelo, on the Paraná river in Argentina. The battle had an adverse effect on the plans of the Paraguayan leader, Francisco Solano López, who had hoped to advance down the Paraná in support of his allies in Uruguay.

Solano López had hoped to use political rivalries in Argentina in order

The two fleets met at a wide point known as Riachuelo. The Brazilians had larger ships with more powerful guns, the Paraguayans more nimble vessels better suited to fighting on a river.

to gain access to Uruguay, but the Argentines were suspicious of his long-term ambitions and refused to allow his army passage. Instead, Solano López created a small riverine fleet and attempted to annex Argentine provinces. Brazil, already fighting Paraguay along their common border, sent ships up the Paraná to help the Argentines. With poor roads in the region, the rivers were the main routes of access, and control of them was vital to military success.

The two fleets met at a wide point known as Riachuelo. The Brazilians had larger ships with more powerful guns, the Paraguayans more nimble vessels better suited to fighting on a river. In the end, in spite of having a couple of ships run aground in the shallow water, the more powerful guns of the Brazilians won the day.

Ships and honour

A **Spanish attempt to** seize control of the guano-rich Chincha Islands resulted in the bombardment of the important Peruvian port of El Callao on 2 May 1866. A powerful Spanish squadron including the ironclad frigate *Numancia* spent nearly five hours firing on the batteries defending the port.

The Spanish were rumoured to be seeking to re-annex Peru and Chile and benefit from the wealthy guano trade from which these two countries profited. However, the British and Americans

At Callao, Méndez Núñez led his ships into the harbour in a V formation to engage the Peruvians. For five hours the two sides battered one another until the Spanish withdrew.

opposed the Spanish ambitions, and at one point a confrontation between American and Spanish ships in Valparaiso harbour resulted in the famous quotation from Admiral Casto Méndez Núñez that "Spain, the Queen and I prefer honour without ships than ships without honour."

At Callao, Méndez Núñez led his ships into the harbour in a V formation to engage the Peruvians. For five hours the two sides battered one another until the Spanish withdrew. Both sides claimed victory, but the Spanish had suffered more heavily – Méndez Núñez was wounded nine times himself – and in the end the war was abandoned.

The Spanish bombardment of the Peruvian port of Callao on 2 May 1866. Spain attempted to reassert a measure of control over Latin America by its seizure of the Chincha islands in 1864.

WAR OF THE TRIPLE ALLIANCE

DATES:	1864-1870
COMBATANTS:	Paraguay and Uruguayan rebels vs Argentina, Brazil and Uruguay
FORCES ENGAGED:	Unknown
CASUALTIES:	Paraguay, 300,000; Allies, 125,000
RESULT:	Allied victory

Paraguayans fend off Triple Alliance

An attempt by the Triple Alliance of Argentina, Brazil and Uruguay to break through a key Paraguayan fortress at Humaitá, Paraguay, failed on 22 September 1866. Allied morale has collapsed and it is clear it will be some time before they are ready to advance again.

The allies faced a serious problem in taking Humaitá as the Paraguayans had constructed a series of successive trench lines and batteries that made it difficult to use their naval superiority on the Paraguay river. On 2 September, a heartening success was achieved when after some hard fighting the battery at Curuzu fell to the allies. The fort

at Curupayty was the obvious next target.

On 22 September, after a brief truce, the allies launched their assault on Curupayty. It was preceded by a lengthy naval bombardment, but this had little initial effect the Paraguayans had constructed a moat in front of their first trench line. Once the allies had finally achieved a breach there, they discovered the Paraguayans had constructed a second trench line, packed with artillery. This unexpected development threw the allied attack into confusion and they were forced to retreat. The allies lost about 5,000 men, the Paraguayans less than a hundred.

Irish Nationalists invade Niagara

A group of Civil War veterans, members of an Irish Nationalist movement known as the Fenian Brotherhood, withdrew from the Niagara peninsula following a raid on Canada that resulted in the Battle of Ridgeway on 2 June 1866. However, many of the Fenians were subsequently arrested, after they returned to the United States on 3 June.

US authorities attempted to intercept the raiders at Buffalo, once they had assembled there. However, about a thousand of them succeeded in crossing the Niagara river. Canadian militia advanced from Port Colborne and met the Fenians. The Canadians were defeated when a few Fenians on stolen horses were mistakenly identified as cavalry, and a move into square formation and back to column was misinterpreted by a neighbouring Canadian regiment as a retreat.

General Winfield Scott in 1861: his physical appearance belied a shrewd, tactical mind.

OBITUARY
WINFIELD SCOTT (1786-1866)

General Winfield Scott has died at West Point, New York. He was aged 79.

Scott was one of the most influential American generals in history. He entered the army in 1807 as a militiaman and served in the War of 1812 between Britain and the United States. During this conflict, he established that the main problem confronting American forces was a lack of discipline. He instituted a stern regime of training and uniform and earned the sobriquet "Old Fuss and Feathers". On 5 July 1841, he became commander-in-chief of the army, a position he would hold for the next 20 years. He captured Mexico City in the Mexican-American War of 1846-48 and was the defeated candidate in the presidential election of 1852.

In 1861, during the American Civil War, the now elderly Scott found himself the target of a press campaign that called for his removal and replacement by a younger, more energetic man as Federal army commander. However, the broad outlines of Scott's strategy, the Anaconda Plan, which envisioned capturing the Mississippi and blockading southern ports, actually proved to be the winning strategy for the Federal in the war.

He never married.

France's Mexican adventure ends tragically

The French attempt to establish a puppet government in Mexico ended on 19 June 1867 with the execution of Maximilian Habsburg, who had volunteered to become emperor of a regime backed by Mexican conservatives and foreign investors. On 20 June, Maximilian's last significant concentration of supporters surrendered in Mexico City.

In June 1864, when Maximilian arrived in Mexico City, the French army was victorious on all fronts against the republicans of the country. However, with the end of the civil war in the United States, the republicans began receiving substantial amounts of weapons from the Americans, who opposed the French intervention.

Throughout 1866, the republicans began reversing the gains of the French and the imperialists. The French had already planned to withdraw their troops, preferring Maximilian to use his own resources and those of his Mexican allies to defend their regime. These troops, however, were for the most part unreliable, and American pressure ensured that the volunteers Maximilian

The execution of Maximilian Habsburg by Mexican republican forces brought to an end the attempt by France to create an empire by proxy in Latin America.

had recruited in Belgium and Austria were forced to leave. Local Mexican troops tended to switch sides depending on who was winning.

In February 1867, the last French troops left Mexico. In April, the city of Puebla, an important conservative centre, fell to the republicans and Mexico City was placed under siege. Maximilian was captured in May, trying to escape from the siege of Querétaro where most of his army had been trapped.

OBITUARY
ROBERT E. LEE (1807-1870)

The most successful Rebel general in the recent civil war in the United States has died at the age of 63 in Lexington, Virginia.

Robert E. Lee's father, Henry Lee, was a hero of the Revolutionary War and Lee grew up in Virginia. He considered that his first loyalty was to his state and when it left the Federal in April 1861, so did he. Lee had been a career army officer prior to Virginia's secession. He distinguished himself in the Mexican War of 1846-48, and also served as superintendent of West Point.

He could have been a very senior officer in the Federal army, but instead created a legendary career for himself as commander of the Rebel Army of Northern Virginia. On some occasions he was helped by the poor calibre of the opposing generals, rather than his own brilliance as a tactician.

He died of complications following a stroke, and is survived by his wife and seven children.

Paraguayan dictator killed, ending war

The dictator of Paraguay, Francisco Solano López, was killed in the Battle of Cerro-Corá on 1 March 1870. His attempts to wage a guerrilla war against the predominantly Brazilian occupiers of his country have ended in failure.

After the battles of 1866, the War of the Triple Alliance became bogged down in front of the Paraguayan fortress of Humaitá. The defences were so strong that the Allies abandoned any attempts at a frontal assault and spent the best part of a year gradually extending their siege lines around the sprawling fortress. Solano López thought an assault on the allied base at Tuyutí might break the siege, but his attempt in November 1867 only succeeded in seizing some allied artillery and supplies. In March 1868 Solano

According to some estimates, only 29,000 male Paraguayans of military age remained after the war's end.

López withdrew most of the garrison of Humaitá, leaving just enough troops to delay the allies. The inevitable surrender occurred in August 1868.

The allies now advanced toward the Paraguayan capital of Asunción and in December 1868, the Paraguayans attempted to halt the advance, but were defeated in three battles. Asunción was occupied on 5 January 1869. Solano López continued the struggle with a small force, but he had no secure source of supplies and the heavy casualties from previous battles had dramatically reduced the number of men in the population of Paraguay. According to some estimates, only 29,000 male Paraguayans of military age remained after the war's end, out of a pre-war population of half a million.

OBITUARY

DAVID FARRAGUT (1801-1870)

Civil War admiral David Farragut has died in Portsmouth, New Hampshire.

He was born in Tennessee, but his parents were residing in Louisiana when his mother died of yellow fever in 1808. He was then adopted by Commodore David Porter, who offered him the chance of a career in the navy. Farragut accepted, aged 11, served with Commodore Porter in the War of 1812 and commanded several vessels between 1834 and the outbreak of the American Civil War. He also founded the naval base at Mare Island, in California.

Farragut had no sympathy for the Rebels so there was no question in his mind of siding with the Rebel cause, but he was limited to shore duties until December 1861, when he was given command of the expedition against New Orleans. He was also active in campaigns along the Mississippi river after the fall of New Orleans. In November 1864 he effectively left war service.

In 1866, Farragut was made a full admiral, the first in US naval history. His last active service was a cruise of European waters in 1867.

IN BRIEF

❧ The capture of the Ethiopian fortress of Magdala on 13 April 1868 by British troops was followed by the suicide of the king, Theodore II, who had believed the place to be impregnable, and the release of his hostages. A British army had invaded Ethiopia in January 1868 to release British hostages taken by Theodore, who believed Queen Victoria had insulted him. After advancing inland from the coast across hot lowlands and into mountainous countryside, they defeated the Ethiopian army and assaulted the fortress.

The Franco-Prussian War (1870-71)

This conflict between the French empire and a confederation of German states began as a war reminiscent of the eighteenth century, over the possibility of a relative of the Prussian king becoming king of Spain. In its aftermath came a revolutionary moment that was to be an inspiration for generations of socialists.

The quick Prussian victory over the Austrian empire in 1866 had not only alarmed the French emperor, Napoleon III, it also created a new rival to France as the leading European military power. Since the fall of Napoleon I in 1814–1815, successive French governments had established their country as something of an arbiter of Europe's destiny. In the 1820s, troops had been sent to Spain to resolve a civil war there; in the 1830s, a crisis in Belgium had similarly been resolved in the French interest; in the 1850s, Napoleon III had fought and won wars with both Russia and the Austrian empire, imposing his French-oriented solution on European problems involving these nations.

However, while France was attempting to establish an empire of its own in Mexico, the Prussian Minister-President Otto von Bismarck was turning Prussia into the dominant power in Germany, then a collection of independent kingdoms and principalities, nominally owing allegiance to the Austrian emperor. When Leopold, a distant cousin

The close-quarters fighting in this romaticised image was a rare event during the war, as most of the combat took place at long range.

On 16 August 1870, at the Battle of Mars-la-Tour, an out-numbered force of Prussians, believing it was engaging the rearguard of Bazaine's army, halted the withdrawal of the French forces.

of King Wilhelm, was offered the Spanish throne in February 1870, Napoleon III saw an opportunity for a showdown between the growing power of Prussia and the traditional power of France. An ambassador was sent to Wilhelm, who reported the results of the talks to Bismarck by telegram. Bismarck edited the text of the telegram before releasing it. The edited words were far more offensive to the French than the original text and the outraged French government declared war on 19 July 1870.

Both countries mobilized their armies. The French expected to find support from Denmark and Austria, who had both recently lost wars against Prussia and other German states. Little had been done beforehand to organize an alliance against Prussia among them, and the German states of Baden, Bavaria and Württemberg joined with Prussia, but Austria and Denmark remained neutral.

The mobilization of the French army was chaotic; by contrast, the Prussian mobilization proceeded efficiently. The armies were on the move by the beginning of July, and three crucial battles were fought in succession on 4–6 August at Wissembourg, Spicheren and Froeschwiller, as a result of which the French forces retreated from the frontiers. These early battles demonstrated the technical superiority of the French infantry's rifle, the Chassepot, while the Germans also discovered their artillery to be far superior to that of the French. The pattern for all future engagements was established: the French soldiers would halt German attacks with rifle fire, until they were swept from their positions either by superior numbers or by shelling from the Prussian guns.

The opening battles shocked the French leaders. Napoleon III appointed a new commander of the Army of the Rhine, Marshal Achille Bazaine, and went to Châlons to organize a new army to counter the Prussian invasion of France. All French commanders realized the army at Metz was at risk of being trapped. Bazaine pushed his army in the direction of Verdun, from where it could co-ordinate attacks with the new force organized by the emperor.

But Bazaine did not move fast enough. On 16 August 1870, at the Battle of Mars-la-Tour, an outnumbered force of Prussians, believing it was engaging the rearguard of Bazaine's army, halted the withdrawal of the French forces. The battle was fierce and marked by Bazaine's inability to recognize the weakness of the army opposed to him. The Prussians succeeded in blocking the road to Verdun and Bazaine decided to withdraw, resupply his army and advance again. He therefore retired to positions around the village of Gravelotte, where he was attacked by two Prussian armies on the 18th.

The Battle of Gravelotte foreshadowed the carnage of the First World War, with attacking forces suffering heavily from the fire of defenders, the Prussians thinking there were far fewer Frenchmen present than there actually were. Generals on both sides showed operational incompetence, using tactics that would condemn thousands of their soldiers to death or wounding, and failing to take effective advantage of such success as was achieved. Mars-la-Tour and Gravelotte resulted in 36,000 Prussian and 28,000 French casualties, but at least the Prussians had the consolation of victory.

> The decisive engagement of the war was fought at Sedan on 1 September 1870. MacMahon's forces were on the verge of being encircled as the battle began and by nightfall were indeed surrounded.

An early combat photograph showing part of the battlefield of Sedan on 2 September 1870. The battle was a masterpiece of Prussian staff work, as the French army was pinned and encircled, and eventually surrendered.

Bazaine withdrew to Metz, where he was besieged and played no further part in the war, until his surrender in October.

Napoleon's second army, the Army of Châlons, now faced the urgent task of retrieving the situation – the Prussians had to be kept away from Paris, while Bazaine needed to be released from the siege of Metz. The Army of Châlons' commander, Marshal Patrice MacMahon, eventually was given orders to attempt the relief of Bazaine and moved north, aiming to catch the Prussians advancing on Paris on the flank. The Prussian commander, Helmuth von Moltke, left about half his forces to besiege Bazaine and with the other half advanced against MacMahon, placing his forces between the French army and Paris. The decisive engagement of the war was fought at Sedan on 1 September 1870. MacMahon's forces were on the verge of being encircled as the battle began and by nightfall were indeed surrounded, including among their number, Napoleon III. The battle had been one-sided, with 17,000 French casualties to 9,000 Prussian; Napoleon and his army surrendered the next day.

With the head of state in Prussian hands, the French might have been expected to capitulate, but they overthrew the regime and established a Government of National Defence. When Paris was besieged on 19 September, the Government of National Defence attempted to organize armies outside Paris that would attack the besiegers and free the city. One government minister, Leon Gambetta, left Paris in a balloon for Orléans to co-ordinate the effort.

This phase of the war saw makeshift French armies desperately trying to cut Prussian supply lines and fight their way through to Paris, but each attempt was defeated. There were too many trained, battle-experienced Prussian soldiers, with too much artillery, for the French to overcome them. On 28 January

> When Gambetta received the news on 30 January at Tours, he at first refused to give up and launched another failed attack directed at Orléans, which had fallen to the Prussians in December.

1871, the government in Paris secured an armistice. When Gambetta received the news on 30 January at Tours, he at first refused to give up and launched another failed attack directed at Orléans, which had fallen to the Prussians in December. Gambetta resigned under pressure from the Government of National Defence on 6 February, and the war finally ended.

Parisian Communards behind a barricade. The collapse of French national political authority brought the first attempt to establish a socialist regime in world history.

Russians battle winter, Ottomans to victory

A
Russian army stands on the brink of a major victory over the Ottomans as it occupies Adrianople on 20 January 1878, after a brief but successful battle three days earlier. Constantinople will almost certainly be captured if the British are not prepared to go to war with Russia over the fate of the Ottoman Empire.

The war developed from a series of revolts, beginning in Bosnia and Herzegovina in the summer of 1875. In Constantinople, the Sultan was deposed in May 1876 by those opposed to his policies of conciliating the Ottoman Empire's traditional rival, Russia. This was followed in June 1876 by the claimed massacre of up to 12,000 Bulgarians after a revolt. Serbia and Montenegro, supporters of the rebels, in turn declared war on the Ottomans, having secretly been assured of the support of Russia. However, in September 1876 the Serbs were badly beaten by the Ottomans, to the surprise of the Russians, who now threatened the Ottoman Empire with war. A diplomatic conference could not avert the conflict and the Tsar declared war on the Sultan on 24 April 1877.

The Russians miscalculated the strength of the Ottoman army. An advance into Bulgaria brought them to the town of Plevna, where they attacked on 20 July and were badly beaten. Both sides sought reinforcements and the Ottomans dug extensive entrenchments before a second Russian attack was driven off again with very heavy casualties. The Russians now retreated from some of their gains to concentrate on the siege of Plevna, and then it was the turn of the Ottomans to attack at Shipka Pass, in August, where they in turn suffered heavy losses.

A third assault on Plevna was made on 11 September, before the Russians settled for a blockade hoping that hunger would end Ottoman resistance. In December 1877, the garrison of Plevna capitulated and in January 1878 the Russians broke through the Shipka Pass, opening the way to Constantinople.

RUSSO-TURKISH WAR

DATES:	April 1877–March 1878
COMBATANTS:	Russia (with Rumanian and Serbian support) vs Ottoman Empire
FORCES ENGAGED:	Russia 240,000; Ottoman Empire 190,000
CASUALTIES:	Russia 47,000; Ottoman Empire 71,000
RESULT:	Russian victory

The long siege of Plevna began on 20 July 1877, when the Russian army attacked Ottoman positions. It only ended five months later with the Ottomans' capitulation.

Defeat of the last Samurai

Takamori Saigo, the last Samurai, summons his troops to fight the invading army of the Japanese government, coming aboard ships to land at Kagoshima on the island of Kyushu. The artist Yoshitoshi created this print, one of popular series on the subject of the Satsuma Rebellion.

A rebellion of traditionalist samurai in Japan has been crushed by the imperial government after the last remnant of the insurgent army was defeated at the Battle of Shiroyama on 24 September 1877 and the leader of the rebels, Takamori Saigo, committed suicide.

The rebellion broke out in the Satsuma region of Kagoshima province on the island of Kyushu, when government troops attempted to disarm the samurai in January 1877. Takamori had originally supported reforms, but turned against the government when he recognized their logical conclusion.

He blundered early on when he preferred to lay siege to a government garrison instead of countering the concentration of the government army on Kyushu. In battle, the samurai were remarkably effective fighters, but they were badly outnumbered and did not have as many modern firearms.

IN BRIEF

On 28 March 1873 the Netherlands declared war on Atjeh, an independent kingdom at the north-western tip of Sumatra. Six days earlier a military expedition had left Batavia to occupy the kingdom and bombarded the capital at Banda Aceh, although this achieved little before the expedition departed to avoid the coming monsoon. A second expedition, sent at the end of 1873, captured the Sultan of Atjeh's main stronghold in January 1874, but resistance continued as Atjehnese tribesmen conducted guerrilla war against the Dutch until 1908.

The Carlist faction won two victories over their liberal opponents in a civil war in northern Spain. On 5 May 1873, they defeated liberal troops at Eraul and on 9 July, they defeated another liberal force at Alpens in Catalonia.

The defeat of a Carlist army at the Battle of Elgueta on 13 February 1876 seemed likely to condemn the Carlist movement to its third defeat in a history of rebellion against the Madrid government stretching back to the 1830s. Now that the Spanish monarchy had been restored under the liberal Alfonso XII, Carlism has lost its biggest aid to recruitment – opposition to a republican form of government.

America's centennial celebrations have been marred by the news that on 25 June 1876 the 7th Cavalry Regiment, commanded by Civil War hero Major General George Armstrong Custer, was badly defeated by an alliance of Indians camped on the Little Bighorn river. Custer and some 200 men were massacred by a band possibly numbering as many as 15,000.

A rebellious conservative army in the Colombian state of Antioquia was defeated by the pro-government forces in the state of Cauca at the Battle of Los Chancos on 31 August 1876. The brief rebellion, over secular education, ended in April 1877 with a treaty.

Wars against the American Indians

The million-man army mobilized by the Federal government in 1865 had been reduced to 55,000, just two years on, when its main mission was policing the frontier. Here, it was scattered across a vast area, virtually unsettled except for a few hardy pioneer farmers and miners. The spanning of the American West by railways, and the urge to find farmland in the West and on the Pacific Coast, brought conflict with the original inhabitants, the American Indians.

General George Crook was the most effective American general in the Indian Wars, but spent his last years denouncing the poor treatment of his opponents.

More Indians appeared on hills to the south and south-east of the soldiers' camp. Again they attacked; again the US troops deployed into a skirmish line and chased them off. The Battle of Wolf Mountain raged to and fro for five hours, with the Indians unusually fighting on foot on account of the terrain. In the end, the Indians had to withdraw as they were running low on ammunition and the soldiers were using cannons against them, to which they had no answer. Casualties, in the end, were surprisingly light: three Indians and two soldiers. The main result of the battle was a huge expenditure of ammunition by the Indians, who found it much harder to replace than the US soldiers.

This apparently minor engagement, some six months after the more notorious Battle of the Little Bighorn, where Major General George Armstrong Custer and part of his 7th Cavalry Regiment were massacred, is not only far more characteristic of the kind of warfare the US army waged against the American Indians, but was in many ways a more decisive battle. The commanders on both

> The preferred tactic was the ambush, whether of a group on the move or of a group in camp, although the Indians were not above taunting their intended victims beforehand, as happened to Colonel Miles's men.

sides were among the most famous of all: the US soldiers were led by Colonel Nelson A. Miles and the Indians by Crazy Horse. Miles demonstrated that no matter what time of the year it was, the army would find bands of Indians who had wandered off the reservation. Many Indians already argued that they needed to make peace with the "bluecoats", whose successes of the previous autumn, together with a shortage of game during this particular winter had meant the roaming bands were finding life hard. In the spring, Crazy Horse surrendered, and in September 1877, while trying to escape arrest, he was killed. Miles, meanwhile, went on to a successful military career, which included the capture of another important Indian chief, Geronimo of the Apache.

Miles stood at the apex of the considerable experience the US army had acquired over many years of dealing with American Indians. In part thanks to being better supplied and able to fight in all seasons, the army eventually defeated every American Indian tribe that challenged the unequal treaties they were required to sign with the "white man". The contest began even in pre-Independence days, as American Indians resisted attempts by European settlers to take away land they viewed as a common resource, and not something that could be traded as if it were a flint or a bow and arrows.

The army's experience began with wars against the American Indians living in the Great Lakes area, including the worst defeat ever suffered against them, the St Clair debacle of November 1792. However, the overall approach to dealing with American Indians was largely established during these early conflicts. A military base would be established near to where the Indians lived. If the Indians violated any treaty, an expedition would be sent out to capture those responsible. Targeting the Indians' food resources and campaigning during seasons when the Indians needed to go hunting, or were tending crops, or faced a shortage of game, was generally advantageous in getting a quick end to any conflict. In a fight, technological superiority (at first firearms, later artillery) needed to be brought to bear as quickly as possible.

A fort on an Indian agency in the American West shows the traditional structure of American frontier forts with blockhouses at the corners.

This all amounted to a war of small units (usually a few companies) scattered widely across a large area, which were often constantly on the move. If anything, it resembled police work more than military operations.

The wars against the Indians followed a particular pattern. Normally, they coincided with the establishment of some kind of white settlement in the area, which usually reduced the Indians' access to their hunting grounds or hampered the free movement of buffalo. In the case of the Custer massacre, the causes of the war began out of a wish on the part of the white man to mine gold in the Black Hills, a sacred area to the Sioux.

The Indians, by contrast, viewed war differently. The tribes of the plains had been fighting each other long before the white man arrived, and the main effect of whites on Indian warfare was to raise the level of technology as they acquired rifles, metal knives and hatchet blades.

For the Indians, war was an *ad hoc* affair, hardly different to hunting, except when large war parties gathered. They would travel in small groups and attack any enemy that they found. "Enemy" was an indiscriminate term, as anyone of the opposing tribe was an enemy, whether or not wearing a uniform, or holding a government commission. Men would be killed, unless made captive in which case they would be tortured for sport. Women

> For the Indians, war was an ad hoc affair, hardly different to hunting, except when large war parties gathered. They would travel in small groups and attack any enemy that they found.

A photograph possibly showing Crazy Horse, a Lakota chief, who was one of the best commanders of the American Indians in all their wars against the United States. He helped defeat Major General George Custer's force at the Battle of the Little Bighorn on 25 June 1876.

of childbearing age were preferably taken prisoner, as were children, who were brought up in the tribe in order to increase its numbers. Women not of childbearing age were also likely to be killed, as were other women and children if the war party was not in a position to transport its captives back to a camp.

War parties were gathered together under the control of a war chief, who was not necessarily the same man as the chief of a band. The war chief was simply the acknowledged leader of the war party, and the choice depended on who was actually a member of the war party in question. However, when the tribe's council had agreed to a general war party, the head of the band was likely to be the war chief. The preferred tactic was the ambush, whether of a group on the move or of a group in camp, although the Indians were not above taunting their intended victims beforehand, as happened to Colonel Miles's men in the Battle of Butte. A volley

or two of gunfire and arrows announced the ambush; this would be followed by a rush to close quarters, where it was hoped the Indians' skill at hand-to-hand fighting would prevail.

There were never very many Indians as a hunter-gatherer lifestyle cannot support a large population. They were therefore very reluctant to take casualties, and if too many warriors were lost it could mean the death of the tribe itself. Consequently, the ambush and hit-and-run tactics were almost forced on Indian leaders to minimize losses.

The end of Zulu power

Members of the Natal Native Contingent, a force of African volunteers who were recruited to fight against the Zulus with British forces during the Zulu War.

The defeat of the Zulu army at Ulundi on 4 July 1879 forced the Zulu king, Cetewayo, to flee his own capital, bringing to an end the dynasty of Zulu kings founded by Shaka Zulu in 1828. The Zulu army has been shattered by the defeat, its regiments scattered across the countryside as warriors flee the battlefield.

The war began in January 1879 with the invasion of Zululand by three columns of British and colonial troops. One of the columns was surprised by a much larger Zulu force at Isandhlwana on 22 January and almost completely wiped out. However, the Zulu forces following the fleeing remnants of this force were in turn halted at Rorke's Drift, where 139 British soldiers beat off repeated assaults by around 4,000 Zulu warriors.

The decisive battle of the campaign took place in March, when the British offensive was renewed. One target of the British attack was a Zulu strongpoint at Hlobane, but the British failure there on 28 March had the unfortunate result for the Zulus of making them overconfident and they attacked a British camp nearby at Kambula the next day. Although they attacked for most of the day they were repeatedly driven off, suffering heavy casualties in the process.

The Zulu army was exceptionally well disciplined and highly skilled tactically, but the warriors were only equipped with short stabbing spears. The rifles and artillery of the British gave them such an advantage that even when the Zulus succeeded, as at Isandhlwana, it came at a high cost.

IN BRIEF

❧ The surrender of Cuban rebels at the town of Zanjon on 10 February 1878 brought to an end to the Ten Years' War, a guerrilla conflict between Cuban nationalists and their Spanish overlords. The nationalists have received considerable support from their friends in the United States, but no official diplomatic aid. Spain was forced to send 25,000 troops to the island to reinforce the garrison in order to suppress the rebellion.

Chile rules the waves

The Chilean fleet achieved a key naval victory at the Battle of Angamos in its war against the small Peruvian navy. On 8 October 1879, the Peruvian ironclad *Huascar* was captured after a long battle against three powerful Chilean vessels; her commander, Rear Admiral Miguel Grau, was killed. Chile now has complete command of the shipping lanes along the coast of the contested Atacama desert.

Chile's growing economic power in the Bolivian territory of Litoral, on the Pacific coast, led to a demand for increased taxes from Chilean companies operating in Bolivia. When these were not paid, the Bolivian government announced its intention to auction off the properties concerned. The taxes violated a treaty, so the Chilean government sent troops to occupy Antofagasta to prevent the auction on 14 February 1879, forcing Bolivia to declare war on Chile on 1 March. At this point, the contents of a secret treaty between Peru and Bolivia became public knowledge. Peru attempted to mediate in the crisis, but Chile rejected the offer and declared war on both Bolivia and Peru.

By this time, Chilean troops had already successfully occupied Calama, having defeated a small Bolivian army at Topáter on 23 March, but from this point the war shifted to a confrontation at sea. The roads along the coast of the Atacama Desert were poor so much of the resupply of troops there needed to be done by sea. The naval war was one of small actions, since neither Peru nor Chile had a large navy. The naval Battle of Iquique on 21 May pitted two Peruvian ironclads against two Chilean wooden ships, each side losing one ship, which had a greater effect on the Peruvian navy, since it was smaller. The surviving Peruvian ironclad, the *Huascar*, spent several months sailing up and down the coast looking for Chilean ships and cutting submarine telegraph cables, until her final battle on 8 October.

WAR OF THE PACIFIC

DATES:	1879-1884
COMBATANTS:	Chile vs Bolivia and Peru
FORCES ENGAGED:	Chile, *c.*30,000; Bolivia and Peru, *c.*36,000
CASUALTIES:	Chile, *c.*7,500; Bolivia and Peru, *c.*9,000
RESULT:	Chilean victory

The Peruvian ironclad *Huáscar* engages Chilean vessels during the battle of Angamos on 8 October 1879. The *Huáscar* was captured, outnumbered by six ships to one.

Afghan adventure proves costly

British troops occupying Afghanistan succeeded in withstanding a nationalist revolt there, having defeated an army led by Ayub Khan, a claimant to the emirate of that country, on 1 September 1880, at Kandahar. However, the British intend to withdraw rather than continue with a military occupation that has been expensive in both money and lives.

The British invasion of Afghanistan began in November 1878 as three columns rushed to cross the Hindu Kush before winter set in. They were successful at forcing their way over and reached Kabul, where a puppet ruler was put in place of the previous emir who fled to Mazr-i-Sharif, where he died. A treaty, signed in January 1879, gave the British considerable control over the country. However, in September the British resident and all his staff were assassinated at Kabul in an uprising as Afghan religious leaders proclaimed a holy war against the invaders. British troops occupied Kabul, but the unrest of its citizens eventually forced the commander, General Sir Frederick Roberts, to withdraw to his encampment at Sherpur. For a time he was besieged there, but the Afghans could not capture the camp and Roberts eventually reoccupied Kabul, where he was sent reinforcements from the other main British base at Kandahar. Here the British put forward their own claimant to the emirate, Abdur Rahman. Ayub Khan's supporters defeated a British column at Maiwand before advancing on Kandahar, which they laid siege to. General Roberts, however, came to the aid of the garrison of Kandahar, and broke the siege.

Afghan warriors sniping at British forces from the side of an Afghan mountain. They were good shots, but lacked artillery and the formal tactics sufficient to stand up to British forces.

Chilean army occupies Lima

Chilean troops entered the Peruvian capital of Lima after defeating the defenders at the Battle of Miraflores on 15 January 1881. The government has fled, vowing to continue the struggle.

Chile has achieved considerable success in this war. After rapidly occupying Bolivia's Litoral province, and securing command of the sea, an army was landed at the town of Pisagua in Peruvian territory on 2 November 1879. The Peruvians, with their Bolivian allies, attempted to drive the Chileans back, but suffered a significant defeat at the Battle of San Francisco on 19 November, when most of the Bolivian army deserted. A measure of revenge was achieved when the rallying Peruvians defeated a pursuing Chilean force in the Tarapacá valley on 27 November, but this did nothing to alter the course of the war.

After rapidly occupying Bolivia's Litoral province, and securing command of the sea, an army was landed at the town of Pisagua in Peruvian territory on 2 November 1879.

After a Chilean force landed at Pacocha Bay in February 1880, several months were spent securing control of the Peruvian provinces of Tacna and Arica. The final battle in these provinces occurred on 26 May when a Chilean army completely overwhelmed the main allied force at the Battle of Tacna, with the town of Arica being secured after an assault on 7 June.

After diplomacy had failed to achieve an end to the war, the Chileans decided to seize Lima; troops were landed at Pisco on 20 November 1880 and advanced north. The Peruvians constructed a line of trenches based on the town of San Juan, but these entrenchments were successfully carried by a Chilean attack on 13 January 1881 and the Peruvians withdrew to the Miraflores line, the last defence before the capital itself.

Boers beat British

A **Boer force only** 500 strong badly defeated a similar sized British force at the Battle of Majuba Hill on 27 February 1881. The victory will secure the independence of the Afrikaners (Boers) of the Transvaal Republic (also known as the South African Republic).

From the beginning of the war in December 1880, the British suffered setbacks at the hands of the Boers, with all their garrisons in the country under siege. On 28 January 1881, the British attempted an assault on a Boer position at Laing's Nek, a pass that led from Natal on the coast into the Transvaal, but the Boers easily fended off the British attacks.

General Sir George Colley, the commander of British forces during the 1880–81 Boer War, seriously underestimated the capabilities and determination of his opponents.

The British, under General Sir George Colley, retreated back to their Natal colony, but once reinforced he chose to make another attempt to enter Transvaal before his replacement, General Sir Frederick Roberts, could arrive with further reinforcements.

Colley moved back toward Laing's Nek, this time taking part of his force to a position on Majuba Hill overlooking a Boer camp. When morning came, the Boers, initially apprehensive, were surprised when Colley did nothing with his advantage so they advanced up the hill, keeping the British under fire. On reaching the summit they were able to occupy higher ground than the British and eventually routed them. Colley was killed in the action.

British troops flee down Majuba Hill after defeat at the hands of Boer forces, 28 January 1881. The British neglected to take proper precautions in securing high ground around their camp.

IN BRIEF

✤ A bloody but brief civil war in Argentina in June 1880 ended with victory for the government forces of the president, Nicolas Avellaneda, after the battles of Los Corrales on 17 June, Puente Barracas on 20 June and Puente Alsina on 21 June. The government of Buenos Aires province, under Carlos Tejedor, had sought to reject Avellaneda's authority and possibly even secede from Argentina altogether.

✤ Basuto guerrillas defeated a British cavalry column at Qalabani in October 1880. The victory preserved Basuto self-government, a rare example of an African military victory in the field ultimately leading to political success.

British hero killed in Khartoum

British general was killed and Islamist nationalists seized power in the Sudan, after Khartoum was successfully assaulted by a rebel army on 26 January 1885. The rebellion was led by a religious leader who called himself the Mahdi, believing himself to be the Prophet Mohammed's expected successor.

The Mahdi's rebellion began in 1881 when he raised an army to secure the independence of Sudan from its Egyptian suzerain. He took a small army to Kordofan in the centre of Sudan where he gathered further recruits. The Egyptian government selected a former Indian Army officer, General William Hicks, to take command of military operations, but he and almost all his army were massacred at the Battle of El Obeid on 3 November 1883.

The British government, which effectively controlled Egypt, now insisted

The rebellion was led by a religious leader who called himself the Mahdi, believing himself to be the Prophet Mohammed's expected successor.

on the abandonment of the Sudan and sent General Charles Gordon to organize the evacuation of Khartoum. Gordon arrived in Khartoum in February 1884, but concluded that there was no possibility of safely evacuating the city with the troops at his disposal, and began organizing its defence instead, hoping that either the British or the Egyptians would send reinforcements to help.

Public pressure in Britain forced the government to act in August and General Sir Garnet began organizing a column to advance to the relief of Khartoum. While the main force laboured up the Nile, a brigade of camel-borne troops was sent on ahead at the beginning of January 1885. The Mahdi in turn sent a force to at least slow down their advance and battles were fought on 17 January at Abu Klea and on 19 January at Gubat. Leading elements of the relieving column only reached Khartoum on 28 January 1885, two days after the city's fall.

General Charles Gordon stands on the steps of the Governor-General's mansion in Khartoum, after the successful assault by the Mahdi's army on the town's defences.

IN BRIEF

⇛ A British army defeated the Egyptians at Tel-el-Kebir on 13 September 1882 after a night march across the desert to hide their plan from the Egyptians. A British fleet had already bombarded Alexandria on 11 July. The victory will enable the British to take control of Egypt, after a crisis provoked by the nationalist policies of Colonel Ahmed Urabi.

⇛ A French naval officer, Captain Henri Riviere, was captured and killed at Halong Bay, Tonkin, on 19 May 1883, by the Black Flag army (Chinese Taiping rebels who had become mercenaries serving the Vietnamese emperor). Riviere had been sent to Vietnam to halt the depredations of Black Flag pirates and seized the citadel of Hanoi on 25 April 1882.

⇛ The Chilean victory over Peruvian resistance at the Battle of Huamachuco marks the defeat of the last effective opposition to the Chilean occupation of the country on 10 July 1883. With

The burst barrel of an Egyptian gun after the bombardment of Alexandria in July 1882 by a British fleet.

a Peruvian government determined on peace, it seems only a matter of time before a treaty is agreed.

French abandon Lang Son, keep Annam

A French expeditionary force on the border between China and Tonkin abandoned its position at Lang Son on 28 March 1885, but may have achieved enough to secure French possession of Vietnam.

After the death of Captain Henri Riviere in the spring of 1883, the French government sent a larger military force to Vietnam in order to extend French control north from Cochin China through Annam and into Tonkin. A French fleet bombarded the Vietnamese capital of Hue in August 1883. The emperor was notionally a vassal of the Chinese and China objected to the annexation of Vietnam to the French empire. Although the Chinese signed treaties acknowledging the fact, they later objected to the French moving troops into their new conquest. War broke out and the French navy sank the Fukien squadron of the Chinese fleet at Foochow on 23 August 1884. The French also blockaded Taiwan.

However, the main battlefield was in Tonkin where a battalion of the French Foreign Legion was besieged at Tuyen Quang for nearly three months. These men were eventually relieved by the expeditionary force that reached Lang Son and then pressed on for Tuyen Quang. On 23 March 1885, this column engaged 10,000 Chinese troops in the Battle of Zhennan Pass on the border between Tonkin and China. Heavily outnumbered, and having shot off most of their ammunition, the French had to retreat after a two-day battle.

A Chinese woodcut claims the victory of their forces over the French during the battle of Foochow on 23 August 1884. In fact, the French wiped out half the Chinese fleet.

Japan seizes Korea

A print in traditional Japanese style depicts the fall of Port Arthur to the Japanese. The port was the key objective of the Japanese in the war, which gave them a base from which to intervene in Manchuria and northern China.

The **Japanese defeated** the last major Chinese army attempting to contest the invasion of Korea at Tienchuangtai in Manchuria on 6 March 1895. With the destruction of this army, and of the Chinese North Ocean Fleet at Weihaiwei, the war – which began because of Japanese anger at the dispatch of Chinese troops to resolve a political problem in Korea – is now effectively over.

The two armies clashed in Pyongyang on 15 September, when the Japanese launched a night assault on the walls of the city, which was occupied by the Chinese. The Chinese were driven out of the city, leaving the Japanese in control of Pyongyang, in addition to Pusan, Chemulpo and Seoul.

The Japanese opened the war with what would become their traditional method of surprise attack. When a Japanese squadron encountered a Chinese steamer, escorted by two small warships, on 25 July 1894, the Japanese sank the steamer, which was carrying troops to Korea, and one of the warships, and machine-gunned the survivors in the water. War was declared only seven days later, on 1 August.

With both sides having rushed armies to Korea in support of their respective political allies, the main campaigns of the war were fought there and in Manchuria. The two armies clashed in Pyongyang on 15 September, when the Japanese launched a night assault on the walls of the city, which was occupied by the Chinese. The Chinese were driven out of the city, leaving the Japanese in control of Pyongyang, in addition to Pusan, Chemulpo and Seoul, which they had already occupied.

After the defeat of the Chinese fleet at the Battle of the Yalu River on 17 September, the Japanese gained command of the seas. They landed troops on the Liaotung peninsula in October and these forces occupied Port Arthur (Lüshun) on 21 November, massacring most of the city's Chinese residents.

The Japanese then moved against the Chinese naval base of Weihaiwei which they captured on 12 February 1895 after a 23-day siege in harsh winter weather.

Chile's president overthrown in civil war

The **armed forces** supporting the Chilean president, José Manuel Balmaceda, were defeated by supporters of the Chilean congress in the Battle of Placilla on 28 August 1891. The president had begun the year attempting to rule without the agreement of Congress to a budget, resulting in an act of deposition being passed against him on 6 January 1891.

Most of the navy gave its wholehearted support to Congress, while the army's sentiments were more divided. The navy withdrew most of its ships, together with the congressmen, to Iquique in the north of the country. The Congressionalist victory over the "Gobernistas" at Pozo Almonte on 7 March secured the northern part of the country as a base for Congress's military forces.

President Balmaceda sent the only ships he controlled, two torpedo gunboats, to attack the Congressionalist fleet in the north. On 23 April, these attacked the ships in Caldera Bay and sank one old ironclad with a self-propelled torpedo.

President Balmaceda sent the only ships he controlled, two torpedo gunboats, to attack the Congressionalist fleet in the north. On 23 April, these attacked the ships in Caldera Bay and sank one old ironclad with a self-propelled torpedo, the first such sinking in naval history.

The Congressionalists were better able to get military supplies and in August succeeded in transporting a strong force to Valparaíso. Landing north of this port on 10 August, the Congressionalist army beat the defending Gobernista force at Concon. The Battle of Placilla has given them control of Valparaíso; it was now only a matter of time before they occupied the capital, Santiago, and toppled President Balmaceda.

IN BRIEF

❧ Some 150 Sioux Indians and 25 American cavalry troopers were killed in a shoot-out at Wounded Knee, Dakota Territory, in the United States, on 29 December 1890. The shooting began as cavalrymen were searching for weapons among the Indians, who were about to be transported to Omaha, Nebraska, and were therefore thought of as prisoners. According to the army, the Indians opened fire on the troopers, before in turn they were fired at by the cavalry.

❧ A column of armed volunteers in the employ of the British South Africa Company invaded Matabeleland in southern Africa and defeated the Ndebele army in two battles on 25 October 1893 and 1 November 1893. In both cases, the artillery and machine guns of the volunteers cut down many of the Ndebele, who were already weakened by an outbreak of smallpox. Matabeleland has been occupied by these whites and much of the land divided up among them.

❧ A revolution broke out in Cuba after 23 February 1895, as Cuban nationalists raised the standard of rebellion when Spain suspended constitutional guarantees in Cuba. The Spanish had some foreknowledge of the event and managed to defeat a number of uprisings in the west of the island, around Havana, but the rebels are waging guerrilla war from bases in the east, with support from exiles in the United States.

The body of Big Foot, Lakota chief, after his death at Wounded Knee, 29 December 1890. The exact circumstances that led to American soldiers opening fire on the Indians remain disputed.

The war against civilians

On 21 October 1896, General Valeriano Weyler y Nicolau, the commander of the Spanish forces in Cuba, opposed by Cuban nationalists involved in guerrilla warfare, instituted a new policy to help him win the war. "All the inhabitants of the country now outside the line of fortifications of the towns, shall within the period of eight days concentrate themselves in the town so occupied by the troops." The policy went under the name *reconcentrado*, which has passed into the English language as the term "concentration camps". The aim of this procedure was to keep the war as short as possible, albeit at the cost of dramatically increased hardship for those in the war zone.

Federal forces destroy a Georgia railroad during Sherman's March to the Sea in the autumn of 1864. Sherman was determined to apply a harsh policy of pillage and destruction that left many citizens destitute and hungry.

vulnerable – the very young, the very old and those already in poor health – were soon dying in large numbers, even in the streets, giving further cause for resentment by the resettled inhabitants. Perhaps as many as 200,000 Cubans died because of this policy.

Making war on civilians was nothing new in military historical terms. As recently as thirty years earlier, Federal soldiers invading the southern states had devastated parts of Virginia and Georgia specifically to deny the resources of those areas to the enemy. In addition to that, the encouragement of slaves to desert to Federal lines had a considerable impact on the plantation economy of the South, by denying them their source of labour. There are also earlier examples of armies such as Napoleon's living off the land, which effectively meant taking whatever they wanted from the people it belonged to. Sometimes the military paid for what they took – normally if it was in their own territory or land they wished to subsequently occupy – but this was not common. In the medieval era, pillaging and destroying villages was standard practice

Weyler required all civilians in the countryside to relocate from their homes and move into the fortified localities constructed by the Spanish, together with any farm animals, food reserves or anything else that Weyler believed might help to sustain the guerrillas in their fight against the Spanish. Those who remained outside the new camps after eight days would be treated as guerrillas and shot.

As a way of solving Weyler's problem, the idea no doubt seemed reasonable – the camps were not intended to be prisons, and people were intended to be properly fed and housed by the army. After a year or two, the war would probably be won and they could go home again. However, from the point of view of those being moved, it seemed very different. They were being taken from their homes and

put in a camp where they would be subject to a degree of military discipline, which meant they would not necessarily be free to come and go as they pleased. Furthermore, their homes and land were likely to be destroyed or damaged in order to deny them to the guerrillas. In practice, the camps were far removed from Weyler's idea of civilized, if inconvenient, temporary accommodation. The officers and men of the Spanish army had enough to do, simply ensuring they had food, were in reasonable health and not the easy targets of Cuban guerrillas, let alone look after a large number of civilians whose sympathies lay more with the guerrillas than with Spain. Consequently, the *reconcentrados* were not well run, and soon disease and hunger were commonplace. Shanty towns emerged within the fortified areas. In these circumstances, the

> The concentration camp and scorched-earth policy in the end reached its logical conclusion in the Second World War with the introduction of strategic bombing as a tactic, and massacres of civilians as part of reprisals.

– such as the Sack of Limoges in 1370 – as it demonstrated the local overlord was incapable of offering the protection to his people that was implicit in the feudal contract.

However, with his Cuban experiment, Weyler was the first to regard civilians as a legitimate target of war. The whole

A Boer mother and her son at a concentration camp in South Africa in 1901. The Boer commandos' hit-and-run campaign against British forces relied on receiving food and help from farms. The British rounded up Boer civilians, putting them in camps where poor sanitation caused many deaths.

implication of his policy was that his army was in a hostile country, and as the occupying army had the right to subject enemy civilians to a form of martial law. This ceased to be an implication and became an established fact in the incidents of this kind that followed in southern Africa and the Philippines.

The British rounded up Boer families and placed them in what they called "concentration camps", while burning down their homes and often shooting farm livestock. Nutrition and hygiene in these camps were very poor, and many women and children died, which led to lasting bitterness on the part of the Afrikaners (as they were later called). However, the policy did work in the end as the Boers conceded defeat in part because they had nowhere to draw supplies from.

A similar policy was instituted on 7 December 1901 by American general J. Franklin Bell, in the Philippines. Here, however, having burned down the villages, alternative accommodation for those who had lived there was not always provided.

The concentration camp and scorched-earth policy in the end reached its logical conclusion in the Second World War with the introduction of strategic bombing as a tactic, and massacres of civilians as part of reprisals. Although notionally the civilian was not the target of these attacks, the limitations of targeting technology condemned those who lived in the wrong neighbourhood to being the target of a cascade of bombs from hundreds of aircraft. By the time the V-1s and V-2s were launched in 1944–45, a city became an indiscriminate target. Modern precision munitions have had the dubious effect of both making it less likely that civilians are targeted directly, while still subjecting them to the health risks of losing electrical power or clean water, as was done by coalition forces attacks on Iraq in both 1991 and 2003. In a sense, these acts demonstrated to the people the fact that their overlord could no longer protect them – not so far removed from the Black Prince's sacking of Limoges in 1370.

French civilians were victims of the Germans on three occasions in a hundred years – during the Franco-Prussian War, during the First World War, and during the Second World War.

America conquers a Spanish empire

The **United States** emerged victorious on all fronts war against Spain declared on 25 April 1898, fought largely among Spanish colonial possessions and concluded by the fall of Manila on 13 August 1898.

The war broke out after the destruction of the USS *Maine*, an American battleship, which exploded in Havana harbour on 15 February 1898. At the time, the Americans believed that the ship had been destroyed by Spanish sabotage. The American public was also sympathetic with the Cuban rebels and the American decision to send troops to Cuba was very popular. The Spanish objected to this interference in their imperial affairs and broke off diplomatic relations on 20 April, leading to war.

Cuba was invaded on 22 June and after a short siege the Americans captured Santiago on 17 July. Although the Spanish squadron based there had attempted to escape the blockading American fleet, it was destroyed in a naval battle on 3 July.

Eight days after Santiago fell, a force landed on Puerto Rico and in four days had secured the island. At the same time American forces landed in the Philippines, having left California in May and June. Philippine nationalists had been fighting the Spanish colonial forces since American Commodore George Dewey had sunk the Spanish Asiatic Squadron in the Battle of Manila Bay on 1 May 1898. On the arrival of American troops, the city of Manila was placed under siege and the first assault was made on 13 August, although a peace protocol had been signed the day before.

A view from the American lines of the assault on San Juan Hill, the heights that overlooked the Cuban town of Santiago on 1 July 1898, during the Spanish–American War.

SPANISH–AMERICAN WAR

DATES:	April–August 1898
COMBATANTS:	Spain vs United States of America
FORCES ENGAGED:	Spain, 43,000; United States, 40,000
CASUALTIES:	Spain, c.7,500; United States, 2,446 combat deaths
RESULT:	US victory

The 21st Lancers charge the Dervish army during the battle of Omdurman, 2 September 1898, the last full-scale cavalry charge of the British Army.

Britain conquers Sudan

On **2 September** 1898, a British force, equipped with machine guns and artillery, decisively defeated a large force of Sudanese warriors equipped with spears and muskets near the town of Omdurman.

Sudan had effectively had independence from imperial rule since 1885 when it achieved its liberation from Egypt, which had ruled the region since 1820.

The British began their campaign to reoccupy the Sudan on behalf of Egypt in 1896 when they took control of Dogala province. Supported by Egyptian troops, the British continued a steady but very slow advance southward, delayed by the need to construct a railway line across the Egyptian desert to help supply the troops.

IN BRIEF

⚜ The Italian army suffered a crushing blow at the Battle of Adowa on 1 March 1896. The Italians were badly outnumbered by their Ethiopian opponents and were caught on the march so they could not bring their considerably superior firepower to bear effectively. Half the Italian army was killed or captured, while the Ethiopians lost even more heavily. The Italian attempt at conquering Ethiopia has been abandoned.

⚜ An attempt to provoke an uprising of foreign workers in the Transvaal Republic over the New Year holiday of 1896 has failed. A group of armed volunteers from Matabeleland under the command of the administrator-general of Matabeleland, the British official Leander Starr Jameson, crossed the border into the South African Republic on 29 December 1895. At Krugersdorp, on 1 January 1896, the raiders encountered stiff resistance and changed their route before surrendering to a large Boer force at Doornkop on 2 January 1896. The Boers suspect the involvement of the British government in the raid.

⚜ On 5 August 1896, a small army of British volunteers attacked a Ndebele army in the Matopo hills of Matabeleland, driving them out of the positions they had occupied overlooking the Tuli Road. In March, the Ndebele had rebelled against their recently arrived British conquerors, together with the neighbouring Shona people. The far more numerous Ndebele and Shona could not defeat the modern weapons of the white settlers, however, and the rebellion was largely over by the autumn.

⚜ The withdrawal of a Greek army from Epirus on 15 May 1897 brought to an end a short and disastrous war against the Ottoman Empire. The Greeks attempted to take advantage of a rebellion in Crete at the end of 1896 by fomenting a similar uprising in Macedonia in March 1897. However, the stronger Ottomans benefited from the lack of discipline in the Greek army and defeated it at Mati in April, capturing the town of Larissa, while driving the Greeks to Pharsala. Both the Greeks and the Ottomans attempted to invade one another's territory in Epirus, but neither side was successful.

The Italian soldiers' last stand at the Battle of Adowa, 1 March 1896. The Italian army was caught on the march, and overwhelmed by a far larger enemy in a rare native victory in a war against an imperialist power during the second half of the nineteenth century.

Black week for the British Army

After war broke out between Britain and the two Boer republics of South Africa – the Orange Free State and the South African Republic (also known as the Transvaal Republic) – over the rights of foreigners living in the Boer lands, the British army suffered its third major defeat at the hands of irregular Boer forces at the Battle of Colenso on 15 December 1899.

The British had massed troops on the borders of the Transvaal but the Boers struck first after the declaration of war on 11 October 1899, crossing the border to besiege the towns of Ladysmith, Mafeking and Kimberley. British military efforts focused initially on breaking the sieges of these towns.

The first major battle came at Stormberg on 10 December 1899, when a British force assaulted a strong Boer position defending an important railway junction they had captured in the Cape Colony.

The overconfident British suffered heavy losses when attacking the expert Boer marksmen. At Magersfontein, the next day, another British column attempting to relieve Kimberley attacked a Boer position, believing it to be on top of Magersfontein Hill. The Boers, however, had entrenched at the foot of the hill and surprised the British as they advanced across the plain, inflicting heavy casualties.

A third column, attempting to relieve Ladysmith in Natal, was stopped at Colenso when it attempted to assault a Boer position overlooking a loop in the Tugela river. The British assault force was deploying in some confusion when the Boers opened fire. A second advancing column was also halted when its artillery went into action within range of Boer riflemen and many of the gunners were shot.

THE SECOND BOER WAR

DATES:	1899–1902
COMBATANTS:	British Empire vs Orange Free State and South African Republic (Boers)
FORCES ENGAGED:	Britain, 250,000; Boer republics, 70,000
CASUALTIES:	Britain, 22,000 (both combat and disease); Boer republics, 6,500
RESULT:	British victory

A Boer commando deployed in a simple trench on the South African veldt. The Boers seriously embarrassed British forces, who did not expect to fight an army of expert marksmen armed with the most up-to-date magazine breechloaders.

Revolution in Colombia

An economic crisis in Colombia produced a political uprising in several provinces dominated by the opposition, which led to a stalemate after the victory of the Liberal faction in the Battle of Peralonso in the north-east of the country on 15 December 1899.

The uprising was originally scheduled for 20 October, but once it became common knowledge the date was advanced to 18 October. The Liberals attempted to block the Magdalena river, an important thoroughfare from the heartlands of the country to the coast.

A political crisis after a collapse of coffee prices provoked the Liberals – who believed themselves to be victims of fraud in the 1897 presidential election – to attempt a coup, taking advantage of deep divisions in the ruling Conservative-Nationalist alliance. However, the Liberals are themselves divided into "peace" and "war" factions, which has restricted their recruitment of fighting men.

The uprising was originally scheduled for 20 October, but once it became common knowledge the date was advanced to 18 October. The Liberals attempted to block the Magdalena river, an important thoroughfare from the heartlands of the country to the coast, along which much valuable international trade travels. However, their fleet of converted barges was sunk in a naval battle on 24 October.

Two Liberal armies assembled in the departments of Santander in the north and Cundinamarca in the centre of the country, but both of them suffered defeat. The Santander force, under Rafael Uribe Uribe retreated toward Venezuela until it made a stand at Peralonso.

An American view of their role in the Philippines, squashing the potential dictatorship of Emilio Aguinaldo, the Philippine nationalist who sought to found an independent Philippine republic.

Americans conquer Luzon

An American brigade landed in the Lingayen Gulf on Luzon in the Philippines, and advanced to San Jacinto where it defeated a Philippine force on 11 November 1899. Once this brigade links up with American forces advancing from the south, the Philippine nationalists will no longer be able to keep a large concentration of troops in the field.

Philippine nationalists, led by Emilio Aguinaldo, had initially welcomed the arrival of the Americans, seeing them as liberators from their Spanish colonial overlords. However, the Americans had every intention of occupying the Philippines themselves and replacing the Spanish as colonial overlords. Fighting broke out between the two sides around Manila on 4 February 1899 and spread throughout Luzon. The nationalists organized their forces around localities, and found it difficult to gather them for any length of time away from their bases, so the American army adopted a policy of sending columns to attack specific objectives, such as the Philippine nationalist capital at Malolos, north of Manila, which fell on 31 March. These columns divided the Philippine forces, making it impossible for them to unite in large enough numbers to challenge the more mobile American forces.

Legations siege brought to an end

A 55-day siege of the foreign legations in Peking finally ended on 14 August 1900 as a relief expedition from the coast reached the small garrison that was defending the embassy compound against far superior numbers of Chinese nationalists. The Chinese forces are known to Westerners as "the Boxers", although their Chinese name is the Righteous Harmony Society. Their aim is to end the increasing control over Chinese internal affairs by foreign countries.

Tension between the Chinese imperial government and foreigners had increased throughout the course of the year. Chinese officials regarded the Boxers as ideal for challenging the foreign powers' demands for special treatment – which only encouraged the violence the Boxers directed towards foreigners, towards Chinese Christians and towards those Chinese who worked for foreigners.

In May 1900, while anti-Western riots became commonplace in northern China, reinforcements were rushed to Peking, although this did not prevent the Boxers burning down the Western-owned racecourse on 9 June. On 20 June, the German minister was murdered by Chinese troops and later that same day Chinese forces opened fire on the foreign legation. The next day China declared war against the Great Powers.

Sniping, shelling and attempts to mine under the walls protecting the legation were more common than set-piece attacks, although the Boxers did make one major assault on the Cathedral, not part of the legation, which was driven off with heavy losses.

The first attempt to send a relief column from Tientsin to Peking by train failed when the Chinese cut the railway line. A second column of troops landed on the coast and lifted the siege of Tientsin on 23 July, having been delayed owing to the rumour that all the legation defenders had been massacred earlier in the month. Only after a letter reached Tientsin from Peking did the relieving force set off.

The force marched out of Tientsin on 4 August. The next day it made a dawn attack on a Chinese army at Yang Zun and swiftly defeated it, thereby ending any meaningful attempt by the Chinese to halt the advance. Once outside Peking, on 13 August, the allies quickly breached the walls and reached the legation.

The ruins of Old Tientsin after the Great Powers' bombardment of the city during the Boxer Rebellion in 1900. The allied soldiers were merciless toward the northern Chinese populace.

The Huns

In July 1900, Kaiser Wilhelm II of Germany gave a speech to German soldiers being sent to China to defeat the Boxers. German sentiment was already outraged by the murder of their minister in Peking, and Wilhelm played on this when he gave a speech that included the following: "Once, a thousand years ago, the Huns under their King Attila made a name for themselves, one still potent in legend and tradition. May you in this way make the name German remembered in China for a thousand years so that no Chinaman will ever again dare to even squint at a German!" Although these words did not appear in the official text, a reporter noted down a shorthand copy of his words, much to the later embarrassment of the German ministry of foreign affairs when it was later used in Allied propaganda in 1914.

Great Powers seize Tientsin

The **international settlement** at Tientsin has been relieved by an allied force that has been marching up from the coast since 14 July 1900. Eight nations have contributed troops to this expedition: Austria-Hungary, Britain, France, Germany, Italy, Japan, Russia and the United States.

Fighting between Boxers and foreigners began even before the legations siege. An attempt was made to seize the railway station on 15 June, but the presence of some 1,700 Russian troops made it impossible for the poorly armed Boxers.

The international settlement at Tientsin was put under siege on 17 June. Between 25,000 and 50,000 Boxers and Chinese troops surrounded the settlement, well equipped with field guns and cannons, but limited to mostly swords and spears as personal weapons. They were opposed by about 2,400 well-armed foreign troops in the international settlement, who were more than a match with their rifles, machine guns, artillery and the Taku forts. The foreign troops managed to destroy the Tientsin arsenal on 27 June, which seriously hampered the Chinese military effort in both Tientsin and against the force assembled by the "Eight-Nations Alliance" of the Great Powers on the coast.

Officers from the different contingents who defeated the Boxers in north China, 1900.

Stalemate into victory in Colombia

The **Colombian Liberals** suffered a morale-destroying defeat after a long battle against their Conservative rivals at Palonegro. The battle opened on 11 May 1900, and only on 25 May did the Liberal forces finally admit defeat in a decisive action of their country's civil war.

Both sides went into battle near Bucaramanga in the east of the country confident of victory. However, the Conservatives were both better equipped

The battle opened on 11 May 1900, and only on 25 May did the Liberal forces finally admit defeat in a decisive action of their country's civil war.

and outnumbered the Liberals two-to-one. Nonetheless, the Liberals more than held their own and after three days of fighting looked to be on the verge of victory. The Conservatives held the Liberals over the next two days and stalemate ensued until a timely resupply of ammunition for the Conservatives forced the Liberals to retreat rather than risk total defeat.

Boers beaten

After **reverses at** Spion Kop in January and Vaal Krantz in February, the British offensives of 1900 have succeeded in capturing the two capitals of the Boer republics, Bloemfontein and Johannesburg. Mafeking, Ladysmith and Kimberley have all been relieved. A skilful operation was carried out by General Lord Roberts along the Orange river, where he fooled the Boer commander about his line of march, eventually surrounding the Boer force and forcing its surrender.

In spite of these defeats, the Boers show no sign of giving up the struggle. Instead they are withdrawing as the British advance, only to reoccupy the countryside after the British have moved on.

A London crowd celebrates the relief of Mafeking in May 1900, ending a 217-day siege that captivated national attention.

Boer War ends

The long and at times bitter struggle between Boers and British officially came to an end on 31 May 1902 with the Treaty of Vereeniging. They have sustained a war almost without battles for nearly two years, relying on mobility and hit-and-run tactics to wage a guerrilla resistance against the occupiers of their countries.

The guerrilla war opened in September 1900, although battles were still fought occasionally when Boer commandos gathered together in larger groups in order to make a major raid on a British garrison or marching column. One of the most successful of these raids occurred in March 1902 when the Boers attacked the British at Tweebosch and captured the second-in-command of the British forces, General Lord Methuen.

The British responded harshly to the Boers' ability to move among a sympathetic population, establishing "concentration camps" where Boer civilians were interned to prevent them from assisting the Boer commandos to live off the country. In parallel with this, farms were burned as families were moved out of them, restricting the supplies available to the Boers. These harsh policies eventually succeeded in driving the commandos to surrender to the British.

A blindfolded Boer prisoner is escorted into captivity by British soldiers. The war between Boer commandos and British forces was an ugly matter. Shooting prisoners was not uncommon.

"Mad Mullah" threatens British Somaliland

The self-proclaimed Mahdi of Somaliland, Abdullah Hassan, known to the British as the "Mad Mullah", suffered a serious defeat at the hands of British-officered Ethiopian troops on 31 May 1903. His four-year campaign of resistance against the British, and against Somali clans co-operating with the British, looks to be in jeopardy.

Sayed Mohammed Abdullah Hassan was born in 1864 a Dulbahanta, a clan of the protectorate of British Somaliland in the Horn of Africa. A pious Moslem in a puritanical tradition, the story of Sudan's Mahdi revolution had a strong influence over him, prompting him to get Somalis to return to their Islamic heritage, and to urge them to expel the infidel British from the territory. He found a following among the nomads

of the interior and in 1899 began to resist both the British regime and the Ethiopian monarchy that controlled the Ogaden, a region considered by Somali nomads to be their own.

In just over a year, a column of troops, about 1,500 strong, managed to inflict a significant defeat on [Abdullah Hassan], capturing about 800 of his followers.

Abdullah Hassan initially targeted Somalis who benefited economically from the British regime, regarding them as "collaborators". In April 1901 the British launched an expedition against him. In just over a year, a column of troops, about 1,500 strong, managed

to inflict a significant defeat on him, capturing about 800 of his followers, with even more of them becoming casualties. Abdullah Hassan renewed his efforts at recruitment and resumed his raids in early 1902, this time with some 1,500 riflemen, necessitating a second British expedition in June. In October 1902, the British forces clashed with Abdullah Hassan's followers at Erigo and inflicted another severe defeat, capturing many of the animals so important to nomadic life.

The British sent more troops to Somaliland and in 1903 co-ordinated operations with the Ethiopians. The campaign had mixed results, as Abdullah Hassan's warriors achieved one or two successes against isolated reconnaissance patrols, although in the end they were forced to flee and disband.

America declares victory over Filipinos

The establishment of a civilian administration of the Philippines on 4 July 1902, under William Howard Taft, coincided with the declaration by the United States that the war against Philippine nationalists resisting the American takeover of the former Spanish colony was at an end.

The American campaign against the Philippine nationalists was a brutal affair. Torture was standard operating procedure for the American troops, and they also applied a "concentration camp" policy similar to that used by the British against the Boers. "Kill and burn! The more you kill and burn the better you will please me," stated General Jake Smith after Filipino irregulars massacred a patrol in the town of Balangiga on Samar Island.

After the capture of Emilio Aguinaldo on 23 March 1901, following a stratagem by General Frederick Funston using Filipino scouts who pretended to surrender, removing any central coordination of the resistance. Isolated nationalists continue to resist and the Moros – Moslems living on Mindanao seeking independence from any non-Moslem regime – are nowhere near being subdued.

American soldiers in the Philippines stand around their Gatling gun. The American army fought a very vicious war against a guerrilla foe who resented the replacement of a Spanish overlord with an American one.

IN BRIEF

❧ Macedonian nationalists, with the support of the Bulgarian government, staged an uprising in September 1902 against the Ottoman administration of this Balkan region. The Ottomans employed systematic massacres to suppress the revolt.

The Russo-Japanese War (1904-05)

At twenty-eight minutes past midnight on 9 February 1904, at Port Arthur, a Russian naval base in Manchuria, two explosions occurred, which were later followed by a third.

They heralded the beginning of the Russo-Japanese War, as Japanese destroyers, under cover of darkness, launched a surprise attack on the Russian Pacific fleet based here, damaging two Russian battleships and a cruiser. The results could have been worse, as the Japanese fired 16 torpedoes altogether that night, but the other 13 either missed or failed to explode.

With the sun up, the Russians prepared to put to sea for battle. The Japanese intended to

> [T]heir surprise attack marked a departure from traditional warfare by the European powers. Countries were expected to declare war, with a reasonable interval prior to beginning military operations.

oblige the Russians, as their fleet, commanded by Admiral Togo Heihachiro, approached, hoping to finish off the reduced Russian squadron. However, although the Russians had been badly mauled, they were still full of fight and the Japanese beat a hasty retreat, unwilling to risk their ships against both the naval guns of the Russian ships and the shore-based ones that defended the harbour.

While nothing new to the Japanese, their surprise attack marked a departure from traditional warfare by the European powers. Countries were expected to declare war, allowing a reasonable interval prior to beginning military operations, but the Japanese ignored this. Although they had broken off diplomatic relations, feelings between Russia and Japan had been bad since the Russians had forced the Japanese to relinquish Port Arthur, a trophy of their victory over China in 1895, only to compel the Chinese to grant them a lengthy lease. Furthermore, after the Boxer Rebellion, the Russians had put a considerable number of troops into Manchuria, where they protected the Chinese Eastern Railway, built by the Chinese at Russia's behest using French money. Japan negotiated for some time to get the troops withdrawn, fearing Russian

ambitions toward Japan's own territorial target of Korea, and the Russians repeatedly made promises which they did not keep to pull the troops out of Manchuria. Nor did they seem willing to negotiate with the Japanese over Korea. Having decided a conflict was inevitable, Japanese leaders chose to strike at a time of their own choosing.

The Russian war effort was hampered by a variety of problems. The average Russian soldier or sailor was less well educated, than the Japanese, and even those of officer class. At a more fundamental level, the Russians still trained their troops in outdated volley-fire methods better suited to muskets than bolt-action rifles, while the Japanese had adopted individualized training on rifle ranges, with each soldier taking aim on his own initiative once ordered to fire. Only in artillery did the Russians have an advantage, but even here they were unable to make full use of it thanks to an artillery doctrine that exposed batteries to enemy fire, and a lack of training for its artillerymen. The situation in the navy was just as bad, perhaps worse – training was hampered by the ice-bound nature of most Russian ports, and

the Russians were clearly unfamiliar with the rangefinders and telescopic sights which were just entering naval service.

By contrast, the Japanese presented a comparative picture of efficiency and enthusiasm for the task at hand, which they demonstrated at the very first battle on land, at the Yalu river in April 1904. The Russians made no attempt to conceal their positions, while the Japanese disguised some of their scouts as fishermen to get a clear picture of Russian deployment. They then began building bridges, even while under enemy fire, to get across the river.

As is always the case in a prolonged war, procedures and tactics changed as both sides adapted to new technologies, hitherto only partly understood in the context of training manuals and exercises. The use of artillery was transformed by what the two armies demonstrated on the field to observers from other armies. Previously, artillery's main task had been to disable the enemy's artillery but the war showed that artillery was far more effective bombarding enemy infantry, especially as superior technology meant that guns could be deployed out of sight, and

The Russian battleship *Tsesarevich* in Tsingtao harbour shows damage caused during the Battle of the Yellow Sea, August 1904. She was the only battleship to escape from Port Arthur in the war.

Russian warships in Port Arthur harbour after being damaged by Japanese shelling during the siege. The war revolved around this key naval base, but the Japanese also sought to eliminate or reduce Russian influence in northern China.

battleship and two cruisers. Mines were also very effective during the war, even claiming a Russian battleship during an engagement on 13 April 1904. Finally, and perhaps most telling for the future, both the Battle of the Yellow Sea on 10 August 1904 and the Battle of Tsushima illustrated that naval actions would take place at far longer ranges than had been foreseen. Accurate gunnery with large-calibre guns was possible at ranges of 12,000 yards (11,000 m), twice the distance anticipated as the maximum effective range for naval combat. Furthermore, experience showed that the heaviest shells, from 12-inch guns, were far more effective than lighter guns of 6-inch or 8-inch calibre that were also carried by battleships. These two factors had a key effect on warship design, leading to the building of the first "all big gun" battleship, HMS *Dreadnought*.

By the war's end, both sides were ready for peace. Defeat had shaken the very foundations of the Russian political system and even for Japan, victory had been costly. Her economy could not have withstood continuing the war for much longer when the treaty of Portsmouth, New Hampshire, was signed on 5 September 1905, bringing the war to an end.

indirect fire could be brought down on the enemy's infantry positions.

Machine guns also came to prominence for the first time. The Japanese gave up an attempt to capture Port Arthur by frontal assault because Russian machine guns caused such heavy casualties, and turned to siege operations instead. In defending Port Arthur, the Russians also deployed barbed-wire obstacles to protect their trenches and slow attacking infantry, forcing them to spend more time under fire. By the time of the Battle of Mukden between 21 February and

twentieth century. At the Battle of Tsushima on 27 May 1905, just like the attack on Port Arthur in February 1904, the Japanese used destroyers armed with torpedoes as part of their combined operations, firing no fewer than 74 torpedoes at the Russians in one all-out attack that claimed a Russian

> [T]he Japanese used destroyers armed with torpedoes as part of their combined operations, firing no fewer than 74 torpedoes at the Russians in one all-out attack that claimed a Russian battleship and two cruisers.

10 March 1905, the Russian army was dug in in lines of trenches, with machine-gun strongpoints, protected by a belt of barbed-wire obstacles. To counter this, the Japanese introduced a system of attacking by rushing forward in alternating small groups, keeping close to the ground. It was a clear portent of the coming First World War.

As on land, the war at sea showed the direction combat would take in the

Japanese infantry on the hills overlooking Port Arthur. The ordinary Japanese soldier displayed the dogged determination of the Samurai to win or die trying.

Aircraft used to drop bombs

Italian soldiers display Turkish flags captured during operation in Libya. Italy secured a small Mediterranean empire during this war.

Italian troops occupied Rhodes and the other islands of the Dodecanese in May 1912, after their troops had captured Tripoli and Tobruk in Libya in October 1911 against weak opposition. The war was started by Italy with the express intent of annexing Ottoman territory – specifically the provinces of Tripolitania and Cyrenaica in North Africa, known to Italian nationalists as the "fourth shore".

The first use of an aircraft in war occurred in October and November 1911, when Italian aeroplanes carried out reconnaissance and bombing missions during their war against the Ottomans in Libya. A reconnaissance was made by air for the first time on 23 October, while the first bomb was dropped from a Nieuport IV on 1 November.

Balkans in turmoil

The Bulgarian army inflicted a significant setback on Greek troops approaching Sofia when it attacked down the Sturma and Mesta river valleys at the end of July 1913. The action resulted in a general armistice in the second of two Balkan Wars that have transformed the map of the region.

The wars began in October 1912, when the Balkan countries almost as one declared war on the Ottoman Empire. Greece, Montenegro, Serbia and Bulgaria all claimed parts of the European portion of The Ottoman Empire. Faced with a united alliance, the Ottomans were rapidly driven back almost to Asia, holding only Adrianople and Constantinople and the territory in between. The fighting halted until the spring of 1913, when Adrianople fell. Crete was claimed by Greece, and a treaty ended the war on 30 May 1913.

The treaty did not cover the distribution of the conquered territories, and Serbia and Greece both coveted parts of Macedonia that had been occupied by Bulgaria. The Bulgarian government thought its best chance came in striking first and at the end of June 1913 the Bulgarian army launched unsuccessful attacks on Serbia and Greece, which ended with the Turks even regaining some of their former European territory.

Balkan irregulars in characteristic mountainous terrain. The Balkan wars ended Turkey's European empire, leaving only a small area to the west of Constantinople in Turkish hands.

OBITUARY

SIR REDVERS BULLER (1839–1908)

The man who was perhaps late-Victorian Britain's most archetypal soldier passed away on 2 June 1908, aged 68. Sir Redvers Buller was the holder of the Victoria Cross, an old Etonian and a veteran of some of the most significant campaigns of the 1860–99 period.

His most meritorious conduct on the battlefield came during the Zulu War, when he won the Victoria Cross during a battle at which he rescued no fewer than three men on separate occasions from the Zulus.

Buller was undeniably brave and was popular with both troops and the British public, but his tactical record as a commander during the opening stages of the second Anglo-Boer War in 1899 was less impressive. Defeated twice by the Boers – at Colenso on 15 December 1899 and at Spion Kop on 24 January 1900 – he was replaced as commander-in-chief by General Lord Roberts, although he retained command of the Army of Natal. Nevertheless, Buller showed great concern for the welfare of his men, always ensuring they were fed, adequately housed and received proper medical attention.

When newspapermen asserted he was incompetent in 1901, Sir Redvers Buller answered their criticisms in a speech in London, but was deemed to have breached military discipline and was dismissed on half pay. He retired to his Devon country estates where he lived out his retirement.

He is survived by his wife and daughter.

Sir Redvers Buller was a brave man and a fine military administrator, but his career ended in controversy.

IN BRIEF

❧ On 3 August 1904, a British force reached Lhasa after several battles against a hopelessly inferior Tibetan army. The war began over British territorial demands along the Indian-Tibetan border.

❧ A Uruguayan landowner attempted to overthrow the government but was defeated at the Battle of Masoller on 1 September 1904. Aparicio Saravia had gathered together an army of farmers and ranchers, but when his cavalry charged against regular army machine guns they suffered typically heavy casualties.

❧ A three-year rebellion by Herero tribesmen in the German colony of South-West Africa that began in October 1904 was brutally suppressed by German military forces. The Germans used concentration camps, forced labour and even massacres to intimidate the Herero into surrendering.

❧ A revolution in Mexico that began on 20 November 1910 overthrew the long-standing regime of Porfirio Diaz, and led to a state of civil war after the army assassinated the revolutionary president Francisco Madero in 1913.

Americans bombard Veracruz

Mexican soldiers defend Veracruz, which was attacked by the American navy and marines in April 1914, after one of the factions in the Mexican Civil War detained some American sailors.

A **Mexican city was** turned into a battleground as a consequence of a perceived "insult" to the American flag a few weeks earlier, as Veracruz was bombarded by a large US fleet on 21 April 1914. At the end of the day, the United States had taken control of the port, and brought the two countries to the brink of war.

The troubles began at Tampico where a squadron of US ships had gathered to

At the end of the day, the United States had taken control of the port, and brought the two countries to the brink of war.

offer some protection to the numerous US citizens living there, mostly working in the oil industry. Mexican soldiers arrested a group of US sailors who had come ashore to get some fuel. Although they were later released, and in spite of a formal apology, the US admiral on the spot demanded a 21-gun salute to the American flag. The Mexicans declined.

On 20 April, US president Woodrow Wilson requested approval from Congress to use US military and naval forces to secure recognition of US rights from General Victoriano Huerta, commander of one of the factions in the Mexican civil war, whose soldiers had arrested the sailors.

The day after, the commander of the US Atlantic Fleet opened fire on Veracruz and landed nearly 800 US Marines and sailors to seize the customs house in the hope of finding some guns that were due to be imported that day. Street fighting broke out, with the Mexican Naval Academy a key strongpoint in the battle.

Austro-Hungarian Archduke shot, European crisis ensues

The embassies and foreign ministries of Europe were hives of activity as the clouds of war appeared on the horizon following the assassination of the heir to the Austro-Hungarian empire's throne. The assassination tipped the Continent into a political crisis. It seems likely that the ultimatum delivered to Serbia by the Austro-Hungarian government on 23 July 1914 will to lead to war between the two states, which the various alliances between European states may well transform into a general war.

On 28 June 1914, a Bosnian Serb, Gavrilo Princip, a member of a nationalist group aiming to create a united South Slav state based on Serbia, fired three shots at the car carrying Archduke Franz Ferdinand and his wife the Countess Sophie, killing both. It was not the first incident that day as a bomb had detonated behind the car killing those in the following vehicle in the motorcade.

Archduke Franz Ferdinand with his wife and the car that will carry them to their assassination in Sarajevo, 28 June 1914.

War in Europe, Belgian fortresses fall

The last forts defending the Belgian city of Namur surrendered to German forces on 23 August 1914, the forts of Liège having surrendered seven days earlier, after a siege lasting ten days.

German troops invaded Belgium as part of their operations against France, after Germany declared war on 3 August. The German government sent an ultimatum to the Belgian government demanding free passage through Belgian territory, but Belgium preferred to remain neutral, so the Germans invaded on the 4th and invested Liège, bombarding the fortresses around the city and launching an assault during the night of 5/6 August. Once heavy 420mm guns arrived on 12 August, the bombardment of the fortresses quickly forced them to surrender and the city, with its crucial bridges over the Meuse river intact, fell into German hands.

From Liège, the Germans advanced on Namur, reaching that city on 21 August. As their heavy guns had been so successful at Liège, they promptly deployed them again and forced the surrender of the forts in two days.

A still from a film taken of Belgian troops by a British film cameramen shows their defence of a roadblock hastily thrown together in the town of Alost.

OBITUARY

JOSHUA CHAMBERLAIN (1828–1914)

This hero of Gettysburg and college professor died on 24 February 1914, from the effects of a wound he suffered during the siege of Petersburg in 1864.

Chamberlain was born in Brewer, Maine, and grew up with strong abolitionist views. At the time of the American Civil War, he was a professor of rhetoric at Bowdoin College, and enlisted in the 20th Maine Volunteers. He saw action at Fredericksburg, Antietam, and Chancellorsville, but achieved his greatest fame for his conduct of the defence of Little Round Top, a hill on the Gettysburg battlefield that was a key point in the Federal lines, for which he received the Medal of Honor. He continued on active service until the end of the war.

After the war, he was four times elected governor of Maine and served as president of Bowdoin College.

He is survived by three children.

Allied disaster on the frontiers

After a series of engagements in Alsace, Lorraine and in the Ardennes, the French and British armies are for the most part in headlong retreat from a sizeable German force that has crossed Belgium and is entering France, its objective apparently Paris. The Battles of the Frontiers ended on 24 August 1914.

Germany's war plan seems to have been ideally suited to the French one. While the French plan envisaged an attack into Alsace and Lorraine, with covering forces stationed on the Belgian frontier, the German plan wheeled a large invasion force through Belgium to strike at the rear of the French armies. The effect was to trap the French between the Germans in Alsace and Lorraine, and those advancing through Belgium.

The early actions occurred in Alsace, around Mulhouse, on 7 August, but the main French offensive took place on 14 August, by which time the Germans were advancing through Belgium after capturing Liège.

French tactics relied on shelling the German positions with 75mm field artillery using shrapnel, followed by an infantry assault. The Germans, however, were well dug in and were well supplied with machine guns. Shrapnel was not effective against the entrenchments and the French assaults in skirmish lines were badly cut up by German machine guns. Not only did the French attacks fail, the Germans were able to switch over to the offensive in Alsace and Lorraine and force a general retreat.

Further north, in the Ardennes and Belgium, the French fared even worse. With the Germans advancing, the two armies met on 22 August, but it only took a day of fighting for the same results to occur as in Alsace and Lorraine. In Belgium, around Charleroi, the French forces were heavily outnumbered and almost overwhelmed. Only at Mons, where the British Expeditionary Force was deployed, did the Germans receive a setback on 23 August, although just as at Charleroi, the Germans had superior numbers and were able to outflank the British position.

German infantry muster in a French village. The Germans fended off French attacks on their common border with France while sending their main strength on a flanking march through Belgium and Luxembourg into northern France, pivoting their advance on the city of Verdun.

Russian army surrenders at Tannenberg

German soldiers stationed in a trench. The Germans were heavily outnumbered on the East Prussian front, but were able to use railways to give them far greater mobility than the Russian army, which had to march toward its objectives.

A **Russian army has** been destroyed by a German one at Tannenberg, East Prussia, during a battle that lasted three days, 23–31 August 1914.

The Russian offensive was slow in coming, owing to the difficulties of mobilizing the large Russian armies with a relatively poor system of transportation in a vast country. However, after the first

Of a strength of 150,000, some 125,000 Russians were killed, wounded or captured. The Germans lost 20,000.

troops crossed the frontier on 15 August, the first battle was fought at Gumbinnen on 20 August. The Russians won and the situation looked precarious for the Germans.

The commander of the German Eighth Army defending Prussia, General Maximilian von Prittwitz, was removed from command after this defeat and was replaced by General Paul von Hindenburg and General Erich Ludendorff, who devised a plan to deal with the situation.

As the Russians advanced with two armies, one east of the German forces and the other to the south, Ludendorff decided to attack the left wing of the southern army with a small part of his army, at the furthest point possible from the eastern one. If this developed well, he reckoned he would be able to shift his forces southward and attack the right wing, too. The plan, set in motion on 24 August, went almost to perfection, as the Russian army to the east remained almost motionless. Meanwhile, the southern army was ordered to move ever further west, increasing the gap between it and the other force, which the Germans quickly exploited. The Russians effectively advanced into a trap, were surrounded and thousands surrendered. On 29 August, the commander shot himself rather than report the defeat. Of a strength of 150,000, some 125,000 Russians were killed, wounded or captured. The Germans lost 20,000.

IN BRIEF

❧ The Germans killed an estimated 5,521 civilians in Belgium during their march through that country. The most notorious incidents occurred at Louvain on 25 August 1914 where the university library and other buildings in the town were destroyed by fire, and at Dinant on the same day, where 896 inhabitants were killed.

❧ A strong British naval force overwhelmed German light naval forces (cruisers and destroyers) at the Battle of Heligoland Bight on 28 August 1914. Three German light cruisers were sunk, out of six committed to battle. The British lost no ships.

Germans withdraw after threatening Paris

Parisian taxis helped rush reinforcements from the French capital's garrison to the front line at the Marne.

The Germans are in retreat after being outmanoeuvred by French and British forces in heavy fighting to the east of Paris on 6–10 September 1914. The battle took place along the Marne river and the campaign involved a million men on both sides.

As the Allied retreat neared Paris, after they had failed to withstand the Germans in the Battles of the Frontiers, the French government fled on 2 September.

[A] withdrawal to Soissons was ordered by the German command, which became more general as the Germans sought a new line of defence along the Aisne, having suffered some 250,000 casualties to the Allied 263,000.

The French overall commander, General Joseph Joffre, had received word that the Germans were sending troops from the West to the East, and so, gambling that the enemy had thus weakened his army,

ordered a counter-attack which had been suggested by the military governor of Paris, General Joseph Gallieni.

Troops from Paris were sent to attack the Germans in the flank as they bypassed the city, which they did at the river Ourcq on 5 September. The following day the attack resumed, but the German commander of the forces directly engaged, General Alexander von Kluck, shifted troops from his left to defeat this threat to his right. What he did not realize was that the British Expeditionary Force and the French Fifth Army were in a position to move into the gap thus created between von Kluck's army and the German Second Army.

The two Allied armies, once in this position, turned to attack the flanks of the German forces, threatening to cut von Kluck off from his line of retreat. On 9 September, a withdrawal to Soissons was ordered by the German command, which became more general as the Germans sought a new line of defence along the Aisne, having suffered some 250,000 casualties to the Allied 263,000.

Germans repel the Allies

During the middle of September 1914, the German army defending the Chemin des Dames in the Champagne region of France repelled several Allied attacks on their position overlooking the river Aisne. Both sides then prepared to try outflanking moves across the largely undefended terrain reaching northwards from the Aisne to the North Sea.

As the Germans dug in on 11 September, the French and British built pontoon bridges across the Aisne and continued with the attacks they had begun after the Battle of the Marne ended two days earlier. The main attack was carried out by the British and the French Fifth and Sixth Armies, but by this time the Germans were beginning to receive reinforcements from troops left to mop up enemy forces in Belgium and around Mauberge. These handily filled the gap that still existed between General Alexander von Kluck's First Army and the German Second Army.

The main attack was carried out by the British and the French Fifth and Sixth Armies, but by this time the Germans were beginning to receive reinforcements.

The Germans deployed their machine guns and artillery to blunt the French and British assaults, which made some progress but were hindered by the lack of good positions for supporting artillery. Once the Germans came under steady shellfire, though, they began digging in and the battle turned into two weeks of shelling and sniping as both sides began using the spade more than the rifle. Local attacks and counter-attacks replaced larger-scale operations involving corps and armies as both sides attempted to secure small advantages. Meanwhile, the hot, dry weather of August and early September changed to rain with a cold north wind.

Russians gain victory, and Lwow

The Russian army has succeeded in its opening campaign against Austro-Hungarian forces in Galicia. The city of Lwow, known as Lemberg to the Austro-Hungarians, fell to the Russians on 3 September 1914, leaving most of Galicia in Russian hands.

The Austro-Hungarians initially adopted a defensive posture toward the larger Russian army, waiting for the Germans to finish off the French before joining an offensive, as had been agreed before the start of the War. However, with the Russian mobilization proceeding slowly, the Austro-Hungarian commander, General Conrad von Hötzendorf, decided to risk an attack and allowed his troops in northern Galicia to make a general advance toward the River Bug. One group pushed north-eastwards, in the vague direction of Brest-Litovsk, the other due east.

At the same time, the Russians also attacked on two fronts. One pushed westward toward Galicia, and the other south-westward from the area of Warsaw toward Lwow, so that both sides were effectively advancing head on toward one another. The Russian south-western advance ran into difficulties almost at the beginning and was forced to pull back in fighting around Krasnik and Komarow in late August. General Conrad grew overconfident and attempted to reinforce his army advancing directly eastwards, which had been badly beaten by Russian forces at the River Zlota Lipa. His troops, however, advanced straight into a trap of his own making, and his reinforcing army was caught in a hard battle to the west of Lwow, while the Russians reinforced their armies to the north. When these attacked, they easily broke through the weakened Austro-Hungarian front and forced a hurried retreat that virtually degenerated into a rout. Only the poor roads saved the situation, as the Austro-Hungarians lost 400,000 men to the Russians' 250,000.

Russian gunners aim their gun at Austro-Hungarian positions around the town of Przemysl in October 1914. The Russian victory in the opening campaigns in Galicia enabled them to lay siege to this key fortress.

Trench warfare and technology

In the fighting along the Aisne in September 1914, the spade became as important a weapon of war as the rifle for the average infantryman. In part this was a deliberate decision by the German Chief of the General Staff, the recently appointed General Erich von Falkenhayn. He realized that the onus for offensive action was on the French, British and Belgians, who needed to evict the Germans from France and Belgium. He therefore put his armies in a defensive posture almost straightaway, which meant digging entrenchments and constructing wire and other types of obstacles. Subsequently, the French and British followed suit, not because they were intent on fighting a defensive war, but because the entrenchments offered better protection against artillery and snipers while offensive action was planned and prepared.

Hiram Maxim, the inventor of an automatic firearm, aims his Maxim gun. The ability to fire several hundred rounds a minute from a single weapon had a dramatic effect on warfare.

1914, shrapnel shells were still extensively used by artillery because they were so effective against infantry and cavalry in the open. The Germans had realized this at the start of the war and tactically deployed in defensive positions against the French attacks along their common border. Once dug in they did not

> War experience in both the Boer War of 1899–1902 and the Russo-Japanese War of 1904–05 had shown that artillery firing shrapnel shells was not particularly effective against dug-in infantry.

suffer the level of casualties that French officers believed they would when subjected to rapid bombardment of shrapnel shells from the vaunted French 75mm gun.

Furthermore, almost all the combatants underestimated the need for heavier guns, especially howitzers that delivered the kind of plunging shellfire – often using high-explosive rounds – that was most effective against infantry in trenches. The British and French, however, had shown less foresight than the Germans and so particularly suffered from the German decision to dig in.

Tactical views on the correct way to conduct an infantry assault also played into the hands of those choosing to entrench their forces. It was apparent from the time of the American Civil War that in certain circumstances, infantry on the attack ought to move forward in rushes, preferably with supporting troops on the flanks firing at the defenders, forcing them to keep their heads down. What was true of armies still fighting with muzzle-loading muskets was even truer of armies equipped with breechloaders, as

Von Falkenhayn's decision made perfect sense in the light of military understanding in 1914. All armies were aware that various technological developments, mostly concentrated in the second half of the nineteenth century, had changed infantry tactics significantly. The development of rifling, followed by reliable breech-loading mechanisms, magazines and smokeless powder meant that soldiers no longer needed to stand up to ram down a cartridge and bullet into a musket, were not enveloped in clouds of smoke when they fired – which meant they could see targets clearly for longer – and could achieve accurate fire at far longer ranges. Attacking forces, therefore, were subjected to enemy fire for a longer period, and frequently from an opponent who was invisible to them

for much of the time, lying prone or in a trench, often with overhead cover.

The machine gun had most of these advantages and furthermore allowed the equivalent firepower of a platoon to be wielded by two or three men. Each German division had 24 machine guns, effectively increasing their firepower by an extra 24 platoons, or about 12 per cent. However, machine guns were not particularly mobile. In attack, they were utilized mainly as a relatively static support weapon, although they were more effective in defence, where there was less need for them to be mobile.

War experience in both the Boer War of 1899–1902 and the Russo-Japanese War of 1904–05 had shown that artillery firing shrapnel shells was not particularly effective against dug-in infantry. When war came in

the mobile warfare that characterized the first six weeks of the war.

Trench warfare did occur on the Eastern Front, but it was invariably a transitional stage in the fighting. It normally occurred either around an important objective such as

> It was apparent from the time of the American Civil War that in certain circumstances, infantry on the attack ought to move forward in rushes, preferably with supporting troops on the flanks firing at the defenders.

As the numerous used propellant containers show in this image of an US gun crew from 1918, field guns like the quick-firing French 75mm were able to fire many rounds accurately, because only the barrel recoiled, whereas the whole carriage of earlier weapons rebounded.

the Prussian troops found out in the Franco-Prussian War of 1870–71. The Boer War and the Russo-Japanese War only reinforced these lessons, emphasizing how much more effective modern firearms were compared with those of the 1870s.

However, this form of rushing assault ran contrary to the need to keep an infantry force under effective command. The fear was that without the officers being able to control the movements of their men, and without NCOs bringing up the rear enforcing discipline on any man hanging back, any attack would go to ground as soon as it came under fire, instead of closing on the enemy position and capturing it. The ordinary infantryman was

could overwhelm the defenders. In reality, it made good target practice as the French, who adopted the densest formations, found out in the war's opening battles.

Falkenhayn's recipe in the West, however, was not applied in the East to the same extent. Here was the key to the effects of technology on warfare in 1914, the explanation as to why trench warfare evolved on the Western Front, and why commanders believed that a "Big Push" offensive, applied correctly, would bring about a restoration of

a town or city, or else on terrain that already offered advantages to the defender, as in the area between Gorlice and Tarnow, between two relatively open areas. The basic reason for this was the average frontage a division occupied in a quiet sector of the front line was 6 miles (10 km), whereas in the East it was 12 miles (20 km). It was far easier to punch through such a thinly held position. Trench warfare was only inevitable where the battlefield was as crowded as in France and Belgium. The fighting on the Eastern Front remained as the generals envisaged war being fought prior to the stalemate in the West, and as they believed it could be once the trench line was broken.

> Each German division had 24 machine guns, effectively increasing their firepower by an extra 24 platoons, or about 12 per cent.

not entrusted with the ability to summon up the will to fight, or with the skill to keep moving forward from cover to cover in the most effective way to achieve the objective.

All the armies entering the First World War planned to advance to the attack in "skirmish lines" – long lines of men placed from 1–5 yards (1–4½ m) apart, depending on the army. The idea was that such a thick formation would maintain a "density of firepower" that

Field telephones were the only means of communicating with headquarters behind the lines, but were connected by fragile lines that could be disrupted by artillery barrages.

The British were forced to call up Royal Marine pensioners to make up the strength for reinforcements sent to Antwerp to help the Belgian army there resist a siege by the Germans.

Antwerp falls after siege

The German army occupied Antwerp on 10 October 1914. The fall of the city was followed by chaotic scenes as hundreds of thousands of soldiers and civilians attempted to escape either by sea, or by land to the Netherlands and France. A dense cloud of black smoke hangs over the port, after oil tanks were set alight by German shelling.

The Belgian army had withdrawn into Antwerp, designated the National Redoubt, after the Germans captured Liège in August. The Germans had left a couple of corps to surround the city and in September the new Chief of the General Staff, General Erich von Falkenhayn, reinforced this force with heavy guns and an additional division. A general bombardment of Antwerp began on 27 September and three days later the Germans began an assault aimed at breaching the first ring of forts and entrenchments that had been erected around the city. The Germans achieved early successes and the Belgians withdrew behind the River Nete.

In Britain, First Lord of the Admiralty Winston Churchill was alarmed by these developments, and was given Cabinet permission to go to the city. He took with him men of the Royal Naval Division, as well as 6,000 other soldiers – 12,000 in total.

Only four days later, however, after the defences along the Nete had been forced, the Belgian government decided to evacuate the city and withdraw the bulk of its army to the north-eastern corner of the country, around Ostend. When the Germans started bombarding the city, the Belgians again began to pull back.

Turkey enters the war

Turkey entered the war against the Allies on 29 October 1914. Turkey had received considerable investments from Germany in the years leading up to the war, most famously the "Berlin to Baghdad" railway. However, one of the biggest coups by the Germans was the transfer of two German vessels to the Turkish navy, making up for the seizure by Britain of two battleships being built in British yards.

The commander of the German Mediterranean squadron, Admiral Wilhelm Souchon, had been well aware of the tense European situation as it developed during July 1914, and had laid plans in keeping with his instructions to attack French bases in Algeria prior to a race into the North Atlantic with the intention of rejoining the German High Seas Fleet there. However, during the night of 3/4 August, Souchon received orders to sail for Turkey. Being already off the Algerian coast, Souchon opted to complete his planned shelling of French

bases at Bona and Philippeville, before setting sail for Turkey.

The British commander in the Mediterranean, Admiral Sir Archibald Berkeley Milne, was aware of the German movement, but in the first days of August it was still uncertain whether Britain would go to war with Germany – the British cabinet had not decided its policy even at the time of the German shelling of Algerian ports. However, it was assumed that war would come and British ships were assigned both to observe the Straits of Otranto (between Albania and Italy), from which Austro-Hungarian ships could reach the Mediterranean shipping lanes, and also the *Goeben* and *Breslau*, which were known to be a threat to the convoy routes between French North Africa and France.

The British divided their forces, and two battlecruisers went after the Germans while four smaller cruisers and accompanying destroyers observed the straits. The Admiralty in London concluded that the German ships would make their way to

the Atlantic and ordered the battlecruisers to move at speed toward the Straits of Gibraltar. In so doing, they accidentally intercepted the two German ships now sailing east. The British, still not yet at war with Germany, began shadowing the German vessels. Souchon, on the *Goeben*, found himself in a difficult position because he would probably lose an action against the two battlecruisers, so he accelerated to 26 knots and evaded the British.

The *Goeben* and the British then played a cat-and-mouse game, although at times it was difficult to tell which was the cat. All the British vessels involved were weaker than the German vessel, but for two days pursued the *Goeben* vigorously. The commander of the British cruiser squadron eventually decided that he stood no chance against the *Goeben*, which in turn could do no effective damage to British interests in the Eastern Mediterranean, and turned back to the Straits of Otranto. The *Goeben* escaped to Turkey, arriving in Turkish waters on 11 August.

The German battlecruiser *Goeben*'s flight to Turkey saved the ship from the futile gesture of an unwinnable confrontation against the far superior British Mediterranean fleet.

Austro-Hungarian cavalry advancing across the plains of Poland. The greater area in relation to the number of troops on the Eastern Front meant that warfare remained mobile.

Russians recover ground in Poland

On 27 October 1914, the chief of staff of German armies on the Eastern Front, General Erich Ludendorff, ordered his Ninth Army to withdraw from its advanced positions on the Vistula river in Russian Poland. This marks the end of the Central Powers' autumn campaign in Poland, with the Austro-Hungarians in Galicia already in retreat, and enables the Russians to retrieve much territory that they had surrendered only a few weeks before.

The Germans began their advance at the end of September, aware that the Russians had abandoned western Poland, which was surrounded on three sides by German and Austro-Hungarian territory at the outset of the war. The Austro-Hungarians were also due to advance northwards to relieve the siege of the fortress of Przemysl and regain both banks of the San river. However, by 9 October the Austro-Hungarian offensive had ground to a halt at the San itself.

The Russians were so confident that they could hold off the Austro-Hungarians that they withdrew three armies from the front and marched them to Warsaw and a line along the Vistula river. As they arrived, the Germans were approaching and some fierce fighting took place along the Vistula and around Ivangorod from 9 October with the Battle of Ivangorod continuing until 20 October. The Germans needed reinforcements, and took them from Ivangorod, with Austro-Hungarian troops replacing them in the line. These were defeated in short order by the Russians, and by 16 October the German army in front of Warsaw was threatened by the Russian advance. Two days later the Austro-Hungarians were in full retreat again as the Russians attacked along the

The Russians were so confident that they could hold off the Austro-Hungarians that they withdrew three armies from the front and marched them to Warsaw and a line along the Vistula river.

San, and the Germans chose to withdraw from Warsaw, returning to their original positions of September after a renewed Russian attack on 26 October threatened their forces.

Race to sea ends in draw

German forces face their French, British and Belgian counterparts the entire length of a line stretching from the North Sea to the Swiss border, after the Germans captured Ostend and Zeebrugge on 15 October 1914. The Belgian army has flooded the area around the Yser river, stopping any further advance westward, while French and British troops have been moved rapidly by rail to cover such major centres as Ypres, Dixmude and La Basée.

The "race to the sea", as the campaign has become known, was started with an attempt to turn the flank of the German position along the Aisne by an attack by French troops in the area between Arras and Compiègne. The Germans countered this with a pincer attack on the northern part of this French attack, with advances north and south of Arras. In order to cover the flank of this manoeuvre, a mass of German cavalry advanced on a great sweep further north around Bethune, aiming to scythe down behind French lines toward Amiens.

Given this strategic situation, with some possibilities for manoeuvre, the British Expeditionary Force was transferred northwards from the Aisne front, to where it could be supplied more easily from the Channel ports, slotting into the line south of Bethune. At Ostend, another British force covered the withdrawal of the Belgian field army from Antwerp, which subsequently took up position along the Yser, to the east of Dunkirk. The only gap in the line now stood between Ypres and La Bassée.

Russian rumours in Britain

A false story has swept Britain this autumn about a mysterious Russian expeditionary force that supposedly arrived in Scotland in August. Some of those who claim to have seen the force say the men were speaking a foreign

The numbers reached astronomical levels for a force that no one has actually seen.

language and had "snow on their boots". The numbers reached astronomical levels for a force that no one has actually seen. The generally accepted figure is a quarter of a million and the rumour has even warranted comment in the humorous magazine *Punch*.

French soldiers occupy a trench. The attempts by both sides on the Western Front to outflank one another only created a line of trenches that cut like a scar across the French countryside.

British hold upper hand around Ypres

A **German attempt to** break the Allied lines at Ypres in Flanders was abandoned with the onset of bad weather on 22 November 1914. Both sides have suffered unexpectedly heavily in just over three months of continuous fighting in France.

The flat countryside of Flanders offered von Falkenhayn what appeared to be his best chance of achieving a significant victory. There was only a scattering of troops between the small Belgian army hugging the coast and the French forces in front of Lille. After the fall of Antwerp on 10 October, von Falkenhayn ordered two German armies to advance through here and reach the Channel ports of Dunkirk, Calais and Boulogne. The race was on between the Germans, attempting to thrust a large army through the gap and to the ports, and the French and British scrambling to plug the hole with troops drawn from other parts of the front.

By 22 October, the French and British had won the race, filling the gap with infantry. The main weight of the Prussian attack came at Ypres, where seven British infantry and three cavalry divisions,

together with a similar number of French troops, faced two German armies amounting to some 24 divisions. However, eight of the German divisions were made up of reservists, student volunteers at the outbreak of war, who were badly trained, with officers called out of retirement and unfamiliar with the latest tactical thinking.

With such an advantage in numbers, the Germans believed they could achieve a breakthrough. The student volunteers were sent into action on 31 October, advancing in skirmish lines more appropriate to the Franco-Prussian War, with flags flying and singing "Deutschland über Alles". They advanced into the rifle fire of professional British soldiers trained to fire 15 rounds a minute and were cut down as if they were walking into machine-gun fire. Where they did achieve their objectives, the British counter-attacks eventually drove them out.

The Germans made their last attempt at breaking the British line on 11 November, sending eight regiments of the Guard along the Menin Road. Just as the reservists suffered heavy casualties, so did the Guard, who similarly ignored the lessons of recent conflicts.

Britain's first naval defeat of the century

Admiral Sir Christopher Cradock died in the Battle of Coronel, after challenging a much stronger German force on 1 November 1914.

T **wo British armoured** cruisers were sunk by a stronger German squadron in a battle off the coast of Chile on 1 November 1914, representing the first British naval defeat since the Napoleonic period.

The German East Asiatic Squadron, consisting of two armoured cruisers and three light cruisers, had moved to the Marianas Islands prior to the outbreak of war, and on 14 August sailed east across the Pacific hoping to raid British shipping off South America. A British squadron consisting of two armoured cruisers, a light cruiser and a converted liner intercepted them off Coronel, Chile, on 1 November at around 4.30 p.m. Fighting began around 7 p.m. and accurate German gunfire quickly sank the two British cruisers.

British soldiers dig a trench in muddy Flanders ground. After being churned up by an artillery bombardment, the soggy ground quickly turned into a quagmire during periods of heavy rain.

German victory in East Africa

The German garrison of German East Africa defeated an attempt by the British Indian army to take control of the port of Tanga, an important seaport in the colony, forcing the British to withdraw on 5 November 1914. The British forces have suffered about a thousand casualties, to the Germans' 150.

The British landed 8,000 men from boats on 3 November, a few miles south of the city, but they had poor quality maps and did not reconnoitre the area. When they marched toward Tanga on 4 November they were ambushed by about a thousand German troops and brought to a halt. Skirmishing during the afternoon was periodically interrupted by attacks from swarms of angry bees.

The British forces have suffered about a thousand casualties, to the Germans 150.

The German counter-attack the next day drove the British troops back to their boats, leaving behind considerable amounts of weapons and ammunition, which were invaluable booty to the isolated German colonial force.

Japan captures Tsingtao

The German-leased port of Tsingtao, in China, surrendered to a predominantly Japanese force on 7 November 1914. The siege had lasted two months.

The Japanese sent a force of 23,000 men, heavily equipped with artillery, to besiege the town. A steady bombardment was maintained throughout the siege, with the Japanese very active in conducting night raids on the German defences and in using seaplanes to scout over the German positions, as well as dropping small bombs.

The Japanese assaulted the German defences on 7 November and once their lines had been broken, the Germans agreed to surrender the port and its garrison of 6,000 men.

British soldiers pass their Japanese allies as they come ashore at Tsingtao to help capture Germany's China treaty port in the autumn of 1914.

Russia and Germany claim victory

Both Russian and German generals claimed victory after their latest engagement around the city of Lódz, which sputters on after a German withdrawal on 24 November 1914. The German commander of the Eastern Front, General Paul von Hindenburg, has requested reinforcements from the Western Front in order to launch further offensive operations during the winter.

The Russian armies in central Poland, after securing Warsaw from a German attack in October, began advancing toward the German region of Silesia which has vital industrial resources. Von Hindenburg's chief of staff, General Erich Ludendorff, withdrew German troops from further south and sent them against the slowly advancing Russian armies on 11 November. One corps of the northernmost army was in an isolated position, and the Germans took advantage of this to defeat it before reinforcements could arrive. With a gap opened in the Russian line, the Germans streamed through it with the intention of capturing Warsaw. The flank

of a second Russian corps was exposed by the retreat of the first and the Germans turned their attention on it as well, forcing it to retire.

Russian commanders were slow to react to the crisis, but when they did they managed to march rapidly to establish a strong defensive position at Lódz, an important supply centre for them. The Germans attempted to attack the city on 18 November, but instead found themselves in a position where they were about to be cut off by a Russian flank attack. Recognizing the seriousness of the situation, they withdrew, taking with them many Russian prisoners. The Russians suffered total losses of 95,000 in these battles, to the Germans' 35,000.

A battalion of Russian soldiers on the march in the winter of 1914. Russian forces have abandoned their traditional defensive strategy and adopted an offensive one, that has so far brought them only serious defeats at the hands of the Germans.

Commerce raider sunk

The German light cruiser *Emden* was destroyed off the Cocos Islands by the Australian cruiser HMAS *Sydney* on 9 November 1914. The *Emden* had cruised the Indian Ocean after parting company with the associated ships of the German East Asiatic Squadron in the Marianas on 14 August. Between 10 September and 28 October, the *Emden* captured or sank 25 Allied ships, the last two ships being a Russian cruiser and a French destroyer in Penang harbour, as well as shelling oil installations at Madras in India, . The *Emden* often disguised her appearance by means of a false funnel, which made her resemble a British vessel.

The hulk of the German light cruiser *Emden* in the Cocos Islands after the ship was defeated by a more powerful Australian light cruiser.

British invade Mesopotamia, hold Basra

An expeditionary force drawn from the British Indian army occupied Basra on 22 November 1914 after a siege lasting two weeks. The expedition is an attempt to attack Turkey from the Persian Gulf, hoping to take advantage of Arab nationalism, and also to protect Britain's vital petroleum industry investments in Persia.

The British had anticipated Turkey's entry into the war on 29 October, having dispatched 7,000 troops from Bombay in mid-month. On 7 November a portion of this force landed on the Fao peninsula. The British had won support from a local sheikh, who supplied intelligence of the Turkish military movements in return for a bribe, thus enabling the British to counter an attempt by the Turks to push them off the peninsula.

With the support of a flotilla of gunboats, the British succeeded in forcing the evacuation of Turkish troops from Basra, and have now secured control of the Shatt al-Arab estuary after driving the Turks away from the vital oil refinery at Abadan.

OBITUARY
LORD ROBERTS
(1832–1914)

Lord Roberts, the last commander-in-chief of the British army, has died of pneumonia after visiting troops at St Omer.

Lord Roberts was the most highly regarded general of the Victorian era, having led British forces to success in Afghanistan and during the Boer War, being showered with honours as a result. He won the Victoria Cross during the Indian Mutiny and in 1901 became commander-in-chief of the British army. After he retired in 1904, the post was abolished and replaced by the Chief of the Imperial General Staff.

He was granted an earldom in 1901, which has been allowed to pass to his surviving daughter, his only son having been killed in action during the Boer War.

Falklands victory

On 8 December 1914, the odyssey of the German East Asiatic Squadron came to an end off the Falkland Islands when four of its five ships were sunk in combat with two British battlecruisers.

The victory of the German East Asiatic Squadron over the British West Indies squadron at Coronel in November 1914 had come as a shock to the Royal Navy. Two powerful battlecruisers were therefore sent to the South Atlantic to find the German squadron and destroy it. Meanwhile, the commander of the German ships, Admiral Graf Maximilian von Spee, planned a raid on the Falkland Islands, a British colony where a coaling station and a radio station were situated. As von Spee's ships neared the islands, they sighted the telltale tripod mast of a British capital ship – the British battlecruisers were coaling at Port Stanley, a coincidence that was to prove fatal to von Spee's ships. Unable to outrun the faster British vessels, the German warships came under fire at about 1.00 p.m., after a three-hour chase. The two German armoured cruisers were sunk first, then the two light cruisers. Nearly 2,000 German sailors, including von Spee and both of his sons, were lost in the battle; the British losses were just 29.

HMS *Invincible* picks up the few survivors from the defeated German East Asiatic Squadron, which was sunk in an engagement in December 1914. Only 215 German sailors survived.

Friendship in the front line

Troops on the Western Front have spent some of the Christmas holiday period fraternizing with the enemy. German, British and, in rare instances, even French troops declared local truces and even exchanged whatever gifts they could with one another. Impromptu football matches are reported to have been played.

Most of the truces occurred in the area around Ypres in Belgium. Shouted Christmas greetings and the singing of carols preceded troops from both sides getting out of their trenches and walking into no-man's-land to visit their enemy. German troops placed candles on small pine trees and put these along the parapets of their trenches. Soldiers also used these truces to bury the dead who had been left lying out in the open, and both sides mourned and prayed for the fallen. There were some instances where individuals appeared to be trying to get a better view of their opponents' entrenchments, but these were discouraged in a respectful manner in order to avoid any possibility of fighting suddenly breaking out. The truces for the most part started on Christmas Eve and continued throughout Christmas Day, although some extended even to the New Year.

British and German soldiers greet one another on Christmas Day 1914. The truce was not uniform across the front, but was widespread.

The German armoured cruiser SMS *Blücher* capsizes after being pummelled by British battlecruisers for nearly two hours. Of her crew 792 were killed, and only 260 were rescued.

Intelligence the key at Dogger Bank

On **24 January** 1915, British ships from the Grand Fleet engaged a smaller German squadron from the High Seas Fleet. The Battle of the Dogger Bank originally started as a raid by the German warships, which had successfully bombarded ports on England's east coast in December. British naval intelligence intercepted and decoded German signals advising ships of the impending raid, and Vice Admiral David Beatty sailed out to meet the enemy. Once the German commander, Admiral Franz von Hipper, saw the more powerful British squadron off the Dogger Bank, he turned his ships to withdraw, but after a two-hour chase, the British came within range and both sides exchanged gunfire. Two German ships were damaged, as was the British flagship, which eventually came to a halt. Beatty tried to order the rest of his ships to continue pursuing the Germans, but this was misinterpreted and the British ships concentrated on one of the damaged German ships, SMS *Blücher*. While the *Blücher* was being sunk the rest of the German ships escaped.

IN BRIEF

⁂ An Austro-Hungarian offensive into Serbia, launched on 8 November 1914, came to an ignominious end on 15 December, when the Austro-Hungarians give up all their gains and allowed Belgrade to be reoccupied by Serbian forces.

⁂ German warships bombarded the British towns of Scarborough, Whitby and Hartlepool on 16 December 1914. The raid resulted in the death of 122 civilians in total and damage to buildings in all three places.

⁂ British Imperial forces began an invasion of the German colony of South-West Africa. On 25 December 1914, Walvis Bay, on the coast, was occupied by units from the Dominion of South Africa and Rhodesian colonies. The decision to invade was a controversial one in South Africa, where the Boers had received support from Germany during their war with the British. In September 1914 there had been a brief rebellion by the Boers against the decision to invade the colony, and martial law was proclaimed in parts of the dominion. The rebellion ended on 28 December.

⁂ Great Yarmouth, Sheringham and King's Lynn were all bombed on 19 January 1915 by German zeppelins. These raids were authorized personally by Kaiser Wilhelm II, the German emperor, earlier in the month. Four people were killed and buildings were damaged.

Ethnic cleansing

At the end of December 1914, the Turkish Third Army attacked Russian forces in Russian Armenia. Enver Pasha, the Minister of War and a member of the triumvirate that provided the effective government of Turkey, took personal charge of this force. His initial target was the town of Sarikamis and he divided his army as it marched toward the objective, expecting the two columns to arrive simultaneously. They did not, however, and the Russian defenders defeated each of these forces separately, preventing the Turks from taking advantage of their numerical superiority. The Turks faced a difficult winter retreat and at least half the army died during the march or in the fighting.

One of the organizers of the crime against the Armenians in Turkey was Kouzi Bey, seated at the table second from the left, here having a drink with some officers of his country's German allies, in a photograph published in a French newspaper.

Kurdish troops were given a free hand against Armenians and killed the men wholesale. The Armenian labour battalions

> On 18 February 1915, Enver Pasha ordered all ethnic Armenian troops in the Turkish army to be assigned to labour battalions. It was the beginning of what was later described as the Armenian Genocide.

The defeat was a tremendous embarrassment for Enver Pasha so he looked for a scapegoat, and found one in the Armenians. The Armenians, who were concentrated around the border with Russia in eastern Turkey, shared a Christian faith with the Russians, who made every effort to emphasize this shared heritage as they planned an invasion for the spring.

On 18 February 1915, Enver Pasha ordered all ethnic Armenian troops in the Turkish army to be assigned to labour battalions. It was the beginning of what was later described as the Armenian Genocide. Gradually the Turkish authorities tackled what they perceived as an "Armenian problem". In March 1915, Armenians were evacuated from the important port of Dörtyol on the Mediterranean coast. In April, the governor of Van province, Jevet Bey, who was also brother-in-law to Enver Pasha, executed five Armenian community leaders, at about the same time as a revolt of Armenians broke out in the province. To this day, historians debate whether the

leaders were executed in an attempt to head off the revolt, or whether the Turks were implementing a plan to remove ethnic Armenians from Anatolia. Whatever the motives, the effect of Turkish policies was the wholesale destruction of the Armenian community in the Turkish Empire.

suffered a terrible rate of attrition as they carried out tasks assigned them by the Moslem authorities. Hundreds of the Armenian intelligentsia were arrested and were allegedly executed.

The Turkish government went further in May. At the end of the month, an order was issued forcing the evacuation of Armenians from all of Anatolia, except the Aegean coast, these people being sent to concentration camps in the deserts of Syria and Mesopotamia. No

Hungry Armenian children await the distribution of food at a camp in northern Syria. The Turks did not kill masses of Armenians outright, but transported them to camps where they starved.

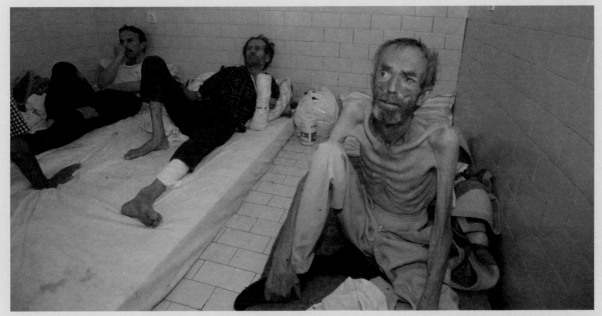

Victims of the Bosnian genocide. Bosnian Moslems and Croats were subjected to systematic murder and starvation by Bosnian Serbs between 1992 and 1995.

attempt was made to provide these displaced people with adequate care during the arduous journey, or even after they had arrived at their new camps. There were widespread accusations of robbery, rape and murder by the guards, many of whom were members of the Special Organization, made up of prisoners released on government orders. If Armenians were not rebelling before these policies were adopted, they were certainly ready to revolt afterwards, and did so in towns such as Edessa.

The exact total of victims is also subject to debate. Although Turkish sources named figures ranging from 200,000 to 600,000, other historians estimate between 1 million and 1.5 million. Whether as a matter of deliberate policy, or as a result of suppressing rebellious activity, the Armenian community of eastern Anatolia was effectively removed from the region during the First World War.

Without doubt, in the past, massacre was a standard practice of Turkish repression of rebellion. In 1876, 15,000 Bulgarians were massacred after they had attempted to assert their independence, an action that ultimately led to the Russo-Turkish War of 1877–78 after which the Russians began agitating for Armenian rights. This Bulgarian massacre shocked the other great powers of Europe at the time, as well as the United States. In

1903, Macedonians were massacred after an uprising, although estimates of the dead were much lower, around 7,000, than in the case of the Bulgarians or the Armenians.

The Armenians themselves had been victims of massacres in 1896, after a terrorist raid on the Turkish Bank in Istanbul in August 1896. Armenian political organizations were repressed, and somewhere between 80,000 and 300,000 Armenians were murdered at the order of the Turkish Sultan of the time.

> The exact total of victims is also subject to debate. Although Turkish sources named figures ranging from 200,000 to 600,000, other historians estimate between 1 million and 1.5 million.

Further massacres of Armenians took place in 1909, after the coup that had brought Enver Pasha to power led to demands for more liberty and autonomy; another 15,000 to 30,000 died.

The coup was a nationalist one and Islam was identified as a key element of the empire under Enver Pasha's regime. According to

those who support the idea that the Turks were engaged in a genocide of the Armenians, the aim of Turkish policies at the time was to remove the Armenians altogether from Turkish territory, by the simple expedients of forced relocation and death. The Turks were not the first to implement such policies, nor would they be the last. The United States' government had forcibly moved several Indian tribes from south-eastern and mid-western states to an Indian territory on the Great Plains. This would be home to tribes from across the country, regardless of their native habitats which had such a deep influence on American Indian culture. Others were restricted to reserved territories closer to home, such as in the Dakota territories or Arizona and New Mexico, during the later nineteenth century. Hitler used the example of the Armenians to justify his own intentions toward the Jews, in his acrid comment in August 1939 about no-one now remembering the Armenians any more. In Rwanda, as in the Balkans of the 1990s, "ethnic cleansing" eradicated groups who were inconveniently on the wrong side of a border. Today, the UN Convention on the prevention and punishment of the crime of genocide, agreed in 1948, established a standard under which individuals such as Enver Pasha can be brought to account for their crimes.

Russians fend off Austro-Hungarians and Germans

Two **winter offensives** on the Eastern Front have forced the Austro-Hungarians and Germans to fight in harsh winter conditions of cold and snow, and both have failed to deal a knockout blow against Russia. It is the first significant setback to the wartime career of German General Erich Ludendorff, the prime mover of the campaign.

One offensive was directed at the Russian armies in East Prussia, while the other was a drive from the Carpathians to break the Russian blockade of the important fortress of Przemysl, which had been under siege since September, apart from a month's hiatus in October. The Austro-Hungarian attacks started on 23 January 1915, but the winter weather and difficult terrain slowed

their advance so that by 5 February they had more or less ground to a halt, and it was the Russians' turn to attack in the Carpathians. The Austro-Hungarians resumed their attacks on 17 February, in the hope of reaching Przemysl, but these failed and in mid-March the garrison finally surrendered.

The German offensive in East Prussia began on 7 February when both the Germans and the Russians had to battle through a snowstorm. The bad weather reduced the effectiveness of the attack, but once the weather abated on 10 February the Germans made great gains, including the destruction of a corps – some 56,000 men – until a Russian counter-attack on 21 February brought the offensive to an end.

French dead on German barbed wire. The French suffered heavy casualties, and owed any gains to a considerable superiority in numbers.

Futility in the Champagne

A **French offensive against** the German-held Sayon salient in the eastern Champagne was called off on 17 March 1915, after they had suffered an estimated 90,000 casualties. General Joseph Joffre had hoped that an advance of about 50 miles (80 km) would cut an important railway line that supplied German forces between Thionville and Valenciennes. With the massive French bombardment on the German trenches having little effect on the German machine-gun emplacements, the massed French infantry assaults soon ground to a halt after an advance of barely 2 miles (3 km).

A new era: unrestricted submarine warfare

On **4 February** 1915, the German emperor, Wilhelm II, declared the seas around the British Isles to be a war zone, and that any shipping found there would be sunk without warning by submarines of the German navy as from 18 February 1915.

German submarines, known as U-boats, had already achieved a number of successes during the war. Being able to attack warships on sight enabled U-9 to sink no fewer than three Royal Navy armoured cruisers, the *Aboukir*, *Hogue* and *Cressy*, on 22 September 1914. They also began attacking merchantmen in October 1914, following the accepted practice of commerce raiding by boarding a vessel and enabling the crew to escape in lifeboats before sinking her. The first such incidents occurred off the coast of Norway.

However, this kind of conduct was not practical around the British Isles, where many warships were able to patrol from nearby ports. In order to take advantage of the submarine's ability to conceal itself underwater, German admirals therefore decided it was necessary to sink ships in the war zone on sight.

Action at Aubers Ridge

On **13 March** 1915, Field Marshal Sir John French called off his attack on Aubers Ridge after three days of heavy fighting, during which the British captured several German trenches, with about 13,000 casualties on both sides.

The British attack had originally been part of a combined offensive with the French, who were to assault Vimy Ridge, while the British moved against Aubers Ridge. It was hoped that the two operations would force the Germans back from Noyon, but the heavy casualties the French had suffered around the Sayon salient prevented them from carrying out their part of the plan. In spite of this, General French continued to press ahead.

The British gambled on a heavy barrage shortly before their advance on a very narrow front. The three German battalions defending the trench line were confronted by 14 British ones and the attack was launched after a 35-minute barrage on 10 March. Although it was initially highly successful, the Germans rushed reinforcements forward. Not being used to the conditions of trench warfare, advancing across torn-up ground and having to form up to take a second line of trenches after securing the first caused fatal delays for the British.

FIRST BATTLE OF CHAMPAGNE

DATES:	December 1914–March 1915
COMBATANTS:	France vs Germany
CASUALTIES:	France, 90,000; Germany, 20,000
RESULT:	German victory

Guns in the Dardanelles

On **18 March** 1915, an Anglo-French fleet attempted to force a passage of the Dardanelles in Turkey, hoping to destroy the forts on either side of the straits and sail into the Sea of Marmara, prior to an attack on the Turkish capital, Constantinople. However, the operation ended in failure after four warships struck mines that had been laid by the Turks only ten days before.

The French battleship *Bouvet* sinks after it had struck a mine on 18 March 1915. The sinking resulting in the loss of almost her entire crew.

Australian troops disembark from longboats at Anzac Cove on the Gallipoli peninsula. Landing at the wrong place, they could not advance as aggressively inland as they might have liked.

Allied troops land at Gallipoli

British Imperial forces and French troops landed on the Gallipoli peninsula on 25 April 1915. The campaign is intended to knock Turkey out of the war, give Allied forces control of the Dardanelles and open a year-round supply line to Russia.

The landings were made at two places on the peninsula. At Cape Helles, British troops landed at five separate beaches on the tip of the peninsula, while soldiers from Australia and New Zealand went ashore at so-called Anzac (Australian and New Zealand Army Corps) Cove, on the western coast of the Gallipoli peninsula, just over 10 miles (16 km) away. From here the Anzacs were to advance across the narrow

peninsula and both prevent the Turkish forces at the southern tip from retreating, and also prevent them being reinforced.

The landings on both beaches were difficult affairs. At Cape Helles the British had mixed fortunes – they were successful on the flanks, but the main landings at V and W beaches resulted in heavy loss of life, with the landing forces suffering between 60 and 70 per cent casualties. The Anzacs landed further north than planned and had to race for the high ground overlooking the cove, against Turkish troops being rushed forward to drive them into the sea. The Turks won the race, although they were unable to drive any of the invaders back into the sea.

DARDANELLES & GALLIPOLLI

DATES:	February 1915–January 1916
COMBATANTS:	British Imperial forces and France vs Turkey
CASUALTIES:	Britain Imperial forces and France, 214,000; Turkey, 300,000
RESULT:	Turkish victory

Predatory pilot captured

Frenchman **Roland Garros,** a pre-war aviator, was captured on 18 April 1915 by German troops after his aircraft had to crash-land behind German lines. Garros developed a set of deflector blades that enabled him to mount a machine gun on the

The bullets, instead of shooting off part of the propellor blade, bounced off the deflectors instead, enabling Garros to shoot down three German aircraft.

front of his plane and fire forward to shoot down enemy aircraft. The bullets, instead of shooting off part of the propellor blade, bounced off the deflectors instead, enabling Garros to shoot down three German aircraft, the first on 1 April 1915.

Roland Garros created a system of deflectors allowing him to fire through the propellor arc.

Germans employ poison gas

Casualties of a gas attack rest at a hospital behind the lines. The use of chlorine gas surprised Allied defenders at Ypres, but the aggressive tactics of the 1st Canadian Division averted a major breakthrough.

German forces used chlorine gas against French colonial troops in the Ypres sector of the Western Front on 22 April 1915. The gas resulted in breathing troubles or blindness to the troops affected, causing death in many cases. Some 5,000 troops died as a result of this attack, opening a gap in the Allied lines 4 miles (6½ km) wide. The Germans' success was so unexpected that in the end it proved to be advantageous to the Allies. The 1st Canadian Division that rushed to replace the French troops soon realized that the enemy's lines were uncontaminated and decided that they would be safer fighting there than in the old French trenches. After soaking their handkerchiefs in urine – the ammonia of which negated the effects of chlorine – the Canadians used them as crude respirators and advanced, with heavy casualties, to capture German positions.

This was not the first time the Germans have used poison gas in the war – on 31 January 1915 they fired chemical shells against Russian positions, but cold temperatures on the day rendered the gas ineffective.

Crucified Canadian rumour circulates

Canadian soldiers are saying that one of their comrades has been "crucified" to a tree or barn door by German soldiers using bayonets to pin him up by his arms and legs. The incident is alleged to have occurred on 24 April 1915, and it has been asserted that the victim was a Harry Banks. The first eyewitness account described the incident as occurring near St Julien, in the Ypres area of the front, but no crucified body has yet been discovered.

Turks routed in Mesopotamia

The British have won a victory at Shaiba, in Mesopotamia, over Turkish forces defending the region between Basra and Baghdad after a three-day battle ending on 14 April 1915.

The British campaign in Mesopotamia originally had the limited objective of protecting British oil installations in Persia, although it was too far from the main centres of the Turkish Empire to be a decisive region in the war. However, the victory at Basra came so easily that the British decided that it would be a simple task to advance to Baghdad.

On 9 April, General Sir John Nixon arrived at Basra to take command of the British forces in Mesopotamia. He had his plans, but the Turks decided to strike first. Using hordes of Arab irregulars to support some regular regiments, the Turks attacked on the night of 11 April. The British lines held and the Turks planned a withdrawal after two days of fighting. On the third day, however, the British cavalry attacked, catching the Turks and their irregular allies unawares, causing them to retreat in some confusion.

Boats carry British artillery along the Euphrates river.

Lusitania sunk, 1,195 lost

The last known photograph of the *Lusitania*, a Cunard liner carrying war munitions when she was torpedoed by the U-20.

The **British liner** RMS *Lusitania* was sunk by a German submarine off the Old Head of Kinsale on 7 May 1915. The Germans claim the ship was a legitimate military target; the British insist that it was not.

The *Lusitania* left New York on 1 May and arrived off the coast of Ireland on 7 May, where it was sighed by the German submarine U-20. The commander of the U-20, Walter Schweiger, ordered the firing of a torpedo in accordance with Germany's declaration of a war zone around the British Isles, making all ships legitimate targets for German warships. After the torpedo exploded, a second explosion occurred. It is not clear what this explosion was, although the *Lusitania* was carrying over 4 million rifle rounds and many cases of shrapnel shells and fuses. Among the dead was American motivational author Elbert Hubbard. Only 774 out of almost 2,000 passengers and crew survived.

Ammunition shortage halts attack

While **a British** offensive at Aubers Ridge near Arras on 9 May 1915 ground to a halt due to a shortage of artillery shells, a French attack at Vimy Ridge on the same day succeeded in attaining limited objectives thanks to better support from their guns.

The 40-minute British bombardment began an hour after sunrise, German machine guns scythed down whole lines of advancing troops and the lack of high-explosive shells resulted in the German barbed-wire entanglements not being breached. After 20 minutes, most of the attacking force lay trapped in no-man's-land. The British attempted to retrieve the situation with several artillery bombardments and a second attack was made in the afternoon, but also failed with heavy casualties. On 10 May an attempt to renew the attack was abandoned owing to a further shortage of shells. The French attack at Vimy gained its initial objectives, but could get no further.

German officers reconnoitre enemy trenches from a house in the spring of 1915. German officers led their army with great efficiency at all levels of command.

IN BRIEF

In 1915, the Germans introduced a system enabling a machine gun mounted on an aircraft to fire through the propellers' blades without hitting them. Designed by Anthony Fokker and based on Franz Schneider's work, the technique was first used successfully on the Western Front on 1 August 1915, when Lieutenant Max Immelmann forced down a British aircraft while flying his Fokker E.1 monoplane.

The German Fokker E.1 monoplane, armed with a single Spandau machine gun.

No gain at Vimy Ridge and Festubert

French and British attacks at Vimy Ridge and Festubert achieved mixed results, the British operation finishing on 25 May, the French on 18 June. After a four-day bombardment, British and Indian troops went over the top shortly before midnight on 15 May. They made some rapid initial gains, but the Germans then withdrew to a new position some 1,200 yards (1,100 m) behind their original front line. This new line held firm against the initial British attacks. The battle then petered out into more limited attacks aimed at making the new Allied line more defensible. A simultaneous attempt by the French to take Vimy Ridge ended with 100,000 casualties – all for little gain.

German South-West Africa campaign

British Imperial forces completed the conquest of German South-west Africa on 9 July 1915 with the signing of a truce between the German military and civil administration, and the South African commanding the British Imperial force, General Louis Botha.

At first, the German defenders had proved successful against South African probes and had even captured the British colony at Walvis Bay on 10 September 1914. But when British forces were beaten at Sandfontein on 26 September, a rebellion by Boers in South Africa put a halt to operations in the German colony.

While the Germans believed that the Namib deserts would prevent South African military forces from mounting an effective attack on the colony from the south, the South Africans had been aware of this problem and had made provision for a regular supply of water to their soldiers, by means of rebuilding the railway destroyed by the Germans. They also developed existing wells to provide more water. The South Africans were ready by late March and began their advance, forcing the Germans to retreat in the face of superior numbers.

The main South African effort was made from Walvis Bay, which was recaptured on Christmas Day 1914. Supply problems, in this case of both food and water, delayed the South African advance until late April. The Germans did not have a sufficiently strong force to resist a co-ordinated advance and retired, more in hope than with any serious prospect of success. The colony's capital, Windhoek, and its powerful radio transmitter, part of a global network that broadcast German news to the world, fell on 12 May 1915, and in the end the Germans surrendered without fighting a major battle.

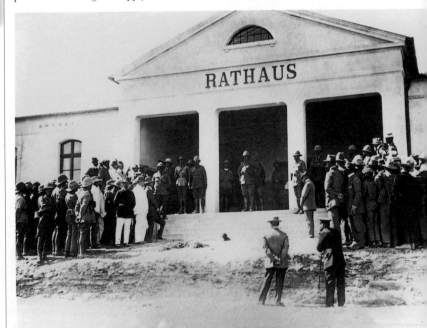

General Louis Botha formally takes possession of the city hall at Windhoek, the capital of the German South-West Africa colony.

Gallipoli

On **21 August** 1915, British forces halted offensive operations around Suvla Bay, an abortive assault landing there two weeks earlier having failed to capture the high ground overlooking the beachhead. After four months of campaigning, the British and French have little to show for their daring operation against the Turks on the Gallipoli peninsula.

Following the April landings, the British tried several times to break through the Turkish lines, but in each case the attacks failed to achieve any kind of breakthrough.

One initial target was the village of Krithia, to the north of the main British landing site at Cape Helles. British patrols came within 500 yards (460 m) of the village on the day of the initial landings, but further attempts on 6–8 May and 4–6 June got nowhere near this distant objective. The best results came in the June attack when the advance totalled 1,000 yards (920 m), but these attacks resulted in between 25 and 50 per cent casualties.

After a last attempt on Achi Baba Nullah, operations from Helles ceased, and the Suvla Bay landings were planned.

Suvla Bay was to the north of the initial landings. By sending troops there and seizing the heights around the bay, the British commander, General Sir Ian Hamilton, hoped either to weaken the Turks opposing the beachheads at Helles and Anzac Cove as they redeployed to face the new threat, or even to trap Turkish forces altogether. However, the 61-year-old commander on the spot, Lieutenant General Sir Frederick Stopford, was concerned about attacking without artillery support, even though few Turkish troops were present. Instead of pressing forward to capture and hold the high ground, he kept his men on the beach, giving the Turks time to rush reinforcements there, and a stalemate ensued, just as at Anzac and Cape Helles.

A view from Turkish positions over the British landings at Suvla Bay in August 1915. The British moved far too slowly to take advantage of Turkish disarray, after the masterful strategic stroke opening a second front in the battle here.

French offensive in the Champagne

French troops in a dugout. The familiar Adrian helmet was first issued in 1915. Long artillery bombardments and a lack of mobile warfare were encouraging troops to dig more deeply into French soil.

Two **Franco-British offensives** were called off on 13 October 1915, after achieving minimal success with high casualties. The year 1915 has been marked by a succession of futile assaults on German positions on the Western Front, with little to show for them other than heavy casualties.

The French attempted once again to achieve a major strategic breakthrough in the Champagne, only to fail against strongly held German positions. A three-day bombardment by 2,500 guns heralded the French offensive by some 500,000 men. On 25 September the troops attacked the German lines in pouring rain, taking the first German line with some ease; but it took another ten days of hard fighting for limited objectives before the Allies were ready to take on the second, main, German line. French artillery observers could not spot the fall of shot on this second line as easily as they had the first, and a general shortage of howitzers, with their steep trajectory, hampered such efforts as could be made. When the

French soldiers attacked, they achieved little. The offensive was abandoned with the loss of 145,000 men killed, wounded or captured.

Also on 25 September, the British launched an attack around Loos, using gas, but unfortunately for the British soldiers, the gas cloud did not move forward as expected and hampered the assault in places. Some success was achieved near the village of Auchy, but the British Expeditionary Force's commander, Field Marshal Sir John French, had not placed

his reserve divisions close enough to the line for them to arrive in time to capitalize on it. When they did finally attack, there were 8,000 casualties out of 10,000 who went over the top. As in the Champagne, the German second-line defences were stronger than the first-line ones, and the absence of an adequate preliminary artillery barrage only made the carnage even more futile. Whereas the British lost about 50,000 men in the Battle of Loos, total German losses in the two battles were only half of the Allied total.

SECOND BATTLE OF CHAMPAGNE AND BATTLE OF LOOS-ARTOIS

DATES:	September–October 1915
COMBATANTS:	France and Britain vs Germany
CASUALTIES:	France, 191,000; Britain, 50,000; Germany, 115,000
RESULT:	Germans stopped British and French from obtaining their objectives, leading to stalemate

Austro-Hungarian infantry collect Russian rifles from a captured trench. Russian failures in the summer campaigns of 1915 led Tsar Nicholas to risk his prestige by taking personal control of the war.

Tsar takes charge after disasters

As the Tsar of all the Russias, Nicholas II, replaced his uncle, Grand Duke Nicholas as overall commander of the Russian armies on 5 September 1915. Since May, the Russians have been pummelled by German-led offensives that have pushed them out of Galicia, Russian Poland and Courland.

When the Germans began an offensive in western Galicia on 2 May, they tried new artillery bombardment tactics. Beginning with a steady rate of fire on 1 May, the barrage was intensified in the final hour before the actual assault. These tactics proved remarkably effective as for the most part the dazed Russians were unable to defend their positions, a huge gap was torn in their lines and a steady retreat that would last all summer began.

Subsidiary offensives followed in East Prussia and across the San river in late May and early June, and by 17 June over 500,000 Russian soldiers had been killed, wounded or captured.

In July, the Germans and Austro-Hungarians invaded Russian Poland. At first the Russian reserves slowed the German advance enough to give some hope of halting it altogether. However, the risk of standing and fighting was that if something went wrong a huge number of troops would be cut off west of Warsaw. Instead, a

Subsidiary offensives followed in East Prussia and across the San river in late May and early June, and by 17 June over 500,000 Russian soldiers had been killed, wounded or captured.

retreat was ordered by the then overall Russian commander, Grand Duke Nicholas. Warsaw fell on 4 August, and the retreat continued throughout the month.

Italy joins war

The Italian army called off its fourth offensive of the year, along the Isonzo river, on 2 December. The Italian commander, General Luigi Cadorna, has been trying all year to achieve a strategic breakthrough here in order to capture the cities of Gorizia, and ultimately Trieste. The Italians have suffered heavy casualties, some 175,000 men, to the Austro-Hungarians' 115,000.

After the government of Italy declared war on Austria-Hungary on 23 May 1915, the Italian army faced a perplexing problem in devising a war. The border between the two countries is effectively the Alps, for the most part extremely difficult terrain for fighting battles and favourable to the defender. The two main places for military operations were east of Udine, along the Isonzo river and east of Lake Garda, in the valley of the Adige river.

A series of battles of the Isonzo began on 29 June 1915, in which the Italians were at a dramatic disadvantage. The Austro-Hungarian army had almost a year's worth of military experience of modern warfare, and had been digging defensive positions along the border for some time after the political crisis had developed between the two states. The Italians, on the other hand, had paid little attention to the effectiveness of machine guns, the futility of massed infantry assaults and the need for heavy howitzers.

An Italian propaganda photograph suggests the Alpini mountain troops use all means at their disposal to defeat the enemy.

IN BRIEF

On 18 September 1915, Kaiser Wilhelm II ended the campaign of unrestricted warfare using submarines against shipping around the British Isles, having already imposed limits on attacks in August.

British troops were halted in their advance up the Euphrates at Ctesiphon on 22 November 1915. Although the 11,000-strong British force, well equipped with artillery, drove a larger Turkish force of 18,000 men out of their entrenchments around the city, both sides suffered heavy casualties. After the battle, the British commander, Major General Charles Townshend, concerned about the security of his supply line, withdrew to Kut al-Amara, which he had captured in September.

The arrival of King Peter of Serbia at Brindisi in Italy on 15 December 1915 marked the end of the conquest of his kingdom by Austro-Hungarian, German and Bulgarian troops in a two-month campaign that began on 11 October 1915, the day after Bulgaria entered the war.

Fighting at Verdun grinds on

A German soldier, next to the remains of a French soldier, peers up from a ruined trench toward French lines. The determined French defensive slowed the Germans decisively.

German forces attacking French defences at Verdun captured the village of Malancourt on 31 March 1916. Major German operations ceased on 23 March, but local attacks aimed at securing limited objectives continue on the Verdun sector of the front.

After capturing Fort Douaumont, German troops became more involved in small operations aimed at taking French positions. On 25 February, the commander of the French forces,

General Frédéric Herr, was relieved and General Henri Philippe Pétain was appointed in his place. The next major battle was fought for the village of Douaumont. Pétain requested his troops to fight to the last in this and other positions that constituted the main line of resistance, in order to buy time for reinforcements, especially of artillery, to reach the front. Every shell hole, every basement of ruined houses, every tree stump became a strongpoint to

the French, and the Germans suffered heavy casualties in their advance. Only when flamethrowers were deployed on 29 February did the Germans turn the tide in their favour at Douaumont. On 2 March the village was in German hands, and the first phase of the Verdun offensive ended.

As the Germans switched their attention to the flanks of the original sector for attack, French artillery on the left bank of the Meuse subjected the main German thrust to enfilading fire. The fighting here revolved around Côte 304 and Le Mort Homme, hills that the French were using to observe their fall of shot. After attacks on Le Mort Homme were halted by French artillery fire, the Germans switched their attention to Côte 304. On 20 March, the assault began, but heavy rain on 21 March turned the battlefield into a quagmire, forcing the Germans to abandon their attacks on 23 March. On the right bank of the Meuse, the Germans restricted themselves to attacks around Fort Vaux that achieved little, although at one time it was claimed the fort had fallen. Medals were awarded, only to be withdrawn later when the truth was learned – the fort was still in French hands.

Mexican guerrillas invade United States

Pancho Villa, a guerrilla leader in northern Mexico, crossed the Mexican-US border and occupied the town of Columbus, New Mexico, on 9 March 1916. The US government has responded by ordering a punitive expedition to conduct an incursion into Mexico.

Mexico has suffered instability and civil war since 1910, when the long-standing regime of Porfirio Díaz was challenged by an alliance of forces of which Villa was a part. Díaz was forced into exile, but civil war continued as Francisco Madero, then Victoriano Huerta and finally Venusitano Carranza in turn became president after coups and further civil conflict. Villa turned against his former ally, Carranza, whose regime had been recognized by

Pancho Villa rides with members of his Division del Norte. Villa's anger with the US government's intervention in the Mexican civil war provoked his attack on Columbus, New Mexico.

the United States government in October 1915. The guerrillas took a hundred horses

and mules, burned Columbus and killed 17 Americans and 67 Mexicans.

German offensive at Verdun

The Germans occupied Fort Douaumont, the strongest of the forts built around the French city of Verdun, on 25 February 1916. The fort had virtually been abandoned by the French and it needed only a small patrol of German soldiers to capture it.

The German offensive at Verdun began on 21 February, having been delayed for ten days by bad weather. The German supreme commander, General Erich von Falkenhayn, viewed the attack not as an attempt to achieve a strategic breakthrough, but rather a means of knocking France out of the War through a battle of attrition. Heavy French casualties in 1915 had already sapped the French army's will to fight, and von Falkenhayn correctly believed that the French would go to great lengths to defend Verdun, a city of considerable historic importance to the country.

Von Falkenhayn's plan envisioned the battle as one largely fought by German artillery, the role of the infantry being to fight for limited objectives, using tactics and weapons that reduced the risk of heavy casualties. After the bombardment lifted from the French positions, specially trained assault battalions, armed with grenades and flamethrowers, would rush forward to seize the trenches. They would be followed closely by German infantry advancing in traditional skirmish line formation, who would occupy the ground gained and defend it against the expected counter-attack.

German tactics have worked very well in the battle so far, although the Verdun front is defended largely by French second-line troops. However, as von Falkenhayn hoped, the French have decided to defend Verdun with all possible resources, and are rushing troops to reinforce their lines.

BATTLE OF VERDUN

DATES:	February–December 1916
COMBATANTS:	France vs Germany
CASUALTIES:	France, 542,000; Germany, 434,000
RESULT:	French victory

French troops advance across a part of the moonscape that was created around Verdun as a result of the heavy shelling that had occurred over the course of the battle.

IN BRIEF

✤ The last British troops were withdrawn from the Helles beaches, Gallipoli on 8 January 1916, ending the attempt to seize control of the Dardanelles and Constantinople from the Turks, following the withdrawl of the last forces at Suvla Bay and Anzac Cove on 20 December.

Surrender of Kut

The British army suffered its worst defeat since surrendering to American rebels at Yorktown in 1781, when a 10,000-strong force besieged at Kut al-Amara for four months surrendered to the besieging Turks on 29 April 1916. The Turks then massacred the 4,000 surviving Arab residents of the Mesopotamian city.

The British commander, Major General Charles Townshend, had retreated to make a stand at Kut after his attack on the Turks at Ctesiphon in November 1915 failed to achieve a breakthrough. On 3 December, he established his defences, which the Turkish commander, General Nureddin Pasha, probed but declined to assault. However, on Christmas Eve, Nureddin ordered a full-scale attack, which was repulsed with heavy losses. He was then replaced as commander by Enver Pasha's uncle, Mohammed Khalil Bey.

Townshend sent word to General Sir John Nixon at Basra that he needed help in order to break out, but Nixon ordered him to hold on until relief arrived. When Townshend reported that his supplies would run out within a month, when in fact they could have been made to last four months, Nixon ordered the urgent organization of a relief column. The British made several separate attempts to raise the siege in January 1916, before their main attack on 8 March. However, too much time was spent in dressing lines for the attack, on the expectation that the Turks had their defences fully manned, when in fact they only had small outposts in place when the British arrived. By the time the attack went in, the Turks had reinforced the threatened sector and the British were badly defeated.

Townshend allowed too many Arab residents of the town to remain, and also discovered that his predominantly Indian force was unwilling to eat horse meat. By the end of April, after an attempt to bribe the Turks to let Townshend and his men go, Townshend had no choice but to surrender.

Major General Charles Townshend (seated, centre) together with his Turkish captors after he had surrendered his army at Kut al-Amara in April 1916.

War comes to Dublin

British troops around the main strongpoint of the Irish insurrectionists, the Dublin General Post Office building.

Irish nationalists, who had taken control of several important buildings in Dublin and proclaimed the independence of an Irish republic, surrendered on 29 April 1916 to British forces who had spent five days fighting in the streets to evict them.

Ireland had been on the verge of civil war at the outbreak of war, as supporters of Home Rule were threatened by Unionists who did not want a parliament for Ireland, but direct rule from Westminster. A Home Rule law was passed just as Europe went to war, and its provisions were shelved until the end of the conflict. Many of those who had been training to fight one another in Ireland joined the British army instead, although some of the most radical proponents of Home Rule, who did not believe the law went far enough, stayed out of the army. Armed with German weapons, they took control of the Dublin General Post Office on Easter Monday, 24 April.

The uprising was limited to Dublin, although the rebels had hoped for units of Irish Volunteers, as they called their army, to take up arms throughout the country. The nationalists had some successes within the city, including an ambush at Mount Street Bridge that caused 250 casualties, almost half the total British losses during the uprising. The British army had artillery, which the nationalists did not, and used incendiary shells that caused fires difficult to put out. The British also used armoured cars mounted with machine guns to patrol the streets. Some 1,200 people were killed or wounded during the fighting, over 800 of them civilians.

German gains at Verdun

The German army has achieved some small successes at Verdun, but at the cost of horrific casualties. Fighting has continued here throughout the months of April and May, with both sides attempting offensives during this time.

The worst fighting occurred at Le Mort Homme ridge and neighbouring Côte 304. The Germans focused their main attack in April on Le Mort Homme, on 9 April 1916. The fighting was the most savage so far and was immediately followed by twelve days of rain. At the end of this wet spell, the French counter-attacked and recovered their positions, thanks in part to their control of Côte 304. The Germans then decided that the fall of Côte 304 would ensure the capture of Le Mort Homme. A night attack, which was preceded by an intense 36-hour bombardment, was successful and on 4 May, the whole of Côte 304 was in German hands. Le Mort Homme fell during subsequent fighting.

Like Le Mort Homme, Fort Vaux also remained the focus of German attention. Following a failed attack on 7 May, the munitions stored at captured Fort Douaumont exploded on 8 May, so the Germans had to spend some weeks restocking with ammunition before they could attack again. A new French commander, General Robert Nivelle, replaced General Pétain on 1 May, and immediately planned an attack on Douaumont. After a six-day bombardment starting on 16 May, two regiments assaulted the fort. At first the French commander in charge, General Charles Mangin, believed himself to be successful and announced the recapture of the fort, but in the event the Germans were able to recover their position, and the French suffered very heavily.

Russian offensive goes wrong

A badly organized Russian attack at Lake Naroch in Belorussia ended on 30 April 1916 when a German counter-offensive recovered all the ground that had been lost in two days. The Russians had launched their attack on 18 March to relieve the pressure on the French at Verdun, but they did not have a proper artillery fire plan, nor had any serious reconnaissance been carried out on the German positions. The result was an ineffective barrage that missed most meaningful targets, and infantry assaults that were cut down in swathes by German

[T]hey did not have a proper artillery fire plan, nor had any serious reconnaissance been carried out on the German positions.

machine guns. In the end the Russians lost over five times as many casualties as the Germans – 110,000 to 20,000.

Russian prisoners captured during the Lake Naroch fighting in 1916. The Russian assault was an object lesson in how not to conduct a battle.

Major Sylvain-Eugene Raynal (in dark coat), commander of the defenders at Fort Vaux, in German captivity.

Fort Vaux falls

The gallant defence of Fort Vaux came to an end when the garrison surrendered on 7 June 1916. The French commandant, Major Sylvain-Eugene Raynal, raised the white flag after four days without water in the face of overwhelming odds.

The Germans had 23,000 men against Major Raynal's 400 in the fort, which was surrounded on 2 June. The fort's heaviest weapon, a 75mm gun, had been knocked out of action in February.

As initial German attacks captured parts of the fort, Major Raynal established a defence in depth. He positioned machine guns in the fort's communication tunnels so that even though the Germans controlled several key gun emplacements, they could not advance further without taking heavy casualties. Raynal also positioned further tunnel blocks behind the forward ones. Once the Germans had killed or captured the forward posts, the support groups were able to blunt the attack before it could make further progress.

For three days the Germans advanced slowly through the tunnels, suffering heavy casualties. The Germans couldn't use flamethrowers effectively in the closed, airless tunnels, and instead had to pour the weapons' inflammable liquid down the tunnel and try to ignite it with grenades. Meanwhile, the

The Germans had 23,000 men against Major Raynal's 400 in the fort, which was surrounded on 2 June.

French defenders had nothing to drink except condensation off the walls or their own urine.

The lack of water also made hygiene impossible and filth built up alongside the wounded and dead in the tunnels. When the thirst became too much, Raynal sent his last carrier pigeon out to his superiors with a message saying he was about to surrender, and on 7 June he raised the white flag. The heir to the imperial throne, Crown Prince Wilhelm, offered his personal congratulations to Major Raynal and gave a sword to him. Raynal proudly commented, "Sir, you did not defeat me; thirst defeated me."

OBITUARY
LORD KITCHENER
(1850-1916)

The British Secretary of State for War, Field Marshal Lord Horatio Herbert Kitchener, was lost at sea on 5 June 1916. He was en route to Russia aboard HMS *Hampshire* when the cruiser struck a mine in the middle of a gale near the Orkney islands and sank.

Kitchener made his reputation serving with British forces in Egypt and the Sudan in the 1880s and 1890s, and also had a key role commanding British forces during the latter half of the Second Boer War, presiding over the defeat of the Boers in 1901–02. He believed the First World War would be a long one, and that Britain needed considerable reinforcement of its small peacetime army. His image famously appeared on a recruiting poster pointing aggressively at the viewer, and insisting that "Your country needs You."

He never married.

Kitchener had become Britain's War Minister on 6 August 1914.

Troops mass at the Somme river

Men of the 4th Battalion, Worcestershire Regiment, before the Battle of the Somme. The battalion had been part of the 29th Division at Gallipoli in 1915.

The **steady rumble** of artillery filled the air of Picardy in north-eastern France for a week from 24 June 1916, heralding the coming onslaught against German trenches either side of the Somme river.

The British army had amassed the largest number of guns in their history, and had stockpiled nearly two million shells for the bombardment of the German positions. However, two-thirds of the British guns were lighter

Huge plumes of smoke and dirt were blasted high into the air, and it seemed, as the British Fourth Army commander, General Sir Henry Rawlinson, put it, that "nothing could exist at the conclusion of the bombardment in the area covered by it".

divisional weapons, whereas it was only the heaviest artillery that had any effect on the German trenches. In spite of this, the bombardment appeared to produce an impressive effect. Huge plumes of smoke and dirt were blasted high into the air, and it seemed, as the British Fourth Army commander, General Sir Henry Rawlinson, put it, that "nothing could exist at the conclusion of the bombardment in the area covered by it".

"There's something wrong with our bloody ships"

The **largest naval** battle of the First World War in the North Sea has pitted the German High Seas Fleet against the British Grand Fleet in a running action that nearly brought catastrophe to the German squadrons. The result was a strategic victory for the British, but with heavy losses of both ships and men.

A Royal Navy intercept of German messages together with other signs of German naval activity led them to conclude that the Germans would be putting to sea with a significant part of their fleet. Just as Scheer wanted to find part of the British fleet, so the British commander, Admiral Sir

John Jellicoe, sought to concentrate the whole of his markedly larger squadron. Consequently, he put to sea with all his ships, even before the Germans had left port.

The two sides sighted one another at 3.20 p.m. on 31 May 1916, and battle was joined between each fleet's battlecruisers. In just over an hour, the British had lost two battlecruisers, leading to the comment by Vice Admiral Sir David Beatty that "There's something wrong with our bloody ships today." He turned back to lure the Germans toward Jellicoe's dreadnoughts. At 6.30 p.m., the Germans realized that they were heading for the main British

fleet, and did the first of three about turns that eventually saved them from catastrophe. The British, meanwhile, lost another battlecruiser. The Battle of Jutland continued even after nightfall, with the Germans racing for home, while the British attempted to locate their main force in order to engage it and sink some enemy warships. In this action, both sides sustained further losses, but the Germans escaped relatively lightly.

In all, the British lost over 6,000 crew, three capital ships and 11 smaller ships; the Germans, on the other hand, lost 2,500 crew, one capital ship, and 10 smaller ships.

Warfare's new higher dimension

The death of the Eagle of Lille, Lieutenant Max Immelmann, on 18 June 1916, marked the end of the career of Germany's first air ace. He was awarded the German empire's highest decoration, the *Orden Pour Le Mérite*, in January 1916, by the Kaiser, together with his main rival, Oswald Boelcke. Immelmann invented an aerial manoeuvre, the Immelmann Turn, which was either a chandelle (a steep climb and bank) or a half loop and half roll. Whichever the actual manoeuvre, the result was a change of direction that helped him toward his total of 15 kills.

Immelmann's career as a pilot can stand as a symbol of the development of aviation in the First World War. He joined the Imperial German Air Service, the *Luftstreitkräfte*, at the outbreak of war. The military use of aircraft had been the subject of theory for several years even

> The first pilot to shoot down an enemy aircraft using a Fokker monoplane equipped with the interruptor gear was Immelmann's great rival, Oswald Boelcke, on 1 August 1915.

before the formation of such pioneering air services as the German one, or France's Aéronautique Militaire. It was generally assumed that they would have an important role in reconnaissance, as well as a lesser one as aerial artillery, dropping explosive devices. However, what hampered the effectiveness of those early aircraft was their under-powered engines, as well as their fragile structures of canvas, wood and wire. While Immelmann flew such planes on reconnaissance missions, the first ace, Frenchman Roland Garros, was shooting down similar aircraft, thereby introducing aerial combat to war.

These reconnaissance missions had already proved invaluable in the war. On the Western Front, the victory at the Marne was in part the result of French and British generals taking note of what an aerial patrol had discovered about German troop movements. Similarly, the German victory at Tannenberg was partly made possible by successful aerial reconnaissance missions. Aircraft were also able to assist with artillery fire, providing a means of spotting the fall of shot, and communicating back to the gunners by means of wireless telegraphy. By the time of the Battle of Verdun, aerial artillery spotting had become so important that the Chief of the German General Staff, General Erich von Falkenhayn, gave a high priority to shooting down French observation planes and balloons.

The Junkers J2 was a highly innovative, all-metal aircraft, although it was very heavy and therefore did not fly very well.

The first aerial combat was a matter of pilots taking rifles or pistols up with them and taking potshots as they flew past an enemy plane. Two-seater aircraft were subsequently adopted to carry rearward-firing machine guns. The first aerial victory

> The popular idea of individual pilots jousting in the skies like modern versions of medieval knights provided a glamorous contrast to the dour proletarian struggle half-fought underground in the trenches.

was the shooting down of a German aircraft by a French two-seater biplane on 5 October 1914. Attempts were made using pusher aircraft (with the engine behind the crew) to develop a forward-firing system, but the pushers were slower than the tractor, front-engined aircraft, on which aiming a machine gun proved difficult. Garros, however, introduced a system that enabled him to fire through the forward propeller blades. A more sophisticated system was

The Fokker Dr 1 triplane is possibly the most famous aeroplane of the First World War. It was highly acrobatic, but consequently difficult to fly. It was also comparatively slow.

Top 10 Aces

Manfred von Richthofen	German	80
René Fonck	France	75
Billy Bishop	Canada	72
Ernst Udet	Germany	62
Mick Mannock	Britain	61
Raymond Collishaw	Canada	60
James McCudden	Britain	57
Andrew Beauchamp-Proctor	South Africa	54
Erich Löwenhardt	Germany	54
Donald MacLaren	Canada	54

underground in the trenches. However, the reality of aerial warfare was considerably different, especially by the end of the War. There was considerable danger for the pilots and observers in the air, with aircraft engines being unreliable, and fire having such rapid and catastrophic consequences that it was not unusual for men to hurl themselves

René Fonck was the leading Allied air ace of the First World War. He became a pilot in 1915, and began flying fighters in the elite Escadrille des Cigognes two years later.

introduced by Anthony Fokker on German monoplanes, entering service in mid-1915. These Fokker monoplanes used a single machine gun firing forward and proved highly effective.

The first pilot to shoot down an enemy aircraft using a Fokker monoplane equipped with the interruptor gear was Immelmann's great rival, Oswald Boelcke, on 1 August 1915. Immelmann's ten-month career in Fokkers marked a period of transition for aerial warfare. Hitherto, aircraft normally flew singly or in pairs, but Boelcke and Immelmann introduced larger formations of three or four aircraft that were able to use their technical superiority more effectively by also having a numerical superiority. The French and British responded with a set of better aircraft than the Fokker – the De Havilland DH2, the FE2b and the Vickers Gunbus, all pusher aircraft, and the French Nieuport 11, a tractor aircraft with a gun mounted above the wing – and larger flights of four or five. The Fokkers' domination of the skies from August 1915 ended in the summer of 1916, and the death of Immelmann in a sense marked the end of the second phase of the air war.

Fighter pilots became celebrities during the First World War, with Immelmann and Boelcke being joined by such individuals as Baron Manfred von Richthofen (the "Red Baron", so-called because he painted his aircraft a bright red), Georges Guynemer of France and Albert Ball of Britain. The popular idea of individual pilots jousting in the skies like modern versions of medieval knights provided a glamorous contrast to the dour proletarian struggle half-fought

out of blazing aircraft and plummet to their deaths in these pre-parachute days, rather than burn alive. Oily filth streamed into their faces and the cold at altitude was highly uncomfortable. Furthermore, the majority of the aircraft were not single-seat fighters, but planes with two or more crew places, flying slowly to take photographs or drop bombs. Formation flying was almost universal by the end of the war, and even in 1916, Boelcke's famous rules of fighting, which are still studied by pilots, recommended attacking in groups.

Larger and heavier aircraft were built during the war, including big bombers such as the Handley-Page O/400, capable of flying from bases in France all the way to Germany and back in a night. Engines became more efficient, while metal began to replace wood in aircraft such as the Junkers J1 and Junkers J2; monoplane designs were found to be aerodynamically preferable to the biplane or triplane. The pioneers of military aviation in 1914 had blazed a trail that was now followed by bigger and better aircraft that flew faster, higher and further than ever before.

The Handley-Page O/400 was typical of the large bombers built during the First World War. These could deliver around 2000 lbs (900 kg) of bombs to a range of 750 miles (1,200 km).

"Big push" on the Somme, 20,000 killed on first day

A still from the film *Battle of the Somme* depicting British troops going "over the top" during the battle. British generals did not believe the volunteer "New Army" was capable of any more sophisticated tactics than a marching advance toward the enemy lines.

A major Anglo-French offensive along the Somme river was fought through July and August, resulting in the removal of the Chief of the German General Staff, General Erich von Falkenhayn, who was replaced by Field Marshal Paul von Hindenburg on 29 August 1916.

At 7.20 a.m. on 1 July, the infantry assault on the Somme began as a large mine was detonated under Hawthorn Ridge, and the infantry went over the top ten minutes later. The British advanced at a walking pace, partly due to lack of training for the men, and partly because they were heavily burdened with some 66 lbs (30 kg) of equipment. It was believed that the heavy artillery bombardment would kill enough Germans and leave the remainder too disorganized to man their trenches and fire their machine guns effectively.

The best success of the day came on the southern sector of the front, around the village of Montauban, and further south where the French XX Corps advanced. More characteristic of the day's successes

was the attack on Thiepval in which the 36th (Ulster) Division advanced against the Schwaben Redoubt and seized both the German front line and then the second line. But German artillery fire made it impossible to reinforce these successes and the British were forced abandoned these positions. One of the worst disasters came at Hawthorn Ridge, where the attackers following up the explosion were halted in no-man's-land, failing even to reach the German barbed-wire entanglements.

General Sir Douglas Haig now ordered a series of limited attacks along the front, attacking such places as Mametz Wood, to keep constant pressure on the Germans.

Thousands died for little gain in these actions, as they lacked the strength needed to achieve a major success. In the first two days, had the British reconnoitred more effectively, they might have made gains around Ovillers and Longueval, but these opportunities were missed.

More ambitious attacks followed at Bazentin Ridge and at Pozières on 14 July, and over the days that followed the fighting continued, with even a cavalry charge on High Wood. But Haig accepted that the likelihood of a major breakthrough had passed and once again reverted to small-scale assaults that were intended to keep pressure on the Germans.

THE SOMME

DATES:	July–November 1916
COMBATANTS:	Britain and France vs Germany
CASUALTIES:	Britain, 420,000; France, 200,000; Germany, 600,000
RESULT:	Stalemate

"They shall not pass"

On 12 August 1916, the German offensive at Verdun was effectively called off after nearly two weeks of fighting between Fleury and Thiaumont. Further fighting in this sector now depends on the French ability to launch counter-attacks.

The Germans had focused on the Fleury–Thiaumont area since 23 June, when they used phosgene gas against French artillery batteries in an attempt to occupy Fort Souville, Fleury and a fortification at Thiaumont. The French line was nearly breached, but company and battalion officers managed to organize enough troops to halt the Germans.

When the Somme offensive began, the Germans moved troops from Verdun to reinforce their front lines against the British, and on 12 July General Robert Nivelle, the French commander, praised the resistance

Further fighting in this sector now depends on the French ability to launch counter-attacks.

of his soldiers, ending with the slogan "They shall not pass." The French defence of Verdun owed much to a continuous flow of supplies and reinforcements, driven by trucks along a single road, La Voie Sacrée, with a truck passing every 14 seconds in one direction or the other.

British heavy howitzers bombard German lines during the Somme offensive.

Le Voie Sacrée

One important target of the German offensive at Verdun was the road that ran almost due south between Bar-le-Duc and Verdun, as it had become the main road route of supply for the French army that was defending the city. The road was guarded by reservists, who also maintained the surface, and by fighter squadrons intended to intercept any attempt by the Germans to bomb the road. Traffic flowed constantly along the road, bringing around 7,000 tons of ammunition each day, as well as reinforcements. A truck passed a given point along the road every 14 seconds. Curiously, food did not travel along the road, but along a parallel, narrow-gauge, single-track railway, known as Le Meusin. During the campaign, the road was known as La Route.

Le Voie Sacrée, at its peak, used 12,000 vehicles and sustained the French defence. A full division's worth of men was employed on keeping it in repair, mostly shoveling gravel on the road. Troops were not allowed to march on it, to ensure the steady parade of trucks continued.

Success at Gorizia

Italy **achieved its** first major success of the war when their sixth offensive on the Isonzo front led to the capture of the town of Gorizia on 8 August 1916.

By restricting the operation to a much narrower 8-mile (13-km) width of front, and concentrating ten divisions there, with excellent intelligence work concealing these movements, General Luigi Cadorna launched his attack on 6 August, capturing Mount Sabatino and Mount Padgora on the first day. Control of the mountains helped the Italians take Gorizia. An earlier attack in March in the same area had failed, although the Italians achieved some gains on the Asiago Plateau, north-west of the Isonzo, in May.

Austro-Hungarian forces travel along a road behind the Italian front. The Austro-Hungarians faced an easy task of defence, with the terrain heavily favouring them.

Russia's last throw of the dice?

Russian artillerymen ford a flooded river with a horse-drawn field gun. The Brusilov offensive effectively broke the Austro-Hungarian army on the Eastern Front, at the cost of the Russian one.

A **two-month offensive by** the Russians on the Eastern Front came to an end on 17 August 1916. Russian losses were very heavy, with over half a million casualties, but they achieved great gains, largely at the expense of Austria-Hungary in the Carpathians.

The attack was the idea of General Alexei Brusilov, who was given command of the whole South-Western Front, from Lwow to Bukovina. He adopted an operational plan of a short, but very intense bombardment, followed by a rapid infantry assault spearheaded by special units of shock troops. The plan worked extremely well and when the attack began on 4 June, was immediately successful.

The rapid advance ensured that by 12 June the Russians had taken over 200,000 prisoners, but the Russian steamroller soon ran out of steam as it outran its supply lines and artillery cover, typical of the offensives of the First World War. When Brusilov tried to restart his attack on 28 July, his gains were much more limited.

More deadly than battle

The continued resistance during 1916 of a small German army in German East Africa, even though outnumbered by three to one, prevented the British from reinforcing their effort on the Western Front with troops deployed against Colonel Paul von Lettow-Vorbeck and his largely native German colonial army.

The British appointed the South African General Jan Smuts to command the army in East Africa, and he arrived at Mombasa, Kenya in February 1916. Smuts had 40,000 men against Lettow-Vorbeck's 16,000-strong force, and sent four columns into German East Africa. One advanced from Kenya, another from Nyasaland, a Portuguese force entered from Mozambique and a Belgian force from the Congo. Lettow-Vorbeck simply dodged them all, employing a "scorched earth" approach against railways and bridges that badly hampered the Allied advance. In an ironic reversal of the British experience on the Western Front, Smuts was able to capture a lot of territory, but could never inflict casualties on his German

> *British troops were plagued with diseases and parasites that severely affected their ability to keep an army in the field, and lost considerably more men to these natural dangers than to the enemy's forces.*

opponents. British troops were plagued with diseases and parasites that severely affected their ability to keep an army in the field, and lost considerably more men to these natural dangers than to the enemy's forces.

Small-scale catastrophes on the Somme

General Douglas Haig's "big push" on the Somme ground down into the kind of attritional battle that the French commander-in-chief, General Joseph Joffre, believed would occur. Allied attacks during the month of August were a number of small-scale attacks that achieved even less overall at a higher cost than the disastrous first-day attack. The Australian Corps attacked around Mouquet Farm on 8 August 1916 in the hope that it would lead to the capture of Thiepval, a key German redoubt on the front line. Mouquet Farm had itself been transformed into a fortress that showed signs of the new German tactic of defence in depth using linked strongpoints, in place of the continuous trench line of the first two years of war. That same day an attempt was made to capture Guillemont, a key position on the part of the line where the French and British sectors met. Neither attack was successful.

South African troops ford a river in Africa. The terrain, the climate and the diseases were more dangerous than German colonial forces to the British Imperial troops.

Rumania crushed in lightning campaign

The Rumanian capital of Bucharest fell into German hands on 6 December 1916, after a 10-week offensive masterminded by General Erich von Falkenhayn swept the Rumanian army into Moldavia.

Rumania declared war on Austria-Hungary on 27 August, having been promised territorial gains by Britain, France and Russia at the expense of the Austro-Hungarians. Rumanian soldiers crossed the border between the two countries that very day. However, Rumania overestimated the success of the Brusilov offensive, believing Austria-Hungary stood on the brink of capitulating. Rumania was almost isolated by its enemies. Its long borders with Germany's allies Austria-Hungary and Bulgaria were difficult to defend, and Russia had little aid to give.

In this weak position, Rumanian resistance was easily overcome. The Germans and Austro-Hungarians first attacked in the Dobrudja, then drove the Rumanians out of Transylvania and seized the main passes through the Carpathians. A renewed offensive in November scattered the Rumanian defenders with relentless pressure and frequent shifting of the point of attack.

German soldiers celebrate their victory over the Rumanians and the fall of Bucharest by celebrating atop the Great Bell of Bucharest, which marks the highest point of the Rumanian capital.

A new weapon

The British have deployed a new weapon on the Somme. Thirty-two of these "landships", armed with two 6-pounder naval guns and two machine guns, were on the start line on 15 September 1916, the opening day of the Battle of Flers-Courcelette, although a third failed to make it into action owing to mechanical unreliability. The landships, or "tanks", proved very effective in overcoming the main obstacle causing needlessly heavy casualties among attacking British infantry: barbed wire. They are also impervious to small-arms and machine-gun fire, but vulnerable to artillery and suffer frequent mechanical breakdowns.

The landships' real purpose has been concealed by the story that they were designed as mobile water tanks for British troops in Mesopotamia.

Attrition on the Somme ends

The British commander, General Sir Douglas Haig, has finally called off the Battle of the Somme, when the Battle of the Ancre ended on 18 November 1916. The campaign has lasted since 1 July 1916, marked by periodic offensives aiming to create a major breakthrough in the German trench lines, interspersed with periods of assaults to attain limited objectives as part of a plan to maintain the pressure on the German army.

The Somme campaign, after its first day, was a succession of battles along smaller fronts, the last major offensive being the Battle of Flers-Courcelette in September. The British finally achieved some first-day objectives, in fighting over the course of 26–28 September, capturing Thiepval and the Schwaben Redoubt, which became known as the Battle of Thiepval Ridge.

In October, the weather turned wet, hampering British efforts even further. Some small gains were made but British progress since July had been so slow that the Germans had ample time to construct further trenches behind

The campaign has lasted since 1 July, marked by periodic offensives aiming to create a major breakthrough in the German trench lines, interspersed with periods of assaults to attain limited objectives.

those that the British soldiers had captured with so much loss. The Battle of the Ancre, begun on 13 November, secured Beaumont Hamel and some other objectives at the northern end of the front.

A wounded soldier from the British armies fighting on the Somme is helped to the rear by two of his comrades. The battle ended with both sides heavily affected by high casualties.

German army concedes defeat at Verdun

On 19 December 1916, the German army found itself back in the same positions from which it had started in February in the great battle of attrition launched to knock France out of the War. When the Germans halted offensive operations in August, the French army refused to leave the Germans with their gains. A series of offensives recovered Fort Douaumont (24 October) and Fort Vaux (3 November) and a final offensive on 13 December captured the few positions left in German hands. The German high command views the battle as a defeat in terms of the objective of "bleeding France white", and with their own losses far too high, no strategic advantage has been achieved.

Arabs in revolt

The Hashemite Sherif of Mecca, Hussein ibn Ali, was proclaimed king of the Hejaz and Arabia on 29 October 1916 at Mecca, having formally proclaimed his independence from Turkey on 5 June. Whereas the Turks have been imprisoning Arab nationalists throughout their empire since they entered the war, both France and Britain have been in contact with Hussein, promising an independent Arab state after the war has been won. Hussein's soldiers have been skirmishing with the Turkish garrison at Medina since June.

1915–16: The futility of war

On 31 December 1916, the people of Europe had little to look forward to that would be "happy" in the New Year, after two years of extremely heavy casualties in the war. The only front on which there was any clear sign of victory was that between the Germans and the Russians. The Austro-Hungarian front to the south had turned into another disaster with the success of the Russian summer offensive. Austria-Hungary looked to be on the brink of collapse, thanks to her losses in that campaign. In Italy, the front line had hardly moved in either direction after a year-and-a-half of war. Allied forces had come and gone in European Turkey. The Western Front was apparently the most futile of all, with little movement since the trenches were originally dug in 1914.

Yet, in spite of all this comparative lack of movement, there had been a tremendous amount of activity, with millions of men suffering death or injury as a result. The last war between two of the world's great powers, the Russo-Japanese War of 1904–05, had claimed 210,000 killed or wounded men. The last war between two of Europe's great powers, the Italo–Turkish War of 1911–12, had casualties on both sides amounting to 20,000. There had been 250,000 dead or wounded in the Franco-Prussian War of 1870–71. Four years of the American Civil War had killed or wounded 600,000. At the end of two-and-a-half years of war between Britain, Germany, Russia, France and Austria-Hungary any reasonable estimate of the likely casualties based on previous experience would have been in the order of 750,000. Turkey, Italy and Japan might have added an additional 350,000 given the more limited opportunities these nations had of fighting massed enemy formations. Yet in 1916, at the battles of the Somme and Verdun alone, 2,196,000 men were killed, wounded or missing – and these two battles only represent about one-quarter of the total casualties suffered during 1915–16.

These two years arguably represent the greatest waste of life in military history, in terms of comparing strategic gain with human loss. The cause of it is straightforward. Commanders were confronted with fighting battles using technology that they did not fully understand, and had to expend the lives of their men in order to acquire this understanding. By the end of 1916, for example, British commanders were

A swathe of dead Rumanian soldiers testify to the power of machine guns firing at dense columns of troops. People of all nations were shocked at the casualties experienced in the war.

well aware that shrapnel shells fired from lighter artillery such as the standard 18-pounder field gun were incapable of cutting the barbed-wire obstacles strewn in front of trenches. They had not experimented beforehand to find this out, and many of the dead and wounded of the Somme paid the price.

Looking for an answer

The generals and leaders of all the countries involved were in a difficult position. They had to do something in order to win the war, and the officer class of all the armies recognized that only by attacking could a war be won. For the French, who hurled a generation of young men to their deaths outside the German trenches in Champagne in 1915, attack was the only way to evict the enemy from their country. The British had to attack because their allies the French were attacking, even if the attacks were believed by British officers, such as General Haig and Field Marshal French at Loos in the autumn of 1915, to be more likely to fail than to win. The British attacked at Gallipoli to help the Russians and keep the Turks away from Egypt. The Germans attacked in the East, because the Russian numerical superiority had to be kept away from German territory, while they attacked in the West at Verdun in 1916 because they believed that was the decisive theatre.

The courage (or foolishness, some might say) of those marching out of the trenches in the face of likely injury or death on such a scale is astonishing. Even more astonishing is the blithe spirit with which the men of 1915 and 1916 went in to battle. German soldiers advanced singing "*Deutschland über alles.*" At Gallipoli, soldiers in a British unit went forward dribbling a football amongst them, until the Turkish machine guns cut them down. It was the same at the Battle of the Somme.

Beastly Hun

As the war dragged on, another motivation for risking one's life was founded on the image of the enemy created by both rumour and actively promoted through the press. The British emphasized the beastliness of the "Hun", who had shot civilians and burned villages in Belgium. The Germans, meanwhile, believed that the British would fight to the last Frenchman, while the French had forced this war on Germany because they had been unwilling to accept the verdict of 1870–71. For Germans, the war

Casualties and Achievements, 1915–16

1915

Chemin des Dames	285,000	French gain little territory
Second Ypres	104,208	Stalemate
Gallipoli	503,000	Turks drive off British
Second Artois	186,000	Stalemate
Second Champagne & Third Artois	440,000	Stalemate
Eastern Front	3,000,000	Major advances for Germans and Austro-Hungarians
Italian front	415,000	Stalemate

1916

Verdun	976,000	Germans are driven back to start line
Asiago	250,000	Austro-Hungarians advance
Brusilov Offensive	1,600,000	Russians drive back Austro-Hungarians
Somme	1,215,000	Stalemate
Rumanian Campaign	240,000	Rumanian defeat
Italian front	230,000	Stalemate
Total	9,444,208	

became one of national survival, especially as the British blockade began to affect their economy and food supplies severely. The pinch was already apparent to Germany's political leaders in late 1916 and they began pondering what measures could be taken.

The futility of this war had been suspected by political thinkers on the Left from the outset. It was the most radical elements who observed with a jaundiced eye their more conservative colleagues voting eagerly for war credits to prove their loyalty to a ruling class that would never accept them or offer the reforms they fought for. The Russian, Vladimir Lenin, wanted the war to be transformed from one of nation against nation into an international struggle of the working class against the rulers. After 1915, Lenin's vision began to take shape as industrial unrest started to affect war production. In April 1916, British

jute workers at Dundee went on strike, not for peace, but for wage increases to combat the price inflation that affected their living standards severely. Food shortages in Germany caused shipyard strikes in June 1916. On 30 October 1916, troops in the Russian capital of Petrograd joined strikers at arms factories, and fought with the police and Cossacks, while British workers struck in protest at the conscription of one of their engineer colleagues in November. One glimmer of light for the warmongers, however, was the rejection by a substantial majority of a resolution at a Labour party conference in early 1917 calling for an immediate end to the war.

So long as the Labour movement was split in all the warring countries, Lenin's dream remained impracticable, and more men chose to die for their country, as opposed to their class.

Peace feelers rebuffed

Various attempts to find some kind of common ground to begin peace negotiations by both the Central Powers (Germany, Austria-Hungary, Turkey) and the Entente Powers (Britain, France, Russia and Italy) failed during January 1917 owing to incompatibility of war aims. France demanded the restoration of the Alsace and Lorraine regions, which Germany refused to surrender. Russia demanded Constantinople, the Turkish capital, which was naturally highly objectionable to the Turks. Italy and Austria-Hungary also had conflicting territorial requirements.

The German industrialist Hugo Stinnes was part of an attempt in January 1917 by German and Austria-Hungary to see if a negotiated settlement could be attained.

OBITUARY
GEORGE DEWEY (1837–1917)

George Dewey, the victor of Manila Bay, died at Washington DC on 16 January 1917, aged 79.

Dewey was born in Vermont and graduated from the US Naval Academy in 1858. He was a veteran of Admiral David Farragut's battle against the rebels in the American Civil War at New Orleans in April 1862, and of the attacks on Fort Fisher in January 1865. After the war he remained in the navy.

In 1897, Dewey, by then a commodore, was given command of the US Asiatic Fleet. As tension between Spain and the United States increased, he sent spies to reconnoitre the locations of the Spanish fleet and fortifications in their Philippine colony. When war came, he sailed into Manila Bay, sank the Spanish naval vessels there and established control of the political situation until American troops arrived in August 1898.

After the war he was eventually promoted to Admiral of the Navy, the only man to hold the rank in American history, and was allowed to remain on active service even past retirement age.

He is survived by his second wife and the son of his first marriage.

British return to Kut

British soldiers recaptured Kut al-Amara on 23 February 1917, where thousands of their comrades had surrendered nearly a year earlier.

When General Sir Frederick Maude took command of British forces in Mesopotamia in July 1916, he spent several months reorganizing and resupplying them. Much effort was put into improving Basra as a base of operations. On 13 December 1916 he began advancing north again towards Turkish positions in the Khadairi Bend, a loop of the Tigris river, which were attacked on 9 January 1917; it took nearly two weeks of hand-to-hand fighting to clear them. A supporting trench network astride the banks of the Hai river, which flowed into the Tigris, was attacked on 11 January and captured on 4 February. The Turks retreated into the Dahra Bend, but on 10 February the British forced them to retreat once more. On 23 February, the British attacked at Shumran and threatened to cut off the Turks on the eastern bank of the Tigris from their base in Baghdad. The withdrawal of these forces opened up the way to Kut and the city fell to the British for the second time, the battle ending on 24 February.

Germany renews unrestricted submarine campaign

The United States broke off diplomatic relations with Germany on 3 February 1917 after Germany resumed unrestricted submarine warfare on 1 February, declaring that any ship in British waters would be subject to torpedo or other attack. The plan had been agreed on 9 January at a conference of war leaders at Pless in Germany and was announced to the United States on 31 January. The previous attempt at this strategy was abandoned after it appeared the United States would enter the war on the side of Britain and France.

During 1916, a combination of heavy military losses and increasing privation among civilians thanks to Britain's highly effective blockade of Germany had revived enthusiasm for unrestricted submarine warfare. At the same time, analysis produced by German naval officers established that a loss rate of 695,000 tons (630,000 tonnes) of merchant shipping would force neutrals to reduce their trade with Britain, causing the British government to sue for peace within six months. This would mean American entry into the war would have little effect. German leaders adopted the verdict at Pless, expecting to force a decision before the harvest of 1917.

A German U-boat torpedoes a merchantman at sea during daylight. The use of unrestricted submarine warfare was Germany's best chance of defeating Britain.

IN BRIEF

֍ German troops on the Western Front began a strategic withdrawal to a new position between Arras and St Quentin, christened the Hindenburg Line. Experience on the Somme indicated that German entrenchments could be better constructed and organized, and the Hindenburg Line embraced these ideas, as well as offering a strong strategic position from which to fight off future Allied offensives.

֍ British and Arab troops co-operated to attack the town of Wejh in the Hejaz, an important link on the railway supplying the Turkish garrison in Medina.

֍ Alexander Kerensky, a Social Revolutionary member of the Russian parliament, spoke in the *Duma* on 27 February against a peace involving annexations.

Tsar abdicates, Russia becomes a republic

Tsar Nicholas II of Russia in internal exile following his abdication from power. He was moved to Siberia in August 1917.

Nicholas II, Tsar of all the Russias, abdicated on 15 March 1917. Russia is now under the control of a provisional government containing moderate democrats and socialists. Although the provisional government intends to keep Russia in the war, far Left socialists are arguing for peace.

Workers' strikes, largely in the Petrograd area, had been ongoing since the autumn of 1916. The situation worsened as food shortages occurred in February, causing a strike at the key Putilov armaments factory. When the workers there were fired by management, those in other factories went out on strike in sympathy. Protests beginning on 8 March led to troops being sent to suppress the meetings, but the troops shot their officers instead and joined the protestors. As a result, the Tsar rushed back from the Russian army headquarters, where he had been acting as commander-in-chief. Confronted with the views of his ministers that he ought to abdicate, Nicholas signed the paper on behalf of himself and his son.

German telegram threatens America

A telegram transmitted by the German foreign secretary, Artur Zimmerman, to the German ambassador in Mexico City, that was released to the press on 1 March 1917, has angered Americans. British code-breakers in the Room 40 unit (the British cryptography unit, originally based in Room 40 in the Admiralty building) had partially cracked the code used by the German foreign office and were able to decipher the Zimmerman telegram. The British foreign secretary, Arthur Balfour, presented it to the American ambassador to London on 23 February.

The telegram stated that while Germany would try to keep America neutral, the ambassador should offer the Mexican president an alliance against the United States conditional on the US declaring war on Germany. Mexico was offered the opportunity to recover territory lost to the US in the nineteenth century.

America declares war

The Congress of the United States voted in favour of a resolution declaring war on Germany on 6 April 1917. The resolution had been requested by President Woodrow Wilson on 2 April, in response to the German resumption of unrestricted submarine warfare. Neither the vote in the Senate nor that in the House of Representatives was unanimous, reflecting a strong anti-war movement that had been a key element in the re-election of Wilson in November 1916 to a second term. The publication of the Zimmerman Telegram had swung opinion among many in favour of war.

With the German resumption of unrestricted submarine warfare in February 1917, Wilson reluctantly accepted America would almost certainly have to enter the war on the Allied side.

Canadian troops working on a plank road as traffic moves along through a French village. The road was constructed after the capture of Vimy Ridge in April 1917 to help move supplies up to the new position.

"Ah, les Canadiens! C'est possible!"

The Canadian Corps of the British Expeditionary Force captured Vimy Ridge from the Germans on 12 April 1917, after four days of fighting following a week-long bombardment. A French soldier is reputed to have remarked

The Canadians constructed an elaborate replica of the ridge, on which they trained. Tunnels were dug to allow troops and supplies to be brought into the front line without being observed, and a comprehensive artillery fire plan was prepared.

on hearing of the ridge's capture, *"C'est impossible."* He then changed his mind when told it was the Canadians who had carried out the attack.

The ridge had remained in German hands despite heavy French and British attacks during 1915, at the cost of 150,000 men. As this was the first operation that would see the four Canadian divisions fighting together as a unit, officers and men were determined to succeed where their allies had failed. The Canadians constructed an elaborate replica of the ridge, on which they trained. Tunnels were dug to allow troops and supplies to be brought into the front line without being observed, and a comprehensive artillery fire plan was prepared.

On the day, the troops performed the "Vimy Glide", advancing in hundred-yard (90-m) rushes every three minutes, as the barrage moved up the slope of the ridge. The three German trench lines were captured in hard fighting and most of the ridge was in Canadian hands by the end of the first day of the attack on 9 April. The battle ended on 14 April.

Double defeat at Gaza

The British army was twice defeated in frontal assaults on a Turkish defensive position at Gaza in Palestine on 26 March and 19 April 1917. The second assault was supported by tanks and naval gunfire, yet was repulsed with heavy losses.

The fighting in Palestine is along the only border between the Ottoman empire and the British that separates Egypt and Palestine. The Turks launched an attack on the Suez Canal in 1915, but the British had been warned of their approach by aerial reconnaissance, and the Turks were badly beaten and retreating across a trackless, waterless desert.

After another attempt by the Turks was beaten off in the summer of 1916, the British decided that a policy of forward defence was the best option. A force marched across the Sinai, capturing the fort at Magdhaba on 23 December 1916, before confronting the main Turkish position at Gaza.

Plan Nivelle fails

The offensive planned by the over-confident General Robert Nivelle failed to deliver its hoped-for breakthrough and full-scale attacks were called off on 20 April 1917. The main attacks were made between Soissons and Reims, along the Aisne river, and some 1.2 million soldiers were involved.

Nivelle had replaced Marshal Joseph Joffre in December 1916, having built his reputation in the second and third phases of the Battle of Verdun, where he first made the Germans pay heavily for their gains and then forced them back to their start line, albeit at a heavy cost in French lives. Nivelle placed great faith in the "creeping barrage", which shifted the bombardment forward, isolating the German positions while allowing French soldiers to advance in rushes under the cover of the bombardment.

The plan was an open secret along the halls of government and somewhat controversial. Some French leaders believed Verdun had taken far too much fighting spirit out of the French army to give the project any chance of success. Nivelle's willingness to talk to journalists and carelessness about distribution of the plans meant that the Germans had plenty of warning of the attack and prepared accordingly.

One 16 April, when the attack opened, 40,000 Frenchmen became casualties. The barrage was not executed properly, and the Germans has reduced the number of men in the front line where the barrage fell, knowing in advance the time and place of the attack. Nivelle had promised a breakthrough in 48 hours, but on 17 April the front line had barely even moved.

French soldiers at a listening post in 1917. Listening posts were extensions of the trench line in the direction of the enemy, and were valuable sources of intelligence about enemy plans.

Sickness, casualties and heat halt British attacks in Mesopotamia

General Sir Frederick Maude's offensive in Mesopotamia has been brought to a halt as losses in fighting for the important railway junction of Samarra and, more importantly, too much sickness, necessitated a pause in operations. Samarra finally fell into British hands on 23 April 1917, whereupon Maude announced his intention to delay further operations until after the summer's heat.

The British forces in Mesopotamia occupied Baghdad on 11 March. The

The British continued their attacks on the Turks from Baghdad, resuming their offensive on 13 March. Falluja was captured on 19 March and an abortive attempt was made to surround the retreating Turks.

Turks attempted to block the British advance at the confluence of the Diyala river and the Tigris, and in fact defeated the first British attack on 9 March. Maude then attempted to outflank the Turks, only to achieve a breakthrough against the original Turkish position which had been largely evacuated in order to counter the British outflanking manoeuvre.

The British continued their attacks on the Turks from Baghdad, resuming their offensive on 13 March. Falluja was captured on 19 March and an abortive attempt was made to surround the retreating Turks. Whenever the Turks tried to make a stand, Maude was either able to manoeuvre them out of position or to cause heavy enough casualties that they were forced to retreat.

Crisis in the Atlantic

The German submarine blockade of the British Isles seriously threatened the British capacity to wage war in its first three months of operation in 1917. In February, 520,000 tons (530,000 tonnes) of shipping were sunk, in March 560,000 tons (570,000 tonnes) and in April 860,000 tons (875,000 tonnes). By contrast, from November 1916 to January 1917, the total tonnage of shipping sunk amounted to only 916,000 (930,000 tonnes). German analysts calculated that such loss rates would rapidly bring Britain to her knees, owing to a poor wheat harvest in North America in 1916.

A troop convoy en route to Europe from the United States. The introduction of a convoy system for merchant as well as military vessels, brought the crisis in submarine warfare to an end.

"Bloody April" for Royal Flying Corps

The battle for command of the air over the Western Front has taken a serious turn for the worse for the British Royal Flying Corps. The Imperial German Air Service received new Albatros D.IIs and D.IIIs last autumn, aircraft that were markedly superior to the Nieuport XVII, Spad VIII and Bristol F.2 Fighter, all aircraft in service with the Allies. When the Royal Flying Corps began operations in support of the British offensive at Vimy Ridge and around Arras in April 1917, involving many reconnaissance flights and fighter patrols, German aerial supremacy quickly established itself. Of some 365 aircraft deployed by the British, 245 of them were lost, two-thirds of the total. One squadron, Jasta 11, commanded by Manfred, Baron von Richthofen, claimed about one-third of these victims.

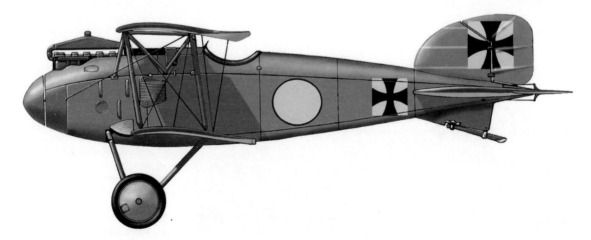

An Albatros fighter aircraft of the Imperial German Air Service. The Albatros was the main fighter aircraft used during the years 1916–17.

Mutiny

The French army was badly affected by mutiny in May 1917, as nearly three years of heavy casualties sapped the troops' willingness to fight. The scale of casualties suffered so far has taken a heavy toll of the nation which had so effectively mobilized its male population to fight the war. In 1914, 754,000 Frenchmen became casualties; in 1915, the total exceeded a million; and in 1916 another million were added to the list. Yet all this sacrifice had produced little apparent change – the German army still occupied about the same area of France that it had at the end of 1914. There was no sign that German morale was near breaking point, nor any sense that one more attack on them would win the war.

The Nivelle offensive of April 1917 seemed to French soldiers to be their last chance. General Robert Nivelle himself had been highly optimistic of success, predicting a breakthrough in 48 hours and there was good reason for the soldiers to believe that Nivelle did have some kind of secret formula, with his combination of specially trained troops and the creeping barrage. The troops who had been taken out of the line to undergo training had been told that many more guns than ever before would be used to support them and were aware that more troops than ever before were being massed on a narrow front; in some sectors of the front they even saw that the newfangled armoured fighting vehicles – tanks – were being deployed with them. Yet crossing no-man's-land to find the wire uncut yet again, and realizing the Germans had been expecting them all along – thanks to the discovery of a copy of the plan by German trench raiders – shattered the last hopes French soldiers had in their leaders. They had warned of 10,000 casualties on the first

day; the men suffered ten times that. They had promised a 6-mile (10-km) advance; the soldiers went 600 yards (550 m).

Troops being rotated out of the front line after the attack warned those replacing them that nothing had changed and that they were marching toward likely death. Officers became aware in the rear areas that the troops were behaving unusually sullenly, finding more solace in drink than normal. One battalion refused to return when their expected assignment to a quiet sector turned into a return to the scene of battle where they had just lost three-quarters of their strength. On 3 May, a whole division refused to attack. They would defend their trenches, but they saw no point in an assault that meant death or maiming for so many.

Russian example

Throughout May and June mutinous conduct persisted in the French army. The recent example of the Russian army, which had joined with Petrograd workers to overthrow the tsarist regime, gave inspiration

to some agitators, although the troops were unable to convert their dissatisfaction into anything approaching revolution. Most of the mutinies amounted to little more than protest marches, although the situation was alarming to French leaders. What perhaps saved France was the existence of a Zone of the Army around the front where the

> [T]he rate of desertion from the French army offered an index to the mounting crisis that resulted in the April mutinies: in 1914 there were 409 desertions; in 1915, 2,433; in 1916, nearly 9,000; and in 1917, 21,871.

soldiers were stationed, either in the front line or in rest and training camps in the rear. The revolutionary impulse was contained in this zone. Thus, what was a source of grievance to the troops, who resented their isolation from the rest of France, may well have saved the country from the kind of revolution that was under way in Russia.

General Philippe Pétain, who replaced General Nivelle at the end of April, worked very hard to stop the mutiny from expanding beyond the stage of a statement of grievances. He arranged for changes to French military practices which had allowed a somewhat tortuous process leading to the execution of mutineers. Instead, a system of rapid trial, sentencing and execution was employed. Great leniency was shown to units that returned to military discipline, with "only" five or so per company being shot. However, rumours persisted of a whole battalion being shelled by French guns, which hinted at a ruthless iron hand in a studded-leather glove. Pétain also took care of a number of other grievances that

Firing squads were used to enforce discipline in armies during the American Civil War, although desertion rather than mutiny was more likely to be the cause of a capital charge in that conflict.

Russian cavalry on the streets of Petrograd. The army remained loyal to the war effort until late 1917, and the collapse of their loyalty to the post-tsarist regime opened the way for the Bolsheviks to take power.

the men had expressed, as well as promising that future attacks would be for more limited objectives and would show greater concern for the lives of the men. Pétain had to solve a problem that all armies experience to one degree or another in war. All the Allied armies were affected by mutiny in one way or another during 1917. The British experienced trouble at the camp at Étaples, while the Russian army brought about the downfall of their government.

Danger at hand

Mutinies represent the most extreme manifestation of discontent on the part of soldiers. When military discipline breaks down, a dangerous situation threatens. A body of armed men, trained to be resolute in the face of danger, can do much to upset civil society. A mutiny represents an organized rejection of military discipline, which means that the mutineers may well not have abandoned the military structure, but are prepared to turn it to their own purposes. Fortunately, other types of indiscipline are far more common and a well-officered army can

avoid mutiny by handling the early symptoms with the correct combination of harshness and sympathy.

Desertion represents the rejection of military discipline by individuals or small groups of soldiers, who flee the camp to escape the authority of the armed forces. Desertion is an index of an army's discontent. During the First World War, the rate of desertion from the French army offered an index to the mounting crisis that resulted in the April mutinies: in 1914 there were 409 desertions; in 1915, 2,433; in 1916, nearly 9,000; and in 1917, 21,871.

Firing squad

Desertion is normally treated harshly, especially when it takes place near or on the battlefield, when execution is the traditional punishment. During the American Civil War, executions for desertion were not uncommon. The problem confronting officers in the field concerns distinguishing desertion from the more common, but somewhat less dangerous threat to military discipline represented by "skulking" – the act of hiding from battle.

A skulker is a soldier who can potentially be returned to duty, for he remains close to the men he fights with, whereas a deserter is trying to leave them behind.

However, desertion far behind the lines was normally and appropriately treated more leniently, and probably many cases of desertion were hidden under the rubric

> Desertion represents the rejection of military discipline by individuals or small groups of soldiers, who flee the camp to escape the authority of the armed forces.

of "absent without leave" or some other less severe charge. Prison was the normal punishment, although other punishments might have been employed. Much depended on the temperament of the officers in charge, and Pétain's generous handling of the soldiers' grievances excused much of the peremptory nature of such executions as did take place.

A barrage of shells crashes into Messines Ridge. The carefully planned attack on the German positions achieved a dramatic success.

Blast heard in London heralds offensive in Belgium

A **British attack on** German positions at Messines Ridge in Flanders successfully captured the high ground and held out against all German counter-attacks until these were called off on 14 June. One key reason for the success of the attack lay in the detonation of a series of large mines under the German trenches, creating a rumble heard across the Channel in London.

The operation was the brainchild of General Sir Herbert Plumer, who ordered digging to commence in the summer of 1916, 22 mine shafts being sunk under the German lines. Both British and German engineers were digging under the ridge, the latter in an attempt to stop the British. The Germans did discover one mine, but the British succeeded in completing the others which extended right under the German position.

The now traditional lengthy artillery bombardment began on 21 May and continued until 2.50 a.m. early in the morning of 7 June. Twenty minutes later, nineteen of the 21 mines were detonated. It was the largest artificial explosion in the war so far and blew the crest off the ridge. The British attackers found only dazed Germans in their trenches and reached all their limited objectives on the first day. The German counter-attacks starting on 8 June were unsuccessful and not unexpectedly, total casualties were higher for the Germans than for the participating French and British units: 25,000 to 17,000.

At first gains, then stalemate at Arras

A **British offensive timed** to divert German reserves away from General Robert Nivelle's planned attack in the Champagne was finally brought to an end on 23 May 1917, showing limited gains overall, in spite of early successes. The focus of the attack was on German trench lines either side of the town of Arras, where the new German Hindenburg Line met the old trench system in Flanders.

On 12 April, a "massed" attack at Bullecourt involving 11 tanks and Australian troops was astonishingly successful at first, although the British did not realize that the Germans had deep dugouts from which flank attacks were made.

The attack was preceded by a week-long artillery bombardment that was far more successful than hitherto at cutting the barbed wire in front of the German trenches, mainly due to better fuses and more shells being made available. When the main attack went over the top on 9 April, the British made some of their furthest advances of the war on the Western Front to date – up to 4½ miles (7 km). On 12 April, a "massed" attack at Bullecourt involving 11 tanks and Australian troops was astonishingly successful at first, although the British did not realize that the Germans had deep dugouts from which flank attacks were made, capturing many of the Australians. In spite of these early successes, the British were unable to sustain the momentum beyond the initial week and Field Marshal Sir Douglas Haig spent the next month ordering small-scale subsidiary attacks until calling the offensive off.

Arabs capture Aqaba

The port city of Aqaba, on the gulf of the same name, was captured by Arab irregulars led by the British officer Colonel T.E. Lawrence on 6 July 1917. Turkish troops garrisoning the city were in a position to attack the supply routes to Egypt used by British forces outside Gaza. When Lawrence visited

Lawrence, with about 30 Arabs, left Wejh and crossed the desert to Wadi Sirhan, where he used 20,000 gold sovereigns to buy an army of 500 Arab irregulars.

Aqaba before the War he learned that the main Turkish defences were in the Wadi Itm, with the aim of stopping anyone who seized the port from moving inland. He realized that a force moving inland on a wide sweep through the desert could approach Wadi Itm from the rear and capture the defences, thereby seizing Aqaba itself. Lawrence, with about 30 Arabs, left Wejh and crossed the desert to Wadi Sirhan, where he used 20,000 gold sovereigns to buy an army of 500 Arab irregulars – enough to surprise the Turks and capture Aqaba.

British Major T.E. Lawrence helped organize the Arab revolt and the attack on Aqaba. The capture of this port cut the Turks of Arabia off from their main forces in Palestine.

To and fro, stale-mate on the Isonzo

Italian troops with heavy guns. The Italian attacks begun in May 1917 accomplished small gains, but no strategic breakthrough was made.

An initially successful Italian offensive, was called off on 8 June 1917, having been driven more or less back to its start line. The Tenth Battle of the Isonzo had opened on 12 May, as Italian guns pounded Austro-Hungarian trenches. The Italian commander, General Luigi Cadorna, returned to his original idea of advancing on a broad front, instead of his 1916 style of concentrated punches. Several mountains were captured, but the Austro-Hungarians kept control of the Tolmino bridgehead and beat off an attack on the Carso, a stony plateau where ricocheting bullets sent showers of rocky splinters over the troops on both sides. Total casualties amounted to over 200,000, 60 per cent of them being Italian.

Wet weather hampers British attack

After three weeks of fighting ending on 18 August 1917, the British army made small gains in Flanders, complicated by a wet August and ground that is in any case reclaimed marshland.

Field Marshal Sir Douglas Haig, the commander of the British Expeditionary Force in France, launched the campaign around Ypres intending to distract the Germans from taking advantage of the disciplinary problems of the French army, as well as offering the possibility of threatening German U-boat bases on the Belgian coast. The bombardment began on 18 July, the heaviest and longest of the war so far, the shells ripping up an ancient system of drainage that had hitherto kept the reclaimed marshland between Ypres and Passchendaele reasonably dry. The ground soon turned into an appalling quagmire that was to cause the attacking British serious problems throughout the offensive.

The infantry attacks began on 31 July, on a front of approximately 14 miles (22 km). The length of the bombardment had made the Germans well aware of the location of the attack and they had reinforced their troops in the area. In spite of these difficulties the British achieved some success, although at a cost of 32,000 casualties. These dead and wounded bought an advance of up to 2,000 yards, (1,830 m) as Pilckem Ridge to the north of Ypres was captured. After two days of fighting, it began to rain and these heavy downpours continued as August has had double the normal monthly rainfall.

A few days of drier weather in mid-month allowed the renewal of the offensive around Langemarck. The rain made it difficult to put supporting guns into position and wooden platforms had to be constructed to keep them from sinking into the mud. Similarly-built plank roads were the only means of bringing up reinforcements, although they were especially easy for German artillery to target. After two days of fighting, the wet weather and lack of success convinced Haig to shift responsibility away from the Fifth Army of General Sir Hubert Gough to the Second Army of General Sir Herbert Plumer, which has led to a pause in offensive action.

Italians finally gain ground

General Luigi Cadorna halted his eleventh offensive along the Isonzo on 12 September 1917 after over three weeks of fighting brought the kind of success he had expected to achieve in the previous ten attempts. The Italian troops had gone beyond the point where they could easily be resupplied or supported by artillery. For the Austro-Hungarians, Cadorna's halt offered a welcome breathing space.

Cadorna assembled his largest force to date for this offensive, deploying over 50 divisions and 5,000 artillery pieces. The attacks began on 17 August with two main thrusts, one around Gorizia and in the plateau of the Carso, the other far to north at the Tolmino bridgehead. Both proved to be successes, although the more northerly push achieved far greater territorial gains, advancing in places to a depth of over 6 miles (10 km).

A British stretcher party struggles to bring a casualty through the muddy fields of Flanders, as heavy rains and damaged drainage systems create a quagmire.

THIRD BATTLE OF YPRES

DATES:	July–November 1916
COMBATANTS:	France and Britain vs Germany
CASUALTIES:	Allies, 325,000; Germany, 260,000
RESULT:	Stalemate

Change of command brings progress at Ypres

German prisoners captured during the battle for Ypres.

New tactics have brought some success to the British as the fighting around Ypres resumed after a period of dry weather. Operations aimed at limited objectives along the Menin Road and Polygon Wood were begun on 20 September and have made much more rapid headway using new tactical methods than the older systems had produced.

The commander of the Second Army, General Sir Herbert Plumer, has been instructing his divisions in combined arms tactics to tackle the German defensive system, after the old methods had led to extremely heavy casualties in the fighting at the Somme. The Germans now use a system of defence in depth, with a forward line of outposts, preferably in the form of concrete pillboxes, supported by trench lines behind, from which counter-attacks can be organized against any breaches in the outpost line.

Plumer's tactics involve sending a skirmish line forward, followed by small teams of infantry equipped with grenades and light machine guns. These groups attack pillboxes or other strongpoints from the flanks, while the troops in the skirmish line identify the same objectives and offer a degree of fire support to the attacking groups. Machine guns and artillery are intended to offer support to break up the inevitable German counter-attacks that follow any loss of ground to British or French attacks.

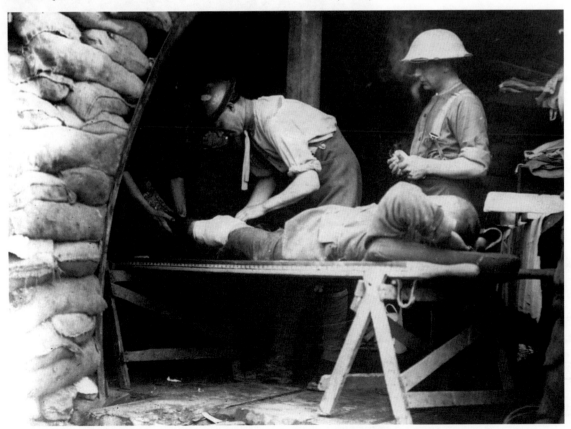

A British soldier receives medical treatment at a field hospital. The stretcher has been placed on a pair of trestles to provide a rudimentary bed.

Advance at Broodseinde, then rain halts offensive

General **Sir Herbert** Plumer's Second Army made some important advances in attacks on 4 October and 9 October, before the weather once again intervened to halt the British in the Ypres salient. Field Marshal Sir Douglas Haig has conferred with his commanders and set an ultimate objective of Passchendaele Ridge for the offensive.

The Germans had been worried by the previous attacks on the Menin Road and at Polygon Wood, which had seen their defensive front line fall more easily than they had anticipated and their counter-attacks to be readily broken up by artillery supporting the British infantry. Therefore, they had reinforced their front line at Broodseinde, which merely resulted in heavier casualties from the British bombardment. Plumer's "bite and hold" approach did not aim at achieving a breakthrough, but instead sought to make gains that kept the advancing infantry within range of the supporting artillery. The combination of the revised German tactics and the British limited objectives was turning the battles into attritional combats.

The offensive on 4 October secured some important gains around Broodseinde, while on 9 October the village of Poelcapelle fell to the British.

British anti-aircraft gunners prepare to fire their weapon.

Germans depart their East African colony

Kashmiri gunners in East Africa. The British force in German East Africa drew heavily on Imperial troops, especially from the African colonies and India.

After a struggle against the British imperial troops lasting nearly two years, the German field army in German East Africa abandoned their colony for Portuguese Mozambique, following fighting at Mahiwa on 15–18 October 1917. The German commander, Colonel Paul von Lettow-Vorbeck, used Portugal's declaration of war against Germany as a justification for raiding the Portuguese colony, where he secured supplies and avoided the considerable British army that had been deployed against him.

Lettow-Vorbeck had repeatedly beaten the British in his campaigns, using an army largely of African askari native troops. In 1914, he had delivered a crushing defeat against a British landing at Tanga, while in 1915 he won a second victory at Jassin. Lettow-Vorbeck preferred to fight a guerrilla war thereafter, as the casualties he suffered at Jassin uncomfortably exceeded his easy victory at Tanga.

The British had made considerable territorial gains in 1916, but had still not defeated Lettow-Vorbeck in the field. At the end of that year, General Jan Smuts, the South African commander of the British Imperial forces in East Africa, had driven Lettow-Vorbeck south, but could not achieve final victory despite his forces outnumbering the Germans by eight to one. The elusive Lettow-Vorbeck remained at large throughout 1917, while Smuts declared imminent victory and departed for London.

Lettow-Vorbeck finally stood and fought at Mahiwa, where 5,000 British soldiers, many of them King's African Rifles, attacked 1,500 troops under Lettow-Vorbeck. The battled lasted three days and the Germans inflicted some 1,600 casualties on the British while suffering a minor loss of 100 of their own.

Ships clash in Gulf of Riga

A **German landing on** the islands in the mouth of the Gulf of Riga has succeeded in clearing the Russian fleet from its advanced base in the area.

The Russians had constructed batteries on Ösel island, the largest in the archipelago, before the war, blocking the southernmost entrance to the gulf. Moon island, on the eastern shore of Ösel island, blocked the northernmost entrance. Seeking to control both these islands and thereby trap part of the Russian fleet in Riga, German battleships bombarded the batteries on Ösel island on 12 October. Troops landed under the cover of the bombardment and succeeded in isolating the Russian batteries.

The Ösel island batteries surrendered to the Germans on 15 October, allowing the German navy to use most of its ships for an attack on Moon island, where two German dreadnoughts clashed with two smaller Russian battleships and an armoured cruiser. The greater firepower of the Germans was too much for the Russian vessels, one of which was sunk while two were badly damaged and fled northwards to the Gulf of Finland.

The naval war in the Baltic was one of small vessels and landings.

Dancer shot as spy

Mata Hari's exotic reputation preceded the war. She was shot by firing squad on 15 October 1917, and passed into legend.

T **he Dutch dancer** Margarethe McLeod (née Zelle), better known by her stage name of Mata Hari, was executed by firing squad as a German spy on 15 October 1917. Mata Hari was born in the Netherlands and spent several years with her husband in the Dutch East Indies. When the couple returned to Europe, she divorced her husband and took up a career in 1905 as an exotic dancer using the name Mata Hari. She had a number of lovers with links to military circles and was in Germany just before the war, as a result of which she was dogged by rumours that she was a spy. In Spain during 1916 she became involved in swapping information between German and French spymasters, as neither side fully trusted her. On 13 February 1917, the French arrested her. She was tried in July, found guilty and received the death sentence.

Passchendaele falls, ending campaign of misery

Canadian forces captured the village of Passchendaele on 6 November 1917, giving the British Expeditionary Force control of Passchendaele Ridge. The British Second Army launched two offensives in October, although a period of wet weather made moving through the mud of Flanders' fields extremely difficult during this fighting.

The first attack was made around Poelcapelle on 12 October, but little ground was gained and casualties were heavy.

British attacks were resumed on 30 October, again with little to show in terms of ground gained, until on 6 November the Canadian troops finally secured the village and Passchendaele Ridge, capturing the objectives from the Bavarian troops defending them.

Marxists seize power in Russia

The Petrograd Soviet (or council) of Workers', Soldiers' and Peasants' Deputies seized power on 7 November 1917 in a coup that overthrew the Provisional Government which had ruled Russia since the abdication of the Tsar in March. The Provisional Government had kept the country in the war against the Germans, giving the radical leftists of the Soviet a useful propaganda tool. In July, the same left-wingers, led by the Bolshevik Party leader Vladimir Lenin, had attempted to overthrow the government. Using soldiers and workers' militia, they seized many key installations in Petrograd and successfully attacked the Winter Palace.

Caporetto, a black day for Italy

Austro-Hungarian troops pause in the town of Conegliano during their advance to the Piave river in November 1917. German and Austro-Hungarian forces used infiltration tactics to drive the Italians out of all their gains captured during the previous two years of war.

The Italian army suffered a massive defeat on the Isonzo front. A combined German and Austro-Hungarian offensive unleashed on 24 October 1917 has driven Italian troops not only out of all their gains won with such difficulty over two years of fighting on the Isonzo front, but also well back into Italy. Treviso and Venice are now threatened with occupation by enemy troops, as the front line has been along the line of the Piave river since 12 November.

The success of the Italian army in the Eleventh Battle of the Isonzo back in August alarmed the Germans, who had found the Austro-Hungarian army a weak partner during the fighting against the Russians on the Eastern Front. German soldiers arrived at the Italian front and when the Italian commander, General Luigi Cadorna, learned of this through aerial reconnaissance, he called off an offensive planned for late September.

The collapse of a serious Russian effort on the Eastern Front allowed the transfer of nine German divisions, six of which put in their main assault in the vicinity of the town of Caporetto. The Germans used gas shells which wreaked havoc among the Italian artillery and enabled their infantry to move forward with relatively few casualties from what shelling the Italians could manage. The Germans also used a very short bombardment, lasting about two hours, unlike the traditional one over several days before an offensive. The Germans also used the storm troop tactics they had practised on the Eastern Front, with companies advancing with little regard for maintaining touch with their comrades on the flanks, and tackling strong points by using machine guns to keep the Italians' heads down, while troops armed with grenades worked around the flanks to destroy the position.

The Germans succeeded in destroying the Italian defences in a couple of days, taking some 270,000 prisoners, thereby starting an all-out retreat that lasted until 11 November. Cadorna was dismissed on 7 November and was replaced by General Armando Diaz.

Tanks and storm troops clash at Cambrai

A **British offensive and** a German counter-offensive around Cambrai left the front line almost entirely unchanged when the fighting ended on 3 December 1917. However, the use of massed tank formations when the British attacked on 20 November, and the German employment of elite assault troops in their counter-offensive launched on 30 November, made this two-week period one of the most mobile on the Western Front since the first trenches were dug in 1914.

The British offensive took place on a 5-mile (9-km) front between the Canal du Nord and the St Quentin Canal, using 19 divisions, with 200 tanks in the first wave and over 400 overall. The British achieved a major breakthrough on the first day, although the Germans held out in some key locations, such as Flesquières, and demonstrated the effectiveness of artillery against tanks. The main objective of Bourlon Ridge was still being contested on 28 November when the British called off their offensive.

The German response contrasted with the British technological advantage by using more sophisticated infantry and artillery tactics which proved devastatingly effective and achieved their breakthrough more rapidly than the British tanks. In the end, the battle was a major disappointment for the British, whose early success produced no lasting gains.

Allenby breaks through at Gaza

G **eneral Sir Edmund** Allenby's Egyptian Expeditionary Force succeeded in breaking through the Turkish defensive line that was anchored on the coastal town of Gaza, and eventually captured Jerusalem on 9 December 1917.

The attack at Gaza was launched on 31 October with a cavalry attack at Beersheeba, by a predominantly Australian force. The Turks had not suspected anything, having been deceived by British into thinking that the main blow would fall on the coast.

The British advance attained a depth of 2 miles (3 km) while at the same time repeated attacks were made on the other end of the Turkish line, pushed back from Beersheeba to El Khuweilfe.

On 2 November, British operations against the Gaza trench lines began with a night-time infantry assault. The British advance attained a depth of 2 miles (3 km) while at the same time repeated attacks were made on the other end of the Turkish line, pushed back from Beersheeba to El Khuweilfe. By 6 November, the Turkish line had been breached in several places and the Turks abandoned it on 8 November. The pursuit continued until Jerusalem was reached and captured.

General Sir Edmund Allenby enters the holy city of Jerusalem on foot, with his staff, Allied officers and political attachés.

IN BRIEF

On 2 November, British foreign secretary Arthur Balfour issued a typed letter, addressed to Lord Rothschild, to give to the Zionist Federation. Balfour stated in this letter: "His Majesty's Government views with favour the establishment in Palestine of a national home for the Jewish people ... it being clearly understood that nothing shall be done which may prejudice the civil and religious rights of existing non-Jewish communities in Palestine." It represented the handing over of territory Britain did not own to people who did not live there, and was incompatible with statements being made by the British government to Arab leaders at the time.

Russian Soviets comes to terms with Germany

On **3 March** 1918, Germany and her allies signed a peace treaty with the revolutionary government of Russia, at the city of Brest-Litovsk. Negotiations began on 22 December 1917, but had been interrupted at several points, mainly to allow the Russian delegates to return to Petrograd to debate the terms under discussion. In February 1918, the armistice was terminated by the Germans, who for a few days resumed military operations against Russian forces until the Russians agreed to resume talks. The treaty pushed the western border of Russia eastwards, creating an independent Ukraine, renouncing Russian rights over Courland and Lithuania and a part of Belorussia, and allowing German troops to occupy Latvia and Estonia. Parts of the Caucasus were conceded to Turkey, notably Kars and Batum. The Russian government also accepted the requirement to pay for the feeding and housing of Russian prisoners of war, but no other financial penalties were required.

Allied reaction to the treaty was one of alarm. The Provisional Government, overthrown by the Bolsheviks and their allies in November 1917, had kept Russia in the

Russian revolutionary leader Vladimir Lenin was brought from Switzerland to Russia by the Germans in the hope that he would succeeded in disrupting the Russian war effort.

war, even though the Russians conducted little offensive action. The Bolsheviks had instead taken Russia out of the war, releasing thousands of German troops for duty on the Western Front.

Russian and German negotiators at Brest-Litovsk. The Soviet government conceded much to the Germans because ultimately they believed the Germans would lose the war in the West.

IN BRIEF

❧ The Germans began shelling Paris on 21 March 1918 using a long 210mm artillery weapon called the Kaiser Wilhelm Gun. The shells fired by this huge railway gun attained a height of 20 miles (32 km), and a range of 80 miles (129 km).

❧ Manfred, Baron von Richthofen, was killed in action on 23 April 1918, while flying near Bapaume, France. Canadian pilot Captain Roy Brown was credited with the victory, but two Australian machine gunners, Popkin and Weston, were also given credit for bringing down the "Red Baron".

❧ The British Dover Patrol naval force attacked the port of Zeebrugge in Belgium, together with Royal Marines, on 23 April 1918. The purpose of the raid was to sink three blockships in a canal that linked the coast with Brugge inland, which was being used as a base for U-boats. The innovative operation made use of a converted cruiser, HMS *Vindictive*, to deliver the Royal Marines to the harbour mole.

Baron von Richtofen was made a celebrity on the German home front to popularise the war.

Germans call off "Michael"

German troops advance across a war-torn battlefield. The essence of infiltration tactics was to bypass strongpoints and attack the supply and communications network that sustained them.

The German army on the Western Front called off Operation Michael, an offensive against the British Third and Fifth Armies, on 5 April 1918. The Germans had used troops transferred from the Eastern Front in an attempt to break through the British lines and swing north to capture the town of Arras. However, they have fallen short of this objective.

A refined version of the methods used in the autumn at Cambrai by the Germans were employed in this attack. The assault plan envisaged a short, highly intense bombardment that would target communications and headquarters, then artillery positions and finally the front line; this would be followed by an infantry assault that was spearheaded by units bypassing any centres of resistance to get into the enemy's rear zones.

The first day saw big gains in the Fifth Army sector, where thick fog aided the Germans, but lesser ones against the Third Army, although in both cases the Germans fell short of their first-day objectives. However, by this time the British command system was in disarray, with orders from higher echelons such as corps taking a long time to reach lower-echelon divisions and brigades, and often being out of date by the time they arrived. By nightfall on 23 March, the Germans appeared to have torn a large gap in the British lines, but

weariness began to affect them. As long as fresh troops could be fed into the line, the German advance continued apace. After three days of fighting in some places the assault troops were finding distractions in the food and drink available in British supply dumps. After years of blockade, German troops were undernourished, and could not resist temptation. Drunkenness probably caused as much delay as British defensive measures.

Although the Germans had broken through the British lines, it had taken them two days longer than they had expected. The British had sufficient motor vehicles for them to rush troops out of reserve to plug the gaps in the line. By 29 March, the Germans could no longer maintain forward momentum and the British were able to re-

Engineers attempt to extract a tank from a ditch. Although a tank's tracks helped them to cross the battlefield, they remained vulnerable to deep holes.

establish a defensive line. Allied losses in the fighting amounted to 255,000 dead, wounded and prisoners, plus 1,300 artillery pieces. The Germans lost 239,000.

SPRING 1918 OFFENSIVE

DATES:	March–June 1918
COMBATANTS:	France, Britain, the United States, Portugal, Belgium and Italy vs Germany
CASUALTIES:	Allies, 537,000; Germany, 509,000
RESULT:	Allied victory

Georgette, in Flanders, meanders to a close

Soldiers of the Middlesex Regiment man a barricade in the streets of Ballieul, a small town on the border between France and Belgium.

General Erich Ludendorff's second offensive of 1918 was called off on 30 April. The attack, launched on 9 April, attempted to achieve a strategic breakthrough by the German army to the Channel ports.

Ludendorff's offensive, code-named Georgette, was aimed at the key rail junction of Hazebrouck, only 15 miles (24 km) behind the lines. The deepest advance achieved by Operation Michael amounted to 50 miles (80 km). If Hazebrouck fell to the Germans, it was likely that the British would have to evacuate their army from this area. The best opportunity for an important breakthrough offered to Ludendorff was an attack that fell on the Portuguese Corps, the centre of

"With our backs to the wall and believing in the justice of our cause, each one of us might fight on to the end."

whose line lay at Neuve Chappelle, southeast of Hazebrouck. A secondary attack would strike at Messines Ridge.

The bombardment on 9 April shattered the Portuguese morale and they broke for the rear, where some were fired on by British troops advancing to their support. The Germans kept up the pressure and on 10 April Armentières and Ballieul were captured. Field Marshal Sir Douglas Haig's Order of the Day on 11 April contained the famous sentence: "With our backs to the wall and believing in the justice of our cause, each one of us must fight on to the end." However, in spite of this rhetoric, the crisis of the battle was still a week away, coming on 17 April when a German attack struck the Belgian Army at Merkem and Kippe, but the Belgians held. A pause in the battle ensued until 25 April, when a fierce bombardment launched the battle for Mount Kemmel. By this stage both sides were exhausted by three weeks of fighting, and the battle petered out in half-hearted offensives. The Allied line had held.

Ludendorff's third try

Flooded to defeat

German officers observe the countryside in the Aisne valley from the Chemin des Dames. The high ground had been fought over in September 1914.

The third German offensive of 1918, unleashed on the Chemin des Dames and Aisne river on 27 May, was called off on 15 June by General Erich Ludendorff. Once again great territorial gains were made, but the Allied line, though stretched, did not break. American troops have entered the fray in substantial numbers for the first time, fighting to halt the Germans at Cantigny, Château-Thierry and Belleau Wood.

The method established in the first two offensives continued in the third. The French suffered worst in this offensive, whereas the first two had been directed against British forces. One corps of British troops, moved out of Flanders for rest, was hit by their second major offensive of the year.

On the first day the German attackers made the longest single-day advance recorded by any combatant army on the Western Front up to that point. The retreat continued. The German army pushed the Allied lines back as far as the Marne, before they were halted. Ludendorff had not intended such a signal success, but rather to draw off troops from Flanders or Picardy in order to facilitate his planned offensive there. However, such was the success of his advance that he decided to let the battle continue, until on 4 June the same factors of tiredness and ill-discipline that had affected the other offensives slowed the attacks. A subsidiary offensive took place in the area between the first and third Ludendorff offensives on 8 June, but this was halted by French counter-attacks.

Having got to within 35 miles (56 km) of Paris, the Germans stopped. Ludendorff intended to regroup, prior to a new offensive in Flanders.

A brief lull on the Italian front in June 1918 preceded an attempt by Austro-Hungarian forces to emulate the success of the Ludendorff offensives on the Western Front. The Austro-Hungarians were forced into the operation by their refusal to offer any more than a few heavy guns to support the German attacks in France. Instead of using their limited resources on a single front, the Austro-Hungarians attacked both in the Asiago and along the Piave on 15 June. Although the Asiago front was a total failure, the Austro-Hungarians made some headway on the Piave. However, the river flooded after a couple of days, and washed away the temporary bridges used to supply the forces across it, so the Austro-Hungarians were forced to withdraw their troops, having lost 150,000 casualties for no gain.

A devastated town on the Italian front, showing the power of artillery bombardment.

Le Hamel, model operation

An attack by British and US 33rd Division troops on the village of Le Hamel on 4 July 1918 achieved some success, spear-headed by 60 tanks. The plan of the British commander, Australian General John Monash, provided a new model for others to learn from. The infantry and tanks were trained beforehand in working together, the artillery support was carefully camouflaged and the bombardment was kept very short. A large proportion of the guns were allocated to firing on enemy artillery and the attack achieved most of its objectives at relatively little cost to the attackers.

Ludendorff fails, Foch succeeds

A German offensive along the Marne was halted by fierce French, British and American resistance. The German attacks on 15 July were east and west of Reims and were preceded by the heaviest artillery barrage yet, but only the latter made any progress at all, crossing the Marne. However, once on the south bank of the Marne the German attackers were unable to go further. The storm troops had suffered heavy losses since March, and were no longer the elite force they had been.

The day after the Germans halted their attacks, Marshal Ferdinand Foch launched the Allied counter-offensive, with troops from France, Britain, America and Italy participating, and supported by 350 tanks.

No preparatory bombardment preceded the Allied attack, except for the creeping barrage that opened at 4.35 a.m. With some advantage of surprise, the main French push achieved a 5-mile (9-km) advance on the first day, and by 20 July the Germans withdrew to the heights north of the Ourcq river where they held for a few days, until on the night of 1/2 August they began a second retreat. They were eventually more or less back where they had begun their offensive in the Champagne, north of the Aisne, in June. Here, on 6 August, they halted the Allies. The three weeks of fighting ended with 95,000 French casualties, 13,000 British and 12,000 American, against 168,000 German.

The German offensive carried them beyond the war zone of the trenches into relatively untouched French countryside. Mobile warfare was restored, which was not necessarily to the advantage of the numerically inferior German forces.

A black day for the German army

A column of German prisoners makes its way to camps in the rear. The British victory at Amiens on 8 August 1918 was a huge blow to German hopes of sustaining the war in France.

The **British offensive** at Amiens on 8 August 1918 achieved gains beyond all expectations as the German army experienced what its commander General Erich Ludendorff described as "a black day for the German army".

As had happened with the German attack on 21 March, fog aided the British as they advanced at zero hour, 4.20 a.m. on 8 August. The fog hid the tanks, which were vulnerable to artillery fire, until the leading elements of the British attack were already into the German defensive line. The British succeeded in creating a 15-mile (24-km) gap, into which they poured men, tanks, cavalry and armoured cars. German soldiers began to surrender in large numbers, causing General Ludendorff to make his remark. When the offensive was halted on 11 August, the Germans had been pushed back up to 10 miles (16 km) in depth. The British suffered 22,200 casualties, the Germans 74,000.

RUSSIAN CIVIL WAR

DATES:	April 1918–November 1920
COMBATANTS:	Bolsheviks vs Whites plus Allied supporters vs nationalists
CASUALTIES:	8 million in total
RESULT:	Bolshevik victory

Tsar shot after civil war breaks out in Russia

The Bolshevik government that took power in Russia in November and brought about peace with Germany now found itself confronted with a growing civil war. After the signing of the peace treaty with Germany, a group of Russian army officers and soldiers gathered along the Don in southern Russia, and started an uprising. At first their forces were small, numbering perhaps 10,000 at most, and their equipment was in short supply. An attempt to capture the town of Ekaterinador in April 1918 failed but the army survived and gathered strength.

The presence of such counter-revolutionary organizations encouraged Russia's former allies to intervene, largely for political reasons. The Czechoslovak Legion, formed by the Russians from Czech and Slovak prisoners captured from the Austro-Hungarian army, joined the opposition to the Bolsheviks in May 1917. They gained control of the Trans-Siberian Railway, and two centres of anti-Bolshevik government emerged at Samara and Omsk. By accident, in June, the Imperial Russian gold reserves fell into their hands.

On 6 July, some of the Bolsheviks' allies, the Left Social Revolutionary Party, staged a revolt. The German ambassador to Moscow was assassinated, and Left Social Revolutionary militia attempted to take control of Moscow. At the same time, a group of former army officers seized the city of Yaroslavl', expecting eventually to be reinforced by French troops due to land at Archangel the same day.

However, the landings never occurred, the Bolshevik forces suppressed the Moscow rebels in a day, and the Yaroslavl' ones by 21 July. Tsar Nicholas II and his family were shot as a consequence of this rebellion during the night of 16/17 July.

Allied armies sent to Russia

After British, Japanese, French and American soldiers and sailors had landed at several ports in Russia on both the Arctic and Pacific coasts, fighting between these troops and the Bolsheviks broke out during the summer of 1918, increasing the tension between the hostile governments of Russia's former allies and the Bolsheviks.

Japanese forces were the first to intervene, landing at Vladivostok in April after the murder of Japanese nationals. Having been joined by American soldiers and more Japanese in August 1918, they soon began moving along the Trans-Siberian Railway, ostensibly in support of the Czechoslovak Legion, but in fact intent on achieving some measure of Japanese influence in the Russian Far East.

The other major incursion began on 6 March, when British Royal Marines landed at Murmansk, on the Arctic Ocean, to protect the supplies that had been shipped there to sustain Russian participation in the war. In May, the British and French forces in the area skirmished with anti-Bolshevik Finns around Petsamo, and major reinforcements arrived on 23 June. Fighting broke out between the British and the Bolsheviks in July after the Bolsheviks had decided to assert their authority by expelling the foreigners from Russian territory. On 1 August, Archangel was seized by a mixed British and American force, and reinforcements were sent here throughout September to prepare for a more powerful advance south and east.

American troops arrive in Vladivostok, Siberia. The Allied countries sent armies to intervene in the Russian civil war, either to support their wartime friends or to gain territory at the Bolsehvik government's expense.

Allenby's armageddon

British General Sir Edmund Allenby delivered a crushing blow to the Turkish army in Palestine at the Battle of Megiddo, which concluded on 25 September 1918. Allenby had captured Jerusalem in December 1917, whereupon his most experienced troops were withdrawn to the Western Front and he had to spend the spring and summer of 1918 training new, inexperienced divisions. The attack was eventually launched into the Jezreel valley (where the Bible's Book of Revelation predicts the final battle, Armageddon, will be fought) after Allenby had completely deceived the Turks as to where the main stroke would occur. Once the infantry had quickly

German and Turkish prisoners, in this case a column of 3,000, captured during the battle of Megiddo march toward Ludd, Palestine, in September 1918.

broken through the Turkish defences, Allenby used his cavalry to push through the gap and swing eastwards toward Beisan intending to cut off the Turkish retreat. After the Turks had been forced to abandon their defences, they were harried by cavalry and aeroplanes during their long retreat into Syria. Australian cavalry entered Damascus on 30 September.

Plan Foch swings into action

Allied forces on the Western Front brought the dour trench conflict to an end, after a series of offensives pushed the Germans steadily back throughout August and September. The Allied Supreme Commander, Marshal Ferdinand Foch, envisaged a steady widening of the offensive from its initial focus in Champagne and around Amiens, until the whole front was in motion. British Field Marshal Sir Douglas Haig's aggressive conduct of the campaign has played an important part in bringing Foch's ideas to fruition.

After two years of unimaginative attempts to bludgeon a gap through the German lines, Allied commanders are showing a good deal of imagination. The British combination of guns, tanks and aircraft proved effective in attacks on the old Somme battlefield on 21–23 August and in breaking the formidable Drocourt-Quéant line in September. The Australian Corps secured Mont Saint Quentin using similar methods. General Charles Mangin, who had been characterized as a "butcher" by his men, achieved further success around Compiègne by varying the start time of his attacks. On 12 September, Pershing's American Expeditionary Force began pushing back the great German salient around St Mihiel. By this time the Germans

German troops in a trench in 1918. The German army continued to fight on, even though it was clear the war was lost.

were in general retreat, attempting to retire to a stronger position that they hoped to hold through the winter. But Foch was already preparing his great stroke, under the motto *"Tout le monde à la bataille"*.

Assassination plot: Soviet Russia in crisis

An attempted assassination of the Soviet leader Vladimir Lenin coincided with the Bolshevik government being pressed hard by its opponents in the civil war. On 30 August 1918 Lenin was shot by Fanny Kaplan, a former member of the Right Social Revolutionaries, who claimed to be acting entirely alone. Lenin was seriously, but not fatally, wounded. Soviet police uncovered a complex group of plots to overthrow Lenin. British officials had been attempting to bribe the Latvian troops garrisoning Moscow, while French and British diplomats had created an informal network among the Bolsheviks' "White" opponents. At the same time, the Red Army launched its first major offensive which recaptured Kazan from the "Whites" on 10 September. There was heavy fighting around several towns along the Volga river and in the Urals, and both sides desperately tried to mobilize recruits from a peasantry that only wanted peace.

British troops enter Lille in October 1918, a northern French town that had been occupied by the Germans since 1914. The soldier with the large gun in the foreground is carrying a Lewis Gun, a relatively lightweight machine gun.

The guns fall silent

An **armistice came** into effect on the Western Front on 11 November 1918, bringing to an end a war that had claimed the lives of millions, and which had been entered into gaily by many young men in 1914.

Marshal Ferdinand Foch's grand offensive, which eventually compelled the Germans to appeal for peace, began in late September. On 26 September, the American First Army attacked in the Argonne region, while French forces attacked between Reims and the American left wing. On 27 September, British forces attacked around Lens, along the River Scarpe; an attack in Flanders followed the day after. Once these had put the Germans under pressure, General Erich Ludendorff and Field Marshal Paul von Hindenburg, the German supreme commanders, visited Kaiser Wilhelm II and informed him of the need to seek an armistice.

The worst blow came the next day, when the British Fourth Army broke through the vaunted Hindenburg Line between Bellincourt and Bellenglise. Although the gap was very fragile around Bellincourt, that near Bellenglise was a disaster for the Germans, who did not expect the Hindenburg Line to be breached so convincingly so quickly.

The Kaiser agreed with his generals and appointed a new government that approached the United States on 4 October with a request for an armistice. By 3 November, a revolution had broken out in Germany, starting with the sailors of the German navy at Kiel. On 9 November the Kaiser abdicated and on 11 November, at 5 a.m., the armistice terms were signed in a railway carriage at Compiègne, coming into effect at 11 a.m. that day.

First World War military dead by country

Country	Dead
Austria-Hungary	1,200,000
Belgium	13,716
Britain and Empire	898, 402
Bulgaria	87,500
France	1,375,800
Germany	1,773,700
Greece	5,000
Italy	650,000
Japan	300
Montenegro	3,000
Portugal	7,222
Rumania	335,706
Russia	1,700,000
Serbia	450,000
Turkey	325,000
United States	126,000

The Paris Peace Conference that resulted in the Treaty of Versailles began on 18 January 1919 and drew up the treaty governing the peace with Germany. Reparations to the victorious powers, especially France, amounted to £6.6 billion.

Italy avenges Caporetto

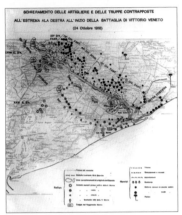

The victorious Italian campaign in the autumn of 1918 recovered all the ground that had been lost after the Austro-Hungarian and German offensive at Caporetto.

On **24 October** 1918, the first anniversary of the combined German and Austro-Hungarian offensive at Caporetto, the Italians launched an attack of their own, targeting Austro-Hungarian troops defending Monte Grappa, a mountain that represented a key "hinge" in the front. The mountain had been heavily fought over during the original Caporetto offensive and in Austria-Hungary's June attacks. Its capture would have led to the surrounding of Italian armies defending the Piave line, so it was a key objective of the new Italian offensive. Things didn't work out the way Italian commander, General Armando Diaz, anticipated.

The Austro-Hungarian generals rushed reinforcements to Monte Grappa from their troops on the Piave as the Italian pressure intensified. When the Italian offensive along the Piave opened on 24 October, the attack at Monte Grappa had not achieved its intended objective. The thinning of the Piave defensive line made the crossing easy for the Italian and British troops attacking. Once this line had been broken the Allies made rapid gains and on 1 November they crossed the next major river, the Livenza. The Austro-Hungarians sought an armistice the next day, which was agreed on 3 November, following the Italian seizure of Trieste. The war in Italy formally ended on 4 November.

Fighting on all fronts

Russia was the setting for fighting between the Bolshevik forces, the "Reds", and their anti-Bolshevik opponents, the "Whites", together with Allied forces, and also nationalists of various peoples who had previously been under the Tsar's rule. Bolshevik Commissar for War, Leon Trotsky, took personal charge of operations on the Volga-Urals front. Samara fell on 8 October, though not before an anti-Bolshevik assembly there established a Directory at Omsk to give political leadership to the White movement on this front. It was ineffective, though, and its war minister, the tsarist admiral, Alexander Kolchak, staged a coup on 18 November and proclaimed himself Supreme Ruler. Though well supported by the British, Kolchak's recruiters were not welcome in Siberia, where people were far enough from Moscow not to notice who ruled them. The Volunteer Army on the Don had far more success, winning control of the Kuban and making a push toward Tsaritsyn on the Volga (later known as Stalingrad).

Meanwhile, the Bolsheviks were on the attack on other fronts. An attempt to evict Allied forces from Murmansk and Archangel, resulted in the Battle of Toulgas, which began the same day that the Armistice came into effect on the Western Front, 11 November. A force of British and American troops held off a Bolshevik attack over three days of fighting. Bolshevik soldiers invaded Estonia on 22 November 1918, where they battled against British and German forces, erstwhile enemies now united against Lenin's regime.

Leon Trotsky addresses troops of the Red Army. Trotsky's ruthless approach and oratorical skills helped organize an army to defend the Bolshevik revolution in Russia.

Greek forces occupy Smyrna

During the First World War, Allied governments had promised the Greek government parts of Turkey if they entered the war on the Allied side. Having eventually done so, the Greeks began to take advantage of those promises in May 1919, with the help of French, British and American ships, by occupying Smyrna, on the Aegean coast of Asia Minor. In 1920, under the terms of the Treaty of Sèvres, the Greeks were given a large area of the hinterland, in addition to Smyrna, which they proceeded to occupy with military forces.

Greek troops with Turkish POWs near the docks of Smyrna. The Greeks hoped to recover the east coast of Asia Minor, which had been dominated by Greek speakers since the 7th century BC.

ANGLO-IRISH WAR

DATES:	1916-1921
COMBATANTS:	Irish Republicans vs Britain
CASUALTIES:	Irish Republicans, 800; Britain, 800
RESULT:	Republican victory

Irish republic goes to war

The shooting of two members of the Royal Irish Constabulary on 21 January 1919 at Soloheadbeg in County Tipperary marked the beginning of a war between irregulars associated with the Irish Republican Army, and the British. On the same day, those Sinn Féin members of the British parliament elected in 1918 assembled at the Mansion House in Dublin as an Irish Parliament, which declared the independence of Ireland from Britain. There were no other incidents in the war until 13 May, when two more constables were killed at Knocklong. When an inquest was held into the killings, the jury blamed the British government for putting the police at risk. After this, any pretence that the Irish Republicans, fighting like Boers in ordinary clothes, were anything other than soldiers, was dismissed by the average Irish subject. A war of ambush and assassination had now begun.

IN BRIEF

Afghan forces attacked British India in May 1919, as the Afghan emir, Amanullah, sought to end British control of his country's foreign policy as established by treaty in 1881. The British responded by invading through the Khyber Pass and bombing Kabul and Jallalabad. The Afghans quickly asked for a negotiated settlement, which the British agreed and an agreement was signed at Rawalpindi on 8 August 1919, restoring a measure of foreign-policy autonomy to Afghanistan.

WAR CELEBRITY
LAWRENCE OF ARABIA

The American journalist Lowell Thomas created a hit with a lecture tour about the seemingly exotic British army intelligence colonel T.E. Lawrence, who has now become known as Lawrence of Arabia.

This former archaeologist, born in 1888, travelled in Syria and the Sinai during the years immediately preceding the war, and subsequently used the knowledge of the Arab people he had gained when he enlisted in the British army and was assigned to British military intelligence in Cairo.

In 1916, Lawrence was part of a mission that attempted to bribe Turkish officers into allowing British soldiers trapped in Kut to go free. In 1917, Lawrence began serving with Arab irregulars who were fighting the Turks in the hope of securing an independent Arab state, with its capital in Damascus, after the war. Lawrence used these irregulars to attack Turkish railways and other supply lines, during the course of which he allowed Lowell Thomas and his camera-man Harry Chase to film some of his activities.

Thomas used film and lantern slides to illustrate his lectures, which opened at Covent Garden Opera House in August 1919. Eventually, some four million people from several countries saw Thomas's show, turning Lawrence of Arabia into an international celebrity.

Red politics menace Europe

Socialists and communists in many central European countries, inspired by the Bolsheviks of Russia and the uncertain political situation created by defeat in the First World War, attempted to establish revolutionary regimes of their own. The biggest outbreak came in Germany where in Berlin in January 1919, the Spartacist League attempted to overthrow the Social Democratic government of Friedrich Ebert. This revolt was suppressed by using right-wing militia of former soldiers to re-establish order, in part through the murder of Spartacist leaders. A similar revolt in Bavaria attempted to establish an independent Bavarian Soviet Republic in April 1919, but this too was suppressed in ferocious street fighting in May. The most successful of these revolutions occurred in Hungary, where a Soviet government was formed on 21 March 1919, after the Hungarian president requested the Social Democratic Party to form a government. The new government promptly established a new republic and dismissed the president. However, a coup attempt in June led to mass executions, while the Rumanian army invaded and defeated the Hungarian forces in a battle outside Budapest in August. The soviet leaders fled, and the Rumanians re-established the old republican regime, which lasted until March 1920.

A German Freikorps (Volunteer) unit during street fighting against socialists.

Crisis in the Russian Civil War

The **Russian Civil** War passed through its crisis during 1919 when White armies threatened Moscow and Petrograd in a crucial campaign for the Bolshevik government.

At the end of December 1918, Kolchak's forces in Siberia succeeded in capturing Perm, an important railway centre north of Kazan. This victory was seen as a sign that the Red victories of autumn were only a temporary setback and a major offensive was launched in the spring. Kolchak's forces launched three armies in the general direction of Moscow in March and made rapid advances for about a month. The Red armies held the Whites through April and May before going on the attack, and by July Kolchak's army was in a retreat that would turn into a rout within a month. Omsk was captured by Red forces on 14 November.

A worse threat was posed to the Bolsheviks by the White forces in southern Russia and in the Baltic states. However, in the absence of a co-ordinating authority for the Whites, Denikin was unable to attack at the same time as Kolchak. He achieved tremendous success, after winning a key victory on 19–21 May in the Ukraine at Velikokhazherskaya. On 30 August Denikin's forces captured Kiev, and by 15 October had taken Orel and was on the brink of capturing Tula. The Bolshevik politburo met that day and decreed that Denikin's forces were the main objective for the Red army. Five days later, the Red Army's counterblow hit an outnumbered army that was worn out by nearly two years of campaigning, outflanked and forced Denikin to order a retreat. On 11 November, the Bolshevik 1st Cavalry Army defeated Denikin's cossacks at Kastornaya, the first time the Reds had got the upper hand on the White cavalry. By the end of the year, Denikin was pondering whether to withdraw to the Kuban or the Crimea to make a final stand.

A poster calling on Russian workers, soldiers, and sailors to help defend the revolution in Petrograd. The Bolshevik government effectively mobilized their territories.

British attack Kronstadt

British coastal motor boats carrying torpedoes attacked the Bolshevik Baltic fleet at its base at Kronstadt on 17 August 1919 in a daring raid. A total of eight boats took part in the raid and they succeeded in passing through the chain of forts guarding the harbour entrance before manoeuvring under heavy fire in the relatively narrow space available. Their torpedoes sank or damaged four ships in total, two of them battleships, and effectively put the Bolshevik fleet out of the war between Whites and Reds in the Baltic states. The Royal Navy lost three boats, fifteen men killed and nine captured.

Polish offensive pushes border east

At the end of 1919, the eastern border of Poland stood on a line roughly from the Daugava river in the north to the Dniester river in the south, running along a line to the east of Minsk. Most of this land had been occupied by the Polish army on the order of Jozef Pilsudski, the army's commander, taking advantage

Skirmishing between Polish and Bolshevik forces took place in February 1919, and Polish forces were also engaged with Ukrainian nationalists.

of anti-Bolshevik sentiment in the region as well as the Bolsheviks' need to counter the White armies advancing on Moscow and Petrograd.

Skirmishing between Polish and Bolshevik forces took place in February 1919, and Polish forces were also engaged with Ukrainian nationalists trying to secure the area around Lwow for the Ukraine. The fighting against the Ukrainians ended in July.

Miracle on the Vistula

A Bolshevik offensive that carried their armies to within 12 miles (19 km) of Warsaw was defeated by Polish forces, whose counter-attack eventually forced an armistice between Poland and the Bolshevik government of Russia.

The war between the Bolsheviks and Poland had been in abeyance for about a year when the Poles renewed it by attacking in the Ukraine in April 1920. Their objective was to create an independent Ukraine that would be an ally of Poland against the government in Moscow. Polish forces managed to capture Kiev on 7 May, but all this territorial success had done nothing to affect the fighting power of the Bolshevik armies. When the Bolshevik counter-attack came, it swept the Poles back across the Ukraine and into Poland.

The Battle of Warsaw, fought between 13 and 25 August, was decisive. The Polish forces first pinned the main Bolshevik attack, while Polish forces struck at the areas of the Bolshevik line where the boundaries between army groups stood. The Poles had the advantage that their plan took perfect advantage of the drawbacks in the Bolshevik plan, which

envisaged sweeping moves north and south of Warsaw attempting to encircle the Polish armies, as well as a diversion from the main Bolshevik effort by troops attacking Lwow. The "miracle on the Vistula" as it became known forced the retreat of the Bolshevik forces from Poland. A ceasefire was agreed in October 1920, and the war came to an end.

BOLSHEVIK RUSSIA VS POLAND WAR

DATES:	February 1919–October 1920
COMBATANTS:	Bolshevik Russia vs Poland and Ukrainian nationalists
CASUALTIES:	Bolshevik Russia, 160,000 (1920 only); Poland, 250,000
RESULT:	Polish victory

Soldiers of the Legion of Polish Women fought in defence of Warsaw during the Bolshevik attack of 1920. The Polish counteroffensive not only halted the Red Army's attack, but drove them back eastwards.

British armoured cars and an aircraft in the mandated territory of Iraq. The British made extensive use of aircraft against the Arab rebels to save the cost of a full-scale occupation.

Revolt in Mesopotamia

The rebellion against the new British mandate over three former areas of the Ottoman empire – given the name Iraq by the British – was finally brought under control in October 1920. The main centre of the rebellion was around Karbala and Ar Ramadi, to the west of Baghdad, which at one point was effectively under Arab control. A second major centre of revolt lay in the north, around Mosul. British operations against the irregular forces of the rebels included the indiscriminate bombing of villages believed to harbour supporters of the Arab nationalist forces, as well as the use of chemical weapons.

The end of the Whites

White forces have largely been crushed by Bolshevik Reds in Russia's long civil war. The evacuation of White forces from the Crimea on 14 November 1920 marked the end of any serious resistance to the Bolshevik government by supporters of either the old tsarist regime or its successor Provisional Government. Admiral Alexander Kolchak, at one time the Supreme Ruler, was handed over to the Reds in January 1920 by the Czechoslovak Legion, after a coup had toppled him from power. He was shot on 7 February 1920. The Whites and associated Allied forces in northern Russia were withdrawn from Murmansk and Archangel in the same month, and American troops left Siberia with the Czechoslovak Legion in April 1920. Only in the Crimea did the remnants of Denikin's forces and the Volunteer Army hold out, now commanded by General Peter Wrangel. During the Polish-Bolshevik campaigning of 1920, Wrangel launched an attack north, but his forces no longer had the strength to sustain an advance even with the bulk of the Red army engaged elsewhere. After the ceasefire between the Poles and the Bolsheviks, Wrangel was forced back into the Crimea, and eventually his forces were evacuated by the French and British navies.

General Peter Wrangel joined the anti-Bolshevik White movement at its start, but failed in his attempts to make it appealing to the Russian masses, as opposed to the rich and the officers.

British troops on the streets of Dublin. The war was an ugly one of betrayals, bombs, arson and street assassinations often carried out by men not in uniform.

Ireland achieves independence

The **treaty establishing** the Irish Free State was signed on 6 December 1921. After three years of an unpleasant war of terror versus counter-terror, the Irish Republican Army had withstood every effort of the British administration in Ireland to suppress them, and exhausted the patience of the London government to continue.

The key to the Irish success lay in the intelligence strategy organized by Michael Collins, who used any means he could to get people with access to information about British plans to reveal them to the Irish republicans. Collins's network included members of the Royal Irish Constabulary, eavesdroppers in pubs or restaurants and infiltrators in the Irish administrative apparatus at Dublin Castle. Collins preferred that people gave information voluntarily, but he also used bribery or blackmail to learn about British plans.

The military campaign involved assassinations and raids, targeting the police and the postal services in 1920. By August, the mail in Ireland had virtually come to a standstill.

Collins's greatest success came on 21 November 1920 when twelve members of the "Cairo gang", intelligence specialists brought in from Egypt where they had been successful against nationalist conspirators, were assassinated. Raids were conducted by active service units who conducted hit-and-run ambushes wherever they could isolate small numbers of British soldiers. Most worryingly for the British was the constant growth of the Irish Republican Army – nothing that they tried could halt the enthusiasm the Irish had for independence. The main British response, the Black and Tans, former English soldiers who were recruited into the Royal Irish Constabulary, was simply a terror force intended to intimidate the Irish into submission. The Black and Tans' most notorious reprisal was "Bloody Sunday", when machine guns were used against a crowd watching a football match in November 1920 after the Cairo gang operation – eleven were killed and eleven wounded. At the same time, parts of Cork were burned. The British government accepted the result of the May 1921 parliamentary elections as a sign that the war could not be won, and agreed a ceasefire in July 1921.

IN BRIEF

◦❧ In July 1920, fighting in China between the Japanese-supported Tuan Ch'i-jui and rival warlords led by Ts'ao K'un, ended in a victory for Ts'ao K'un and his associates.

◦❧ French troops invading Syria defeated an Arab force at the Battle of Maysalun on 23 July 1920. The Arabs were attempting to create a kingdom ruled by King Faisal, the de facto leader of the First World War's Arab Revolt against the Turks. The French had established an independent Lebanese republic under their protection, which the Arabs did not recognize. The French, in turn, were awarded a League of Nations mandate over Syria, which the Arabs also did not accept.

Warlords fall out again

The military men who dominate China's search for a stable central government have fallen into fighting amongst themselves again after the Washington Naval Conference threatened to hand more power over Shantung's railways to the Japanese, to the outrage of Chinese nationalists. The nationalists demanded the resignation of the government, which was supported by Chang Tso-lin, while Ts'ao K'un and Wu Peifu supported the nationalist position. On 28 April 1922, fighting broke out that ended in the defeat of Chang Tso-lin by Ts'ao K'un, Wu Peifu and their new ally Feng Yü-hsiang. Fighting was much heavier than in 1920, although Wu Peifu's skilful handling of his forces ensured victory for his faction. Chang Tso-lin retreated from Peking to his base in Manchuria, which he now declared to be independent.

Troops of the Irish Free State army with artillery pieces aimed at the Dublin Four Courts building which had been occupied by opponents to the treaty with Britain that had ended the War of Independence.

A war for thirty-two counties

Conflict between factions of the Irish nationalists, who recently won dominion status after a two-year conflict against the British, began in June 1922, when anti-treaty republicans seized the Four Courts building in Dublin. The anti-treaty faction opposes the agreement on many grounds, including the loss of six northern counties remaining under British rule, the continued use of a royal seal and oath of loyalty to the British monarch taken by Irish parliamentarians. The British put pressure on the Irish Free State to suppress these irregulars, supplying artillery to the Free State to help. The Four Courts were bombarded and the republicans there surrendered on 30 June, while fighting went on in the rest of Dublin until the new Irish National Army drove them out.

OBITUARY
ERICH VON FALKENHAYN (1861-1922)

Erich von Falkenhayn died in Potsdam on 8 April 1922. He was 60.

Von Falkenhayn joined the German army and participated in the Boxer Rebellion. In 1913, he was appointed Prussian Minister of War. After the failure of the German attack in France in September 1914, von Falkenhayn was appointed Chief of the German General Staff, in effect commander-in-chief.

Von Falkenhayn believed the War required a new tactical approach, one which emphasized the use of artillery, and defensive measures generally. Offensive action was only intended to create situations in which the enemy was forced to counter-attack, exposing themselves to the German guns. Verdun, the battle of attrition he launched against the French in February 1916, was intended to be a model of this, but his commanders in the field misunderstood his wishes and mishandled the battle, causing far heavier German casualties than von Falkenhayn anticipated.

He was removed from his post in August 1916, and afterwards served in the Balkans in the Near East and on the Eastern Front before he retired in 1919.

Atrocities follow Turkish victory over Greeks

Greek forces were driven out of Asia Minor in disorder in September 1922 after their defeat at the hands of Turkish nationalists. The Greeks had been awarded Smyrna and an area of the hinterland around the port under the Treaty of Sèvres, signed in August 1920, by the representatives of the Ottoman sultan. The sultan's rule was at an end, though, as Turkish nationalist republicans assembled in Ankara and rejected the treaty, as well as setting up a government of their own. The Greek government believed that an attack toward Ankara would destroy the republican movement and allow the treaty to take effect, so at the end of March 1921 a Greek army began marching inland from Smyrna, initially forcing the Turks to retreat. However, the Turkish commander, Mustapha Kemal, who had made his military reputation during the Dardanelles

campaign and also fighting the Russians in the Caucasus during the First World War, waited until the Greeks were at the end of a long supply line which could be attacked by irregular forces, then blocked the Greek advance some 60 miles (96 km) from Ankara, at the Sakharia river. On 23 August the Greeks attacked and suffered heavy casualties as they were defeated, forcing them to retreat on 13 September 1921 to a position closer to Smyrna. Mustapha Kemal waited a year to strengthen his army before attacking the Greeks on 26 August at Afyonkarahisar. On the second day of the battle, the Greeks broke and fled back to Smyrna, where they were evacuated in chaos. The Turks arrived on 9 September 1922 and burnt large parts of the town, killing most of the Greek population who had lived there for centuries, while the small number of survivors of the massacre fled.

Smyrna burns as the Turks reoccupy it in 1922. The Greeks of Asia Minor were mostly killed or evicted in the closing stages of the Greco-Turkish war.

The IRA puts down its arms

Civil war in Ireland finally came to an end on 24 May 1923, when the leaders of the Irish Republican Army ordered their men to put down their arms and return to their homes.

The IRA had begun its war in Dublin in June 1922. Defeated there, the republicans continued the fight largely in the south and west of Ireland, using guerrilla tactics of hit and run which had proved successful against the British. Their most successful coup

The IRA had begun its war in Dublin in June 1922. Defeated there, the republicans continued the fight largely in the south and west of Ireland, using guerrilla tactics of hit and run which had proved successful against the British.

was perhaps the killing of Michael Collins, mastermind of the war against the British, in an ambush in Cork on 22 August 1922.

However, what had worked against an occupying power failed against the provisional Irish Free State government. The government's ferocious policy of executing many republicans captured with arms was answered by republican assassinations of parliamentarians who had voted in favour of the law.

The majority of Irish people were tired of war, having just survived the three-year conflict with the British, and were happy with the partial independence they had received, and the republicans found little of the support that had been crucial to their success in the war against the British. At least 3,000 Irish lost their lives in the war.

Christian warlord changes balance of power in China

Chinese nationalists protest against the unequal treaties between China and the Western Powers, as well as the corrupt administrations propped up by Western states and Japan in Peking.

In 1924, fighting between Kiangsu and Chekiang became a war between the warlords Wu Peifu in Peking and Chang Tso-lin in Manchuria. Wu was expected to win easily, but one of his generals, Feng Yü-hsiang, defected to Chang on 30 September 1924, changing the balance of power. Feng was able to occupy Peking on 23 October and appealed to the Chinese Nationalist Party (or Kuomintang) for help. The Nationalist Party had mobilized the anti-Western, yet socialistic spirit of the May Fourth Movement that had emerged during the negotiations leading to the Versailles Treaty of 1919. The Nationalists had established a government in the south claiming to be the actual government of all China, and were supplied with weapons and other military assistance from the Soviet Union. In November, Feng dismissed the president of China, former warlord Ts'ao K'un, and Chang Tso-lin became the de facto ruler of Peking and China. Feng brought out of retirement Tuan Ch'i-jui, who had been Chinese prime minister from 1916 to 1919, and patron of many of the warlords now struggling for mastery of the Chinese Republic.

WAR CELEBRITY
BENITO MUSSOLINI

Benito Mussolini, who was granted dictatorial powers in Italy on 3 January 1925, is a veteran of trench warfare on the Isonzo Front. He began his political life as a socialist, espousing a revolutionary Marxist creed. However, he was an early supporter of Italian entry into the war, and as editor of the newspaper *Il Popolo d'Italia*, promoted a mixture of syndicalist pro-trade union politics and intervention in the war.

Mussolini was drafted into the Italian army and sent to fight on the Isonzo, but in 1917, he was badly wounded in grenade practice and invalided out of the forces. On 23 March 1919 he founded a new political movement, the Fasci di Combattimento. The title "fasci" referred to the fasces, symbols of the power over life and death held by the consuls of the ancient Roman republic. The Fascists attracted many veterans to their ranks, who formed "combat squads" to intimidate leftists. Mussolini's party consequently began to gain support from rich Italians who sought a vigorous opposition to "subversion".

In 1922, Mussolini proclaimed his intention to seize power. Rather than appoint a Socialist prime minister to confront the Fascists, King Victor Emmanuel III offered Mussolini the office. Mussolini, supported by many democratic politicians, quickly established an oppressive regime, and the murder of socialist Giacomo Matteotti by Fascists in 1924 gave a stark warning to all left-wing opponents of their likely fate if they caused trouble.

Spanish artillery during operations against Abd el-Krim, the Rifian leader of a resistance movement seeking to establish an independent state in the mountains of Morocco.

French help Spaniards beat rebels

Spanish and French troops brought to an end the six-year conflict with Moroccan Rifi and Jibala tribesmen when, on 19 July 1927, the 7th Bandera of the Spanish Foreign Legion occupied Bab Tazza, south of the Spanish-held city of Tetuán.

The origins of the war lay in the determination of Abd el-Krim, a Rifi who once worked for the Spanish administration of Spanish Morocco, to create an independent republic for the tribesmen. He had been imprisoned by the Spaniards in 1917, escaped in 1919, and spent two years working to unite the tribes against the Spaniards. On 1 June 1921, a Spanish armed force pursuing a local brigand who had been pillaging Spanish military supply convoys since March 1919 established a military post of 250 men across the Amekran river at Abarrán. Having warned the Spaniards not to cross the river, Abd el-Krim sent a force against it and virtually wiped it out, killing 179 of the garrison. In July, General Francisco Silvestre advanced to Annual to challenge Abd el-Krim but constant sniping prompted Silvestre to order a withdrawal on 22 July, at which point Abd el-Krim ordered an attack. For five days the Rifi harried the Spanish column until it was wiped out and 12,000 Spaniards killed. The survivors escaped to Monte Arruit where they were besieged until they surrendered on 9 August, at which point many were massacred in spite of having been granted terms.

The war turned into a typical guerrilla combat of blockhouses and raids until April 1925, when Abd el-Krim rashly attacked French troops on the Algerian border. The French joined the Spanish in sending a massive army into the Rif, using tanks, aeroplanes and mustard gas against the enemy. Abd el-Krim surrendered in May 1926 after a year of being pursued. With his capture, the conquest of the rest of the Rif was only a matter of time.

Chinese warlords agree to Nationalist rule

A Chinese man faces execution at the hands of soldiers belonging to one of the Warlord armies that have divided China.

Chiang Kai-shek established a national authority over all of China for the first time since 1917, when his government was recognized by China's warlords in October 1928.

The delicate balance established at the end of 1924 between the various warlords and claimants to national authority over China was upset by the death in 1925 of the Nationalist leader, Sun Yat-sen. On 22 November 1925, war broke out between Feng Yü-hsiang and the master of Manchuria, Chang Tso-lin. Wu Peifu, the former northern faction leader now based in Hupei province in the centre of the country, joined with Chang to defeat Feng. Feng had been receiving aid from the Soviet Union, which was at the same time supplying the Nationalist forces. Feng and the Nationalists now combined against the common enemy, the Chang-Wu faction. Once the Nationalists had built up their army, they launched the Northern Expedition from Canton

in July 1926. The advancing armies rapidly gained control of all of southern China, including, by March 1927, the great port of Shanghai, as well as key cities such as Hankow and Nanking. However, at this point, Chiang Kai-shek, who had replaced Sun as leader

The advance on Peking resumed in March 1928, and after some see-saw fighting to the east, Chang admitted defeat and withdrew back to his Manchurian base.

of the Nationalists, broke with the Soviet Union. He now confronted all the rival warlords, including Feng, Chang and Wu. The advance on Peking resumed in March 1928, and after some see-saw fighting to the east, Chang admitted defeat and withdrew back to his Manchurian base. Chang was assassinated by the Japanese in June, and in October, Chiang established his Nationalist government, which brought the twisting tale of Chinese civil wars to an end.

OBITUARY

THE FIRST EARL HAIG
(1861-1928)

Field Marshal Earl Douglas Haig, the commander of the British Expeditionary Force in France during 1916-18 died on 28 February 1928, aged 66.

Haig was a member of the famous whiskey distilling family of the same name. He served with Kitchener in the Sudan in 1898, and in the Boer War. When war broke out in August 1914, he became commander of the British Expeditionary Force's I Corps. During 1915, he campaigned against his commander, Field Marshal Sir John French, continuing as commander of the force, and sought to replace

him. In December 1915, French was removed and Haig became commander.

Haig's term as commander was marked both by disaster and victory. The heavy casualties experienced by the British on the Western Front under his command overshadowed his willingness to innovate and learn from his experiences. He kept the pressure on the German army throughout 1916 and 1917, and deserves some credit for using the tank and for developing the excellent gunnery capability of his army.

After the war, he worked hard to raise funds for ex-servicemen in need and many of his former soldiers mourn his passing. He is survived by his wife, three daughters and one son.

Viva Cristo el Rey

A **negotiated settlement** brokered by the American ambassador to Mexico, Dwight Whitney Morrow, brought to an end the three-year uprising against anti-clerical laws in Mexico on 21 June 1929.

The Cristero Revolt was a reaction to laws signed by Mexican President Plutarco Elías Calles in June 1926 that imposed penalties on priests for speaking against the revolutionary government of Mexico. Initially, the Catholic Church organized boycotts, suspended religious services and lobbied for the amendment of the Mexican constitution to remove its anti-clerical articles. On 3 August, however, a shootout took place between Mexican soldiers and Catholics who had barricaded themselves in a church in Guadalajara. In September, several individual groups of landowners and civic officials declared themselves to be in rebellion, while a group organized by the Mexican Association of Catholic Youth did the same on 1 January 1927.

The rebellion was focused in the states of Jalisco, Michoacán, Colima, Guanajuato and Zacatecas, and featured a range of curious characters including two priests who proved to be natural soldiers, and a cynical mercenary who was hired to command the "Cristero" forces. The fighting was largely between small bands of rebels using guerrilla tactics and the army or local militia, but occasionally the Cristeros would gather in larger forces to take on units of the army. In spite of having inferior weapons, the Cristeros achieved some success and by 1929 the rebellion appeared irrepressible, although not strong enough to defeat the government. However, sympathizers emerged in the army, and the government, now led by President Emilio Portes Gil, recognized the danger and began negotiations.

The Blessed Father Miguel Pro, a Jesuit priest, spreads his arms at the moment of his execution in November 1927. The Cristero War pitted traditionalist Mexicans against a government determined to create a secular republic.

Red Army victory in Manchuria

The Soviet Union has defeated China in a war that showed the Red Army to be an efficient fighting force. On 26 November 1929, the day before Harbin fell to the Red Army, the Chinese warlord in Manchuria, against the wishes of the Nationalist government in Peking, opened negotiations with the Soviet Union to end the war.

The war had ostensibly begun over the arrest of some Soviet consulate staff and visitors to the consulate at Harbin, Manchuria, on 27 May 1929. However, the real cause of the war was control of the Chinese Eastern Railway, a tsarist-era construction that the Soviet Union sought to retain, and which the Chinese Nationalist government wanted to bring under its control.

Negotiations ended when diplomatic relations were broken off on 16 August. The Soviets sent 100,000 of its best troops to various points along the Manchurian-Soviet border, while the Chinese warlord in control of the area, Chang Hsüeh-liang, mobilized his well-equipped forces, which included remnants of the White Russian Siberian army that fought the Soviet regime in the civil war. Soviet troops had already crossed the border on 12 August, seeking advantageous positions around key border cities such as Blagoverschensk and Manchouli, and fighting broke out around the latter city.

No major actions then occurred until 10 October when the Chinese floated mines down the Sungari river into the major trade artery of the Amur river, and also shelled Soviet shipping near Lahasusu, close to where the Sungari meets the Amur. Two days later the Red Army crossed the border in force and laid siege to Dongjiang and Lahasusu. A month later they launched a major assault on Manchouli, and destroyed one of the best Chinese units at Chalainor.

General Chang Hsüeh-liang (centre) fought the Soviet Union for control of the Chinese Eastern Railway, which ran through his fief of Manchuria.

WAR CELEBRITY
ERICH PAUL REMARK

Erich Paul Remark served in the front lines on the Western Front during the Great War. He had been drafted into the German army in 1916, aged 18, and after basic training went into action in June 1917. He was badly wounded by British shelling in November and spent the next ten months in hospital or convalescing. Returned to the army for garrison duties in October 1918, the war ended before he could be sent back to the front, and Remark resumed his studies for a teaching career.

In 1920, however, he published his first novel, and eventually found work in magazine publishing. In 1928, a novel based on his war experiences, *Im Westen nichts Neues*, was serialized in a magazine. Based on its popularity, it was published in book form in 1929, and sold a million copies in its first year in Germany. Translations published abroad sold another million, and a Hollywood film taking the book's English title, *All Quiet on the Western Front*, was released in April 1930. The film won the best film and best director Academy Awards.

Japanese seize three Manchurian provinces

The Kwantung Army, Japan's main military force in China, ended its offensive against Chinese forces in the north-east when it captured Harbin on 28 January 1932 at the request of the government in Tokyo. The three eastern provinces of Manchuria are now in Japanese hands.

The "Manchurian Incident" began on 18 September 1931 when a Japanese officer detonated explosives, damaging the train track near Beidaying, where 7,000 soldiers of Chinese warlord Chang Hsüeh-liang's army were stationed. The damage was superficial and a train successfully negotiated that part of the track moments after the explosion occurred, as observed by a Japanese patrol from the Kwantung Army, stationed along the railway, which was controlled by a Japanese company. However, fighting broke out between Japanese forces and the Chinese at Beidaying near Mukden.

Although only a small group of Japanese officers plotted the bombing, they relied on the fact that after fighting broke out the rest of the Kwantung Army would respond in self-defence to reports of attack by Chinese forces. Reinforcements arrived from Korea, and troops across Manchuria carried out a pre-determined offensive. The Chinese, however, were under instructions from the Nationalist government in Nanking not to resist. Where fighting did occur, it arose in situations where word did not get through to Chinese forces, or where their officers chose not to obey the command. Consequently, the Japanese easily conquered the provinces of Heilongjiang, Chi-lin and Liaoning.

Japanese mounted infantry in a Chinese city. The Japanese found the conquest of Manchuria an easy task, after Chinese leader Chiang Kai-shek opted to avoid battle and rely on diplomacy to restore Chinese control in the end.

Chinese, Japanese clash at Shanghai

Partisan uprising in Peru

Mass executions at Chan Chan in northern Peru in July 1932 marked the end of an attempt to overthrow the government of President Luís Miguel Sánchez Cerro. The uprising had been under preparation ever since the defeat in the October 1931 presidential election of the candidate of the American Popular Revolutionary Alliance, Victor Raúl Haya de la Torre. His supporters (Apristas) believed they had been cheated of victory and rumours circulated for weeks before the inauguration of President Sánchez Cerro that the Apristas would stage an uprising using their sympathizers in the police and armed forces. Once Sánchez Cerro was in office, he moved against the Apristas, firing or reassigning those who held key postings.

Shanghai burns as Japanese forces launch an attack on the city. The Japanese were eventually forced to return the city to Chinese control, although they maintained a sizeable military and naval force in the area.

The uprising had been under preparation ever since the defeat in the October 1931 presidential election of the candidate of the American Popular Revolutionary Alliance (APRA, from its initials in Spanish), Victor Raú Haya de la Torre.

The Chinese army retreated on 3 March 1932 after a month-long battle with Japanese forces in and around Shanghai. The League of Nations called on both sides to stop fighting and dispatched a delegation to broker a negotiation.

The fighting was triggered by Japanese claims that a monk of theirs had been beaten up by Chinese students. This deed was part of a general anti-Japanese movement that had led to a boycott of Japanese goods in China over the invasion of Manchuria. The Japanese sent marines into action and street fighting began. Reinforcements arrived for both sides, with the Japanese sending aircraft carriers and other warships in addition to more marines and soldiers. Japanese superiority in aircraft and naval gunnery eventually gave their troops the decisive advantage, and the Chinese withdrew.

APRA members were subject to repressive laws and arrests, and after an assassination attempt in March 1932 against Sánchez Cerro, Haya de la Torre was imprisoned. On 7 July an uprising in Trujillo, in the north of Peru, resulted in the capture of the army barracks there. Sánchez Cerro sent aircraft as well as ships and soldiers to bomb and attack the rebels until they surrendered on 9 July. A handful of rebels escaped to begin a guerrilla campaign against the government, but most were captured and many subsequently shot.

Sandino ends his revolt

Augusto **Sandino agreed** to accept the presidency of Juan Bautista Sacasa of Nicaragua and to lay down his arms, in an agreement signed on 2 February 1933. The American military forces who had been fighting him for almost six years had already departed in January.

The mystical rebel leader emerged during the Constitutionalist War that broke out in Nicaragua in 1926, after an American-backed coup had installed a Conservative president over the claims of the Liberal Sacasa. Sandino allied with the Liberals, who seemed on the verge of winning the war in April 1927, but at this point, the Americans intervened and got the two sides to sign the Espino Negro accord. Sandino rejected this settlement and when American marines came to Nicaragua to enforce it, his subsequent attacks were directed against them.

Sandino attacked the properties of the Standard Fruit Company and gold mines funded by American investors, attempted to disrupt presidential elections in 1928 and 1932, and achieved a high degree of support from the indigenous peoples of Nicaragua. His early attempts to attack American military bases proved futile and were countered in one instance by the first systematic use of dive bombing tactics to support attacking troops by US Marine Corps aircraft at Ocotal in July 1927.

Augusto Sandino (centre) with two of his comrades. Sandino's guerrilla war against American influence in Nicaragua turned him into a hero to many in Latin America.

OBITUARY

HEIHACHIRO TOGO (1848-1934)

The Japanese admiral Heihachiro Togo, sometimes referred to as "the Nelson of the East", died on 30 May 1934 at the age of 86.

Togo was born in the city of Kagoshima, on the island of Kyushu in southern Japan. His father was of the samurai class. Togo was sent to Britain to study naval science in 1871, along with a number of other young Japanese sailors considered to have potential. After seven years, Togo returned to Japan.

He fought in the Sino-Japanese War of 1894–95, commanding the cruiser Naniwa, in which he sank the British-flagged steamer Kowshing, at a time when it was ferrying Chinese troops to Korea. In 1904-05, Togo commanded the Japanese fleet in the war against Russia, which earned him his reputation. He was successful against two Russian fleets, the Pacific Fleet in Port Arthur, and the Baltic Fleet which had sailed around the world only to face defeat at Tsushima.

He is survived by his wife, two sons and a daughter.

The bloody war for a desert

Wrecked Bolivian tanks in the Chaco region. The Bolivian government spent a substantial amount of money in its efforts to conquer the inhospitable Chaco in belief that substantial amounts of oil could be found.

The ceasefire agreed between Bolivia and Paraguay on 14 June 1935 has halted a three-year war over the Gran Chaco, an arid region between Bolivia and Paraguay valued by the latter for its crop of mate tea leaves, but thought by the former to contain a substantial quantity of oil. This potential drew the interest of the powerful Standard Oil Company of the United States, as well as the nation of Argentina, both of which have given assistance to the combatants.

Skirmishes between the two countries over control of the Gran Chaco had been going on since 1927. Then a pre-emptive attack was made by Paraguayan forces in September 1932. The target of the attack was a small fort named Boqueron, which was besieged and surrendered on 29 September 1932. The Bolivian army was badly weakened by the defeat, losing many of its most experienced troops. In January 1933, the conscripts drafted by the Bolivians after Boqueron went into action at Nanawa, a small fort held by Paraguay near the Pilcomayo river. The Bolivians came close to success, but after five days

of fighting gave up their attacks and settled for trench warfare that resembled a kind of mini Verdun. Skirmishing went on for months until a second assault on 5–6 July, including the exploding of an underground mine (that was 98 feet (30m) short of the enemy positions) and the use of tanks, failed. On 11 July a Paraguayan counter-attack drove the Bolivians out of their trenches and ended the siege of Nanawa.

After the victories at Boqueron and Nanawa, the Paraguayans went on the offensive, having constructed several roads through the Chaco in order to bring precious water more easily to the men at the front. At the beginning of December, Paraguayan forces slipped around the Bolivian flanks at Campo Via, and on 11 December two Bolivian divisions surrendered. When the offensive ended on 19 December, the Paraguayans had occupied about half the Chaco.

Paraguayan successes continued through 1934, and only in 1935 did the Bolivians halt their advance. Both of these poor countries could ill afford to fight such a war, which cost the lives of 100,000 soldiers.

Italians conquer Ethiopia

On 9 May 1936, Italian king Vittorio Emmanuel III was proclaimed emperor of Ethiopia in a ceremony that marked the annexation of one of the two remaining independent African states to European empires. The war had pitted the aircraft and armour of the Italians against the technologically inferior Ethiopian army, which had little chance, especially after the Italians deployed gas.

A dispute between the two countries had arisen in 1934, over the oasis at Walwal in the Ogaden. In December, skirmishes resulted in 200 casualties in total between the two sides, and the matter came before the League of Nations in Geneva. In September 1935, the League refused to declare either party guilty of provoking the conflict. Italian dictator Benito Mussolini at this point decided to risk League sanctions, and sent massive reinforcements to the Italian colony of Eritrea, to the north of Ethiopia.

In October, the Italians invaded. Their advance was slow, but the hapless Ethiopian army had no answer to the machine guns and heavy artillery of the Italians, let alone more advanced weapons, and Ethiopian assaults were fruitless. Addis Ababa was occupied on 5 May 1936, three days after Haile Selassie fled into exile. League sanctions proved inadequate to halt Mussolini, who in any case was being courted by the French and British governments fearing the rise of German military power under Adolf Hitler.

Italian tankettes and infantry on the advance in Ethiopia.

Red Army bloodies Japanese noses

Soviet strategic bombers in flight. The disputed Soviet-Korean border triggered the clash between Japan and the Soviet Union in 1938.

A division-sized battle between the Soviet Red Army and the Japanese Kwantung army ended in a decisive victory for the former when the Japanese requested an end to hostilities on 10 August 1938. The Japanese attacked Soviet forces on the Shachofeng and Changkufeng

The Japanese attacked Soviet forces on the Shachofeng and Changkufeng heights near the Soviet-Korean border. The Red Army reinforced the defenders with tanks and mechanized units, and both sides used aircraft.

heights near the Soviet-Korean border. The Red Army reinforced the defenders with tanks and mechanized units, and both sides used aircraft. Eventually the Japanese were repelled. Although the Japanese withdrew, after suffering 1,200 casualties, the Red Army had suffered comparable losses.

OBITUARY

ERICH LUDENDORFF
(1865-1937)

General Erich Ludendorff, the mastermind of many German offensives during the First World War, has died in Bavaria at the age of 72.

Ludendorff had been an efficient staff officer in the pre-war German army, and played a key role on both the Western and Eastern Fronts in August and September 1914. The tremendous German successes on the Eastern Front in 1915, combined with failures in the West in 1916, to see Ludendorff and General Paul von Hindenburg put in supreme command in August 1916. Germany knocked Russia

out of the war in 1917, then Ludendorff organized the major German offensives of spring 1918 which, in the absence of American reinforcements, might have forced Britain or France to negotiate.

After the war, Ludendorff promoted the idea that the German army was "stabbed in the back" by the politicians at home, and could still have fought the Allies to a standstill in 1918. In 1923 he participated in the attempt to overthrow the German government by the National Socialist German Workers Party, and served as a deputy in the Reichstag, as well as running for president against von Hindenburg. He retired from public life in 1928.

The Civil War in Spain

The army uprising of 18 July 1936 marked the visible challenge to constitutional government in Spain by those rejecting the results of the February election. However, the plotting had begun in the days after the vote was held on 16 February, and received serious impetus when the President of the Spanish republic, Niceto Alcalá Zamora, was removed from office by the parliament. Alcalá Zamora had been removed quite legitimately by the letter of the constitution, but in conjunction with other policies of the leftist majority, it looked to conservatives as if the intention was to overthrow the constitutional order and institute a Soviet regime in Spain.

Members of the XV International Brigade on parade in a Spanish town. The XV brigade included volunteers from Britain, the Balkans, Belgium, France and the United States.

The leading conspirator was General José Sanjurjo Sacanell, and the murder of José Calvo Sotelo, a conservative, on 13 July led him to put his plans into effect. Rebellions occurred across Spain, including the key cities of Madrid, Barcelona, Seville, Cádiz, Jerez de la Frontera, Córdoba, Zaragoza and Oviedo, but the uprisings in Madrid and Barcelona

> Rebellions occurred across Spain, including the key cities of Madrid, Barcelona, Seville, Cádiz, Jerez de la Frontera, Córdoba, Zaragoza and Oviedo, but the uprisings in Madrid and Barcelona failed.

failed. The fighting at Barcelona was the heaviest of the day where paramilitary police and armed workers' militia defeated an attempt to seize the city. Similarly, in Madrid, armed workers combined with loyal artillery and air force units to overcome the rebels, who had taken refuge in the main barracks. However, the rebels ended up controlling a vast swathe of northern Spain and the south-western corner of Andalucia. Isolated outposts of rebel control were at Granada and in the Alcázar of Toledo.

Both sides were ruthless in the slaughter of their opponents. The Nationalists, as the rebels became known, were particularly thorough in settling old scores with leftists in the regions under their control, but in loyalist Spain workers pillaged convents, monasteries and churches, even to the point of tipping the bodies of the dead out into the street. Many priests were killed, but so were civilians of conservative political views, regardless of whether they were rich or poor.

Rebels on the march

The initial phase of the war saw the rebels trying to expand the area under their control, while the government attempted to organize its scattered forces into a coherent army capable of halting the advancing enemy. A substantial portion of the Army of Africa was ferried over the Strait of Gibraltar in German and Italian aircraft loaned to the rebels by the sympathetic leaders of those dictatorships. Ships also carried reinforcements, and soon rebel columns were advancing from Seville, approaching Madrid from the west. On 28 September, the garrison of the Alcazar was relieved when Toledo, on one of the main roads from the south to Madrid, was captured by the Nationalists.

Meanwhile, in the north, the rebels sought to capture the towns of San Sebastian and Irún. The intent was to seal off the border here from France, which would prevent arms reaching the one area in the north still in loyal hands, the Basque country. On 13 September, San Sebastian fell to the Nationalists.

The Nationalists' "final assault" on Madrid began on 7 October 1936. Nationalist commanders expected the same easy victories over Republican militia that had been won since July. In fact, the

The ruins of Guernica. The Basque town was bombed in April 1937 by German aircraft with the intention of destroying the town completely.

A Republican soldier throws a grenade. The majority of the Spanish army in Spain sided with the Republican government.

Republicans had learned from their mistakes – this time militia units did not retreat at the first bombardment or assault and slowed the rebel advance. Once arms from the Soviet Union, especially tanks and aircraft, began to reach the front in some quantity, the tide began to turn. It took a major assault in November, using all the resources the Nationalists could spare from all fronts, to reach the suburbs of Madrid, and even here the Republicans' stout defence prevented the fall of the city.

Army of Africa

In spite of their apparent success, gaining control of half the country, the Nationalists' owed everything to the support they had received from Nazi Germany and Fascist Italy. The Army of Africa had been crucial in gaining control of the south-west, and the rebels would probably have found it impossible to transport them without German and Italian aircraft. By contrast the Republicans quickly found themselves the victim of an arms boycott that was intended to affect both sides, but in fact only worked against the Republic. Only the Soviet Union was willing to give them arms and charged a high price for them. Supporters of the Republic from abroad were more readily available, and the International Brigades were key shock troops in 1936–37, until casualties took their toll on the units' effectiveness.

"Volunteers" from Germany and Italy also joined the rebels, although many were military personnel under orders. The Italian dictator Mussolini was particularly keen to see Italians play an important role in a rebel victory, and virtually forced the rebel leader, General Francisco Franco y Bahamonde, to use them in an attack toward Guadalajara. The Italians were badly beaten in this battle, in March 1937, following an earlier rebel defeat in the Jarama valley, in February. With more and more Soviet arms reaching the Republic, and the rebels apparently stalemated, it looked as if the government was likely to win the war.

Franco shifted his strategy to conquering those industrial cities of the north that still held out for the Republic. Chief among them was Bilbao, capital of the Basque region. The rebels' plans for a post-war Spain did not concede the degree of autonomy that the Basques, who linguistically were not Spanish-speaking, had gained from the Republic. Hence, in spite of their moderate politics and Catholic faith, they were staunch Republicans. On 26 April 1937, the Condor Legion, Franco's German air force, bombed the Basque town of Guernica, virtually obliterating it, in the hope of intimidating the Basques. The gesture had the opposite effect and Bilbao did not fall until July, largely owing to the superior artillery and air power of the rebels. Santander, another important northern city, fell to the rebels in August.

Republican attacks

By the summer of 1937, the Republicans had finally trained a large enough army to attack the rebels. The results in two offensives were the same, as officers' inexperience hampered initial successes, and gains were quickly reversed by the arrival of rebel reinforcements. A desperate winter battle for Teruel ended with little actual change in the front, although the town changed hands twice.

By the spring of 1938, the tide of battle was now running definitely in favour of the rebels. The last gamble of the Republic came in the fierce battle of the Ebro, from 24 July to 18 November. At this stage, the Republicans' one hope was to hang on long enough for the war between Germany and Britain and France that seemed inevitable. They would surely then

> By the spring of 1938, the tide of battle was now running definitely in favour of the rebels. The last gamble of the Republic came in the fierce battle of the Ebro, from 24 July to 16 November.

receive the aid needed to defeat the rebels. The offensive had as much a political objective in demonstrating the continued viability of the Republican war effort as a military operation, designed to reverse the steady rebel advance. However, the attacks ended in failure, as Franco reinforced the threatened areas and then recovered all the lost ground. Barcelona fell to the rebels on 26 January 1939 and Madrid surrendered on 28 March, bringing the war to an end.

General von Richthofen directs the gaze of a German observation post. He was commander of the Condor Legion, the German air and tank force sent to Spain to fight with the Nationalists.

Poland overrun by Germans, Soviets

The **German dictator**, Adolf Hitler, was finally forced to fight when Poland refused to accept an ultimatum. Hitler had demanded an extra-territorial road through Polish territory separating East Prussia from the rest of Germany, as well as the German annexation of the Free City of Danzig. The Poles rejected this in March 1939, and Hitler waited until August 1939 before launching a military attack to secure his goals.

The German army crossed the Polish border in force on 1 September 1939, with three main axes of attack: from East Prussia toward Warsaw, from north-eastern Germany towards the Vistula, and the main attack from Upper Silesia. The mobilization of Polish forces was incomplete at the time of the attack,

and the Polish defensive plan was based on the assumption that Poland's allies France and Britain would mount a rapid attack on Germany's western border. In the event this did not occur and the Polish army was consequently poorly positioned to sustain a long campaign against the Germans.

Once the Soviet Union, which had signed an alliance with Germany a week before the attack, invaded Poland on 17 September, the Poles had no hope of holding out even in the south-eastern corner of the country, where Polish generals had hoped to make a stand against the Germans. The capital, Warsaw, fell on 27 September and the last large formation of the Polish army, Independent Operational Group Polesie, surrendered on 6 October.

A German motorized column on the move through a Polish village. The German superiority in modern military equipment, especially radios, was decisive in the war against the Poles.

Soviets, Japanese skirmish in Mongolia

The **Red Army** inflicted a major defeat on Japanese forces in a border dispute along the river Halha in Outer Mongolia that ended on 16 September 1939 with a ceasefire. The campaign began in May when Japanese and Mongolian troops clashed along the river, followed by subsequent fighting

The campaign began in May when Japanese and Mongolian troops clashed along the river Halha, followed by subsequent fighting between the Red Army and the Japanese.

between the Red Army and the Japanese. The Japanese decided to launch a major offensive on 1 July.

Japanese forces assembled east of the river, then crossed it in force driving back the Red Army. However, the Red Army general commanding, Georgi Zhukov, used a tank attack unsupported by infantry to halt the Japanese, who were forced to withdraw because of their inability to support their troops. Skirmishing and patrolling followed for about three weeks while the Japanese brought up reinforcements. Their artillery was no match for that of the Soviets as the offensive stalled again, and a war of attrition began as the Red Army reinforced its forces with tanks and mechanized troops.

The Red Army's attack on 20 August was strongly contested by the Japanese, but the commanding general mistook the main point of the assault and reinforced the wrong sector of the line, allowing the Soviets to make an easy breakthrough that led to the encirclement of an entire Japanese division. Some Japanese soldiers fought their way out of the pocket, but most were killed or wounded.

German naval defeat off South America

The German pocket battleship *Graf Spee* was scuttled by its commander in the estuary of the River Plate on 17 December 1939, four days after a battle between her and British warships. The *Graf Spee* was at sea at the time of the declaration of war on 3 September and in the three months that followed had sunk nine merchant vessels. On 13 December, the *Graf Spee* was located off the River Plate estuary by three Royal Navy cruisers. In a naval battle lasting about an hour and a half, the *Graf Spee* succeeded in badly damaging the British cruiser HMS *Exeter*, but suffered light damage herself and took refuge in Montevideo, Uruguay. Here, her captain, Hans Langsdorff, concluded that the British were massing a large fleet outside and chose to scuttle his ship rather than risk heavy loss of life to no military purpose. In fact, he was a victim of a masterful deception plan and committed suicide on 19 December.

The Graf Spee burns in the River Plate. Clever deception measures convinced German Captain Langsdorff that a much stronger British squadron awaited him than was actually the case.

Plucky Finns halt Red Army

An attempt by the Soviet Union to compel Finland to surrender territory resulted in a disastrous showing by the Red Army in a winter campaign. After the Finns rejected Soviet demands for territorial exchanges, the Red Army severely underestimated the fighting ability of its opponent. The Red Army was halted by the "Mannerheim Line", a chain of concrete bunkers erected since Finland gained its independence in 1918 in an area between Lake Ladoga and the Baltic coast.

A worse defeat was suffered further north, as the Red Army attempted to capture the town of Oulu. At the Battle of Suomussalmi, beginning on 8 December 1939, the Finns skilfully defeated a Red Army column strung out along a road, first by blocking it and its line of retreat, then slicing it into sections that could be defeated piecemeal.

Red Army dead lie beside one of their tanks in a Finnish forest. The Red Army's performance in the war left much to be desired.

IN BRIEF

☞ US President Franklin Delano Roosevelt declared a limited national emergency on 8 September 1939. It was soon clear that he favoured the Allied powers of France and Britain. In November the US Congress passed a Neutrality Act that allowed belligerent countries to buy arms from the United States as long as they could transport them from the country themselves – which effectively limited sales to France and Britain. This was just one thing Roosevelt manipulated to favour the Allied powers.

Flying accident changes plans

The engine failure of a German Messerschmitt Bf 108 on 10 January 1940 allowed German plans for the invasion of Belgium and the Netherlands to fall into the hands of the Belgian army. The two-seater plane was carrying a pilot and a Luftwaffe adjutant who had in his briefcase the German plans. He was trying to burn the documents when Belgian border police arrived on the scene and took both him and his papers into custody. The plans revealed the German intention to carry out a modified version of the First World War's Schlieffen Plan, as the Allied High Command had anticipated.

German dictator Adolf Hitler therefore ordered his commanders to create an alternative plan. The Chief of Staff to Army Group A, General Erich von Manstein, had proposed an alternative at the time of the creation of the original plan, and suggested it again at the

The Chief of Staff of Germany's Army Group A, General Erich von Manstein, developed a new plan for the German attack on France.

The two-seater plane was carrying a pilot and a Luftwaffe adjutant who had in his briefcase the German plans. He was trying to burn the documents when Belgian border police arrived on the scene and took both him and his papers into custody. The plans revealed the German intention to carry out a modified version of the First World War's Schlieffen Plan.

meeting with Hitler. Von Manstein's plan gave Army Group A the key role in the offensive, with an armoured thrust through the Ardennes, reaching France in the vicinity of Sedan and Hirson. This time, mainly out of necessity, the German generals accepted von Manstein's plan, and prepared to move a large mechanized army through the Ardennes, a wooded area believed to be too difficult to be negotiated by such a force.

Red Army forces Finland to yield

Finland signed a peace treaty with the Soviet Union on 12 March 1940, bringing to an end the war between the two countries that had begun in the preceding November. The treaty yielded parts of the Karelian isthmus, including Finland's second-largest city, Viipuri, plus other areas of the country including about 12 per cent of the population, all of whom had to be evacuated under the terms of the treaty.

Soviet leader Josef Stalin had appointed General Semyon Timoshenko to take charge of a renewed Red Army offensive against the Mannerheim Line in the Karelian isthmus. Timoshenko's probes began on 1 February and his main attack on 11 February. The Russians now used heavy artillery bombardments to precede their infantry and tank attacks, and also had command of the air. By contrast, the Finns had such limited supplies of ammunition that they could only open fire when a breakthrough appeared to be imminent, allowing the Red Army to mass its forces unhindered.

The Finns began seeking terms from the Soviets, only to receive encouragement from Britain and France, who hoped to send military forces both to aid the Finns but also to occupy iron ore mines in northern Sweden that were of key importance to the German war effort. The Germans, in their turn, encouraged the Finns to make peace with the Soviets, hinting that the border could always be adjusted in a future conflict. By 5 March the Red Army had broken through the Mannerheim Line and kept pressing westwards. The Red Army, on Stalin's orders, kept the pressure on up to the very last minute of fighting.

Germany invades Denmark, Norway

A **German invasion has** not only succeeded in defeating Denmark, but has also taken control of key regions in the south of Norway, as German troops continue to advance north up the sea coast. German dictator Adolf Hitler believed that if he had not invaded Scandinavia first, the British would have occupied the ports, both to threaten Germany from the north and to interfere with the export of iron ore from Sweden to Germany. Control of Norway would also make it easier for German warships and U-boats to enter the Atlantic to raid British merchant shipping.

The German plan emphasized the importance of securing surprise and of using fast warships to transport German troops, since merchant ships were too slow to ensure surprise and there were not enough aircraft to transport the troops needed. Denmark was quickly overrun by the Germans, but Norway presented a greater problem.

On 9 April, German troops landed by air and sea at Oslo, Bergen, Kristiansand, Trondheim and Narvik. The attack on Oslo was significant for the Norwegian defenders who were able to sink the German cruiser *Blücher* with torpedoes fired from a shore installation.

While the Germans succeeded in attaining their objectives fairly rapidly in the south, they had more problems in the north. Half the entire German navy's destroyers were caught in Narvik harbour by a strong British squadron and sunk on 13 April. Allied landings at Namsos and Andalsnes followed this victory, for drives on Trondheim and Narvik. As April ended, Allied forces in Norway were pressing on Narvik and Trondheim.

German soldiers in Norway manhandle a heavy gun through a muddy field. The Germans fight against the Norwegian army continued for two months after the initial invasion.

Daring assault captures Eben Emael

German paratroopers after their successful assault on the Belgian fortress, Eben Emael.

German airborne assault troops made a landing on Fort Eben Emael in Belgium on 10 May 1940, as part of the general German offensive against France and Britain. It represents the first military use of gliders in war and was also the first time that shaped-charge weapons were used to penetrate armour.

Fort Eben Emael stands near the Albert Canal and was intended to prevent the capture of three bridges that offered access to Liège from the south. The German army had constructed a full-scale replica of the fortress in Czechoslovakia following the annexation of the western part of that country in 1939. The fort was largely underground, with defensive cupolas and pillboxes poking out to provide positions from which to shoot at attackers.

The assault was made by about 90 German paratroopers who landed directly on the fort and took control of the bridges. They held their positions for a day, until reinforcements arrived in sufficient numbers to force the surrender of the fort. About 1,200 Belgian soldiers were captured.

Allies advance to Dye river and Gembloux Gap, fight massive tank battle

The largest tank battle yet in history broke out in the Gembloux Gap, Belgium, on 12 May 1940, and lasted two days until the French withdrew, having halted the German advance and caused heavier casualties to the attackers. The Battle of Hannut, between elements of the French First Army and German XVI Panzer Corps of two divisions, bought valuable time for the French and British forces entering Belgium in support of the Belgian army, enabling them to establish their main defensive position along the Dyle river by 15 May.

A French tank passes through a Belgian town. The French plan was designed on the assumption the German army would repeat its manoeuvre of 1914.

Allies abandon attempt to capture Trondheim

German air attacks and determined resistance on the roads between Namsos and Trondheim have caused the Allies to abandon their bases at Andalsnes and Namsos, and give up any hope of capturing the key city of Trondheim, which divides north and south Norway. General Kurt Woytasch handled his troops aggressively in blocking the roads vital to the Allied advance and

General Kurt Woytasch handled his troops aggressively in blocking the roads vital to the Allied advance and stopped the cautious Allied approach in its tracks, although losses on both sides were light.

stopped the cautious Allied approach in its tracks, although losses on both sides were light. German aircraft supported Woytasch's operations by launching major bombing raids on the Allied bases at Andalsnes and Namsos. Unable to advance, and learning that Woytasch was receiving reinforcements from the south, the Allied commanders chose to evacuate Namsos, surrendering southern Norway to the Germans.

German breakthrough at Sedan reaches coast

The lead elements of a German panzer division reached the Channel coast at the Somme estuary on 20 May 1940, dividing the main part of the Allied armies in Belgium and northern France from the remainder of the French armies to the south. Amazingly, this advance was achieved in the space of only seven days, far faster than the French commanders had

French generals were too slow and their tanks did not reach the German breakthrough fast enough to seal it off.

anticipated, and therefore beyond their capacity to challenge effectively.

The Germans made their main attack through the Ardennes, aiming to cross the Meuse river at three points: Dinant, Monthermé and Sedan. The Germans struck the French defences where second-rate troops had been positioned, since French generals did not believe a major advance through the heavily wooded Ardennes forest was practical.

The Germans made effective use of dive-bombers against the French troops defending the line of the Meuse, most of whom were older reservists, recalled to the army at the outbreak of war, and with no experience of such attacks. Panic was greatest at the Sedan crossings where the Germans managed to establish a bridgehead of about 3 miles (5 km) deep. Smaller penetrations were achieved north of Dinant and at Monthermé.

French counter-attacks over the following two days were ineffective. Two French tank divisions were sent to halt the Germans. The Germans blocked the advance of one, and pivoted in front of it before heading west at speed; a second was defeated when it rushed its attacks piecemeal; the third, even more

A German Pazkpfw II light tank beside a demolished bridge in a Belgian village. The German advance was little delayed by enemy action, as engineers rapidly erected suitable replacements.

futilely, was assembling in support when the German tank columns drove through its assembly area, separating its fighting formations from the support units.

IN BRIEF

❧ A debate in the House of Commons of the British parliament on 7–8 May 1940 resulted in a victory for the Conservative government of Neville Chamberlain, though with a much reduced majority of 281 to 200. A visibly shaken Chamberlain left the chamber after the result had been announced and the very next day invited the minority Labour party to join forces with him to form a new coalition government. On 10 May, as the Germans launched their offensive in Western Europe, it became apparent that the Labour party were not prepared to serve under Chamberlain, but would instead serve under the leadership of First Lord of the Admiralty, Winston Churchill. Chamberlain consequently resigned as prime minister (although remained leader of the Conservative Party), and Churchill received the royal commission to form a new coalition government that included members of the Labour Party and the Liberal Party.

❧ The Dutch army fought a short campaign from 10 to 14 May against invading German forces, until the bombing of Rotterdam convinced the Dutch authorities that continued resistance would only lead to further massive damage affecting the civilian population. German attacks had moved too quickly, making it impossible for the Dutch to carry out their role in the French plan to aid them.

British and French forces evacuated from Dunkirk

Operation Dynamo, a nine-day operation to rescue the British Expeditionary Force from the Continent, finished on 4 June 1940, having removed over 300,000 British troops from the beaches at Dunkirk. It received significant assistance from the order by German dictator Adolf Hitler to his forces in France to halt in order to give follow-up forces time to catch up with the advanced spearheads.

The evacuation began on 26 May, two days after the British army began to pull out of a salient it had created near Arras. An armoured attack against the advancing German columns on 21 May had succeeded in disrupting the German advance, but an accompanying French attack from the south did not occur and the British forces were not strong enough to achieve more than a local success. A renewed offensive was being prepared when on 25 May the commander of the British Expeditionary Force, General Lord Gort, opted to abandon the plans when the Germans broke through the Belgian army's defensive line near Courtrai, threatening to cut the British off from the Channel.

Gort withdrew to Dunkirk to form a defensive perimeter, while the Royal Navy assembled a fleet that mixed together warships and small ships and boats from ports around Britain to carry the soldiers from the beaches to Britain. The operation was marred by confusion between British officials and their French allies. The French had agreed to the operation on the understanding that their troops would also be evacuated, but by 31 May, of 120,000 soldiers carried off the beaches, only 6,000 had been French. The British were expected to provide a part of the rearguard that held off the Germans from the beaches, but the bulk of this effort was in fact provided by the French army. At one point the French admiral in command of the bridgehead, Jean-Marie-Charles Abrial, asked for the three British divisions he had been promised by Lord Gort, but the British general on the spot, after Gort had left, refused, and put his men aboard the ships.

The last British troops were evacuated on 2 June, and the following two days were devoted to getting French soldiers out of the bridgehead. In the end, 338,226 soldiers were evacuated, nearly 140,000 of whom were French or Belgian.

The Germans did not prosecute their attacks on the bridgehead effectively, as the order to halt issued on 24 May prevented them from advancing aggressively with their armour from the south. The German high command might also have wished Army Group B, which had invaded Belgium and the Netherlands, to carry out the destruction of the Allied forces around Dunkirk. However, the fleet and the beaches were subject to constant aerial bombardment, as the German air force attempted to stop the evacuation.

IN BRIEF

❧ Allied forces were evacuated from Narvik on 8 June 1940, having captured the town from its German defenders on 28 May. The Norwegian armed forces signed an armistice with Germany on 9 June, allowing the country to fall under German occupation.

❧ Italy declared war on France and Britain on 10 June 1940. Italian forces attacked along the border, gaining a little territory along the Riviera, before an armistice came into effect on 22 June.

A Norwegian civilian in Narvik.

France surrenders at Compiègne

Humiliated French officers were forced to sign an armistice on 22 June 1940 in the same carriage used by the victorious Allies in November 1918. The decision to seek an armistice had been taken by the new premier of France, Marshal Philippe Pétain, on 17 June, and the signing was attended by Adolf Hitler.

The French army had fought on even after the evacuation of Dunkirk and the surrender of Belgium, in the face of superior German air power and now a numerical advantage in terms of armies. The French commander, General Maxime Weygand, who had replaced General Maurice Gamelin on 20 May, had prepared careful defences against the Germans, using a chequerboard pattern of strongpoints, known as hedgehogs, in depth along the Somme river. At the tactical level, French anti-tank gunners were now ordered to fire at enemy vehicles on sight, replacing the earlier doctrine of centrally controlled barrages which had seriously hampered French efforts to counter German armour in the earlier battles of the War.

In the opinion of their German opponents, French soldiers fought better in the battles along the Somme and Aisne that opened on 5 June, as German casualties per day doubled during this phase of the battle. Gallant stands were made at Saumur by the cadets of the cavalry school for two days, ending on 19 June, and along the Loire by the 109th Infantry Regiment. In spite of these achievements, the Germans entered Paris on 14 June. The French government had fled to Bordeaux and declared the capital an open city on 10 June. By 17 June, the Germans had advanced as far south as Caen, Orleans, Nevers and Besançon.

The Germans insisted on using the same railway carriage for signing an armistice as had been used in 1918 when Germany sought an end to the First World War.

Former Allies battle at Mers-el-Kébir

A **powerful British squadron** in the Mediterranean attacked a French squadron at Mers-el-Kébir, Algeria, on 3 July 1940, sinking one ship and damaging two others.

Operation Catapult was the Royal Navy's plan to neutralize the powerful French fleet which, when the armistice was signed between France and Germany on 22 June, was liable to fall into the hands of the Germans, eliminating at a stroke the considerable naval advantage possessed by the British. Several small ships in British ports were easily captured. Another squadron, in port at Alexandria, in Egypt, submitted to British control after lengthy negotiations. The strongest concentration of naval power outside European France were the battleships and destroyers at Mers-el-Kébir.

The Royal Navy assembled a force of three battleships, an aircraft carrier, two cruisers and 11 destroyers to deal with the French flotilla. On 2 July, an emissary from the British admiral in command, James Somerville, offered the French commander,

Admiral Marcel-Bruno Gensoul, a choice of options ranging from joining the British to sailing to the French West Indies, out of German reach. Admiral Gensoul declined any of these alternatives and Admiral Somerville ordered his ships to open fire late the next afternoon. The French battleship *Bretagne* blew up when her magazine caught fire, and two more battleships were badly damaged. French ships were unable to reply effectively from their berths in port and nearly 1,300 French sailors perished.

French battleships under bombardment in Mers-el-Kébir. The British action was considered unnecessary by the French, who had no intention of their vessels falling into German hands.

OBITUARY
LEON TROTSKY (1879–1940)

Leon Trotsky was assassinated in his office at home in Mexico City. He was stabbed in the head with an ice pick on 20 August 1940 and died of his wounds the next day.

Trotsky is better known to the world as a revolutionary leader of 1917, but he played an important military role during the Russian Civil War. He was appointed Commissar of War on 13 March 1918, and reinvigorated an army that was an unhappy mixture of revolutionary militia and former officers. He instituted a system of political commissars accompanying each unit, in order to prevent the "military experts" (former tsarist officers) from using the army against the government. Once the campaigns had begun, Trotsky toured his forces in his famous armoured train, appearing wherever a crisis occurred in order to ensure the victory of the Red Army.

He is survived by his second wife. His first wife, his two daughters by his first marriage, and his two sons by his second marriage all predeceased him.

Germans attack Britain by air

Six weeks of steady air combat over Britain has seen RAF Fighter Command keep the upper hand over German opposition flying from airfields in France and Norway. The Germans are hampered by the short flying range of their best fighter aircraft, the Messerschmitt Bf 109, and by many of their aircraft losses occurring over Britain, where surviving aircrew are virtually impossible to rescue.

The Royal Air Force began its defence of Britain on 10 July, as German photo-reconnaissance flights and attacks on convoys began. The Germans were hopeful initially that Fighter Command would be drawn into dogfights over the Channel and lose vital fighters, but the British declined to engage the Germans in strength, using hit-and-run tactics that focused on the bombers.

The weather delayed the official opening of the campaign until 13 August, although the Germans in fact began attacking the radar stations along the south coast that were a crucial part of Fighter Command's defence network on 12 August. These raids took some of the stations off the air for a few hours, except for the one at Ventnor on the Isle of Wight, which was out of action for four weeks.

The first heavy day of attacks came on 15 August, when over a thousand German aircraft crossed the Channel, as well as a long-range raid from Norway and Denmark. The Germans suffered heavy losses, without achieving lasting damage, but they did cause problems, prompting Churchill to comment in the car on the way back from Fighter Command headquarters where he had spent much of the day, "Never … have so many owed so much to so few", which would eventually work its way into one of his famous speeches. The heaviest casualties of this opening phase occurred on 18 August, when a total of 69 German aircraft were lost to 33 RAF.

British fighers at an airfield in southeastern England. The well-developed air defence system covering London and the South East succeeded in defeating the German air attacks both against the airfields and against the metropolis.

The truth about blitzkrieg and the Finest Hour

The word "blitzkrieg" was first used to describe the German approach to warfare, not in some tactical manual studied carefully by panzer commanders in German military schools in 1938, but in a magazine. *Time* magazine, an American weekly, had established a reputation for its literary style, which strove to make news "interesting" through writing that emphasized the drama of the situation. A journalist, describing the war Germany had unleashed on Poland, seized on the idea of "a war of quick penetration and obliteration – Blitzkrieg, lightning war". The author of the article, which appeared in the issue dated 25 September 1939, had given a name to something that, at the time, was still being developed.

The Chain Home radar stations along the British coast were a primitive version of radar, but successfully gave sufficient early warning of German attacks for the superior British fighters to get airborne and mass for an attack.

The *Time* **writer** was trying to find a way to describe the speed of the German invasion of Poland, compared with the static warfare familiar to readers in the United States from the First World War. Although he emphasized the German tanks

> As in Poland, the German army benefited from short-comings in the opposition that perfectly complemented their advantages. The French army was outgeneralled even before any newfangled war-fare could have an impact.

moving through the rear areas of the Polish army, racing ahead of infantry and artillery, and preceded by bombing raids, the reality of the German offensive was different.

While tanks were important to German success in Poland, they did not deliver the decisive blows that the *Time* author implied. The German victory in Poland owed as much to the infiltration tactics of the First World War as to the panzer divisions of the Second. There were no massed armoured formations in addition to the attacking divisions during the Polish campaign. The greatest concentration came with the Tenth Army, which was in the centre of the German line and made use of a panzer corps, the XIX, in addition to its four infantry corps. This was where the main German attack came, and the Corps Commander, General Heinz Guderian, made the most of his opportunities. His units pierced the Polish front and prevented the formation of any cohesive defensive position to seal the gap they had created.

These successes were not, however, entirely a product of some new operational approach, but also owed much to the technological

shortcomings within the Polish army. The Poles did not have many radios in their army, and it was a slow process to transmit information to headquarters or orders from the commanders. Thus, once the Germans had made a breakthrough, the Polish forces couldn't catch up with developments fast enough before the Germans could exploit them with infantry divisions that had considerably more transport than their Polish equivalents. An opponent better equipped with radios and artillery might have made the campaign difficult for the Germans.

Massed formation

The French and British were better equipped than the Poles, but the journalistic impression of blitzkrieg applies better here than in Poland. The Germans massed a

Winston Churchill boosted British morale, but his only hope of victory lay in Britain becoming financially dependent on the United States.

substantial part of their armoured forces in the centre of the front, seven out of ten armoured divisions advancing between Dinant and Sedan. At the point where the crossings of the Meuse were made, however, tanks played a less significant role. The attack on the French positions at Sedan were carried out by assault infantry and engineers, assisted by artillery and aircraft, and the tanks only came into action once the infantry had created a gap in the line.

Even after this, the Germans were greatly aided by the failure of the French generals to hold back a large enough

> On 18 June 1940, the day after Marshal Pétain announced his intention to seek an armistice, Churchill gave a long speech in the House of Commons that ended with the phrase, "This was their finest hour."

reserve to deal with a major breakthrough. The Allied plan was based on rushing their main force forward into Belgium, gambling the whole future of the campaign on guessing correctly the German plan. Having guessed wrong, French generals did their best to seal off the breach, but miscalculated both the direction of the German attack and the speed of the advance. As in Poland, the German army benefited from shortcomings in the opposition that perfectly complemented their advantages. The French army was outgeneralled even before any newfangled warfare could have an impact.

Money and war

Journalistic turns of phrase were second nature to British Prime Minister Winston Churchill. On 18 June 1940, the day after Marshal Pétain announced his intention to seek an armistice, Churchill gave a long speech in the House of Commons that ended with the phrase, "This was their finest hour." The words came to embrace the campaign fought in that summer of 1940, when the British armed forces rose to the challenge issued by Churchill to 'brace ourselves to our duties' and fended off the German onslaught.

Another phrase-maker of times past, the

The success of the German offensives in 1939 and 1940 owed less to dive bombers and tanks, and more to radios and superior generalship, than was thought at the time.

Reverend E. Cobham Brewer, the creator of *Brewer's Phrase and Fable*, characterized money as the sinews of war, and for all the heroism of the British people when they stood alone against Nazi Germany during 1940–41, they needed to pay a tremendous amount to carry on the war. Two months after Churchill's speech to the House of Commons, it was apparent that Britain could no longer finance the war. The money, it was calculated, would run out by December. The Lend-Lease Act passed by the US Congress in March 1941 was vital to Britain continuing the war against Germany, as it allowed the American government to finance the British war effort. Lend-Lease did not just pay for weapons, it also covered food, trucks, transport aircraft and landing craft.

Had it not been for this American aid, it is quite possible that Britain would have been forced to open peace negotiations in early 1941. That the aid would come was never in real doubt, unless President Franklin Roosevelt lost his bid for an unprecedented third presidential term in November 1940. In 1945, most of the outstanding loans were consolidated in a fifty-year loan granted in 1945 at 2 per cent interest, due to be paid off in December 2006. The "Finest Hour" myth was ultimately sustained by the dollars of American taxpayers, willing to wait over sixty years to get their money back.

Hitler calls off invasion, RAF defeats Germans

On 17 September 1940, Adolf Hitler, Germany's dictator, postponed indefinitely the planned invasion of Britain after the German air force had been unable to secure command of the air over the English Channel.

The air campaign by Germany against Britain effectively began on 12 August with attacks concentrating on radar stations. On 24 August, the campaign switched to a new phase, as the Germans, under orders from Göring, intensified their efforts by launching a concentrated series of attacks against British airfields supporting Fighter Command. These raids continued through to 4 September, except on those days the weather prevented flying. Fighter Command was stretched to its absolute limit by these raids, as the Germans relentlessly sent bombers across the Channel. Pilots of Fighter Command's squadrons were carrying out up to four sorties per day, and tiredness must have badly affected them. However, the Germans were suffering just as much, and at the end of August morale was very low among German aircrew.

Nevertheless, the attritional battle was being won by the unhappy Germans. Not because they were killing British pilots or destroying British planes faster than they could be replaced, but because they were damaging the airfields and command facilities that were the vital support for the pilots and aircraft. At this point, the Germans switched their main target to London, where they believed that they could destroy Fighter Command in the air. The first London raid occurred on 7 September, targeting the docks, with the heaviest raid a week later on 15 September. But the strategy was flawed. The RAF had reserve squadrons just to the north of London which had largely been kept out of the battle, and these deployed in large formations, inflicting heavy casualties on the German attackers. London was also further from the German airfields, so the bombers received more limited fighter cover, increasing their losses. On 15 September, the Germans lost twice as many aircraft as the British and Hitler effectively called off the daylight bombing offensive as a result.

America swaps destroyers for bases

One of the American destroyers transferred to the Royal Navy, the *USS Laub* became *HMS Burwell*.

The United States and Britain signed an agreement on 2 September 1940 under which 50 old US Navy destroyers would be transferred to the Royal Navy. In exchange, the United States would receive 99-year leases on bases in the Bahamas, Antigua, St Lucia, Trinidad, Jamaica and British Guiana, in addition to gifts of bases in Newfoundland and Bermuda. President Franklin Roosevelt had mentioned the deal in his press conference on 16 August.

German airpower, symbolized by the Stuka, was unable to achieve superiority over southern England. The German losses outpaced their production of aircraft and aircrew, while British factories churned out plenty of fighters.

Italy defeated in Egypt

Italian soldiers in rifle pits in the Western Desert. The Italian army lacked enough trucks and tanks to take on the smaller, but more mobile, British Western Desert Force.

A **British offensive that** began on 8 December 1940 drove Italian troops out of Egypt, in a daring operation that has netted thousands of prisoners. Benito Mussolini, the Italian dictator, had hoped his offensive would coincide with the German invasion of Britain, but after Hitler postponed that operation from mid to late September,

Mussolini ordered his offensive to proceed on 13 September. The ponderous Italian advance halted on 17 September, after a mere 60 miles (96 km). The British counter-attack passed around the south of the Italian defensive position and attacked from the rear. By 11 December, nearly 40,000 prisoners had been taken as the advance continued west into Libya.

Italy invades Greece, achieves little

I **talian troops crossed** the border with Greece on 28 October 1940, moving at their customary slow pace. The Greek army mobilized quickly and by 9 November had begun chasing the Italians back to their bases in Albania. The Greeks infiltrated Italian positions by moving through the mountains overlooking the valleys in which the Italian forces had confined themselves. The heaviest phase of the fighting began on 14 November, over the town of Koritsa, and on 21 November Greek troops occupied the town, while all Italian forces withdrew from Greece.

Dramatic raid in Italy opens new era of warfare

B **ritish aircraft, flying** from the aircraft carrier HMS *Illustrious*, attacked Italian warships at Taranto, Italy, on 11 November 1940, and sank or damaged four of them using torpedoes. Never before in history had such an attack been made, and fears that a harbour like Taranto was too shallow for using air-dropped torpedoes were shown to be false. A total of 21 aircraft took part in the raid, attacking in two waves. The battleship *Conte di Cavour* was sunk, and two others were badly damaged.

IN BRIEF

⁜ A German submarine torpedoed the SS *City of Benares*, sinking her on 17 September 1940. Ninety of the passengers were children being evacuated under a government scheme to Canada, and 77 of them perished.

⁜ A British and Free French attack on Dakar, French West Africa, begun on 23 September 1940, ended on 25 September with the withdrawal of the British and Free French forces after the Vichy French defenders had resisted strongly. Casualties on both sides were light.

⁜ Japan signed a Three-Power Pact with Germany and Italy in Berlin on 27 September 1940, in which they agreed to assist one another if one of the three was attacked by a country not currently involved in the war. The treaty was aimed at the Soviet Union and especially the United States.

⁜ German troops occupied the oil wells in Rumania on 7 October 1940. The occupation was with the consent of the Rumanian government.

British offensive crushes Italian army in North Africa

The **British offensive** against the Italian invaders of Egypt concluded with a stunning victory for the Imperial and Commonwealth forces at Beda Fomm on 8 February 1941.

The offensive, which had begun in Egypt in December 1940, carried on into Libya in January 1941. The city of Bardia fell on 5 January and Australian troops captured Tobruk on 22 January. By the end of the month, British forces had reached as far west as Derna. An armoured thrust sent toward Beda Fomm crossed the Libyan desert to arrive on the coast there on 5 February, cutting off the line of retreat for the Italian army and trapping the bulk of it in a pocket. These troops surrendered on 8 February, bringing the campaign to an end. Between the beginning of January and 8 February, an additional 90,000 Italian prisoners were taken. British Prime Minister Winston Churchill ordered a halt to the British attack at El Agheila and sent troops from the Western Desert Force, which had carried out the operation, to Greece, to assist the Greeks against the Italians.

Huge numbers of prisoners were captured during the battle of Beda Fomm, as the British forces based in Egypt drove the Italian invaders out of both Egypt and eastern Libya.

German sunflower blossoms in North Africa

German forces arrive at Tripoli, Italy's main port in its Libyan colony. Hitler sent a small mechanized force to help stabilize the situation in North Africa.

A small **German military** force, commanded by General Erwin Rommel, whose daring exploits at the head of the 7th Panzer Division in France in the spring of 1940 played an important part in the German victory

A second division, the 15th Panzer, is due to be transported to North Africa in the next few weeks.

there, arrived in the Italian North African port of Tripoli on 14 February 1941. Operation *Sonnenblume* (Sunflower) brought the 5th Light Division of the German army to reinforce the Italian forces and help stop the British from advancing from Cyrenaica to Tripolitania in Libya. A second division, the 15th Panzer, is due to be transported to North Africa in the next few weeks.

Italy's East African empire vanishes under attacks from British troops

On 26 March, after 11 days of fighting, the British captured the strongly held position of Keren, Eritrea. Columns of British forces are also driving into Italian Somaliland on the Indian Ocean, and into Ethiopia from Sudan.

The war came to East Africa in August 1940, when the Italians invaded British Somaliland with 175,000 soldiers. The heavily outnumbered British force fought from a defensive position at Tug Argan, but it was inevitable that they would be forced to retreat, and the Italians took control of Berbera, the capital of the colony, on 19 August, about two weeks after entering the country.

The British gradually mobilized forces from India and their African colonies to recover British Somaliland as well as to invade Italian Somaliland. The Italians could do little to reinforce the territory as it was isolated by British control of Egypt and Gibraltar, preventing Italian shipping from reaching the Red Sea or Indian Ocean ports.

On 19 January, the British invaded Eritrea from the Sudan, using troops transferred from the victorious Western Desert Force that had triumphed over the Italians in Libya, and from India. This column succeeded in advancing rapidly through Eritrea and captured the key fortress of Agordat by the end of the month. The Italians then tried to make a stand at Keren, holding up the British advance.

The Ethiopian emperor, Haile Selassie, arrived back in Ethiopia on 20 January, when he crossed the border with Gideon Force, a column of irregular soldiers, many of them Ethiopian exiles, advancing from Sudan under British command.

The invasion of Italian Somaliland from Kenya began on 29 January. The Italian commander, General di Simone, was so short of petrol that he could not concentrate his forces anywhere near the frontier and be sure of their being able to move again, and so he has decided to entrench along the Juba river, about 60 miles (96 km) from the border, in the hope of forcing the British into positional warfare. However, the Italian line was easily breached. Mogadishu was captured on 25 February and most of the country was under British control by 5 March. British forces then entered Ethiopia and began racing for the capital, Addis Ababa.

Royal Navy victory at Cape Matapan

The Royal Navy defeated a small Italian fleet off Cape Matapan, in southern Greece on 28 March 1941. The engagement began at 8.30 a.m., when a British cruiser squadron covering troop movements to Greece encountered an Italian cruiser squadron. At midday, an Italian battleship, the *Vittorio Veneto*, arrived and began firing at the British cruisers. The British themselves were expecting to rendezvous with a British battle squadron from Alexandria, and the aircraft carrier HMS *Formidable* sent a torpedo-plane strike against the *Vittorio Veneto* that succeeded in distracting it long enough to allow the British cruisers to escape. A second torpedo-plane strike at 3 p.m. successfully damaged the *Vittorio Veneto*. A third air strike damaged the Italian cruiser *Pola*. The British squadron eventually encountered the Italian cruisers and damaged two of them plus two escorting destroyers. The four damaged ships were sunk by British destroyers during the night, and the *Pola* the following morning.

British sailors during a gunnery drill in harbour at Alexandria. The British Mediterranean Fleet won a victory at Cape Matapan through good training and aggressive pursuit of the enemy.

Yugoslavia conquered in lightning campaign

German troops play tourist in Sarajevo. The German blitzkrieg against Yugoslavia was the most rapid and decisive of such campaigns, although both the strategic situation and the balance of forces heavily favoured the Axis powers.

Two **German armies,** with Hungarian and Italian support, have overwhelmed the unprepared Yugoslavian forces in a campaign that lasted a mere 11 days. The Yugoslav armed forces surrendered on 17 April 1941.

On 27 March, the Yugoslav government had just joined the Tripartite Pact, the alliance between Italy, Japan and Germany that was agreed in 1940, when a coup overthrew the government and installed a predominantly Serbian, anti-German government under the authority of the heir to the kingdom's throne, King Peter. At the time, the Germans were planning an invasion of Greece, after the arrival of British troops to support the Greeks in their war against the Italians. It was therefore a relatively simple matter to transfer a second army to Austria to join with forces advancing from Bulgaria and incorporate an invasion of Yugoslavia in the same plan.

The German campaign commenced on 6 April with air attacks and two days later ground forces invaded from four directions. The Yugoslav army only put up a serious defence in the south-east of the country, around Paracin and Kragujevac. Its Croatian units were particularly unenthusiastic about resisting the Germans, whom they perceived as supporting them against a Serb-dominated government. A separate Croatian government was established on 11 April. The rest of the Yugoslav army seemed unable to co-ordinate its actions in the face of the German blitzkrieg, and through the lack of preparedness on the part of their troops. Once Sarajevo surrendered on 15 April, it was impossible for any organized resistance to continue.

German forces in Africa go on the attack

General **Erwin Rommel,** commander of German forces in Africa, has achieved considerable success with an offensive originally designed as a probe to test the British positions around El Aghelia. On 27 April 1941, German forces captured the Halfaya Pass, on the border between Libya and Egypt.

Rommel commanded two divisions of German troops: the 5th Light Division and, at the end of his campaign, the 15th Panzer Division. On 24 March, elements of the 5th Light engaged British forces near El Aghelia and, when the British failed to put up much of a fight, he decided to expand his operation with an attack on Mersa Brega, where the British at El Aghelia had withdrawn to. The British in this area were too scattered to defend the position effectively and as a result the concentrated force of German tanks easily broke through the British line. The British commander of the Western Desert force, General Sir Philip Neame, ordered a withdrawal to Benghazi, but, at the same time, he ordered the garrison there to prepare to evacuate its positions.

In fact, the British did not bother to make any effort to make a stand at Benghazi or Mechili, but continued their retreat.

Neame and General Richard O'Connor were captured on 6 April, two days after the fall of Benghazi, while on a staff reconnaissance. On 7 April, a whole brigade of British troops surrendered after being surrounded at Mechili. The 9th Australian Infantry Division was surrounded at Tobruk on 12 April. The Germans pushed on eastwards until they were halted by British defences at Sollum the next day. After three weeks continually advancing, the German troops were exhausted and their vehicles needed urgent repairs. As Rommel's offensive ground to a halt, the British began building a defensive line at Mersa Matruh.

Germans chase British out of Greece

The last British soldiers evacuated Greece on 30 April and a German army now occupies the country. The invasion was in part prompted by the arrival of British forces in mid-March 1941, which the Germans feared posed a long-term threat to their vital oilfields in Rumania.

The German invasion began on 6 April, when the Twelfth Army crossed the border from its bases in Bulgaria. The border was long, however, and difficult to defend against an attack from the north. The Greeks had constructed the Metaxas Line, named after a Greek dictator, who died on 29 January 1941, but the Germans were able to bypass this by sending their armoured columns through Yugoslavia, entering Greece behind this line.

Meanwhile, three divisions confronted the Metaxas Line, and fought with difficulty through the Greek position. Once German tanks entered the port of Salonika on 8 April, Greek troops in this area surrendered.

The Germans then attacked the next main defensive line along the Varda river without much difficulty, as neither the Greeks nor their British allies had secured the valley through the mountains on the border between Greece and Yugoslavia – the Monastir Gap. Again, German armoured forces were able to reach the area behind the defensive line, although the British forces were able to put up some resistance in a tank battle around Kozani on 13 April.

The British had always intended to make their main stand along the Aliakmon river, only fighting delaying actions beforehand, but the Germans easily breached this line on 16 and 17 April. After this, British operations were limited to rearguard actions to cover the withdrawal from Greece.

A German infantry support gun. The German army was liberally supplied with artillery pieces at all levels, but rarely was able to mass the weight of barrage achieved by the British.

"Brevity" fails in the desert

The British **XIII** Corps attack "Operation Brevity" on the German and Italian positions around Halfaya Pass failed to accomplish its objective of relieving the Australian soldiers surrounded at Tobruk when it was called off on 27 May 1941. The British attacked with two divisions, the 7th Armoured Division and the 4th Indian Division, on 15 May and succeeded in breaking through the Italian defenders of Halfaya Pass. German commander General Erwin Rommel, however, rushed armoured forces to the threatened sector and these halted the British attack. A short pause ensued before a German counter-attack on 27 May forced the British to withdraw from the Pass.

German battleship sunk in Atlantic

The **German battleship** *Bismarck* was sunk by a British squadron, including three battleships, on 27 May 1941. The *Bismarck*, in company with the cruiser *Prinz Eugen*, left the German naval base at Bergen, Norway, on 21 May, heading for the Atlantic to raid the convoys sailing between North America and the British Isles. She was sighted north-west of Iceland on 23 May, and intercepted in the Denmark Strait early on 24 May by HMS *Hood* and HMS *Prince of Wales*. The *Hood* was sunk in the engagement, while the *Prince of Wales* was damaged and had to break off the action. However, one of the *Bismarck*'s fuel compartments was damaged, forcing the battleship to head for France for repairs. The *Prinz Eugen* went on a separate route, needing to refuel before heading for France.

On 26 May, an RAF flying boat spotted the *Bismarck*, whereupon she became the target of British carrier-borne aircraft flying from HMS *Ark Royal*, and was damaged by a torpedo. The *Bismarck*'s rudder was jammed and she could only sail in circles, making it a matter of time before British warships reached her for the final battle.

The German battleship Bismarck failed abysmally as a commerce raider, owing to its efficient pursuit by the Royal Navy, which spared nothing to hunt her down.

Iraq plotters flee, leaving British in charge

British armed forces completed a two month campaign to remove from power a pro-Axis regime in Iraq that threatened a key route for supplies to British forces in Egypt and Libya. An armistice ending the fighting was signed on 30 May.

Pro-Axis Iraqi officers had staged a coup on 1 April 1941 and named Rashi Ali al-Keilani, a staunch nationalist who supported their schemes, head of the government.

Under the terms of a treaty agreed when Britain granted independence to Iraq in 1930, British armed forces had the right to cross Iraq and two British bases were established in the country, at Habbaniya in the centre, and at Basra on the Gulf coast. A few weeks after the coup, on 18 April, British troops from India landed at Basra. For Rashid Ali, who had been waiting for the arrival of a substantial supply of weapons from Germany before abrogating the treaty, the time had come to act. A brigade of troops equipped with artillery was sent against Habbaniya. The British in response flew in more men and additional aircraft, which successfully attacked Rashid Ali's force on 2 May. By 6 May, the Iraqis were in retreat.

Five days after the "siege" of Habbaniya ended, a force of 7,000 British troops entered Iraq from Transjordan, hurrying to topple Rashid Ali and restore the previous pro-British regime. It took only six days for them to cross the desert before they reached Habbaniya on 18 May and continued their advance, now aimed at Baghdad. They arrived outside the city on 30 May, at which point Rashid Ali, his Iraqi officers, and German and Italian diplomats all fled, ending the revolt.

Soldiers of the Arab Legion, operating from Palestine into Iraq, were part of a two-pronged invasion of that country that toppled its pro-Axis regime.

Large-scale airborne operation captures Crete

Using gliders and paratroops, the German Army seized the island of Crete from the Allied forces defending it. The Royal Navy lost several valuable ships in the evacuation of British and Commonwealth forces from the island, the last of whom left Crete on 30 May.

The German attack began on 20 May with glider-borne and parachute forces landing around Maleme Airfield on the western end of the island. Other landings were made at Khania, and later in the day at Rethimnon and Heraklion.

British forces resisted the German paratoopers well during the first day of battle, to the extent that the Germans abandoned the idea of reinforcing besides landing other than the one at Maleme, and even here their situation was precarious. However, the British withdrew the defenders of Hill 107, overlooking the airfield at Maleme, during the night, allowing the Germans to occupy this commanding position. German aircraft then began using the airstrip late in the afternoon of 21 May, even though it was still under observed artillery fire. The German air force largely controlled the skies over Crete, which hampered British efforts to fight back. During the next two days, the Germans rushed reinforcements to Maleme and steadily increased their forces on the island. On 23 May, the British general staff in London decided the battle was lost and ordered the evacuation of the island, which began on 28 May.

A German transport aircraft burns during a parachute drop on Crete, May 1941.

A German Panzer III tank, adapted for short journeys underwater, emerges from the River Bug during Operation Barbarossa, the invasion of the Soviet Union.

Leaderless Russia invaded

A **little more than** a week after invading the Soviet Union, the Germans achieved an astonishing degree of success, with advanced spearheads nearing Riga in the north, past Minsk in the centre, and in control of Lvov in the south.

German armies crossed the border with the Soviet Union on 22 June 1941 in an attack that caught the Red Army almost unaware. In spite of several warnings, the Red Army was still deployed largely in its peacetime garrisons, and not in the field according to its wartime defensive plans for the

homeland. German armoured forces were therefore easily able to bypass any concentrations of troops. The German air force successfully destroyed a significant portion of the Red Air Force at its bases, and was subsequently able to provide vital support to the troops on the ground in preventing the Soviets from organizing any coherent resistance to the German onslaught.

The Soviet dictator, Josef Stalin, disappeared from public view. The announcement of the German invasion to the Soviet peoples was instead made by the Commissar for Foreign Affairs,

Vyacheslav Molotov, on 22 June. On 28 June, after learning the Germans had captured Minsk and surrounded 400,000 Red Army troops, Stalin

German armies advanced across the border with the Soviet Union on 22 June 1941 in an attack that caught the Red Army almost unaware.

abandoned his commissars by moving to his country house in Kuntsevo, effectively paralysing the government.

"Battleaxe" fails to break through

A British offensive intended to relieve the siege of Tobruk failed in its attacks on German and Italian positions at the Halfaya Pass. The battle was won on 17 June 1941 by the German commander, General Erwin Rommel, who successfully outmanoeuvred his British opponents with a daring battle plan. British Prime Minister Winston Churchill was so disappointed by this turn of events that he removed General Archibald Wavell from command in the Western Desert and appointed General Claude Auchinleck in his place on 1 July.

The arrival of Tiger Convoy at Alexandria on 12 May, after a difficult journey through the Mediterranean lasting about a week during which it was subjected to frequent air attacks, provided the tanks and aircraft needed for a second offensive to drive Rommel back from the Egyptian borders. Almost 240 tanks arrived aboard these ships.

The offensive began on 15 June, but ran into a carefully constructed anti-tank screen of 37mm, 50mm and, most effectively, 88mm anti-tank guns. The armour of the British Mk II infantry tank, the Matilda, was impervious to the 37mm and 50mm guns, but the 88mm guns – anti-aircraft weapons brought into the front line – could penetrate the thick frontal plate of the Matilda.

The German anti-tank gunners estimated they had knocked out some 60 of the British tanks but the German counter-attack on 16 June fared little better than the original British assault as the British managed to halt the Germans, causing 50 per cent casualties to the 15th Panzer Division. Rommel then decided that, based on intelligence from British radio traffic and dispositions, his enemy was more worried about being attacked in the flank than about how to break through the German lines. He disengaged his main armoured strength and, leaving a weak screening force between the British and their goal of Tobruk, sent his tanks into the desert to strike the British in their left flank.

The Germans deployed 88mm anti-aircraft guns, such as this, to great effect during Operation Battleaxe to defeat the heavy armour of some of the British tanks.

British forces invade Vichy mandates

A British soldier shows how German aircraft flying under French colours had arrived in Syria.

D amascus, the capital of the French League of Nations mandate territory Syria, fell to an Allied invasion force on 21 June 1941. The British had become concerned when German aircraft used the Vichy-controlled territory to support the Iraq coup in April 1941, and chose to invade and secure the territory for the Free French forces based in London.

The invasion began on 8 June 1941, involving 34,000 Allied soldiers, the largest contingent being Australian, with Palestinian Jewish, Free French, British and Indian units too. During the first ten days of the campaign, the Vichy French resistance kept the Allied forces from advancing far. French submarines also attacked British ships protecting a convoy carrying a large force of troops to Sidon.

The British, however, succeeded with a commando raid in the Lebanon that disrupted the French defence of the crossings over the Litani river, which effectively opened the way for the Australians to reach Damascus. By the middle of the month, General Archibald Wavell, in Egypt, decided to send further forces from the Western Desert to aid the troops attacking Syria, as well as ordering some of the occupation force in Iraq to advance on Palmyra.

Army Group Centre in heavy fighting around Smolensk

The area around Smolensk was the scene of heavy fighting throughout July as Panzer Group 2, commanded by General Heinz Guderian, strove to gain ground for the coming attack on Moscow.

For the Red Army, the fighting between the Dniestr and Dnepr rivers marked their first serious attempt to thwart the advance of the German Army Group Centre toward Moscow. The armies on the border had been overwhelmed, and the invaders moved rapidly, even over bad roads. The Red Army had retained a powerful reserve behind the main line, intended originally to attack an invading enemy on the flanks. While some of these troops were rushed into small-scale attacks whose main purpose was to delay and divert rather than to halt the German thrusts, the others gathered along the Dniestr in concentrations at Orsha, Mogilev and Rogachev. The commander of the Red Army's Western Front, Marshal Semyon Timoshenko, was organizing forces that were intended to crush the German bridgeheads as soon as they crossed the Dniestr.

Guderian studied the situation and took a calculated risk. True to "blitzkrieg", he decided to cross the Dniestr in between Timoshenko's concentrations, between Orsha and Mogilev. These were bypassed while he hurried toward Smolensk, which fell on 16 July, the fifth day of this offensive.

However, as Guderian's tanks advanced, their southern flank stretched out vulnerably in front of the Red Army's reserves, leading Guderian to call for reinforcements. Panzer Group 2 captured Yelnia, a key road junction overlooked by high ground, and came to a halt. Guderian's ambitions, though, prevented his army from joining Panzer Group 3 to encircle the Soviet forces east of Smolensk.

On 23 July, Timoshenko launched attacks that aimed at both widening the gap that remained, connecting the Soviet forces nearly trapped east of Smolensk, as well as cutting off Guderian's Panzer Group in a reverse encirclement. Although the offensive failed, and Hoth's Panzer Group 3 finally closed the ring on 27 July, German commanders were increasingly nervous about the degree of resistance they encountered.

Stalin's broadcast calls for "no mercy to the enemy"

Josef Stalin, Soviet leader, emerged from the seclusion he had occupied since the German invasion began on 22 June, to broadcast to the nation on 3 July 1941. The speech called for the Soviet people to "mobilize yourselves and reorganize all your work on new wartime bases, where there can be no mercy to the enemy".

Stalin had spent some of the time between 22 June and 30 June in a depression at his country dacha at Kuntsevo, outside Moscow, having seemed to have given up the fight. On the night of 30 June, a delegation of high-ranking Soviet leaders approached him and offered him chairmanship of a State Defence Committee. The gesture roused him from his depression and the next day he resumed leading the defence of his country.

German engineers assemble a pontoon bridge across the Dniepr River. The rivers were the main obstacle to their advance into the Soviet Union during the summer of 1941.

German gains in north and south

Army Group North reached the shores of Lake Ilmen, south of Novgorod, on 31 July 1941. Most of the fighting took place in the Baltic States, occupied by the Soviet Union in 1940. All the capitals of these countries were captured by German forces, starting with the Latvian capital of Riga, on 1 July 1941. The wooded terrain and marshy areas hampered the Germans' armour from the kind of deep thrusts that characterized their advance in the centre, although the distance to the main objective was less.

The sluggish advance of Army Group South during Operation Barbarossa has been the cause of some concern to the German High Command. The army group has had the largest front to attack across and was confronted the strongest part of the Red Army, so its relative slowness is understandable. Early in the campaign, Army Group South came into contact with the newest Soviet tank designs, the T-34 medium tank and the KV-1 heavy tank, which are far superior

to anything in the German army. The Red Army deployment of these was ineffective and the German air force's concentrated bombardment of the concentration areas also disrupted Russian counter-attacks. Once the Germans got past Lvov,

however, their advance accelerated. The Sixth Army broke through the Stalin Line, a pre-war defensive position, on 5 July, and a Red Army counter-attack at Korosten was beaten off by Panzer Group 1. By 11 July, leading elements of Panzer Group 1 were within 10 miles (16 km) of Kiev. By the end of the month, a large group of Soviet forces was encircled at Uman, and all Soviet attempts to break through to the pocket had been beaten back by the Germans.

German reconnaissance motorcycles drive across a bridge past a wrecked T-34. German forces made great gains, but Russia's vastness left the Red Army plenty of room to reorganize.

KV-1 Tank

The Germans were surprised to encounter two new Soviet tanks during Operation Barbarossa. The T-34 was a medium tank, while the KV-1 was intended to become the standard heavy tank. German anti-tank guns in service in 1941 couldn't knock out the KV-1.

IN BRIEF

⚜ Finland, having been bombed by Soviet warplanes in June, and after allowing German troops to enter their territory, launched an offensive on 9 July 1941, which pushed Red Army troops back along the shores of Lake Ladoga and in the Karelian Isthmus.

⚜ The French Vichy commander defending Syria requested an armistice on 12 July 1941, from the invading Free French, British and Commonwealth forces.

Germans turn from Moscow to make big gains in the Ukraine

A horde of Red Army prisoners in German hands. Although the Germans rounded up a huge number of captives, they also faced some determined resistance from men and women determined to sell their lives dearly.

PPD-40

The PPD-40 sub-machine gun was the standard sub-machine gun of the Red Army in 1941. The large ammunition drum helped to make it effective with its rapid rate of fire. The Red Army valued the sub-machine gun more highly than other armies and issued them in large numbers. The PPD-40 was replaced by the PPSh-41.

The German dictator, Adolf Hitler, redirected his army's main effort away from Moscow after the surrender of the Soviet armies trapped in the Smolensk pocket on 5 August 1941. He issued a directive on 12 August that urged the conquest of the economically valuable Ukraine, a decision capped by the surrender of over 600,000 soldiers around Kiev on 19 September.

Hitler's attitude in part changed because of his army's own intelligence estimates. These, on 8 July, suggested that two-thirds of the Red Army had been destroyed in the engagements so far, and that what remained lacked officers. As the month wore on, the continued German success could only mean that even more Soviet formations had been destroyed. Hitler's directive of 12 August redirected General Heinz Guderian's Panzer Group 2 toward the south. Guderian's tanks had already halted their drive on Moscow to tackle the concentration of Soviet forces around Roslavl on their southern flank. Once this operation was completed, Panzer Group 2 continued to push southward, past the Soviet Bryansk Front which was too busy preparing defences for the expected attack on Moscow to hit Guderian's columns in the flank.

As the German offensive developed, the Soviet commanders concluded that the real target of Guderian's panzers was now Kiev, and the Soviet forces around it. General Georgi Zhukov advocated giving up Kiev in order to save the armies by their withdrawal, but Soviet leader Josef Stalin believed Kiev was too valuable and opted for offensive action to deter Guderian from continuing his advance. Nothing, however, seemed to halt Guderian. The Red Army rushed reinforcements, organized new armies and withdrew troops from exposed positions in order to stem the progress of Panzer Group 2. None of these initiatives were co-ordinated effectively, however, and inadequate counter-attacks against the panzer divisions were brushed aside as Guderian continued his advance. By the time Stalin ordered withdrawals to the east bank of the Dnepr on 7 September, it was too late – Guderian's leading forces were already in the rear areas through which the Soviet armies must withdraw. Once Army Group South's Panzer Group 1 attacked from a bridgehead at Kremenchug on 12 September, the jaws of a trap began to close around the Soviet forces defending Kiev. At some point, Stalin must have decided that the armies would be surrounded anyway, and it was better for them to fight where they stood in the hope that a counter-offensive could relieve them, or that they would last long enough to buy vital time for organizing the defence of the rest of the Ukraine. The encirclement was completed on 12 September.

Leningrad placed under siege

The **German Army** Group North reached the shores of Lake Ladoga on 8 September 1941, cutting off the city of Leningrad from communication by land with the rest of the Soviet Union. To the north of Leningrad, Finnish troops fighting in Karelia also advanced far enough along the Ladoga coast to cut off the city. The first German shells fell on the city on 4 September. On 6 September, German dictator Adolf Hitler issued a directive ordering Leningrad to be isolated rather than assaulted, in order to move units from Army Group North and redeploy them for the assault on Moscow.

Advancing German infantry pass a fortress on the Narva river. The German thrust toward Leningrad was the weakest of Barbarossa's three thrusts, but came closest to success.

Churchill, Roosevelt meet, agree charter

Franklin Roosevelt (left) and Winston Churchill on the HMS *Prince of Wales*.

An **Atlantic Charter,** embracing eight principles for a post-war world, was agreed between British Prime Minister Winston Churchill and American President Franklin Delano Roosevelt, during a three-day meeting in Placentia Bay, in the British colony of Newfoundland, on 9–12 August 1941. Several governments-in-exile subsequently agreed to the Charter's principles at a meeting in London in September 1941.

WAR CELEBRITY:
SERGEANT YORK

In September 1941, a Hollywood film commemorating the heroic deeds of Sergeant Alvin York was released. York was an average backwoods Tennessee farmer in April 1917, when the United States entered the First World War. He had been something of a hell-raiser in his teens. Drinking and brawling were commonplace activities but the death of a friend of his in a bar-room fight in 1914 affected York deeply. He found religion, becoming a member of evangelical sect the Church of Christ in Christian Union. On 5 June 1917, York received a draft notice, to which he responded with a claim that his religion forbade him from fighting. However, the Church of Christ in Christian Union had only been founded in 1909 and was not recognized by the authorities as a Christian sect. York went to war. On 8 October 1918, while serving with the 328th Infantry of the 82nd Infantry Division, York and sixteen of his comrades captured part of a German machine-gun nest in the Argonne forest. When more Germans opened fire on the Americans and their prisoners, York, who had hunted in Tennessee's woods since boyhood, accounted for nine of the enemy dead, and helped capture 132 prisoners. He was awarded the Congressional Medal of Honor for his exploit. Ironically, York's own church viewed the movies as sinful.

America's undeclared war

On 17 December 1940, President Franklin Roosevelt gave a press conference at the White House, a frequent occurrence, his first major topic of the day being the war situation in Europe. At great length, Roosevelt emphasized the importance of keeping the British fighting the Germans for the national security of the United States. He then came up with his famous "garden hose" metaphor: the lending of a garden hose to fight a fire, with it being returned once the crisis had finished. This was the introduction to the American people of the idea of Lend-Lease, part of a chain of increasingly partisan moves by the United States in the war that ultimately resulted in the loss of the USS *Reuben James* to a U-boat's torpedo on 31 October 1941, with the loss of 100 American sailors' lives, at a time when no state of war existed between the United States and Germany.

An American M3 tank is lifted by a crane. American-supplied tanks were vital to the British Army's military strength in battles in North Africa and Europe.

Roosevelt's re-election in November 1940 released him from most of the political restraints that had governed his actions up to then. The isolationist lobby in the United States had been strong and had mounted a powerful campaign against the interventionists during 1940, until in June, at the nominating convention of the Republican Party, Eastern power brokers secured the nomination for Wendell Willkie, a man of internationalist views. Willkie gained in the polls late in the campaign when he gave voice to isolationist sentiments, at a time when about 80 per cent of Americans were opposed to going to war. But it was too late. Roosevelt won the election, and the last best chance of the isolationists was lost for good.

Roosevelt had already taken interventionist

> In November, the British made the United States aware of their financially precarious position. They had about $500 million to finance further war purchases, having spent $6 billion since September 1939.

measures as early as June 1940, when Army Chief of Staff General George C. Marshall joined with the Chief of Naval Operations Admiral Harold Stark to recommend that the United States cease shipments of arms to Britain. Roosevelt turned them down and in September traded 50 older destroyers to the British in exchange for leases on bases in the Western hemisphere. In November, the British made the United States aware of their financially precarious position. They had about $500 million to finance further war purchases, having spent $6 billion since September 1939. Britain could no longer finance the war; she had been defeated, even though she had won the Battle of Britain.

Britain fights, America pays

Roosevelt chose to finance Britain's ability to continue in the war using American taxpayers' money. The vehicle was the Lend-Lease Bill, presented to Congress on 10 January 1941, which was enacted in March 1941, after secret staff talks between American and British officers had been going on for six weeks. At the end of March, 28 Italian ships and two German merchant vessels in American ports were seized and subsequently handed over to the British to help make up for losses to German submarines. In April, in violation of traditional neutrality understandings, the British were allowed to repair and refuel their ships in the United States. In May, American aircraft and pilots assisted the British in locating the German battleship *Bismarck*, which was subsequently sunk in part owing to this activity. In July, American Marines first replaced British soldiers in Iceland, allowing the British to be transferred to war zones.

Each of these incidents violated traditional norms for the conduct of neutral countries in a war. The Germans were angered by them, but there was little they could do about it. Hitler was focused for most of this period on his impending invasion of the Soviet Union, and his main concern was to avoid American entry into the war. Three days before the invasion took place, a German submarine

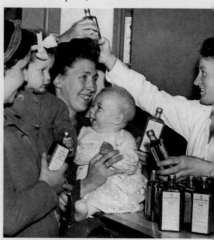

Lend-lease transfers were not limited to arms, as these mothers receiving orange juice knew.

Depth charges rolled off USS *Greer* explode in the Atlantic. The *Greer*'s attack on a German U-boat in September 1941 was part of an undeclared naval war fought between the Germans and the US Navy in the mid-Atlantic.

incident, as at the time German U-boats were in transit from their bases in France to stations in the Atlantic and around the British isles. Convoy SC-48 was less lucky in this respect. This slow convoy left Halifax on 5 October, and was spotted by a U-boat ten days later. Eight more U-boats concentrated

On 17 October, the USS *Kearny*, while manoeuvring among the merchant ships of the convoy, was hit by a torpedo fired by U-568; 11 American sailors were killed and 22 wounded.

on attacking the convoy, and a squadron of four American destroyers came to aid the British and Canadian escort ships. The American vessels depth-charged a couple of U-boats on contact, but sank none. On 17 October, the USS *Kearny*, while manoeuvring among the merchant ships of the convoy, was hit by a torpedo fired by U-568; 11 American sailors were killed and 22 wounded. The *Kearny* was able to reach Reykjavik for repairs. The *Reuben James*, torpedoed in similar circumstances on 31 October, became the first American warship to be lost in the Second World War.

It was only a matter of time before some incident would lead to a declaration of war between the United States and Germany.

shadowed the battleship USS *Texas*, and an accompanying destroyer, for about 140 miles (225 km), in an attempt to torpedo her. Only bad weather prevented the German captain from carrying out his attack.

When Roosevelt met British prime minister Winston Churchill in Newfoundland in August 1941, the two leaders put much more emphasis on signing the Atlantic Charter, and less on a second agreement, which Roosevelt even chose to keep secret from the American people. This agreement created a zone in the western Atlantic (that in fact extended to the east of Iceland) in which convoys would be escorted by American warships. Roosevelt wanted to get it into operation before informing Americans of its existence.

Destroyers vs U-boats

On 4 September, an American destroyer, the USS *Greer*, in a position 150 miles (240 km) south-west of Iceland, received a report from a British aircraft of a submerged German U-boat nearby. The *Greer* began trailing the submarine, which was subsequently depth-charged by the British aircraft. After being trailed by the *Greer* for about two hours, the German captain fired a torpedo at her, prompting the *Greer* to drop her own depth charges on the German submarine. On 11 September 1941, in response to this incident, Roosevelt authorized US warships to attack German vessels appearing in waters

deemed necessary for America's defence. An undeclared naval war had now broken out between the United States and Germany.

The first convoy to be given American warships as escorts was HX-150, sailing from Halifax, Nova Scotia, to Liverpool, England. An American destroyer squadron rendezvoused with it and replaced the Canadian escorts on 16 September. This convoy reached its destination without

American soldiers on parade in Iceland in October 1941. In January 1941, the American army and navy agreed the strategic interests of the United States required them to aid the British war effort.

Typhoon fades before Moscow

Soviet anti-tank defences in the streets of Moscow. The NKVD played the key role in preparing the defense of Moscow, including arranging "stay-behind" resistance in case of the fall of the capital.

The **German offensive** to capture Moscow, Operation Typhoon, stalled within 20 miles (32 km) of the capital on 28 November 1941. The transfer of many Red Army divisions from Siberia to Moscow, together with an especially harsh winter and lack of preparation for it on the part of the German army, were the main causes of the defeat.

German dictator Adolf Hitler once again changed the strategic direction of his offensive against the Soviet Union in September, after it became apparent that a large part of the Red Army's strength in the Ukraine would be destroyed or captured in the fighting around Kiev. Believing that the conquest of the key industrial area in south-eastern Ukraine, the Donbass, would fall easily to his armies, Hitler

MG-34

The MG-34 machine gun was the standard German squad light machine gun, but also served as the crew-served heavy machine gun at company level. In the latter role it was provided with a tripod mounting to make it more accurate.

restored Moscow to its position as the main objective for the German army in 1941. He ordered Panzer Group 2, commanded by General Heinz Guderian, to again come under the control of Army Group Centre, the main German military force before Moscow, and also Panzer Group 3, commanded by General Hermann Hoth, which had been sent to aid Army Group North in the battle for Leningrad. Army Group Centre was also assigned Panzer Group 4, which had previously been part of Army Group North.

With its armoured forces restored and reinforced, Army Group Centre was able to resume its offensive toward Moscow, which had been suspended at the end of July in order to allow Guderian's panzer divisions to attack in the Ukraine. Panzer Group 2 was one of the three spearheads aimed at Moscow, racing forward once the breach in the Soviet lines had been made; it reached the town of Orel in a matter of four days, so unexpectedly that the town's residents, thinking the tanks driving through the streets were Red Army ones, waved. By 5 October, the leading German spearhead was not much further from Moscow than Orel had been behind the front line at the start of the offensive. The next day, however, the first snow fell.

Initially, the problem for the Germans

was not snow, but mud. The daytime temperature was not cold enough to keep the snow on the ground, and it melted. The mud was only made worse as the unpaved roads became quagmires under the tracks of tanks, the wheels of vehicles and the tramping feet of thousands of marching men. The German advance slowed markedly, although progress was still made. On 14 October the city of Kalinin, north-west of Moscow, fell, cutting the railway line with Leningrad. The offensive had already created two large encirclements of Red Army forces, at Bryansk and Vyazma, and the Germans claimed another 600,000 Soviet prisoners were taken in these. The three weeks it took to eliminate these pockets, with the last troops surrendering on 20 October, caused the Germans a delay they could not really afford.

By this time reinforcements from Siberia were arriving, at first as a trickle, but a portent of things to come. Furthermore, as November arrived, the effect of the Russian winter began to impair the Germans' ability to move. While the freeze-up hardened the previously muddy roads, the engines of tanks and trucks froze. On 15 November, the Germans made a final attempt to push on to Moscow, and the 7th Panzer Division of Panzer Group 3 got as close as the Moscow-Volga canal, but the German commanders knew that any Soviet counter-attack would force them to pull back.

German machine gunners firing from a shell hole during street fighting in a southern Soviet city in the autumn of 1941.

A British Crusader II tank rolls past a burning German Panzer IV tank in the Western Desert. The Crusader tank gave its name to the British offensive to relieve Tobruk.

Tobruk siege lifted

Thirteen days of fighting at the end of the November have raised the long siege of Tobruk where German and Italian forces have had British and Commonwealth troops surrounded. The British Eighth Army launched an offensive from its base in Egypt, having received some 700 tanks, and built airfields and roads in inhospitable desert terrain.

The commander of the German Panzer Group Africa, General Erwin Rommel, was caught unawares by the British attack on 18 November. He had refused to believe any signs of the impending attack having to some extent been the victim of a British intelligence operation to deceive him. Rommel only accepted that he was under attack on 20

November and, with his characteristic energy, immediately threw himself into organizing a counter-attack.

The battle that followed over the next four days was a chaotic one, with tank forces manoeuvring wildly in the desert south-east of Tobruk. British thrusts here suffered heavy casualties, but in reality these were only feints. While Rommel drove them back into Egypt and then moved against rear-echelon units near the border, the New Zealand Division successfully advanced along the coast road to open a corridor to besieged Tobruk. Tank losses on both sides were heavy, but the British had more tanks to lose than the Germans, so the attrition favoured them.

IN BRIEF

❦ The Japanese government of Prince Fuminaro Konoye resigned on 16 October 1941, and a new government, which was headed by the former War Minister, General Hideki Tojo, was then appointed by Emperor Hirohito.

❦ The last Italian forces in Ethiopia surrendered on 27 November 1941 at Gondar, a defensive position high atop a mountain.

Sino-Japanese War 1937–41

On 7 July 1937 a telegram reached the colonel commanding the Chinese 219th Regiment, stationed at Wanping town outside Peking (Beijing), and responsible for the security of the Lugou bridge (known to Westerners as the Marco Polo Bridge, on account of the belief that it was described in the works of the Venetian explorer). The telegram came from Japanese forces conducting an exercise in the area and who believed that one of their soldiers had deserted to Wanping Town. They wished to search the town in order to locate him.

Japanese troops take cover behind a barricade during the fighting in Shanghai in November 1937. The Chinese fought hard to retain this port, but failed despite putting their best troops into the battle.

After a conference with General Song Che-yuan, commander of the Twenty-Ninth Army, of which the 219th Regiment was a part, the colonel rejected the Japanese request. That night, the Japanese began a bombardment of Wanping town, and on 8 July tanks and infantry crossed the bridge as fighting broke out between the two sides. The Japanese were unable to hold the bridge after the Chinese received reinforcements, and the Japanese withdrew and offered to negotiate.

Army in China

In spite of the setback, the Japanese were in a strong position in this part of China. The Japanese army had already largely surrounded the city of Peking even before the outbreak of fighting, under rights granted by the treaty ending the Boxer Rebellion in 1900, as well as in subsequent agreements. Their army was much better equipped

than the Chinese forces, with artillery and tanks, while the Chinese armies rarely had more powerful weapons than mortars and heavy machine guns. Japanese leaders were concerned, though, that this disparity would soon change. China's leader, Chiang Kai-shek, had already instituted reforms intended to give China armed forces capable of standing up to the Japanese by 1940, buying equipment in Germany and developing a Chinese arms industry. In the meantime, Chiang had preferred to focus on disciplining dissidents within his government and opponents outside it, primarily the Chinese Communist Party, who urged that all China unite to fight the Japanese first, and worry about a central government for China after the invader had been expelled. The Xian Incident, Chiang's arrest by Chang Hsüeh-liang and Yang Hu-cheng, allies of his in northern China, in December 1936, forced changes to his plans. Like the Communists, Chang

and Yang believed that Japan was the main enemy. Instead of supplanting Chiang, however, they forced him to negotiate an agreement for a united anti-Japanese front, including an abandonment of his anti-Communist campaign. Chiang, once released, imprisoned Chang and Yang, but held to the treaty.

> The Japanese army had already largely surrounded the city of Peking even before the outbreak of fighting.

The Xian Incident frightened the Japanese government. Lacking raw materials, their aggressive attitude towards China could only be pursued cheaply if the Chinese were disunited. Tension increased during 1937 and the Lugou Bridge Incident led to mobilization orders. It seemed to provide the perfect opportunity to attack Chiang and topple his regime. Full-scale war broke out in northern China on 26 July, and both Peking and Tientsin were in Japanese hands within the week.

Japanese artillery fire at Chinese positions while the accompanying infantry wait to go on the assault.

Mitsubishi Ki-21 bomber aircraft over China on a raid. The Japanese army and naval air forces gave Japan a considerable advantage over the Chinese, having more modern aircraft and better-trained pilots.

For Chiang, the north was a bad place to fight as most Chinese troops in the area had been members of other warlords' armies. However, it was vital to make a stand somewhere and he chose to attack Shanghai, where the Japanese already had some 8,000 soldiers and marines stationed, even before the outbreak of war. The assault began on 13 August and the siege lasted three months, with Chiang's German-trained forces fighting ferociously. The superior Japanese artillery, mainly provided by the large fleet in the harbour, eventually proved too much for them. They withdrew to a defensive position between Shanghai and the capital at Nanking, along the Yangtze river.

In November, German mediation produced an offer of negotiations from Japan to China, but Chiang rejected the offer unless the situation was restored to where it had been in July. The Japanese generals had already sent three columns marching on Nanking. As the battle began on 8 December, Chiang left the city, ultimately to establish a new capital at Chungking. After three days, the Chinese garrison of Nanking tried to retreat across the river, but a lack of boats meant few escaped. An orgy of violence by the Japanese soldiers then took place that became known as the Rape of Nanking. This followed attacks on British and American Yangtze gunboats and

any remaining sympathy for Japan in the West now vanished.

The Japanese now turned from their victories north and south to tackle the region around the city of Hsuchow, about halfway between Peking and the Yangtze Valley. This was the decisive battle of the

> By the beginning of 1941, Japan's war effort had reached a crisis. The war had been costing as much as $5 million a day in 1938, yet there was nothing of value left to conquer to defray the cost.

war and Chiang Kai-shek concentrated his best armies in the north here, even winning a minor victory at Taierhchuang in April 1938. The Japanese response to this defeat was a massive reinforcement of their troops, and the Chinese gave up the fight around Hsuchow on 15 May. The Japanese now instituted a strategy to cut off the Nationalists from the most valuable parts of China and from supplies from the West, an advance up the Yangtze from Nanking culminating in the fall of Hankow. All the major ports remaining

in Chinese hands were occupied during 1939, including Wenchow, Foochow, Amoy, Swatow and Pakhoi. Partly in response, the Chinese constructed a road from Kunming to Lashio in Burma through difficult mountain terrain, to allow war materiel to be shipped to Rangoon and then upcountry. Supplies also came through French Indochina, until the Japanese occupied the north of that colony in September 1940.

New enemies

By the beginning of 1941, Japan's war effort had reached a crisis. The war had been costing as much as $5 million a day in 1938, yet there was nothing of value left to conquer to defray the cost. Guerrilla warfare in Japanese-occupied areas was endemic and impossible to defeat. In June 1941, the Japanese armed forces agreed to occupy the rest of French Indochina, which brought a trade embargo and freezing of assets from Britain, the Netherlands and the United States. At this point, the Japanese lacked the resources to continue the war indefinitely – Chiang's determination to keep China fighting until help could come from some quarter had succeeded. The Japanese, in the face of the embargo, decided to attack Western countries. By default, they would enter China's war on China's side.

Wrecked German vehicles on a Russian road in winter give mute testimony to the German defeat before Moscow in November and December 1941. The Germans came tantalizingly close to the Soviet capital, but they had been asked to do too much in the time available.

Soviets drive Germans from Moscow

The **Red Army** won its first significant victory of the war after unleashing an offensive on 5 December 1941 that drove back the German forces attempting to encircle Moscow. The commander responsible for the defence of Moscow, General Georgi Zhukov, had learned from questioning prisoners and from Soviet partisans that the German armies near Moscow had no reserves in support, and concluded that they could not resist a major attack.

The Russian offensive consisted of two major operations north and south of the embattled Soviet capital. Having achieved some success north-west of Kalinin and Klin, the Russians broadened their offensive by attacking in the direction of Vitebsk-Smolensk, which placed strong forces behind the German troops nearest the city, as well as against the main strength of the German divisions further east. On the West and Bryansk Fronts south of the city, the Red Army hit the flank of General Heinz Guderian's Panzer Group 2 which had been fighting to get round strong Russian resistance at Tula. But the Red Army forces were better prepared for the cold than the Germans, and carefully husbanded reserves of aircraft were deployed to give them local air superiority for the first time since the start of the invasion. At the same time, partisans operating behind the German lines seriously disrupted the already fragile German supply network.

In their weakened state, the German armies could not withstand these fresh Soviet forces. As their flanks gave way, the troops directly in front of Moscow had to retreat to avoid being encircled. The only point where the Germans were able to hold up the Soviets significantly was at a bend in the Volga river at Rzhev.

US Pacific Fleet attacked

The **Japanese navy** launched a surprise attack against the American Pacific Fleet while it was at anchor at its base at Pearl Harbor, Hawaii. Two hundred Japanese aircraft launched from six carriers attacked at 7.55

Two hundred Japanese aircraft launched from six carriers attacked at 07.55 a.m. on 7 December 1941.

a.m. on 7 December 1941. The Japanese had not made any declaration of war, although one was due to be delivered in Washington DC at the time of the attack. In spite of indications of an impending Japanese attack, the American ships were completely taken by surprise. American losses were high, with 347 aircraft being destroyed or damaged, four out of seven battleships sunk, but only nine other warships badly damaged. An additional Japanese attempt to attack using midget submarines failed completely, with all five vessels being lost.

Two Pacific Fleet battleships at Pearl Harbor on 7 December 1941, victims of a surprise Japanese attack from aircraft carriers.

Japanese surprises in Malaya

The Japanese armed forces supplied an object lesson in combined operations and the use of speed and aggression by an outnumbered force to inflict serious defeats on the British defenders of the colony of Malaya in December 1941. The Japanese sent an invasion force of 50,000 men overland through Thailand and by sea across the South China Sea from bases in French Indochina. The air bases in northern Malaya were heavily bombed on 8 December and on 10 December two British ships, the battleship HMS *Prince of Wales* and battlecruiser HMS *Repulse*, were sunk by Japanese aircraft while hunting the Japanese invasion fleet.

The Japanese also landed troops on the coast of Malaya at Kota Baru and at various points along the coast of Thailand. The troops in Thailand quickly moved to the western side of the peninsula, along which ran the main north-south road, and by 12 December had driven the British defenders out of a key position at Jitra.

Pacific island war

Japanese forces occupied the Pacific islands of Guam and Makin on 10 December 1941, and attempted to invade Wake island on 11 December. This was preceded by bombing and strafing raids by Japanese aircraft flying from the Marshall islands, but the US Marine Corps garrison on the island held out. When a naval force consisting of 11 warships and two transports arrived it was driven off by accurate close-range gunfire from 5-inch guns on Wake, sinking two Japanese destroyers and damaging most of the rest of the flotilla. A much larger force, including four heavy cruisers, arrived off the island on 23 December and a landing force of 1,000 men overwhelmed the marine garrison of 500 men.

Japanese infantry capture an oil refinery in the British territory of Hong Kong in December 1941. The British garrison had no chance of sustaining a lengthy defence of Hong Kong, isolated as they were from the rest of the empire.

IN BRIEF

⚬ Germany declared war on the United States on 11 December 1941.

⚬ Japanese landings on the island of Luzon in the Philippines took place between 9 and 12 December 1941. The main attack came on 22 December, with the landing of a reinforced division at Lingayen Gulf.

⚬ The British crown colony of Hong Kong surrendered to the Japanese on Christmas Day 1941, after a battle lasting 17 days. The Japanese drove the British garrison off the mainland in five days of fighting, but the attack on Hong Kong island itself produced a desperate struggle in which Japanese air supremacy was a key factor in the final victory.

⚬ Panzer Group Africa, the German-Italian army in Libya, retreated all the way to El Agheila, where it had begun its offensive in 24 March 1941, and halted on New Year's Eve. Its commander, General Erwin Rommel, had chosen to withdraw after discovering that he was on the verge of being surrounded in the first week of December.

Withdrawal to Bataan

The **Filipino-American army** defending the Philippines against the Japanese invader retreated into the Bataan peninsula at the mouth of Manila Bay on 5 January 1942. Initially, the commander in the Philippines, General Douglas MacArthur, had wanted to stop the Japanese invasion on the beaches. However, when their landings on 22 December 1941 succeeded against weak opposition, he opted to implement the pre-war plan of defending Bataan in order to deny the Japanese the use of Manila Bay.

After Japanese troops occupied Manila on 2 January 1942, their commander, General Masaharu Honma believed the defenders to be a broken army. The Japanese advance had been easy, in part because it was confronted by a fighting withdrawal, but when their offensive against the Bataan position began, Japanese commanders were surprised at the toughness of the resistance they encountered.

General MacArthur's men were eventually forced out of their initial position on the peninsula, the Main Line of Resistance (MLR), when Japanese troops managed both to fend off a counter-attack and position strong forces threatening the line of retreat to the Rear Battle Position (RBP). On 22 January, MacArthur ordered a general withdrawal to the RBP after a disappointingly short battle on the MLR.

American troops on the Bataan peninsula, enduring a Japanese bombardment in 1942.

Soviet offensive widens

On **5 January** 1942, the Red Army, having repelled the German attempt to capture Moscow, widened its offensives, first to attempt

A Soviet poster encourages recruitment by showing Mother Russia holding the Red Army Oath of Allegiance under the slogan, "The Motherland Is Calling".

Red Army machine gunners aim at German positions in the snow. The Germans made little preparation for the winter, limiting their ability to resist the Soviet counter-offensive.

a double envelopment of the German forces before the Soviet capital, and then to attack both near Lake Ilmen and in the Ukraine. Attacking on such a wide front was the idea of Soviet leader Josef Stalin, who believed that a major strategic victory could be won. The Germans around Demyansk were encircled by the Red Army, as German dictator Adolf Hitler insisted that they were not to retreat under any circumstances, an order that resulted in the resignation of the commander of Army Group North, Field Marshal Wilhelm Ritter von Leeb.

British troops make final stand in Singapore

A column of British troops withdraws from mainland Malaya to the island of Singapore. The Japanese had completely outmanoeuvred the British, forcing them to make a final stand in difficult circumstances.

The last British troops evacuated the Malay peninsular on 31 January 1942, leaving the British commander, Lieutenant General Arthur Percival, under direction from the British prime minister, Winston Churchill, to defend Singapore "until after protracted fighting among the ruins of the city".

The British defence of the Malay peninsula has been marked by good intentions suffering from poor execution, while the Japanese by contrast have shown immense skill and imagination. Japan's Twenty-fifth Army, commanded by General Yamashita, was given a hundred days to secure the conquest with an army that includes extra engineering troops to cope with the numerous bridges that were expected to need rebuilding quickly in order to maintain the speed of the offensive. The Japanese infantry were also given large numbers of bicycles to assist them to move rapidly around the flanks of any British defensive positions. Before the invasion, the Twenty-Fifth Army trained on Formosa, where mountainous jungle terrain resembled what the troops would find in Malaya.

By contrast, the British defenders received almost no training for operations in the jungle either side of the roads in Malaya. The effects of this unpreparedness were apparent in the first major engagement, around Jitra on 12 December, when the British forces withdrew after a Japanese attack, supported by tanks, achieved a small tactical success on the right of the British defensive position. The British hastily withdrew when in fact their counter-attack had halted the Japanese. The effect was to hand the initiative permanently to the Japanese, who kept harassing the retiring British, not allowing them to prepare strong defensive positions as they retreated down the peninsula.

By the beginning of January 1942, Percival decided that there was little hope of the British being able to hold central Malaya against the Japanese, and planned to make a stand in Johore, at the southern end of the peninsula. However, the same day that he drew up his plan, the 11th Indian Division, which Percival expected to hold the Japanese for about three weeks, was decimated by the Japanese. Percival therefore had to assemble his forces to defend northern Johore sooner than expected, but he succeeded in creating a defensive position

that cut diagonally eastwards from Muar on the coast to Gemas in the hilly centre. Japanese attacks on this line began on 15 January and while the position held in the highlands, on the coast the superior quality of the Japanese Imperial Guards was decisive against the 45 Indian Brigade, which was entering the battle for the first time. On 22 January the British again began withdrawing and Percival began preparing to continue the retreat to Singapore island.

IN BRIEF

❖ Japanese landings on Borneo and the Celebes in the Dutch East Indies on 10/11 January 1942 opened their campaign to secure the most coveted territory in their offensive in the Pacific. The oil in the Dutch East Indies is vital to the Japanese war effort and is the main reason that the Japanese government chose to go to war against countries whose industrial resources far exceed their own capability.

The Final Solution

On 20 January 1942, 15 German public officials, including the Himmler's deputy, Reinhard Heydrich, and representatives from several ministries, including the Reich Chancellery, attended a meeting at a villa overlooking the Wannsee lake in Berlin. The minutes of this meeting refer to "the discussion about the final solution of the Jewish question". In them, Heydrich declares that he has been delegated by Hermann Göring to prepare the arrangements for the Final Solution, a matter that would be handled by Heinrich Himmler and the SS.

Jewish children behind the barbed wire of the Auschwitz concentration camp in southern Poland. The German government's genocide of European Jews was comprehensive in its search for victims.

Göring specifically referred to eliminating Jews from the German economy and from this point onward the Nazi regime officially began the persecution of Jews as a matter of national policy.

> On 9 November, "Crystal Night", Nazi activists went around burning or wrecking buildings, breaking shop windows or beating up Jews. As many as 200 Jews were killed that night.

Nazi dictator Adolf Hitler owed his rise to power in part to his fierce anti-Semitic views, which found sympathy among many nationalist-minded Germans. The "stab in the back" by "International Jewry", together with its allies the Bolsheviks, was a myth widely held. Once war broke out in Europe in 1939, any restraints on Nazi anti-Semitic policy by the need to follow legal norms were lifted. In January 1939, Hitler stated in a speech to the Reichstag that "if international finance Jewry … should succeed once more in

After nine years in power, the Nazi Party had already acquired considerable experience of using the police, judges, other civil servants and the army, to persecute and even murder their victims. The main targets of the Nazis were Jewish people, but Communists, Poles and other Slavs, freemasons, gypsies, homosexuals and people with disabilities were also persecuted. In fact, the original German concentration camps, set up in 1933 during the first year of Nazi rule, were aimed more at political opponents than for Jews and other racial groups. These concentration camps became places where prisoners could and would be malnourished, tortured and turned into slave labour. Then

in 1935, the Nazi government denied German citizenship to Jews.

In 1938, Heydrich organized a brutal terror campaign, mostly taking place in a single night, directed against synagogues, Jewish cemeteries and shops, and Jews themselves. On 9 November, "Crystal Night", Nazi activists went around burning or wrecking buildings, breaking shop windows or beating up Jews. As many as 200 Jews were killed that night and 2,000 more died in concentration camps after they were arrested. Three days later, Hermann Göring presided over a meeting of Nazi officials at which he stated: "I have received a letter written on the Führer's orders requesting that the Jewish question be now, once and for all, co-ordinated and solved."

An SS man searches through the coat of a newly-arrived Auschwitz inmate.

Reinhard Heydrich was the mastermind behind the Nazi schemes, until his assassination in June 1942.

plunging nations into another world war, the consequence will [be] the annihilation of the Jewish race in Europe."

A directive issued by Heydrich on 21 September 1939 referred to "as few concentration points as possible are to be set up, so as to facilitate subsequent measures". The directive was issued to the chiefs of special squads known as *Einsatzgruppen*. In October 1940 Jewish ghettos were established throughout the General Government – the area of pre-war Poland that had not been annexed by Germany or the Soviet Union. The Jews here were isolated from the rest of

> The most notorious incident occurred at Babi Yar, out-side Kiev, on 30 September 1941, when 33,700 people were killed. The brutality of these executions was felt even by those carrying them out.

the population by a wall and were plagued by starvation and disease.

The Einsatzgruppen shot many educated Poles, such as teachers and priests, during the invasion of 1939. In 1941, new Einsatzgruppen were organized for the German invasion of the Soviet Union, to carry out similar mass executions of Jews and Communist Party officials: Heydrich wanted the Einsatzgruppen

to shoot most of the Jews of Russia and the Baltic States, as opposed to confining them in ghettoes to await death due to natural causes. The corpses would be buried in mass graves outside cities. The most notorious incident occurred at Babi Yar, outside Kiev, on 30 September 1941, when 33,700 people were killed. The brutality of these executions was felt even by those carrying them out: an account exists of Himmler himself being shaken after watching 100 Jews executed. The Reichsführer-SS subsequently demanded that a different form of execution be found. In September 1941, at the concentration camp of Auschwitz, Poles and Red Army prisoners were used in poison gas experiments using a pesticide, Zyklon B. The success of this test provided the means Himmler sought for a method of mass killing that would be less traumatic for the perpetrators. On 10 October, it was decided to transport German Jews to the labour camps already existing in occupied Poland.

On 12 December 1941, the day after Germany declared war on the United States, Hitler spoke to a number of high-ranking Nazi leaders, referring to the destruction of the Jews being "a necessary consequence" of the conflict. The Wannsee Conference of January 1942 was intended to put Hitler's wishes into effect, by bringing together top-level officials from various ministries. The minutes of the conference describe exactly what was planned, subject to Hitler's approval. The Jews of Europe would be moved to camps in the East, where the able-bodied would be put to work, "in the course of which action doubtless a large portion will be eliminated by natural causes". The conference minutes are oblique in referring to what would happen to those who were not able-bodied, but a vast deportation of an estimated 11 million Jews was clearly planned. More detail was given about how to determine who would be included in the Final Solution and the minutes specify exact treatment of different categories of persons of "mixed blood". The meeting at Wannsee took about an hour and a half.

Meanwhile, a camp at Chelmno, near Lodz, had already opened in December 1941, exclusively for the purpose of exterminating Jews from Lodz and the surrounding area. The Wannsee conference now gave impetus to the building of more camps. Some, such as Birkenau, were built near existing prison and labour camps, in Birkenau's case Auschwitz. Others, such as Treblinka, were specifically constructed to carry out the plan outlined at Wannsee. Subsequently, waves of deportations of German and Austrian Jews to the camps in Poland began.

A pile of skulls found by Soviet troops at the Majdanek concentration camps. The liberation of occupied territories confirmed exactly what was happening in the camps.

Singapore surrenders

The British Empire experienced its worst defeat since the loss of the American colonies when the army defending Malaya surrendered to the Japanese on 15 February 1942, putting Malaya and its considerable natural resources under Japanese control. Prime Minister Winston Churchill was very unhappy with the result of this campaign, cabling Lieutenant General Arthur Percival beforehand saying: "Battle must be fought to bitter end. Commander and senior officers should die with their troops." Some 130,000 British and Empire soldiers became prisoners.

The Japanese attacked the north-western part of the island on the night of 8–9 February, overwhelming the Australian defenders here by sheer weight of numbers. Reserves that might have halted the Japanese did not arrive quickly enough to stem the assault. When the Australian commander, Major-General Gordon Bennett, misinterpreted orders he had received from Percival and withdrew from his position before Percival had intended, the only chance the British had of delaying the Japanese victory was lost.

The Japanese, by contrast, had done almost everything right. They aggressively fought round the flanks of every British position they encountered, and made a point of seizing the reservoirs and pumping stations that supplied fresh drinking water to the city of Singapore. Once these had been captured by the Japanese, the lack of water in the chaotic situation of Singapore – a city packed with refugees and drunken deserters – made the end inevitable.

Japanese heavy artillery covered by camouflage nets in Malaya in 1942. Superior artillery was a key reason for the success of the Japanese crossing to Singapore island.

The British surrender party makes their way to the Japanese lines on 15 February 1942. The loss of Singapore's water supply had doomed the defence.

Major-General Gordon Bennett escaped the surrender; his troops went into captivity.

Naval and air battles doom Allies

The decisive Japanese victory at the Battle of the Java Sea on 27–28 February 1942, together with their occupation of key airfields in the Dutch East Indies, ensured that their conquest of this resource-rich colony would be complete. Java Sea was the largest fleet action since the Battle of Jutland in 1916.

The Japanese invasion of the last major island in the archipelago controlled by the Allies was preceded by an attempt to locate the Japanese invasion fleet beforehand, in order to sink some of the transports. The Allied commander, Admiral Karel van Doorman, had five cruisers and 11 destroyers, which he took on a sweep east of Java. The invasion fleet consisted of 41 transports escorted by four cruisers and 14 destroyers. Van Doorman encountered the transports with two cruisers and 12 destroyers in close escort late on 27 February and immediately attacked. Considering himself to be in a tactically disadvantageous position, he manoeuvred to reduce the Japanese advantage rather than to close with the transports – which in the end did little to protect his ships and less to achieve his objective. The Japanese experienced gunnery that was accurate enough to straddle their vessels, but was not accurate enough to score hits, while Allied torpedoes also seemed ineffective.

Just after 5 p.m., three-quarters of an hour after the beginning of the battle, the Japanese hit HMS *Exeter* in the boiler room, causing the ship to lose power and disrupting the Allied formation. Two Allied destroyers were also sunk before the day ended. Under the cover of night, van Doorman again tried to find the transports and although his force was reduced to four cruisers when his destroyers had to depart, he still pursued the invasion convoy. Soon after 11 p.m., he found the Japanese escorts again,

this time losing his life and his two Dutch cruisers as Japanese torpedoes struck home around 11.30 p.m. The two remaining cruisers withdrew, in accordance with van Doorman's last orders.

The invasion of Java was the last stage in the conquest of the Dutch East Indies, which the Japanese had begun in January with the seizure of Tarakan, a small island off the coast of Borneo, on 10 January. The next day, landings from the sea were supported by the first-ever Japanese airborne assault when paratroopers were dropped during the

operation to seize Menado, on the northernmost tip of the island of the Celebes. These two operations typified the Japanese strategy in the Dutch East Indies. Naval landings, supported sometimes by paratroopers, seized vital airfields and harbours that would supply the next stage of the conquest. Using the airfields, the Japanese then swept the small Dutch air force in the archipelago from the skies; having command of the air meant that any attempt by Allied warships to halt the invasion fleets would be countered by mass bombing attacks.

The cruiser HMS *Exeter* sinks after attacks by Japanese cruisers on the morning of 1 March 1942, while attempting to withdraw to Surabaya after the battle of the Java Sea.

Japanese bomb Australia

The **port city** of Darwin, in Australia's Northern Territory, was the target of Japanese air raids on 19 February 1942. The Japanese aircraft contained a mixture of land-based bombers and aircraft flown off four of the carriers that had been used in the attack on the US Pacific Fleet at Pearl Harbor in December 1941. Over 200 aircraft were involved, starting their attacks just before 10 a.m., the main targets being shipping in the harbour and port facilities, as well as a nearby Royal Australian Air Force base. Over 200 people were killed, and between 300 and 400 wounded. The port was put out of action for several weeks. Many thousands of people fled the town, fearing an impending Japanese invasion.

Smoke rises from Port Darwin in Australia's Northern Territory after Japanese aeroplanes flying from aircraft carriers attacked the town on 19 February 1942.

Burma: British defeat, Japanese delay

Japanese Type 89 tanks cross a bridge thrown together across a demolished structure in June 1942. The Burmese campaign was a long retreat for the British army.

The **British army** suffered a major defeat on the Sittang river in Burma, yet caused a serious delay to the advancing Japanese when they blew up the bridge over the river on 23 February 1942. Since the main Japanese attack on Burma began on 22 January, British forces had been conducting a series of fighting withdrawals, hoping to make a stand on the Sittang. However, as the fighting neared the river on 16 February,

Most were either captured or killed trying to ford the swift-running Sittang.

the 17th Indian Division's plans could not be fully implemented. The supposedly orderly withdrawal had turned into a chaotic one, and when on 22 February small Japanese infiltration groups appeared to be on the verge of capturing the Sittang bridge, the divisional commander ordered it to be blown in spite of the majority of his men still being on the wrong side of the river. Most were either captured or killed trying to ford the swift-running Sittang. The Japanese faced the problem of whether to attack toward Rangoon, with its oil terminal and port facilities, or to drive northwards toward the remaining concentration of British and Chinese forces in the central region of the colony.

Channel dash stuns British

The German battlecruisers *Scharnhorst* and *Gneisenau*, together with the heavy cruiser *Prinz Eugen*, daringly raced up the English channel from the French port of Brest on 11–13 February.

The ships left Brest during the night and reached the Straits of Dover without being sighted. This daring operation made a mockery of the supposed command of the sea held by the Royal Navy.

The ships left Brest during the night and reached the Straits of Dover without being sighted. This daring operation made a mockery of the supposed command of the sea held by the Royal Navy.

British withdraw in Libya

British forces, poised at El Aghela to attack into the western Tripolitanian portion of the Italian colony of Libya, withdrew to the Gazala-Bir Hacheim line on 1 February 1942 to avoid attacks by Panzer Army Africa which threatened to encircle large portions of the British Eighth Army. Among the booty captured by General Erwin Rommel's German and Italian forces were 1,300 trucks.

General Erwin Rommel speaks to some of his officers during the Western Desert campaign in early 1942. Rommel drove his subordinates hard, and won victories by doing so.

Dutch surrender Java

The Japanese completed their conquest of the Dutch East Indies when the Dutch defenders of the island of Java, the last centre of resistance in the archipelago, surrendered on 8 March 1942. The Japanese had landed at three points on the island on 1 March: Kragan, in the east, Eerten Wetan in the centre and Bantam Bay in the east. The Kragan landing was virtually uncontested and the Dutch defenders in the region were too few to withstand the advance on the key naval base of Surabaya, although they did manage to hold out long enough for the demolition of many of the port installations to be carried out successfully. The Japanese reached Surabaya on 7 March, effectively ending any resistance in this part of the island.

The Bantam Bay landing, by contrast, was attacked by air and naval forces, including the cruisers HMAS *Perth* and USS *Houston*. In the resulting naval engagement, four Japanese transports were damaged or sunk, but both Allied cruisers were sunk, with heavy loss of life. On advancing inland, Japanese troops encountered stern resistance from the Australians at Leuwiliang, which held them up for two days before they managed to turn a flank and force a fighting withdrawal.

The centre landing proved the most significant. A reinforced Japanese regiment faced little resistance on the ground, but Allied air attacks proved effective in disrupting the advance inland. Enough trucks were landed for a Japanese force to drive 30 miles (48 km) inland to the aerodrome at Kalidjati and capture it, hampering Allied efforts to continue attacks on the landing beaches. A Dutch tank unit attempted to retake the airfield on 3 March, but by this time Japanese aircraft had arrived. First they attacked the front and rear vehicles in the long column, destroying them and thereby blocking the road which ran through paddy fields, then they shot up the remainder of the column. With the airfield in Japanese hands, air superiority passed to the Japanese and the Allies' defeat was only a matter of time.

Japanese army vehicles on the streets of Jakarta. Japan's main objective in launching its attacks in late 1941 was the Dutch East Indies, and its extensive oil resources.

New British strategy

British heavy bombers, such as the Avro Lancaster I, that began to enter service in early 1942, made possible massively destructive raids by night on German cities.

The British bombing of Germany took a new turn on 28/29 March 1942 when 234 bombers attacked the city of Lübeck. The town, largely built of wood and militarily unimportant, had most of its centre destroyed by fire from incendiary bombs. Britain's Bomber Command has explicitly adopted a strategy of "area bombing". A 14 February 1942 directive from the Air Ministry to Air Marshal Arthur Harris, instructed him that "Operations should now be focused on the morale of the enemy civilian population and in particular the industrial workers." This was to be a direct attack on civilians, regarded by many as an unethical form of war, but Bomber Command nevertheless adopted this strategy because its previous efforts at precision bombing by day had resulted in very heavy loss of aircraft, while precision bombing by night had proved ineffective. The scale of operations Harris has in mind for the rest of the war was demonstrated on 30/31 May when 1,046 aircraft attacked the German city of Cologne, in which 3,300 houses were destroyed, leaving 45,000 people without homes or workplaces. Civilian casualties were relatively light, with only 384 deaths.

Mud and blood in northern Russia

A slow, attritional struggle in northern Russia during the spring of 1942 produced no clear-cut advantage for either side. The fighting took place largely in swampy terrain to the south of Leningrad, as Soviet attempts to lift the siege of that heroic city were thwarted by fierce German resistance.

At the end of the Soviet winter offensives in February 1942, two German corps were encircled around the town of Demyansk. Adolf Hitler ordered that the defenders fight to the last, while supplies were flown in and either landed on airstrips or dropped by parachute. Meanwhile troops on the western face of the pocket fought in both directions to reopen a corridor that would allow the besieged German troops to be resupplied by road. Any thought of retreat was abandoned on the Führer's orders.

Meanwhile, the Germans in turn tried to trap the Soviet Second Shock Army in an operation of their own to the north-west of Novgorod. This swampy terrain was better suited to defence than the open area around Demyansk and progress was very slow, but the Soviets were reliant on two supply routes out of the swamp, and these were cut on 20 March after five days of fighting. A Soviet counter-attack quickly regained control of these roads, and it was the only the effects of the rain and thaw turning the highways to clogging mud in April that effectively cut off the Second Shock Army from outside help.

Around Demyansk, the Germans succeeded in breaking through the Soviet lines and re-establishing a supply route on 21 April 1942.

The bitter cold of a relatively severe winter in Russia during 1941–42 took a heavy toll of the German soldier on the Eastern Front.

Japan bombed by Americans

One of Doolittle's sixteen B-25 bombers takes off from the aircraft carrier USS *Hornet* for a morale-boosting raid on the Japanese home islands.

Sixteen American medium bombers flew off the aircraft carrier USS *Hornet* on 18 April 1942 on a one-way mission to bomb Japan, attacking targets in Tokyo and Nagoya before attempting to fly to Chinese airfields. No aircraft reached the Chinese bases, but most crew on the bombers, including their commander Lieutenant Colonel James H. Doolittle, succeeded in either crash-landing or bailing out over Chinese territory. One bomber landed at Vladivostok, in the Soviet Union, where the crew was interned. The Japanese captured eight prisoners, of whom three were executed. A further two crew were killed in a crash-landing.

Japanese raid Indian Ocean

A powerful Japanese fleet, which included five aircraft carriers and four battleships, made a successful raid into the Indian Ocean that was completed on 20 April 1942 when the ships returned to Japanese waters without significant loss, having left for Ceylon and the Bay of Bengal on 26 March. The British were alerted to the approach of the enemy a few days later and on 31 March ordered shipping to leave Colombo harbour. About two-thirds of the merchant ships present there had fled by the time Japanese aircraft attacked on 5 April, but the Japanese focused their attacks in any case on the harbour installations, causing significant damage. In the afternoon of the same day, the Japanese sank two British heavy cruisers. The port of Trincomalee was hit on 9 April, the same day that Japanese aircraft sank the light aircraft carrier HMS *Hermes*, which at the time had no aircraft aboard.

At the same time, a smaller Japanese flotilla, including a single light carrier and several heavy cruisers, raided the key shipping routes along the Bay of Bengal, sinking a substantial number of merchant vessels, and raiding the ports of Cocanada and Vizagapatam.

The heavy cruiser HMS *Dorsetshire* was sunk off Ceylon on 5 April 1942 in company with her sister ship HMS *Cornwall*, by Japanese dive bombers.

Augustus Agar, VC

The Japanese raid on Ceylon brought the last seagoing assignment of a British naval hero, Augustus Agar. As captain of the cruiser HMS *Dorsetshire*, he suffered a leg wound and lung damage when his ship was sunk. In 1919, he had won the Victoria Cross after attacking Soviet warships in port at the Kronstadt naval base. He also attempted some daring raids using oil tankers against the invasion barges assembled by the Germans at Boulogne for their intended cross-Channel invasion in 1940.

Fall of the Philippines

The last surviving elements of the American Far Eastern Army, surrendered to the Japanese on the island of Corregidor in the Philippines on 6 May 1942. Japan has now completed its conquest of south-east Asia, which it has accomplished in five months.

American forces had withdrawn into the Bataan peninsula, and here, although driven from their Main Line of Resistance (MLR) toward the north of the peninsula, successfully withstood the Japanese assault on their Rear Battle Position (RBP) in early January. On 8 February, the Japanese commander of the Fourteenth Army, General Honma Masaharu, called off further attacks in Bataan until reinforcements could be sent. His forces had lost heavily in the fighting, especially an attempt to land a

flanking force on the south-western side of the peninsula, known as the Battle of the Points. Two battalions of his 20th Regiment were decimated in this attack, while the third met the same fate in an attempt to break through the RBP.

The next month was spent bringing in reinforcements from the East Indies and French Indochina, especially artillery units. Honma resumed his attacks on 3 April, beginning with a five-hour artillery bombardment that preceded the infantry assaults. The American forces by this stage had spent over three months on half rations with limited medical supplies, malaria and dysentery were widespread and the troops were too weak to fight effectively, so that the Japanese broke through with ease. The original commander of the army,

General Douglas MacArthur, had left the Philippines on 12 March on orders from Washington DC, and travelled to Australia to take command of Allied forces there. From army headquarters on the island of Corregidor, his successor, General Jonathan Wainwright, refused to allow the surrender of the forces on Bataan, but on 8 April the commander of the American units there ordered his men to lay down their arms.

The garrison of Corregidor held out under constant bombardment for another month, before Japanese landings on the island on 6 May succeeded in establishing a foothold. With the Japanese pressing hard on the Malinta Tunnel, where American wounded were hospitalized, and fearing for the lives of these men, based on the reputation the Japanese soldiers had acquired for wanton butchery, Wainwright sought terms from the Japanese.

American troops, who had surrendered to the Japanese, march under escort across the Bataan peninsula in the Philippines. Many died en route, as the Japanese treated captured soldiers harshly.

Japanese-Americans consigned to internment

Japanese-Americans interned at the Santa Anita camp. Americans of Japanese origin were treated far more harshly than German-Americans or Italian-Americans.

American citizens of Japanese ancestry were rounded up by the American military and deported from the Pacific coast of the United States by Civilian Exclusion Order No. 346, which was issued on 3 May 1942. This followed the authorization of Executive Order 9066 by President Franklin Roosevelt in 19 February 1942.

The Civilian Exclusion Order No. 346 programme relocated some 112,000 Japanese-Americans to camps in eastern California and the Rocky Mountain states, as well as Arkansas.

Japanese-Americans were singled out for this treatment from among American citizens whose ancestors were from one of the Axis countries, although German-Americans and Italian-Americans were allowed to continue living in their homes, and were subject to the draft. As a result of the programme, over 5,000 Japanese-Americans renounced their citizenship; however, the vast majority remained loyal to the United States, with a small minority volunteering for military service.

Madagascar base occupied

Allied troops invaded the Vichy French colony of Madagascar on 5 May, successfully occupying the naval base of Diego Suarez on the northern tip of the island. The Allies were concerned that Japanese naval forces might now make use of the island as a base from which to attack Allied shipping in the Indian Ocean. The Allied invasion was completely unexpected and the Vichy garrison on the island was totally unprepared when the landings occurred. The British forces undertaking the operation did not have sufficient strength to attack other Vichy garrisons on the island, and the Vichy

The Allied invasion was completely unexpected and the Vichy garrison on the island was totally unprepared.

authorities continue to rule over central and southern Madagascar.

British Commandos sail toward Diego Suarez on the island of Madagascar aboard a boat crewed by Royal Navy personnel.

The "Lady Lex", the USS *Lexington*, on fire and sinking after being struck by two torpedoes in her port side and bombs striking both her main deck and her smokestack. She went down without capsizing, eliciting the comment, "She is going down with her head up, a lady to the last."

Fleets clash without seeing one another

The first naval battle in which the opposing ships of each side did not see one another occurred between American and Japanese warships in the Coral Sea on 7–8 May 1942. The battle occurred as part of a Japanese attempt to capture Port Moresby, the main Allied base in New Guinea, and establish a base on Tulagi, an island in the Solomons chain. The Japanese created three separate fleets to carry out the operation and although some American warships were sunk, the Japanese attack on Port Moresby was averted.

At this time American signals intelligence had broken the main code used by the Japanese Combined Fleet. The commander-in-chief in the Pacific, Admiral Chester Nimitz, was aware by the end of February that the Japanese were planning to seize Port Moresby and the two aircraft carrier task forces in the Australia–New Zealand area were alerted in March.

The Japanese fleets left their key central Pacific naval base at Truk island on 30 April–1 May. The Tulagi group succeeded in occupying the island, with the aim of establishing a seaplane base there, only to be attacked the next day, 4 May, by aircraft from the USS *Yorktown*. During the next two days, both sides became aware of one another's presence, but poor visibility prevented either from locating the other. On 7 May, however, the American and Japanese admirals launched major air attacks against one another, but on the basis of mistaken reports. The Japanese attacked and sank an oil tanker and a destroyer, thinking they were an aircraft carrier and a cruiser, while the Americans attacked a light carrier, thinking it was a fleet carrier. All these ships were sunk. The next day, the fleet carriers were attacked. The Americans badly damaged the *Shokaku*, while the Japanese damaged both the *Yorktown* and the *Lexington*. The damage to the USS *Lexington* was at first not thought to be severe, but an aviation gasoline leak exploded, damaging the ship so severely that she was abandoned at 5.07 p.m., and that evening the *Lexington* was torpedoed and sunk by an American destroyer to prevent her capture by the Japanese.

British and Chinese forces retreat from Burma

By **20 May** 1942, Allied forces completed their two-month retreat from Burma, in which hundreds of thousands of civilian refugees were also involved. An estimated 750,000 more died en route, in one of the worst civilian disasters of the war so far.

The Japanese, having crossed the Sittang river in southern Burma on 2 March, resumed their offensive which had been temporarily delayed by the British defence of the bridge at Sittang. By this time the Allied commander in India (which now included Burma), General Sir Archibald Wavell, had replaced Lieutenant General Sir Thomas Hutton with Lieutenant

A Japanese soldier races through the Burmese jungle during an attack. The Japanese had far better training in jungle warfare than their British counterparts.

Pilots of the American Volunteer Group, a mercenary force recruited to help the Chinese against the Japanese before the latter's attack on the United States, in front of one of their P-40 fighters.

General Sir Harold Alexander. Wavell ordered Alexander to hold Rangoon at all costs but it quickly became apparent to Alexander once he arrived on the spot that this would end in a crushing defeat for the British. The Japanese assumed that the British would defend the city, but instead Alexander withdrew his forces, after destroying the oil refinery there. Once Rangoon fell on 7 March, the Japanese paused to await reinforcements from the East Indies and Malaya. Meanwhile, the British received some support from China, when three armies (equivalent to a British division) arrived to protect the Burma Road, a highway through mountainous terrain that was China's sole route for receiving supplies for its war against the Japanese.

The Japanese chose to attack Allied air forces on 21 March, and in six days established air supremacy over Burma, which made it easy for them to break through the Allied defences in central Burma and the retreat began. Lashio, the Burmese end of the Burma Road, fell on 29 April, Mandalay on 1 May and Kalewa on 11 May.

Red Army crushed around Kharkov

An encircled force of Red Army soldiers was finally overwhelmed by German attacks on 30 May 1942, bringing to an end a short campaign that began with a Soviet attack and ended with a German victory. The Soviet offensive aimed to continue the round of victories that had been won along the front during the winter of 1941/42, by keeping the pressure on the Germans to prevent them from carrying out an offensive of their own. Soviet leader Josef Stalin and his commanders chose the Kharkov area thinking it to be the weakest link in a series of key supply centres for the German army on the Eastern Front.

The offensive began on 13 May. On the northern part of the front, around Volchansk, the Red Armies involved immediately ran into tough resistance from the Germans. Here, in order to achieve any significant advance, the Soviet commanders had to commit their second echelon of divisions, normally held in reserve until a key breakthrough was made, to support the first echelon in attacking the original German front.

Greater gains were made in the south, around Barvenkovo. The commander of the German army group here, Field Marshal Fedor von Bock, convinced Adolf Hitler that the Soviet offensive represented an opportunity rather than a problem. Conceding ground in the south would enable them to counter-attack, turning a setback into a key victory; Hitler enthusiastically embraced von Bock's idea. The Germans used air power to harass the advancing Soviet forces, rather than committing substantial numbers of ground troops, in order to save the

A Red Army soldier armed with a PPSh-41 sub-machine gun peers cautiously at a possible enemy position during street-fighting in wet spring weather.

latter for the coming attack. Once the momentum of Red Army attacks slowed on 15 May, the Germans prepared for their counterstroke.

On 17 May, the First Panzer Army was unleashed on the Red Army forces around Barvenkovo. Its armoured spearheads pushed northwards, while troops from VIII Corps of the German First Army supported them with a drive southwards. After five days of fierce fighting, the two forces met west of Izyum, trapping two Soviet armies. As usual, Soviet soldiers resisted fiercely as the German attacks gradually squeezed the encirclement, fanatical among them being a battalion of Red Army women soldiers who were especially determined to kill as many Germans as they could before they themselves died. Over 200,000 Red Army soldiers were taken prisoner. German losses in the whole operation were relatively light, about 20,000 men being killed or wounded.

Lieutenant-General Nikita Khruschev (left), a Politburo member, and Colonel Leonid Brezhnev (right), discuss the military situation around Kharkov in the spring of 1942.

Rommel battles in Cauldron

The Germans in North Africa attacked the British defensive line between Gazala on the coast and Bir Hakeim inland, making some progress by the end of May 1942. The British, expecting an attack, had laid around half a million landmines to create artificial barriers, and deployed their forces in a series of "boxes", with anti-tank weapons

The British, expecting an attack, had laid around half a million landmines to create artificial barriers.

carefully sited to provide supporting fields of fire and plenty of wire entanglements to give protection from attacking infantry.

Rommel, however, decided to outflank this strong position by attacking around its southern flank. Initially, on 27–29 May, his attacks faltered when they met unexpected concentrations of armour and lost communication with their supporting air force squadrons. However, the British deployed their tanks badly, siting the formations so that they were unable to support one another and sending in counter-attacks piecemeal so that Rommel was able to beat them off. Once he re-established communication with his air force counterparts, Rommel's offensive resumed and in a major battle known as The Cauldron, delivered a crushing blow to British armoured formations, capturing 3,000 prisoners when he secured the surrender of one of the boxes.

British prisoners of Rommel's Panzer Army Africa await transportation to camps. Rommel's victory in turning the British line based on Gazala, in Libya, enabled an invasion of Egypt.

M3 Tank

Grant was one of the names given by the British to the American M3 medium tank, which had entered service with the US Army in 1939. These vehicles first saw action at the Battle of Gazala in May 1942. Its high silhouette was a major drawback, and in the Red Army, which also received versions of the M3 tank, it was known as "the coffin for seven brothers".

Commando raids

After Dunkirk, the British military was in an awkward predicament. Traditionally, the British army waged war against a Continental enemy by placing its comparatively small military forces either directly alongside an ally with a large army, as in France during the First World War, or else in a theatre where the enemy might not be able or willing to deploy the full weight of its army, as in Spain during the Napoleonic Wars of the early nineteenth century. In the summer of 1940, there was no Continental ally for the British to fight alongside, nor any likely theatre of war where the British could engage a fraction of the German forces effectively.

An oil factory in the Vaagso islands goes up in flames after demolition work by British commandos who attacked the German base there in December 1941. The British also captured materials to assist with breaking the German Enigma code.

The army searched for an effective answer to the question of how to strike at the enemy in these circumstances and, with Prime Minister Winston Churchill's encouragement, arrived at the idea of "combined operations". Harassing raids on the coasts of France and Norway were seen as a way of both engaging the enemy and learning about amphibious warfare. Units of volunteers to receive training in these special operations were created in July 1940, the name "commando" coming from the hit-and-run Boer War formations of the Afrikaaner republics. In October, the original Commandos were reorganized into Special Service Battalions, each of two Commandos, and made their first raid on the Lofoten islands, off the Norwegian coast, on 4 March 1941. Five destroyers escorted two amphibious warfare ships, especially adapted to carry landing craft. Herring oil factories manufactured glycerin that was used in explosives there, while the possibility of capturing a German Enigma cypher machine and other encryption intelligence also existed. The raid was a success, in that the factories were blown up and Enigma machine rotor wheels were captured without casualties, but it was a small operation and of extremely limited strategic impact.

During 1941 raids were still limited. The island of Spitzbergen was occupied in August, in order to destroy the coal mines there and evacuate the miners who worked in them; no German troops present. In North Africa, a

During the attack on Vichy French Syria in June 1941, men of Combined Operations were landed to seize key installations ahead of troops advancing overland from Palestine. This proved effective, although casualties were heavy.

raid on Bardia in April 1941 was ineffective, while an attempt to assassinate the German commander, General Erwin Rommel, failed owing to poor intelligence, with the loss of Lieutenant Colonel Geoffrey Keyes (who was awarded the VC for the action), the son of the first Director of Combined Operations, Admiral Sir Roger Keyes. Two raids in Norway in December 1941, at Maaloy and Vaagso, and the Lofoten Islands, were carried out as experiments and for diversionary effect, as well as bringing aircraft into Combined Operations with the participation of Bomber Command and Coastal Command.

Apart from raids, the Commandos participated in one other operation that offered traditional-minded military men a glimpse of how commandos might be used in traditional operations, as opposed to hit-and-run raids. During the attack on Vichy French Syria in June 1941, men of Combined Operations were landed to seize key installations ahead of troops advancing overland from Palestine. This proved effective, although casualties were heavy.

The wreck of HMS *Campbeltown* in the *Normandie* dock at St Nazaire. The successful demolition of this warship put the dry dock out of action and prevented the Germans from utilizing the port facilities for their large warships.

The year 1942 saw the most dramatic Commando operations of the war so far. Perhaps the most incredible was that conducted against a German radar installation at Bruneval in France in February. Paratroopers from the 1st Airborne Division jumped over France and then made their way to a Würzburg radar installation that had been there since the autumn of 1941. Under fire, they removed components of the station, as well as photographing its specifications painted on the radar's dish. These components were loaded on landing craft and brought back across the Channel for intelligence experts to reconstruct and analyse.

The raid on St Nazaire at the end of March was equally successful, and more dramatic. The target of the raid was a large dry dock built for the use of the liner *Normandie*, but which it was thought would allow the battleship *Tirpitz* to attack Atlantic convoys after being transferred to the French coast from its Norwegian

hideouts. A destroyer, HMS *Campbeltown*, was adapted as a huge bomb, with her bow packed with explosives; timed fuses ensured that the crew and escorts could

> The year 1942 saw the most dramatic Commando operations of the war so far. Perhaps the most incredible was that conducted against a German radar installation at Bruneval in France in February.

escape before the explosion. On the night of 26–27 March, about 250 Commandos and 14 motor launches accompanied the *Campbeltown* across the Channel. The dry dock was successfully rammed, but casualties among both the Commandos and crews of the launches were very heavy;

only five launches made it back to Britain. The explosives did not go off until 28 March, killing nearly 500 Germans trying to work out how to remove the vessel. The dry dock was put out of action for the duration of the war.

The appointment of the Chief of Combined Operations, Commodore Lord Louis Mountbatten, to the Chief of Staff's Committee, with the acting rank of Vice Admiral, in March 1942 marked the end of the Commandos' uncertain status within Britain's military and naval forces. However, to some extent their raiding role had never been fully developed before the war's events made the original concept outdated. Just over three months after the first Commando raid, the Germans invaded the Soviet Union, and by the end of that same year the United States had been drawn into the European war, and its military leaders were eager to mount a full-scale invasion of Continental Europe. The Commandos subsequently adapted themselves to the new environment.

Japanese carriers sunk

Four Japanese carriers were sunk by three American carriers at the Battle of Midway island on 4 June 1942. Japan will find it difficult to replace both the ships and aircrew at this stage of the war.

The Americans became aware of Japanese plans by 6 May, nearly three weeks after Japanese commanders had decided to undertake the operation. The Americans were initially unsure of the ultimate target of this large Japanese fleet concentration, believing it either to be the Hawaiian islands or Midway. Eventually it was concluded that both might be targets, and Admiral Chester Nimitz, the commander of the American Pacific Fleet, chose to send all his available carriers to

defend Midway. The Americans also used intelligence gained from signals intercepts to prevent the Japanese from gathering information about the location of the American aircraft carriers.

The Japanese carriers left home waters on 26 May and reached Midway on 4 June, when they mounted a raid on the air base there. However, the Japanese reconnaissance around Midway was inadequate and they never located the American carriers until the reserve aircraft on Japanese flight decks were already being rearmed with bombs for use against land targets. Rather than fly these off against the US warships, the Japanese carrier commander, Admiral Nagumo, chose to let the Midway attackers land

before launching the reserve aircraft.

While his aircraft were refuelling and rearming, there was an American air strike. Dive-bombers hit the Japanese aircraft carriers while vulnerable fuel hoses and munitions were still out on the decks. Three aircraft carriers were effectively destroyed in six minutes. The fourth carrier, the *Hiryu*, managed to launch an air strike that damaged the American carrier *Yorktown*, but the *Hiryu* was hit by a second American air attack that destroyed her. Japanese losses in the battle were 2,500 men and 332 aircraft; the Americans lost 307 men and 147 aircraft. Four Japanese carriers and one cruiser were lost; the Americans lost the *Yorktown* and one destroyer.

Japanese occupy Aleutian islands

On 6/7 June 1942, Japanese army and naval forces landed on two islands in the Aleutian chain west of Alaska, representing the first invasion of American territory since 1814. The Japanese forces were part of a larger operation including the attack on Midway island in the Pacific.

The Aleutians operation began on 3 June when carrier-borne aircraft attacked Dutch Harbor, the biggest port in the Aleutian chain, on Amaknak island, where an air base and naval facilities were located. The raid accomplished little, damaging some of the facilities and killing 25 service personnel and the aircraft carriers then sailed away.

Meanwhile, the landings took place on 6 June, when Japanese marines landed on Kiska, and on 7 June, when Japanese soldiers seized Attu. A weather and radio station on Kiska was the sole forces installation on either island, but that did not stop the Japanese brutalizing the 50 people they found there, who were taken from the islands and sent to prisons and labour camps in Japan.

Dutch Harbor, in the Aleutian islands, after a Japanese bombing raid on 3 June 1942. The Japanese subsequently occupied two islands further west in the chain, Attu and Kiska.

OBITUARY
REINHARD HEYDRICH
(1904–1942)

SS-*Obergruppenführer* Reinhard Heydrich (above, far left), Deputy Reich Protector of the protectorate of Bohemia and Moravia, died on 4 June 1942 from wounds inflicted by a British-sponsored assassination attempt on 27 May.

Heydrich was the archetype of the evil Gestapo officer, and earned such nicknames as the Blond Beast and the Hangman of Prague. Born in Halle in Saxony, he entered the German Navy in 1922, but nine years later was dismissed from the service for "conduct unbecoming to an officer" allegedly over a love affair with the daughter of an industrialist.

Heydrich joined the Nazi Party and the SS in 1931, as a member of its intelligence unit that monitored individuals thought likely to be a danger to the Party. In 1932 he became head of the Nazi security service, which was eventually merged into German state security following Adolf Hitler's accession to power in 1933. In 1936, Heydrich also became chief of the security police. As Himmler's deputy, he became a key architect of the Final Solution of the "Jewish Question", beginning in 1938, when he was given overall charge of the agency that encouraged Jews to emigrate from Germany. In September 1941, he was named Deputy Reich Protector of Bohemia and Moravia (the Czech part of Czechoslovakia), and consequently became the target of Czech resistance fighters, who were sent from Britain, ambushed his car and wounded him with a grenade. The wounds became infected and Heydrich died.

He is survived by his wife, two sons and two daughters.

Germans capture general

The capture of General Andrei Vlasov on 12 July 1942 marks the end of the trapped Soviet Second Shock Army, caught in the swampy terrain southwest of Leningrad between Novgorod and Gruizino. This army had been under siege since 20 May, when the narrow corridor that had kept it supplied for months was finally cut by German attacks. Vlasov had

This army had been under siege since 20 May, when the narrow corridor that had kept it supplied for months was finally cut by German attacks.

been appointed its commander in order to extricate it from its precarious situation, but ultimately he and his men were abandoned to their fate. They were not allowed to withdraw and in the end, after the Germans had cut them off from their comrades, they were reduced to extreme measures to feed themselves, including reportedly cutting off the hooves of dead horses, boiling them and eating the scrapings. By the beginning of July, most of the survivors had surrendered to the Germans.

Sevastopol falls in display of German might

German forces captured the Crimean naval port of Sevastopol on 4 July 1942 after a siege lasting 250 days. The final assault was intended to show the world the capability of the German army to overcome any fortress, no matter how strong.

The German Eleventh Army, under the command of General Erich von Manstein, was reinforced by some of the most powerful artillery pieces found in European arsenals in 1942. These included 600mm mortars and a 800mm railway gun known as Dora. Over 1,500 men were needed to prepare the ground for the latter, in addition to a gun crew of 1,420. Five or six rounds from Dora demolished enough of a concrete or brick fort to allow the infantry to attack and capture it.

Manstein had subjected Sevastopol to a constant bombardment by aircraft and artillery from 3 June, until on 7 June the infantry assaults began. The fighting lasted the rest of the month as the Germans and their Rumanian allies gradually forced their battle line closer and closer to the city. Some 90,000 Soviet soldiers and sailors survived the siege to be taken prisoner.

A group of Red Army soldiers rest after the surrender of Sevastopol. The Germans captured some 90,000 prisoners after the city's fall.

MP38

The German MP38 sub-machine gun was developed from the earlier MP36 and was first used in combat during the 1940 invasion of Poland. Although reliable and inexpensive, it had a relatively slow rate of fire. The combination of a slower rate of fire and a less powerful cartridge, however, helped make it more accurate.

Luftwaffe personnel practice their firearms skills with MP38 sub-machine guns.

Hitler takes revenge

Rows of murdered citizens of the village of Lidice laid out in a field. The Czech village was destroyed on Hitler's orders as a reprisal for the assassination of Reinhard Heydrich.

Angered by the death of Reinhard Heydrich, Deputy *Reichsprotektor* of Bohemia, on 4 June 1942, German dictator Adolf Hitler ordered reprisals against all Czechs believed to have assisted his assassins. On 10 June, the mining village of Lidice was destroyed, and its inhabitants shot or sent to concentration camps.

After Lidice had been surrounded by German police to cut off all escape routes, the population was rounded up and segregated by sex and age. All males over the age of 15 were placed in a barn and shot on 11 June. Most of the women were sent to Ravensbrück, a concentration camp, where many died. The children were divided into those who were considered suitable to be raised as Germans (mostly by their physical appearance), and those who were not, the latter being murdered in a gas chamber. In all, 340 residents of Lidice were killed by the Germans. All buildings in the village were dynamited, the rubble bulldozed and the land subsequently planted with trees. The village of Lezaky was subjected to similar treatment two weeks later.

Rommel's repulse in Egypt

Field Marshal Erwin Rommel, commander of Panzer Army Afrika, suffered a setback when his attempt to force his way through the British Eighth Army at El Alamein ended on 3 July 1942 with the abandonment of offensive operations. The run of victories for Rommel that began in January have come to an end.

The battle began on 1 July and lasted three days. Auchinleck had massed his artillery and the Germans were subjected to a steady barrage that blunted their enthusiasm for advancing

Rommel planned a two-pronged attack between El Alamein, a railway halt on the coast, and Ruweisat Ridge, a piece of high ground running west to east along the same line as Rommel's advance. The British commander, General Sir Claude Auchinleck, had anticipated the location of Rommel's attack and arranged his troops to attack the German thrusts from the flanks. The battle began on 1 July and lasted three days. Auchinleck had massed his artillery and the Germans were subjected to a steady barrage that blunted their enthusiasm for advancing. Tanks clashed around Ruweisat Ridge, the crews of both sides' armoured vehicles fighting desperately in the hope of avoiding the fate they had seen so often of comrades incinerated in their tanks, turning into charred corpses whilst still sitting in the driver's seat or manning the turret.

By 3 July, Auchinleck was confident that he had halted Rommel and positioned his mobile reserve, the 1st Armoured Division, behind Ruweisat Ridge. Rommel again urged his tanks forward on 3 July and the British were pushed slowly but steadily backwards throughout the day. But the Germans did not have the strength to break through and when Rommel called off the action that night, Auchinleck knew he had won the battle.

Halfway around the world

An Italian aircraft flew from southern Russia to China, and then Japan and back in a remarkable aviation feat. The purpose of the mission was to deliver diplomatic codes to Tokyo to ensure that radio communications among the Axis powers could be secure, a method that would be much faster than the normal transfer by submarine.

A Savoia-Marchetti S.75 GA carried out the flight, leaving Italy on 29 June 1942, and staging through to Zaporozhe, where the Italian army in the Soviet Union had established an airfield. The next night, the aircraft departed for China, flying at 2,500 feet (760 m), north of the Caspian Sea, the Aral Sea and Lake Balkhash, then the Altai Mountains and the Gobi Desert, until it reached Paotou in Inner Mongolia on 1 July. The aircraft finally arrived in Tokyo on 3 July. The return flight was made from 16 to 20 July.

The Malta convoys

Malta had at one time been a key base in the chain that stretched around the world for use of the British fleet. It had only been under British control since 1800 and had been vital for the defence of British interests in the Mediterranean throughout the nineteenth century. Its position almost at the exact centre of the sea along its east–west axis was the key to its importance; ships based there could strike in both directions. Once Italy sided with Germany, Malta's location between the Italian peninsula and the Italian colony of Libya only served to increase its strategic potential.

German Messerschmitt Me 109s give fighter cover during a bombing raid on the island of Malta. The Germans and Italians chose to try to neutralize the island with airpower, rather than attempt its capture.

to constant air attack in the waters of the Mediterranean, as well as threatened by torpedo boats and other light naval forces.

Between July 1940 and January 1941, the resupply of Malta was relatively easy. The Royal Navy was able to provide strong escorts to the convoys, including aircraft carriers which neutralized Italian air power to some degree. Modern aircraft were flown in from the decks of aircraft carriers, greatly increasing the strength of the island's air defence. However, the arrival of German

> Between July 1940 and January 1941, the resupply of Malta was relatively easy. The Royal Navy was able to provide strong escorts to the convoys, including aircraft carriers which neutralized Italian air power to some degree.

aircraft in January 1941 increased the difficulty of getting supplies to the island, although attacks on the convoys affected the escorts more than the vital supply ships. It wasn't until the summer of 1941 that the effects of Malta-based submarines and aircraft on Axis supply convoys to North Africa produced an intense air assault on the island and any attempt to supply it.

Malta's ideal position was partly negated by modern aerial warfare – it was only valuable as a fleet or air base so long as the airspace around it remained dominated by its defenders. The British had therefore made no plans to mount a determined defence of the island in the pre-war period and at the outbreak of war, the few aircraft that were present in 1940 were biplanes still in their crates.

Regardless of Malta's strategic vulnerability, British Prime Minister Winston Churchill was determined to defend the island against the Italians, mindful of its old strategic value and ignoring its modern strategic vulnerability. Malta was to be a base for air and naval forces that could threaten Italian convoys to North Africa. Thanks to Churchill, Malta arguably played a decisive role in the conflict in North Africa, both as a diversion of Axis air power from the land battle, and as a threat that reduced the amount of supplies reaching Rommel and his men.

Hard work

Maintaining this threat was an arduous task. Malta had no natural resources of fuel and was not even self-sufficient in food. Ships bringing these much-needed supplies, as well as anti-aircraft ammunition that was vital to the defence of the island, had to be brought by naval convoy to the main port of Valetta. Between 1940 and 1943, when the threat to Malta finally abated, several convoys made the dangerous run to Malta, often subjected

The George Cross

The George Cross was instituted in September 1940 by King George VI for heroic acts by civilians in highly dangerous circumstances. It ranks next to the Victoria Cross among British decorations. The award to the island of Malta was the first collective award and was received on behalf of the Maltese by the island's governor, Lieutenant General Lord Gort VC.

British soldiers in Malta walk past a building reduced to rubble by an Axis bombing raid. The people and garrison of the island remained under a virtual siege between July 1940 and March 1943.

Night and day

During 1942 the battle for Malta intensified, as the Germans and Italians, on Hitler's orders, sought to destroy the island as an offensive base. A convoy attempting to bring supplies at this time might be attacked any time during night or day. By night, the Axis attackers would drop flares to light up the scene. Ships had to search both the skies for air attacks and the horizon for motor torpedo boats, as well as the tracks of torpedoes fired from submarines. Dive-bombing was the most accurate method of attack and the successive screaming dives of the aircraft produced an unnerving effect on the men on deck.

The most famous of all Malta convoys was Operation Pedestal, in the summer of 1942. At this time, Malta's situation was desperate. The rations had been cut to less than 1,500 calories per day, a diet that doomed its recipients to slow starvation. Aviation fuel, spare parts and ammunition were all running low. The ships assembled at Gibraltar and included the oil tanker SS *Ohio*. To ensure the survival of the convoy, a powerful escort was organized, with over 40 warships escorting 14 merchant vessels. The Straits of Gibraltar were passed on 10 August and enemy attacks began on 11 August.

Desperate fight

The Germans and Italians spared nothing in trying to halt the convoy. Over 700 aircraft flew missions against it, while submarines and torpedo boats attacked by sea. An experimental drone aircraft packed with explosives was even tried, although it failed. Only five of the merchantmen reached Malta by 15 August, including the *Ohio*, which had been badly damaged by a torpedo and reached Valetta very low in the water. The escorting force lost one aircraft carrier, two cruisers and a destroyer sunk. Three more warships were badly

> The most famous of all Malta convoys was Operation Pedestal, in the summer of 1942. At this time, Malta's situation was desperate. The rations had been cut to less than 1,500 calories per day, a diet that doomed its recipients to slow starvation.

damaged, including another aircraft carrier. The convoy might have been wiped out had the Italians been ready to risk an attack by cruisers and destroyers, but German and Italian air force officers were unwilling to supply the fighter cover the naval officers considered essential. Malta survived.

The entire island received the highest civilian honour bestowed by the British during the war, the George Cross on 16 April 1942, but, after the success of Pedestal, the situation was never quite so desperate again.

British warships in action during one of the Malta convoys in 1942. The island could have been forced to surrender had the Royal Navy not secured passage of merchant ships bringing supplies.

Fighting on Guadalcanal

Battles on land, sea and in the air raged intermittently during the month of August 1942 around the island of Guadalcanal in the Solomons. US Marines initially faced no opposition when they landed there on 7 August. Instead, the Japanese responded later that day with air raids on the American beachhead, and a naval sortie. The latter, on the night of 8/9 August, in the Battle of Savo island, inflicted the worst defeat on the US navy in its history, the Japanese sinking four heavy cruisers for little loss, although they failed to attack the vital transport vessels.

For the Japanese military and naval commanders in Tokyo, Guadalcanal came to resemble a line drawn in a playground. Having had it crossed, they had no choice but to put up their fists and fight; a military detachment was dispatched to the island.

A combination of poor Japanese intelligence and the ambition of Colonel Ichiki, the detachment commander, led to defeat. Ichiki believed there were 2,000 Marines on the island (there were, in fact, 11,000). He attacked with the 800 troops he had, after writing diary entries for future dates that included: "August 21. Enjoy fruits of victory."

Unfortunately, when the Ichiki Detachment charged the Marine positions across the Ilu river on the night of 20/21 August, they were mown down by machine guns and anti-tank guns firing canister. The Marines then counter-attacked. After three days, the Ichiki Detachment was wiped out and Ichiki himself committed suicide.

Knee Mortar

The Japanese Nambu Type 89 Grenade Thrower was one of the best weapons in the Japanese infantryman's arsenal. It was small and light, 24 inches (60 cm) long and 10 lbs (4½ kg) in weight, with a maximum range of 700 yards (640 m). Its barrel was rifled and its curved base plate rested on the ground to fire it, a feature that led the Allies to give it the name "knee mortar", although it would severely injure anyone who tried to use it like that.

Battle of Eastern Solomons

American and Japanese carrier fleets clashed in a naval battle off the Eastern Solomons on 22–25 August 1942. Neither side gained its strategic objectives, but the Americans caused heavier losses to the Japanese.

The battle began in the late afternoon, after a small Japanese carrier, the *Ryujo*, had been spotted by a scout plane.

Admiral Jack Fletcher ordered a major strike against this target, but the carrier was a decoy sent out by Admiral Kondo Nobutake to reveal the Americans' position.

Admiral Jack Fletcher ordered a major strike against this target, but the carrier was a decoy sent out to reveal the Americans' position. Having given themselves away, the American carriers were attacked by 36 dive-bombers. The USS *Enterprise* was badly damaged and only kept afloat by expert damage control, while the *Ryujo* was sunk by American planes. Japanese aircraft losses were substantial.

US Marines landing on Guadalcanal on 7 August 1942 to capture a Japanese airfield. This had been begun by the Japanese as part of a campaign to capture Port Moresby, New Guinea.

Canadian misery at Dieppe

A wrecked Churchill tank and dead Canadian infantry lie on the shingle beach at Dieppe after the defeat of the Allied landing there on 19 August 1942.

The landing by Canadian troops and British commandos at the French port of Dieppe on 19 August 1942 ended in disaster. The purpose of the landing, described as a raid, remains uncertain.

Three co-ordinated landings were made. Commandos came ashore on the flanks of the main assault to tackle German gun emplacements that threatened the beaches around Dieppe itself. Only the left flank attack, to the north of Dieppe, achieved any success at all, whilst the right flank attack ran into German light naval forces that sank several landing craft before withdrawing. None of the main attacks made any serious headway, each of them being halted short of their objectives. On one beach, 60 German soldiers managed to hold off an entire regiment. Of 4,963 Canadian soldiers who crossed the Channel, 2,753 were either killed or taken prisoner.

Rommel fails at Alam Halfa

On 30 August 1942, Panzer Army Afrika, commanded by Field Marshal Erwin Rommel, failed in an attempt to envelop the British Eighth Army in its El Alamein position. The Eighth Army had been given a new commander two weeks before Rommel's offensive, Lieutenant General Bernard Montgomery, who had taken command of the Eighth Army, after his predecessor, Auchinleck, had lost the confidence of Prime Minister Winston Churchill. In the event, Montgomery used Auchinleck's plan for fighting the next battle, with some small adjustments.

Rommel launched one of his familiar right hooks around the southern end of the British line on the night of 30/31 August, but a shortage of fuel prevented him from launching a sufficiently strong attack on the main concentration of British tanks on Alam Halfa ridge on 1 September. With

his men suffering constant harassment by the Desert Air Force's bombing and strafing attacks, Rommel abandoned his plans and withdrew.

The most successful Australian air ace of the Second World War, Wing Commander Clive Caldwell (nicknamed "Killer"), shot down a total of 28 German aircraft in the Western Desert.

Germans near Caucasus, but winter forces halt

German infantry supporting a tank attack on the steppes of Southern Russia during the great advance of the summer of 1942.

Armoured columns of the German First Panzer Army neared the town of Ordzhonikidze, in the Caucasus region of the Soviet Union, at the end of October 1942, but the approach of winter forced a halt in operations.

On 26 July, German tanks crossed the Don river to advance on the main objective of the Germans' 1942 summer offensive, the oilfields of the Caucasus. The German economy was desperate for oil, not just to fuel the considerable number of ships, vehicles and aircraft needed to sustain naval, military and air operations in modern war, but also for the tractors used in the harvest, including in the newly conquered Ukraine. Within a couple of days, the Germans had torn a large hole in the Russian defences, 100 miles (160 km) wide, and raced into the Kuban region.

On 9 August, the oil town of Maikop, together with the important road and rail centre at Krasnodar, fell into German hands, although Soviet engineers denied the oil wells of Maikop to the Germans by dynamiting those they couldn't seal with concrete. German engineers estimated it would take a year to bring them back on line.

In spite of this setback, the Germans pressed on toward the mountains, in the face of strong Soviet resistance. By the end of August, the First Panzer Army was still 60 miles (96½ km) from Grozny, another important town, but after a month of fighting they were little closer and went over to the defensive. A final effort was launched on 25 October and got to within 5 miles (9 km) of Ordzhonikidze, but the Germans could go no further, and Hitler ordered the Luftwaffe to bomb the oilfields of Grozny and Baku, concluding they would never be his.

OBITUARY

HANS-JOACHIM MARSEILLE (1919–1942)

The death of the "Star of Africa" in a flying accident on 30 September 1942 brings to an end the career of a most remarkable pilot.

Marseille's idiosyncratic approach to aerial combat was highly successful, but his character alienated him from many of his commanding officers during the early months of his career in the Luftwaffe. He was transferred from his original unit, after service in the Battle of Britain, to North Africa, where he was finally able to blossom into a talented fighter pilot. Through practice, training and a disciplined lifestyle, he became an expert at high-deflection shooting (firing at aircraft from a sharp angle), whilst maintaining pilot skills under high G-forces, and marksmanship.

Marseille liked to fly with a single wingman, believing that in the desert this offered a better chance at avoiding detection than flying in formation. His most famous exploit came on 1 September 1942 when he shot down 17 enemy aircraft in a single day. He died when his Me-109's engine caught fire and he was knocked unconscious while bailing out, consequently being unable to open his parachute.

Fighting on two fronts in New Guinea

A sick American soldier is carried across a stream in New Guinea. American and Australian forces gathered to defend Port Moresby against the Japanese.

Australian troops, with American support, inflicted two defeats on the Japanese in fighting in New Guinea. The Japanese had landed about 1,500 men at the north end of Milne Bay on 26 August, while a largely Australian force defended three airstrips at the head of the bay with over 6,000 combat troops. The odds were evened, however, by the Australians need to hold a reserve to cover any subsequent landing elsewhere in the bay. The Japanese got as far as Airstrip No. 3, the

Australian troops march from the front line to rest after some hard fighting on the Kokoda Trail.

nearest to their landing beaches, before the superior firepower of the Allied forces halted their night-time assaults. The Japanese withdrew and in spite of 700 reinforcements, were evacuated on 4–6 September after heavy rains and lack of supplies had caused the outbreak of many jungle diseases, ulcers, fevers and trench rot.

Along the Kokoda Trail, the Japanese resumed their successful advance against the Australians on 26 August. Initially, General Douglas MacArthur, overall commander of the New Guinea operations, couldn't understand why the Australians were being pushed out of the Owen Stanley Mountains, but he had underestimated the Japanese strength. However, having realized his mistake, he planned a flanking movement at the same time as increasing the bombing of the Japanese supply lines. The Japanese had chosen to halt and go over to the defensive at Ioribaiwa, almost within sight of Port Moresby, but on 18 September, the Japanese high command switched their emphasis from New Guinea to Guadalcanal, and when the Australians attacked on 26 September, the Japanese withdrew what forces remained at Ioribaiwa.

Firepower halts Japanese on Guadalcanal

Two **Japanese infantry** attacks launched against the US Marines defending Henderson airfield on Guadalcanal have ended in defeat with heavy casualties, as American artillery and machine guns took a heavy toll. The Japanese army had long placed its faith in night attacks against an enemy liable to be superior in firepower. During the nights of 13 and 14 September 1942, a brigade-strength Japanese force numbering about 3,000 men attacked the 19,000 Marines. Neither attack succeeded and casualties were so severe that the battle became known as "Bloody Ridge". The Japanese then sent a full division as reinforcements. The Sendai Division began its attacks with probes on 21 October and continued to hurl itself against the Marines' position until the night of 25/26 October, after which the shattered remnants withdrew. As an example of the kind of punishment the Japanese experienced, a single regiment lost about a third of its men.

The USS *Hornet* under attack by Japanese torpedo planes and dive bombers during the battle of Santa Cruz on 26-27 October 1942.

The Japanese navy co-ordinated with the army in an attempt to isolate the Marines on Guadalcanal by seeking a decisive battle with US naval forces in the vicinity.

The Battle of the Santa Cruz islands on 26/27 October 1942 resulted in defeat for the American fleet and the loss of a carrier, although once again Japanese pilot losses were heavy.

Stalingrad

The battle waged for Stalingrad through the autumn and early winter of 1942 produced one of the epic confrontations of military history, to be ranked among such names as Austerlitz, Gettysburg and Verdun. The Red Army's defence of this city has been desperate and determined, matched only by the Germans' attempts to seize it, but gradually their expectation of victory has turned into despair.

German infantry finally occupy the Tractor Factory, which had been the focus of the fighting in the city during October and November.

On 5 April, the German dictator Adolf Hitler issued a war directive setting out his plans for the summer offensive on the Eastern Front. The main effort would be made in the south, where the first stage of an attack would aim at capturing Voronezh. The subsequent advance would proceed in two directions: towards the Volga river at Stalingrad, and southwards toward the Caucasus Mountains. The armies would dig in along the Volga and the Caucasus to sit out the winter. Throughout the directive, Hitler harped on the fact that speed was essential to victory. Although his generals were aghast at the vast distances their troops must cross to attain their objectives, Hitler believed he understood the key to surmounting this obstacle.

German optimism

A week before Operation Blue – as the offensive was code-named – began on 28 June, the plans for the operation accidentally fell into Soviet hands after a light aircraft carrying a staff officer crashed behind Soviet lines. When their details were reported to the Soviet leader, Josef Stalin, he duplicated his mistake of the previous year and refused to believe in this intelligence. With the German offensive falling on the Soviet armies that had been weakened in the Kharkov offensive, the same rapid advance of the year before was achieved, although the Germans were unable to repeat the great encirclements of 1941. Having been constantly astonished at the extent and recuperative powers of the Red Army during the previous year, they became optimistic that they had finally exhausted the Soviet reserves.

Stalin even implied the same, replying to Marshal Semyon Timoshenko's request for more divisions: "If they sold divisions in the marketplace I'd buy you one or two, but unfortunately, they don't." However, the reality was that he had learned from his mistakes of the preceding summer and allowed the withdrawal of armies threatened by encirclement. The old Stalin only emerged after the fall of Rostov-on-Don on 25 July, when he issued his new order: "Not One Step Backwards. Panic mongers and cowards must be liquidated on the spot." Special units were created to shoot anyone headed for the rear without authority.

Reduced to rubble

As German ground troops neared the city of Stalingrad, the bombardment of the third-largest city in the Soviet Union began. Luftflotte 4, commanded by the man who had ordered the savage destruction of Guernica during the Spanish Civil War, General Wolfram Baron von Richthofen, sent wave after wave of bombers that reduced one of the model cities of Soviet development

> The old Stalin only emerged after the fall of Rostov-on-Don on 25 July, when he issued his new order: "Not One Step Backwards. Panic mongers and cowards must be liquidated on the spot."

to rubble. That same day, German tanks reached the banks of the Volga and their crews looked with a mixture and pride and amazement at the eastern bank, from which the steppes of Asia stretched into the distance. The order now came from Stalin to turn the city into a fortress, and it fell each successive stage. The fight for the Mamaev Kurgan, a burial mound that served as a public park, and for the grain silos in the south of the city, marked the first stage. Then the focus shifted northward to take in the Tractor, Red October and Barrikady factories. Throughout the battle

> "Quiet night" replaced good night as the Nazi soldiers tried to rest in the dark. For the Red Army, snipers became the legends of the battle, most famously Vasily Zaitsev, who was reported to have killed 149 Germans with his rifle.

the Germans sought to cut the lifeline for the Sixty-Second Army at the ferry across the Volga. Whereas the Germans fought by day, counting on the dive-bombing Junkers Ju 87 Stukas to provide accurate air support, the Soviet soldiers ruled the night, with their raids on foot and by little U-2 biplanes that dropped flares and bombs. "Quiet night" replaced good night as a polite parting for Nazi soldiers. For the Red Army, snipers became the legends of the battle, most famously Vasily Zaitsev, who was reported to have killed 149 Germans with his rifle.

By the time of the Germans' final assault of the battle, on 12 November, the Red Army only controlled about 10 per cent of the city in two narrow pockets, with their ferry across the Volga under fire from German machine guns. But the nerve of the German troops was cracking and they were increasingly attempting to desert, or exposing themselves to the risk of minor wounds that would earn them a respite from the battle. It was at this point that the Red Army's counter-offensive, in preparation for months, was unleashed on the flanks of the Sixth Army's advanced position. The battle in Stalingrad was now irrelevant to the future of Paulus and his men.

Red Army infantry engage the enemy in a block of flats during the fighting. The Soviet forces attempted to defeat the German superiority in artillery and aircraft by keeping their front line close to that of the Germans.

to General Vasily Chuikov and his Sixty-Second Army to defend it.

Chuikov took charge of the army the day before the German Sixth Army commanded by General Friedrich Paulus began its main effort to capture the city on 12 September. The battle quickly descended into what the Germans called "*Rattenkrieg*", war of the rats. The grenade, the sub-machine gun, the sniper's rifle and the flamethrower became the most valuable weapons in fighting at close quarters amidst buildings and rubble. The armour of tanks was more vulnerable to anti-tank rifles (almost useless in open country at anything except suicidal range), which could stay under cover until their crew could aim at the tops and rear of the tank, normally less thickly protected.

Landmarks
The fight for Stalingrad was in fact something of a Russian doll of conflict, one battle inside another. The smallest battle was that between small squads of soldiers, or even single snipers, taking place in a street or building. The fighting swirled around the landmarks of the battle in

Civilians remained in the city, and still had to find a way to survive the fighting, taking cover in basements and, once houses had been reduced to rubble, in shell holes.

Monty defeats Rommel at El Alamein

General Bernard "Monty" Montgomery's offensive at El Alamein began with a powerful night bombardment of the German positions. Here a 140mm field gun shells likely enemy tank positions.

The **British Eighth** Army, having halted Rommel's Panzer Army Afrika at El Alamein, has driven the Germans and Italians out of their defensive positions with a set-piece offensive.

The attack began at the first full moon, after the British had completed their careful preparation, on the night of 23 October. General Bernard Montgomery, who had carefully fostered an image of the solder's friend as "Monty", favoured a night attack. The attacks would concentrate on two points: in the north, the main blow would fall near the coast, south of Tel el Eisa; in the south, a diversionary attack would press along the Himeimat Ridge. In both cases, infantry would make the breach, and once they had "crumbled" the Axis defences, the tanks would break through and advance westwards.

The British had to cross huge minefields that the Germans and Italians had spent much of September busily laying, and used specially adapted tanks known as Scorpions to clear a path. These used a rotating drum at the front, with flails attached, that detonated mines before the tank's tracks could do so.

In the event, Montgomery's attack was initially delayed by problems getting the tanks through the advances made by the infantry. On 26 October, when Montgomery halted to regroup, the Germans took the opportunity to counter-attack. These attacks also failed, so that when Montgomery renewed his advance on 1 November, the Germans did not have sufficient tanks to hold their line, and on 4 November they began to withdraw.

"Anton" brings all France under German control

German and Italian military forces began occupying the remainder of France on 11 November 1942 following the Allied invasion of French North Africa. Italian troops advanced into the Riviera and landed on Corsica, while German forces pushed east and south-east from the coastal strip they occupied along the Bay of Biscay, and south from central France towards Vichy and Toulon. German tanks reached the Mediterranean coast that very evening.

German dictator Adolf Hitler ordered Operation Anton in order to forestall an invasion of southern France and Corsica by Allied forces, which he believed would follow the landings in North Africa. The action was denounced by the French government at Vichy as a violation of the 1940 armistice.

When it became apparent that the Germans intended to seize the powerful French squadron at Toulon, in the early hours of 27 November 1942, as German tanks were smashing down the gates of the naval base, the French began scuttling those ships that could not escape to the Allies. The Germans ended up with a naval base with a number of sunken ships in it.

The French destroyer *Chamois*, scuttled to prevent capture, rests in Toulon harbour.

Americans and British land in French North Africa

In **the most** complex amphibious operation of the war so far, on 8 November 1942 American and British troops landed in Morocco and Algeria, and secured significant portions of the French North African colonies. The troops in Operation Torch landed at three points on the coast: at Casablanca, on the Atlantic coast, and at Oran and Algiers in the

The French fired at the American and British troops at Casablanca.

Mediterranean. At Casablanca, the landings were made at three separate points, to avoid the concentration of French forces there. The response of the French to the invasion was uncertain. In the event, they initially fired at the American and British troops who landed on 8 November, but subsequently agreed to ceasefire arrangements. By 11 November, combat between Vichy French and Allied forces had ceased. Two days later, the Commander in Chief of French armed forces, Admiral François Darlan, who was in Algeria visiting his sick son, came to an agreement giving the Allies French support in North Africa. It took another nine days, before the final agreement was achieved.

1st Infantry Division

The American 1st Infantry Division, the Big Red One, was established in May 1917, and was the first American division to land in France to enter combat, and to suffer casualties. Unlike many American divisions organized during the First World War, the 1st Infantry Division remained in service throughout the inter-war period.

American soldiers aboard a landing craft wait for it to take them to the beaches of North Africa. The US Army's first large combat operation in the European theatre went relatively smoothly.

US victory in Ironbottom Sound

A **series of naval** engagements on 13–15 November 1942 resulted in a decisive victory for the US navy in the campaign for Guadalcanal. Afterwards, the Japanese abandoned any further operations to drive the American forces from the island.

The Japanese had assembled a convoy of eleven ships at Rabaul to deliver 12,000 soldiers and 11,000 tons (10,000 tonnes) of supplies to the haggard, hungry force on Guadalcanal island. The reinforcements and supplies would enable a renewal of the offensive against the American army and Marines there. However, unloading the ships would take some time, so Admiral Yamamoto ordered two battleships with supporting cruisers and destroyers to bombard Henderson Field, the American air base on the island, to knock it out long enough to allow the unloading to take place

without harassment from the air. As the raiding force proceeded down the Solomon chain, it was spotted by American aircraft patrols, and American naval forces in the vicinity moved north by night to intercept the Japanese.

In the early hours of 13 November, the two squadrons discovered each other. The American warships had sailed into the midst of the Japanese formation and the night was lit up by gun flashes as the ships fired at point-blank range. The Americans had no battleships, but were at such short range that their 8-inch gun cruisers achieved key hits on one of the Japanese battleships, and torpedoes couldn't miss. Two American admirals with the force were killed and all but two of the 13 American warships were sunk or damaged. The Japanese commander, Admiral Abe, aborted his mission, even

though one of his battleships was still capable of the bombardment. The next day, the damaged Japanese battleship was abandoned and sank.

Yamamoto was furious, and effectively dismissed Abe from the service, then ordered a second mission with the surviving battleship, the *Kirishima*, but this also failed and the *Kirishima* sank after a duel with two American warships on 14 November. So many ships had been sunk in the area north-east of Guadalcanal that it became known as Ironbottom Sound. The Japanese convoy was badly battered by air attacks and the surviving four vessels were run aground on Guadalcanal on the morning of 15 November. However, air attacks from Henderson Field prevented the ships being unloaded, destroyed such supplies as they carried, and killed or wounded many of the reinforcements.

A wrecked Japanese transport on the coast of Guadalcanal, one of four merchant ships beached after the naval battles fought between 13 November and 15 November 1942.

Race to Tunis

Admiral François Darlan, the
high commissioner for French
North Africa, was shot in the
Summer Palace at Algiers,
on 24 December 1942 by a
young man named Ferdinand
Bonnier de la Chapelle. He
died at the hospital. Amazingly, the original, detailed
confession that Bonnier de la
Chapelle gave to the investi-
gating police commissioner
was burned and at a subsequent inquest he asserted
that he had acted alone. He
was found guilty on Christmas Day and shot on Boxing
Day after writing a shorter
confession that claimed the
existence of a plot to restore
the French monarchy. There
are now several rumours laying blame for the assassination on various American and
British political and security
personnel, including General
Dwight Eisenhower, President
Franklin Roosevelt and Prime
Minister Winston Churchill.

A mechanized column in Tunis. The city was the main supply base for German and Italian forces in North Africa, and therefore the target of the Allied advance in late 1942.

Admiral Darlan had secret dealings with Allied leaders over the future of French forces in the colonies.

In response to Operation Torch, the Axis countries rushed their own troops to Tunisia, first to arrive being Italian fighter aircraft in Tunis on 10 November 1942. With an airfield under control, a sizeable airlift rapidly brought tanks, guns and supplies to Tunisia, as well as a division-sized force of German and Italian troops. These forces established two defensive perimeters around the port of Bizerta and the city of Tunis. The Axis build-up continued in these two areas until on 25 November, the Allied forces in Algeria advanced into Tunisia in three separate columns. The northernmost column was halted at Djefna, about 30 miles (48 km) from Bizerta, on 28 November, while the two southern advances met near Djedeida, less than 20 miles (32 km) from Tunis, where they met heavy German resistance, and were also halted. On 1 December, the Germans counter-attacked and drove the Allies back, thanks in large part to having air superiority over the battlefield. On 10 December, the Allies finally halted the Germans near Medjez el Bab. A second attempt on Tunis beginning on 22 December similarly failed.

Allies take Buna

The **Japanese bridgehead** at Buna was eliminated in an assault beginning on New Year's Eve 1942, with Japanese troops attempting to flee in the water being machine-gunned by Allied aircraft. It was the end of a two-month campaign that finally secured Papua for the Allies, ending the threat to Port Moresby.

Initially, the Allies planned to send a strong force on a flank march to the west of the Kokoda Trail, over the forbidding Owen Stanley Mountains. The march took a terrible toll on the men forced to carry it out, who were unable to get sufficient fresh water to drink and ended up exhausted by stomach disorders such as diarrhoea or dysentery. Coincidentally, as the troops neared their objective, where they paused to recuperate, word reached the Allied commanders of a potential airstrip further east of the Laruni–Jaure path that had proved so difficult. Troops had already been flown to the Cape Nelson area, further west along the coast from the Japanese bridgehead at Buna, so a second flanking force was sent to the newly constructed airstrip at Abel's Field.

By mid-November, the Australian and

"Take Buna, or don't come back alive," was MacArthur's advice to Major-General Robert Eichelberger (left).

American forces were poised to attack Buna and Gona. The Japanese had strongly fortified their position, using well-camouflaged coconut-log bunkers. Fighting began on 18 November but by the end of the month the Allied forces had made little progress, and the combination of enemy firepower and disease had done much to reduce the Allied three-to-one advantage in numbers. The American 32nd Division in particular had disappointed General Douglas MacArthur in its attacks on Buna. Although the division had suffered from insufficient preparation for operations in jungle terrain, and had lost one of its main sources of supplies, some coastal luggers, to air attack, MacArthur regarded its setbacks as a failure of leadership, and sacked its commander, Major-General Edwin Harding. In his place he sent Lieutenant-General Robert Eichelberger, who received many of the supplies, men and air support that MacArthur had refused to send Harding.

Supported by extra artillery, tanks and supplies, the Australian and American forces penetrated the Japanese lines with ease. The renewed offensive began in mid-December, and the Japanese defences around Buna and Gona were overrun by 14 December with the fighting finally finishing on 2 January 1943.

An American soldier stands over the bodies of Japanese who have killed themselves rather than be prisoners, after the Japanese position at Buna, New Guinea, was captured by Allied forces.

Red Army traps Germans

Soviet forces unleashed an offensive on the German armies in two sectors of the front in late November 1942. Operation Uranus struck at the Rumanian forces guarding the flanks of the German Sixth Army then embroiled in the battle for Stalingrad. Operation Mars attacked Army Group Centre around Rzhev.

Both operations had been carefully planned and co-ordinated, together with massive superiority in tanks, artillery and men. Mars was intended to keep the Germans from transferring forces from the Moscow front to Stalingrad, while Uranus was intended to seal the Germans in Stalingrad into a pocket.

The Uranus attack began on 19 November. The Rumanian forces had already been identified by Red Army intelligence as the weak link in the German lines, with the officers being inefficient and the men indifferent to the policies that had brought them far from home in a war they wanted no part of. Furthermore, bad weather prevented the Germans from offering any effective air support. It only took four days for the

Soviet thrusts to achieve the encirclement, as the pincers met at Kalach on 23 November.

Hitler responded with a "stand fast" order, perhaps partly inspired by the resolute resistance his own troops had encountered among Red Army soldiers during the great successes of the Barbarossa offensive. He hoped to relieve this army with a counter-offensive of his own. The Red Army's relative inactivity during the weeks following the creation of the Stalingrad pocket allowed the Germans to assemble a new military force under Field Marshal Erich von Manstein. This attack began on 12 December and made some gains. However, a second Soviet offensive was unleashed on 16 December, again against a non-German army protecting the flank, in this case the Italian Eighth Army. Now both von Manstein's Army Group Don and Army Group A, the German forces in the Caucasus region, were threatened with entrapment just as was the German Sixth Army at Stalingrad. On 29 December, von Manstein abandoned the effort to relieve Stalingrad.

RGD 33 HE Grenade

The Red Army's RGD 33 HE Grenade resembled the stick grenades used by the German army, but with a metal throwing handle. The grenade was potentially lethal within a radius of 30 yards (27 m).

Operation Mars involved more troops than Uranus and four separate thrusts were launched on 25 November. The Germans, however, had been in this position for almost a year, in contrast to the weeks the Italians and Rumanians in the south had to prepare for attacks. German forces were well dug in and skilfully disrupted the Red Army's attacks. Eventually, Reich Marshal Georgi Zhukov, the overall commander for Mars, called off the attacks on 15 December. By this time it was apparent that better chances for success were available in the Stalingrad theatre.

Red Army soldiers on the advance in Stalingrad after the beginning of Operation Uranus, the 1942 Soviet winter counter-offensive. The bad flying weather, which grounded German aircraft, was a great help to the attacking Red Army.

Big Two at Casablanca

President Franklin Roosevelt made the first flight overseas by an American president while in office, in order to attend a conference with British Prime Minister Winston Churchill and Fighting French chiefs Generals Charles de Gaulle and Henri Giraud at Casablanca on 14–24 January 1943. The conference took several important decisions, including a requirement that any peace negotiations with the Axis countries would be conducted only on the basis of their unconditional surrender.

The conference also defined some key objectives for the Allies. Following victory in North Africa, the next Allied objective would be the invasion of Sicily and Italy; the invasion of France would be delayed until 1944. A combined Anglo-American bomber offensive against key economic targets in Germany would be conducted, and the manufacturing priorities were defined, giving priority to submarine construction and the aircraft industry.

President Roosevelt and Prime Minister Churchill brought their staffs to Casablanca, Morocco, and drew up the strategic plans of the Western Allies for the rest of the war.

Surrender at Stalingrad

The last surviving troops of the German army defending Stalingrad surrendered on 2 February 1943. They had not eaten or slept properly for months, almost all suffered from lice, and many of those with frostbite lost fingers and toes. The Soviets claimed a total of 91,000 prisoners.

The final Red Army offensive against the defenders of Stalingrad was unleashed on 10 January 1943, the main initial objective being the airfield at Pitomnik, which fell on 15 January. The Germans resisted fiercely with what weapons they had, but they lacked anti-tank ammunition; their counter-attacks were quickly broken up by Soviet artillery fire. The struggle continued as the Soviets squeezed the pocket more and more tightly until a pause in the action followed the fall of the airfield as the Soviets regrouped. Then the Red Army assaults resumed. The Germans were deployed in "hedgehog" defences with overlapping fields of fire. White-coated troops surged forward towards the German lines, to be met by a withering fire that killed and wounded many of them. When these tactics failed, they pulled back to assault from a flank, trying to get in the rear of the German strongpoints.

At the end, the Sixth Army's commander, General Friedrich Paulus, was promoted by Hitler to Field Marshal on the assumption he would commit suicide, but he was captured anyway on 1 February. Although von Paulus refused to sign a surrender document, the next most senior German officer surviving on 2 February did so that evening. The wounded who could not walk were machine-gunned, as were any Germans who were believed to be Gestapo, SS or military police. The remainder were marched off into captivity, which meant a ten-year sentence to the Soviet labour camps.

A column of German and Rumanian prisoners, stretching across the southern Russian steppes, is herded into captivity after the surrender at Stalingrad.

German soldiers look forlornly up at a solitary Ju 52 on a resupply mission. The Luftwaffe high command made promises that could not be kept, dooming the German army at Stalingrad.

Supplying Stalingrad by Air

The successful operation to deliver supplies to German troops trapped in the Demyansk pocket during the early months of 1942 convinced Adolf Hitler that a similar operation could sustain the Sixth Army trapped by the Red Army at Stalingrad. But the scale of the Stalingrad operation was considerably greater as Sixth Army estimated it needed 770 tons (700 tonnes) each day. When Reich Marshal Hermann Göring consulted with his staff, he put in a request for 550 tons (500 tonnes), to be told that 385 tons (350 tonnes) were the maximum possible, and that could not be sustained indefinitely. Nonetheless, while a relief counter-attack was organized, the Luftwaffe attempted to keep the Sixth Army supplied. However, the poor weather, heavy anti-aircraft concentrations on the route to the main airfield at Pitomnik and Soviet air sorties all limited the amount, which barely reached 440 tons (400 tonnes) per week, let alone 385 (350) per day. By the middle of December, men began to die of starvation; by the middle of January, it was clear to all that the airlift had failed.

IN BRIEF

❧ 14th Indian Division advanced into the Arakan region of Burma, where it was halted by the Japanese at the end of December 1942. Attacks on the Japanese at Donbaik during January 1943 failed to push them out of strongly defended positions.

Atlantic convoys

The crucial campaign in the European theatre of the Second World War featured few set-piece battles, but a relentless campaign of hit-and-run raids against supply lines. The Battle of the Atlantic pitted the naval forces of Britain, Canada and, later, the United States against German ships and submarines.

The convoy system was implemented by the Royal Navy immediately on the outbreak of war to protect the transport of supplies for the war effort.

Between January and March 1943, the Battle of the Atlantic reached crisis point as the impact of three-and-a-half years of war began to take its toll on Britain's imports. Before the war, the average amount of imports to Britain totalled more than 50,000,000 tons (50,800,000 tonnes) deadweight. During 1942, these had been more than halved to 23 million tons (23,700,000 tonnes) deadweight. With Britain in genuine danger of being unable to sustain its war effort, shipping losses began to rise again. These reached a total 1,189,000 tons (1,200,000 tonnes) for the first quarter of 1943, a rate of loss which would exceed 4,500,00 tons (4,570,000 tonnes) for the entire year. This rate of loss was far less than had occurred in 1942, but the 1942 figure had been boosted by losses to American merchant shipping sailing between domestic ports. The 1943 losses were predominantly to ships crossing the Atlantic. Furthermore, if there was to be any possibility of a Second Front in Western Europe, the quantity of shipments to Britain would actually have to rise, not fall. What was coming to Britain now represented the minimum to continue the war effort at existing levels, not expand it to encompass a major campaign in France. Britain greeted the

New Year with food stocks that would only last another three to four months.

Shifting balance

Yet there were signs, for those who were sufficiently far-sighted, that the tide of battle might be turning. One advantage the Germans had in 1942 was the security of their Triton code used to transmit messages to and from U-boats at sea. It took almost a year after the code was introduced for American and British code-breakers to decrypt it, the breakthrough finally coming in December 1942 after the capture of a codebook from U-559 in the Mediterranean. At the same time, the Allies introduced a new code for sending messages to their convoys – being completely unaware that the Germans had broken the old code. Another Allied advantage came from the impending introduction of microwave radar for aircraft – U-boats had the means to detect shortwave radar, but not microwave emissions. A third development was the discovery through

operational analysis that large convoys were more efficient than smaller ones, and formed part of a general overhaul of convoy management implemented in early 1943.

At this time, there remained two key gaps in the system of convoy defence

> Convoy ONS-154, for example, travelling via the southern route, was roughly handled in the Azores gap, losing 14 of its 45 ships, for the loss of only one U-boat, in December 1942. This was one of the greatest U-boat victories of the war.

– the area between zones where air patrols were possible, the Greenland and Azores gaps. Admiral Karl Doentiz, the German navy's commander-in-chief of its U-boat arm and later overall commander-in-chief,

Salvos of depth charges were the main anti-submarine weapon used from warships during the early part of the war, rolled off the ship astern, and set to explode at various depths.

sinking ship and for the lucky survivors hours in an open boat or raft, heaving on freezing salt water until rescue arrived. U-boat crews found life just as nerve-wracking. Little could be done except to sit out a depth-charge attack and an extended period

> For the crews of the merchant ships and escorts, convoy duties were nerve-wracking – to sleep below decks was to take a terrible risk, as a ship could sink in as little as two or three minutes.

submerged resulted in breathing stale air fouled by persistent engine smells.

As February 1943 came to a close, the Royal Navy became increasingly concerned about the outcome of the Battle of the Atlantic. German U-boats had had a successful month, winning key convoy battles against SC-118 and ON-166, sinking 140,000 tons (142,250 tonnes) of shipping from these two alone. For the Royal Navy and Coastal Command, the crisis of the war in the Atlantic had arrived.

Convoy systems were even used for coastal vessels sailing on the inshore waters of the British Isles, in this case to protect against both air and submarine attack.

deployed his U-boats here in wolfpacks that could attack almost with impunity. Convoy ONS-154, for example, travelling via the southern route, was roughly handled in the Azores gap, losing 14 of its 45 ships, for the loss of only one U-boat, in December 1942. This was one of the greatest U-boat victories of the war. German U-boats attacked mainly by night, although they did pick off stragglers by day. In the case of ONS-154, all the attacks but one were made under cover of darkness.

Peril on the sea
A few days immediately after leaving port, the rations aboard ship or U-boat consisted of dull, tinned food and a lack of fresh bread, fruit or vegetables. For the crews of the merchant ships and escorts, convoy duties were nerve-wracking – to sleep below decks was to take a terrible risk, as a ship could sink in as little as two or three minutes. The merchant ships could do nothing to protect themselves except sail in a straight line in formation and hope the escorts would drive off any attackers. Flower Class corvettes, such as HMCS *Battleford* escorting ONS-154, were dreadfully wet, both from sea water and from condensation, and rolled horribly in the rough water of

the Atlantic, causing severe sea sickness among a crowded crew. Action was actually welcomed in offering some distraction from the overall misery, but could result in a

Aircraft were the best anti-submarine weapons of all, and the construction of small escort carriers closed the "Mid-Atlantic Air Gap", the zone of the ocean where land-based air cover could not reach.

Japanese evacuate Guadalcanal

Japanese destroyers embarked the surviving 13,000 Japanese soldiers off the island of Guadalcanal during 1–7 February 1943. The operation followed several weeks of debate among Japanese leaders in Tokyo in which army generals favoured continuing the fight on Guadalcanal, in spite of the tremendous problems sending supplies and reinforcements to the island. However, naval officers believed that the losses that the convoys would suffer from American air and naval attacks would be too costly

Although this operation was a tremendous success with 13,000 Japanese soldiers escaping, fighting on the island had cost the lives of 25,000.

for any possible gain that could result from recapturing the island. In the end, the view of the navy prevailed, and the evacuation was ordered. On 23 January, Japanese troops began withdrawing from their advanced positions on Guadalcanal, the American failure to patrol aggressively preventing them from learning what was going on. Although this operation was a tremendous success with 13,000 Japanese soldiers escaping, fighting on the island had cost the lives of 25,000 Japanese to enemy weapons, disease and malnutrition. It was the greatest defeat the Japanese army had experienced in its history.

Rommel sweeps into Kasserine Pass

American armoured infantry advance to the crest of a ridge from their halftracks during the Kasserine Pass battle.

In February 1943, German and Italian forces, under the command of Field Marshal Erwin Rommel, clashed with American troops in a major engagement for the first time during the war at Kasserine Pass in Tunisia. After a nine-day battle, the Germans withdrew, having achieved a major tactical victory, but without substantially altering the strategic situation.

Rommel's ultimate objective was the town of Tebessa, an important supply dump on the Algerian side of the border, and he was given two armoured divisions with authority to go as far as he could. When the main German attack struck toward Sidi bou Zid on 14 February, it caught the Americans badly deployed and unsuspecting of a major German attack, intercepted German signals having led the Allied commanders to believe that the Germans were going to attack further north.

There followed three days of American defeats as first they were driven out of their original positions, then their counter-attack failed and finally they were driven out of their fall-back positions. The American commander, Major-General Lloyd Fredendall, then set up a new defensive line at Kasserine Pass. This line was driven back as well, but did not collapse, and when Rommel's last attack was held off on 21 February he declined to resume the offensive the next day.

M1 Garand rifle

The first semi-automatic rifle in military service was the American M1 Garand rifle. All other armies used weapons that had to be reloaded using some kind of bolt action to chamber a new round and could only be fired when the trigger was pulled. Ammunition for the rifle was held in 8-round clips, the empty clip being ejected with a distinctive ping.

Small battle, large consequences

A**Japanese convoy bringing** much needed supplies for Lae, a town in New Guinea occupied by the Japanese but now under Allied attack, was wiped out by Allied air power in the Bismarck Sea on 1–3 March 1943. One Japanese naval officer later said, "This defeat was the biggest cause of the loss of New Guinea."

The convoy consisted of eight transports and eight destroyers, with 6,500 soldiers and marines on board, together with supplies. A patrol aircraft spotted the convoy the same day after it had left Rabaul, the main Japanese base in the region, but cloudy conditions prevented the Allies from attacking. However, an improvement in the weather on 2 March saw the attacks begin. On 2 March, high-level bombing struck one of

the transports, the *Kyokusei Maru*, forcing her abandonment. On 3 March a co-ordinated attack by light and heavy bombers, escorted by fighters, swept in. The light bombers flew in low, using a technique known as skip-bombing, to bounce the bombs into the enemy ships. The heavy bombers flew high; their bombs would be easy to avoid, but turning to avoid them would present the broadside of the ship to the threat of the skipped bombs. The results were devastating. In fifteen minutes, seven transports and two destroyers were crippled or sinking. Less than half the soldiers and marines were rescued by the surviving ships and by submarines, whereupon all but one of the remaining destroyers retreated to Rabaul. The *Asashio*, left behind to help survivors, was sunk by air attack later that day.

Skip-bombing

Skip-bombing proved a remarkably successful method for attacking ships. It was normally performed by light bombers such as the Douglas A-20, or by medium North American B-25s; even heavy Boeing B-17s performed skip-bombing attacks by night. The aircraft flew in at an altitude of 175–300 feet (50–90 m), and in level flight, so that the bombs would "skip" along like a flat stone across water. The release point was at least 60 feet (18 m) from the target, but up to four bounces were achievable. Even a near miss could damage the hull of a ship.

An American B-25 bomber performing skip bombing techniques against a Japanese escort vessel. The battle of the Bismarck Sea pitted American air power against the Japanese navy.

Clash in the North Atlantic

U-boats achieved a major victory after three days of attacks in the North Atlantic which began when patrolling U-boats spotted a convoy in the early hours of 16 March 1943. Three groups of U-boats were directed against convoy HX-229, reaching it in the late afternoon and torpedoing eight merchant ships under cover of darkness that night. Meanwhile, a U-boat travelling to intercept HX-229, detected another convoy about 120 miles (193 km) to the east. Convoy SC-122, which had left New York three days before HX-229, was a slow convoy and the Germans' good fortune in spotting the two relatively close together ensured that every available U-boat within cruising range was sent after them. (In fact, at the time there were no less than seven convoys in the North Atlantic.) SC-122 lost a total of nine merchant ships over three nights, while HX-229 lost thirteen ships. Both convoys were given strong escorting forces, but the lack of air cover in the Greenland Gap (also known as the Black Pit) proved decisive. The one success came when a Flying Fortress (the British name for the B-17) flying from Iceland spotted U-384 on 19 March and sank her with depth charges.

German submarines practicing "Wolf Pack" tactics during training. The German Navy massed its submarines against Allied convoys hoping to overwhelm the escorts with numbers.

RAF attacks Ruhr

Bomber Command began an extended series of raids against the German industrial heartland of the Ruhr on 5 March 1943, with one on the town of Essen carried out by 442 aircraft, four-fifths of the available Bomber Command front-line strength. The raids

The raids made use of Oboe, a system of directional navigation that transmitted a signal used by a pathfinder aircraft which led the way for the bombers.

made use of Oboe, a system of directional navigation that transmitted a signal used by a pathfinder aircraft which led the way for the bombers. For the attack on Essen, de Havilland Mosquito light bombers carried the transponders used to receive the signal. A second raid was made on Essen on 12 March, damaging the Krupps plant there.

The versatile de Haviland Mosquito light bomber gave the British a fast attack aircraft that relied on speed to elude the enemy.

Cracking the Mareth Line

British stretcher bearers of the Indian Medical Service rush to help wounded Gurkhas during the fighting on the Mareth Line in Tunisia. British Imperial forces, including New Zealanders and Indians, made key contributions in the Western Desert.

British and Commonwealth forces advanced inland around the flank of the Mareth Line, a fortified position stretching from the coast to the mountains in south-eastern Tunisia on 26 March 1943, forcing the German and Italian soldiers defending it to withdraw.

The Eighth Army, under its commander General Bernard Montgomery, had initially reached the border between Libya and Tunisia in mid-February. Montgomery then paused in order to build up his forces for one of the set-piece attacks that he favoured, but while he built up his forces, intercepted German communications revealed an impending attack near Medenine. Montgomery chose to meet this attack with artillery, and on 6 March his forewarned troops halted the German and Italian tanks in their tracks, destroying 52.

Two weeks later, Montgomery launched his own offensive. The British were initially successful, penetrating the Mareth Line (a pre-war defensive position built by the French colonial authorities in Tunisia), but a German counter-attack drove them back. A "left hook" by the 2nd New Zealand Division had made some progress while the frontal attack was under way and after being reinforced by 1st Armoured Division, the New Zealanders resumed their advance on 26 March. The attack was preceded by a heavy aerial bombardment and was directed at El Hamma, a town on the road to the larger city of Gabes on the coast. With the line turned, the Germans and Italians hastily withdrew.

IN BRIEF

⚜ The Gloster Meteor, the first British jet fighter aircraft, made its maiden flight on 5 March 1943.

⚜ American and Japanese ships clashed in the Battle of the Kommandorski islands in the North Pacific on 26 March 1943. Both sides had small, mixed, cruiser-destroyer forces, but the Japanese were escorting two transports bringing supplies to their garrison on Kiska island. No ships were lost, but the Japanese retreated, returning to base with the transports.

German soldiers at Katyn Forest. The Germans uncovered the site of a massacre of Polish officers by Stalin's secret police, but the Soviet government accused them of carrying out the killings.

Polish officers massacred

Berlin Radio announced on 13 April 1943 that the bodies of 3,000 Polish officers had been discovered in a forest near Smolensk, Russia. According to the broadcast, the massacre had been carried out by the Soviet secret police, but two days later, the Soviets claimed that the victims had been killed by the Germans, who then blamed the Soviets for propaganda purposes. The Germans selected an international commission of forensic scientists, mostly from Axis countries but including a representative from Switzerland, to inspect the corpses, to be made up. They concluded that the deaths had occurred between March and April 1940, but did not assign responsibility for the killings, although at that time the territory was part of the Soviet Union.

Squadrons battle over Solomons

Aerial battles between Japanese and American aircraft took place near Guadalcanal in April 1943 as the Japanese tried to sink some of the large fleet of cargo vessels and transports off the island, and warships using nearby Tulagi as a naval base. On 1 April 1943 a three-hour engagement over the Russell islands between about 40 American fighters against a large Japanese raiding force resulted in the loss of 20 Japanese fighters to only six American. A week later, a second assault involving 160 Japanese aircraft actually reached the anchorage used by the ships, to be met by a mixed American and Australian force that included every available aircraft on Guadalcanal, 76 in all. The Japanese again lost heavily, this time a quarter of their force, against only seven Allied aircraft shot down, of which all but one pilot was saved. Throughout the whole month the Japanese sent groups of two or three bombers every night to attack the airfields on Guadalcanal, and occasionally these succeeded in destroying aircraft tightly packed in the limited space on the ground.

Japanese Aichi D3A dive bombers on the attack. The D3A was adapted specifically for operations in the Solomon islands from bases in New Britain by the addition of extra fuel tanks.

Wingate's long-range raid

Major General Orde Wingate in March 1944 talking with officers of his Chindits in prior to the launching of their second raid into Burma.

A **British brigade that** had travelled deep into Burma, hoping to disrupt Japanese supplies and communications, struggled back to India through the jungle over a number of days in late April 1943. The plan was the idea of Brigadier Orde Wingate, who believed it was possible to place a large formation of troops behind enemy lines and keep it supplied by air. His force initially made a stealthy crossing into Burma, avoiding contact with the Japanese whenever possible. Wingate's troops achieved some success, including the destruction of railway bridges and damage to railway tracks, but casualties were high. Half of 77 Indian Infantry Brigade were killed, wounded or debilitated by a long stay in the jungle.

Assassination of an admiral

Following the interception and decoding of a signal describing the itinerary of an inspection tour by Admiral Yamamoto, commander of the Japanese navy, the US navy's Pacific Fleet commander-in-chief approved a mission to assassinate him in April 1943. The 339th Fighter Squadron sent 18 P-38 Lightnings to intercept Yamamoto's flight on 18 April. The aircraft used larger-than-normal drop tanks to extend their range and flew at under 500 feet (152 m) to avoid radar detection, the 430-mile (692-km) flight being the longest fighter interception undertaken during the war. In a brief air battle, the bomber carrying Yamamoto was hit by a burst of fire and crashed in the forests of Ballale island, the first stop on his tour. Everyone on board the bomber was killed as a result.

OBITUARY
ADMIRAL YAMAMOTO (1884–1943)

Admiral Yamamoto, commander of the Japanese navy and mastermind of their strategy in the naval war against the United States, was killed when the Mitsubishi G4M bomber carrying him was shot down by American aircraft on 18 April 1943. He had just celebrated his 59th birthday.

Isoroku entered the navy in 1901 and fought at the Battle of

Tsushima in 1905, when he lost two fingers on his left hand. He was a student at Harvard University in the United States in 1919–21, which gave him a good understanding of American people and society; he returned to the US as naval attaché at the embassy in Washington for the period 1926–28. During the 1930s, Yamamoto was an enthusiast of naval air power at the expense of battleship construction, and an opponent of closer relations with Nazi Germany. As with the rest of the navy, he did not agree with the war against China which began in 1937; he was also opposed to any conflict with the United States, correctly believing that the disparity in industrial power between his country and the US was too great.

Once war began, Yamamoto implemented a strategy of a surprise attack against the US Pacific Fleet, followed by a decisive naval engagement. While the first part of his strategy was a success, he lost the vital Battle of Midway on 4 June 1942.

He is survived by his wife, two sons and two daughters.

Axis defeat in Africa

German and Italian troops in Africa surrendered on 13 May 1943, after a final offensive that captured their main supply ports at Tunis and Bizerte. The Allies took 275,000 prisoners, which represented a major victory.

The offensive began with an attack by the British Eighth Army at Wadi Akarit on 6 April which, after painstaking preparations by General Bernard Montgomery, proceeded very slowly, with poor co-operation between tanks and artillery. Furthermore, a supporting attack at Fondouk Pass, that was intended to cut off the Italian First Army's retreat, was mismanaged and the Italian and German forces escaped.

In the end, the massive superiority of the Allied forces in tanks and aircraft proved decisive as they forced the enemy back in a second series of attacks beginning on 19 April.

A massive holding camp for the thousands of German and Italian prisoners who surrendered in May 1943 to the Allied forces in Tunisia. Nearly 300,000 men were captured.

Famine in Bengal

A famine broke out in Bengal, India, in May 1943. The food situation there had been growing increasingly serious as a lot of rice was imported from Burma, now under Japanese control. This was made worse when the rice crop was destroyed by a storm in late 1942. The lack of concern by the government in London, despite warnings from British officials in Delhi, together with the mismanagement by local authorities in the Bengal region, meant that remedial action to reduce the effects of the famine were not taken quickly enough to prevent the situation from worsening rapidly.

British retreat from Arakan

The British troops that had begun a limited offensive in the Arakan region of Burma were forced to retire in early May 1943 after several Japanese moves threatened to cut off their line of retreat back to India. When the main forward base at Buthidaung was attacked by the Japanese on 3 May, the order for a general withdrawal and the abandonment of the Arakan offensive was given by the new commander of British troops in the theatre, General William Slim.

Warsaw ghetto uprising defeated

Although sniping continues, the Germans successfully crushed the uprising of Jews in the Warsaw ghetto, with the capture of the headquarters bunker at 18 Mila Street on 8 May 1943. The uprising began on 19 April, when the Jews in the ghetto chose to resist rather than be shipped off to concentration camps, 2,000 German troops were deployed and have spent nearly three weeks fighting them in the streets; the ghetto's buildings have now been razed to the ground. A very small number of Jews succeeded in escaping under cover of the fighting.

Two Jewish resistance fighters are taken away by German soldiers during the fighting in the Warsaw Ghetto.

The Eder Dam, breached by the famous Dambusters raid in May 1943, the day after the raid. The bombing technique, the "bouncing bomb", defeated the German torpedo nets arranged in front of the dam.

Lancasters breach dams

Eleven **RAF Lancaster** bombers of 617 Squadron succeeded in damaging two German dams on the Eder river in the Ruhr region of Germany on 17 May 1943. The "Dam Busters" used a unique bouncing bomb that skipped along the surface of

The "Dam Busters" used a unique bouncing bomb that skipped along the surface of the water.

the water until detonating behind the torpedo nets placed by the Germans to protect against just such an eventuality. The commander of the raid, Wing Commander Guy Gibson, was awarded the Victoria Cross for the action.

IN BRIEF

The civilian government of Argentina, under President Ramón Castillo, was overthrown by the army on 5 June 1943. Castillo's government had followed a neutral line in the war, but the army was resolutely pro-Axis. The choice of General Pedro Pablo Ramírez as president was powerfully influenced by the United Officers Group, with Colonel Juan Domingo Perón among its leaders.

The island of Pantelleria, an important fortress for the Italians, was forced to surrender following heavy bombing on 11 June 1943. The operation was commanded by American General Dwight D. Eisenhower.

Large numbers of Japanese aircraft attacked American naval forces supporting a landing on the island of Rendova in the Solomons, on 30 June 1943. The Japanese suffered heavy losses in these attacks and according to Allied claims have lost over a thousand aircraft in the fighting over the Solomons during the past year.

As the RAF continued its 'Battle of the Ruhr', with large-scale attacks on key Ruhr industrial targets such as Düsseldorf, Bochum and Gelsenkirchen, American daylight bombing raids hit submarine yards at Wilhelmshaven, Cuxhaven, Kiel and Bremen during the month of June 1943.

Espionage and cryptography

Learning what the enemy is up to, without revealing one's own plans and strengths, has been a major objective of warfare for millennia. However, in the last 150 years, the emphasis given to espionage has shifted to cryptography.

The American Civil War was in some respects the last major war in which the efforts of human intelligence – spies working behind enemy lines – were generally more valuable than discovering the enemy's plans through intercepting and decoding messages. There were several important spy networks developed by both Union and Confederate governments. On more than one occasion, a spy got word from Washington DC of important news related to Union military plans. In July 1861, Rose Greenhow alerted General P.G.T. Beauregard of the planned Union advance on Bull Run. In late 1862, Thomas N. Conrad sent word of General Ambrose Burnside's advance to Fredericksburg to General Robert E. Lee. Each of them acquired their information by listening to what people were telling them or were saying among themselves. Rebel spies based in Canada also engaged in sabotage, attempting a bank robbery in St Albans, Vermont, and burning hotels in New York City.

Hidden words

A pointer to the future was provided by the use of coded messages. These were sent using flags (or torches/lanterns by night) or over military telegraph systems. Messages were encoded, since anyone within sight could see the flags. The rebel code, using a method of letter substitution, was broken by Union cryptanalysts, but the Union code, which

> Mata Hari was typical of many First World War spies in being a woman – the British maintained a large network of female spies in Belgium and northern France, who transmitted information about railway transport.

substituted words for people and places, and was padded with extra words and rearranged into a rectangle, was never broken because the rebels never devoted enough attention to doing so.

The increase in the scale of warfare coinciding with the evolution of flight contributed mightily to the greater emphasis on cryptography over espionage. As armies became larger and more dependent on machinery to move supplies, so the amount of materiel stockpiled to support movements increased to the point where it was clearly visible both from the ground and from the air. During the American Civil War balloons were already being used to look toward the enemy positions from a great height. The Wright brothers believed that the best potential customers for their flying machine would be the armed forces of

Human spies, such as the notorious Mata Hari, were still sought by all sides in war, but the increasing use of telecommunications, allowed the interception and reading of messages.

various countries, specifically to observe the movements of enemy forces. During the First World War, the value of aerial observation was immense and the shooting down or protection of reconnaissance aircraft became vitally important.

Listening in

Meanwhile, the development of wireless telegraphy was having an impact in a different way. Whereas it was possible to tap into a telegraphic cable and listen to messages being sent down it, the problem for the military was to get a small group of men to a position behind enemy lines where messages could be detected, and then for them to return in time for the information to be useful. The convenience of wireless telegraphy was also its drawback – messages could be sent anywhere a receiver was located, but anyone with a receiver within range could also pick up the information being sent. Codes were therefore adopted to conceal the content, but a code can be broken given enough time, although in wartime this is often at a premium. Furthermore, a lucky break, such as the recovery of German cipher keys after the wreck of a cruiser in the Baltic in August 1914, gave Allied codebreakers the ability to read German messages. The French created a very large cryptanalysis department, the Bureau de Chiffre.

> The Germans created a powerful encryption machine known as Enigma, while the Japanese created a similarly difficult code to crack in JN-25. Both were broken, though in different ways.

Espionage networks did function in the First World War. Mata Hari is one of the most famous spies of all, executed for being a double agent. She claimed to be an agent of French intelligence, but was discovered (through cryptanalytical methods) to be passing information to the Germans. Mata Hari was typical of many First World War spies in being a woman – the British maintained a large network of female spies in Belgium and northern France, who transmitted information about railway transport.

Richard Sorge went to Tokyo to collect information about German and Japanese intentions toward the Soviets in September 1933. As a journalist, he soon made contacts among the highest circles of the Japanese government.

Machines at work

By the time the Second World War broke out, all combatants were well aware of the dangers of cryptanalysis. The Germans created a powerful encryption machine known as Enigma, while the Japanese created a similarly difficult code to crack in JN-25. Both were broken, though in different ways. The Allies were able to read Enigma messages after more traditional human intelligence – a disgruntled employee who sold information – gave French intelligence some key documents about Enigma in the 1930s. During the war, the Germans changed the codes periodically, which meant continued cryptanalysis was required throughout the conflict, but by understanding how the machine worked, the amount of effort was considerably reduced. The information was managed under the name ULTRA, which Eisenhower described as having "simplified my task as a commander enormously [and] saved thousands of British and American lives".

JN-25, or "Purple" as the Americans called it, was broken exclusively by means of cryptanalytical methods. Tabulating machines assisted mathematical analysis, and once the code was cracked the codebooks could be laboriously recreated by the Americans. The human element in cryptanalysis really comes in interpreting the information uncovered. For example, in April 1942, the Americans only understood about a third of the code, but this was enough to conclude that an amphibious attack was planned against Port Moresby, and the Battle of the Coral Sea ensued.

> The convenience of wireless telegraphy was also its drawback – messages could be sent anywhere a receiver was located, but anyone with a receiver within range could also pick up the information being sent.

People networks

There were also a number of successful espionage networks during the Second World War. Richard Sorge, a German who spied for the Soviet Union in Japan, befriended a journalist who was able to pass him secret documents from the Japanese government. He reported the impending German attack in June 1941, but his information was ignored by Soviet leader Josef Stalin. Another German, Rudolf Roessler, lived in Switzerland and also passed information to the Soviet Union, but although it remains unclear how he got his material, it was uncannily accurate and was used to prepare against the German attack on Kursk.

An example of an Enigma coding machine, used by the Germans to encrypt their messages.

German Pzkpfw IV tanks, with additional armour to reinforce their turrets and sides against high-velocity rounds, roll across the Russian steppes on their way to engage the enemy in the Kursk salient.

The largest tank battle

The largest tank battles of the war so far were fought around the Russian city of Kursk in July 1943, when German and Red Army tanks battled as the Germans attempted to inflict a major defeat on the Red Army in their summer offensive.

The front around Kursk curved out westwards to form a salient that was vulnerable to an attack on either side. The German plan was to pinch it out by striking toward Ponyri in the north and Prokhorovka in the south. Great faith was placed by the German generals in their new self-propelled guns known as Ferdinands, and in the Tiger tanks that would spearhead the armoured thrusts. However, the Soviets' own intelligence analysis suggested as early

as March 1943 that the German blow would fall at Kursk, and they also received confirmation via their Lucy network of spies. Marshal Georgi Zhukov convinced Soviet leader, Josef Stalin, to let the Germans attack first and then destroy them with a massive counter-attack.

The Red Army's strategy required substantial defensive preparations and regrouping, with some 40 per cent of Red Army rifle divisions being sent to the Kursk salient, along with every single tank army. Huge belts of mines and wire obstacles, backed by thousands of anti-tank guns, were put in place.

When the German attack began, on 5 July 1943, it ground forward slowly, delayed

by the Soviet defensive belt. A massive tank battle was fought at Prokhorovka on 12 July, when the Red Army chose to go on the offensive after absorbing German pressure for a week. SS tanks clashed with the Fifth Guards Tank Army in the largest tank battle of the war. Soviet commanders had no qualms about ordering their armour to charge pell-mell into German formations, ramming the enemy tanks aside. After a day of close-quarter combat, with over 800 tanks destroyed or damaged, both sides dug in for the night. The German offensive had been halted.

The Red Army counter-attack in the Orel salient, to the north of Kursk, began on 13 July, and with the Allied invasion of Sicily, the Germans called off their offensive.

Tiger Tank

The German Pzkpfw VI Tiger I tank was first used in service in September 1942, but it was not easy to produce quickly and it did not enter service in large numbers until the first half of 1943. The tank was much heavier and better armoured frontally than previous German tanks, but was expensive and early models were prone to breakdown. Its 88mm gun could penetrate the armour of most Second World War tanks.

Operation Gomorrah destroys Hamburg

The city of Hamburg was turned into a raging inferno on the night of 27 July 1943 when over 700 RAF bombers attacked the city. The raid was part of a series of attacks which began on 24 July and ended on 3 August. The US Army Air Force attacked the city during the day, while the RAF wreaked havoc by night. The total death toll from Operation Gomorrah amounted to 50,000 and a substantial part of Hamburg's buildings were destroyed.

The raid saw the first use of "Window", strips of aluminium dropped to create a confusing mass of radar signals in order to defeat the radar-controlled German night fighters from being directed toward the RAF bomber stream. Three major raids were made by night: 24/25 July, 27/28 July and 28/29 July. On the night of 27/28 July, firefighters could not reach one area allowing the fires to take hold and spread rapidly through the city, which had already been experiencing a dry summer. The flames turned into a massive firestorm that reached temperatures of 815°C (1,500°F) and there were swirling winds that sucked people into it like a tornado.

The crew of a Lancaster bomber walk away from their plane after a night raid on Germany. Losses among the aircrew of Bomber Command were considerable, in spite of the use of night-time flying to make detection by sight more difficult.

Allies take Sicily

American tanks advancing through the narrow streets of Palermo after the fall of the city to the Allies in July 1943. Sicily was the first Axis home territory occupied by the Allied forces in the war.

The last Axis troops left Sicily on 17 August 1943. Shortly after the final boatload left Messina for the Italian mainland, American troops arrived in the city. The invasion of the island on 10 July was the largest amphibious operation of the war so far, and involved the large-scale use of airborne troops for the first time during the war.

The Allied forces included veterans of the North African campaign, as well as newly arrived divisions from the United States and Canada. They were opposed by German and Italian troops, but the sternest resistance came mostly from the former. Allied forces landed in the south-eastern corner of the island, intending to advance northwards to Messina up the eastern coast, but the advance had stalled by 13 July. The commander of the US Seventh Army, General George Patton, achieved the breakthrough when he interpreted his orders liberally and sent a strong force westwards toward Palermo. The Axis forces defending this area had been withdrawn after the landings on 10 July, so Patton's men captured Palermo with ease on 24 July. That same day the Grand Council of the Fascist Party met and, after an adverse vote against him, Italian dictator Benito Mussolini was deposed by King Victor Emmanuel the day after. The Allies now advanced on Messina from both the west and the south.

Operation Tidal Wave over Ploesti

On **1 August** 1943, American bombers of the Eighth and Fifteenth Air Forces made a daring long-range raid on the Rumanian refinery complex responsible for 60 per cent of Germany's oil supplies. The Americans suffered heavy casualties in the raid, but did temporarily reduce output by 40 per cent.

The bombers dropped down to an altitude of 500 feet (150 m), but an error during the flight staggered the formation and ended up scattering it in such a way that aircraft attacked Ploesti from several different directions. (The German defenders initially believed this was intentional, admiring the skill with which the pilots avoided one another.) Flying almost at tree-top level, the B-24s were able to drop their bombs with great accuracy.

An American B-24 flies over the oil refinery of Ploesti, Rumania. The bomber streams fell into disorder and casualties were heavy.

MacArthur, Halsey cartwheel toward Rabaul

US infantry struggle through the mud of a track. By selectively seizing islands in the Solomon islands, the main Japanese base at Rabaul, New Britain, was isolated.

Australian and American forces began Operation Cartwheel, which achieved its first significant success on 5 August 1943, with the fall of Munda, and its airfield, on the island of New Georgia.

Operation Cartwheel was intended to capture the key Japanese base at Rabaul via a two-pronged advance up the Solomon islands and across New Guinea. The landing on New Georgia deprived the Japanese of the airfield at Munda, which they had built up into their most important forward air base in the region. Three separate landings were made on the island: the first at its easternmost point on 21 June; the next on 2 July at Zanana, a little over 10 miles (16 km) from Munda; and the third on the north-west of the island at Rice Anchorage.

The jungle terrain on New Georgia provided many hiding places for the Japanese defenders, who skilfully built pillboxes out of logs and camouflaged them with foliage. Much of the fighting had to be carried out by small groups of unsupported infantry. With the humid, wet weather making the air foetid, and diseases quickly spreading among the troops, it was only after reinforcements arrived for the original division assigned to the task that the Americans made any progress.

Kharkov liberated as Red Army punches through German lines

The most important city in the eastern Ukraine, Kharkov, was liberated by the Red Army on 23 August 1943, an event celebrated by a 224-gun salute in Moscow. The victory comes toward the end of the six-week Red Army offensive that has followed on from the defeat of the Germans at Kursk.

The main weight of the Soviet attack hit the Germans south of the Kursk salient. With an overwhelming superiority in men, tanks and guns, and a huge number of aircraft in support, the Soviets easily made a breach in the German line west of Belgorod, when they unleashed their attack on 12 July. Throughout the month they widened this breach to the west, while at the same time putting in concentric attacks toward Kharkov. The German dictator, Adolf Hitler, imposed a "stand fast" order on his troops defending Kharkov, but the army group commander, Field Marshal Erich von Manstein, eventually prevailed on Hitler to allow the Germans to withdraw.

Soviet attacks north of the Kursk salient have also been successful, liberating the city of Orel on 4 August and driving westwards toward the key railway centre at Bryansk.

German troops retreat through a burning town in southern Russia. The German defeat at Kursk was turned into a massive Red Army counter-attack.

An Australian radioman tries to fix the battery of his radio near Lae during fighting on New Guinea in September 1943. The Australians bore the brunt of the fighting on New Guinea, from which the Japanese threatened their country directly.

Australians capture New Guinea ports

The capture of Finschafen on 2 October 1943 threatened New Britain, an important Japanese naval and air base in this part of the Pacific theatre. General Douglas MacArthur, supreme commander of the theatre of operations, combined landings by sea with advances over land and a parachute drop to achieve this success.

The operation was conducted in three stages. The first secured Salamaua, the second captured Lae and the third was directed at Finschafen. The campaign began on 17 August 1943, when the Allied air forces launched a series of raids on Japanese airfields in the area. The main blows fell when a brigade of the Australian 7th Infantry Division made a landing near Lae on 4 September 1943. This was followed by a parachute drop by the US 503rd Parachute Infantry Regiment at Nadzab on 5 September, to secure the key airfield there. Other troops from the 7th Infantry Division

were flown into Nadzab starting on 7 September.

The Japanese had trouble keeping their forces supplied. The effect of all these Allied operations closing on the Vitiaz Strait which separated New Britain from New Guinea was to threaten their already straitened supply lines. Most Japanese soldiers lacked a proper diet which in the tropics left them even more badly affected by disease than the Allied forces. Meanwhile, the high command in Tokyo was reconsidering where to establish its main line of resistance and in the end General Adachi Hatazo, commander of the Eighteenth Army, decided to abandon Salamaua and Lae. Australian soldiers occupied the former on 12 September and the latter on 16 September.

The ease of the success led MacArthur to order a further advance on Finschafen, which could rule out

a landing on New Britain as Allied airpower could effectively isolate the Japanese forces there. The 9th Australian Division landed 6 miles (9½ km) north of Finschafen on 22 September and after beating off a Japanese attack on 26 September, occupied Finschafen.

Fritz-X

The German Air Force used a remotely-controlled glider bomb against Allied shipping off Salerno in September 1943. Delivered by Dornier Do 217 bombers, these had already successfully sunk an Italian battleship, the *Roma*, attempting to sail to an Allied port as part of the surrender of Italy. The bombs damaged a number of warships, and sank a hospital ship and a transport. Fighter aircraft could shoot down the mother aircraft, however, and these missions had to be abandoned once a substantial number of fighters were based at the beachhead.

Italy invaded by Allies at Salerno

Naples fell to American troops on 1 October 1943 after a month of hard fighting in the south of Italy that nearly resulted in an embarrassing defeat for the Allied troops landed at Salerno.

The first Allied troops to enter Italy were men of the Eighth Army, who crossed from Sicily to the toe of Italy, landing at Reggio di Calabria on 3 September. The German and Italian forces in the area were light and withdrew rather than fight. The Allies had planned a large combination of amphibious assaults for 9 September, drawing on their forces in Sicily, Tunisia and Algeria. By far the largest force, the Fifth Army commanded by General Mark Clark, was to land at Salerno, about the furthest point north along the coast that fighters based in Sicily could cover effectively, while the British 1st Airborne Division landed by sea at Taranto in the "heel".

The landings at Salerno suffered problems from the start when the convoys were spotted by German aircraft not long after leaving their ports. There was no preliminary bombardment and the small number of Germans overlooking the beaches were ready to the point of broadcasting a "welcome" message over loudspeakers beforehand. Although casualties would have been heavy had the defenders been more numerous, the Germans were already moving their Tenth Army south, concentrating three divisions around the beachhead by 10 September.

The German counter-attacks that began on 12 September with the seizure of key preliminary objectives, nearly broke through on 13 September. All that stood between them and the beaches was the artillery of the US 45th Infantry Division, whose defensive fire, together with offshore naval gunfire, succeeded in buying enough time to reorganize the beachhead's defences. The next morning, the Allied artillery halted the German advance and the Germans withdrew to a new defensive line along the Gustav Line.

British troops disembark from a landing ship on the beaches of Salerno. The ship is creating a smoke screen to give some protection from possible German air attack during the landings.

Italy surrenders, Mussolini rescued

After secret negotiations, the Italian government agreed to an armistice with the Allies that was announced to the world on 8 September 1943, the day before the landings at Salerno. However, the large number of German troops already in the country seized key strategic points and occupied the capital, Rome, causing members of the government and King Victor Emmanuel, to flee to Allied protection at Bari. German troops disarmed their Italian counterparts, while also calling on them to join them in continuing the war. A few did so, while others fled south to join the Allies or were deported to Germany as prisoners.

The Germans also rescued former Italian dictator Benito Mussolini from arrest. Mussolini had been kept at Gran Sasso, a resort in the Apennine Mountains in the Abruzzo. On 12 September German commandos landed by glider, disarmed Mussolini's guards and flew the former dictator to Vienna. Six days later, he proclaimed the Italian Social Republic, with himself as head of state, and established his government in the resort town of Salò.

The hotel Campo Imperatore from which Mussolini was rescued on the orders of Hitler in September 1943.

Black Thursday follows Black Week for US Army Air Force

Smoke and the flashes of explosions mark the bombing of Schweinfurt in October 1943. The raid was part of a strategic plan to eliminate the German ball-bearing industry.

Heavy losses in a week of bombing raids on Germany over the period 8–14 October 1943 have called into question the US Army Air Force's strategy of daylight precision bombing.

The raids were part of the Combined Bomber Offensive that had been agreed at the Casablanca Conference in January 1943. The targets included Bremen, Gdynia, Münster and Schweinfurt and the scale of losses was severe, the first three missions costing 88 bombers. The raid on Schweinfurt, on 14 October 1943, was the largest of the three, with the target a ball-bearing plant that had already been bombed on 17 August 1943. The Germans defended the target fiercely, with fighter aircraft continuing to engage the bomber formations even though anti-aircraft shells were threatening to do as much harm to them as to the Americans. Over 1,200 bombs were dropped, but only 88 hit their

Over 1,200 bombs were dropped, but only 88 hit their target. The Americans lost 82 bombers out of the 291 that did not abort, and over 600 aircrew were killed.

target. The Americans lost 82 bombers out of the 291 that did not abort, and over 600 aircrew were killed. Although the capacity of the ball-bearing factory was substantially reduced, the effect on its actual production was minimal.

Paratroopers over Kanev

The largest Soviet airborne operation of the war was a parachute drop in late September 1943 on the western bank of the Dnieper to create a bridgehead for the advancing Red Army troops. The whole operation was error-strewn. The force of two brigades was too small for the 20-mile (32-km) circumference intended to be held, the Germans had inadvertently moved substantial forces into the area after it had been selected for the drop, and there weren't enough aircraft to deliver the paratroopers all at once. The drop on 25 September resulted in a chaotic attempt to hold the bridgehead without heavy weapons or equipment. In the end, about a thousand Red Army soldiers survived to conduct guerrilla operations in the area until reached by friendly troops on 14 November.

"Death Railway" opens

The Bangkok to Rangoon railway, crossing the River Kwai, opened on 25 October 1943, having been completed in August 1943. Construction of the railway began in August 1942, using prisoners captured by the Japanese at the surrender of Singapore, or in the campaign in the Dutch East Indies, to supplement the large numbers of labourers drafted from China and other Japanese-occupied countries.

The railway was constructed simultaneously from Thanbyuzayat in Burma southwards, and from Nong Pladuk in Thailand northwards. The rate of attrition among the workforce in the jungle was horrendous as the Japanese were determined to build the railway as fast as possible, and drove the workers hard. Rations were poor and engineering equipment extremely limited. Cranes and trucks were replaced by human muscle as teams carted materials around by hand or by using pulleys and ropes. Some 40 per cent of the 200,000 Asian labourers died in the construction; just over 50,000

Some 40 per cent of the 200,000 Asian labourers died in the construction; just over 50,000 Allied prisoners went to work on the project and just over 20 per cent of them – about 11,000 – died.

Allied prisoners went to work on the project and just over 20 per cent of them – about 11,000 – died.

Allied prisoners at work on the Kwai railway linking Bangkok to Rangoon. The Japanese treatment of captives was harsh, although to some extent the harsh treatment Japanese officers meted out to their own soldiers set the standard for the treatment of captives.

Kiev liberated, Germans fend off disaster

The Red Army's largest offensive of the war so far secured the liberation of Kiev from the Nazis on 6 November 1943 after a heavy bombardment. The victory came one day before the 26th anniversary of the Bolshevik Revolution.

After the capture of Kharkov in August, Soviet commanders, prompted by Soviet leader Josef Stalin, chose to continue their offensive in spite of the considerable losses they had already suffered at the hands of the Germans. These assaults in the south were accompanied by another offensive toward Bryansk, which was liberated on 17 September.

The southern offensives unfurled over several days in August, rolling up from the south. The South-western Front began its drive on 13 August, while the Central Front, the last to begin on 26 August, was delayed by supply problems. The drive forward by the Red Army was relentless and German troops were hampered to a degree by Adolf Hitler's orders not to give up territory. The steady, grinding attrition slowed down the German army. Any hope of drawing reinforcements from another part of the front was prevented by the attacks toward Bryansk. It was apparent to the commander of Germany's Army Group South that their best hope was to stand along the Dnepr river, the western bank of which was surmounted by high bluffs. Hitler, believing the creation of some kind of Eastern Wall could be achieved here, agreed.

But German plans were overturned by the offensive spirit of the Red Army. As its formations reached the Dnepr, they surged across the broad river, using any raft, boat or other floating object that they could; the first bridgehead was established on 22 September. However, continued shortages of ammunition, fuel, trucks and bridging equipment prevented the Soviet forces from exploiting their success effectively as their bridgeheads were held under intense pressure of steady bombing from German aircraft, and were hemmed in by German troops.

Pausing as if to draw breath and to celebrate the liberation of Smolensk on 25 September, the Red Army resumed its relentless advance on 24 October, this time widening its front further to include a drive toward Minsk. A left hook from a bridgehead over the Dnepr at Lyutezh and a diversionary attack near Bukrin on 1 November preceded the main assault on 3 November, which itself involved the heaviest bombardment yet seen on the Eastern Front.

Citizens of Kiev greet their Red Army liberators. Kiev was Russia's oldest city, and its liberation on 6 November 1943 ended a series of small German successes on the Eastern Front.

Landing Vehicle, Tracked (LVT)

The LVT was developed in the 1930s as a rescue vehicle for use in swamps. When an article about it appeared in *Life* magazine in the late 1930s, the US Marine Corps identified it as a vehicle that could be adapted for use in the amphibious landings that were seen as the main duty of the Corps in the approaching war.

Desperate fighting on Tarawa

The American flag was hoisted over Tarawa in the Central Pacific on 23 November 1943, after a three-day battle that pitted some 35,000 American marines and soldiers against 2,600 Japanese marines, plus a similar number of labourers.

The battle opened on 20 November with a naval bombardment from three battleships, five cruisers and nine destroyers, preceded by a half-hour of strafing and bombing by aircraft flying from the accompanying aircraft carriers. Then the landing began. Coral reefs off the island meant that amphibious tractors were used to land the marines. In some parts of the island, they took heavy fire as they carried the troops ashore, and those who leaped over the side to wade the final few yards were shot down in large numbers. Those who did make it ashore were pinned down behind a log sea wall. Casualties to the first wave amounted to 30 per cent.

Breakdowns in communications hampered the Americans' ability to co-ordinate their attacks. The few tanks that landed were knocked out by Japanese gunfire without making significant gains. However, during 21 November, the western side of the island came under American control, as carefully directed naval gunfire destroyed most of the Japanese machine-gun posts. It was only on 22 November that the US Marines succeeded in pushing the Japanese back any considerable distance, and by nightfall it was apparent that the Japanese were doomed. A mass attack by those left at 4 a.m. on 23 November brought the battle to an end.

American Marines behind a sandbag entrenchment erected to provide some cover on the largely flat island. The Japanese were well prepared for the American attack, but the overwhelming advantage in numbers and supporting firepower rested with the Marines.

Big Three assemble in Tehran

The leaders of the three main Allied powers, the United States, the Soviet Union and Britain, met together at Tehran, Iran, between 28 November and 1 December 1943. The leaders took several key decisions concerning the management of the war. While Soviet leader Josef Stalin gave a commitment to enter the war against Japan once Germany was defeated, American President Franklin Roosevelt and British Prime Minister Winston Churchill agreed to launch the Second Front in the spring of 1944.

The troika that ran the Allied countries during the war met at Tehran on 28 November 1943 and after three days had agreed an overall strategy for the rest of the conflict.

900-day siege ends

On **27 January** 1944, the commander of the Red Army's Leningrad Front Military Soviet formally announced the end of the blockade of the city that had lasted since September 1941.

Planning for the offensive to lift the siege had begun in the autumn of 1943, with the stockpiling of supplies. The Germans had frequently drawn on the besieging forces to reinforce more threatened sectors of the front and weaker divisions had replaced the better-quality ones. The offensives began on 14/15 January, striking north and south of Leningrad to encircle a large portion of the German Eighteenth Army. A third phase involved a drive from either side of Lake Ilmen, to the south of Leningrad, toward Pskov.

The short winter days – with only a few hours of daylight between 9.30 a.m. and 4.30 p.m. – slowed the tempo of offensive operations. Nevertheless, Soviet forces made steady progress against German fortifications that had moved little over the past two years, but were now defended by less capable troops. The critical stage of the battle came on 17 January as the Soviets gradually forced their way through the German lines and after two days the Germans began to pull out rather than risk encirclement. The Soviet forces, meanwhile, reinforced their advances with their reserves as they prepared for the mobile phase of the offensive. The Germans pulled back westward and the fighting now revolved around crossroads and towns, instead of fortified positions.

On 20 January the historic city of Novgorod was liberated by the Red Army and once the Moscow–Leningrad railway was cleared of German forces, the blockade had clearly been lifted for good.

Red Army snipers trudge through deep snow in search of a position from which to fire at the retreating German forces. Good camouflage was vital to snipers, and in northern Russia men wore thick white winter coats that would render them just about invisible from a distance when lying down.

Dreary road to Cassino

Heavy fighting in the town of Cassino reduced its buildings to rubble during the spring of 1944. The Germans controlled most of the high ground around the town, most famously the nearby monastery.

After five months of fighting through difficult terrain in cold, wet, winter weather, Allied forces find themselves halted in front of the German defences known as the Gustav Line, which spans the width of the Italian peninsula.

When Allied forces battled their way northwards from Salerno, they were delayed by a combination of the weather, their own ponderous head-on assault tactics, German demolitions, mountainous terrain, and a transport and supply system requiring a network of modern roads that did not exist in this part of Italy. The French divisions that served in the Fifth Army were the only ones to negotiate successfully the terrain and lack of roads, purchasing or requisitioning every available donkey and mule they could find, and bringing supplies up to the forward sectors of the front on foot, while British and American trucks battled for traction on sloping mountain roads turned to mud by the appallingly wet winter weather.

On 17 January 1944, the British Eighth Army launched an offensive around Mintauro which seriously threatened a breakthrough, but in the end was halted after two days by a mixture of British hesitancy and German reinforcements. An attack in division strength across the Rapido river by the US 36th Infantry Division failed as the Germans held the high ground on the far bank. Their artillery spotters rained shells down on US bridging equipment, while rubber boats brought to get the troops across the river had to be inflated in full view of the enemy, thereby removing any chance of surprise. After two days of attempting to batter their way across the river, beginning on 20 January, the Americans had nothing to show except 2,000 casualties.

Wasteful frontal attacks in divisional strength continued to blight Allied operations during the ensuing month. Two American infantry divisions, the 34th and 36th Infantry Divisions, were decimated after a couple of weeks fighting around Cassino. French forces had achieved some gains north of Cassino, but at considerable cost, and troops had to be transferred from the British Eighth Army to reinforce this sector of the front in February, as the battle drew to a close.

Fifth Army

The Fifth Army was one of several formed within the US Army during the Second World War, on 4 January 1943. Unlike most American armies created during the war, it incorporated troops of other nationalities, including at various times Poles, French, Americans, South Africans and British. Lieutenant General Mark Clark took command of the army during the summer of 1943.

The body of General Stemmerman is carried to a coffin for burial after he was killed in action during the battle of the Korsun Pocket. Stemmerman knew his forces were doomed if they did not break out, but encircling Red Army forces were waiting when the Germans made their attempt.

German pocket obliterated by Red Army

The survivors from a strong force of Germans who had been encircled by the Red Army in the Ukraine were rounded up and sent to prison camps after their attempt to break out failed on 17 February 1944. The total cost of the "Korsun Pocket" to the Germans was around 75,000 men.

The pocket had been formed during the stop-start Soviet winter offensive of 1943–44, which had begun on 24 December 1943 with an attack in the Ukraine. Soviet leader Josef Stalin's vision for the winter offensive incorporated a drive into western Ukraine, together with one to end the siege of Leningrad. The Ukrainian offensive continued to be the main thrust of Red Army operations on the Eastern Front during 1943. Although the Germans had been in steady retreat for most of this time, they had eluded any attempt by the Soviets to achieve a sizeable encirclement. The

Germans' luck deserted them when a Soviet offensive launched on 24 January succeeded in surrounding eight German divisions in the Korsun area, including one Waffen-SS Panzer division and a group of Belgian Waffen-SS volunteers. The Soviet advance had been so rapid that the German pocket was formed by 28 January, only four days after the start of the attack.

Short of supplies, the Germans continued fighting, although the end was inevitable as the Soviets squeezed the ring tighter with each passing day. The Germans to the west feverishly tried to open some kind of gap to allow their comrades to escape, committing four armoured divisions to the attack, but the Soviets kept a tight grip. In the middle of a blizzard, the German commander ordered a desperate breakout in the general direction of the nearest German armoured units, but the Soviets carefully

prepared an ambush that caught the Germans by surprise – they believed they had broken through, when Soviet tanks, infantry and cavalry emerged from hiding. Red Army soldiers were more interested in killing than in taking prisoners, and of the 75,000 casualties, perhaps 20,000 were captured.

Fighting in Arakan

A second British offensive in the Arakan, part of three attacks into Burma during early 1944, resulted in the Battle of the Admin Box that ended on 23 February.

The battle lasted 18 days and saw Japanese front-line troops infiltrating the positions of the 7th Indian Infantry Division to engage cooks, clerks and other headquarters troops within the Admin Box. However, with support from tanks held in reserve there and aerial resupply, the rear echelon force successfully held off the Japanese.

Big Week for Allied air forces in Europe

After five days of bombing raids ending on 25 February 1944, the German fighter force lost control of the skies over Germany. The Allied Operation Argument had launched massive attacks on the factories involved in the production of aircraft – not just the aircraft themselves but also of key components, such as the ball-bearing plant at Schweinfurt.

The plan had been prepared some time before the actual attack, but the weather was unfavourable for the kind of sustained operations that were necessary for success. The purpose was not, in fact, to destroy

The fighter escorts were tremendously successful, claiming some 600 German fighter aircraft shot down, although their actual losses were probably smaller.

these factories, but to engage the German fighter force with new long-range fighter aircraft entering service with the American air force.

US aircraft flew over 3,000 sorties from bases in Britain and Italy, receiving support from night raids by RAF's Bomber Command. The fighter escorts were tremendously successful, claiming some 600 German fighter aircraft shot down, although actual German losses were probably smaller. Nevertheless, the number of experienced fighter pilots lost was high enough to affect German air defences permanently.

Following the success of Big Week, American aircraft began a series of raids against Berlin and other targets during the month of March, specifically to draw what was left of the German fighter force out to fight.

The pilot of a B-17 bomber nicknamed "The General Ike" waves from his cockpit. B-17 pilots were required to be exceptionally skilled at formation flying.

"Stranded whale" at Anzio

Stalemate between German and Allied forces ensued around the Anzio beachhead after six weeks of fighting petered out on 4 March 1944. The initial Allied landings took place on the night of 22 January and were intended to open the road to Rome by outflanking the German Gustav Line position.

The commander of the Anglo-American VI Corps, carrying out the landings, General John Lucas, had little faith in the success of the operation. He believed that his force lacked the strength to cut Highway 6, leading south from Rome, and capture the Italian capital; his pessimism was justifiable, having only two infantry divisions in the initial landing force. Once news of the landing reached the German headquarters, Field Marshal Albert Kesselring's request for reinforcements was met by drawing on divisions scattered around the Nazi conquests, and within 48 hours elements of eight divisions were arrayed around the Allied bridgehead.

Lucas had made a point of digging in before pushing forward, so any chance of cutting Highway 6 was lost. On 22 January, a battalion of US Rangers probed the front around the town of Cisterna, the road appeared to be clear, but the loss of key scouts caused a halt. When the advance resumed a few hours later, German troops had taken up previously unoccupied positions, and of 700 Rangers only six returned to Allied lines, the remainder being either killed or captured. Despite being given two more divisions, one armoured, as reinforcements, Lucas called off his advance, contributing to British Prime Minister Winston Churchill's comment that "I had hoped we were hurling a wildcat ashore, but all we got was a stranded whale."

Meanwhile, Hitler characterized the "stranded whale" as "an abscess", and ordered its removal. At the beginning of February, the Germans outnumbered the Allied forces 120,000 to 96,000, and began a month of counter-offensives against Anzio. They came very close to success on 17–18 February, but Lucas's timely reinforcement of the sector under attack along the Anzio to Albano road saved the day. It did not save him, however, as, to his amazement, he was removed from command on 22 February – he believed he was winning the battle. Both sides had suffered heavy casualties in bad weather.

American troops disembark on the sea front at Anzio in January 1944. Anzio owed much to the same Churchillian vision that produced Gallipoli in the First World War, and suffered from the same caution by the generals on the spot in advancing from the landing zone.

Monastery bombed, Germans stand firm around Cassino

The smoking ruins of buildings in Cassino after an Allied bombardment. Firepower failed to defeat the Germans.

A week-long battle around Cassino, that included the destruction of the historic abbey by bombers, ended on 23 March 1944 when Allied forces abandoned their offensive with little to show for it. The Allies used a combination of New Zealand and Indian troops to carry out the attacks.

Over 700 aircraft participated in the bombing raids that pulverized the town of Cassino with over 1,000 tons (900 tonnes) of high explosive on 15 March. The New Zealand advance into the town was badly hampered by the rubble left by the bombing, and hardly made any gains. On the second day, a battalion of Gurkhas succeeded in reaching a hill to the north-west of Cassino, but fire from German paratroopers in the abbey overlooking the town and the hill made contact with them tenuous. The remainder of the battle consisted of attacks and counter-attacks intended to link up with the Gurkhas, or cut them off from help, until General Sir Harold Alexander ordered a halt to operations. German casualties were very heavy; the Allies lost about 2,400 killed.

Chindit leader killed, operation goes on

The death of Major General Orde Wingate in a plane crash on 24 March 1944 deprived the Long Range Penetration Groups, far behind Japanese lines in Burma, of their leader, but not of their mission. The groups, better known as the Chindits, are carrying out mobile operations in the Japanese rear to disrupt the occupying army's supply lines.

Wingate's Operation Thursday established fortified bases in Burma from which mobile columns were able to attack the Japanese as part of an intended larger operation involving the occupation of northern Burma and an offensive in the Arakan, and although a simultaneous Japanese offensive saw some operations cancelled, Operation Thursday went ahead.

The first Chindit brigade entered Burma on foot in February, but most of the force was flown in by air on 5 March. Gliders were used to fly in three more brigades to landing zones where fortified bases would allow resupply and the evacuation of casualties by air. At the time of Wingate's death, a stronghold had been established at White City, threatening the railway between Indaw and Myitkyina, after a fierce battle for Pagoda Hill involving fighting at close quarters, with men clubbing or hacking at one another with knives, bayonets or samurai swords. Wingate's replacement was Brigadier Joseph Lentaigne.

A donkey train carrying heavy equipment is led by Chindits through the Burmese jungle. Most troops were brought by aircraft to their combat zone far behind Japanese lines.

Marauders on the road to Nhpum Ga

The American-inspired offensive to clear northern Burma, over which military supplies were flown to China following the Japanese occupation of Burma in 1942, achieved a key goal when American troops, who had seized the town of Nhpum Ga, successfully held off Japanese counter-attacks until a relief force arrived on 9 April 1944.

The American troops operated in conjunction with the Chinese Army in India, a formation under the operational control of the American General Joseph Stilwell, who believed that properly trained Chinese troops could defeat the Japanese. His attack into northern Burma was in part an attempt to prove his point, but also part of a wider British, Chinese and American initiative.

Only the American prong of the attack went forward as intended, beginning when the Chinese Army in India crossed from its bases in Assam province into Burma in December 1943. A successful engagement with the Japanese at Yupbang Ga on 13 January 1944 gave a needed fillip to Chinese morale. By the time the only unit

of American troops joined the offensive on 24 February, the Chinese had sustained themselves in Burma for two months against strong Japanese opposition, advancing along the Hukawng valley.

The 5307th Composite Unit (Provisional), christened "Merrill's Marauders" after its commander Brigadier-General Frank Merrill, advanced from India to their support. The Marauders adopted the kind of strategy that the Japanese had used so effectively during their conquest of Burma, advancing around the flank of the enemy and setting up a road block behind their position, forcing them to decide whether to defend to the front or attack at the rear to remove the road block. The first battle, at Walawbum, ended on 6 March when the Japanese were forced to withdraw to the south, and again the Marauders moved behind the enemy flank to set up two road blocks at Shaduzup and Nhpum Ga. The battle for Nhpum Ga began on 28 March and ended ten days later with the Japanese forced to retreat.

Members of Merrill's Marauders march Indian-file though the Burmese jungle. The 5307th Composite Unit (Provisional) was made up of soldiers that other units did not want.

Hitler proclaims Narva fortress

Festung Narva (Fortress Narva) was the name given on 23 March 1944 by German dictator Adolf Hitler to the position defended by a Waffen-SS corps incorporating many volunteers from European countries who had joined the Waffen-SS in a "crusade against Bolshevism". Narva is a key position on the Panther Line, a defensive position that follows the eastern bank of the Narva river but which was already partly breached by a Red Army attack in February.

Narva is a key position on the Panther Line, a defensive position that follows the eastern bank of the Narva river but which was already partly breached by a Red Army attack in February.

The offensive had been a secondary phase of the operations that had ended the siege of Leningrad earlier in the year. Among the Waffen-SS units that distinguished themselves in the February battles along the Narva river were the "Nederland" unit of Dutch volunteers and the "Nordland" division, as well as some Estonian Waffen-SS volunteers. Several Soviet bridgeheads and incursions were halted in February. A renewed round of Soviet attacks in March were also fended off. Although the city of Narva had largely been destroyed by bombing and artillery in early March, Hitler designated the defences of the place as a fortress, which effectively meant it had to be defended to the last man. With the arrival of the spring thaw at the same time as Hitler's proclamation, fighting on this sector of the Eastern Front came to a halt in the muddy conditions.

US aircraft pound Truk

Smoke rises from Dublon town on Truk atoll after a bombing raid by American carrier aircraft. Truk was the main Japanese naval base in the central Pacific, and a frequent target for American raids.

After raids in February, a second raid on the advanced Japanese fleet base on Truk, on 29–30 April 1944, effectively destroyed the facility.

The February raids covered the landings on Eniwetok atoll, when six fleet aircraft carriers and seven light carriers brought over 500 aircraft to perform the operation. The Japanese had advanced warning of the American raids, which were planned to hit a substantial concentration of Japanese warships, and withdrew many of the vessels from the harbour to bases elsewhere in the Pacific. The planning for the attack on Truk envisaged multiple raids following a fighter sweep that would secure air superiority over the base. The aircraft of Task Force 58 destroyed 200 Japanese aircraft on the ground and sank 41 ships.

The April raid used US Army Air Force four-engined bombers and focused on the docks, airfield and other military installations that had largely been ignored by the carrier raids.

IN BRIEF

The capital of Dutch New Guinea, Hollandia, was occupied by American forces on 22 April 1944. The Japanese garrison of 12,000 men was largely comprised of reservists and service troops, and fled after the bombardment by Task Force 77 began. General Douglas MacArthur masterminded the largely unopposed landing of 52,000 American soldiers here, as well as at nearby Aitape. Hollandia offered excellent naval and air base potential.

The explosions of American bombs throw up smoke, debris and fountains of water during a raid by the Fifth Air Force on Hollandia in April 1944.

Bombing round the clock

British and American bombers subjected Germany to a constant aerial bombardment intended to destroy the ability of the country's economy to manufacture key products for the war effort. While the Royal Air Force attacked by night, bombing areas of cities where factories and other important economic installations were located, the Americans attacked by day, relying on precision bombing.

The ruins of Dresden, following the great firestorm raid of February 1945. Incendiary bombing raids brought devastation to several German cities, including Hamburg, Darmstadt and Pforzheim.

attack the bombers. Fighter aircraft lacked the endurance to accompany the bombers all the way to their targets and back and bombers did not carry enough defensive weapons to cope with the lightning attacks of interceptors. Bomber Command therefore retreated to the cover of night for its attacks on German targets, which reduced losses to enemy fighters dramatically, but considerably reduced the accuracy of attacks. In August 1941, a report to the War Cabinet showed that only 20 per cent of bombers managed to get their bombs within 75 square miles (194 km²) of the target.

> Between August 1940 and August 1942, when the first American bombers joined in attacks on the Continent, a total of 66,225 tons (67,290 tonnes) of bombs were dropped, or an average of 2,760 (2,800) per month.

Ineffective

To make matters worse, the number of bombers available to attack targets in Germany was small, which meant that few bombs actually fell on the enemy. Between August 1940 and August 1942, when the first American bombers joined in attacks on the Continent, a total of 66,225 tons (67,290 tonnes) of bombs were dropped, or an average of 2,760 (2,800) per month – a little more than half what the Germans managed during the Blitz months of 7 September 1940 to 16 May 1941.

Things only began to change after the Casablanca Conference in January 1943. British Prime Minister Winston Churchill and American President Franklin Roosevelt authorized the Combined Bomber Offensive, a blueprint for bombing Germany round the clock, the Americans doing so by day, the British by night. The Americans believed a combination of the efficient Norden

Before the Second World War began, the consensus of many strategists, especially among high-ranking officers of the Royal Air Force, was that large-scale bombings of cities would prove a decisive factor, but the early years of the war showed that this was far too optimistic an assessment. When tested in wartime conditions, bombers were found to be highly vulnerable to attack from enemy fighters and often unable to hit their targets. One of the earliest large bomber raids, by the British against German ships at Wilhelmshaven on 18 December 1939, resulted in most of the attacking aircraft being shot down.

Part of the problem was that before the war no one in Bomber Command had given much thought to the ability of the enemy to

Lord Cherwell, the scientist Frederick Lindemann, was a key advisor to British Prime Minister Winston Churchill on the development of bombing policy.

bombsight and the much more powerful defensive armament of their B-17 Flying Fortress bombers, would ensure their daylight raids would achieve a level of effectiveness that had so far evaded the British.

Heavy casualties

The reality proved very different. American raids at Ploesti and Schweinfurt damaged operational capacity of industrial targets, but had little effect on production; US casualties were unacceptably high while the effect on the German economy was minimal. British night raids did not achieve much more but killed many more Germans. The impact of the famous Dambusters' raid lasted a couple of months at best, while the bombing of Hamburg killed many civilians and damaged many buildings, but did not have a serious impact on German submarine production.

Accuracy improved by night as the British deployed radar-equipped aircraft to guide bombers to their targets. Various electronic countermeasures such as Window, also limited the Germans' ability to find and destroy the bombers. Nonetheless, German industrial production continued to increase.

Bleak outlook

From the perspective of 1 November 1943, the outlook for the Combined Bomber Offensive looked bleak. In fact, a turning point had been reached and the Allies had inadvertently discovered the "magic formula" that would deliver success.

Substantial numbers of German fighter aircraft had been withdrawn from other fronts to attack Allied bombers throughout 1943, which is why losses were high. But whereas the unescorted raid against Schweinfurt had led to 20 per cent casualties, an American raid on Emden accompanied by P-47 Thunderbolts with drop fuel tanks suffered only 3 per cent loss. From February 1944, bomber streams were escorted by fighters.

The ability of the German air force to defend its homeland was destroyed in a

> The impact of the famous Dambusters' raid lasted a couple of months at best, while the bombing of Hamburg killed many civilians and damaged many buildings, but did not have a serious impact on German submarine production.

few weeks in February and March 1944. Between January and April the Germans lost over a thousand fighters, the heaviest losses coming in February and March. It was not only the Combined Bombing Offensive that benefited. On 12 May 1944, a series of raids against oil targets reduced German output – not capacity this time – by 18 per cent. There were no longer enough German fighters to challenge the Allied air forces for supremacy over the battlefield and by May 1944, it was apparent that the bombing of German cities and industrial targets was finally making a real contribution to the Allied war effort.

A formation of B-17 bombers in formation during a raid in 1943. The vapour trails in the background are of their accompanying fighter escorts. American heavy bombers did not carry as large a load of bombs as their British counterparts, but were far better provided with defensive armament.

Germans driven out of Cassino

Fighting at Cassino flared up again in mid-May when the Allies renewed their offensive around the Italian town. This time attacks were launched along the entire length of the line from the Tyrrhenian coast to the Monte Cassino area. Nonetheless the Polish II Corps suffered very heavy casualties fighting around the abbey of Monte Cassino and just north of it.

The key breakthroughs were made by French North African troops fighting to the south of Cassino when they captured Monte Ceschito on 13 May, the first major breach in the Gustav Line. The French commander, General Adolphe Juin, pushed reinforcements through the gap and began to threaten German rear areas. Meanwhile, some bridges had been erected over the Rapido river in the Cassino area, and each time German artillery attempted to shell them, thereby revealing their positions, they were subjected to massive air attack by fighter-bombers.

On 17 May, French troops reached the road between Itri and Pico, which was the key for supporting German troops around Cassino and in the Liri Valley to the south. The commander of the German Tenth Army, General Heinrich von Vietinghoff, recognized the inevitable and ordered a withdrawal from the Cassino position.

British and South African troops stand with a captured Nazi flag in Cassino. The Allied victory finally came thanks to hard fighting by infantry in the mountains around Cassino, during which Free French troops drawn from France's North African territories played the key role.

Twin victories for British over Japanese in India

British officers confer during the Imphal-Kohima fighting. The Japanese spoiling attack was successfully parried by the British, who then began a counter-offensive into Burma.

British and Indian Army forces successfully defended India against invasion by the Japanese (whose forces included a contingent of anti-British Indian volunteers) in battles at Kohima and Imphal. The Japanese attempted the offensive with limited resources, leaving their heaviest artillery behind in Burma owing to the difficulty of transporting it through rugged terrain, and relied on captured supplies.

The U-GO offensive, devised by General Renya Mutaguchi of the Fifteenth Army, consisted of a main attack toward Imphal, while a subsidiary offensive drove on Kohima, which in Japanese hands would cut off Imphal from road resupply. The advance on Imphal began on 8 March, when three Japanese divisions crossed the Chindwin river. The British succeeded in withdrawing all but one division from their positions here. The 17th Indian Division was caught by the Japanese 33rd Infantry Division, and required support from a second division in order to escape the Japanese on 25 March. That, however, left Imphal exposed to attack

and required the transfer of a British division from the Arakan front.

Meanwhile, the advance on Kohima by this stage was also involving troops that the British commander, General William Slim, had intended to withdraw. Reinforcements were flown in, and the Japanese succeeded in surrounding the British base there on 3 April. Fierce fighting in the hills and mountains surrounding Kohima began and lasted most of the month. The Japanese came close to victory, but on 18 April relief arrived at Kohima and the worn-out defenders received key reinforcements that turned the tide of battle. The Japanese troops were starving by 15 May and withdrew two weeks later.

At Imphal, the Japanese began their assault from three directions at the beginning of April. The northern attack came closest to succeeding when it occupied Nungshigum Hill overlooking the main airstrip, but once again air support and artillery helped the British overcome the Japanese here and further Japanese attacks achieved little.

Myitkyina airfield falls, town still in Japanese hands

After ten days of fierce fighting, stalemate ensued around the northern Burma city of Myitkyina, where Merrill's Marauders and other Allied units have been battling the Japanese for control of this strategic base. By 27 May 1944, the Japanese still held the town, while Allied forces were in control of the airfield. The 5307th Composite Unit, popularly known as Merrill's Marauders, is so worn out by the constant fighting since it entered combat in February that its troops have been known to fall asleep from exhaustion during combat.

The Bren gun

The standard light machine gun used in British infantry sections during the Second World War was a weapon of Czech design. The gun was highly accurate for a light machine gun, but was less effective at suppressive fire, as the rounds fell in too tight a pattern to encourage many soldiers to put their heads down.

D-Day, the greatest operation

After three years of planning, D-Day, on 6 June 1944, placed 130,000 men, supported by 6,000 ships and landing craft and over 10,000 aircraft, in Normandy, France, in the largest combined operation of the war yet. Its success rested, however, on the combat soldiers whose duty was to make a frontal assault against an enemy in prepared positions – the most dangerous of military missions.

American troops wade through low tide off Normandy toward Omaha beach on 6 June 1944. The heights occupied by the Germans can be seen dimly through the smoke. The Americans suffered heavy casualties, but eventually gained the heights thanks in part to naval gunfire support.

The first assault troops came by air, not by sea, as some 25,000 paratroopers and glider-borne infantry landed behind the beaches scattered between the Orne river and the vicinity of the town of Ste Mère-Eglise. The British 6th Airborne Division landed in the east, while two American divisions were dropped in the west.

One of the key British objectives was a bridge over the Caen Canal, that was successfully captured in a textbook assault by three platoons. The firefight was short and sharp, ending with a gallant charge by the British paras, firing from the hip, across the bridge. A second objective, a battery of guns at Merville that commanded the main British beach at Ouistreham, was captured by an airborne battalion. The paras engaged the defenders in hand-to-hand combat and destroyed the guns once they had been captured.

In contrast, the American drop was more chaotic. Anti-aircraft fire and inexperienced pilots led to most of the paratroopers being scattered far from their intended drop zones. Some order was achieved, partly through

> One of the key British objectives was a bridge over the Caen Canal, that was successfully captured in a textbook assault by three platoons. The firefight was short and sharp, ending with a gallant charge by the British paras.

the assistance of a child's toy that produced a distinctive clicking sound when pressed, known as the "cricket". Ad hoc formations emerged around officers and NCOs who gathered together anyone they came across.

The American paratroopers did, however, manage to achieve most of their objectives, in part because the chaotic drop confused the Germans, who were unable to identify where they were heading.

The most daring assault was carried out by Staff Sergeant Summers at Mesières where a German artillery barracks was captured almost single-handedly by the American NCO when he decided to lead by example and charge it, while all but one of the rest of his comrades, whom he had never seen before, waited until he had captured all but the main building. By lunchtime on 6 June, American paratroopers had secured most of the exits off Utah Beach and had captured Ste Mère-Eglise, among other key objectives, but the road between Carentan and Ste Mère-Eglise remained open to the Germans.

The landings were staggered according to the time the tide turned, as the Allied planners co-ordinated their operation with

American paratroopers advance past a French cemetery in the village of St Marcouf. The airborne drops behind the Allied beaches played an important role in disrupting the ability of the German defenders to reinforce the landing beaches.

inland. The Canadians at Juno were even more successful and nearly achieved all their planned objectives by the end of the day. Canadian tanks reached the Caen–Bayeux road, but the lack of supporting infantry meant they were forced to withdraw.

The British 3rd Infantry Division at Sword Beach landed on the narrowest front in order to provide the most concentrated effort in reaching its objective, the capture of Caen. The Germans here were well dug in, however, as at Omaha, and it took a lot of hard fighting to clear pillboxes

> But it was a different story at Omaha, the next beach along. Being the only beach between the Vire river and Arromanches, the Germans knew that it was a likely target and fortified it heavily.

at Ouistreham, Lion-sur-Mer and La Brèche. By mid-morning, German tanks were reported to be assembling north and west of Caen, and these attacked at 4.30 p.m.. Faced with enemy armour, the British had to abandon any hope of reaching Caen that day.

However, from Utah to Sword, the Allied forces were firmly ashore on the Continent, and the long-awaited Second Front for the Liberation of Europe had begun.

the rising of the water, so that the strong belt of obstacles placed by the Germans was rendered ineffective. The American landing at Utah Beach was largely unopposed, in part because it took place 1 mile (1½ km) further south than had been planned. But it was a different story at Omaha, the next beach along. Being the only beach between the Vire river and Arromanches, the Germans knew that it was a likely target and fortified it heavily. Naval gunfire support here was less effective, owing to smoke and haze. Landing on the correct beach, and a strongly defended one at that, many men failed even to get out of the landing craft, as the Germans were already firing at the ramps before they opened. Once they had, the troops were cut down; those who reached the beach found themselves trapped under heavy enfilading fire. Casualties were heavy and at midday General Omar Bradley, in command of the US assault, briefly considered abandoning the beach. He did not, and coincidentally, American infantrymen of the 1st Infantry Division (the Big Red One) were beginning to gain the less well defended bluffs overlooking the beach while destroyers sailed close inshore to give naval gunfire support. It was enough to establish a tenuous toehold ashore by nightfall.

The experience of the soldiers landing at the Anglo-Canadian beaches of Gold, Juno and Sword was far less extreme than for their American counterparts at Omaha. In part this

was because they avoided the problems of drift and heavy seas that afflicted the Americans. But an important role was also played by the more determined effort the British made to get armoured support for their men onto the beaches. A number of specialized tanks, known as AVREs (Armoured Vehicles, Royal Engineers), made bunker busting a far easier task. At Gold Beach, an AVRE played a key role in capturing a sanitorium at Le Hamel that the Germans had converted into a strongpoint. Gold Beach was largely cleared by midday and the British began moving

Canadian troops land on Juno beach from infantry landing craft. In the background are some of the AVRE tanks which made a vital contribution to the relative success of the landings.

D-day engineering

The Allied landings in Normandy required the support of an immense engineering effort in order to ensure enough food, ammunition and fuel reached them, and included artificial ports, underwater pipelines and specialized tanks.

The pipeline laid under the English Channel to Cherbourg delivered a considerable amount of fuel to the Allied armies fighting in northwestern Europe.

An army fighting a modern battle requires a vast amount of supplies and engineering support, yet most observers rarely think about how getting this to the men at the front is probably the most important factor in strategic decision-making. The Normandy Campaign of 1944 provides a good summary of how these considerations are taken into account at each stage of the process starting with planning and ending with combat.

The selection of Normandy as an invasion target was dictated in part by the need for a reasonably sized port nearby. The Axis effort in North Africa had been seriously hampered by the lack of an adequate port to support Field Marshal Erwin Rommel's 1942 invasion of Egypt. At the same time, the raid on Dieppe illustrated how difficult it would be to secure a port by direct assault. The Germans were equally aware of the importance of these dock facilities and all the ports in France were well defended.

The Allies thus isolated several possible locations for an assault, based on their requirement of a port near the beaches. There was the Biscay coast, the north Brittany coast, Normandy, the mouth of the Seine near Le Havre, the Pas de Calais and the Dutch-Belgian coast. The Biscay and Dutch-Belgian coasts were too far from Britain; the Pas de Calais was too well defended. An attack around Le Havre would involve landings either side of a river mouth, which would mean a divided force

> These projects, code-named Mulberry, involved hauling 50,000 tons of steelwork, a million tons of concrete, 6 miles (10 km) of bridging and 120 miles (193 km) of steel cabling across the Channel.

and went against basic military principles. Brittany offered good options, but was the furthest point from Germany. Normandy was the best compromise, although its nearby port at Cherbourg was not well suited to cargo operations.

The problem for the planners was that some 600 tons (544 tonnes) of supplies were needed each day by a single division in combat. While a partial solution was available through parachute drops and using large tank landing craft that could unload directly on the beaches, the British believed that artificial harbours provided an effective long-term solution. These projects, code-named Mulberry, involved hauling 50,000 tons (45,300 tonnes) of steelwork, 1,000,000 tons (900,000 tonnes) of concrete, 6 miles (10 km) of bridging and 120 miles (193 km) of

One of the large casemates used in construction of the Mulberry artificial harbours off the invasion beaches is towed from Portsmouth harbour.

capable of receiving 600 tons (545 tonnes) of fuel an hour, this target was rarely met.

In the long term, ten pipes were laid across the Channel from Sandown Bay to Querqueville, to the west of Cherbourg. The job of laying this Pipeline Under The Ocean (known by its acronym PLUTO) could not be completed until Allied forces had secured most of the Cotentin Peninsula, a job that took all of June. Laying the pipe itself was therefore delayed until August. The pipes were made of flexible metal, with a bore diameter of 3 inches (100 mm), and unrolled from a large drum known as a Conun Drum.

In addition to these large projects, a host of specialized vehicles were also assembled to assist the invasion. The British formed an entire armoured division from these vehicles, the 79th Armoured, known as The Funnies. The Americans had very different attitudes to armoured warfare than the British and largely dispensed with such support, although they did attempt to land "Duplex Drive" tanks. These were adapted Shermans with a canvas screen and two propellers. The screen, when raised, gave enough buoyancy to the tank for it to drive through the water at 4 knots. However, in the event, these tanks were launched too early and many were swamped.

In addition, the British deployed Sherman tanks designed to drive through minefields with flail drums that spun heavy chains, detonating any mines in front of the tank. Another British adaptation was made to their Churchill tank. The standard 6-pdr A/T gun was replaced with a 290mm Petard mortar to create the Armoured Vehicle, Royal Engineers (AVRE). This was specifically designed to knock out pillboxes or other fortifications, proving immensely useful on 6 June and thereafter. The AVRE could also use a flail or carry fascines – bundles of sticks and wood – that could be dropped into ditches to allow tanks or infantry to cross them more easily.

steel cabling across the Channel. Breakwaters were made out of 200-foot (60-m) caissons as an outer ring and 74 sunken merchant ships to provide an inner ring. Construction of the Mulberry harbours began on 8 June 1944 and they were in operation by the end of the week. A total of 74,000 troops, 10,000 vehicles and 17,000 tons (15,500 tonnes) of supplies were unloaded using them in their first week of operation.

The Allied divisions had a lot of trucks and other vehicles – an American infantry division alone contained just over 2,000 vehicles of various types. The fuel consumption of such a force, once on the move, was also sizeable, being around 30,000 gallons (113,500 litres) of fuel in one day. Shipping of fuel clearly ranked high in importance together with food, medical supplies and ammunition. The Allied planners solved this with two solutions, one short-term covering the campaign in Normandy, the other intended to go into effect once the breakout was under way.

For immediate needs, four short pipelines were laid off Port en Bessin, to the east of Omaha Beach, to which a tanker could moor and discharge fuel. This went into operation in mid-June. (Prior to that mobile warfare was thought unlikely and fuel requirements could be met by delivering petrol cans direct to the beach via landing craft.) Although this project, code-named Tombola, should have been

SHAEF

The Supreme Headquarters, Allied Expeditionary Force ran the organization of the Normandy campaign. It controlled the strategic air forces for a time, giving them targeting priorities, as well as co-ordinating the naval operations in support of the troops landed ashore. The American General Dwight Eisenhower was the Supreme Commander, but all his immediate deputies were British: Air Chief Marshal Sir Arthur Tedder as his deputy, Admiral Sir Bertram Ramsay in charge of naval operations, General Sir Bernard Montgomery, the ground force commander, and Air Chief Marshal Sir Trafford Leigh-Mallory, the air commander.

Rome falls

Allied troops entered the first major Axis capital on 4 June 1944 when members of the Fifth Army reached the Eternal City. The fall of Rome marks the end of the linked campaigns of Anzio and Cassino. The force at

The fall of Rome marks the end of the linked campaigns of Anzio and Cassino.

Anzio was on the verge of achieving the significant success it had been intended to achieve when Fifth Army commander General Mark Clark redirected its efforts toward capturing Rome, getting headlines for himself, instead of trapping German troops to the south and bringing about a major military victory. The German forces were already in retreat when their commander, Field Marshal Albert Kesselring, declared it an open city.

Lieutenant-Colonel Charles A. Ellis's 91st Reconnaissance Group were the first Allied troops to enter Rome on 4 June 1944.

"Hurricane" blows over Biak

Wrecked Japanese tanks on the island of Biak. Some of the biggest tank battles of the Second World War in the Pacific occurred here, but the lightweight Japanese vehicles were no match for the Americans' anti-tank weapons.

Operation Hurricane, General Douglas MacArthur's assault on the island of Biak, north-west of New Guinea, achieved control of the island on 27 June 1944. The Japanese had adopted a new approach to defending the island that left troops fighting from dug-in positions even after the American forces had secured all their main objectives, leaving them with having to face more months of hard fighting to finish off the island's garrison.

American forces landed on Biak on 27 May after MacArthur had refused to believe intelligence estimates that placed 11,000 Japanese troops on the island, although many of these were rear-echelon rather than combat troops. The Japanese commander, Colonel Naoyuki Kuzume, chose not to defend the beaches, but to position his forces in depth, occupying positions that would prevent the Americans from using the main target, the airfield, until they had been completely cleared of the enemy. Caves on the island provided natural strongpoints, while camouflaged pillboxes and other entrenchments were constructed using natural resources.

The Americans soon found the Japanese were conducting a different kind of defence. Before, they would hurl themselves against American lines in night-time banzai charges in which human spirit and determination frequently failed to overwhelm American firepower. Now, Japanese attacks were relatively light, although in some cases they were supported by tanks (resulting in the South West Pacific theatre's first tank battle when Japanese Type 95 tanks engaged American Shermans on 29 May). Instead, tenacious defence by the Japanese greatly slowed the American advance, in the end causing the removal of the operation's commander by MacArthur.

Decisive battle turns into a turkey shoot

American and Japanese warships clashed in the Battle of the Philippine Sea on 19 June 1944. The Japanese Admiral Ozawa hoped to use the longer range of his carrier aircraft to good effect by attacking from beyond the range of their American counterparts. However, his pilots were not nearly so well trained and the lack of protective armour that helped Japanese aircraft achieve their longer range made them easy to shoot down. The Japanese attacked the American fleet in four waves and in each case the defending American fighters succeeded in shooting down a large number of them – in the end nearly 350 Japanese aircraft were lost in the fighting. The American counterstrike succeeded in sinking one Japanese carrier, while two more were hit by torpedoes from American submarines patrolling the area and subsequently sank. The battle ended any hope the Japanese had of decisively defeating the American fleet in the war.

A Grumman TBF Avenger prepares to take off from an American carrier. The Japanese were outnumbered in both ships and aircraft.

German rocket hits London

A V-1 flying bomb falls on London. The weapons, using a basic jet engine that produced a buzzing sound, were launched from sites along the Pas-de-Calais or the Dutch coast.

An unpiloted rocket-propelled flying bomb that had been fired from a launcher in the Pas de Calais landed in London on 13 June 1944, its 1,870 lb (850 kg) warhead detonating on impact.

The flying bomb was a *Vergeltung* (German for "reprisal") that German dictator Adolf Hitler hoped would change the course of the war.

Ten V-1 rockets were launched by Flakregiment 155 and for the first time the characteristic buzzing sound of the ramjet engine was heard over England.

Six of the rockets ditched, failing to complete the crossing of the Channel, two landed in Kent, one in Surrey and only one reached the intended target of London.

Flying bombs are sufficiently slow and unmanoeuvrable for them to be attacked by anti-aircraft fire and fighter interception, but they still pose a serious threat to south-eastern England, causing British Prime Minister Winston Churchill to urge Allied forces in Normandy to break out from their bridgehead as soon as possible.

American bombers raid Japan

A group of new heavy American bombers, aircraft with a range of 1,600 miles (2,575 km), succeeded in attacking the Japanese home islands from bases in China. The development of the Boeing B-29 had been hampered by numerous teething problems, especially with the engine, but there were enough aircraft to sustain a strategic bombing campaign by early 1944. Chinese labour constructed bases for the super bomber and these went into operation in May. On 15 June, 68 B-29s took off from bases in Chengu and bombed the Yawata steelworks on the island of Kyushu. Little material damage was done, but Japanese morale suffered a severe blow when it was realized that such large aircraft were clearly able to mount a sustained campaign, unlike the one-off Doolittle raid of 1942.

Japanese sword

Japanese soldiers, especially officers, drew on the spirit of the samurai warriors of Japanese history to inspire them. Like all officers, the Japanese carried swords in full dress, and often in action as well.

A B-29 during a bombing mission over Japan, 1944. The aircraft had a long range, a heavy bombload, a pressurised crew compartment for high-altitude flight, and remotely-controlled machine gun turrets. However, it was not easy to fly and its development had been dogged by accidents.

Defeat marked by mass suicide

A soaked American, possibly a medic or naval gunfire support spotter, crawls along the beach at Saipan on 15 June 1944 under enemy fire, while a Marine crawls in the opposite direction. In the background is a landing vehicle, tracked with 75mm howitzer.

Large-scale fighting on Saipan, one of several Central Pacific islands that have been converted to bastions where garrisons expect to hold out to the last man, ended on 9 July 1944. The last days of the Japanese defence were marked by several actions of mass suicide by Japanese civilian residents of the island.

The initial landings were made on 15 June, and included one army and two US Marine divisions, totalling 71,000 troops. The Americans regarded the islands in the Marianas chain, including Guam and Tinian as well as Saipan, as vital for the eventual invasion of Japan. American naval and air force officers envisioned using them for fleet bases and airstrips suitable for B-29 heavy bombers that could reach Japan's cities.

There was no sophistication in either side's approach to this battle. The American divisions basically formed a line across the width of the island and advanced northwards. The 30,000 Japanese defenders dug in where they could, although materials such as concrete and steel reinforcing were in short supply, and fought until killed or ordered to retreat. Some counter-attacks, with tank support, were made on the American beachheads on the first night after the landing, but these were beaten off by far superior American firepower. Towards

the end of the battle, the Japanese General Igeta Keiji, chief-of-staff of the Thirty-first Army, reported on why they were experiencing defeat. American firepower was relentless and ever-present, not only devastating Japanese positions, but also the rear areas where units were withdrawn to regroup. The Americans also had total command of the air, its planes flying over Japanese positions with impunity. In these circumstances, Igeta protested that the emperor's soldiers had done the best they could.

On 7 July, the surviving Japanese soldiers, numbering 3,000 including walking wounded, made a mass suicide charge which succeeded in penetrating American positions, but could achieve little once reserves were used up in the battle.

There were some 30,000 Japanese civilians on the island when the Americans attacked. About two-thirds of these committed suicide during the battle, out of fear of what the Americans would do to them, many throwing themselves from cliffs on the northern end of the island; mothers even jumped off with their babies.

Admiral Nagumo, commander of the Japanese carrier forces at Pearl Harbor and Midway, was nominally in command of the defence of Saipan, and committed suicide toward the end of the battle.

Americans drive west to Cherbourg

The key port of Cherbourg was largely under American control after the capture of the German officer commanding the defending garrison on 26 June 1944. Its port facilities have been damaged by German demolitions and will take months to repair.

The Americans deployed a complete corps in the attack, beginning on 22 June, under the command of General Joseph Collins. The advance into the Contentin Peninsula had begun on 10 June, and in spite of it being relatively lightly defended, the Bocage countryside of hedgerows and small fields slowed the American advance. On 18 June, American troops reached Barneville on the west coast of the Contentin, cutting the Germans in Cherbourg off from reinforcement, making the capture of the port inevitable.

American GIs escort German prisoners captured at the surrender of Cherbourg on 28 June 1944.

Germans repel British moves toward Caen

General Sir Bernard Montgomery's hope of securing Caen on D-Day remains unfulfilled as June 1944 draws to a close. Two British attacks intended to force the Germans out of the Normandy city failed in the face of German counter-attacks.

The first operation was an attempt to outflank the Germans from the west. The fighting began on 11 June with the 7th Armoured Division heading toward Villers-Bocage. Progress was slow as the Germans were able to exploit the characteristic bocage of Normandy, a succession of small fields bounded by thick, stout hedges, each of which could serve as a defended obstacle, making infantry support from the 50th Infantry Division crucial to any success. The village of Caumont fell on 12 June and an armoured spearhead drove on toward Villers-Bocage, but the Germans attacked the corridor it created in several places, including an advance by an SS tank company of Tigers commanded by Captain Michael Wittmann, who managed to knock out 12 tanks, 13 troop carriers and a couple of anti-tank guns before his own tank was destroyed. He and his crew escaped the wreck, but they had played an important part in halting the British. With their flanks very vulnerable, the British retired to Livery.

Montgomery ordered a second attack on a wider front, with four divisions instead of elements of two, a few miles east of the Villers-Bocage thrust. Taking advantage of Ultra intercepts of German coded communications, he ordered the attack to take place on 25 June to spoil a planned German operation. Assisted by heavy artillery support, Operation Epsom ground slowly in the direction of Brainville-sur-Odon. The British attack was hampered by several problems, including poor reconnaissance, a timidity in the face of light resistance and tactically inept handling of infantry attacks. The advance fell short of Caen when it eventually halted on 1 July, but the combination of naval gunfire and Allied air supremacy ensured that an advance of about 5 miles (9 km) on a width of about 2 miles (3 km) was made.

Caen falls to British

Parts of the city of Caen, deemed an important D-Day objective, fell to advancing British troops a month after the Allied landings, on 9 July 1944 at the end of Operation Charnwood. The previous failures led

[T]he attack was preceded by nearly 500 Allied aircraft subjecting the city to a massive aerial bombardment beforehand.

British General Sir Bernard Montgomery to try something different and the attack was preceded by nearly 500 Allied aircraft subjecting the city to a massive aerial bombardment beforehand. However, the British attack did not go forward for another 18 hours and was slowed by the rubble created by the heavy bombing when it did begin.

The city of Caen was blown to rubble by Allied bombing attacks that preceded major offensives by Montgomery's British and Canadian forces.

OPERATION EPSOM

DATES:	25–30 June 1944
COMBATANTS:	Britain vs Germany
FORCES ENGAGED:	Britain, 60,000 men, 600 tanks; Germany, 35,000 men, 228 tanks
CASUALTIES:	Britain, 4,000; Germany, 2,700
RESULT:	Stalemate

Americans capture St Lô

After six weeks of hard fighting through the bocage of Normandy, American troops captured the important road junction town of St Lô on 18 July 1944. The hardest part of the battle had been along the Martinville Ridge, stretching east of the town. The relative ease with which American troops were now able to capture key high ground to the north and east of the city – Point 122 and Point 192 – which had earlier proved difficult even to reach, demonstrated that the German forces in this sector of the front were at the end of their endurance. German replacements for combat losses had been arriving in a trickle, in contrast to the

American troops captured the important road junction town of St Lô on 18 July 1944.

steady stream of men arriving both as replacements and as new divisions for the Americans.

59th Infantry Division

The 59th Infantry Division of the British army was a Territorial Army formation of mainly part-time reservists from the West Midlands. Although it played an important role in Operation Charnwood, it was broken up in August to provide replacements for other British divisions.

American soldiers shelter in a shell hole in the town square of St Lô in July 1944. The battle for the city was one of the key engagements of the entire Overlord campaign, as an Allied victory here would open the way to terrain more favourable to the deployment of tanks.

Hitler survives assassination attempt, many officers implicated

A bomb exploded during a conference at German dictator Adolf Hitler's East Prussian headquarters, *Wolfschanze* (Wolf's Lair), on 20 July 1944, killing several officers, but not the Nazi leader. A plan to mobilize the Reserve Army to take control of Berlin failed that evening and the attempted assassin, Colonel Claus Count von Stauffenberg, was executed that evening along with four other conspirators.

The plot, concocted by disaffected German army officers, had existed in its basic form since late 1942, but until Stauffenberg was appointed chief of staff to the commander of the Reserve Army, General Friedrich Fromm in July 1944, opportunities to carry out the assassination were limited. Stauffenberg carried a bomb to conferences on no less than three occasions before rumours that the plot had been uncovered convinced him that the next chance must be taken. Stauffenberg carried the bomb in a briefcase which he left under the oak conference table and which went off twenty minutes after Stauffenberg excused himself from the room.

General Ludwig Beck, who would have become head of state had the conspirators succeeded in killing Hitler and taken control of Berlin, committed suicide that night. The conspirators included General Carl-Heinrich von Stülpnagel, commander of German forces in France, General Friedrich Olbricht and Colonel Henning von Tresckow.

The shattered interior of Hitler's East Prussian headquarters testifies to the power of the 2-lb (90g) bomb used in the assassination attempt. "It was the work of a coward," declared Hitler.

Cobra strikes in Normandy

Bourguebus Ridge, tank graveyard

A self-propelled gun of the US 6th Armored Division rolls through Lessay, France, at the base of the Cotentin peninsula. The drive to Coutances, further south, created the opening the Americans needed to sweep west and east.

An American offensive, code-named Cobra, initially with limited aims, has turned into a major break out from Normandy, sweeping into Northern France. A new American army group was formed on 1 August 1944 to co-ordinate the operations of two US armies.

On 25 July, 1,600 Allied strategic bombers struck at the German front lines near St Lô, some of the bombs falling instead on American lines, causing nearly 600 casualties. The offensive had been scheduled to take place a day earlier, but bad weather caused a day's delay and as word had not reached all the Allied squadrons, some bombs had been dropped on 24 July, alerting the Germans. When the American forces withdrew from the front in order to avoid the bombing, in some sectors the Germans moved in to occupy the vacated positions. The American offensive initially therefore found resistance as fierce as ever, in spite of the carpet bombing. But this was merely the tough outer crust to a hollow shell and as soon as the Americans had pierced it, they found further opposition almost non-existent. In spite of the slow progress, General Joseph Collins, the corps commander in front of St Lô, committed his reserves.

On 29 July, American forces had pressed beyond their original objective of a line from Coutances to Caumont, and the new American Army Group commander, General Omar Bradley, believed the German army was on the verge of breaking. He therefore formed a new army, under General George Patton, to achieve the breakout that the Allies had been fighting for over the past seven weeks.

A British offensive preceded by heavy aerial bombardment ground to a halt on 21 July 1944 in the face of strong German anti-tank gunnery. The long-range objective for British General Sir Bernard Montgomery's plan, Operation Goodwood, was the town of Falaise. Initially, the job was to clear the Germans out of the remaining parts of Caen and create a gap in the German front that could be exploited by the three armoured divisions that would spearhead the attack. In the event, bad weather delayed the heavy aerial bombardment intended to precede the assault. The British only jumped off on 18 July, after 2,000 bombers had dropped their loads on the German lines. German defences were at first

The British only jumped off on 18 July, after 2,000 bombers had dropped their loads on the German lines. German defences were at first overwhelmed by this concentration of high explosive, but the front was so narrow that they had time to recover before the British could bring up enough reinforcements to widen the breach.

overwhelmed by this concentration of high explosive, but the front was so narrow that they had time to recover before the British could bring up enough reinforcements to widen the breach. Using the high ground of Bourguebus Ridge as the linchpin of their defence, German anti-tank guns wreaked havoc among the advancing British. Over 400 tanks were lost to these guns before Montgomery went over to the defensive.

Operation Bagration

The Red Army's greatest victory during the Second World War occurred in June 1944, with the liberation of Belorussia, the last major portion of Soviet territory still under German control.

General Ivan Bagramyan's First Baltic Front opened the offensive with a reconnaissance in force. He quickly converted his feint into a major assault when the German positions were revealed to be weak.

The offensive took place on such a vast scale that it has become known either as "the destruction of Army Group Centre", referring to the German force that was its target, or its code name Operation Bagration, selected by Soviet leader Josef Stalin after a Russian general of the Napoleonic era in the early nineteenth century. Planning for the operation began in April 1944 and the Red Army assembled a substantial force to deal with it. A total of 166 divisions were allocated (about a third of their total divisional strength), supported by nearly 7,000 aircraft, most of them fighters and close-support bombers. German formations, though larger, were far more understrength, and amounted to 50 divisions.

Hidden intent

Before the battle, the Soviet commanders organized an elaborate deception campaign to fool the Germans about their plans. The scheme included phoney concentrations of troops both to the north and south of the intended operational area. Radio communications were also curtailed, especially near the front line. Field telephones and written messages were used instead where possible. Soviet commanders also kept a substantial force of tank and mechanized divisions in the northern Ukraine, the region the Germans anticipated was the most likely to be the location of the next major Red Army offensive. Another trick was to reinforce existing units up to full strength, instead of bringing up additional divisions and corps, which had been the policy in the past. For the Germans, it looked as though the number of units was very much the same.

The offensive was preceded by partisan activity behind the German lines. The Red Army put substantial reliance on hit-and-run attacks directed mainly against the transportation network that brought reinforcements to threatened sectors. Volunteers, some of whom were dropped by aircraft behind the German lines, carried out these attacks. The partisans were subject to many of the same military regulations as Red Army soldiers, but the Germans did not regard them as soldiers protected by the laws of war and hanged many that they captured. They had already played an important role earlier in the war, attacking railways before the Kursk offensive and the fighting in the Ukraine in 1943, and carried out the same sorts of missions in the days leading up to the start of Operation Bagration.

Jumping off

The offensive was officially scheduled to begin on 23 June, but was preceded by a day of reconnaissance in force. In the far north of the operational area, this achieved such success that the local Soviet commander, General Ivan Bagramyan, simply sent his assault formations to exploit the breach already created. The main attacks in the central sector went forward on 23 June 1944, but did not achieve the initial degree of success that had occurred further north. The greatest success came on 24 June, when the attacks on the southern end of the front, around Bobruisk, began. The artillery barrage preceding the advance by tanks and infantry virtually obliterated German divisions in some sectors of the front.

The first big encirclement came in the north, when five German divisions were

> A total of 166 divisions were allocated (about a third of their total divisional strength), supported by nearly 7,000 aircraft, most of them fighters and close-support bombers.

surrounded around Vitebsk on 25 June. Although only about 30,000 soldiers were surrounded, it still represented the creation of a huge gap in the German lines. Two days later, a pocket was created around Bobruisk, where 70,000 soldiers were trapped. The city of Mogilev was also surrounded, but many fewer German soldiers were caught here. By the time the Bobuisk pocket was eliminated on 29 June, Army Group Centre had lost about 200,000 men killed, wounded or taken prisoner.

Decisive victory

These successes caused the Soviet high command to rethink its plan and opt for

OPERATION BAGRATION

DATES:	22 June–29 August 1944
COMBATANTS:	Soviet Union vs Germany
FORCES ENGAGED:	Red Army, 1.7 million men, 5,000 tanks; Germany, 800,000 men, 900 tanks
CASUALTIES:	Red Army, 765,815; Germany, 678,000
RESULT:	Soviet victory

Russian civilians freed from Nazi prison camps return to their homes in and around Vitebsk, liberated during Operation Bagration. The Red Army's offensive was not immediately apparent as a major one, but unfolded gradually until the German high command realized its extent on 25 June.

a far more ambitious goal, by sending armoured spearheads to the west of Minsk, instead of to the Belorussian capital's east. German forces everywhere were unable to establish any sort of coherent front to block the Red Army advance. Bagration's major objectives had all been achieved by 3 July once Soviet troops entered Minsk from both the north and the south, creating yet another pocket, this time of 105,000 German soldiers to the east of the city. Very

few German troops now stood between the Red Army and Poland. On 5 July the Red Army began surging westwards in several directions, aiming at the Baltic, Vilnius and Warsaw. The offensive was also broadened southwards, after the Germans had withdrawn divisions from other parts of the front to stem the Red Army tide flooding across the Belorussian plain. On 12 July, the First Ukrainian Front pressed forward toward Cracow and eastern Czechoslovakia;

the Vistula river and the suburbs of Warsaw were reached on 1 August.

By this stage the ability of the Red Army to sustain operations was beginning to deteriorate as the armies outran their supply lines. Further gains were made in the extreme north and south of the front before Operation Bagration effectively ended on 29 August. The German army lacked sufficient resources to recover the immense losses suffered in this two-month campaign.

T-34/85

The backbone of the Soviet armoured force was the T-34 tank. It was designed for mass production and originally carried a 76mm gun. It was so effective that the Germans designed two new tanks specifically to counter it, the Tiger heavy tank and the Panther medium tank, which necessitated the replacement of the 76mm gun on the T-34 by an 85mm one to penetrate the thicker armour of the newer German tanks.

Waffen-SS

The Waffen-SS traced its origins to a few hundred members of the Nazi Party in the 1920s, who had received military training, but by the summer of 1944 had expanded to the size of a small army, numbering over 20 divisions and several independent brigades and regiments.

Adolf Hitler stands flanked by top SS men Heinrich Himmler (right) and Sepp Dietrich (left).

SS units played a leading role in the defence of Normandy against the Allies, six of the ten armoured divisions deployed there being SS. Almost all lost heavily in the fighting. Leibstandarte Adolf Hitler was reduced to 30 tanks, Das Reich lost 450 men and 15 tanks, Hohenstaufen 460 men and 25 tanks, Frundsberg was reduced to battalion size and lost all its tanks, Hitler Jugend to 300 men and ten tanks, and Götz von Berlichingen was completely destroyed. Normandy cemented the reputation for the fanaticism in combat of the Waffen-SS, a reputation that had begun in the savagery of the Eastern Front, but had only been encountered on a limited scale by the Western Allies before June 1944, who had hitherto only fought small formations in France and a single division in Italy.

Battling the left

The SS (Schutzstaffel) had its beginnings in the Nazi Party, originally being a personal armed bodyguard for the party leader. Many of its members were drawn from the Freikorps, the right-wing paramilitary forces that battled socialists and communists in Berlin, Munich and other German cities during 1919, when it seemed that a revolution might take place in Germany, just as it had two years earlier in Russia. Most of these men were veterans of the First World War.

> During the first year of fighting on the Eastern Front, the Waffen-SS established a reputation for being efficient troops, fanatical in combat. Their record prior to that had been more mixed.

The SS, however, did not get access to government-issued weaponry until 1934, a year and a half after Adolf Hitler's appointment as chancellor of Germany. At this time they were still a political organization, but in August of that year the formation of the SS-Verfügungstruppe (Special Troops) created a military organization within the SS, although it was still subject to party as opposed to government control, and was intended mainly for ceremonial and security uses. The SS-Verfügungstruppe received formal recognition as a military unit when conscription was reintroduced in Germany in 1935.

Mixed record

By the time war broke out, the SS-Verfügungstruppe had expanded to incorporate a motorized infantry regiment that saw action during the Polish campaign. In addition to this regiment, a further three divisions were deployed in the campaign in France in 1940, the year during which the Waffen-SS was officially formed. One of

these divisions was broken up and two more divisions were formed from it during the winter of 1940/41.

During the first year of fighting on the Eastern Front, the Waffen-SS established a reputation for being efficient troops, fanatical in combat. Their record prior to that had been more mixed, but the experience of war weeded out the worst political appointees. The general predisposition of the SS towards physical and mental excellence provided good material to work with (the pre-war SS refused any volunteer with physical imperfections, even a dental filling). The Totenkopf Division in particular played an important role in the fighting, preventing the Demyansk Pocket from being overwhelmed by the attacking Red Army.

SS soldiers during the invasion of the Netherlands in 1940. Operation Barbarossa cemented their efficient reputation.

SS troops with a light-infantry gun used for close-support of infantry platoons.

There were many reasons why the Waffen-SS developed its particular *esprit de corps*, perhaps the most important being its treatment of the men who comprised it. It evolved an ethos of valuing merit over the traditional pathway to the top in the German army – membership of the upper class in Prussia or other parts of the country. By contrast, the Waffen-SS drew its officers from talented members of the lower-middle or working classes, as well as the traditional

> As early as 1939, an SS NCO rounded up 50 Jews in Poland and shot them. The fact he was not convicted by the SS authorities was a clear signal that the men of the Waffen-SS were not to be held to accepted standards.

officer class of German society. Those who were friends of high-ranking SS officials, especially SS chief Heinrich Himmler, could rely on their connections to get them favoured promotions, but the average officer got to the top through bravery in combat or talent in the administrative aspects of command.

Fraternal discipline

Furthermore, the meritocracy of the upper ranks extended after a fashion into the lower ones. Officer candidates and enlisted men experienced basic training together, and once posted to their units, officers were expected to earn the respect of their men. The emphasis was on brotherhood and in these circumstances discipline followed naturally.

However, this attractive institutional characteristic went hand in hand with a brutality that attained criminal levels. The SS supervised the concentration camps, with many pre-war SS soldiers serving as guards in concentration camps, particularly those from the original Totenkopf Division. As early as 1939, an SS NCO rounded up 50 Jews in Poland and shot them. The fact he was not convicted by the SS authorities was a clear signal that the men of the Waffen-SS were not to be held to accepted standards of civilisation. In the Soviet Union in particular, the Waffen-SS behaved with murderous callousness towards civilians, although they were not the main perpetrators of atrocities – a role carried out by the SS Einsatzgruppen (mission groups), which were not part of the Waffen-SS.

Top priority

After the German defeat at Stalingrad, the SS played an important role in blunting the Soviet offensive across the Ukraine, recapturing the city of Kharkov in early 1943, and became the German military's elite. Many more SS divisions had been formed in 1942–3, by drawing on ethnically German communities outside Germany, and foreign volunteers. These divisions avoided much of the reorganizations that reduced the combat power of Wehrmacht divisions, and were increasingly given priority for the latest equipment.

The July 1944 bomb plot against Hitler ended any residual respect he had for the army (Hitler had long regarded the army's high command as insufficiently dedicated to his schemes). Himmler was given control over raising new army formations, as well as over the movement of officers between units, and was therefore in a position to ensure favourable treatment for his Waffen-SS.

While early recruits to the SS were all volunteers, and required to be physically perfect specimens, in 1943 recruitment was widened to include non-Germans such as Bosnians, Flemings and Balts.

Paris liberated

The French 2nd Armoured Division entered Paris on 25 August 1944, bringing to an end four years of German occupation. The German commander of the capital, Major-General Dietrich von Choltitz, did not want to commit the acts of vandalism demanded by Adolf Hitler, who wanted many of the monuments of the French capital destroyed. Although von Choltitz was willing to defend the Parisian suburbs, both he and the German commander in the West, Field Marshal Walther Model, considered the long-term defence of Paris doomed to failure. Von Choltitz opted to negotiate a gradual surrender of the city, by first agreeing a truce with the French Resistance organization in Paris, and then carrying out a face-saving skirmish on 25 August before surrendering.

American troops take a look at the Eiffel Tower following the liberation of Paris in August 1944.

Ultra, airpower halts Germans

An attempt by the Germans to cut off the American spearheads advancing towards Brittany, with an armoured attack from Mortain on 7 August 1944, was defeated through the use of Ultra signals intelligence. The Germans, on Hitler's orders, planned a thrust towards Avranches on the coast, but they were unable to mass the eight panzer divisions they had intended and only four were able to carry out the attack. General Omar Bradley, the American overall commander, alerted his forces that a German offensive was impending and also received substantial reinforcement for his air support. Taking advantage of a day of bad weather on 7 August, the Germans attacked and made some gains, reoccupying Mortain and pushing back the US 30th Infantry Division. However, when the weather cleared on 8 August, Allied fighter-bombers resumed their sorties and the German attacks were stopped in their tracks. The Americans counted 100 destroyed German tanks after the battle, at a time when a strong German armoured division might consist of a total of 120 tanks.

US 4th Armored Division

The US 4th Armored Division was formed in April 1941, its first action being on 17 July 1944. The division played an important role in the break-out from Normandy, rapidly taking Coutances on 28 July, and then racing into Brittany before turning east.

A squad of American infantry with a Nazi flag standing next to a knocked-out German self-propelled gun. Allied fighter-bombers converted many German vehicles into smoking wrecks along highway D13 between Trun and Chambois.

Falaise Gap closed slowly

The possibility of the Allies trapping virtually all the German army in Normandy slipped away as both British and American commanders were slow in closing the Falaise Gap. Polish and American troops finally met at Chambois on 19 August 1944, by which time something like two-thirds of the potential prisoner haul had escaped from the pocket. Even so, around 50,000 German soldiers were taken prisoner.

To the east, around Caen, the British engaged a substantial portion of the German armour in France, while to the west, the huge reserves of American soldiers, tanks and guns gradually pushed the Germans back until they were able to turn the flank at Avranches. General George Patton's Third Army then began sweeping into Brittany and eastwards toward Le Mans. Once the latter was reached by the French 2nd Armoured Division on 9 August, the Allies began a general advance to squeeze the pocket north and south, aiming to close it in the area of Argentan and Chambois.

Wary of the situation, the German army group commander, Field Marshal Gunther von Kluge, ordered a withdrawal eastwards on 16 August. In spite of the open neck at the eastern end of the pocket, the Germans still faced a fierce fight to get themselves out of the trap, as elements of Allied units were already advancing into the gap. The Mace, a ridge above Chambois, was the scene of vicious fighting between Polish troops serving with the British and Canadians, and the escaping Germans. The German areas of the pocket were also subjected to relentless attack from Allied fighter-bombers that caused widespread casualties and damage to vehicles. In one instance, German troops even surrendered to attacking aircraft! Some 10,000 German soldiers were counted among the dead, along with nearly 700 armoured vehicles and over 2,000 other vehicles.

French, Americans land in France

Operation Dragoon, the Allied invasion of southern France, took place on 15 August 1944, when three American divisions landed on beaches between St Tropez and Cannes. The Germans in the south of France were ordered by Adolf Hitler to retire northwards, since the forces in Normandy were already withdrawing eastwards, thereby giving up the Seine crossings to the Allies.

Allied troops disembark on the southern French coast. The Americans believed that Marseilles offered them vast port facilities at a reasonable cost in possible combat losses.

Monty's gamble

A daring daylight parachute assault in the Netherlands was an all-or-nothing gamble that demanded good luck and aggressive action for success, with the promise of a major victory.

A mechanized column from 30th Corps rolls through a Dutch town on the way to Arnhem. The British 1st Airborne Division was expected to hold out for four days awaiting the arrival of the tanks and heavy weapons of the Guards Armoured Division.

the Allies in a good position to send an armoured assault across the North German Plain (good tank country) towards Berlin. The main drawback was that Operation Market Garden was scheduled for 17 September, giving only a week to plan the whole operation. However, work had already been in hand on an Operation Comet, which would have resulted in British and Polish airborne troops landing at various key points, including Njimegen and Arnhem.

> Although the airborne commanders had some reservations about the plan, the Allied generals for the most part, in the early autumn of 1944, believed the Germans were a beaten force.

Although the airborne commanders had some reservations about the plan, the Allied generals for the most part, in the early autumn of 1944, believed the Germans were a beaten force. Anything was possible, provided enough resources were thrown at the problem.

Daylight drop

Operation Market Garden embraced 150,000 troops in 14 divisions, a thousand transport aircraft, a thousand bombers and a thousand fighters. The troops would have to secure five major river or canal crossings along a narrow road 64 miles (103 km)

On 10 September 1944, there was a meeting between the commander of Allied forces in north-west Europe, American General Dwight Eisenhower, and the commander of 21st Army Group, British Field Marshal Bernard Montgomery. Eisenhower had adopted a strategy of a broad-front advance, with thrusts driving for Alsace, Lorraine, the Ardennes, and through Belgium towards the Netherlands. Six days earlier Montgomery had proposed that a single powerful thrust would have more chance of ending the war quickly and invited Eisenhower to a meeting at 21st Army Group headquarters in Brussels.

The meeting on 10 September resulted in Eisenhower agreeing to Montgomery's

plan for a combined parachute assault and ground advance that would seize the Dutch town of Arnhem, and the bridge there across the Rhine river. If successful, Hitler's West Wall defences would be outflanked and the Rhine crossed, with

OPERATION MARKET GARDEN

COMBATANTS:	British, Polish and Americans vs Germans
FORCES ENGAGED:	Allies, 150,000 men, 300 tanks; Germans, 89,000 men, 145 tanks
CASUALTIES:	Allies, 18,000; Germans, 13,000
RESULT:	German victory

Transport pilots being briefed before the operation. Not all Allied commanders were convinced that an airborne assault was the best use of the aircraft and men needed for a parachute operation.

long. The airborne landings would take place in daylight, in order to reduce the risk of the night-time disorder experienced in Normandy, and to allow the paratroopers to assemble quickly in their battalions and seize their objectives. The main problem with the plan was that it relied on everything going right, completely ignoring intelligence reports suggesting that II SS Panzer Corps was refitting in the Arnhem area.

Fine weather on 17 September suggested the good fortune the Allies needed to succeed. A stream of aircraft that took an hour the pass overhead flew over the towns and villages of eastern England. Inside sat the paratroopers, about 20 in each C-47 Dakota transport, burdened with about half his own weight in equipment. There was heavy anti-aircraft fire over the Netherlands.

Paras at Arnhem

The initial parachute drops went well, the two American landings in particular being near perfect, although there were mixed results in achieving their objectives. The bridge at Son, over the Wilhelmina Canal, was blown up before American paratroopers could seize it, while at Nijmegen, the German defences were too strong. Meanwhile, bridges at Veghel and Grave were taken. At Arnhem, the railway bridge was blown up, but British paratroopers managed to gain control of the north end of the highway bridge in

battalion strength. The remainder of the 1st Airborne Division was held up by the large number of snipers the Germans deployed to delay their approach to the bridge.

The German defenders of Arnhem were drawn mainly from II SS Panzer Corps, which was indeed refitting in the area. Although the airborne assault had taken the Germans completely by surprise, the likely

> Fine weather on 17
> September suggested the
> good fortune the Allies
> needed to succeed. A stream
> of aircraft that took an hour
> the pass overhead flew over
> the towns and villages of
> eastern England.

objectives were obvious and it was a simple matter of rushing reinforcements to the Arnhem area, as well as the Meuse-Escaut Canal. A copy of the plan had also fallen into German hands via a crashed glider, allowing them to pinpoint the intended drop zones and severely limit the supplies that got through to the 1st Airborne Division.

Sustained harassment

On 18 September, the Germans attempted to rush the bridge with armoured cars and half tracks, but the 2nd Battalion of

the Parachute Regiment used their light anti-tank weapons to considerable effect against the attacking force. The Germans retreated and subjected the area around the north end of the bridge to a sustained bombardment and harassment by snipers. The next day the Germans deployed assault guns to blast selected houses held by the paratroopers in order to ease the passage of German infantry through the streets around the paratroopers' positions.

Lieutenant Colonel John Frost's 2nd Parachute Battalion held out for another two days until, reduced to 140 all ranks, they surrendered on 21 September. Attempts by the rest of the 1st Airborne Division to reach them failed when the Germans used anti-aircraft guns against the British attacks.

Engineers constructed a bridge across the Wilhelmina Canal at Son, while a cross-river assault by the US 82nd Airborne Division at Nijmegen seized enough of the north bank of the Waal to allow the ground advance to continue north of the river. While the Germans strongly defended the direct road route to Arnhem, a final Allied parachute drop, by the Polish Airborne Brigade, secured the nearby town of Driel, which was reached by the British 43rd (Wessex) Division on 22 September, outflanking the German positions astride the Arnhem-Nijmegen road. On 25 September, as the remnants of the 1st Airborne Division escaped the German encirclement, Operation Market Garden ended in failure.

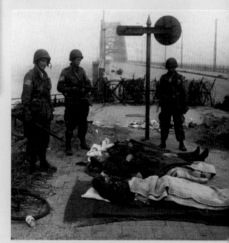

82nd Airborne Division paratroopers guard wounded German prisoners after the fighting around Nijmegen Bridge.

The war in Yugoslavia

Belgrade was liberated by the Red Army and Yugoslav National Liberation Army on 20 October 1944, after nearly a week of hard fighting. Although much of Yugoslavia remained in Axis hands, the victory was the climax of two and a half years of a brutal three-cornered conflict.

Yugoslavia had been created by the Versailles Treaty ending the First World War in 1919, adding several former areas of the old Austro-Hungarian empire to the pre-war kingdom of Serbia. Croatia, Slovenia, Bosnia and Herzegovina were added to a Serbian kingdom that already included Macedonian and Albanian ethnic areas.

Alliance, coup, invasion

After the outbreak of the Second World War in 1939, Yugoslav politicians began to play one side off against another, as pro-Allied and pro-Axis factions emerged. The determination of Germany's ally Italy, under the Fascist dictator Benito Mussolini, to annex substantial parts of Yugoslavia did not help the Axis cause in the country. In the spring of 1941, an alliance signed with Germany was repudiated when the government that had negotiated it was overthrown by a coup. German dictator Adolf Hitler ordered the occupation and dismemberment of the country, which was completed in a short campaign in April 1941. Germany annexed

Yugoslav partisans enter Belgrade on 20 October 1944. Tito ensured his forces played a prominent role in the city's liberation, to prevent the Red Army from thinking they could dictate terms to him.

part of Slovenia, while Croatia was given "independence", less the Dalmatian coast which went to Italy. To compensate for this loss, Bosnia and Herzegovina became part of Croatia. Kosovo was handed over to Italy's puppet regime in Albania, while Bulgaria was given Yugoslav Macedonia.

The first resistance to the Axis settlement came in the form of an ethnically Serbian movement that drew on the pre-1941 royal Yugoslav army for its fighting men. The Chetniks were Serbian nationalists and monarchists, who had little appeal to Croats, Slovenians, Bosnians and other former subjects of the Yugoslav monarchy, and basically fought for a restoration of the pre-invasion state. The Croatian state, ruled by the Fascist Ushtashe, proved one of the best recruiters for the Chetniks, by means of their organized butchery of Serbs within Croatia.

Tito's army

It was only after the German invasion of the Soviet Union released the Communist Party of Yugoslavia from its support of Soviet leader Josef Stalin's alliance with Germany, that a truly national Yugoslav resistance army

Partisan leader Josip Broz, who took the pseudonym Tito in 1934, had been an active member of the Yugoslav communist party since 1920, and secretary-general since 1937.

emerged. A partisan army was officially created on 29 June 1941, by the Communist leader Tito (born Iosip Broz, of Croatian and Slovenian parentage). The partisans began guerrilla activity in July 1941, but their aims

> The first resistance to the Axis settlement came in the form of an ethnically Serbian movement that drew on the pre-1941 royal Yugoslav army for its fighting men.

and those of the Chetniks were incompatible and an attempt by the two to co-operate broke down after a meeting in November 1941. Tito did not want a restoration of the monarchy, while the leader of the Chetniks, Drazha Mihailovich, was appalled by Tito's willingness to tolerate actions that would lead to reprisal massacres by the Germans or their allies, deeds that Tito thought would increase the flow of recruits to the partisan army. With the Yugoslav government-in-exile resident in

Dead Yugoslav partisans, murdered by Nazi forces in 1944. There was no mercy shown by either side in the fighting, as both ideological and ethnic rivalries were given savage expression during the war.

Cairo, Britain (and later the United States) initially supported Mihailovich, while the Soviet Union gave what help it could to Tito.

The war in Yugoslavia was remarkable for its brutality. While the Croats, Bosnians and Albanians massacred ethnic rivals as a matter of policy, the Germans shot a hundred Yugoslav civilians for any German soldier killed by guerrillas. About 1.2 million Yugoslavs are estimated to have lost their lives in the war.

Bosnian bases

Both partisans and Chetniks were mostly reduced to hideouts in Bosnia, from which they periodically launched raids as best they could. The Chetniks were more interested in fighting the Germans and Croats, and gradually developed a strange alliance with Italy, joining the Italians to fight the partisans, while the Italians turned a blind eye to Chetnik attacks on their Croat and German allies. To counter the hit-and-run raiding of the guerrillas, Germans, Italians and Croats mounted seasonal offensives that sought to drive the guerrillas out of their bases. In late 1942, guerrilla attacks were so successful that the Germans mounted a seven-division offensive to drive the partisans out of their Bosnian bases. In this action, the Italians were supported by the Chetniks, and advanced from the Dalmatian coast into Bosnia, while the Germans positioned themselves in northern Bosnia with their Croat allies, and advanced more slowly in order to maintain an unbroken line that would be the anvil on which the Italian hammer smashed the partisans. In the event, the partisans fought so hard that they created a gap in the German line through which thousands of fighters escaped.

In November 1943, at the Teheran Conference, the British and American governments agreed to abandon their support for the Chetniks and acknowledge Tito's partisans as the sole legitimate resistance force in Yugoslavia. In part this was because the Chetniks had largely abandoned the fight, preferring to attack partisans, Croats and Moslems. Later that same month, a conference at Jajce set up a Supreme Legislative Council and an Executive Committee for the Liberation of Yugoslavia, and agreement with the government-in-exile was reached in June 1944.

> While the Croats, Bosnians and Albanians massacred ethnic rivals as a matter of policy, the Germans shot a hundred Yugoslav civilians for any German soldier killed by guerrillas.

Knight's leap

The Germans attempted to kill Tito on 25 May 1944 when an SS parachute battalion was dropped on his headquarters at Drvar in Bosnia, in Operation Knight's Leap. The Germans succeeded in capturing some of his personal possessions, which they put on show in Vienna, but Tito himself managed to reach the coast and resume his leadership of the struggle.

When the Red Army first entered Yugoslavia in September 1944, Tito went to Moscow to liaise with Soviet leaders, including Stalin, before transforming his guerrillas into a field army that participated in the Soviet offensive. The Germans fought fiercely, in part to keep their forces in Greece from being cut off from Germany before they had a chance to withdraw. But with the fall of Belgrade the southern part of Yugoslavia was largely liberated, leaving the Independent State of Croatia to fight on with Germany.

Cetniks hand over a Yugoslav partisan they have captured to the Germans, in Montenegro.

History's biggest naval battle

The largest naval battle in history, a series of engagements around the Philippine islands between American and Japanese fleets, took place on 23–26 October 1944. The Japanese navy had decided to go for a final battle risking most of their strength, hoping to achieve a major victory over the US navy. In the event, in four engagements, the Japanese suffered a defeat that cost them four aircraft carriers, three battleships, eight cruisers and twelve destroyers; American losses were relatively light.

A cloud of smoke and debris obscures the light cruiser USS *St Louis* behind an escort carrier after a Japanese kamikaze bomber in Leyte Gulf struck it.

MacArthur returns

General Douglas MacArthur wades ashore on Leyte in the Philippines in October 1944, making good his promise to return.

Striding through the waters of Leyte Gulf, American General Douglas MacArthur, who had felt a tremendous sense guilt when leaving the Philippines in early 1942, returned

[T]he Japanese forces on the island were reduced to scattered pockets.

to the archipelago on 20 October 1944, when he came ashore on Leyte island. The campaign, the first major step in the American liberation of the Philippines, continued until the end of December, when the Japanese forces on the island were reduced to scattered pockets.

IN BRIEF

⁓ American troops landed on the Pacific island of Peleliu on 15 September 1944, beginning a two-month campaign that ended with the capture of the island and the death of virtually the entire Japanese garrison.

⁓ The first major German city to fall to the Allies was Aachen, when American troops accepted the surrender of its defenders on 21 October 1944.

⁓ RAF bombers succeeded in sinking the last battleship of the German navy, the *Tirpitz*, near Tromsø, Norway, on 12 November 1944, with the loss of 1,000 of her crew. The aircraft used an extremely heavy Tallboy bomb, packing 5 tons (5 tonnes) of explosives.

⁓ The port of Antwerp was opened to traffic on 26 November 1944, after Canadian and British troops cleared the Scheldt Estuary of German troops between 2 October and 8 November. The port eased Allied supply problems, which were reaching a crisis with major port facilities restricted to Marseille and Toulon.

⁓ On 9 December 1944, there was a lull in the two-month-long battle for the Hürtgen Forest, between Aachen and the Roer river, after the American forces had sustained heavy losses. The German defenders in the forest had the advantage of difficult terrain, in which they had built many concrete pillboxes and sown extensive minefields.

Silent killer falls on London

The V-2 rocket was the first weapon to leave the atmosphere, on the way to its target.

The first of a new secret weapon fell on London on 8 September 1944, when a German V-2 rocket, the world's first long-range ballistic missile, fell on the suburb of Chiswick, having made a sub-orbital space flight. Unlike the V-1, which flew at similar speeds to aircraft, the V-2 was a supersonic missile and consequently it arrived without any warning of the sudden explosion as its impact fuse detonated. V-2s were originally intended to be fired from fixed silos, but Allied bombing forced the Germans to fire them from mobile launchers.

German allies knocked out of war

The signing of an armistice between Finland and the Soviet Union on 10 September 1944 marked the end of a second German ally's participation in the war against the Soviet Union, Rumania having already agreed an armistice on 13 September 1944, following a coup in August that removed from power the pro-Axis government in Bucharest.

Finland had joined in the war against the Soviet Union about a week after the German invasion began in June 1941. After recovering territory lost in the Winter War with the Soviet Union in 1939–40, the Finns went over to the defensive, and following the German defeat at Stalingrad in February 1943, the Finns began looking for ways to bring their alliance with Germany to an end. In June 1944, the Red Army began major offensive operations against the Finns, which after a month had the Finnish government actively looking for ways to end their participation in the conflict.

Rising in Warsaw

The Germans defeated an uprising in the Polish capital Warsaw on 3 October that was intended to liberate the city in advance of the Red Army, whose leading units reached the River Vistula on 1 August 1944. The uprising began that day, part of a national rebellion against German occupation. However, the outnumbered and poorly supplied Poles had no chance against the Germans, with their tanks and heavy artillery. The Polish Home Army had relied

[T]he outnumbered and poorly supplied Poles had no chance against the Germans.

on the Red Army continuing its offensive, but Soviet forces were at the end of their supply lines and their attacks in support were of a limited nature. On 22 September, the 1st Polish Army, which had crossed the Vistula earlier in the month, retreated back to the eastern bank, and Marshal Rokossovsky, commander of the Red Army front in this sector, declared that no further attempt would be made to seize Warsaw for four months.

OBITUARY
ERWIN ROMMEL

Field Marshal Erwin Rommel, the highly respected commander of German forces in North Africa and France, committed suicide on 14 October 1944, after being implicated in the plot to assassinate Adolf Hitler on 20 July.

A veteran of the First World War, Rommel commanded the 7th Panzer Division during the campaign in France in 1940, during which he established a reputation for speed and aggression in the attack. Early in 1941 he was sent with German troops to North Africa, where he benefited considerably from poor co-ordination between British tanks and infantry in the Western Desert.

Once the campaign in North Africa had ended, Rommel was given command of Italy then north-west France, preparing for the eventual Allied invasion of France. Although he worked hard at his task, in the end the Allied forces were successful in the Normandy landings of June 1944.

A number of his close aides were involved in the plot to assassinate Hitler, although Rommel himself kept out of it.

The Battle of the Bulge

The biggest battle in the US army's history began when German dictator Adolf Hitler hurled his last significant reserves against American positions in the Ardennes on 16 December 1944, in the hope of achieving a breakthrough that would recapture Antwerp and destroy the British and Canadian armies in Belgium and the Netherlands.

Reconnaissance forces of the 1st SS Panzer Division orient themselves amid the woods of the Ardennes. American resistance at Stavelot blunted the division's main advance during the battle.

Hitler's plan was given the code name The Watch on the Rhine (Der Wacht Am Rhein) and covered an attack by three armies in deepest winter, at a time when bad weather would keep the bulk of the Allied air forces grounded. The German plan envisaged a two-pronged drive that would push toward Namur and Liège in Belgium, before driving on to Antwerp, capturing Brussels on the way.

Tight security

The Germans had massed thirteen infantry divisions and seven armoured divisions to attack six American divisions, most of which anticipated being in a quiet sector of the front. For various reasons, Allied intelligence provided little warning of the German plans. One key factor was a tightening of security by German forces, who made less use of transmitted orders, encrypted using an Enigma coding machine. Consequently, while Allied signals intercepts revealed various movements behind the German lines, there was no apparent structure to these shifts of forces.

The attack began on 16 December, preceded in most places by a short, heavy artillery barrage. Infantry mainly led the attack, the plan being to opening gaps in the American lines through which the tank divisions would advance. The Germans made poor progress in the north, in part because the 2nd Infantry Division had unexpectedly reinforced the 99th Infantry Division shortly before the attack. The next day would be crucial. The Germans had fallen short of their first day objectives, while the Americans still held, precariously, the key road junction at St Vith.

Massacres of prisoners

On 17 December the Germans unleashed their main armoured thrusts, as well as carrying out a parachute jump aimed at blocking the road from Aachen at Monschau. The jump had been delayed for a day by the weather and ended in

The biggest battle in the US army's history began when German dictator Adolf Hitler hurled his last significant reserves against American positions in the Ardennes on 16 December 1944.

total failure, as the inexperienced transport pilots scattered the paratroopers over too wide an area. The tank attacks were more successful and included the advance of the SS battle group commanded by Lieutenant-Colonel Jochen Peiper. This group carried out several massacres of prisoners, most notably near the town of Malmédy. Peiper's advance was delayed by American combat engineers blowing bridges near the town of Trois Points, then his forces were held around La Gleive and Stoumont as the Americans rushed in reinforcements. When an American counter-attack had recovered Stavelot, cutting him off from the rest of his division, Peiper eventually escaped encirclement on 24 December with only

The Tiger II heavy tank equipped battalions that formed the spearheads of German assaults. Although thickly armoured, the tank had severe engine and drive train problems.

American soldiers reload their M1 semi-automatic rifles while fighting from a roof in a Belgian town. The American army fought the biggest battle in its history in the Ardennes.

800 of the nearly 6,000 men with whom he had begun his attack.

Worse still for the German plans, the Americans resisted strongly around St Vith which was still holding out on 19 December, when the 3,000 survivors of two American infantry regiments on the Schnee Eifel east of the town surrendered. St Vith was successfully defended for another two days before the Americans finally withdrew, but the delay in capturing the town contributed to serious traffic jams slowing the German advance.

Bastogne

Further south, the Germans achieved more success, although here, too, they fell short of their first day's objectives, the Clerve river. The US 28th Division could not, however, sustain the constant pressure of five German divisions, and during 17–18 December the Germans captured Clervaux and Drauffelt, opening the road to Bastogne. Several roads through the Ardennes converged on this market town, and American General Dwight Eisenhower rushed the 101st Airborne Division to hold it in the face of the advancing Germans. They began arriving during the night of 18/19 December but were unable to prevent the powerful German armoured columns from surrounding the town. The paratroopers

withstood a siege until relief arrived from Patton's Third Army, reaching them on 26 December. Famously, Brigadier-General Anthony McAuliffe, the acting commander of the 101st Airborne, dismissed a German demand for surrender on 22 December with the curt expression "Nuts".

Though the Germans were held up at Bastogne, St Vith and Trois Points, a large gap existed between Bastogne and St Vith. Two German tank divisions surged into it and at the town of Houffalize, they were well placed to approach St Vith from the rear, to take Trois Points from the rear, or to drive towards the Meuse. The Germans pushed in a north-westerly direction from Houffalize, aimed at Namur and Liège, while one tank division drove south around besieged Bastogne, heading toward Dinant. In the event, the village of Foy-Notre Dame, just short of Dinant, was as far as they got. With their tanks short of fuel, the weather cleared on Christmas Day enough for British Typhoon fighter-bombers to assist American and British tanks in an attack that destroyed this battle group.

On 19 December, at Verdun, Eisenhower met his top commanders, and emphasized that the German offensive presented a valuable opportunity to destroy the enemy army. Rather than cutting the German salient off at its base, Eisenhower opted to push it in. He based his decision on the logistical situation, as speed was of the essence. On 22 December, the American counter-offensive began.

It took several weeks to drive the "bulge" created by the German attack back, but on 26 January 1945, American forces finally completed the operation.

Troops of the US 1st Infantry Division on the march during mopping up operations in January 1945.

Americans land on Luzon, largest Philippine island

Battleships of the US 7th Fleet's Bombardment Group. The American forces ashore relied on support from the guns of destroyers, cruisers and even the 16-in weapons of these battleships.

In one of the largest amphibious operations of the war, rivalled only by the Allied landings in Normandy, 175,000 American soldiers were put ashore in the Lingayen Gulf, onto the Philippine island of Luzon, beginning on 9 January 1945. The initial target of the American landings was the capital, Manila, and General Douglas MacArthur drove his forces hard to get there fast. MacArthur also landed a strong force south-west of Manila on 15 January, and ordered a parachute drop on 31 January at Taygaytag Ridge. Both concentrations of American forces, north and south of Manila, began a race to be first to reach the capital.

The Japanese commander in the Philippines, General Yamashita Tomoyuki, regarded Manila as indefensible, and only left a largely naval force there to delay rather than resist the Americans. On 3 February, the leading elements of the 1st Cavalry Division, approaching the city from the north, won the race. However, those Japanese who had been left behind put up a fierce resistance in street-to-street fighting that kept the city from being secured by the Americans until 4 March.

Last German gasp at Lake Balaton

The failure of a German offensive at Lake Balaton in Hungary led to the fall of the town of Szekesfehervar on 23 March 1945, and the end of German resistance to the Red Army in this country, with its vital oil wells. By 1 April, the Soviets were in a position to threaten Vienna.

As Soviet advances in Hungary during early 1945 threatened the last oilfields supplying the German military, located in Hungary at Nagykanizsa, Adolf Hitler committed his very last reserves to an attack to drive the Red Army back across the Danube and keep the oil flowing to Germany. The Soviets had advanced warning of the German plans when the American General George Marshall sent details to his counterpart, Marshal A.I. Antonov on 20 February. The Red Army forces in Hungary constructed three well-fortified defensive lines, reminiscent of the preparations for the Battle of Kursk in 1943.

The German attack began on the night of 5/6 March and made steady, grinding progress of about 5 miles (9 km) per day through to 9 March, but then gradually slowed. On 14 March, the last reserves were thrown into battle, but attacks on their flanks brought the advancing Germans to a halt; the southern attacks also failed to make any impression on the Soviet lines.

The Soviet counter-attack, unleashed on 16 March, took a week to bring about near encirclement of the attacking forces around Szekesfehervar. On 23 March, the German front suddenly collapsed, with even the vaunted SS being routed.

A Soviet Ilyushin Il-2 Sturmovik flies over Hungary. The Red Air Force by this stage of the war had almost complete command of the air.

Operation Northwind threatens Strasbourg

The French city of Strasbourg was briefly threatened by a German attack in Alsace and Lorraine that struck at the overextended American armies in this sector of the Western Front, until the Americans beat off a final German attack on 25 January 1945.

The Germans sent seven infantry and three armoured divisions against the Americans between Sarreguimines and Bitche, achieving modest gains that led to American General Dwight Eisenhower recommending the abandonment of Alsace east of the Vosges Mountains. After a stormy meeting with French leader Charles de Gaulle on 3 January, Eisenhower relented. When the second phase of German offensives began on 5 January, three German armoured divisions supported by two infantry divisions put three American divisions under such intense pressure that they made a strategic withdrawal to a new line following the Rothbach and Moder rivers, but still protecting Strasbourg. The Germans' third attempt to advance on Strasbourg ended on 25 January when a local American counter-attack outflanked the Germans' forward positions and led to the withdrawal of their forces.

German blow misfires

RAF air crew make their way across a muddy Continental airfield to a Hawker Tempest. Airfields like this were the target of Operation Bodenplatte, a secretly planned series of dawn attacks by the German air force.

The Germans attempted to eliminate Allied close air support, a thorn in their side since the fighting in North Africa, with a desperate blow on 1 January 1945. It was intended that a thousand German aircraft would make surprise attacks on Allied air bases in the Netherlands, Belgium and Northern France. With aviation fuel scarce, this operation needed to be highly successful to make it worthwhile. By attacking at dawn, the German pilots hoped to catch

> *With aviation fuel scarce, this operation needed to be highly successful to make it worthwhile.*

the Allied aircraft on the ground, when aircraft are at their most vulnerable. In the event, the Germans damaged or destroyed nearly 500 aircraft, with comparable losses to themselves. However, the Germans were less able to replace such losses, and many experienced pilots who would be used to train new ones became casualties.

IN BRIEF

❧ On 30 January 1945 the passenger ship *Wilhelm Gustloff* was torpedoed by a Soviet submarine and sank with the loss of 9,000 lives, the worst single maritime disaster in history. Most of the people were refugees fleeing Danzig and East Prussia.

❧ The long-anticipated Red Army offensive across the Vistula was finally launched on 12 January 1945. Warsaw was liberated on 17 January and the Oder river was reached on 31 January.

❧ On 31 January 1945, Private Eddie Slovik became the first American soldier to be executed for desertion since the Civil War.

Big Three meet at Yalta

Plans for the administration of a defeated Germany and the liberated countries of Yugoslavia and Poland were agreed as the top Allied leaders, Franklin Roosevelt of the United States, Josef Stalin of the Soviet Union and Winston Churchill of Britain, met in the Soviet resort town of Yalta in the Crimea over the period 5–11 February 1945.

Germany is to be occupied by the three Allied powers and France, and administered by them, pending the signing of a peace treaty. A secret agreement was also arranged for the Soviet Union to join the war against Japan three months after the war in Europe finished. In addition, the Yalta conference redefined the borders of Poland and proposed the inaugural meeting of the United Nations in San Francisco in April 1945.

Churchill, Roosevelt and Stalin discussed the postwar fates of Poland and Yugoslavia, and what to do with Germany and the Nazis once the Allies had finally occupied the country.

Tokyo burns in firestorm

A large American bombing raid on the night of March 9/10 using incendiary bombs devastated the Japanese capital of Tokyo, with more than 100,000 Japanese killed. The 333 B-29s that participated in the raid flew at low level from bases in Guam, Saipan and Tinian, with maximum bomb load and

[T]he fire reached temperatures of (980°C) 1,800°F whipping up winds that blew the flames throughout the largely wooden city.

little defensive armament to minimize fuel consumption. Pathfinder aircraft dropped bombs at the centre of the intended target area and were then followed by the rest. The centre of Tokyo was the target, but the fire reached temperatures of (980°C) 1,800°F whipping up winds that blew the flames throughout the largely wooden city. When dawn came on 10 March, rivers were seen to have been dried up by the heat and the ground was too hot for digging.

British enter Germany

British and Canadian forces stormed into Germany during Operation Veritable, launched by Field Marshal Sir Bernard Montgomery's 21st Army Group on 8 February 1945. The attack targeted the Reichswald, a low-lying forested area that the Germans hoped would provide excellent defensive terrain. The attack opened with the heaviest bombardment seen on the Western Front, as 1,034 guns pounded the German positions for five-and-a-half hours. Six divisions then attacked over a front 7 miles (11 km) wide, supported by a substantial arsenal of the specialized armour that had proved so valuable during the Normandy landings, helping tanks and men through the mud that developed as the ground thawed with the approach of spring. By 13 February, the Reichswald was cleared.

The British attack was due to coincide with the American Ninth Army's attack across the Roer river, but the Germans had opened the dams and flooded the area, causing a delay until 23 February. By then most of the German reserves in this sector had been drawn into the battle around the Reichswald and when the Americans attacked in overwhelming numbers, they were able to race towards the Rhine. The Germans succeeded in blowing up all the bridges the Americans hoped to capture, but by the beginning of March all of the Allied armies stood on the west bank of the Rhine.

IN BRIEF

⁂The US 9th Armored Division succeeded in capturing a railway bridge over the Rhine at Remagen, Germany, on 9 March 1945 after the demolition charges intended to destroy it exploded but failed to demolish it. General Omar Bradley, the commander of the 12th Army Group, rushed as many divisions as he could to the area. By 13 March, five American divisions were busy widening the bridgehead on the east bank of the Rhine.

Uncommon valour on volcano island

General Harry Schmidt, US Marine Corps, declared on 26 March 1945 that the island of Iwo Jima was secure after over a month of fighting between 70,000 Marines and 21,000 Japanese soldiers and sailors.

The Japanese recognized the danger American control of Iwo Jima might pose in the summer of 1944 after the Americans had successfully invaded Saipan – Iwo Jima would provide a base for both fighters and damaged bombers on the return flight from Japan. General Kuribayashi was sent to take command of the island's defences, and chose to defend almost every square yard, committing his men to a suicidal mission that would eschew the banzai charges of Guadalcanal and Saipan, and instead force the Americans to find and kill every single member of the well-dug-in garrison. Most of these installations were impossible to knock out except with grenades or flamethrowers.

The first wave of US Marines landed on 19 February 1945. Their first objective was Mount Suribachi, a volcanic vent that

A group of Marines raise the American flag atop Mount Suribachi, Iwo Jima, on 23 February 1945, four days after the initial landings. Although there was still a month of fighting before the island was declared secure, control of the mountain was the key initial objective.

dominates the entire island from the south-western corner, but offered an excellent vantage point over the landing beaches for artillery spotting. It took three days to winkle the Japanese out of this position and the mountain's capture was eventually marked by a flag-raising, memorably captured on film by the photographer Joe Rosenthal. Of the six Marines who lifted the flag over Suribachi, only three survived the battle.

[T]he island of Iwo Jima was secure after over a month of fighting between 70,000 Marines and 21,000 Japanese soldiers and sailors.

It took another four weeks of hard fighting through the two main lines of resistance the Japanese had established on the island before it was truly secure. The battle had the highest ratio of American dead to troops engaged in the nation's history and seven Marines earned Medals of Honor for their conduct on Iwo Jima. As Admiral Chester Nimitz, commander of the US Pacific Fleet said, "Among the Americans who served on Iwo Jima, uncommon valour was a common virtue."

Marines leave their landing craft and clamber through the black volcanic sand of the island. Their Japanese opponents used concrete made from the sand to make strong emplacements.

Fighting continues in Luzon

Soldiers of the 1st Cavalry Division enter Manila in February 1945. The Philippines' capital was the scene of the worst street fighting in the Pacific war.

At the end of March 1945, the American Sixth Army on Luzon could look at the month of fighting that had followed the fall of Manila on 4 March as one that had brought all the strategically and economically significant objectives under their control. However, a large Japanese force, commanded by the victor of Malaya, General Yamashita, remained in control of the northern part of the island. The main action occurred east of Manila, in a campaign launched on 20 February to capture two dams that supplied most of the Philippine capital's drinking water. As in other battles in the Pacific, the Japanese had skilfully constructed their defensive positions, taking full advantage of rugged terrain in the hills and mountains of Luzon. The Japanese attempted a counter-attack on 12 March as the American troops threatened their main defences, the mountains of Pacawagan and Mataba, but this were so feeble that the Americans did not even realize the enemy had taken the offensive. The cost in casualties was so severe that the Japanese in this part of Luzon were doomed to eventual defeat. The main question was how long it would take.

Germans surrender in Italy

German troops in Italy officially surrendered to the Allied armies on 2 May 1945, although the agreement was signed four days earlier. The Germans had already agreed in principle to surrender on 31 March, following secret

Former Italian dictator Benito Mussolini was captured by partisans in Dongo and was executed summarily.

talks in Switzerland, but until the final Allied offensives began on 6 April, no further action was taken. Bologna was liberated on 20 April, Modena, Reggio and Parma followed rapidly. Former Italian dictator Benito Mussolini was captured by partisans in Dongo and was summarily executed by a couple of partisan officers, who arrived from Milan having heard he was in custody. His body, along with those of other leading Fascists, was put on display in a Milanese square on 29 April.

The body of Mussolini swings upside down in Piazza Loreto, Milan, along with some of his friends and associates who were executed with him on 28 April 1945.

Hitler dead, Berlin in Soviet hands

The red Soviet banner with hammer, sickle and star is lifted over the Reichstag building in Berlin on 2 May 1945, symbolizing the Soviet conquest of the German capital. Hitler committed suicide in the ruins of the city on 30 April.

The **Second World** War in Europe ended on 8 May 1945 when the Germans capitulated unconditionally to the Allies. Berlin fell to the Red Army on 2 May, when its garrison formally surrendered.

The offensive to capture Berlin began on 16 April. It involved the crossing of the Oder by Marshal Georgi Zhukov's 1st Belorussian Front, and of the Neisse by Marshal Ivan Koniev's 1st Ukrainian Front. With the two marshals both having strong ambitions to be the conqueror of Berlin, Zhukov's forces got off to a bad start. The Seelow Heights, standing between them and Berlin, were stoutly defended, and the terrain was poorly suited to tanks. Faced with slow progress on the first day, Zhukov rushed in his armoured units, creating a terrible traffic jam. With Soviet leader Josef Stalin demanding success, Zhukov put pressure on his subordinates to forge ahead at all costs.

Koniev, by contrast, was successful right from the start. Crossing the River Neisse at 150 separate points, and using lightweight assault bridges to get the infantry across, his men quickly opened a gap in the German lines through which Koniev sent two tank armies. On 21 April both army groups had their forces on the outskirts of Berlin.

On that day, the city was brought under constant artillery fire, and street fighting began. Civilians retreated to the uncertain security of bunkers, where they were often attacked with explosive charges and flamethrowers. Those who avoided this fate suffered severely at the hands of Red Army second-echelon troops, many of whom were brutalized, liberated prisoners having been given a sub-machine gun and a license to rape, murder and loot.

In the event, on 28 April, with troops from both fronts engaged in fighting through the streets of Berlin, the honour of capturing the Reichstag and other key buildings in the German capital was awarded to Zhukov's men. Hitler committed suicide on 30 April and almost immediately afterwards the Germans began trying to reach some kind of truce with the Red Army, until surrender arrangements were agreed on 2 May.

IN BRIEF

The German positions around the city of Colmar, France, were finally captured on 9 February 1945 when the French First Army drove the last of the German forces from Alsace and across the Rhine. The French offensive had opened on 20 January.

A series of raids on Dresden during 13–15 February 1945 produced a horrific firestorm and casualties estimated to be around 30,000 dead.

Allied troops ranged across the North German Plain after Field Marshal Sir Bernard Montgomery's operations Plunder and Varsity brought his 21st Army Group across the German river on 24 March 1945. Varsity was a daylight airborne operation, the largest single-day parachute assault of the war. The careful preparation and narrow frontage of the attack ensured that a hole was punched in the enemy line; German lack of reserves meant that Allied forces were now able to roam freely across Germany.

The Austrian capital of Vienna was captured by the Red Army on 13 April 1945. The offensive began on 6 April and the week-long battle for the city involved vicious street fighting, in which the buildings on the Ringstrasse were badly damaged.

Soviet and American forces established contact on 24 April 1945 and formally began to define their separate zones of occupation at Torgau, Germany, on 25 April 1945.

Typhoon of steel on Okinawa

US landing craft, part of a vast fleet of 1,300 vessels, land supplies in support of the American invasion of Okinawa. The fleet became the target of 1,485 kamikaze aircraft during the five months following the invasion on 1 April 1945.

Japanese forces, heavily outnumbered, defended the island of Okinawa for ten weeks, until their remnants were overwhelmed by American soldiers on 22 June 1945. The battle was marked by ruthless defence on land, while at sea waves of kamikaze attacks were thrown against the Allied fleet offshore, although these achieved no decisive effect in spite of sinking 38 ships.

American forces landed on Okinawa on 1 April 1945, supported by a huge armada of warships; about 60,000 troops were landed on the first day. The Japanese put up little resistance initially, but as the Americans fanned out north and south across the island they found the Japanese waiting for them in the usual carefully prepared positions. The Japanese concentrated their forces in the southern part of the island, where the bays suitable as fleet bases for the planned invasion of Japan were located.

For several days after the landing, the Americans encountered relatively few Japanese. The Japanese commander, General Ushijima Mitsuru, kept his artillery, which was far more numerous than anything the Americans had met in the Pacific islands so far, from drawing counter-battery fire from the huge armada of battleships, cruisers, and destroyers offshore. No serious resistance was met until 7 April as American forces approached the main Japanese defensive line, north of the town of Shuri. The Japanese used their artillery to good effect against the initial advances, disrupting the American infantry-tank tactics that were normally successful against Japanese pillboxes. The American soldiers battered against this line of defence for two weeks, confronted by an enemy relying on skilfully placed positions, often taking advantage of reverse slopes, night infiltrations to harass the Americans and suicidal counter-attacks. The Japanese made the Americans pay a heavy price, but at an even greater cost to themselves. On 23 April, General Ushijima decided to withdraw to a second line of defence, about 1 mile (1½ km) behind the first, whereupon the Americans began assaulting the second line, even stronger. The war in Okinawa turned into a Pacific version of the First World War's Western Front, with the Americans grinding down the Japanese until eventually they would break. By 16 May, General Ushijima had committed his last reserves to the line and a week later he pulled back to a third line, about 7 miles (11 km) further back. The remainder of the campaign was fought amid heavy monsoon rains, until the fighting finally ended on 22 June.

A US Marine aims his M1 Thompson sub-machine gun. The invasion was a combined Army-Marine operation under the command of Lieutenant-General Simon Bolivar Buckner, Jr.

August Storm bursts on Manchuria

Red Army soldiers stand guard outside the railway station at Harbin. Japanese leaders regarded the Soviet invasion of Manchuria as the *coup de grâce*.

The **Red Army's** invasion of Manchuria, launched on 9 August 1945 following the Soviet Union's declaration of war on Japan, finally came to an end on 20 August after a model campaign of manoeuvre in which the mechanized Soviet forces overwhelmed a large Japanese army that had been stripped of most of its combat power (such as anti-tank guns) to aid the war effort in the Pacific. The Chinese region of Manchuria is now occupied by Soviet forces. The Red Army's Operation August Storm incorporated airborne assaults and amphibious landings in Korea, Sakhalin and in the Kurile islands, while the main ground attacks were made in two directions, from Mongolia and from Vladivostok. The former completely surprised the Japanese, who did not believe the Red Army could sustain a large army through the trackless desert of Mongolia without a good railway network.

IN BRIEF

⚜ On 28 May 1945, American forces on Luzon, in the Philippines, captured the Wawa Dam, having already secured the Ipo Dam on 17 May.

New weapon obliterates Japanese cities

American aircraft have dropped two bombs on the Japanese cities of Hiroshima and Nagasaki, in each case utterly destroying two large cities. The Hiroshima bomb, a uranium device, was dropped on 6 August 1945, the Nagasaki bomb, a plutonium device, on 9 August. In both cases, the bombs exploded with a blinding flash. Subsequent experiences depended on where anyone was standing in relation to ground zero. Kimura Gonichi, a man 2½ miles (4 km) from the Hiroshima bomb, felt a searing blast of heat. Morimoto Shigeyoshi was indoors, underground, a few hundred yards from the Nagasaki bomb and felt a tremor like an earthquake (he had also been indoors at Hiroshima). Buildings were transformed into rubble in seconds by the blast wave, and the high temperatures seared skin off, or blistered it so badly that it came off wholesale when the person was moved. A characteristic mushroom cloud rose above the cities, which was as hot as steam to the touch and plastered a film of radioactive dust on anything that it touched. The cloud brought water vapour up high enough for it to condense and fall as heavy black rain. The total casualties killed by the bombings alone were 70–80,000 at Hiroshima, and about the same at Nagasaki, but the subsequent effects of radiation poisoning increased those death tolls substantially.

A mushroom cloud looms over Nagasaki on 9 August 1945, after the dropping of a second atomic bomb on a Japanese city by the Americans.

Zionists attack British at King David Hotel

Members of the militant Zionist group Irgun detonated a bomb at the King David Hotel in Jerusalem on 22 July 1946, killing 91 people, among them civilians. The bombing was part of an extended campaign of terrorism by Zionist organizations against the British in Palestine, where they have held a mandate to administer the territory under the League of Nations since 1922.

Zionists had been trying to organize a "Jewish National Home" in Palestine since the creation of the Zionist Organization in 1897 at a conference in Switzerland. European and Yemeni Jews had begun immigrating into Palestine in significant numbers in the 1880s, although access to the region was controlled by the administrative authorities, at first the Turks and later the British, both of whom, for different reasons, were wary of antagonizing the Arab majority who lived there. At the end of March 1944, the British banned Jewish immigration into Palestine, a plan that had been announced in May 1939. This followed several years of riots and rebellion on the part of Jews and Arabs resident in Palestine, each objecting to the interests of the other. After the outbreak of war, most Zionists agreed to a truce with the British, but the immigration ban led to a revival of the conflict, opening with the assassination of Lord Moyne, the British Minister Resident in the Middle East, in November 1944, by two members of LEHI (from the Hebrew acronym for Fighters for the Freedom of Israel), a Zionist paramilitary group. Although the assassination horrified some Zionists, others took it as a signal that a war to end the British mandate would begin as soon as the war against the Nazis was finished.

In October 1945, Zionist paramilitaries attacked railway lines and police stations across Palestine, opening the terror campaign against the British. The conflict between the two sides escalated until in June 1946 the British mounted Operation Agatha, removing a large quantity of documents from Zionist offices and taking them to the King David Hotel, where various administrative arms of the mandate had offices. On 22 July, several

The King David Hotel in Jerusalem after it was wrecked by bombs planted by Zionist terrorists on 22 July 1946.

Irgun members smuggled bombs packed into milk churns into the hotel, but were discovered. The terrorists killed an unarmed British officer and a policeman, before engaging in a firefight with guards as they attempted to escape, having started the time fuse to their bombs.

Greek Communists fail to take a "capital"

Communist partisans in street fighting during the Greek Civil War. The communists received only half-hearted support from Yugoslavia and Soviet-supported regimes in the Balkans.

On 1 January 1948, a field force of about 2,000 Greek Communist fighters began withdrawing from the town of Konitsa near the Albanian border, in north-west Greece. They had launched an attack, supported by artillery, in the hope of capturing a significant town that would act as the capital of the Communist provisional government that had been proclaimed on 24 December 1947, the same day that the military operation against Konitsa began. The civil war in Greece pitted the two factions in the resistance to the Germans – the Communists and the non-Communists – against one another. Fighting had broken out after a two-year truce in 1946, but until the attack on Konitsa had largely been a drawn-out, hit-and-run campaign of guerrillas against the police and army.

Civil war in China breaks out after Americans leave truce talks

Fighting between Nationalists and Communists occurred in many regions of northern China during 1947, the fighting being concentrated in Manchuria, Shensi province and Shantung province. A large Communist force established itself in the Tapieh mountains to the north-east of Wuhan. Although the Communists preferred to fight a guerrilla war, the battles that did occur were often substantial engagements involving hundreds of thousands of men, and were often instigated by the Communists themselves, demonstrating an unexpected level of confidence in their capabilities.

The end of the war in China brought the rivalry between the two major political factions back into the open. During the

US troops in Tientsin in 1945. American forces were in northern China to help evacuate the large Japanese army stationed in the country, and counter Soviet influence from Manchuria.

Dead Chinese Communist soldiers arrayed underneath the wall of the village of Tsingpu, near Shanghai. The Communists were strong in the country; the Nationalists controlled the cities.

war, for the most part, both sides carefully husbanded resources in anticipation of post-war battles. The Americans, sponsors of Chiang Kai-shek's struggle against Japan, but also including many sympathizers with the Communists, attempted to broker some kind of settlement between the two sides. General George C. Marshall, who had served as US Chief of Staff throughout the war, came to China along with several divisions of American forces to help find some kind of stable solution. However, the situation was complicated by the presence of a large Soviet military force in Manchuria, who did all they could to help the Chinese Communists establish a presence in the countryside and towns, while limiting access by the Nationalists and American forces.

Marshall made repeated attempts to form a power-sharing council which the Nationalists objected to because it offered more control than they were willing to concede to the Communists. In January 1947, Marshall returned to the United States, disgusted with both sides, although he was more critical of the Communists. His replacement, General Albert Wedemeyer, was a more wholehearted supporter of the Nationalists, and did much to secure a substantial quantity of military aid, although only a portion of what Chiang Kai-shek demanded.

A "Red China" for the future

The proclamation of the People's Republic of China in Peking on 1 October 1949 came at the end of a three-year civil war that pitted Nationalist against Communist governments.

The decisive battle in the Communist victory came in the middle of China, when the Communists attacked south from Shantung and achieved a major victory in capturing Suchow, in the course of which several Nationalist armies were destroyed or surrounded. Further fighting to the south of Suchow ended in January 1949 with the destruction of seven Nationalist armies and the loss of 550,000 men killed, wounded or captured. The effect of this Huai Hai campaign was to destroy any chance of the Nationalists preventing Communist control of China north of the Yangtze river. The fall of Tientsin shortly afterwards eliminated the last major concentration of Nationalist troops in northern China, and it was only a matter of time before the far stronger Communist forces conquered the southern part of the country.

Chinese Nationalist troops march through Shanghai in 1948. Nationalist leader Chiang Kai-shek had already gone to Taiwan when Shanghai fell to the communists on 27 May 1949.

La Violencia, civil war in Colombia

The assassination of Liberal politician Jorge Eliécer Gaitán in Bogotá, Colombia, on 9 April 1948, triggered a civil war in this South American country. The assassination followed two years of Conservative government persecution of Liberal Party institutions. The president, Mariano Ospina Pérez, had been elected in 1945 after two Liberal candidates split the normal majority vote for the party. When the Liberals won the 1947 mid-term congressional elections, Conservative-controlled local authorities

In the province of Caldas, a group of paramilitaries known as pájaros (birds) was formed to intimidate local Liberals.

stepped up a low-key persecution of Liberal local politicians that already included some murders. In the province of Caldas, a group of paramilitaries known as *pájaros* (birds) was formed to intimidate local Liberals. With the Conservatives in control of the police, Liberal leaders formed militias to protect themselves, and these quickly evolved into guerrilla groups during 1948-49. Conservative paramilitaries murdered Liberals, especially those associated with Gaitán, while Liberal guerrillas both murdered Conservatives in revenge and also began attacking the police who, to them, seemed indistinguishable from Conservative paramilitaries.

India, Pakistan divide Kashmir between them

A UN-sponsored ceasefire between Pakistani and Indian forces fighting for control of the region of Jammu and Kashmir, north-west of India, in the Himalayas, came into effect on 31 December 1948, ending a year-and-a-half of war between the two new states. Pakistan had separated from the rest of India to include the predominantly Moslem areas of the former British-controlled possession. Jammu and Kashmir had a Moslem majority, but was ruled by a Hindu prince and included large minorities of Buddhists and Sikhs. The fighting began when Moslem irregulars, who received support from Pakistan, began a revolt in June 1947 that culminated in a declaration of a rebel government on 24 October 1947. Three days later the ruler of Kashmir asked the Indian government for protection and Indian forces advanced into the region. Indian troops were brought to the capital, Srinagar, by air and, supported by a handful of armoured cars, turned back the Moslem irregulars who were on the edge of the city. Fighting shifted to the western border with Pakistan, where the irregulars had several cities under siege. When Indian forces advanced in May 1948 to end the sieges of Punch and Uri, they clashed with Pakistani regulars. As more troops entered the fray, progress became limited to short advances and after August 1948 the front barely moved.

Israel secures independence

Israeli soldiers train for street fighting in 1948. The Zionist settlers in Palestine prepared for an Arab invasion.

The state of Israel, officially brought into existence by the United Nations on 15 May 1948, finally came to an armistice agreement with the last of its neighbours on 20 July 1949, ending over a year of fighting in which the Arab states attempted to prevent the partition of Palestine.

When the British mandate ended on 15 May, both sides immediately embarked on military operations. The Arabs invaded Palestine from three directions, in support of Arab forces already active, while Israeli forces fought to secure the areas around Jewish settlements. Some fierce fighting occurred in Jerusalem, where the best of the Arab forces, the Jordanian Arab Legion, succeeded in securing the Old City. A ceasefire on 11 June gave both sides time to recuperate from heavy losses. A ten-day renewal on 9 July ended in stalemate, but in October 1948, a renewal of combat led to significant gains for the Israelis. The first armistice was finally agreed with Egypt on 24 February 1949, and other Arab states followed in quick succession.

Soldiers of the Arab Liberation Army near Jerusalem. The army consisted of Arab volunteers from many countries, with its headquarters in Damascus, and relied on support from Syria.

OBITUARY
JOHN J. PERSHING
(1860-1948)

General John Pershing, commander of American forces in Europe during the First World War, and patron to many of the leading American generals of the Second, died on 15 July 1948.

Pershing's military career began after he graduated from West Point in 1886 and entered a small army that was largely a frontier protection force chasing Indians. He served in the Spanish-American War and also in the Philippines, before leading the Punitive Expedition into Mexico in pursuit of Pancho Villa.

In 1917, he was named commander of the American Expeditionary Force, which he was determined would fight as a separate army, instead of permitting American troops to be distributed throughout the armies of the Allies. He retired from active service in 1924.

His wife and three daughters predeceased him, dying in a fire in 1915. He is survived by one son.

North Korean forces surge across 38th Parallel

The **invasion of** South Korea by Communist North Korean forces began on 25 June 1950, and continued until by 31 July all but a small area around the city of Pusan was occupied by the northerners. The North Korean army's easy victory was partly because they had better equipment – they deployed T-34 tanks while the South Koreans lacked adequate artillery – but also because they

A battalion-sized force made a stand at Osan on 5 July, but withdrew in disarray when threatened with being surrounded.

attacked in far superior numbers (135,000 vs 95,000 that fell to 51,000 within a week as a demoralized army ran away).

On 27 June, the United States offered to send troops and aircraft to support the South Koreans, in accordance with the United Nations' Security Council resolution authorizing international action against the North Koreans. The

North Korean prisoners erect barbed wire fencing for the camp they would be confined to. The North Korean army occupied almost all of South Korea, leaving United Nations' forces in control of a small area around Pusan.

first troops to arrive were rushed from the army of occupation in Japan, but like the South Korean formations, they lacked their full complement of heavy weapons. A battalion-sized force made a stand at Osan on 5 July, but withdrew in disarray when threatened with being surrounded. These men were part of the 24th Infantry Division which attempted to make a stand at Taejon between 16 and 20 July, but again were overwhelmed by an enemy who outnumbered them and were strong in tanks. More worrying was

the fact that the American troops were not causing particularly heavy casualties before they withdrew. It was never likely that the division could stop the North Koreans, but more "fight" was expected from them. However, at Pusan, three American army divisions, later joined by a Marine brigade and British troops, managed to make a stand that did halt the North Koreans, while the United Nations' forces, now under the command of General Douglas MacArthur, prepared their counter-attack.

American landing craft and control of the sea offered them a degree of strategic manoeuvrability that could easily be exploited around the Korean peninsula.

US infantry are driven to the front line around Pusan.

China occupies Tibet

A **Tibetan provincial governor** signed a surrender agreement with Chinese military leaders on 19 October 1950 after a Chinese invasion of the country had begun two weeks earlier. The crisis over Tibet started in May, with skirmishes on the border between elements of the two armies. However, the Tibetans did not have a modern army, and only had about 10,000 men against at least 40,000 Chinese. The Tibetans also had hardly any artillery, only a couple of hundred mortars and a similar number of machine guns, and were easily defeated at Chamdo. The battle was over quickly as the Tibetans more or less gave up, with over 5,000 being taken prisoner, while only 180 were killed or wounded. After this, the Chinese began negotiating with the government of the Dalai Lama, Tibet's ruler, intending to secure the annexation of the country.

MacArthur's bold stroke takes UN forces to Yalu

T **he UN army** in Korea is now on the North Korean border with China, after South Korean troops reached the Yalu river on 25 October 1950. The advance from the far south-east of the Korean peninsula, starting in the embattled

The North Korean army had largely exhausted itself in its drive south and was in no fit state to withstand a determined attack from Pusan.

perimeter around Pusan, was made possible after General Douglas MacArthur chose to make a daring amphibious landing at Inchon, to the east of the South Korean capital Seoul.

MacArthur's idea was greeted with dismay by naval officers, on account of the extreme tides in the Inchon area. There would only be about three hours of sufficiently high water to land a large military force and subsequently supply it. In fact, the area was only lightly defended and the landings on 15 September were completed with ease. However, the street-by-street fighting in Seoul was a much harder battle and it took three days to secure the city. In part this was because the UN troops at Pusan launched an attack of their own to coincide with the landings. The North Korean army had largely exhausted itself in its drive south and was in no fit state to withstand a determined attack from Pusan. The North Korean retreat, while not precipitate, did not halt until UN forces were north of the North Korean capital of Pyongyang, with elements of the UN Eighth Army reaching the Yalu river and the border with China.

Chinese soldiers cross a river during the invasion of Tibet. The Chinese empire had claimed Tibet, and the Chinese communist regime chose to enforce a traditional claim to suzerainty over the priestly Himalayan state.

Chinese surprise United Nations

The **evacuation of** Inchon on 5 January 1951 by United Nations forces marked the successful entry of the Chinese into the Korean War. The Chinese offensive has driven the UN forces back from the Yalu river as far as 30 miles (48 km) south of Seoul.

Chinese soldiers first made contact with South Korean troops of the UN army on 25 October 1950 when they made a number of preliminary attacks that showed how night attacks negated the firepower advantage of the American forces. The American commanders, General Douglas MacArthur and General Walton Walker, both believed that these limited attacks represented a main effort by the Chinese, but the Chinese, with Marshal Peng Te Huai in overall command, had managed to conceal the movement of some 200,000 men from UN reconnaissance aircraft. Interrogation of prisoners and reports by villagers indicated the presence of Chinese troops in large numbers, but without concrete evidence these were ignored.

On 1 November, the Chinese first hit American troops with an attack on the 1st Cavalry Division. The main offensive was unleashed on 25 November and sent UN forces reeling backwards. The American

American Marines stand guard over Chinese Red Army soldiers in Korea in March 1951.

2nd Infantry Division was attacked while trying to withdraw through a pass near Kunu-ri and suffered a major defeat. In contrast, the 1st Marine Division held out against Chinese forces attacking their positions at the Chosin Reservoir, as well as their main supply route south to the coast at Hungnam. The battle for this supply route became a desperate one.

Chinese attacks, both here and elsewhere, were cacophonies of sound. Since they lacked radios and maps, orders and signals were made with bugles and whistles. The sounds of these echoed in the heads of UN soldiers, as well as the blasts of grenades

and the rattle of machine-gun fire, as they fought back against night attacks, which prevented any effective air support.

On 1 December, the most forward units of the 1st Marine Division, around Yudam-ni at the northern end of the reservoir, were ordered to withdraw south to Hagaru at the southern end. The withdrawal took the form of a breakout, as the leading elements of the Marines had to battle their way down a road with mountains either side occupied by Chinese mortars and machine guns. They arrived at Hagaru on 3 December, and on 6 December set off for Hungnam, which they reached on 10 December.

The UN Eighth Army's retreat on the western side of the peninsula was nowhere near as heroic. At Pyongyang millions of dollars of equipment were burned to prevent them falling into the hands of the Chinese and North Koreans when they reoccupied the city on 5 December. One major advantage UN forces had over the Chinese was their numerous trucks. While these tied them to the roads, they also helped them to outrun the Chinese who moved on foot across any terrain, but more slowly. On 23 December, the commander of the Eighth Army, General Walton Walker, was killed in a traffic accident. His replacement, General Matthew Ridgway, arrived in Korea on 26 December. Even though Seoul and Inchon were about to fall, Ridgway believed that UN forces could still halt the Chinese and drive them back north.

British soldiers of a reconnaissance unit wait during the retreat from the Yalu river in 1951. The British supplied a substantial contingent of some 63,000 men to the UN's forces in Korea.

OBITUARY

MARSHAL PHILLIPPE PÉTAIN (1856-1951)

Marshal Philippe Pétain, who twice in his lifetime was called upon to help save France from national crises, died in prison on the Île d'Yeu, off the Atlantic coast of France on 23 July.

Pétain was born in the Pas-de-Calais, just across the Channel from Britain, a country towards which he held a lifetime suspicion. He graduated from the French military academy in 1878 and in September 1914 commanded a division in the Battle of the Marne. He made his name for his dogged defence of Verdun, following the start of the German offensive in February 1916. After mass mutinies in the French army in the spring of 1917, Pétain was appointed commander-in-chief of the French army, and through a mixture of ruthlessness and concessions restored the French military to a measure of effectiveness.

In 1940, Pétain effectively became dictator of France and signed an armistice with Germany. He managed to keep his country neutral, but only by actively assisting the Germans in other ways. As a result, he was tried for collaboration in 1945 and sentenced to death. His sentence was commuted to life imprisonment.

He is survived by his wife and stepson.

Ridgway's ripper recaptures Seoul

The new commander of the UN Eighth Army in Korea, General Matthew Ridgway, achieved some key successes with his first offensive of the war, one that led to the recapture of Seoul on 14 March 1951.

The first tentative UN counter-attack against the Chinese and North Korean forces took place on 25 January. When the attacking forces advanced with ease, Ridgway prepared a much bigger operation. Operation Killer, beginning on 21 February, was a general advance all along the line that re-established a continuous front for UN forces. Operation Ripper, begun on 7 March, had the main objective of driving the communist forces back north of the 38th Parallel, the pre-war boundary, and a more specific hope of securing the "Iron Triangle", an area between three North Korean towns where the main supply dumps and roads south for any attack on the UN forces would be located.

First jet ace

The first jet pilot ever to achieve the title "ace", with five officially confirmed "kills" of enemy jet fighters, accomplished this historic feat on 20 May 1951, when Captain James Jabara of the US Air Force shot down two MiG-15s during a big dogfight near the

Jabara flew an F-86 Sabre, the standard American air force fighter aircraft at this time.

Yalu river. Jabara flew an F-86 Sabre, the standard American air force fighter aircraft at this time. His opponents may have been Soviet airmen flying planes carrying North Korean or Chinese markings, for as well as aircraft, the Soviets also supplied pilots.

Glosters' glory at the Imjin

The see-saw struggle on the Korean peninsula finally failed to tip strongly in any direction when the UN 29 Brigade, a formation of British and Belgian troops, succeeded in blunting a major Chinese attack along the Imjin river on 28 April 1951. Although the British forces eventually had to abandon their positions overlooking the river, the defence was so tenacious, especially by men of the Gloucestershire Regiment, that the Chinese had no further reserves to commit to the attack.

General Matthew Ridgway took command of the UN's 8th Army after General Walton Walker died in a traffic accident.

Crushing defeat at Dien Bien Phu

Viet Minh soldiers charge French positions at the "Dominique" position in the battle of Dien Bien Phu in 1954. Dominique was one of the last French strongholds during the battle.

After the French army experienced a major defeat at the hands of the nationalist Viet Minh, a ceasefire ending the eight-year war in French Indochina was agreed at Geneva, Switzerland, on 20 July 1954. At the siege of Dien Bien Phu, 13,000 French troops were up against 50,000 Viet Minh, and the surrender of the garrison there on 7 May 1954 triggered peace talks that ended in the ceasefire.

Operation Castor, the French plan to parachute a sizeable force into Dien Bien Phu, was the idea of General Henri Navarre, the commander of French forces in Indochina, and was designed to counter the successful Viet Minh offensive in Laos. Any failures the Viet Minh experienced in Laos owed more to their difficulty keeping troops supplied there than French military action. Navarre believed he could turn the tide by parachuting in a large force to occupy Dien Bien Phu, from where

he hoped to supply friendly guerrillas, as well as forcing the Viet Minh to attack and expose themselves to superior French firepower.

The French plans went completely awry soon after the first paratroopers landed on 20 November 1953. Although the guerrillas were not initially well organized, French airpower was unable to halt the Viet Minh from assembling a large force around Dien Bien Phu, which was in the floor of a valley. By 13 March 1954 the Viet Minh began their attack on the base, they had sited plenty of artillery on the high ground around the French base, far more than the French were able to deploy. Furthermore, the Viet Minh unexpectedly deployed anti-aircraft guns which prevented French airpower from being effective either in attacking ground targets or in resupplying the garrison. The 57-day siege rapidly acquired an air of inevitable Viet Minh victory, although they suffered heavy casualties.

French, Viet Minh, battle to stalemate

The successful ambush and pursuit of French troops at Chan Muong, that only ended with their reaching the safety of the Red River Delta near Hanoi on 24 November 1952, ended nearly two years of mobile warfare in the conflict between the French colonial power and the Viet Minh nationalists fighting for the independence of French Indochina.

The Viet Minh had been waging a guerrilla war against the French since 1947. The communist victory in China in 1949 altered the strategic balance by allowing the predominantly communist Viet Minh to receive massive amounts of armaments both from China and the Soviet Union, where before they had been relatively isolated. General Vo Nguyen Giap, the Viet Minh commander, immediately launched a series of attacks against French garrisons along Colonial Route 4, that succeeded in overrunning them before driving the survivors into the Red River Delta around Hanoi.

The situation only changed with the arrival of a new French commander in 1951, General Jean de Lattre de Tassigny, who had volunteered for the task. General Giap was heavily defeated by de Lattre de Tassigny when he launched a series of attacks starting in January 1951 and ending in May, forcing him to give up any hope of breaching the de Lattre Line. De Lattre de Tassigny now counter-attacked with his own forces, driving the Viet Minh out of the delta, and then attempted to capture the key road junction of Hoa Binh, 25 miles (40 km) west of the delta region. In January 1952, however, de Lattre de Tassigny returned to France suffering from cancer, and died soon after. His successor, General Raoul Salan, continued with his plan but Hoa Binh was too far from the de Lattre Line to be supported effectively and in February 1952 it was abandoned. Although Salan ordered a raid on several key Viet Minh supply dumps in November, which ended in a confused retreat and the ambush at Chan Muong, Giap's forces still lacked the firepower to break the de Lattre Line.

Korean ceasefire ends fighting

A ceasefire between the United Nations, and North Korean and Chinese forces was agreed at Panmunjon on 27 July 1953. This ended more than a year of dour attritional warfare as both sides battled over terrain that would aid the defence of any border agreed in a subsequent peace treaty. Most of the fighting was over hills christened by such names as Carson, Vegas, Old Baldy and Pork Chop.

General Mark Clark signs the armistice ending the Korean conflict on 27 July 1953.

French, British fruitlessly seize Port Said

British troops pass a the wreckage of an Egyptian truck during the attack on Port Said.

T he withdrawal of the last British and French troops from the Suez Canal Zone on 23 December 1956 marked the end of an attempt to prevent nationalization of the canal by Egypt's president, Gamal Abd al-Nasser. British marines, and French paratroopers and tanks had landed there on 6 November, after an airborne assault the previous day. The fighting ended abruptly with a ceasefire that night; the political negotiations that ended the fighting also forced the withdrawal of British and French forces.

The declared aim of the attack was to protect the Canal Zone from the fighting going on in the Sinai between Israeli and Egyptian forces, but in fact the Israelis had attacked at the request of the French and British in order to provide an excuse for their military intervention. This had begun on 31 October with a bombing campaign directed against Egyptian airfields, but the largely Soviet-piloted Egyptian air force intended to remain firmly on the ground. Having wasted time on this operation, the allies conducted two parachute drops at Port Said on 5 November; the British captured the airfield while the French took a key bridge. This was followed by the amphibious landings on 6 November, which included the first ship-to-shore helicopter-borne assault in history.

OBITUARY

HEINZ GUDERIAN
(1888-1954)

General Heinz Guderian, a key participant in the creation of German armoured forces before and during the Second World War, died on 14 May 1954.

Guderian joined the army in 1907, entering his father's regiment. He served in mainly signals positions during the First World War, and was one of the few officers from the wartime army who was given a commission in the 100,000-man Reichswehr of the Weimar Republic. While serving in the Reichswehr he began laying the foundations for Germany's Second World War tank divisions, before commanding corps in the invasions of Poland and France, and a panzer army in the attack on the Soviet Union. He was dismissed after the defeat before Moscow and only returned to Adolf Hitler's favour after the defeat at Stalingrad, when he became Inspector-General of Armoured Forces. He was not tried as a war criminal but was kept a prisoner until 1948.

He is survived by his wife and two sons.

The Cold War

The Soviet Union and the United States have been engaged in a hostile confrontation on political, economic and diplomatic levels for 15 years, but have managed to avert the outbreak of a war that would certainly have turned into a nuclear exchange with devastating effects for the world.

The Americans tested the world's first hydrogen bomb on 1 November 1952. The hydrogen bomb used a much more powerful fusion explosion than the fission explosions of 1945.

but probably owed much more to his own determination to remain in control, a passion that had driven a million Soviet citizens to the execution cells, and millions more to hard labour and a starvation diet in harsh, often fatal, conditions in camps scattered across the Soviet Union. He had experienced a nervous breakdown when his former ally, Adolf Hitler, ordered the invasion of the Soviet Union in June 1941, and thereafter only put his trust in what he could control.

> During the Korean War, the Cold War hotted up as American and Soviet pilots clashed in the skies over MiG Alley, but for the most part neither side wanted to go to war with the other.

The Iranian prime minister Mohammad Mossadegh was deposed by British and American covert action in the spring and summer of 1953, out of unfounded fears of him seeking to ally with the Soviet Union.

The origins of the Cold War have traditionally been a matter of considerable debate among historians, but in fact simply continued the same hostility that had existed between the Soviet Union and the leading capitalist powers before 1939. The main difference was that the war had increased dramatically the territorial extent of the Soviet Union by bringing all of Eastern Europe under its influence, while at the same time creating a Soviet military superpower. The more active role played by the United States in world politics, in contrast to its isolationism of the years between 1919 and 1939, combined with its much greater wealth and more powerful armed forces to create a far more serious challenge than the Soviet Union had faced before.

Foreign intervention

Josef Stalin's own paranoid character further fed Cold War tensions. Stalin's view of foreign countries was largely distorted by his experience of the Russian Civil War and the accompanying intervention by Britain, France, Japan and the United States. His hostility was justified by Marxist-Leninist theory,

During the war years, Stalin engaged in power politics with alacrity, even apparently agreeing to a division of influence in the Balkans by ticking a sheet of percentages of influence provided for him by British Prime Minister Winston Churchill. For Britain,

Soviet leader Josef Stalin maintained a strategy of tension with the West that was only somewhat relaxed by his successors.

the fate of Poland, the country which had triggered the war with Germany, was key to their assessment of Soviet post-war intentions. Stalin made no secret of his intent to control it. With hundreds of thousands of Red Army soldiers in Poland, American president Franklin Roosevelt's inclination to postpone consideration of Poland's future until after the war was more realistic. When Roosevelt died in April 1945, his concept of what might happen in the post-war peace conference died with him.

Anti-communism

Roosevelt's successor, Harry Truman, responded to a civil war in Greece between Greek communists and the Greek elite by proclaiming the Truman Doctrine, under which he committed the United States to assist any government threatened by communist movements. Stalin, however, showed little interest in Greece, which he had already conceded to the British. Instead he provoked a confrontation over the status of Berlin in June 1948, by imposing a blockade on the areas of the city occupied by the Western powers. The blockade was a failure, as the Berlin Airlift

The body of a Hungarian secret policemen lies on a Budapest street at the feet of western journalists during the rebellion against the communist regime.

with the Nationalist Chinese over the islands of Quemoy and Matsu in 1958.

Crises

Khruschev fought the Cold War by the means of carefully calculated bluffs. The victory of Fidel Castro in Cuba in 1959 gave him the gift of a revolutionary anti-American nationalism that established his country's credentials as a supporter of the Third World. Faced with the problem of people fleeing East Germany, mainly through the open border in Berlin, Khruschev encouraged the construction of a wall, which began on 13 August 1961. American and Soviet troops and tanks confronted one another at Checkpoint Charlie, and American officials looked at options for a limited nuclear strike. In the end the wall remained and diplomacy averted war. The Berlin Wall crisis was subsequently overshadowed by an even tenser moment when the Soviets deployed missiles armed with nuclear warheads in Cuba, putting most of the United States under threat. Diplomacy retrieved the situation, securing the withdrawal of American missiles from Turkey in return for the removal of Soviet missiles from Cuba.

delivered enough food and fuel to keep the city going over the winter.

The victory of the communists in China and the successful detonation of an atomic weapon by the Soviet Union in 1949 truly escalated the Cold War to a condition of global tension. The defeat of Chiang Kai-shek's Nationalists became a stick with which anti-communists in the United

> Confronted by the problem of people flee-ing East Germany, mainly through the open border in Berlin, Khruschev encour-aged the construction of a wall, which began on 13 August 1961.

States could beat those who seemed less enthusiastic for any confrontation. The supposed Peking–Moscow axis (which was nowhere near as united as was imagined in the West at the time) contributed to the substantial US military reaction to the communist invasion of South Korea, a place hitherto of little strategic interest to the United States.

European uprisings

During the Korean War, the Cold War hotted up as American and Soviet pilots clashed in the skies over MiG Alley, but for the most part neither side wanted to go to war with the other. Stalin's death in March 1953 began a shift away from Europe as the focus of confrontation, in part because his successors believed the cost of maintaining the Soviet position far exceeded the ability of their country's economy to sustain it. Uprisings in East Germany in 1953, Poland and, most disastrously, in Hungary in 1956 underlined how the Soviet presence was sustained by force. The use of tanks against and executions of Germans, Poles and Hungarians was powerful propaganda for capitalist countries.

Stalin's eventual successor, Nikita Khruschev, saw much more fertile grounds for Cold War competition in the nationalist movements that put an end to European colonial empires. The Soviet Union was unstinting in its support for Egyptian leader Gamal Abd al-Nasser in his nationalization of the Suez Canal and in resisting the attempts by France and Britain to recover their control of it. However, most of his support was moral rather than material, even to the point of not supporting his Chinese ally in a confrontation

American tanks at Checkpoint Charlie in Berlin during the 1961 crisis: the world came very close to a Third World War.

Operation Kadesh unleashes Israelis in Sinai

The announcement on 9 November 1956 by Israeli prime minister David Ben-Gurion that Israeli troops would withdraw from the advanced positions within 10 miles (16 km) of the Suez Canal, brought to an end the Israeli attack on Egypt launched 12 days earlier. The Israelis had joined with the French and British to attack Egypt, although in their case it was in order to put an end to cross-border raids from the Egyptian-controlled Gaza Strip. The operation began on 29 October with an Israeli parachute drop that seized the Mitla Pass, closely followed by seven armoured spearheads thrusting into Sinai and the Gaza Strip. The Israeli attacks focused on speed to reach their stop line near the Suez Canal rather than overwhelming the Egyptian forces, most of whom occupied defensive cantonments that were easily bypassed. Egyptian resistance was fiercest at Umm Katef, but the Israelis occupied the entire Sinai Peninsula with ease.

Revolution in Cuba

The arrival of *"El Líder Máximo"* Fidel Castro in Havana on 6 January 1959 marked the culmination of an insurrection in Cuba by left-wing forces. Castro began his revolution in 1953 with an attack on the Moncada Barracks in Santiago de Cuba on 26 July that ended disastrously. Many of his comrades were shot after surrendering and Castro himself was lucky to survive, being tried and sentenced to prison. He was later exiled and organized a new revolutionary movement in Mexico. He led a force of 80 men to Cuba in December 1956 and began an efficient guerrilla struggle that finally attracted a major response from the Cuban army in June 1958. This campaign came close to victory when its commanding general risked negotiating with Castro, allowing the revolutionary leader to extract his forces from a trap at Las Mercedes in August. The fall of Santa Clara in December 1958 prompted the flight of Cuban dictator Fulgencio Batista from Havana on 1 January 1959, and the road to the Cuban capital was now open for Castro.

De Gaulle surrenders Algeria

The announcement on 4 November 1960 of a referendum on the future status of the French colony of Algeria, to be held in January 1961, marked the political victory of the Algerian FLN (Front de Libération National) in spite of the military defeat of its ALN (Armée de Libération National).

The ALN opened its war against the French colonial authority on 1 November 1954, directing its guerrilla campaign against French military and police installations, as well as farms, mines and factories owned by French settlers in Algeria (known as *pieds-noirs*). The conflict intensified in August 1955 after a peasants' revolt near Philippeville and Constantine resulted in the murder of over a hundred *pieds-noirs*. The army, police and *pied-noir* militia took revenge by massacring many more Algerian Arabs. In March 1956, the ALN began a campaign of bombing in Algiers that launched the battle of Algiers as a second front in the liberation war. The French were now confronted by both a war in the countryside and one in the city.

The French army responded by constructing large garrisons in the countryside that patrolled aggressively against the guerrillas. Villages suspected of helping the guerrillas were either attacked by the army or bombed by aircraft. Many Algerian Arabs were forcibly removed from their homes and resettled where the army could ensure they gave no help to the guerrillas. Barbed-wire or electrified fences were erected along the borders with Tunisia and Morocco, preventing guerrillas based there from crossing easily. The arrival of French paratroopers in Algiers in January 1957 ensured the war there intensified as well. Barbed-wire barricades were erected to divide the Casbah, while thousands of detainees were tortured, measures that succeeded in ensuring the arrest or death of the FLN leadership in Algiers by September.

The French army had effectively won the war by January 1958, but the measures it had taken were unpopular in France. The generals in Algeria formed their own junta in May, demanding that General Charles de Gaulle take charge of the French government, and succeeded. De Gaulle intensified the war in 1959, but only as a means of forcing the FLN to the negotiating table on French terms.

French soldiers confront pro-Organisation Armée Secrète (Secret Army Organization) demonstrators in Algiers, March 1962. The organization was created by French officers and politicians who believed that De Gaulle had reneged on promises to maintain a French Algeria.

Exiles defeated at Bay of Pigs

Anti-Castro exiles captured during the Bay of Pigs invasion in April 1961 stand under the watchful eyes of Cuban soldiers. The invasion failed miserably, and could only have succeeded with the direct intervention of American military forces against the Cuban army.

On 20 April 1961, Cuban armed forces defeated an attempt by Cuban exiles, recruited and organized by the United States of America, to start a war to overthrow Fidel Castro's communist government of the island. The exiles and their friends in the American government now blame the reluctance of President John F. Kennedy to offer full support to the invaders for the failure.

The exiles had formed a small military formation of some 2,000 men, named Brigata 2506, with the help of the American Central Intelligence Agency. The plan had been approved in March 1960 before the election of Kennedy, who was unenthusiastic, wanting to avoid too prominent a US involvement.

The battle began on 15 April when Cuban airfields were attacked by B-26 bombers piloted by Americans. Thirty-six hours later, the exiles landed at Playa Girón and Playa Larga. The Americans and exiles believed that there was a genuine possibility of a popular uprising against Castro, but the Cuban leader responded vigorously to the appearance of the exiles, rushing some 40,000 militia and soldiers to the landing areas, supported by aircraft, artillery and tanks. The exiles were only able to hold out until 19 April when the survivors attempted to infiltrate into Cuba. However, they were subjected to an air attack and fled into the nearby swamps where they were mostly rounded up over the next day.

Mercenaries in action in Congo

A bloody uprising in the Congo, in which European hostages were taken, was suppressed by April 1965 with the help of mercenaries commanded by Major Mike Hoare and Belgian paratroopers. The uprising began as a reaction against government corruption, but the Simbas (Swahili word for lion), who served as its military force, soon demonstrated that they were brutal murderers, slaughtering anyone whom they believed served the corrupt central

The uprising began as a reaction against government corruption, but the Simbas (Swahili word for lion), who served as its military force, soon demonstrated that they were brutal murderers, slaughtering anyone whom they believed served the corrupt central government.

government. On 5 August 1964, the Simbas took control of Stanleyville and proclaimed a national government of their own, as well as taking some 1,600 Europeans hostage. The Belgian and American governments believed these hostages would be murdered if they could not be ransomed, and negotiated with the Simbas for over a hundred days. However, a military solution eventually seemed practical and on 24 November, 350 Belgian airborne troops landed at Stanleyville airport and headed into town. Another force, including Hoare's 5 Commando, approached Stanleyville by road. The Belgian paratroopers located the hostages and rescued almost all of them, at the same time killing anyone who appeared to be a Simba. The fighting was quickly over with about 60 hostages killed, together with thousands of Simbas. The Simba revolt was gradually suppressed over the succeeding months.

War at the roof of the world

A **sharp but small** border conflict between India and China ended on 21 November 1962 with a unilateral ceasefire. The war was a legacy of nineteenth-century border issues between China, Tibet and British India.

The seeds of the war lay in the Chinese annexation of Tibet in 1950. They subsequently constructed a military road through an arid region where the borders of China, Pakistan and India met, known as the Aksai Chin. After the completion of this road in October 1957, Jarwahalal Nehru's Indian government pointed out that the road ran through territory claimed by India. Chinese foreign minister Chou En-lai replied that nothing here had been settled, and also pointed out issues China had with the MacMahon Line that the Indians regarded as the common boundary between China and India to the east.

There was skirmishing between Chinese and Indian border patrols in 1959 and India began deploying more troops along the border, albeit in small, scattered garrisons. In 1961, Nehru ordered the Chinese border posts to be isolated, and the Chinese began a military build-up near the border. Sporadic fighting broke out in July 1962 and sustained combat on 10 October. At first the fighting mostly took place in the eastern zone, but on 20 October the Chinese attacked in the Aksai Chin. After four days there was a two-week pause broken on 14 November by an Indian attack at Walong. The Chinese responded by defeating both the detachment at Walong and the main Indian force located in the Bum La and Se La passes. Further fighting also took place in the Aksai Chin. The Chinese were better equipped for warfare at high altitude in the mountains and won decisively on all fronts. Largely because of Nehru's demands for swift action, the Indians were still wearing warm-weather clothing, and were short of ammunition.

Indian officers discuss the tactical situation on the border in Ladakh during the war between China and India.

OBITUARY
DOUGLAS MACARTHUR
(1880-1964)

Douglas MacArthur, a general who commanded American forces in three major wars, died on 5 April 1964 at the age of 84.

His father was a veteran of the American Civil War and Douglas grew up on army posts. He graduated from West Point in 1903 and joined the Corps of Engineers. During the First World War he commanded the 84th Infantry Brigade, and in 1919 became commandant of West Point. In 1930, MacArthur began a term as Army Chief of Staff, before being seconded to the Philippines in 1935 to help organize the Philippine army. As a consequence, when the Japanese attacked in 1941, he commanded the defence of the Philippines, until ordered to leave by President Franklin Roosevelt. He was then put in charge of the South-west Pacific Area, encompassing Australia and New Guinea, and subsequently led the liberation of the Philippines and the occupation of Japan. He finally commanded UN forces in the Korean War from June 1950 until April 1951, when he was controversially relieved for recommending the bombing of China. In an address to Congress in 1951, he memorably said, "Old soldiers never die, they just fade away." He retired from public life after the 1952 presidential election.

He was married twice and had one son by his second marriage.

Israelis triumph in six days

Alightning attack by Israeli armed forces has succeeded in defeating the armed forces of Egypt, Jordan, Syria and Iraq. The fighting began on 5 June 1967 and ended six days later on 10 June.

The war began with an air attack by the Israeli air force. Achieving total surprise and complete success, the Israelis destroyed most of the Egyptian air force on the ground, together with a substantial part of the Jordanian, Syrian and a small part of the Iraqi air forces.

The ground campaign was equally successful, with the key positions of Rafah and Umm Katef falling to the Israelis on 6 June. On 7 June, the Israelis began exploiting their gains, racing across the Sinai and taking up positions overlooking the Mitla Pass, through which the retreating Egyptians would have to pass. Here, a combination of Israeli tanks and aircraft created carnage among the Egyptian columns, and the retreat turned into a rout. On 8 June, Israeli troops reached the Suez Canal, where they halted.

Israeli hoped Jordan would stay out of the war, but commitments to Egypt, the presence of Iraqi troops and a sense of Arab solidarity convinced the Jordanians to take part. The Israelis launched their attack on 6 June and outmanoeuvred the Arab forces on the West Bank, while paratroopers fought their way into Jerusalem, capturing the Old Town. Israeli warplanes destroyed the main strength of the Iraqi divisions in Jordan before they could even cross the river in support of Jordanian forces on the West Bank.

On the Syrian front, the Israelis limited their initial attacks to the air. The Syrians were in a strong position, but did little to relieve the plight of their Egyptian allies. A few bombardments and a minor attack in battalion strength were the limits of Syrian involvement until the Israelis struck on 9 June. In only 27 hours, the Israelis swept the Syrians off the Golan Heights in an attack that involved considerable close-quarter fighting, including hand-to-hand combat, in the trenches and bunkers along the Golan.

An Israeli mechanized column advances through the Sinai desert as a truck carrying Egyptian prisoners of war heads away from the front line.

India gains advantage over Pakistan

India and Pakistan fought a second war over Kashmir, the divided area between the two countries, that ended with a ceasefire that was ordered by the United Nations on 22 September 1965, although fighting continued until 27 September. Neither side could claim a decisive victory, although the Pakistanis had suffered heavier losses.

There had been skirmishing in April 1965 between border police in the Rann of Kutch, an arid area that lies along the border between Pakistan and the Indian state of Gujarat. Several key Pakistani politicians held the belief that the poor showing of the Indian army in the war with the Chinese in 1962 meant that Pakistani forces would easily occupy Kashmir. A special force of infiltrators was then established to enter Kashmir as irregulars and begin a series of guerrilla operations.

On 24 August, Indian forces crossed the border dividing Pakistani-controlled Kashmir from its Indian counterpart. It is not clear whether Pakistani forces had already crossed the border disguised as Kashmiri irregulars or whether the Indian army began its operations in anticipation of the Pakistani attack. The war in Kashmir bogged down after a couple of weeks with neither side having achieved any decisive gains, before the main theatre of operations shifted southwards to the Punjab.

Here the Indians crossed the border and started to threaten the Pakistani capital of Lahore. In two sizeable tank battles, the largest since the Second World War, the Indians were defeated at Sialkot, while they crushed the Pakistanis at Asal Uttar. In the latter battle, so many tanks were destroyed or abandoned that the Indians cannibalized them all to make the Patton Nagar (Patton Village), after the American M47 Patton tank which was the most numerous tank in the Pakistani forces.

The icon of revolution

The death of Che Guevara in Bolivia, where he was captured and then murdered by the Bolivian army at the request of the American Central Intelligence Agency, has not killed the spirit of a man whose career came to symbolize Third World liberation struggles.

Fidel Castro (left) lights a cigar during a conference with Che Guevara during their campaign in the Sierra Maestra mountains in the late 1950s. Guevara, trained as a doctor, turned out to be an excellent military leader during the guerrilla war.

Che Guevara, a leader of the Cuban revolution who subsequently attempted to export the victory of Fidel Castro to the Congo and Bolivia, was killed by Bolivian special forces on 9 October 1967. He had entered Bolivia some time between the second week in September and the first week in November 1966.

Political motivation

Guevara was born in well-to-do circumstances in Argentina, although his family later suffered financial hardship. According to his own account, he was radicalized by a trip that he took through Latin America with a cousin that took them through Chile and Peru, and eventually to Venezuela. During that trip Guevara came to believe that a social revolution was the only means by which ordinary Latin American people could achieve a just share of economic development.

In 1953, a year after his trip and after he had completed his medical studies, Guevara went to Guatemala, where a reformist government under President Jacobo Arbenz was trying to broaden ownership of land. A land-reform policy was bound to antagonize the United Fruit Company, a major US corporation, which was Guatemala's largest landowner. The company's own accounting and management policies made it vulnerable to Arbenz's law reforms, and consequently it appealed to its stockholders to help, including the US secretary of state, John Foster Dulles. The American Central Intelligence Agency organized Arbenz's opponents and he was effectively toppled in a coup. Guevara, who had been working as a medic, joined a militia that was in support of Arbenz, but Arbenz instructed his foreign supporters to leave the country and Guevara took refuge in the Argentinian Embassy.

Cuba

Arbenz's regime had attracted support from radicals throughout Latin America, and the contacts Guevara made with them led him to a Cuban revolutionary group in Mexico. In July 1955, Guevara met Fidel Castro, living in exile in Mexico City. Guevara offered to help make a revolution in Cuba and began receiving military training.

Guevara landed in Cuba together with Castro's little band in November 1956; he was one of the lucky handful who survived their first contacts with the Cuban army and reached the Sierra Maestra. Although Guevara set out intending to be a doctor to the guerrillas, in fact he soon revealed himself to be a natural soldier, and was

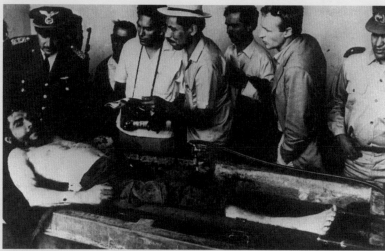

The body of Che Guevara, displayed after his execution. He had possibly expected to be imprisoned and exchanged or ransomed by the Castro regime. Instead, by American request, he was shot.

Time magazine put Che Guevara on the cover of their issue dated 8 August 1960, representing him as a key figure in international Communism.

awarded the title Commandante for his leadership in the field. Guevara's tactical abilities were demonstrated at the Battle of Las Mercedes in July 1958 when he attacked a column of troops reinforcing the Cubans engaged with Castro's force, and rescued Castro from disaster. Guevara also skilfully brought the 8a Columna to the Escambray Mountains and opened a new front against the Batista regime. The Battle of Santa Clara in December 1958 utilized the mobility of a guerrilla force to attack from several directions, although by this stage Guevara was possibly fortunate that the Cuban army seemed to be losing heart for the battle.

With Castro's triumph in January 1959, Guevara established the labour camp system which was used to confine political enemies, as well as supervising a number of executions. Guevara also began offering help to revolutionary movements in other Latin American countries. Castro and Guevara gave support to an attempt by Panamanian revolutionaries in April 1959 that they were eventually forced to disown when the Organization of American States revealed the extent of Cuban support. Another attempt to export the Cuban revolution, a sponsored invasion of the Dominican

Republic by Dominican exiles and leftists, similarly ended in total failure.

Global ambition

For Guevara, the Cuban model for revolutionary war was the one to be followed in other Latin American states. The failures in the Dominican Republic and in Panama did not limit his or Castro's ambition, and with Cuban assistance, groups of guerrillas were infiltrated into Colombia, Peru, Venezuela, Argentina and Nicaragua. Guevara had developed a theoretical basis for guerrilla warfare, believing that an active guerrilla force fighting a dictatorial regime – a *foco* – would in itself attract recruits and widen the basis for an insurrection.

Guevara's developing political thinking directed the next step in his military career. In February 1965, he spoke to a meeting on Afro-Asian solidarity in Algiers, in which he made it clear that to him the struggle

> After recovering his health and brooding over his situation, Guevara decided to establish a *foco* in Bolivia, believing that the United States would be uninterested in this land-locked Andean state.

was no longer one of capitalism against socialism, but the undeveloped world against the developed one. Castro and Guevara believed Africa was the weak link in the global system and Guevara went to organize a revolution in the Congo.

Guevara's Congo experience was depressing. The Congolese forces he joined, initially with Laurent Kabila, were disorganized and disunited by different factions, with the leadership unwilling to make sacrifices in the lifestyle they aspired to. Nor were many in the Congo willing to fight a revolutionary war. After seven months, Guevara left, suffering from dysentery and asthma.

Bolivian dead end

After recovering his health and brooding over his situation, Guevara decided to establish a *foco* in Bolivia, believing that the United States would be uninterested in this landlocked Andean state, the borders of which touched five Latin American countries. He arrived

in the autumn of 1966 and established a camp on land his confederates had bought in the Bolivian jungles. Bolivian communists greeted his arrival almost with open hostility, since neither they nor their Soviet masters believed the country was in any position to attempt a revolutionary insurrection. Perhaps unwittingly, perhaps intentionally, a former agent of the German police allowed a notebook containing complete details of Guevara's urban network of support in La Paz to fall into police hands.

The actual fighting began on 23 March when guerrillas ambushed a Bolivian army patrol. Things went well for Guevara throughout April, but in July the tide of battle began to turn as the Bolivian army defeated the guerrillas in a couple of skirmishes, and by August Guevara and his men were isolated and on the run. In October, Bolivian Rangers located their position and Guevara was captured after a firefight that left most of his men dead. He was executed the next day, officially on the orders of Bolivia's president René Barrientos.

Guevara speaks with a Cuban guerrilla during the Santa Clara campaign in front of a captured tank.

❧ On 30 November 1967, British armed forces withdrew from the South Arabian region of southern Yemen, after four years of terrorism and political agitation against their presence. Trouble had started in December 1963, after a grenade attack on the British High Commissioner, following the merger of Aden into the Federation of South Arabia. A guerrilla war began from bases in the hilly region known as the Radfan, while a state of emergency was declared in the city of Aden. In 1964, the British government announced their intention of granting the Federation independence in 1968, and in 1966 that they would withdraw all their military forces at independence. Mass rioting in early 1967 was followed by a mutiny among the South Yemen army in June that year. The British pulled out early and South Yemen came under control of the guerrillas.

❧ A small-scale guerrilla war between Indonesia and Britain, Australia, New Zealand and Malaysia was declared ended at a conference in Bangkok on 28 May 1966. The Confrontation was President Sukarno's attempt to prevent several British-controlled states on the north of Borneo island – Sarawak, Sabah, and Brunei – from joining the Federation of Malaysia. Indonesian volunteers crossed the border into these areas and raided villages, targeting the garrisons installed by the British. The British, with Australian and New Zealand assistance, countered with cross-border raids of their own.

Superpowers in shooting war

China and the Soviet Union fought a series of skirmishes along their common border that provoked global fears of a nuclear war, until talks opened on 20 October 1969 in the Chinese capital Peking to resolve the dispute.

The fighting occurred at various points along the border in Manchuria and in Xinjiang, but the worst fighting came at Demansk island (Zhen Bao to the Chinese) on the Ussuri river in Manchuria. On the night of 1/2 March 1969, between 200 and 300 Chinese soldiers camped on the island. The Soviet Army kept two outposts on Damansky island, and when word reached one of them its commander, Lieutenant Ivan Strelnikov, took out a patrol to investigate. They found the Chinese waiting for them.

When Strelnikov and his men attempted to disperse them, the Chinese opened fire, both in front and from enfilade positions on the flank. Strelnikov and 24 of his men were killed in the exchange. The firing had attracted the attention of the Soviet Army soldiers at their other outpost and they came to support their comrades, eventually chasing the Chinese off the island.

Soviet forces then built up their strength along their border, moving in tanks and artillery. On 15 March, in a second engagement, the Soviet Army used its multi-barrelled rocket launchers against the Chinese, which included targeting reserve and logistic units on Chinese soil, causing heavy casualties estimated by the Soviets at 800 dead.

"Football War" erupts in Central America

A brief war between El Salvador and Honduras ended in a ceasefire negotiated by the Organization of American States that came into effect on 20 July 1969. Although the conflict was triggered by a football match, tension between the two countries had in fact been intense for some time owing to large numbers of migrant Salvadoran workers being expelled from Honduras. Fighting began on 14 July, with an attack by Salvadoran military forces on Honduras. The Salvadorans occupied parts of Honduras before fuel shortages, caused in part by a Honduran air attack on the country's only refinery, prevented the Salvadoran army from continuing a major offensive.

A Honduran patrol finds the bodies of two Salvadoran soldiers killed during a skirmish on 18 July 1969.

IN BRIEF

◈ The 82 surviving crew members of the USS *Pueblo* were released across the demilitarized zone separating North and South Korea on 23 December 1968. On 23 January North Korean warships had challenged and boarded the US intelligence-gathering ship and detained its crew. The men were subsequently kept in prison camps in poor conditions that included beatings. The North Koreans claimed the ship was in their territorial waters, while the Americans asserted the vessel was in international waters.

OBITUARY

DWIGHT EISENHOWER
(1890–1969)

Dwight Eisenhower, general and president, died on 28 March 1969 of heart failure. He was 78.

Eisenhower's father, an engineer, was working in Texas when he was born on 14 October 1890. He attended West Point and graduated in 1915, but missed action during the First World War. When he was selected to be commander of US forces in the European theatre in 1942, therefore, he had never been a combat commander, having served mainly in staff appointments. Working with his British counterparts in preparations for Operation Torch, he displayed a deft ability to negotiate diplomatic situations that resulted in his appointment as supreme commander of the Allied Expeditionary Force in 1944, for the invasion of France.

During Operation Overlord and the subsequent fighting in France and Germany, Eisenhower ably defused many crises resulting from the natural competitive rivalry of commanders in British, American and French units. His "broad front" advance across France and into Germany does not appear particularly imaginative, but he was a shrewd calculator of logistical problems in modern war and it is consequently difficult to find fault with any of his strategic decisions in the circumstances.

Elected in 1952, his presidency from January 1953 to January 1961 was low-key in many respects, but he ended the Korean War, persevered in resisting the Soviet Union, established American influence in the Middle East and, at its end, warned Americans of the malign influence of a "military-industrial complex".

He is survived by his wife and one son.

Nigeria crushes rebellion

The attempt by the Eastern Region of Nigeria to establish itself as the independent state of Biafra ended in failure as the Biafran army surrendered on 12 January 1970. The people of the Eastern Region are predominantly Ibo, and the war tested the idea whether post-colonial African states could survive borders that did not reflect the pre-colonial ethnic divisions in Africa.

Nigeria had experienced political unrest since 1964 when the second military coup in its history supplanted a predominantly Ibo regime in July 1966. The new regime was dominated by northerners and westerners, and many in the Eastern Region, which contained most of the oilfields of Nigeria, felt they were not getting a fair share of the wealth generated by the oil. When Lieutenant-Colonel Odumegwu Ojukwu proclaimed himself head of state of an independent Biafra on 7 June 1967, the

Nigerian army advanced into Biafra to suppress the rebellion, expecting a relatively easy victory. The Biafrans, however, were led by former Nigerian army officers. Having some idea of their plans, the Biafran army was easily able to counter the Nigerian manoeuvres and followed this up with an invasion of the Mid-western Region, aiming at the capital, Lagos. The Biafran attack delayed the Nigerians, but although it was slow, the Nigerian advance was impossible to stop. The Biafran capital, Enugu, fell in October 1967, but the war dragged on for another two years as the Nigerians were unable to resupply their troops effectively or sustain anything other than short offensives. The Biafrans had few allies in the world, while the Nigerians were supported by both Britain and the Soviet Union.

The war was noted for the effects of a blockade, causing widespread starvation and death among Biafrans.

IN BRIEF

❧ A ceasefire between Egypt and Israel sponsored by the United States of America came into effect on 7 August 1970, ending a short, limited conflict between the two countries that had opened in June 1969 when Egyptian president Gamal Nasser proclaimed a "war of attrition" along the Suez Canal. Egypt and Israel traded artillery bombardments and commando raids. Israeli also launched number of deep-penetration air raids that included a clash with Soviet pilots on 18 April 1970 near Cairo.

Biafran soldiers use commandeered tugboats during the The Biafran War. The war became a long, drawn-out conflict owning to inefficiencies in the ability of the Nigerian army to supply its offensive.

Black September for Palestinian cause

An agreement between the leader of the Palestinian Liberation Organization, Yassir Arafat, and King Hussein of Jordan was signed on 13 October 1970, bringing to an end the conflict known as Black September. Palestinian refugees in Jordan had begun a sustained campaign of guerrilla raids into Israel and the occupied West Bank after the end of the 1967 war. The presence of a large body of armed men not under Jordanian authority, together with Israeli counter-raids, alarmed King Hussein, and sporadic fighting between his supporters and the PLO during the first half of 1970 raised tension considerably. Hussein's opening of negotiations with Israel in the summer

On 17 September King Hussein launched attacks on Palestinian camps and a full-scale civil war broke out in Jordan.

of 1970 was followed by a campaign of hijackings by radical Palestinians, which he interpreted as a direct challenge to his authority. On 17 September he launched attacks on Palestinian camps and a full-scale civil war broke out in Jordan. When Syrian troops tried to intervene with tanks, a battle along the border resulted in heavy losses to the Syrians. Although the PLO had a large force in Jordan, they lacked the heavy equipment and artillery of the Jordanian army and in the end Arafat sued for peace.

An aircraft burns on Dawson Field in the Jordanian desert after its hijacking and bombing by members of the PLO. While the aircraft was destroyed, the hostages were released.

OBITUARY
WILLIAM SLIM
(1891-1970)

Field Marshal William Slim, commander of the British imperial army in Burma in 1943-45, and subsequently Chief of the Imperial General Staff at the time of the Korean War, died on 14 December 1970.

Slim came relatively late to an army career, having been a teacher and a clerk before receiving a commission in the Royal Warwickshire Regiment during the First World War. He saw action at Gallipoli and in Mesopotamia. He transferred to the British Indian army in 1919, where he remained until 1948.

During the Second World War, Slim demonstrated an ability to adapt to his environment and the capabilities of his troops, highly unusual for a British general of his generation. He made extensive use of air resupply operations, rather than rely on difficult routes through the jungles of Burma and India. He also recognized that his troops were more effective in defence than attack, and developed a system of "boxes" that enabled them to withstand Japanese attacks. His triumphant liberation of Burma showed a mastery of logistics the envy of any commander.

He is survived by his wife, a son and a daughter.

The Yom Kippur War

The Arab states of Egypt and Syria suffered another defeat in another war with Israel, in spite of early successes and the deployment of anti-tank guided missiles in large numbers.

An Egyptian soldier brandishes a portrait of President Anwar el-Sadat, the former army officer who took his country to war against Israel in 1973.

The governments of Egypt and Syria had responded to the defeat of their armies in 1967 by a substantial program of re-equipment and training. Both the new equipment and the instruction came from the Soviet Union, the latter reflecting Soviet tactical ideas and experience. During 1972, the Egyptian president, Anwar el-Sadat, made it very plain both to his people, to his government and to the world that he intended to go to war with Israel in order to recover Sinai and the Gaza Strip, which Israel had occupied in 1967, to the extent of being willing "to sacrifice one million soldiers". He found a willing partner in the military ruler of Syria, Hafez Assad, who had his own ideas about making Syria the dominant power in the Arab world, and recovering the Israeli-occupied Golan Heights.

Since 1967, the Israelis had relied on being able to launch a pre-emptive attack of their own, in case of a planned Arab offensive, a kind of policy that depends on accurate assessments of the enemy plans. As the Egyptians and Syrians made their preparations for an attack, however, Israeli intelligence crucially misinterpreted key signs of what was coming. Most importantly, the Israelis expected the Egyptian air force to receive a major reinforcement from the Soviet Union in the shape of new fighter-bombers that would be able to attack Israeli tank formations. As long as these were not delivered, the Israelis were confident that they still had time to prepare for an attack. However, as the religiously important Yom Kippur holiday in October approached, activity on both the Syrian and Egyptian fronts increased, indicating that some kind of military operation was in preparation.

Slow to mobilize

The Arab leaders chose Yom Kippur because of the effect the commemoration of this holy day has on Israeli society. Almost all Jews, whether orthodox or liberal, retreat into their homes on this day, and keep to themselves and their prayers, even to the point of not using electricity; radio stations go off the air. An attack at this point would provide additional time for offensive operations against an only partially mobilized enemy. The Israeli armed forces would find it much harder to contact reservists not already called up, which made the failure of Israeli intelligence to make an accurate forecast of enemy intentions at this time all the more disastrous.

The Egyptian attack across the Suez Canal achieved notable success. Preceded by a supporting barrage of 2,000 guns, the attacking units breached the earthen rampart erected by the Israelis and isolated many strongpoints, while other elements of this first echelon pushed forward to establish a screen of anti-tank missiles. After infantry

An Israeli Centurion tank passes a supply dump in the Sinai Desert. The British-designed tank was the mainstay of the Israeli army's armoured forces during the Six Day and Yom Kippur Wars.

An Israeli jeep drives past a wrecked Syrian tank during the fighting on the Golan Heights. The Syrians faced a harder task than the Egyptian army, since the Israeli Defence Force was fighting very close to key population centres in Israel, and had to defeat Syrian attacks near the border.

and engineers had secured the bridgeheads, massive numbers of tanks began to cross the Canal and fan out to counter the expected Israeli counter-attack. By the end of the first 24 hours of operations, the Egyptians had made the largest single-day crossing of a defended water obstacle in military history – 100,000 troops, 1,000 tanks and over 10,000 other vehicles.

Israeli defence

On the Golan front, the Syrians preceded their own offensive with a heavy air attack, followed by a barrage similar to that used by the Egyptians. They achieved far less success than the Egyptians mainly because the strategic situation demanded that the Israelis defend this line in strength since once breached there was no possibility of trading space for time, as in the Sinai. The only major territorial success for the Syrians came around Mount Hermon, near the border with Lebanon, where they captured an important observation post. Nevertheless, the Syrians decimated two Israeli armoured brigades in the fighting and the Israeli high command believed the Golan front had been stretched to breaking point. Reserve units at platoon level were rushed there as soon as they were available, regardless of whether their higher formation headquarters had

formed. The main strength of the Israeli Air Force was concentrated on the Golan, where it suffered heavy losses from the Syrian air defence network.

Had the Syrians not halted on 7 October,

> By the end of the first 24 hours of operations, the Egyptians had made the largest single-day crossing of a defended water obstacle in military history – 100,000 troops, 1,000 tanks and over 10,000 other vehicles.

they might well have breached the Israeli line. However, their objectives having been reached, like the Egyptians, they shifted to the defensive. On both fronts the Israelis attacked the waiting Arab forces. In the Sinai, anti-tank missiles drove off the Israeli tanks with heavy losses. In the Golan, however, the Israelis first mastered the Syrian air defence screen by flying at low level, and then resumed their traditionally highly effective co-ordinated ground and air attacks. By 11 October, the Syrians were under serious pressure, having been driven back into Syria;

with Damascus under air and artillery attack, the Israelis halted their major offensive on this front and switched their main effort to the Sinai.

Tank battle

Here, the Egyptians resumed offensive operations to relieve pressure on their Syrian allies. On 14 October, the largest tank battle since the Second World War occurred as Egyptian forces attempted to capture the Mitla, Giddi and Khatmia passes. The Egyptians had by now moved beyond the range of their anti-aircraft defences and suffered heavy armoured losses before they were halted. It was now the Israelis' turn.

The Israelis attacked a gap between the Egyptian Second and Third armies, drove to the canal and established a bridgehead on the west bank. A diversionary attack resulted in an Israeli paratroop brigade being in an area known as Chinese Farm where the epic battle of the war was fought. Two days of fighting followed before the Israelis finally established a secure front incorporating Chinese Farm. Israeli armoured divisions on the west bank of the Canal now swept west and south, cutting the Egyptian Third Army off, and even reached Suez city by the time a United Nations' ceasefire took effect on 24 October.

War spawns new nation

The new state of Bangladesh came into being following the signing of a ceasefire on 17 December 1971 between India and Pakistan, following their third conflict since 1945. Unlike the previous two conflicts, the decisive theatre was in the east.

Pakistan incorporated the predominantly Moslem areas of the former British Indian Empire, and as such was divided between the area along the banks of the Indus river (West Pakistan) and the Moslem areas of Bengal (East Pakistan). When an East Pakistani party, the Awami League,

secured a majority of seats in the parliamentary election, the country's dictator, a West Pakistani general, Yahya Khan, suspended parliament. Riots in East Pakistan followed, and on 25 March, a campaign of repression was launched there by the security forces. Millions of East Pakistanis fled to India as refugees, while the Awami League proclaimed the independence of East Pakistan as the state of Bangladesh.

The Indian government lent some support to the Bangladeshis, including helping them organize a guerrilla army that began raids into East Pakistan.

When Indian artillery began firing in support of the guerrillas in November 1971, Yahya Khan opted for war.

A sudden air attack on 3 December 1971 by Pakistani aircraft initiated the conflict. This did not achieve the success the Pakistanis hoped for, and the Indian army launched a swift offensive into East Pakistan that forced the capitulation of Pakistani defenders by 16 December.

On the western front, Indian and Pakistani armoured forces clashed on the traditional battlefields near Chhamb and Sialkot, but both sides were cautious and neither achieved a decisive breakthrough.

Pakistani soldiers armed with a bazooka rifle in position to resist the attack of the Indian army in East Pakistan in December 1971. The third war in 25 years between the two was more decisive than its predecessors, as East Pakistan became the independent state of Bangladesh.

IN BRIEF

A British soldier, Gunner Robert Curtis, was shot dead by a member of the Provisional Irish Republican Army on 6 February 1971, the first British military fatality in Ireland since the end of the Anglo-Irish war in 1922. British soldiers began patrolling the streets of towns and cities in Northern Ireland following ferocious sectarian rioting in Belfast and elsewhere during the summer of 1969. The Provisional IRA was formed in January 1970 after a split in the Irish Republican Army; hitherto its armed actions had been largely directed against Northern Irish police and Protestant rioters.

British soldiers confront a crowd in Northern Ireland in August 1969. The army was ordered to protect Catholics, and ensure that Northern Ireland remained part of the UK.

On 14 August 1974, Turkish troops occupied just over a third of the island of Cyprus, an island with a minority Turkish population, following political turmoil on the island. The original Turkish landings had been made on 20 July 1974, around the town of Kyrenia. A ceasefire went into effect two days later, followed by inconclusive talks broken by the renewed Turkish advance.

OBITUARY

GEORGI ZHUKOV
(1896–1974)

Marshal of the Soviet Union Georgi Zhukov, the leading commander of the Red Army during the Second World War, died on 18 June 1974.

Zhukov was born into a peasant family and became a war hero during the First World War, serving with the cavalry. During the civil war following the Bolshevik Revolution in November 1917, Zhukov became a member of the First Cavalry Army, which was closely associated with Josef Stalin. Zhukov's successful career was in part a consequence of belonging to the "Konarmiya Clique", which also included Marshals Kulik, Timoshenko, Voroshilov, Budenny, and several other leading Red Army officers – one reason why Zhukov escaped Stalin's purges of the army during the 1930s.

During the Second World War, Zhukov was Stalin's favourite man for dealing with a crisis, after winning the battle outside Moscow in November 1941. He played an important role in first breaking, and then relieving, the lengthy siege of Leningrad, as well as preparing the Red Army defences that halted the powerful German tank thrusts at Kursk. He also played a prominent role in the Soviet counter-offensives, and eventually secured the honour of capturing central Berlin. However, his victories often came at a heavy cost as he was indifferent to casualties so long as the objective was reached.

America's first defeat

The story of America's war in Vietnam is one of a battle of wills between two nations, the one with the stronger will paying a very heavy price to secure its existence.

American Air Cavalry move out from a landing zone in Vietnam. The 1st Air Cavalry Division was the first unit to fight a major battle in Vietnam against North Vietnamese regulars.

The **direct involvement** of US military forces in Indochina began following the inauguration of President John F. Kennedy in January 1961. Kennedy wanted to fight the war cheaply, using counter-insurgency special forces directing the effort of Vietnamese troops. Unfortunately, he was backing the regime of Ngo Dinh Diem, a ruthless mandarin who had already toppled his patron, the former French puppet emperor, Bao Dai.

Assassinations

Apart from the Viet Cong, the guerrillas assisted by the communists in North Vietnam, Diem had plenty of enemies at home. Many resented his intensely personal rule and his meddling in military affairs. He did not want a large American force in South Vietnam, but Kennedy's own advisors sought to increase the American commitment to send a public signal to the world that the advance of communism would be resisted everywhere.

American deployments to Vietnam increased rapidly during 1962. As these forces grew, however, the Vietnamese came to rely on American warplanes and artillery to fight their battles. This, together with the political corruption of Diem's regime, led middle-ranking American advisors to conclude that the South Vietnamese would not win the war. American officials at higher levels, however, identified Diem as the problem, and organized a coup to depose him on 1 November 1963, during which Diem was killed. But it was the assassination of Kennedy on 22 November 1963 that really changed the American approach to Vietnam. Kennedy's successor, Lyndon Johnson, who had been committed to the war even before he became president, told the generals he would expand the war using American troops to fight in place of the Vietnamese, delaying only until after he had secured re-election in November 1964.

Meanwhile, the North Vietnamese leadership began making preparations of their own to intensify the struggle. Starting in November 1963, the Ho Chi Minh Trail, a network of jungle tracks that stretched from North Vietnam through Laos and Cambodia, was greatly developed. Parts were turned into roadways suitable for trucks and heavy vehicles, while underground facilities that offered protection against bombing were constructed, including supply depots, extensive barrack accommodation and workshops.

Escalation

Clashes in the Gulf of Tonkin in August 1964 between American warships supporting South Vietnamese raids on North Vietnam led to the US Congress authorizing American action against the North Vietnamese. Johnson launched a bombing campaign against North Vietnam, called Operation Rolling Thunder, after the Viet Cong attacked an American base

American Marines advance up the outer wall of the citadel at Hue during the Tet offensive in February 1968. The battle for Hue lasted 26 days, and was one of the most intense of the war.

American troops engage North Vietnamese forces in forested terrain. The key sector in the war lay in the Central Highlands of South Vietnam, an area of forest and jungle from which the North Vietnamese could threaten the key coastal highway running the length of South Vietnam.

in February 1965. In March, he sent Marines to protect the airfield at Da Nang, South Vietnam, and on 28 July, Johnson announced a massive expansion of the American ground forces. When the American 1st Cavalry (Airmobile) Division began operations in the Ia Drang Valley in October, a large-scale ground war between North Vietnam and the United States was under way.

The fighting in the Ia Drang, especially the battle for Landing Zone X-Ray in mid-November, established the pattern of the war, as a large airmobile force of American troops fought a four-day battle with North Vietnamese regulars. The North Vietnamese rushed the American position repeatedly, trying to get so close to the Americans that their superiority in firepower delivered from the air or by artillery would be negated for fear of hitting their own positions. (The tactic was described as "getting between the enemy and his belt".) It was the only answer the North Vietnamese had to American firepower, and resulted in heavy casualties. However, the American weakness throughout the war was also illustrated here, as they could never secure the initiative from the enemy who would simply break off a battle that was not going their way. American forces could never successfully pin the North Vietnamese long enough to inflict a major defeat on them.

Body counts
In 1966 and 1967, the American commander in Vietnam, General William Westmoreland, used his forces in "search and destroy"

operations, with units being sent out to drive the enemy out of areas deemed important. The Vietnamese usually evaded them, sometimes with serious losses. On 30 January 1968, the Vietnamese attacked across the country, including suicide assaults on the American embassy and a radio station in Saigon. Most critically, they battled for the old Vietnamese imperial capital Hue, shooting 3,000 civilians after they had captured the city, which they held grimly until defeated by American Marines and South Vietnamese forces on 24 February. Although the warning signs of the attack were clear, the American leaders preferred to focus on the siege of Khe Sanh, which began ten days before the Tet Offensive and lasted until 8 April. After Tet, the American political leadership in Washington suffered a crisis of morale. With the American high command demanding more troops, including reservists, in order to cover other American military commitments in Europe and elsewhere, the war was dividing the country sharply into pro- and anti-war camps. At a meeting on 25 March, leading American political figures asked Johnson to find a way out of the war. Instead, Johnson announced on 31 March that he would not seek re-election.

Johnson's successor, Richard Nixon, started with the advantage that on 5 April 1968, North Vietnamese leaders declared their willingness to negotiate. The talks began under Johnson, on 10 May 1968, but there was no common ground. The North Vietnamese refused to withdraw their troops unless Viet

Cong representatives entered the South Vietnamese government. Nixon responded by expanding the war to Cambodia, where the North Vietnamese kept key supply bases, first by bombing and then, in April/May 1970, by a major invasion. In the meantime, fighting continued to rage fiercely in Vietnam itself, notably at the Battle of Hamburger Hill in May 1969 (more Americans were killed in action after Tet than before). But Nixon's plan was to "Vietnamize" the war by reducing the number of American soldiers, and giving a more prominent role to South Vietnamese troops. The failure of their Lam Son 719 operation in February 1971, a raid against North Vietnamese bases in Laos, merely confirmed what American military men had already known in Kennedy's time.

Peace talks
Thanks to American airpower, the South Vietnamese withstood a North Vietnamese offensive in March/April 1972, but by this stage, the decisive battles of the war were being fought between negotiating teams in Paris. When the two sides seemed near a deal in December, the North Vietnamese broke off the talks. Nixon responded with a heavy bombing campaign of the north, which he called Linebacker II. Talks resumed on 8 January 1973, and a ceasefire between the United States and North Vietnam was signed on 27 January 1973.

An American Marine watchfully observes from behind a wall for signs of enemy movement.

Saigon falls, Vietnam united

Saigon, the capital of South Vietnam, was captured by the North Vietnamese on 30 April 1975, with American diplomatic staff making a hurried escape by helicopter from the roof of their embassy. It was the culmination of a two-month campaign that finally reunited North and South Vietnam after 20 years.

The North Vietnamese leaders had concluded that a two-year campaign would bring them control of the south by 1976. In December 1974, they attacked in the relatively unimportant province of Phuoc Long. The ease with which it fell and the lack of any American interest led them to a much larger operation in March 1975, which was intended to capture Ban Me Thuot, a key position from which a further advance could cut South Vietnam in two. Ban Me Thuot fell in two days, partly because the North Vietnamese deployed tanks, but also because the South Vietnamese experienced a shortage of ammunition.

On 20 March, the South Vietnamese

Vietnamese soldiers ride a tank in to Saigon on 30 April 1975, bringing an end to a 30-year war for a united, independent Vietnam.

head of state made a fatal error when he ordered the army to evacuate their positions in the Central Highlands to regroup on the coast and continue the struggle from there. However, the South Vietnamese had never planned for this and the retreat turned into a mad dash for the coast which hundreds of thousands of civilians joined in, resulting in chaos. General Van Tien Dung, North Vietnamese commander-in-chief, saw his opportunity and quickly broadened his offensive, swinging north as well as harassing the retreating South Vietnamese. From then on, effective resistance against the North Vietnamese was impossible as South Vietnamese soldiers expected to retreat if put under pressure, and did so as soon as attacked.

The advance to Saigon and the coast was little more than a procession by the North Vietnamese, preceded by an unruly mob of refugees, mostly those associated with the South Vietnamese regime. The only American involvement was to evacuate its own people and those South Vietnamese whom the United States sought to protect.

South Africans, Cubans clash in Angola

A South African military force withdrew from Angola in January 1976 after a six-month sojourn in that newly independent country, which had

Cuban soldiers fought for the Marxist MPLA faction in the Angolan Civil War, helping defeat the anti-communist FNLA and UNITA.

embarked on a civil war between the rival factions that had fought for independence.

The MPLA (Popular Movement for the Liberation of Angola), the FNLA (National Front for the Liberation of Angola) and UNITA (Union for the Total Independence of Angola) had fought the Portuguese colonial regime since 1962, until a coup in Lisbon in April 1974 unseated the government. Radical army officers willing to grant Angola independence came to power, but the three movements began fighting in March 1975 rather than wait for elections. The MPLA had the advantage of a central position, while the FNLA was based in the north and UNITA in the south. Cuba offered help to the MPLA, which was gladly accepted. Meanwhile, the South Africans had independently offered to help UNITA, who also accepted. South Africa moved a column of armoured cars into Angola from Namibia on 13 October 1975, as the MPLA shifted its army to fight UNITA, after the FNLA was defeated. Cubans and South Africans clashed about 120 miles (193 km) south of the capital,

Soldiers of the FNLA raise their rifles during their advance into Angola from their bases in Zaire in the first months of 1975.

Luanda, in mid-December 1975. When the South Africans failed to break through the larger Cuban forces, they halted, before deciding to withdraw rather than continue an expensive war in a country they had no hope of securing.

IN BRIEF

⁂ In April 1976, a small guerrilla war in the Dhofar, the westernmost region of the Sultanate of Oman, drew to a close. The war had begun in 1965, as Dhofaris demanded greater development of their region. Never large, the insurrection was propped up by neighbouring South Yemen during the 1970s, during which the Sultan deployed a British-led force drawing its troops from Oman, Iran, Pakistan and Jordan, as well as Britain. The SAS fought several important skirmishes in the war.

⁂ On 4 July 1976, Israeli paratroopers succeeded in rescuing most of the hostages from a hijacked Air France airliner that had been flown to Entebbe, Uganda. The operation involved a 2,000-mile (3,200 km) flight from Israel, using three C-130 cargo planes and several airliners.

Lebanon torn in pieces

A **war between communities** in the Lebanon was finally halted when a ceasefire was agreed between the Palestinian Liberation Organization and Syria on 16 October 1976. The conflict had begun on 13 April 1975 in a dispute between a Palestinian fighter and a Christian Lebanese militiaman in Beirut, which was followed by an attack on a local church in which three Christian militiamen, known as Phalangists, were killed. This in turn was avenged by the ambush of a Palestinian bus and the death of 27 Palestinians. Fighting in Beirut then became widespread.

The arrival of numerous Palestinians in the Lebanon following their eviction from Jordan in the aftermath of the war in September 1970, increased tensions in a country where a plurality of Sunni Moslems accepted minority Christian control over portions of the government. However, in the spring of 1975, Lebanese Moslems joined to support the Palestinians against the Phalange, and fighting persisted throughout the summer of 1975, in company with lengthy political negotiations. The murder of four Christians on 6 December, however, elevated the conflict to a new level.

Christian militiamen now set up roadblocks and murdered any Palestinians or Moslems they caught. Once word spread throughout Beirut, tit-for-tat murders became widespread and hundreds died. In January 1976, full-scale war in the Lebanon broke out, with bombardments and sieges of Palestinian camps in east Beirut and Christian towns such as Damour. In March, Moslem Lebanese military forces launched a widespread attack on Christians throughout the country. The ensuing disorder provoked the intervention of its neighbour, Syria, which preferred a stable regime for fear of an Israeli invasion. In April, the Syrian army entered the Lebanon, and in June began attacking the PLO, which Syrian President Hafez Assad blamed for the Lebanese conflict. The country was now effectively partitioned, with over 60,000 Lebanese and Palestinians having died in the 19-month conflict.

An armoured car crewed by soldiers of the Lebanese army patrols the streets of Beirut in late 1975. The Lebanese army generally fought on behalf of the constitutional government.

Israel invades the Lebanon

An **Israeli military** force, which had launched an invasion against PLO camps in southern Lebanon on 14 March 1978, withdrew on 13 June. The Israelis attacked after a group of Palestinian commandos had hijacked an Israeli bus and engaged in a running gun battle with security forces on 11 March. Sending a force of three brigades on a broad front into southern Lebanon, the Israelis drove Palestinians out of camps within 6 miles (10 km) of the border. They also reinforced the position of the Lebanese Christian South Lebanon Army, supplying it with weapons. The SLA had come under increasing pressure from Palestinians, who occupied several Christian strongpoints because of their useful location for bombarding Israeli communities across the border. The actual fighting lasted about seven days.

Israeli tanks withdraw from southern Lebanon in June 1978 after a limited invasion of that country resulted in the creation of the United Nations' Force in Lebanon (UNIFIL).

French Foreign Legion, Belgians parachute into Zaire

French Foreign Legion paratroopers near Kolwezi in Shaba province, Zaire. They were trying to protect European workers threatened by the invasion of the province by secessionist fighters.

French and Belgian paratroops completed their mission of chasing rebels in Zaire's Shaba Province back to their bases in Angola on 21 May 1978. The rebels had briefly invaded the province in 1977 and returned on 11 May 1978. In the aftermath of the earlier invasion, the Zairean army engaged in brutal retaliation toward the Lunda tribe who resided in the area. This second incursion saw wholesale execution of any Zairean military or civil official by the rebels, to avenge the judicial murders of the preceding year. However, the rebels went further, after the Zairean army launched a poorly supported parachute drop on 16 May, executing many employees of European mining firms who worked in the province's mines. The majority of these lived in Kolwezi. Once word reached French, Belgian and American diplomats in the Zairean capital of Kinshasa, their respective governments planned some degree of intervention to rescue their nationals. On 19 May, both Belgian and French paratroopers made airborne drops around Kolwezi, but by this stage the rebels had already begun to withdraw and there was little resistance.

IN BRIEF

A Somali soldier takes position in a trench during the short Ogaden War between Somalia and Ethiopia in 1977–78. Somalia occupied the Ogaden region between the two countries, but the Ethiopians drove out its forces.

Somali forces withdrew from the Ogaden region in March 1978, bringing to an end eight months of military conflict between Somalia and Ethiopia over this disputed area. The Somali government had supported guerrillas belonging to the Western Somali Liberation Front (WSLF) since 1974. In July 1977, the Somali army invaded the Ogaden in support of the WSLF, and captured the town of Jigjiga, among others. However, the Somalis could not capture Harar, which was strongly defended by the Ethiopians, supported by Soviet and Cuban forces. In February 1978, an Ethiopian counter-attack drove the Somalis out of most of the Ogaden.

On 18 October 1977, the German anti-terrorist unit, GSG9, rescued 86 hostages held by Palestinian terrorists aboard a Lufthansa passenger plane hijacked to Mogadishu, Somalia. The terrorists demanded the release of a number of members of the German terrorist group, the Red Army Faction, who had been tried and jailed for their crimes. Three hijackers were killed.

The self-appointed president-for-life of Uganda, Idi Amin, left the capital, Kampala, for Libya on 11 April 1979 before the arrival of Tanzanian troops who had invaded the country in support of Ugandan exiles in November 1978. Idi Amin had ruled the country for nine years, having overthrown President Milton Obote, who became the leader of the exiles.

Tanzanian soldiers and tanks advanced into Uganda toward the city of Jinja in April 1979, in support of Ugandan exiles opposed to the dictatorship of Idi Amin.

Three-cornered war in South East Asia

As the monsoon rains reached Cambodia in May 1979, a war involving three of the states in the region came to a pause. A border conflict that began between Cambodia and Vietnam in 1975. Pol Pot, the Cambodian prime minister, had been a key leader in the civil war that brought the Khmer Rouge (Red Cambodian) movement to power in 1975. During 1976, an internal power struggle put Pol Pot in complete control of party and state. Pol Pot's nationalist politics, combined with historic Cambodian claims to parts of South Vietnam, took practical effect in January 1977, when Cambodian soldiers attacked Vietnam. Fighting continued throughout the year, but the Vietnamese made no significant response until September 1977, when they launched an offensive against some of the Cambodians in Vietnam. On 16 December 1977, the Vietnamese began a much larger offensive, driving the invaders back into Cambodia and even crossing the border to attack bases. The Vietnamese then withdrew from Cambodia in early January 1978.

The war continued, as the Cambodians repeatedly launched raids into Vietnam to destroy villages and disrupt the economy. Pol Pot rejected every attempt by the Vietnamese to find a diplomatic solution. The Vietnamese decided to give their support to those Khmer Rouge leaders who had lost out in the factional conflict of 1976. At first, the Vietnamese lent support to those internal rivals who remained, but Pol Pot's army crushed these in the middle of 1978. In December, the Vietnamese launched a large-scale invasion of Cambodia and drove Pol Pot's forces out of Phnom Penh in disorder, establishing a new government under exiles who had to Vietnam.

The Chinese government had made an ally out of Pol Pot's regime and threatened to punish the Hanoi regime. However, this anger owed more to the Peking government's wish to ensure that Vietnam recognized China as the dominant power in East Asia than to its support for Pol Pot. On 17 February 1979, a force of about 100,000 Chinese troops, supported by tanks and artillery but not aircraft, crossed the border and invaded Vietnam. The objective of the Chinese was the capture of the provincial capitals of all Vietnamese provinces bordering China. The Vietnamese held back their regular forces, using a paramilitary militia and border guards to battle the Chinese in hill and jungle terrain that favoured the defender. Through sheer weight of numbers the Chinese reached the vicinity of Cao Bai, Hang Lien Sen, Lai Chou, Quang Ninh and finally Lang Son, where they faced the fiercest resistance of all, although the city eventually fell. On 2 March, the Chinese announced their intention to withdraw, which was accomplished by 16 March, but with further Chinese operations failing, and with heavy casualties, there was no let-up in the fighting in Cambodia.

A Khmer Rouge soldier carries an RPG-7 grenade launcher during the fighting with Vietnam in October 1979.

Pol Pot, the leader of the Khmer Rouge, gives an interview to Western journalists. Pol Pot masterminded both the victorious strategy of the Khmer Rouge and their horrific attempt to remake Cambodian society, resulting in the deaths of two million Cambodians.

Nicaraguan dictator falls

Sandinista militia stands to in a Nicaraguan town. The Sandinista victory in 1979 transformed the hopes of marxist guerrillas in Central America.

A brief national insurrection toppled the 40-year-old dictatorship of the Somoza family in Nicaragua when President Anastasio Somoza Debayle fled Managua on 17 July 1979. The insurrection, which began after Somoza had the opposition leader and newspaper editor Pedro Joaquin Chamorro assassinated in January 1978, developed from an eighteen-year guerrilla war against the Somoza dictatorship, fought by the Frente Sandinista de Liberación Nacional (Sandinista Front for National Liberation). The assassination was followed by a general strike lasting two weeks, and an uprising in the town of Momimbo that required a sizeable military force to suppress it. The Sandinistas began organizing a second uprising that took place in August 1978, but the badly equipped rebels were no match for Somoza's National Guard, who used aircraft to bomb their own people. The Sandinistas now took six months to prepare a major national guerrilla offensive that they unleashed on 29 May 1979. Within a month, the guerrillas had succeeded in isolating and overwhelming National Guard positions across the country.

Rhodesia defeated by African guerrillas

On 12 December 1979 the new British governor general of Rhodesia arrived in the colony's capital, Salisbury, to prepare for the immediate independence of the country with a black African majority rule constitution. For 14 years a white-dominated government had attempted to maintain its independence from Britain.

The white regime had been opposed by two groups of African majority rule guerrillas, the Zimbabwe African National Liberation Army (ZANLA) and the Zimbabwe People's Revolutionary Army (ZIPRA). Both operated from bases in neighbouring countries, attempting to infiltrate into Rhodesia to attack white farms and other economic installations. The war began on 24 April 1966, when a group of seven ZIPRA guerrillas were caught and killed by the Rhodesian security forces. For many years, the guerrilla struggle was ineffective as their movements from bases in Zambia were too easily predicted. However, in 1973, the chance arose to establish bases in the Portuguese colony of Mozambique, which was also subject to an African-rule insurgency. ZANLA moved to Mozambique and the Rhodesian forces now had to defend their borders from attacks on two sides.

The Rhodesian security forces attempted to counter this with more aggressive use of flying columns to enter Mozambique, most notably in the attack on ZANLA's Nyadzonya base in August 1976. Over a thousand guerrillas were killed for the loss of a few wounded, after an armoured column raided the camp.

The effect of sanctions, which severely limited the amount of military supplies available, and the inability of the small Rhodesian army to secure the country's long border, doomed the white regime to defeat.

A Rhodesian army instructor lectures members of the Pfumo ReVahnu ("Spear of the People"), an auxiliary force drawn from the black African population.

The Falklands War

The conflict between Argentina and the United Kingdom over the Falkland/Malvinas islands resembled the Second World War more than the messy guerrilla conflicts that have dominated warfare since 1945.

The explosion of a bomb on HMS *Antelope* on the night of 23 May 1982 destroyed the Royal Navy frigate. The daring raids by Argentine aircraft on the British naval forces in San Carlos Water failed to disrupt the British landings.

On 2 April 1982, Argentine commandos and other forces landed on the Falkland islands and overwhelmed the small British garrison of 80 Royal Marines at Port Stanley. The move had been planned by the Argentine military junta, and also included the landing of a small military force on South Georgia, an island between the Falklands and Antarctica. General Leopoldo Galtieri, the junta chief, believed the action would rescue his regime's popularity, which was falling in the face of economic troubles and dissatisfaction with the lack of human rights and democratic government. Britain also faced severe economic problems and Galtieri gambled that the cost of recovering the islands would be too high for British Prime Minister Margaret Thatcher to tolerate.

Task force

Thatcher herself faced almost the same problems as Galtieri, and the invasion was a heaven-sent opportunity for her to rally support for her government, which was presiding over a massive increase in unemployment. British officers focused on what a deployment of naval, air and land forces could achieve, rather than the difficulties faced, which temperamentally suited Mrs Thatcher, and she agreed to send a task force to the South Atlantic. Ships exercising off the coast of North Africa formed the core of the first wave sent south, while other vessels, carrying Royal Marines and paratroops, departed from British ports. The task force consisted of 2 aircraft carriers, 15 escorting frigates and destroyers, two amphibious assault ships, 43 merchant ships and three submarines. They carried about 7,000 marines and soldiers. Further forces were sent out subsequently. The Argentines deployed about 13,000 soldiers to the Falkland islands, but the bulk of these forces were conscripts and reservists, unlike the professionals making up the British military force.

On 12 April, the British proclaimed a total exclusion zone extending out 200 miles (321 km) from the Falklands. The first British

> On 2 May, the sinking of the aged Argentine cruiser *General Belgrano* by a British nuclear submarine really brought home to both sides the seriousness of the conflict. Some 323 Argentine sailors died in the sinking.

landings occurred on 21 April on South Georgia, which the British believed might convince the Argentines that they were in earnest about fighting for the Falklands, and would encourage them to withdraw. However, bad weather forced the withdrawal of the landing force before any contact was made with the Argentinian garrison. The arrival of an Argentine submarine on 24 April further delayed the British attack, but on 25 April, British helicopters sank the submarine off Grytviken harbour, and British special forces captured the harbour buildings as the Argentine garrison put up no resistance.

Diplomatic disaster
Galtieri had hoped that the British would receive little support from the United States and other countries in this war. He seemed to expect that the United States' involvement would be limited to some kind of diplomatic mediation that would ensure a face-saving settlement for all concerned, and the transfer of the islands to Argentine sovereignty. In fact, the administration of President Ronald Reagan was split into pro- and anti-Argentinian factions, but the top officials were in favour of Britain, and perhaps Reagan's natural inclination was to favour the British. In any case, at the end of April, he declared his full support for Britain, and at this point the whole rationale behind Galtieri's invasion collapsed. Britain had opted to fight and the United States refused to remain neutral.

The British riposte first reached the Falklands on 1 May, when an aged Vulcan bomber conducted the first of what were known as the Black Buck raids, bombing the airfield at Port Stanley. The Vulcan's attack required several mid-air refuelling rendezvous, and was followed up by an attack by Sea Harriers flying from the Task Force's carriers. Vulcan bombers made four further raids on the Argentine occupation force.

The same day as the first Black Buck raid, the Argentine air force itself attacked British ships shelling Argentine positions. The Argentine attack failed to damage any British ships, and they lost two fighters, one in combat with British Sea Harriers, and the other downed by friendly fire when trying to make an emergency landing.

Sink the *Belgrano*
On 2 May, the sinking of the aged Argentine cruiser *General Belgrano* by a British nuclear submarine really brought home to both sides the seriousness of the conflict. Some 323 Argentine sailors died in the sinking, while the event was infamously celebrated by a British newspaper with the headline "Gotcha!". On 4 May, the Argentine air force scored a major victory when it badly damaged the British destroyer HMS *Sheffield* with an Exocet air-to-surface missile.

The first British landings were made at San Carlos Water on 21 May, the littoral area between the two largest islands of the archipelago, which provided a reasonably safe anchorage for the vessels of the Task Force. However, it became something of a bomb alley as it offered Argentine aeroplanes a chance to attack ships that were unable to manoeuvre out of the way. A fierce air battle followed, and three British ships, one of them a merchant transport, were lost in the four days after the landings.

The first land battle of the campaign came at Goose Green on the night of 26/27 May, when British paratroops made a night attack on the Argentine force stationed there. The capture of Goose Green allowed British troops to march across West Falkland from San Carlos Water to Port Stanley, to engage the main Argentine position. On 11 June, the British launched simultaneous attacks on Mount Longdon, Mount Harriet and Two Sisters, heights overlooking Port Stanley. At this point, the British clearly looked likely to win, and the fall of Wireless Ridge and Mount Tumbledown on 13 June led to the fall of Port Stanley on 14 June. British casualties during the war amounted to 1,035 killed and wounded, Argentinian losses to 1,717 killed and wounded.

Argentine PoWs in the streets of Port Stanley after the surrender on 14 June 1982. The majority of Argentine forces in the Falklands were drawn from conscripts.

Iran-Iraq war enters new phase

The Ayatollah Khomeini's call for Moslems across the Islamic world to imitate his revolution in Iran alarmed Arab leaders, who welcomed Saddam Hussein's Iraqi invasion.

An **Iranian offensive** against the Iraqi port of Basra, launched on 13 July 1982, heralded a new phase in the ongoing war between Middle Eastern neighbours Iran and Iraq. Although the Iranians were defeated with heavy losses, the war had been fought entirely in Iran prior to Iraqi leader Saddam Hussein's unilateral ceasefire declared on 10 June, and the subsequent withdrawal of Iraqi forces.

With the tacit support of the United States, Saddam Hussein sought to take advantage of the upheavals brought by the 1979 Iranian Islamic revolution, by seizing parts of Iran bordering on the Shatt-al-Arab, where the Mesopotamian rivers flow into the Persian Gulf. On 22 September 1980, five of Iraq's 12 army divisions crossed the border into the area of south-western Iran known as Khuzestan. The offensive aimed at the capture of the cities of Khorramshahr, Abadan, Dezful and Ahwaz, but moved so slowly against minimal opposition that they could only isolate Dezful and Ahwaz before engaging in a major battle for Khorramshahr. The Iranian army was in disarray in part owing to purges of its officer corps by the theocratic dictatorship of Ayatollah Khomeini. Khomeini sent the paramilitary Pasdaran (Guardians), a parallel army to the regular forces intended to guard the Islamic revolution. Khorramshahr fell on 24 October 1980, after heavy Iraqi losses, and Saddam Hussein chose to blockade Dezful and Ahwaz rather than risk further high casualty rates.

The Iranians attempted several offensives starting in the spring of 1981, but the army failed abysmally and Khomeini directed more resources toward the Pasdaran, even calling up the Basiji, a militia force that received a bare two weeks' military training. In November 1981, these were used in fanatical "human wave" attacks that included children. These achieved some success, the tactic was repeated on several occasions and Khorramshahr was recaptured on 22/23 May 1982. Faced with a war of attrition in Iran, which an Iraq with a population perhaps a third of Iran's was bound to lose, Saddam Hussein opted for his ceasefire in search of peace.

The body of an Iranian soldier lies in the desert, after the defeat of one of their 1982 offensives. Despite heavy casualties, Iran's larger population advantage gave them a long-term advantage over Iraq, forcing Iraqi dictator Saddam Hussein to try for a diplomatic settlement of the war.

A hostage in the Iranian embassy in London creeps along from one balcony to another, during the British Special Air Service's assault that brought the siege to an end on 8 May 1980. The secretive SAS became a media star after this operation.

IN BRIEF

An American attempt to rescue 52 hostages who had been taken prisoner by Iranian students in the US Embassy compound in the Iranian capital of Tehran failed on 24 April 1980 after two helicopters broke down at Desert One, the code name given to an area used as a rendezvous in Iran. The mission involved eight helicopters piloted by Marines, six C-130 aircraft and the Army's Delta Force anti-terrorist Special Operations unit. The helicopters flew from US Navy ships in the Persian Gulf.

Members of the British Special Air Service regiment successfully rescued 19 hostages held by six Iranian terrorists at the Iranian embassy in Prince's Gate, London, on 5 May 1980. Parts of the action were recorded and shown live by British Broadcasting Corporation news cameramen present at the scene.

Israeli aircraft bombed and destroyed a nuclear research reactor near Baghdad, Iraq, on 7 June 1981. The bombing prevented the reactor, named Tammuz by the Iraqis, from going into operation. The Israelis feared the Iraqi research was intended to produce a nuclear weapon.

Two American fighters engaged two Libyan warplanes over the Gulf of Sirte on 19 August 1981, shooting down both. The Libyans had claimed most of the Gulf of Sirte as their territorial waters, but this was not recognized by the US government.

Palestinians withdraw from the Lebanon

An Israeli armoured personnel carrier drives through a Lebanese street in the Bekaa Valley in June 1982. The Israeli invasion of the Lebanon was intended to end the Palestine Liberation Organization's terrorist and guerrilla threats to northern Israel.

The **withdrawal of** the majority of Palestinian fighters from the refugee camps in the Lebanon on 1 September 1982 achieved the key military objective of Operation Peace for Galilee, the Israeli invasion of the Lebanon. Israel, however, suffered a major diplomatic defeat, especially after the massacres of an estimated 2,000 men and women at the refugee camps of Sabra and Chatila, on 16 September, an act carried out by Israel's allies in the Lebanon, the Phalangist militia.

The Israeli invasion began on 4 June 1982 with a series of air raids, following the attempted assassination of the Israeli ambassador in London. Israeli aircraft bombarded Palestinian camps, preceding a three-pronged offensive into the country that began on 6 June, involving two thrusts from northern Israeli and an amphibious landing near the Alawi river.

Peace for Galilee involved the Israelis in a campaign against two opponents:

the Palestinian Liberation Organization (PLO) and its camps scattered around the country; and the Syrian forces that had been stationed in the country since intervening in the civil war in 1976. The war against the Syrians was short and concluded with the signing of a ceasefire on 11 June. The main action was an

attack on an anti-aircraft missile site in the Bekaa Valley on 9 June that saw 17 out of 19 missile batteries knocked out, a model operation that used electronic warfare techniques together with missiles designed to destroy radar installations. The destruction of the strong Syrian anti-aircraft defences opened the way for powerful aerial support for the ground attack against the Syrian army in the Lebanon.

By contrast, the war against the PLO was a long one, the longest fight the Israeli Defence Force had thus far undertaken. This was in part a deliberate decision. The Israelis had little trouble driving north through Palestinian-dominated territory between the border with Israel and the Lebanese capital, Beirut. On 12 June, the Israelis were within sight of Beirut airport. The Israeli defence minister, Ariel Sharon, was unwilling to allow Israeli forces to engage in street fighting in Beirut, and instead laid siege to Beirut, hoping that the population would turn against the PLO and demand the political solution the Israelis wanted. Artillery shells and aerial bombs rained down on Beirut, while the Israeli army stood back. The steady bombardment affected civilians and PLO fighters alike, and a twelve-hour heavy bombardment on 12 August forced the Lebanese government to act. They demanded that Arafat should leave and on 21 August, following his orders, PLO fighters began departing for other Arab countries, such as Tunisia. The Israelis allowed them to go.

1982 ISRAELI INVASION OF LEBANON

DATE:	June–September 1982
COMBATANTS:	Israeli and Lebanese Phalangists vs the Palestinian Liberation Organization and Syria
FORCES ENGAGED:	Israelis and Phalangists, 76,000; PLO and Syrians, 37,000
CASUALTIES:	Israelis and Phalangists, 676; PLO and Syrians, 9,800
RESULT:	Israeli victory

Bloody Guatemala

A Guatemalan peasant receives rough treatment from military forces during the counter-insurgency campaign in this Central American republic.

The government of Guatemala gained the upper hand in a long war against Marxist guerrillas after a brutal military dictator was toppled by a coup on 8 August 1983. When General Efraín Rios Montt came to power in March 1982, the guerrillas were increasingly gaining control over the countryside of this rural country. Rios Montt instituted a policy of "*frijoles y fusiles*" ("beans and rifles" in Spanish), intended to win over the countryside by helping the peasants with handouts, or violently punishing those who preferred the guerrillas. One of the most notorious crimes committed during the policy was the massacre of about 250 Mayans by Guatemalan soldiers at Plan de Sanchez on 18 July 1982. Thousands of Guatemalans, mostly indigenous peoples, were killed until Rios Montt was himself removed from power in 1983 by the army. However, his policy achieved a marked success against the guerrillas, who lost most of the gains they had won since beginning their struggle in 1966.

IN BRIEF

◦§◦ The Goukouni Oueddi regime abandoned the capital of Chad, N'djamena, to the rival faction led by Hisséne Habré on 7 June 1982. Oueddi retreated to northern Chad, while Habré established a stable government with French support. The civil war began in February 1979, and included intervention by the Libyan dictator Muammar Gaddafi.

◦§◦ The island republic of Grenada in the Caribbean was declared secure on 3 November 1983 after an invasion by approximately 6,000 US soldiers and Marines that toppled the country's Marxist regime, and evicted a large number of Cubans who were present on the island constructing an airport. US forces had begun landing on the island from helicopters, by parachute and from the sea on 25 October.

American troops firing a machine gun during the invasion of Grenada in October 1983.

Iranians fail in assaults on Basra

Renewed Iranian attacks intended to capture the Iraqi city of Basra have failed to achieve any significant victories except for the capture of Majnoon island in March 1984. In response, the Iraqi air force launched missile attacks against shipping using Iranian ports, targeting vulnerable oil tankers in particular.

During 1983, the Iranian army began a hit-and-run strategy that attempted to make use of the superior numbers of the Iranian army. Their heaviest attacks came in Iraqi Kurdistan, 400 miles (644 km) north of the main theatre of operations along the Shatt-al-Arab waterway, where the population deeply resents rule from Baghdad. The Iranian generals hoped that these raids, as well as others elsewhere along the border, would stretch the Iraqi forces to the point where a well-timed attack would achieve a decisive breakthrough. However, the Pasdaran (Guardians), an Islamic military force in parallel to the army, preferred to attack at Basra, and used their greater political influence to secure a switch in Iranian strategy.

Dead Iranians in foxholes on the bank of a waterway near Basra, the main city along Iraq's small coastal zone in the Persian Gulf.

Iraqi soldiers fight in the open desert terrain characteristic of the border regions between Iraq and Iran. The Iraqis used roads and helicopters to shift troops quickly to different sectors threatened by Iranian offensives throughout the war.

US intervention in the Lebanon ends

The announcement by American President Ronald Reagan on 7 February 1984 that the American component of the Multi-National Force in Beirut would be gradually withdrawn brings to an end an attempt by Western powers to create some stability in war-torn Lebanon. When the force came into existence in August 1982 it consisted of French and Italian soldiers and American Marines; a British contingent joined in February 1983. The original purpose was to keep the warring Lebanese factions and Israeli forces around Beirut from fighting one another, but the Americans in particular saw their duty as re-establishing the authority of the government of the Lebanon.

The first sign of serious trouble came on 18 April 1983 when a car bomb destroyed the American embassy, killing 57 staff. Worse followed once Israeli forces finally began withdrawing from the Lebanon in the summer of 1983. The Lebanese army was drawn into a fight with militia of the Druze community in the Shouf mountains, which spread to Beirut. US Navy ships bombarded Druze and other Moslem positions in the Shouf from September onwards.

US Marines clear the destroyed Beirut barracks in October 1983. A suicide truck bomber killed over 200 American Marines, part of the Multi-National peace-keeping force.

Having taken sides, the Americans now became subject to regular attacks. In the early hours of 23 October, a yellow Mercedes-Benz crashed into the Marine barracks at Beirut airport and the driver detonated his explosive load, killing himself and the Marines. A similar attack was made on the French contingent. In retaliation, both American and French aircraft attacked Syrian and Iranian positions in the Lebanon, since these two countries were held responsible for the

attack. An American attack on Syrian anti-aircraft missile sites after they had been used to fire at American reconnaissance aircraft on 4 December 1983 resulted in the loss of two American aircraft. By this stage, it was very clear that only a massive commitment of American military and naval resources would have any impact. President Reagan decided that the price of success would be too expensive for the benefits to be gained, and announced the withdrawal of American forces.

OBITUARY
ARTHUR HARRIS (1892-1984)

Marshal of the Royal Air Force Arthur "Bomber" Harris died on 5 April 1984 at the age of 91.

Harris commanded Bomber Command from 1942 until the end of the war.

He was living in Rhodesia when the First World War broke out. After joining the army, he volunteered for the Royal Flying Corps, and served both on the Western Front and in the air defence of Britain against attacks by German zeppelins and bombers. After the end of the war, Harris chose to make a career of the air force, and took part in the bombing campaign in Mesopotamia against Arabs opposing British rule. When the Second World War began, Harris commanded No. 5 Bomber Group and conducted many raids on Germany.

Harris was appointed commander of Bomber Command in February 1942, at a low point in the arm's wartime experience. It was the sole

means the British possessed of hitting directly at Germany on a large scale, and Prime Minister Winston Churchill was eager to hear of its effectiveness. Unfortunately, night-time bombing was remarkably ineffective, and Harris chose a new approach, which was to send large numbers of bombers to attack the general vicinity of a target. The questionable legality of this tactic was brushed aside, and Harris's reputation was tarnished by his enthusiasm for it. This, and the very heavy casualties suffered by Bomber Command in the war, ensured Harris remained controversial right up to his death.

He was married twice.

Reagan's secret war failing in Nicaragua

The defeat of the Contras, an army of anti-Sandinista Nicaraguans based in Honduras and Costa Rica, in December 1984 has imperilled the long-term US objective of toppling the Cuban-supported Nicaraguan government. Following the victory of the Sandinistas in a rebellion against the dictatorship of Anastasio Somoza, a number of Somoza's supporters fled to neighbouring Central American countries. The Nicaraguan government's friendly relations with Cuba, and its support of

Marxist guerrillas in El Salvador, were of great concern to President Ronald Reagan's administration in the United States. On 23 November 1981, Reagan signed a directive authorizing the Central Intelligence Agency to support the resistance to the Sandinista regime.

A secret war now began. Contras had already begun incursions from Honduras, but until July 1982 the war was a small-scale guerrilla conflict. In July 1982, the first large engagement of the war resulted in a defeat of the Contras near the border with

Honduras. However, American support was lavish, and included repeated exercises between American and Honduran forces that were perceived as threatened invasions by the Sandinista government.

The war intensified in the second half of 1983, when 30 helicopters arrived in Honduras to help the Contras in their fight, together with light motor boats that were used to attack oil storage tanks at Corinto, Nicaragua, in October. However, the revelation that the CIA had mined Nicaraguan harbours a few weeks earlier in April 1984 caused an uproar in the US Congress and led to a law banning aid to the Contras. By December 1984, the Sandinistas clearly had the upper hand, and used their strength to drive the bulk of the Contra forces out of Nicaragua.

Contras march through high grass in northern Nicaragua. The Contras could not defeat the Sandinista government militarily, but the Sandinistas could not win politically so long as the Reagan administration was prepared to offer support, even if it was against American law.

El Salvadoran army gains upper hand in civil war

A **meeting of guerrilla** leaders belonging to the Farabundo Marti National Liberation front (FMLN) in May 1985 conceded the advantage in the civil war that has been raging in the country to the government forces.

On 10 January 1981, the guerrillas launched their "final offensive". Salvadoran military forces had suffered from a boycott by the United States government under President Jimmy Carter after repeated human rights violations. The guerrillas believed that the weakened state of the army left it vulnerable to a popular uprising. However, no general strike or other form of popular resistance to the government occurred, and instead the rebels now found themselves fighting a major conventional war with the Salvadoran armed forces. After the inauguration of President Ronald Reagan on 20 January 1981, American policy changed and support was resumed.

Salvadoran troops stand watch at an outpost in Suchitoto, El Salvador, in November 1982. The Salvadoran army came close to losing the war against marxist guerrillas, but extensive American aid ensured that they survived setbacks.

Nonetheless, the rebels' assessment was correct, and they inflicted many spectacular defeats on Salvadoran armed forces over the next four years. These included a raid on Ilopango air-base in January 1982 that destroyed 70 per cent of the Salvadoran air force, the destruction of two key bridges at Puente de Oro and Cuscatlán, and a lengthy siege of the city of San Miguel beginning in September 1983.

American aid, especially in the form of helicopters and military advisors, came just at the right moment to assist the surprisingly resilient Salvadoran army, which suffered no major loss of morale in spite of its difficult situation.

IN BRIEF

❧ A group of about 100 guerrillas fighting for independence for the Tamils living on the island of Sri Lanka attacked a Sri Lankan army base at Kokkilai on 13 February 1985. It was the first large-scale operation mounted by guerrillas during a period of civil strife that began on 17 August 1981 when a state of emergency was declared. In July 1983 between 1,000 and 3,000 Tamils lost their lives in riots triggered by the guerrilla ambush of an army patrol.

❧ The Iraqis defeated an Iranian offensive at Badr in March 1985. The Iraqis and Iranians began nuisance raids using missiles and bombers on one another's major cities, while the Iraqis launched a series of air raids on Iran's main oil export terminal at Kharg island.

❧ On 6 November 1985, Colombian M-19 guerrillas attacked the Colombian Palace of Justice in Bogotá, holding Supreme Court justices and palace staff hostage. Army forces attacked the next day, setting fire to the building. Over 100 died.

Workers from the Palace of Justice in Bogotá, Colombia, flee after guerrillas belonging to the M-19 revolutionary movement seized control of the building on 6 November 1985.

Americans bomb Libya, but miss Gaddafi

Over 40 American aircraft bombed targets in Libya on 15/16 April 1986, including an attack on the Azizyah Barracks that may have been intended to kill the Libyan dictator Muammar Gaddafi, who kept a residence nearby.

The attack capped several weeks of increasing tension between Libya and

President Ronald Reagan held Gaddafi responsible for terrorist attacks against America and its allies.

the United States. President Ronald Reagan held Gaddafi responsible for terrorist attacks against America and its allies, including at the Rome and Vienna airports on 27 December 1985. In March 1986, US Navy vessels went on manoeuvres in the Gulf of Sirte, an area claimed as territorial waters by Libya, seeking a confrontation. On 24 March, an engagement resulted in the destruction of Libyan missile boats and air defence radar systems. When a bomb went off on 5 April at a Berlin disco frequented by American servicemen, killing two, the United States claimed Libyan agents planted it.

The bombing raid was in direct retaliation for the Berlin disco bombing. The US assembled a substantial air and naval force, including F-111 bombers flying from bases in Britain. These were forced to take a roundabout route because both France and Spain refused to allow them to fly across their air space. The attack only lasted ten minutes, and included several different targets including the Benghazi and Tripoli air defence networks, as well as Tripoli airfield, Jamahiryah Barracks, as well as Azizyah Barracks. The total number of Libyan casualties is still uncertain, but one American F-111 was shot down by a Libyan missile, with the loss of its two-man crew.

A Libyan man stands next to an unexploded bomb after the American raid on Tripoli in April 1986.

Libyan soldiers stand beside shrapnel from American anti-personnel bombs dropped on Libya in April 1986. In addition to bombing Gaddafi's compound in Tripoli, American aircraft attacked Libyan air force and military bases.

IN BRIEF

Iranian soldiers achieved two important victories in the war with Iraq. On 10 February 1986, they captured al-Faw, an abandoned oil terminal in the Shatt-al-Arab. In response, the Iraqis seized the town of Mehran on 12 May, which the Iranians had occupied earlier in the war, although an Iranian counter-attack recaptured the city on 10 June.

A ferocious battle around Fish Lake in southern Iraq between Iranian militia and the Iraqi army ended on 2 February 1987 with the complete defeat of the Iranian forces, outmanoeuvred by their Iraqi counterparts. The operation, named Kerbala 5 by the Iranians, was intended to bring the war to an end. The

Iranians used human-wave attacks that the Iraqis had prepared for by constructing massive earthworks used by both infantry and tanks. The Iraqis subjected the attacking Iranians to heavy artillery bombardments that shattered the impetus and eventually drove them back across the Shatt-al-Arab waterway.

On 5 July 1987, a suicide bomber of the Liberation Tigers of Tamil Eelam drove a truck through the wall of barracks used by the Sri Lankan army, before detonating a large bomb that killed 40 soldiers.

South African and Angolan forces clashed along the River Lomba on 12–16 September 1987 during Operation Modular, an invasion of Angola by the South

Africans in support of guerrillas fighting the Angolan government.

Indian peacekeeping troops began fighting the Liberation Tigers of Tamil Eelam on 9 October 1987, after the Tigers rejected the peace agreement negotiated in July that allowed Indian troops to act as peacekeepers while other Tamil organizations and the Sri Lankan government implemented autonomy proposals.

US warships shelled Iranian oil platforms in the Rostam oilfield in the Persian Gulf on 19 October 1987, in retaliation for Iranian missile attacks on tankers. US special forces boarded one of these platforms and demolished it with explosives.

Shia Lebanese siege of PLO camps ends

The **Syrian-sponsored Amal** (Hope) movement raised its siege of Palestinian refugee camps around West Beirut on 7 April 1987, effectively ending a second round of the Lebanese Civil War.

The fighting began as Palestinian refugees in the Lebanon began rearming after the withdrawal of the Multi-National Force from the country in early 1984. All Palestinian fighters had left the country in August and September 1982, but the PLO sought to recreate its network, since most of the refugees remained behind. However, many Lebanese blamed the Palestinians for the civil war and the Israeli invasion, and among them the Shia Moslem Amal movement took the lead in resisting a renaissance of PLO strength in the country. On 19 May 1985, Amal and its Druze allies attacked the Palestinian camps at Sabra, Chatila and Burj el-Barajneh. The fighting lasted until a ceasefire on 17 June, with Sabra and much of Chatila in Amal hands, but the other two camps still controlled by the PLO.

Two more rounds of sustained fighting,

together with desultory skirmishes in between, occurred in May 1986 and in September 1986. On the latter occasion the camps around Tyre were the flashpoints for the conflict's beginning. However, Amal was still unable to gain control of the Palestinian

camps, even after deploying tanks given to them by the Syrians. During the third round their rivals for the loyalty of the Lebanon's Shia, the Iranian-sponsored Hezbollah, gave some aid to the Palestinians. In February 1987, the Syrian army occupied West Beirut and Amal eventually handed most of its positions over to them.

A Shia militiaman fires an RPG-7 grenade launcher from the back of a motorcycle during fighting around the Palestinian refugee camps in 1986.

The Afghan crucible

The Soviet intervention into Afghanistan not only led to the defeat of the Soviet Army, but also spawned a new network of Moslem radicals who were determined to build on their victory and defeat all enemies of the Arab world.

The war in Afghanistan began as a wish by the Soviet Union's leadership to act as kingmaker during a political dispute between factions of the ruling Marxist party in Afghanistan. The Afghan People's Democratic Party had seized power in April 1978. Its reform programme, which included more rights for women and a redistribution of land, provoked a rebellion of traditional-minded rural Moslems in mid-1978 in eastern Afghanistan. The rebellion turned into civil war as the Americans began covert operations in support of the rebels, after the Afghan government had signed a friendship treaty with the Soviet Union in December 1978.

Coup

Hafizullah Amin overthrew the original Marxist leadership in September 1979. By this time the Afghan army had lost control over much of the mountainous countryside, although its control over the country as a whole remained unthreatened. However, Amin was unwilling to take Soviet advice on how to fight the war. Faced with his increasing demands for supplies, the Soviets turned to his rivals and deposed Amin on 27 December 1979, killing him in the assault

As Soviet forces withdraw from Kabul in May 1988, Afghan soldiers hand the departing commander of a tank flowers. They had cause to regret the departure of their Red Army allies, who had largely sustained the war against Moslem Afghan guerrillas opposed to the Marxist regime.

on the presidential palace. Large numbers of Soviet troops then entered the country at the request of the new president, Babrak Karmal, on the same day. About 40,000 Soviet soldiers and airmen arrived in Afghanistan, and the war against the guerrillas intensified.

However, most Afghans did not welcome the arrival of the Soviet Army forces. The average Afghan was deeply religious and unsympathetic to the secular socialism of the ruling party. A very public demonstration of their attitudes came on 23 February 1980, when a substantial portion of the population of Kabul went up to their rooftops one night and almost as with one voice proclaimed the basic tenet of Islam, "*Allah akbar*" – God is great. Many Afghans withdrew to the more remote mountain regions of the country and assembled in bands that used hand-crafted Lee Enfields or even older models, widening the war that the Afghan government had been fighting for over a year.

Armoured operations

The Soviet Army undertook offensive action both in support of its Afghan allies and to maintain its communications between the cities of Afghanistan. The Soviet forces initially relied on artillery and aerial firepower, and armoured columns, but these proved incapable of defeating the guerrillas, who simply withdrew when brought under heavy fire to places where armoured vehicles could not follow easily, and returned once the Soviet soldiers had moved on.

A column of Soviet armoured cars crosses a bridge in Afghanistan: the Red Army's initial tactic was to send columns of armoured vehicles across country to find and destroy the guerrillas.

It took over a year of ineffective armoured operations before the Soviet Army began to adapt itself better to the conditions of the campaign. The key development came with an expansion of the use of the helicopter. The Soviet Army had an excellent helicopter gunship, the Mi-24, which carried a powerful armament of rockets and machine guns. Armoured forces were now used to fix the location of Afghan guerrillas, and the soldiers then summoned helicopters to attack from the air. Where jet aircraft flew too quickly to target a group of guerrillas on a ridge accurately, helicopters travelled slowly enough to rake the Afghan positions, or the fleeing groups of guerrillas headed for better cover. Furthermore, the Mi-24 could transport a squad of troops, allowing them to engage the guerrillas, if appropriate.

Combat zones

The main areas of operation initially were the Kunar Valley, the site of the first major Soviet Army offensive in 1980, and the Panjsher Valley, an area 40 miles (64 km) north-east of Kabul dominated by the guerrillas, where the Soviets launched repeated offensives throughout their occupation of the country. Later in the war, the area around Khowst, Kandahar and Paktia province dominated the fighting. The Soviets were never able to sustain the size of force their own analysis deemed necessary to subjugate Afghanistan (30 divisions), in part owing to the inability of the roads of the country to make

An Afghan army rocket launcher fires a barrage against guerrillas near Jalalabad in March 1989. After the withdrawal of the Soviets, the war against the occupation turned into a civil war.

supplying a force of such size feasible.

The Afghan guerrillas received support from several sources. At first, they relied on traditional social networks, remaining close to their villages and using them for food and medical assistance. The Soviet forces, however, soon denied them this resource by means of a bombing campaign, forcing the rural population of the main war zones to flee to refugee camps. The Islamic governments of Iran and Pakistan also viewed the guerrillas

favourably, offering them safe havens in their countries, which the Soviets were reluctant to enter. Finally, the United States soon saw Afghanistan as the best way to fight the Soviet Union by proxy. The Central Intelligence Agency organized a lot of arms and finance for the guerrillas. Most importantly, they supplied them with Stinger anti-aircraft missiles, which enabled them to take on the Mi-24 Hind helicopters with greater success than merely shooting at the unarmoured tail.

Al-Qaeda

The guerrillas did not only need to rely on Afghans for manpower. The war also attracted combatants from the Islamic faithful around the world, but especially from Saudi Arabia. It was considered a jihad, a war in defence of Islam directed against unbelievers. Wealthy Saudi Arabians donated sizeable sums to the struggle, and the funds were used to buy arms, to pay for training, and to help Moslems from other countries to travel to Pakistan and Afghanistan to join the war. In 1988, the Soviet Union announced it would leave Afghanistan. For one eager fundraiser, however, the Afghan model provided a means, he believed, to help Moslems in other conflicts. Osama bin Laden, a wealthy Saudi Arabian himself, used the experience he had gained supporting the war in Afghanistan to create a network, al-Qaeda, that would fight on behalf of Islam against unbelievers around the world.

An Afghan guerrilla, or mujahideen, aims an RPG-7 grenade launcher. The mujahideen initially fought with outdated firearms, but acquired surface-to-air missiles and other advanced weaponry.

Iran-Iraq war comes to an end

The acceptance of a United Nations' ceasefire by the Iranians on 20 August 1988 brought to an end the eight-year war with Iraq. The Iranian religious leadership had concluded in early 1988 that the war would take at least another five years to win. The Pasdaran (Guardians) Islamic military force and Basiji militia had been using very primitive human-wave tactics that the Iraqis had learned to counter with massive firepower, with consequently extremely heavy casualties to Iranian forces. By early 1988, the Iranian military power had effectively been destroyed, and the Iranians were unable to launch a spring military offensive. In response, the Iraqis recaptured Al-Faw in April and Majnoon island in June, eliminating all the major gains the Iranians had achieved since 1982. Saddam Hussein had been offering peace to the Iranians since June of that year, and the Iranian religious leadership finally accepted his offers in July 1988.

Palestinian intifada rages against Israel

The year 1988 has been marked by constant fighting between Palestinians and the Israeli Defence Force, although this has been confined to mobs throwing stones or burning tyres. Rioting broke out on 9 December 1987 in the Jabalya refugee camp in the Gaza Strip between Palestinians and Israeli police and soldiers. The Palestinians were angered by a traffic accident in which an Israeli army truck had killed four and injured seven Palestinians. The riots marked the beginning of the intifada (uprising) against Israeli rule by Palestinians.

Peace in Nicaragua

The acceptance on 15 January 1988 by Nicaraguan president Daniel Ortega of the peace plan proposed by Costa Rican president Oscar Arias began a peace process to end the war in Nicaragua. The war had been waged since 1981 between the Sandinista

The war had been waged since 1981 between the Sandinista government of Nicaragua and the Contra insurgents sustained by financial and military aid from the United States.

government of Nicaragua and the Contra insurgents sustained by financial and military aid from the United States. The Contras had been unable to secure widespread support from the Nicaraguan people, and had been defeated repeatedly in the field whenever they attempted large-scale invasions intended to secure a major city in which they could proclaim a provisional government. The last attempt, to capture Rosita, achieved only temporary success. The involvement of US government officials in a conspiracy to raise funds illegally for the Contras, together with various scandals such as the capture of American mercenaries working for the Contras and the murder of American civilians by the Contras in Nicaragua, contributed to their willingness to pressure the Contras to settle with the Sandinistas.

Festooned with bandoliers of ammunition, a Contra machine-gunner patrols the hills of Chontales province in Nicaragua in June 1987.

IRAN-IRAQ WAR

DATES:	1980-1988
COMBATANTS:	Iraq vs Iran
FORCES ENGAGED:	Iraq, 190,000 men, 8,500 armoured vehicles; Iran: 805,000 men, 2,000 armoured vehicles
CASUALTIES:	Iraq, 375,000 (estimated); Iran, more than 500,000 (estimated)
RESULT:	Iran defeated Iraqi invasion

Abu Nidal

One of the leading terrorists of the 1980s was Abu Nidal, a Palestinian from Jaffa, who became active in the Palestinian Liberation Organization after the 1967 Six-Day War. Abu Nidal split from the PLO in 1971, eventually forming a Fatah Revolutionary Council to conduct his own terror campaign. Among the terrorist attacks attributed to him and his organization were the attempt on the life of Shlomo Argov that precipitated the 1982 Israeli invasion of the Lebanon, the 1985 Rome and Vienna airport attacks and a 1988 car bombing of the Israeli embassy in Cyprus. He also reputedly supplied the bomb used in the Lockerbie bombing.

He died in 2002, in Baghdad, although whether murdered or by suicide is not clear.

IN BRIEF

⁓ Abu Jihad, a Palestinian guerrilla leader believed to be the moving force behind the intifada, the popular uprising in the Gaza Strip and on the West Bank, was assassinated in his home on 16 April 1988. The assassins are believed to have been Israeli commandos, although the Israeli government has never claimed responsibility for this.

⁓ A bomb destroyed Pan Am Flight 103, en route from London to New York on 21 December 1988, while the aircraft was flying over the town of Lockerbie in Scotland.

The cockpit and nose of Pan Am Flight 103, a Boeing 747 airliner that was destroyed by a bomb placed by Libyan agents in December 1988 over Lockerbie, Scotland.

The bomb had been planted in the forward cargo hold, where it was being carried as unaccompanied baggage. All 243 passengers and sixteen crew were killed.

⁓ The Republic of Panama, which was created out of Colombian territory by the United States in 1903, was occupied by US forces in a short invasion that began on 20 December 1989. The Panamanian dictator, General Manuel Noriega, was overthrown and a new civil administration installed.

An American soldier stands guard in Panama City after the invasion of 20 December 1989 that overthrew the regime of General Manuel Noriega.

The First Gulf War, 1990-91

Saddam Hussein's invasion of Kuwait unleashed the most modern military forces in the world against his ill-prepared army in terrain perfectly suited to the mixture of airpower and tank forces that would lead the way for the coalition forces.

Scud surface-to-surface missiles parade down an avenue in Baghdad in January 1990. Iraqi Scuds were fired at both allied bases in Saudi Arabia and at Israel, which was taking no direct part in the war to liberate Kuwait.

Like most other Middle Eastern problems, the Gulf War owed its origins to the British actions following the defeat of the Ottoman Turks in the First World War. The British effectively recognized the independence of Kuwait, and established a protectorate over it, while also creating a separate Iraq under a League of Nations mandate. However, under the Ottomans, Kuwait had been part of Iraq. The Iraqi authorities at no time recognized the British separation of Kuwait from Iraq, but the British protectorate left the Iraqis with no realistic possibility of pursuing their territorial claim.

Iraqi debts

In January 1990, General H. Norman Schwartzkopf, of the United States Army Central Command, declared to a Congressional committee that Iraq was now the strongest military power in the Gulf region, and theoretically posed a serious threat to oil-rich Arab states of the Gulf. The Iraqi dictator, Saddam Hussein, faced a serious financial problem. His country had run up a sizeable debt in fighting an eight-year war with

Iran, and hoped to pay it off by capitalizing on its considerable oil revenues. However, whenever Iraq tried to reduce supply in order to boost prices, Kuwait would simply increase production to offset the Iraqi reduction. For Saddam Hussein, the Kuwaitis were acting selfishly in their own interest, since part of the debt was owed to them. In his view, Kuwait had eagerly paid for Iraqis to die in order to protect them from Iranian Islamic radicalism, but was unwilling to allow Iraq to pay off its debt quickly. In mid-July, after accusations that the Kuwaitis were engaged in slant-drilling (sinking oil wells at an angle) into Iraqi oil fields, Saddam Hussein ordered General Ayad Futayih al-Rawi to plan the invasion of Kuwait.

Al-Rawi's attack began in the early hours of 2 August 1990, with an armoured division and a mechanized division crossing the land border, while three brigades of the elite Republican Guards were carried by helicopter to Kuwait City. Four infantry divisions followed up the armoured advance, and within two days Iraqi tanks were deployed along the border of Saudi Arabia and Kuwait. The same

day as the invasion, the United Nations Security Council passed Resolution 660, which required Iraq to withdraw from Kuwait. Meanwhile, US President George Bush was meeting with his security advisers, who coincidentally had been planning for operations in the Gulf area just a few months earlier. At the request of King Fahd of Saudi Arabia, Bush committed the United States to defending the desert kingdom, and American troops began arriving on 7 August.

Desert Shield

The Americans christened the deployment of troops to Saudi Arabia Operation Desert Shield. In addition to army forces, US Navy battle groups and US Air Force fighting wings also arrived. While the United States assembled military forces to defend Saudi Arabia, its diplomats were also hard at work bringing together a coalition of countries under the auspices of the United Nations. On 29 November, the UN's Resolution 678 authorized the use of force against the Iraqi occupation of Kuwait. Although American forces represented about three-quarters of those deployed, there were also important contingents from 34 other countries, including

Precision bombs, using laser guidance technology, blasted these holes in aircraft hangers at an Iraqi-held Kuwaiti airport.

An M1A1 Abrams tank makes a smoke screen during Operation Desert Storm in February 1991. The US tank forces completely overwhelmed their Iraqi opponents in every battle they fought.

Argentina, Australia, Britain, Canada, France, Germany, Honduras, Italy, New Zealand, Poland and Spain. Resolution 678 imposed a deadline of 15 January 1991 for Iraq to withdraw from Kuwait. When this passed, the coalition air forces went into action.

The air bombardment strategy made extensive use of precision munitions, such as laser-guided bombs and cruise missiles. The use of such weapons reduced the risk of civilian deaths, although those living near key installations remained much more likely to be killed or wounded than other residents of Iraq. The key targets were initially the Iraqi air defence system, and communications and leadership targets. Once these had been knocked out, the air forces turned to attacks on railways, bridges, port facilities and troops in the field. Finally, the third stage of the air offensive included attacks on Iraqi troop positions, which proved very vulnerable in spite of their extensive engineering efforts.

Firing wildly

On 16 January, Iraq responded to the coalition attacks by firing eight Scud missiles at Israel. The Israelis had not participated in the coalition at all, but Saddam Hussein presumably hoped to draw them into the fighting and thus disrupt the coalition by alienating its Arab members from the United States. It was greatly feared that the Iraqi missiles would make use of chemical or biological weapons, but in the event this fear proved groundless. The Iraqis also triggered the first ground combat of the war, when they struck at the US Marine positions around Khafji in Saudi Arabia on 29 January. Advancing in three columns, the tanks and personnel carriers were halted by Marine outposts using TOW anti-tank missiles and calling in close air support. A third column succeeded in entering the town of Khafji itself, but the coalition forces' air supremacy prevented the Iraqis from reinforcing this success, and after two days they withdrew.

The coalition ground attack went forward at 4 a.m. on 23 February (EST), two days after Iraq accepted a Soviet ceasefire proposal. The one concession made by the American commander, General Norman Schwartzkopf, was to declare no attacks would be made on retreating Iraqi units. The advance was conducted on a broad front, with armoured columns driving into the desert before turning to trap the Iraqi forces in Kuwait. Meanwhile, advances were made directly into Kuwait to drive the Iraqis back in the direction of the armoured thrusts. The Iraqis lacked sufficient troops to extend their front far into the desert, and their open flank in the west was easily turned. Iraqi troops put up little resistance to the initial offensive. Even the vaunted Republican Guard preferred to surrender if they were given the chance. On 26 February, the Iraqis began to retreat from Kuwait. The long convoy out was constantly bombed and strafed by coalition aircraft, giving the road along which it travelled the nickname "the Highway of Death". A few major battles were fought, including 73 Easting, on 26 February, and the Battle of Medina Ridge on 27 February, which was the largest tank battle in American history. Both of these battles were fought in poor visibility, the US night-vision equipment giving them a significant advantage over their Iraqi opponents. Combat operations ended on 28 February.

The Iraqis suffered 25,000 dead during the war. Estimates of the wounded run into six figures. Coalition losses amounted to 345 (battle and non-battle) and about a thousand wounded.

Pillars of smoke and flame mark Kuwaiti oil wells sabotaged by retreating Iraqi troops in March 1991.

Croatia secures independence

The admission of an independent Croatia to the United Nations on 22 May 1992 split the former Yugoslav federation in two, as the second largest ethnic group within its borders had its secession recognized internationally.

The Croatian government had declared independence on 25 June 1991, but found that ethnic Serbs residing within

In September a battle erupted over the town of Vukovar, a Croatian city within the predominantly Serbian region of Krajina.

its borders were unhappy with their new status as a minority, no longer part of the same country as their cousins in Serbia. In September a battle erupted over the town of Vukovar, a Croatian city within the predominantly Serbian region of Krajina. When Croatian forces attempted to capture barracks occupied by the Yugoslav People's Army in September, the Yugoslavs rushed an armoured column from Belgrade to Vukovar. The siege lasted six weeks, and ended with the capture of the city by the Yugoslavs and the eviction of many Croat residents. However, the Yugoslavs had suffered heavy losses in the battle, and approached the next city along their line of advance, Osijek, more cautiously. Osijek was larger, and initially the Yugoslav army relied on artillery shelling to prepare the way for its advance. However, Yugoslav president Slobodan Milosevic was unwilling to risk the conquest of hostile Croat areas, and withdrew his army.

Yugoslav federal troops follow a tank across a Slovenian field. The leaders of the Federal Army were unwilling to risk serious fighting in Slovenia after its declaration of independence.

American special forces engage militia in Mogadishu

An American soldier watches passers-by carefully at a checkpoint on a road outside Mogadishu in December 1993.

Eighteen American soldiers were killed, and two helicopters were lost during street fighting in Mogadishu on 3–4 October 1993 in an attempt to detain two members of the Somali warlord Mohammed Farrah Aideed's government. Estimates of Somali casualties range as high as a thousand dead.

In a second incident, a number of soldiers were killed while participating in the United Nations' operation to establish a degree of order in chaotic Somalia. On 5 June, 24 Pakistani soldiers died in fighting militia controlled by Aideed while attempting to disarm them. The bodies of some of the Pakistanis were horribly mutilated. On 12 July, US helicopters attacked a building believed to be the site of a meeting of Aideed's militia leaders, killing 50 men who turned out to be clan elders seeking to mediate between Aideed and the UN forces.

Somalia searches for order

United Nations forces arrived in Somalia on 9 December 1992 to attempt to restore a measure of order in the war-torn country where the population stood on the brink of an humanitarian disaster. The government of Somalia had collapsed after the former dictator, Mohammed Siad Barre, fled the country in January 1991, after a coalition of his opponents, led by Mohammed Farah Aideed, unleashed massive protests against his murderous regime. However, the coalition quickly fell apart and the country collapsed into chaos as clan-based militias and bandit gangs vied to grab control of various parts of Somalia. In the fighting that followed, about 20,000 people died. Only the far north, which proclaimed itself the independent state of Somaliland, avoided the disaster. Without any recognized central authority, the distribution of food and other resources around the country failed. Around 300,000 people were estimated to have died from food shortages. Food distributed by the United Nations was seized by local warlords.

A group of Somali militiamen repair their "technical", a converted jeep equipped in this case with a recoilless rifle, but heavy 12.7mm machine guns were also mounted.

IN BRIEF

❧ An alleged Tamil suicide bomber succeeded in assassinating Indian prime minister Rajiv Gandhi and 14 others on 21 May 1991. The bomb was presented to him in a basket of flowers.

❧ A brief war between the government of Slovenia, which declared its independence from Yugoslavia on 25 June 1991, and Yugoslavia ended with a victory for Slovenia. The Yugoslav army was reluctant to carry out any major action that threatened civilian casualties. Furthermore, much of its strength in Slovenia was widely scattered in barracks that were easily isolated and surrounded by Slovene forces, and the Yugoslavs relied on armoured columns advancing along predictable routes to re-establish the government's authority. Casualties amounted to 62 fatalities for both sides, demonstrating that both avoided intense combat.

❧ A peace conference in Addis Ababa on 1–5 July 1991 brought to an end a 30-year guerrilla war fought by Eritrean independence movements against the Ethiopian government.

❧ A campaign in northern Sri Lanka between Tamil Tigers and the Sri Lankan army see-sawed for the first eight months of 1991 until the army re-established control over Jaffna in early August, but found its military units in the north isolated and frequently surrounded by Tamil Tiger guerrillas.

Bosnia's agony ends

The **Dayton Peace** Accords, signed on 21 November 1995, brought to an end the three-year ethnic war that pitted Serbs against Croats and Bosniaks (Bosnians who are not ethnic Serbs or Croats) in Bosnia-Herzegovina.

The war began in the spring of 1992, when Bosnian Serbs attacked to gain control of key strategic positions in the east and northwest of Bosnia. The Bosnian Serbs were far better equipped and organized than the nascent army of a Bosnian government that had proclaimed independence on 5 March 1992.

International perception of the war was dominated by the "ethnic cleansing" that went on. The Serbs in particular rounded up Bosniaks or Croats who mingled in neighbourhoods where Serbs were a plurality or majority, and either killed them or forcibly evicted them, sending them to live in areas where Bosniaks or Croats were predominant. The most notorious incident was the killing of 7,000 Bosniaks at Srebrenica in July 1995. The Serbs' conduct led to an alliance between Croats and Bosniaks that became effective in 1995, together with massive arms shipments from Iran to the Bosniaks. Around 38,000 civilians from all sides were killed in the war, together with some 60,000 soldiers.

A house in Sarajevo burns fiercely after the city had been shelled by Bosnian Serb militia.

Chechens fight for independence

A Chechen man searches for water in Grozny during the winter of 1994–95. The effects of Russian shelling of the town are visible on the building in the background. Virtually the entire city had been turned into a fortress by the Chechen nationalists.

After a campaign lasting over a year-and-a-half, Chechen nationalists secured a truce with the Russian government in August 1996 that offered them the real possibility of independence. The Chechen government had unilaterally declared independence in November 1991. The Russian government did little about reasserting its authority until the spring of 1994, when they began supplying arms to the pro-Russian Chechens. As this failed to end the insurgency, Russian forces, including both army units and paramilitary internal security forces, advanced into Chechnya in December 1994.

The military operation had been planned hurriedly, and the troops chosen to carry it out were those based near Chechnya, and not necessarily the best available for the task. Even naval infantry, whose expertise is in amphibious landings, were included in a country lacking a coastline or large rivers. Two Russian columns were delayed by political protestors in the Chechen towns nearest the border. A Chechen counter-attack on 13 December badly delayed the third. By the time they reached the Chechen capital of Grozny, political pressure from President Boris Yeltsin's government was such that they rushed to the attack before isolating the city and its defenders. The Russians made an elementary mistake by allowing their tanks to push ahead of the supporting infantry when they began their attack on Grozny on 1 January 1995. On 19 January, the Presidential Palace fell, but large areas of the city remained in control of the Chechen defenders. Russian forces only now began trying to blockade these troops by capturing the roads leading from Grozny to Dagestan, along which Chechen supplies travelled.

On 8 February, during a truce, the Chechens withdrew from Grozny. The war now descended into an interminable guerrilla campaign as Chechen fighters withdrew to the mountains of southern Chechnya. Although the Russians controlled the towns and cities, the Chechens manoeuvred freely through much of the rest of the country, frequently isolating and attacking Russian military columns. Occasionally the Chechens launched raids into communities on the other side of the border, notably Budyonnovsk on 14 June. Casualties during the war amounted to around 5,000 Russian dead, 3,000 Chechen fighters killed, and possibly as many as 100,000 Chechen civilians.

IN BRIEF

A car bomb exploded in the parking garage underneath the North Tower of the World Trade Center on 26 February 1993. The bomber was a Kuwaiti national, Ramzi Yousef, who was a part of the al-Qaeda terrorist network. He was helped by an American citizen of Iraqi descent, Abdul Rahman Yasin, who built the bomb. Six people were killed, and 1,042 injured.

A Tamil Tiger suicide bomber assassinated Sri Lankan president Ranasinghe Premadasa and 23 others on 1 May 1993. Tamil guerrillas defeated the Sri Lankan army at Pooneryn on 11 November 1993, killing some 750 soldiers.

The signing of the Oslo Accords at Washington DC, on 13 September 1993 brought to an end the Palestinian intifada, an uprising that pitted stone-throwing gangs against Israeli tanks and soldiers armed with automatic rifles.

Sri Lankan forces completed the key objective in a military operation against the Tamil Tigers, begun on 17 October 1995, when on 5 December they captured the city of Jaffna.

The Republic of Nagorno-Karabakh, once part of the Soviet Republic of Azerbaijan, had its independence acknowledged in 1994, in a ceasefire that ended a lengthy war between neighbouring Armenia and Azerbaijan. Nagorno-Karabakh's predominantly Armenian population had seceded from Azerbaijan in February 1988, resulting in ethnic fighting between Azeris and Armenians in Nagarno-Karabakh.

Rescue workers help an injured man from the World Trade Center after a car bomb exploded in the underground parking garage in February 1993. The bomb had been planted by a Kuwaiti Islamic fundamentalist with the help of an American of Iraqi descent.

NATO launches war from air

An 11-week bombing campaign directed against Yugoslavia finally succeeded in forcing the Yugoslav president Slobadan Milosevic to accept a United Nations' peace-keeping force in Kosovo on 11 June 1999, and the return of some 500,000 ethnic Albanian refugees to the province, together with an autonomous status for its administration. The military campaign was unique in modern warfare for being conducted almost entirely by aircraft and anti-aircraft weapons.

Albanians in Kosovo began a guerrilla war against the Yugoslav federation in 1996. As the crisis worsened, more Kosovars fled to nearby Albania and NATO demanded that the Yugoslavs allow a peacekeeping force to enter Kosovo and restore order. Milosevic refused, and the bombing of Yugoslavia began on 24 March 1999. Most of the air operations were carried out by the US Air Force. British, Canadian, German and Spanish aircraft also took part. The Yugoslav air defence system was initially targeted, but when this failed to compel Milosevic to accept NATO peacekeepers, the targets were gradually widened to military ones such as barracks and weapons factories, and finally to include civilian targets such as utilities and the state-owned radio and television broadcast offices.

A collapsed span of the Liberty Bridge, at Novi Sad, Yugoslavia, rests on the bottom of the Danube river after being bombed by NATO aircraft during the air war against Yugoslavia in 1999.

Battle in the mountains

The eviction of the last fighters from the Kargil area of the disputed Kashmir region between Pakistan and India on 26 July 1999 brought a three-month conflict between the Asian neighbours to an end. The trouble began when the Pakistani army chose to reoccupy its forward bases in the mountainous Kargil earlier than normal in the spring. In addition, they moved into more advanced positions, crossing the Line of Control that divides Kashmir into Pakistani and Indian areas. The infiltration was conducted in part by Kashmir irregulars and Afghan mercenaries. When these forces ambushed an Indian patrol, it alerted the Indian military and government to the advance across the Line of Control.

The main target of the Pakistanis was Highway 1A, which was the main avenue for supplies to reach the Indian forces. The Indians were forced to make some difficult frontal assaults on Pakistani positions, most famously at Tololing, a key position overlooking Highway 1A. These attacks often had to be made under cover of darkness, when the temperature falls well below freezing in the high winds of the Himalayas.

In July, the Indians prepared to expand the war by blockading Pakistani ports, while the Pakistanis seriously considered a nuclear strike on India. US president Bill Clinton made it very clear that such a move would not be welcome, and the Pakistanis opted to withdraw their forces back across the Line of Control.

IN BRIEF

Colombian Marxist guerrilla leader Manuel Marulanda co-ordinated a long guerrilla war.

❧ A suicide bomber detonated a truck in front of the Sri Lankan Central Bank on 31 January 1996, killing 91 people and wounding 1,400 others.

❧ A group of 13 leftist urban guerrillas, who had occupied the Japanese embassy in Lima since December 1996, were killed when Peruvian special forces assaulted the building on 22 April 1997, rescuing the remaining hostages.

❧ Laurent Kabila took power in Congo (formerly Zaire) on 17 May 1997 after a war that had pitted troops of the government of Mobutu Sésé Seko against rebels supported by Uganda and Rwanda. The rebels initially based their military forces on ethnic Tutsis living in Zaire, who became alarmed at the large number of Rwandan Hutus, who had carried out a campaign of genocide against Tutsis in Rwanda. Mobutu had allowed the Tutsis to find refuge in Zaire. The Zairean army was unable to defeat the rebels near the border with Rwanda, and many Zairean soldiers soon switched sides, causing Mobutu to flee.

❧ The Fuerzas Armadas Revolucionarias de Colombia, the main Colombian guerrilla group that has been fighting since 1964, attacked a military base at Las Delicias on 30 August 1996, and overran it. This marked a new stage in the war as the guerrillas switched over to a campaign to establish "no-go" zones in which the army was unable to assert the national authority.

❧ The American embassies in Dar es Salaam, Tanzania, and Nairobi, Kenya, were attacked by car bombs organized by al-Qaeda on 7 August 1998. In Nairobi 224 people were killed, and 11 in Dar es Salaam. On 20 August, US armed forces launched cruise missile attacks against suspected al-Qaeda facilities in Sudan and Afghanistan. The attacks, however, did not do much damage to al-Qaeda's ability to continue planning further operations.

A wounded man is lifted from the American embassy in Nairobi, Kenya, after an al-Qaeda bomb had badly damaged it on 7 August 1998.

Russia conquers Chechnya

A **Russian offensive against** the Chechen secessionist republic finally ended on 29 February 2000 when the Russians secured control of the village of Shatoi, and the Vedeno and Argun gorges in southern Chechnya. Although many Chechen guerrilla fighters remain active, the Russian army is now in complete occupation of the main cities of the country, including the capital Grozny.

The second war was launched after Chechens began fighting for the independence of the neighbouring republic of Dagestan in March 1999. Russian prime minister Vladimir Putin first ordered the army to halt the Dagestani insurgency, which included attacks on bases in Chechnya used to support the insurgents. On 4 September 1999, bombs exploded in Moscow, Volgodinsk and Dagestan, killing 300 people. The Russian security forces blamed Chechen rebels, whose extradition was demanded from Chechnya. When the Chechens refused, the Russian army attacked.

Their advance into Chechnya began on 30 September, the capital Grozny was

Russian marines move through close terrain near the village of Khatuni in the Vedeno gorge of southern Chechnya during operations against Chechen guerrillas in February 2000.

surrounded in November and a long siege begun. This time the Russian army relied on the use of airpower and artillery to defeat the Chechens in the city, which was by now heavily fortified. After over two months of bombardment, the Russians began attacking toward the city centre in January 2000. Chechen counter-attacks had succeeded in opening a supply route into the city on 4 January, but the long period of isolation left stocks low. By 1 February, the Chechens knew they faced defeat and opted to flee Grozny. Many key leaders and other fighters were killed or wounded in the escape. An estimated 1,000 Chechen fighters died, with Russian casualties about twice this number. Many Chechen citizens had also been killed, while others were rounded up in internment camps to prevent them from supporting the fighters.

IN BRIEF

❧ On 22 April 2000, Tamil Tiger guerrillas succeeded in capturing the Elephant Pass military complex that separated the Jaffna peninsula from the mainland of Sri Lanka. This catastrophe for the Sri Lankan army resulted in its losing most of the territory gained in offensives during 1995–96.

❧ A two-year war between Ethiopia and Eritrea over a disputed border ended on 18 June 2000 with the Eritreans accepting the Ethiopian claims. The fighting broke out in May 1998 when the Eritreans sent an armoured force into the disputed region of Badme after one of its patrols had been fired on by local police. The subsequent combat was intense, as both sides mobilized large armies: In May 2000 the Ethiopians used 'human wave' assault tactics against the Eritrean trenches, which enabled them to make a major breakthrough and Ethiopian forces occupied a substantial portion of Eritrea's territory.

A Russian BMP-1 armoured personnel carrier patrols the streets of Grozny after the Chechen defenders fled the city in February 2000.

SECOND CHECHEN WAR

DATES:	1999–2000
COMBATANTS:	Russian Federation vs Chechen separatists
FORCES ENGAGED:	Russian Federation, 94,000; Chechnya, 25,000 irregulars
CASUALTIES:	Russian Federation, 4,000; Chechnya, 1,400
RESULT:	Russian victory

Al-Qaeda plots foiled, except one

The USS *Cole*, a destroyer, was attacked by al-Qaeda terrorists in Aden harbour in Yemen on 12 October 2000. Two terrorist suicide bombers blew a large hole in the side of the ship, and injuring 39 people.

The concept was originally part of a series of plots directed at targets in Jordan and elsewhere in the Middle East, part of al-Qaeda's plan to mark 1 January 2000. This included four attacks on tourist sites in Jordan, a car bombing of Los Angeles International Airport and an attack on a US Navy destroyer in Yemen. The Jordan and Los Angeles operations were foiled by active police forces, while the Yemen attack failed when the terrorists packed too many explosives in their boat and it sank.

Islamist war in Algeria near end

A ten-year civil war between radical Moslems and the military government of Algeria appears to be nearing its end after the Islamic Salvationist Army agreed to an amnesty from the government and disbanded on 11 January 2000. The war had its origin in the refusal of the army to allow elections in 1992 that seemed likely to lead to the victory of the Islamic Salvationist Front, a political movement that seemed unlikely to continue with democratic elections once it had achieved political power. The war was in part a low-key guerrilla struggle directed against the army and police, but the Armed Islamic Group, another more radical formation, used a terror campaign directed against anyone deemed not supporting the struggle in Algiers and other cities of the central coast. A series of massacres in 1997, apparently carried out by the Armed Islamic Group, completely destroyed any sympathy for the guerrillas among civilian Algerians, and even caused fighting to break out between the two main guerrilla groups.

Sri Lankan soldiers investigate the scene of a Tamil Tiger suicide bombing in Colombo in October 2000. The Tamil Tigers have made some of the most extensive use of suicide bomb volunteers in their war for an independent Tamil state in the northern part of the island of Sri Lanka.

Americans occupy Afghanistan

Smoke streams from the north tower of the World Trade Center as United Air Lines Flight 175 flies toward the south tower at about 9.00 a.m. on 11 September 2001.

American military forces in association with Afghans fighting the Islamic fundamentalist Taliban regime in Afghanistan took power after a short campaign when Taliban leader Mullah Omar retreated from the city of Kandahar on 7 December 2001.

The American intervention was a consequence of the Taliban giving refuge to Osama bin Laden and his al-Qaeda network of terrorists. Al-Qaeda was held responsible for the attacks on Washington DC and New York city on 11 September, in which around 3,000 people lost their lives. President George W. Bush demanded that the Taliban hand Osama bin Laden over to the United States to stand trial for the attacks. After the Taliban refused to accept the American demand, American special forces and air force began supporting the Taliban's main opponent in an Afghan civil war, the Northern Alliance.

The Northern Alliance had been waging war against the Taliban since 1996, and was still the most widely recognized government of the country, controlling about 30 per cent of the territory, with military support from Iran and Russia. On 7 October 2001, American and British air forces began bombing Kabul, Kandahar and Jalalabad. Special forces soldiers were already in the country helping organize an air campaign. Two weeks later, close support missions to assist the Northern Alliance's army began, including the use of massive 15,000 lb (6,800 kg) daisy cutter bombs. The fall of Mazr-e-Sharif

A US Special Forces soldier rides on horseback patrol in Afghanistan on 25 August 2002.

on 9 November marked the beginning of the final phase of the campaign, with the Northern Alliance advancing toward Kabul, which was abandoned by the Taliban three days later.

By the end of the month, the Taliban were restricted to the area around Kandahar, while al-Qaeda forces were regrouping in a complex of caves near the Pakistan border in the Tora Bora mountain. US Marines established a base near Kandahar on 25 November. The attack on Tora Bora was carried out by Afghan militia supported by American aircraft and artillery, while in Kandahar US ground forces assisted the Northern Alliance. Both Mullah Omar and Osama bin Laden decided that the struggle could continue if they escaped, and both made their way out of their respective refuges in December.

One of the prisoners captured during the fighting in Afghanistan is escorted into detention at Guantanamo Bay in January 2002.

IN BRIEF

⚛ The war between the Tamil Tigers and the Sri Lankan government was ended by a ceasefire agreed on 24 December 2001.

Sierra Leone's descent to chaos and back

President Ahmad Tejan Kabbah of Sierra Leone declared on 18 January 2002 that the civil war in his country was at an end.

The war had begun in 1991 when the Revolutionary United Front (RUF)

[O]n May 2000, with the RUF on the verge of capturing Freetown, around 2,000 British troops were deployed to evacuate foreigners and stabilize the government.

attacked villages in eastern Sierra Leone from its bases in Liberia. The Sierra Leone armed forces were incapable of blocking the advance of the RUF, which used brutal tactics to terrorize the people, and relied heavily on child soldiers and mercenaries from Burkina Faso for its operations. An attempt to incorporate the RUF in the government by an agreement signed in July 1999 failed, and in May 2000, with the RUF on the verge of capturing Freetown, around 2,000 British troops were deployed to evacuate foreigners and stabilize the government. When 11 British troops were held hostage by a gang believed to be associated with the RUF, the British mounted a rescue operation called Operation Barras on 10 September 2000. The hostages were rescued. Subsequently, the RUF was gradually disarmed, thanks to additional attacks from Guinea on its bases.

IN BRIEF

❧ Three bombs detonated by terrorists in the resort town of Kuta on the island of Bali in Indonesia on 12 October 2002 claimed the lives of over 200 tourists and hospitality workers. The bombs were believed to have been planted by Indonesian Islamic radicals.

❧ The seizure of a Moscow theatre by Chechen rebels on 23 October 2002 ended with an attack by Russian security forces on 26 October, preceded by the use of a mysterious gas that apparently claimed the lives of around 150 people, including all 42 of the rebels.

A British paratrooper patrols a neighbourhood in Freetown, Sierra Leone, during the British intervention in their former colony. The Blair government sent a small force of troops to Sierra Leone in May 2000, to protect foreigners at risk from factions in Sierra Leone's civil war.

Saddam Hussein toppled in Iraq blitzkrieg

Soldiers of the 101st Airborne Division of the American army clear houses in the city of An Najaf, Iraq. The 101st Airborne was deployed to Kuwait and supported the advance of the 3rd Infantry Division along the western bank of the Euphrates river.

A 600-hour war brought to an end the dictatorship of Saddam Hussein over Iraq. The arrival of US Marines of Task Force Tripoli at Tikrit, in the centre of the country, on 13 April 2003 put coalition troops in the last region holding out against the occupation.

The election platform of American president George W. Bush during the 2000 campaign had included calling for the eviction of Saddam Hussein from office. After the invasion of Afghanistan broke the al-Qaeda network of bases there, Bush alleged that Saddam Hussein had ties to terrorism directed against the United States. The Bush administration made unverified claims of Iraq's possible possession of materials used in biological and nuclear weapons to justify an invasion. On 17 March, Bush gave Saddam Hussein 48 hours to leave Iraq or face invasion. When the deadline expired on 20 March, the bombing of Baghdad began, and the next day British and American ground forces attacked Iraq.

The bombing concentrated on Iraqi government buildings and various utilities such as electricity and water, and used both cruise missiles and precision-guided munitions.

The ground attacks included armoured thrusts from bases in Kuwait, US and British Marine landings at the Faw peninsula in the Shatt-al-Arab, and US airborne troops landing in western Iraq around al-Rulba and in the north-east around Sulaymaniyah and Arbil. While the British Royal Marines secured the area around Basra, US forces drove on Baghdad in a two-pronged advance, at first following the line of the Euphrates river and then with the 1st Marine Division crossing over toward the Tigris at Kut.

Saddam Hussein's forces offered little resistance. The army had never recovered from its disastrous defeat during the Gulf War 12 years earlier, and most resistance was put up by Ba'athist party militia. Saddam Hussein's strategy seemed to rely on some kind of sustained guerrilla resistance, until something turned up that would retrieve the situation.

On 6 April, American forces had established a perimeter around Baghdad. It was feared that the Iraqi forces would make a last-ditch stand here, turning the city into a Middle Eastern Stalingrad, but apart from some Republican Guard diehards, there was little sustained resistance and the Iraqi capital was secured on 9 April.

Clouds of dust and smoke mark explosions in Baghdad during the air raids and cruise missile attacks on the second night of the American campaign to overthrow Saddam's dictatorship.

Liberian capital besieged

A member of a Liberian rebel movement brandishing a rocket launcher. The rebels received support from Liberia's neighbours to sustain their war against the government in Monrovia.

A renewed round of civil war in Liberia came to an end with the agreement to send UN peacekeeping troops in September 2003. The war was fought between the Liberian government and two groups of rebels, who had managed to lay siege to the Liberian capital, Monrovia, in June 2003, but lacked the strength to launch an assault. Instead, they bombarded the town, killing many civilians, while leaving the security forces of President Charles Taylor largely untouched. One group, the Liberians United for Reconciliation and Democracy, had been formed with the support of the government of neighbouring Guinea. The other, the Movement for Democracy in Liberia, was believed to be supported by Côte d'Ivoire.

Congo civil war ends

A complicated war in Congo, that had been christened "Africa's great war" by some analysts, came to an end on 18 July 2003, with the appointment of a transitional government to take control of the divided country.

The war had its origins in a falling out among the rebel factions who took power after former dictator Mobutu Sésé Seko fled the country in May 1997. In August 1998, President Laurent Kabila felt sufficiently confident in his political strength in Congo to dismiss his Tutsi sponsors, who had supported his rebellion against Mobutu. This move alarmed the Tutsis living in Congo, who had frequently been treated badly by Mobutu, as well as having seen their ethnic relations in Rwanda butchered by Hutus, who were then given refuge by Mobutu. The Tutsis took control of dams and diamond mines in their area while the government began mobilizing local militias against them.

Kabila was able to mobilize support from other countries, including Angola, Zimbabwe, Chad and Libya, that led to Angolan and Zimbabwean soldiers arriving in Zaire to defend the capital, Kinshasha, against rebels who received support from Rwanda and Uganda. Zaire was divided into three areas and the war continued as a clash of militia groups more interested in looting, rape and protecting valuable resources, such

Militia battle in the street of a Congo town in June 2003. The vast African country had been riven by ethnic rivalries since its inception, and these were exacerbated when it gave asylum to refugees fleeing Rwanda's civil war.

as diamond mines, instead of a military affair with front lines and carefully planned offensives.

Kabila was assassinated in January 2001, but until a series of agreements produced the withdrawal of foreign military forces during 2002, the war continued in its chaotic way. The death toll from this war has been estimated in excess of 4 million.

Horror on the Madrid line

The explosion of ten bombs on four commuter trains on Spanish railways leading into Madrid on 11 March 2004 claimed the lives of 191 people. The bombs detonated between 7.37 and 7.40 a.m. Initially, the Spanish government claimed the bombs were the work of ETA, the terrorist organization fighting for independence for the Basque region of Spain. It soon became clear that the attacks did not conform in several ways to the traditional pattern of ETA bombings. The police subsequently identified a group of Moroccans as responsible, and arrested a number while others died when an explosive device detonated in their residence as the police attempted to arrest them. Other suspects escaped. No clear link to al-Qaeda was ever established.

The wreckage of a commuter train at Atocha station in Madrid after a terrorist bomb exploded on the morning of 11 March 2004.

West African crisis spreads to Côte d'Ivoire

Another West African country found itself at risk of civil war as political dissent in Côte d'Ivoire turned into a geographical division. A peace agreement signed in Pretoria, South Africa, on 6 April 2005, halted a conflict that at one time had threatened to draw in France and the United States.

The crisis began in September 2002 when a group of soldiers in the capital, Abidjan, rebelled and withdrew to the Moslem north where they found many sympathizers. Throughout September and October, the rebels expanded the number of communities under their control. France and the United States both sent troops. While American special forces rescued US nationals, the French forces gave protection to the many French citizens living in Côte d'Ivoire, as major battles erupted in the towns of Tiebissou and Bouaké.

During November and December, new rebel groups emerged in the west of the country, including some who drew on the many refugees from Liberia living in camps near the border. The government of President Laurent Gbago had blamed immigrants for the crisis almost from the start. In December, the French expanded their forces in the country from 1,000 to 2,500, and the conflict decreased in intensity except in the west.

Skirmishes continued through 2003 and 2004. In November 2004, two aircraft of the Ivorian Air Force attacked the French base at Bouaké, killing nine French peacekeepers. The French retaliated by attacking the Ivorian Air Force base at Yamossoukro, and destroying two aircraft and installations.

Moroccan peacekeeping troops arrive at Yamoussoukro airport in the Côte d'Ivoire on 22 May 2004. Rebels had been fighting the government of Côte d'Ivoire since September 2002.

IN BRIEF

⌁ A group of 32 armed terrorists occupied a school in Beslan, in the Russian republic of North Ossetia, on 1 September 2004. All but one was killed in an assault on 3 September by Russian security forces. Over a thousand people were killed or wounded in the incident, most after one or two of the terrorists' bombs exploded and shooting became general during the assault.

⌁ The Australian embassy in Jakarta, Indonesia, was attacked by a car bomb on 9 September 2004. Eleven people were killed and over 140 injured.

A Daihatsu minivan used in a bomb attack on the Australian embassy in Djakarta in September 2004 was captured on a security video before the car bomb was detonated.

Volunteers carry a wounded child from the school at Beslan, in North Ossetia, part of the Russian Federation, during the Russian special forces attack on the hostage-takers who had seized the school in September 2004.

Iraqi insurgency threatens Middle East

A mercenary guards Iraqi election officials and American diplomats at a meeting in Mosul, Iraq, in the 2005 election campaign in Iraq. Iraq's elections were free and fair, but the difficult ethnic and religious patchwork in the country meant they settled little about its future politics.

In **spite of** the successful conduct of elections to a national assembly in December 2005, the continued terror and guerrilla campaign against the predominantly American coalition military force and its Iraqi allies threatens not only the future of a sovereign, united Iraq but also hopes for a lasting general peace in the Middle East.

The Iraqi insurgency began almost immediately after the Coalition had successfully occupied Iraqi in April 2003. The initial fighting was conducted largely by Ba'athist party militia and Saddam Hussein's fighters, which may have been the Iraqi dictator's intent all along. The death of his two sons and grandsons in a shootout with members of the American 101st Airborne Division on 22 July, and his own capture on 13 December, did not end the insurgency, but offered hope that it would eventually end in the absence of any serious political alternative to the administration established by the coalition. The only major setback was the Canal Hotel bombing on 19 August, which killed the UN General Secretary's special representative, Sergio Vieria de Mello.

A wave of car bombings in early 2004 was followed by the murder of four mercenaries working for the US government in Fallujah on 31 March 2004. Fallujah now became the focus for

American Marines take cover from sniper fire in Fallujah, Iraq, in December 2005. The insurgency gradually drew in radical Islamic terrorists from across the Moslem world.

Iraqi resistance, and US military forces operating in the so-called Sunni Triangle in the centre of Iraq. A siege lasting over a month began on 3 April. At the end of it, American forces only occupied about half the city and a truce was signed that effectively handed over policing of the city to a "Fallujah Brigade", whose membership probably included many of the insurgents. Fallujah turned into an anti-American stronghold, where

the authority of the provisional Iraqi government did not apply, and Moslem clerics ruled by Islamic law, until a second US-Iraqi attack in November re-established the government's authority.

In spite of the Fallujah crisis, the insurgency was largely one of sniping attacks and improvised explosive devices that targeted US vehicle movements. During the fighting for Fallujah, it became apparent that radical Moslems

from across the Middle East, including al-Qaeda leader Abu Musad al-Zarkawi, were drawn to Iraq for the opportunity of joining the war against the United States. The attack on the Golden Mosque at Samarra on 22 February 2006 represented the opening of a new phase in the war as sectarian violence escalated between the different factions, with militias increasingly infiltrating Iraqi security forces as volunteers.

A sniffer dog checks a car for explosives before the car is driven off. The dog's handler is a mercenary employed by a company based in Illinois, USA. Foreign companies and government organizations make extensive use of mercenaries, called "security contractors", in Iraq.

Second intifada peters out

A second uprising by Palestinians against Israel appeared to have lost all momentum following a meeting on 8 February 2005 between the Israeli prime minister Ariel Sharon, Palestinian Authority president Mahmood Abbas, King Abdullah II of Jordan and Egyptian president Hosni Mubarak. The ostensible cause of the renewal of the intifada was the visit by Ariel Sharon to Jerusalem on

28 September 2000 to the mosque at Temple Mount. This was followed the next day by widespread rioting by Palestinians, and on 12 October, two Israeli reservists who had been detained by Palestinian Authority police were murdered by a mob. The Israelis launched air strikes against Palestinian Authority buildings, and a steady series of tit-for-tat riots, bombings and shootings ensued, pitting Israeli forces

against secular Palestinian nationalists and radical Moslem political movements. Suicide bombings directed against Israeli civilians became commonplace, while Palestinian Authority officials became involved in arms smuggling. In 2002 ferocious battles at the Jenin refugee camp resulted in at least 55 deaths, while a standoff between Israeli soldiers and armed militants in the Church of the Nativity in Bethlehem resulted in Israeli snipers shooting seven militants within the church.

INDEX

PICTURE CREDITS

The publishers would like to thank the following sources for their kind permission to reproduce the pictures in this book.

Key: T = Top, B = Bottom, L = Left, R = Right and C = Centre

AKG-Images: 62t, 70, 83t, 105, 129, 138t, 161t, 169b, 178t, 208, 250, 259t, 316b; /Ullstein Bild: 193l, 244 t, 272t, 278b, 308t, 308b

Corbis Images: 14b, 23b, 24t, 30, 31, 34, 39t, 49t, 51b, 57, 59b, 61, 65, 66t, 67, 72t, 72b, 91, 97b, 136b, 142b, 150, 153b, 157, 164t, 183, 215t, 227, 230t, 233l, 240, 249br, 260b, 263, 264b, 266t, 268l, 281b, 288, 297t, 298b, 299b, 300, 301t, 309t, 313t, 314t, 319b, 319t, 320t, 323t, 332br, 334t, 334b, 338l, 350, 378b, 379t; Sean Adair/ Reuters: 388 tl, /Asia Art & Archaeology, Inc.: 71; /Sergio Barrenechea/Epa: 392t; /Bettmann: 13t, 17 , 25, 48, 56t, 58, 69b, 75, 76, 79b, 81, 82, 83b, 87, 93b, 100 , 100 , 102, 110, 111r, 151b, 153t, 155t, 158br, 165t, 166, 169t, 171, 180t, 184t, 185t, 187b, 195, 197, 199, 205, 207t, 210, 213b, 214l, 218 b, 219, 220b, 228b, 229t, 231tl, 233r, 241, 255b, 256t, 258t, 262t, 264t, 265, 281t, 281c, 291b, 294, 299t, 301b, 314b, 316t, 323b, 326t, 326b, 328t, 329b, 331b, 331tl, 332bl, 333, 335b, 337b, 339b, 344, 345t, 345b, 351t, 352, 353t, 354b, 355b, 355t, 359b, 360l, 360r, 369t, 389; /Bernard Bisson: 372b, 372t; /Henri Bureau/Sygma: 358b, 359t; /Bryn Colton/Assignments: 366, 377t; / Steven Clevenger: 370; /Durand: 375t; /EFE: 187t; /Francoise de Mulder: 356t; /Hulton-Deutsch Collection: 18t, 95, 98, 99, 122, 126b, 155b, 158bl, 158t, 175, 177, 181, 182, 185b, 186t, 191, 196b, 204, 214r, 215b, 234, 242t 267t, 274b, 285, 289l, 298t, 302, 304, 313b, 322, 329t, 332t, 342t; /Jon Jones/Sygma: 382b, /William Karel/Sygma: 358t; /Ed Kashi: 384; /Alain Keler/Sygma: 364t; /Yevgeny Khaldei: 325, 327t, /Yuri Kochetkov/epa: 386b; /Jacques Langevin/Sygma: 380t; /Benjamin Lowy:

390t,; /Wally McNamee: 367b; /Medford Historical Society Collection: 26t, 43, 56; /Ali Meyer: 9; /Museum of Flight: 132t; /Oliver Coret-Antoine Serra/In Visu: 390b; /Jacques Pavlovsky/Sygma: 364b, 368t, 368b, /Peter Russell; The Military Picture Library: 231b; /Philadelphia Museum of Art: 80; /Reuters: 373, 376, 386t, 387, 392b; /Reza; Webistan: 375b, /Patrick Robert: 374t, 391b; /Patrick Robert/Sygma: 119; /Seamas Culligan/ZUMA: 53; /Sean Sexton Collection: 173; /Christian Simonpietri: 348t; /Les Stone/Sygma: 377b; /The Corcoran Gallery of Art: 66b; /The Mariners' Museum: 260t, /David Turnley: 382t; /Peter Turnley: 381; /Underwood & Underwood: 88, 159r, 179.

Getty Images: 271t; /AFP: 225b, 346, 356bl, 371b, 385b; /Vitaly Armand/AFP: 374b; /Spencer Arnold: 178b; /Felice Beato: 17t, 21; /Central Press: 189, 196t, 337t, 362; /J. Cuinieres/Roger Viollet: 132b; /Myron Davis/Time & Life Pictures: 276; /Harry Dempster: 237b; /Jack Esten: 339t; /Evening Standard: 290; /Stephen Ferry/Liaison: 385t; /Terry Fincher: 343; /Terry Fincher/ Express: 354t; / /Fox Photos: 223, 273, 296; / David Furst/AFP: 394t; /R.Gates/ Hulton Archive: 194; /Van Hoepen: 86; /Harlingue/Roger Viollet: 96t; /Hatch/ MPI: 311b, /Henry Guttmann: 69t, 147t; /John Hoagland: 361t; /John Hoagland/ Liaison: 371t; /Hulton Archive: 12, 16, 32b, 33, 44, 51t, 84r, 89t, 92, 93t, 108t, 112b, 130b, 142t, 144t, 144b, 145, 146, 162, 172b, 172t, 174b, 180b, 209b, 238, 257, 270, 275t, 282, 287b, 309b, 338b, 342b, 346t, 353b; /Hulton Archive/US Navy: 254, /Imagno:186b, 224b, 337tr; /Alexander Joe/AFP: 380b; /Nicholas Kamm/AFP: 379; /Keystone: 190, 200b, 201, 211t, 218t, 222t, 224t, 225t, 226bl, 226t, 228t, 230r, 235t, 237t, 243, 255t, 261t, 267b, 268b, 315b, 328b, 340, 347b, 351b, 357; /Keystone/Hulton Archive: 133b, 245t, 286, 293t, 320b, 361b; /Keystone/MPI: 327b; /LAPI/Viollet: 335t; /Laski Diffusion:

222l; /M. McNeill/Fox Photos: 369b; /MPI: 29b, 32t, 42b, 73, 295t; /Mansell/ Time & Life Pictures: 77l, 284, /Mansell/ Time Life Pictures: 154b, 232; /Mauricio Lima/AFP: 394b; /Shane McCoy/Mai/ Time Life Pictures: 388b; /Carl Mydans/ Time & Life Pictures: 226br, 283, 292, 324, 338tr; /Sgt J A Marshall: 103t; /Pictorial Parade: 188; /Ralph Morse/Time Life Pictures: 303; /Scott Nelson: 388t; /Fred Ramage/Keystone: 291t; /Kenneth Rittener: 293r, /Robertson: 14t; /George Rodger/Time Life Pictures: 235b, 287t; /Daniel Rosenblum: 349; /Issouf Sanago/ AFP: 391t; /Issouf Sanogo: 392b; /Slava Katamidze Collection: 151; /George Strock/Time & Life Pictures: 256b; /Allan Tannenbaum: 383; /Reinhold Thiele: 90; /Three Lions: 317t; /Time Life Pictures: 176b, 347t; /Time Life Pictures/Mansell: 10-11, 77r; /Topical Press Agency: 94b, 125, 136t; /Yuri Tutov: 393, /US Army: 274t; / Miguel Vinas/AFP: 341; /Ian Waldie: 271b; /Walshe: 174t

Imperial War Museum: 96b (Q 81831), 97t (Q 100136), 103b (Q 5095), 104 (Q 53230), 106 (Q 53523), 108b (Q 57380), 109 (Q 52827), 111 (Q 22178), 112 (Q 20896), 113 (Q 22687), 111l (Q 22178), 116 (Q 107445), 117 (SP 682A), 118t (Q 112876), 119 (Q 106217), 119t (Q 114867), 120b (Q 53879), 120t (Q 108330), 120 (Q 106227), 121b (Q 90475), 123 (Q 49296), 124 (HU 68589), 126t (Q 23760), 127 (Q 69585), 128b (Q 34370), 128t (HU 55527), 131 (Q 718), 134 (Q 1142), 135b (Q 78038), 137 (HU 64215), 138 (HU 024888), 140 (HU 72105), 143 (Q 20343), 150 (Q 2295), 152 (Q 5935), 154t (Q 15457), 156 (Q 45338), 159r (Q 47997), 160 (Q 6530), 163 (Q 9178), 165 (Q 95579), 184 (HU 47654), 192t (PC 449), 198t (A 6), 202t (E 1579), 207 (Q 4154), 212 (HU 39578), 213l (HU 39619), 213tr (A 4815), 217 (HU 5065), 217 (E 6751), 221 (HU 780), 222b (RUS 1124), 246 (HU 36275), 247b (CF 90), 251t (HU 5138), 252t (E 14775), 253 (A 12661), 258b (MH 9701), 275b (HU 60392), 277 (K 5287), 295b (MH 4505), 310 (OWIL

35108), 312 (BU 945), 318t (EA 47958), 321 (CL 1598), 324 (HU 50242),

Emory University: 37; /Jean Restayn: 147b, 280, 307b, 318b; John Hess: 24b, 42t; Library of Congress: 26b, 47t, 54; Mary Evans Picture Library: 62b, 85; National Archives: 46; Naval Historical Foundation: 41, 200t, /Courtesy of Mr Elmer Jackson, Capital Gazette Press, Annapolis, MD: 49 b, /Courtesy of Radm Ammen Farenholt, USN (MC) 1931: 55; /Watercolour by R. G. Skerrett, 1904: 3b; New York Historical Society: 47r; PA Photos: 363; /AP: 202b; Photos 12.com :118b, 133t; /Ann Ronan Picture Library: 193r; /Hachede: 45t, 192b; /Oasis: 45b, 130t; /Oronoz: 64; Picture-Desk: The Art Archive/Culver Pictures: 29 t, 35, 52, /Imperial War Museum: 135t; Private Collection: 244b, 262b, 297b, 317b; Rex Features: /Sipa Press: 336, 378t; Rodina Archive: 216, 220t, 256b, 251b; TRH Pictures: 236t, 242b, 266b; /Cody Images: 211b; The Bridgeman Art Library: /Chateau de Compiegne, Oise, France: 20; /Collection of the New York Historical Society, USA: 78; /Library of Congress, Washington D.C., USA: 8, 84l; /Museo Historico Nacional, Buenos Aires, Argentina: 63; /Private Collection: 13b, 27, 39b; Topfoto.co.uk:18b, 68, 89b, 118b, 139, 151t, 164b, 167b, 167t, 168, 170, 176t, 198b, 203, 206, 209t, 229b, 231c, 239, 245b, 248, 249bl, 249t, 259b, 261b, 278t, 279, 305, 306, 307t, 330, 389; /AP: 289l, /Alinari: 161b; /Collection Roger-Viollet: 19, 74, 94t, 107, 118, 247t, 252b, 311t, 331tr; /Public Record Office/HIP: 15, 269; USAMHI: 22, 23t, 28, 36, 40, 50, 59t, 60t, 60b, 79t; Ullstein Bild: 248b; /Walter Frentz: 315t

Every effort has been made to acknowledge correctly and contact the source and/or copyright holder of each picture and Carlton Books Limited apologises for any unintentional errors or omissions which will be corrected in future editions of this book.